Penguin Business
Even More Offensive Marketing

Hugh Davidson graduated in Economics and Law at Cambridge
and subsequently qualified as a barrister-at-law at Gray's Inn.
A former Procter & Gamble marketing manager, later a marketer
with United Biscuits, he first went into consulting with
Glendinning in the USA, then became Director of European
Consulting. He returned to line management, first as President
of Playtex in Canada, then President of Playtex Europe, and was
a member of the International Management Committee in New
York.

He has contributed articles to many publications, including the
*Harvard Business Review*, the *Japanese Diamond Business Review* and
*Management Today*, and is the author of *Offensive Marketing*, also
published in the Penguin Business Library. He is a Visiting
Professor of Marketing at Cranfield University School of
Management, a Fellow of the Chartered Institute of Marketing,
and a Fellow and past Chairman of the Marketing Society, and
conducted the 1997 Marketing Society Masterclass on 'How
Marketers Can Win the Future'.

Hugh Davidson is co-founder and Chairman of Oxford
Corporate Consultants, the leading-edge strategic marketing
consultancy. During his consultancy career, he has worked
globally for many of the world's leading companies, including
British Airways, Corning, Shell, Halifax, Volkswagen, SmithKline
Beecham, Prudential, Allied Domecq, Mitsubishi, PepsiCo and
H. J. Heinz.

D0063426

# EVEN MORE OFFENSIVE MARKETING

## An Exhilarating Action Guide to Winning in Business

Hugh Davidson

**Penguin Books**

PENGUIN BOOKS

Published by the Penguin Group

Penguin Books Ltd, 27 Wrights Lane, London W8 5TZ, England
Penguin Putnam Inc., 375 Hudson Street, New York, New York 10014, USA
Penguin Books Australia Ltd, Ringwood, Victoria, Australia
Penguin Books Canada Ltd, 10 Alcorn Avenue, Toronto, Ontario, Canada M4V 3B2
Penguin Books (NZ) Ltd, 182–190 Wairau Road, Auckland 10, New Zealand

Penguin Books Ltd, Registered Offices: Harmondsworth, Middlesex, England

First published 1997
10 9 8 7 6 5 4 3 2

Copyright © Hugh Davidson, 1997
All rights reserved

The moral right of the author has been asserted

Filmset in Bembo and Gill Sans

Printed in England by Clays Ltd, St Ives plc

# Contents

To my parents

# Foreword
## By Dr Anthony J. F. O'Reilly

Chairman, President and Chief Executive Officer
H. J. Heinz Co., Inc.

Chairman
Waterford Wedgwood

Since Hugh Davidson and I first collaborated in 1971, on the threshold of my US career with H. J. Heinz, much has happened to both of us. Our original collaboration was on *Offensive Marketing*, which proved to be a bestseller. *Even More Offensive Marketing* is its sequel. It retains the enduring principles of the original, takes their application forward beyond the millennium, and is a new book, not a new edition.

Hugh Davidson is an iconoclast. He is also an immensely readable writer, with a strong commercial sense. The strategy of his book underlines the belief that successful marketing, or, in his view, Offensive Marketing, comprises certain attitudes and practices towards marketing, competition and planning which are, unfortunately, rare.

The rapid rate of marketing change has further accelerated in the past five years. One aspect is the development of Relationship Marketing. This involves an individual and long-term approach to customers, and has been of particular importance to both H. J. Heinz and Waterford Wedgwood. However, new product and brand development, appropriate investment in efficiency, technology and communication, and commitment to quality, value and service, remain critical to future marketing success.

Good marketing practice is based on freedom of consumer choice, which is an essential element in a democracy. Supermarkets are a better model of the democratic process in action than Congress or the Houses of Parliament. Customers impose their will on the producer and retailer by exercising their right to make choices in a competitive market. Hugh Davidson's book highlights the process of co-operation between consumer and producer and illustrates how mutual responsiveness can benefit both.

His definitions are refreshing and simple. He believes that professional marketing involves a determination to achieve all the major innovations in a given market, a freedom from the shackles of industry tradition or interruptive bureaucracy, and a view of marketing as a profit-oriented approach to business that permeates not just the Marketing Department, but the entire business. Above all, he believes that Offensive Marketing requires a dedication to strategy and planning.

Hurray! It has all been said before, but it has rarely been said so succinctly and so refreshingly. Not above employing popular gurus to bolster his case, he quotes Levitt tellingly: 'When it comes to the marketing concept today, a solid stone wall often seems to separate word from deed.' His answer is, 'Kill the bureaucratic plague; dis-establish the maintenance men; stop talking about Offensive Marketing and DO something about it.' He observes, in my view accurately, that good marketing is not so much a matter of intelligence and ability (as good and bad companies seem to have an abundance of both), but more a question of attitudes, organization and technique.

Hugh Davidson has a certain elegance in his choice of mnemonics. He says that Offensive Marketing is a matter of POISE, that it should be Profitable, Offensive, Integrated, Strategic (embracing short- and long-term corporate plans) and Effectively Executed. The book unashamedly assumes that the right attitudes and organization structures have a profound effect on corporate profit, and essays only one real definition of marketing (and a very good one it is), that it 'involves every employee in building superior customer value very efficiently for above-average profits'. He also stresses that if you don't balance the short-term-profit/consumer-benefit equation against your long-term ambitions, you won't have a business to realize those long-term ambitions against.

Offensive Marketing is quite simple to describe. A company's offerings must be so attractive to customers that they will want to buy and go on buying. The offerings must also be developed and marketed so efficiently that the company will make handsome profits. To succeed, both sides of the equation have to be matched. Good customer value or low-cost operation on their own are not enough in today's very competitive market-place.

The only way I know of achieving this simple formula is to have winning strategies, and strong, well-motivated people to execute them. In Chapter 7 Davidson explains how to develop winning strategies. He also warns that they wear out quickly unless they are updated to meet changing customer needs and new competitive moves. The world is full of lagging companies which used to have winning strategies. I am a strong believer in the importance of attitudes and was glad to see a whole chapter devoted to this. Qualities we encourage at Heinz are ingenuity, dedication, willingness to chance risk and ability to spot a problem and pursue it doggedly.

Talking about corporate culture is much easier than creating or sustaining it. From hard experience, I know that 'making it happen' requires example, emphasis and evangelism from all managers every day of the week.

The author is at his best in describing marketing misfits. He instances five: *Markeaucrats*, who are a cross between genuine marketers and bureaucrats; *the new Luddites*, who view production people as an inferior form of human life; *the egotistical employees*, who pander to the company president, knowing that the latter believes that sales volume is more important than profits; *the milker*, who cuts everything, particularly above-the-line expenditure, and then runs for it; and finally a superb title, *the galloping midget*, whose exploits are worth the purchase price of the book.

What Davidson wants is integrated marketing, believing that it is an approach to business rather than a specific discipline. He states that the main benefits which successful companies gain through Offensive Marketing are higher profits, a longer life-cycle on existing products and services, and a better success rate with new products and acquisitions. Could we ask for more?

My own experience suggests general accord with these principles, and great difficulty in implementing them. In particular, it is extremely difficult to graft policies of innovation and imagination on to big, successful organizations. The entrepreneur, by definition, is almost a loner. Large businesses have a certain civil-service-like quality about them. Promotion in many instances is by non-mistake rather than by visible victory. Additionally, the gestation period required for new ideas to mature to profitability is often hampered by the internal accountancy disciplines of the organization. An idea, product concept or joint venture may take three to four years to mature to profitability. The normal reporting system of a business is the monthly account, followed by the quarterly report, the half-yearly review and the annual assessment. Unless such systems are intelligently interpreted, they can sound the death-knell for a slowly maturing but potentially profitable idea, and I was glad to see Hugh Davidson calling for broader measures of business performance in Chapter 2.

One answer is the venture management team, free from the shackles of the system. Quite simply, a multi-discipline venture team can bypass much bureaucracy and operate on a discrete timescale, free from monthly interruption and quarterly execution. This is not to write a blank cheque for venture managers, but it is an attempt to position them in a manner which allows imaginative distillation of new ideas, without the interference of systems which are appropriate to successful ongoing business, rather than embryonic activity.

Additionally, new business development, which I define as any new product concept, initiative or liaison which can create a new and viable profit centre for the company, should be directly accountable to the Chief Executive. This does two things:

1. It involves the Chief Planning Officer of the corporation, the Managing Director/President, in that area where planning is most important, i.e. the development of new business.
2. It elevates the whole concept of new product/new business development on the corporate totem pole, and gives a thrust and vigour to this aspect of the company's activities which it will otherwise not achieve.

From practical experience at Heinz, I can say that this structure has provided us with a rapid and apparently successful system of new business and new venture development. The drawbacks are that it is time-consuming, and for long periods of time sterile in terms of results achieved. Nevertheless, it remains among the most important responsibilities of any Chief Executive. The same is equally true of acquisitions, both in terms of defining the area of search, and in terms of participating in the negotiations for the acquisitions candidate.

Despite being an iconoclast, Hugh Davidson is old-fashioned in some of his beliefs. He believes that consumers buy product and service benefits rather than advertising or promotions. He believes the surest way to corporate growth is through product or service superiority. He believes that marketing is irrelevant unless supported by efficient low-cost operation. Additionally, he believes that all the other members of the marketing mix, such as communication, pricing and presentation, respond most amiably to a superior product and service, and will work hardest on its behalf. How many times have we all neglected this truism!

I found his book stimulating, provocative and original – or maybe it was that I was secretly flattered by his agreement with most of my pet prejudices.

**Tony O'Reilly**
Pittsburgh, USA, 1997

# Acknowledgements

Oxford
August 1997

Dear Contributors,

'Acknowledgements' is a cold and formal heading under which to record my warmest thanks to the many very busy people who have contributed substantially to this book. Since it does not do justice to the help you have given me, I am therefore writing this letter personally to you all. The comments you made were very useful and constructive, and indeed I adopted over 90% of them.

My wife, Sandra, acted as editor-in-chief and secretary, a role in which her degree in publishing proved most useful. She greatly improved the clarity and style of the book, pouncing on jargon and unnecessary complexity, while also typing and laying out three versions of the book – of which this is the final one. Much of her work was done in the small hours.

My brother, Ewan Davidson, head of finance at RNLI and previously for many years Treasurer of J. Sainsbury, commented constructively on Chapter 2; and my son Ian Davidson, a product manager at Cereal Partners, made many valuable points, particularly on Chapter 1 and the 'Bulletin Board'.

My friends at SmithKline Beecham Consumer Health provided excellent feedback, especially Peter Jensen, European Chairman, and Chris Harley-Martin, Marketing Manager, Horlicks, who read the first draft in full. As a result of Peter's comments, I changed the structure of the book. Martin Dreger, Vice President Category Management, read half the book on a bumpy flight to the USA and made a number of useful suggestions.

I was very fortunate that Alan Mitchell, a leading journalist on marketing topics, agreed to read the first draft. With typical thoroughness, he produced ten pages of high-quality comments, accurately identifying weaknesses and inconsistencies and making many constructive suggestions. He greatly influenced the final version.

Matt Housden, Senior Lecturer at the University of Greenwich, also went through the first draft. His key points, especially on Relationship Marketing and Customer Lifetime Values, led me to make fundamental changes.

My colleagues at Oxford Corporate Consultants were helpful both in making comments and in minimizing recent interruptions to my literary efforts. David Hill read the first half of the first draft, and his beneficial comments were characteristically direct and succinct. Gina Banns read the whole book and scored each chapter against a number of criteria, enabling me to focus effort on the weaker ones.

Colleagues at Cranfield University School of Management have provided helpful input in various conversations, especially Professors Malcolm McDonald, Martin Christopher and Simon Knox. Malcolm has a particular fund of knowledge on how to market business books, read this one in full over Christmas, and identified some key areas for improvement, which I took action on.

Nigel Worne, Managing Director of Fox's Biscuits, Hamish Taylor, Managing Director Eurostar, and previously Brands Director at British Airways, stimulated new thinking during various conversations over the years leading up to and during the writing of this book, as have Martin Grant, Managing Director of Allied Domecq Leisure; Peter Glynn-Jones, Managing Director Strategic Management, SmithKline Beecham; Jacques Blanchard, Chairman of Novaction; John Hooper, Director General of ISBA; Dr John Mills, Corporate Vice-President of Covance, and my colleagues, Jonathan Turner, Julian Thomas and Marina Foxlee of Oxford Corporate Consultants.

I had very profitable discussions on branding with Sandra Blaza, Marketing Director of Pedigree Petfoods; on a variety of topics with Jürgen Hintz, previously Senior Vice President, Procter and Gamble, and CEO Carnaud Metal Box; with Chris Moss, Lloyds TSB, on his prior experience as Marketing Director of Virgin Airways and Orange; and with Malcolm Little, Chief Executive, United Biscuits, UK.

Michael Reyner, and McKinsey & Company, were most helpful in constructing charts on PC industry profitability.

Diana Woodburn of Business Development Unit, as well as Doug Henderson and Andrew Cross, went to a great deal of trouble to brief me fully on the Sharp Electronics case example, which appears in the last chapter.

Alastair Rolfe, Director of Business Publishing at Penguin, has been consistently constructive and supportive, and, together with Helen Drake and Andrew Welham, contributed much to the (Offensive) Marketing plan for the book.

I appreciated the extensive facilities of the library at Templeton College, Oxford, and would like to thank Gill Powell, Manager of the Information Centre and Library.

Finally, I am most grateful to my consulting clients from whom I have learned so much (especially in South Humberside, the Great West Road, Birmingham and Bühl).

Thank you all again, for your generosity of time and thinking. If this book does not meet its objectives after the involvement of so many able people, I deserve to be put down for five years' hard marketing labour – working exclusively on sales forecasting and customer complaints.

Sincerely

*Hugh Davidson.*

# Bulletin Board

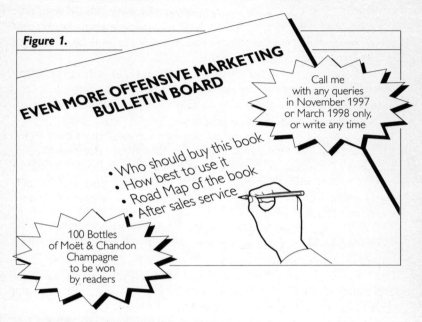

**Figure 1.**

EVEN MORE OFFENSIVE MARKETING BULLETIN BOARD

- Who should buy this book
- How best to use it
- Road Map of the book
- After sales service

Call me with any queries in November 1997 or March 1998 only, or write any time

100 Bottles of Moët & Chandon Champagne to be won by readers

## 1. Who should buy this book

*Even More Offensive Marketing* is targeted at competitive people who are serious about strengthening their marketing skills and developing their career, and who are committed to marketing as an approach to business. Its purpose is to impart practical learning, to communicate leading-edge approaches and to stimulate new thinking. Some of you will be studying marketing, many will be practising business people. I have attempted to make the book interesting and clear to all readers. However, applying the practices and processes will require some commitment on your part, since facile shortcuts and illusory 'easy solutions' have been avoided.

I hope this book, and especially the first five chapters, will be read by Chief Executives and Board members, since Boards of Directors, not marketing people, determine whether or not their companies apply the five principles of Offensive Marketing.

## 2. How best to use this book

I would like everyone who buys this book to read and benefit from it. Otherwise you have wasted your money and I have wasted my time.

However, like myself, you may not read all the books you buy. Indeed, Tom Peters, joint author of *In Search of Excellence*, which sold over five million copies, estimated that only 10% of buyers read even the first five chapters.

I would therefore advise different people to use this book in different ways. Students and those taking business courses should benefit from reading the total book. Directors and senior executives are likely to find Chapters 1 to 9 most valuable, while marketing practitioners will also derive much practical advice on execution from Chapters 10 to 16.

However, it should be emphasized that *Even More Offensive Marketing* is a total package, and even if you only read a few chapters in detail, it is worth skip-reading the rest to get the full story.

## 3. The Road Map of the book

*Even More Offensive Marketing* is the sequel to *Offensive Marketing*, the first edition of which was published 25 years ago. While the principles of Offensive Marketing have proved enduring, the environment and techniques have obviously changed dramatically.

*Even More Offensive Marketing* is a new book, not a new edition. It retains the enduring principles of *Offensive Marketing* but the material is new, containing many fresh approaches and tools. It takes clear positions on issues and is deliberately practical, with many checklists, examples and step-by-step processes. Each chapter has an opening summary and a closing flow chart, and some have detailed practical exhibits at the end.

Many of the examples are taken from my own business experience, but some of these have been presented anonymously, for reasons of confidentiality. Others are fictional constructs, derived from a range of experiences. The category into which each example fits is either indicated in the text of the book or referenced.

The five key principles of Offensive Marketing – Profitable, Offensive, Integrated, Strategic and Effectively Executed, as summarized in the mnemonic POISE – have been retained, since their relevance appears to have increased over time. 'Integrated', in particular, is now very much in vogue, *though I wish people would talk less and do more about it*, and there is growing recognition of the prime importance of 'Effective Execution'.

*Even More Offensive Marketing*, therefore, is constructed around POISE.

| **Table 1.** | | |
|---|---|---|
| **P:** | Profitable | ● Proper balance between firm's need for profit and customer's need for value |
| **O:** | Offensive | ● Must lead market, take risks and make competitors followers |
| **I:** | Integrated | ● Marketing approach must permeate whole company |
| **S:** | Strategic | ● Probing analysis leading to a winning strategy |
| **E:** | Effectively Executed | ● Strong and disciplined execution on a daily basis |

Chapter 1 covers the need for Offensive Marketing, defines it and outlines its five key principles – P–O–I–S–E – which the remainder of the book develops. Here is the Road Map:

| **Table 2.** | |
|---|---|
| **P**<br>**Profitable**<br>→ | ● Chapter 2 suggests that the traditional financial view of profit is outdated and describes how Offensive Marketers can develop measures of company performance more suited to contemporary business practice.<br><br>● It shows how Offensive Marketers maximize profitability by matching their assets and competencies to the most appropriate opportunities for their companies or brands. Efficient matching of the two enables companies both to provide superior customer value and to generate superior profits. |
| **O**<br>**Offensive**<br>→ | ● Chapter 3 demonstrates the importance of vision, attitudes and values in establishing the right environment for Offensive Marketing. Even the most brilliant marketers will fail if Board attitudes towards quality, service, investment and innovation are shallow and half-hearted. |
| **I**<br>**Integrated**<br>→ | ● Chapter 4 is the most important in the book. It illustrates how in the Offensive Marketing company everyone is a marketer, and it outlines practical steps for making this happen. |
| **S**<br>**Strategic**<br>→ | ● 'Strategic' comprises 4 chapters, covering the main elements in preparing and developing Offensive Strategies, then translating them into effective plans.<br><br>● It starts with the strategic foundation, 'Offensive Business Analysis' (Chapter 5), which outlines the requirements for effective analysis and suggests a five-step process for applying them;<br><br>● Progresses to 'Developing a Distinctive View of the Future' (Chapter 6), which shows how marketers can anticipate the future and *lead* the development of the Strategic Plan;<br><br>● And culminates in 'Developing Winning Strategies' (Chapter 7), which describes the various types of competitive advantages, and how to convert them into winning strategies.<br><br>● The final chapter (Chapter 8) in the 'Strategic' section deals with turning strategies into marketing plans and incorporates an example of a fully worked plan for Rasputin Vodka. |

> **E**
> **Effectively**
> **executed**
> →
>
> ● Chapter 9 to 15 outline how to execute Offensive Marketing Strategies and Plans. Each chapter is a mini-book, covering offensive principles governing each topic, then outlining a disciplined process for implementing them on a step-by-step basis.
>
> ● There are seven best practice guides to:
>   ✓ Offensive Segmentation,
>   ✓ Offensive Brand Development,
>   ✓ Offensive New Product and Service Development,
>   ✓ Offensive Communication,
>   ✓ Offensive Market Research,
>   ✓ Offensive Pricing,
>   ✓ Offensive Channel Management.
>
> ● The important topic of Relationship Marketing is not given a separate chapter, since it permeates the whole of Offensive Marketing and appears in most chapters.

## 4. After Sales Service and Relationship Marketing

To encourage you to read the book, we have included a reader competition, with 100 prizes of Moët et Chandon champagne. You will find the entry form somewhere in the middle of the book. To enter, all you need to do is answer a few one-line questions on the book, and submit a 100–150 word example of **Even More Offensive Marketing**, either from your own experience or from published sources. All qualifying entries will be included in a random draw, to be made on 25 September 1998. Your chance of winning should be pretty good, since few successful business books sell more than 10,000 copies per year, and, as you know, only a minority of readers will participate.

Finally, to reinforce my commitment to Relationship Marketing, we are setting up special phone, fax and e-mail lines in November 1997 and March 1998 only, to enable you to contact me personally to discuss any queries, criticisms or suggestions about this book. To take advantage of this opportunity, buy your copy now. You will find details within the book.

At any other time, please feel free to write to me at Penguin Books, 27 Wrights Lane, London W8 5TZ. You will of course receive a reply. I will be particularly interested to receive examples of either Offensive or Inoffensive Marketing.

I hope you feel this book has met its objectives from your viewpoint.

Hugh Davidson

# 1. The Offensive Marketing Approach: POISE

## Chapter Summary

Marketing and marketers are under attack. Managing and Financial Directors are questioning whether marketing is working. They point to the lack of innovation in their companies, the high failure rate of new products, and their inability to develop sustained competitive advantage.

Marketing people in turn criticize their own companies for short-termism, unwillingness to invest or take risks, and for loading Marketing Departments with such a weight of day-to-day tactics that they have neither time nor opportunity to lead the direction of corporate strategy.

At the same time, new and old industries are enthusiastically hiring marketing people, while the business establishment exhorts companies to adopt the marketing approach and build long-term customer relationships.

Why the paradox? Because even companies claiming to be marketing-orientated often only go through the motions. They make aggressive noises, but continue to run on the spot with 'Me too' and 'Me three' products and services, seeking, like slimmers, magic short-term cures which require little effort. They have only a vague vision of the future, lack the determination to develop and invest in winning strategies and consistently overstate their real state of health.

This is partly because their functional structure inhibits a company-wide approach to marketing, partly because Marketing Departments themselves often adopt a narrow and inward-looking role, failing to spearhead the company's future vision and strategy.

Yet marketing and marketers have never had a bigger opportunity to realize their full potential, as companies seek innovation and profitable growth, as new financial measures more favourable to marketing, like shareholder value and the balanced scorecard, gain in popularity.

Offensive Marketing is designed to help you exploit this opportunity. It is a set of attitudes, approaches and processes practised by only a handful of consistently successful companies.

Offensive Marketing enables marketing to achieve its full potential, leading rather than following, and viewing every employee as a marketer.

## Is Microsoft an Offensive Marketer?

Bill Gates was only technically a dropout when he left Harvard University in his second year. He left because, together with Paul Allen, he had developed the software language for the first personal computer, the Altair. Some of the experts at Intel, who produced the 8080 microchip for the Altair, said it was impossible to develop BASIC language for it, but Microsoft Basic was written in eight weeks, without even the benefit of an Altair computer for reference. Indeed Gates and Allen only saw a working Altair for the first time when Microsoft Word was (successfully) run on it, in Albuquerque, New Mexico.[1]

In a turbulent industry with over 75,000 competitors worldwide, and for two difficult decades, Microsoft has consistently grown sales and profits at a dramatic rate. It overtook IBM in market capitalization after only seventeen years in business.

### Why has Microsoft been so successful?

Here are some reasons:[2]

- The company has a clear and easily understood vision – 'Microsoft software on every desktop PC.'
- It hires a very specific type of person with strong technical background, high intelligence, a drive to succeed and ability to handle pressure.
- It has a distinctive management style, built around informality, speed, hard challenges and stock options – directed towards making better products quickly and winning.
- Microsoft always wants to be ahead of competition in every way. It competes both in the market-place and the law courts. The drive to win is very strong.
- The company invests heavily in its vision of the future. R & D costs are 14% of sales, sales/marketing investment is 32%, while cost of goods is only 15% of sales.
- Deal-making has always been a strength. The agreement of IBM, to use MS–DOS as the operating system in its PCs, established MS–DOS as the industry standard and enabled Microsoft to build dominance in this critical strategic area.
- Microsoft takes controlled risks and places high priority on speed to market-place.

## Offensive Marketing

You have just read an example of **Offensive Marketing**. Both Microsoft and Bill Gates are Offensive Marketers.

This book is about Offensive Marketing, which combines the age-old virtues of risk-taking with a modern approach to marketing. Offensive Marketing is practised by only a handful of successful companies, and the phrase has been coined to differentiate the contents of this book from the sluggish and specialized concept that passes for marketing in many companies.

Offensive Marketing is not a neat concept capable of instant encapsulation in an elegant one-liner. It describes particular attitudes and methods that cover the whole marketing spectrum, so its boundaries are widely spread and ragged. In essence, it involves aiming to innovate every major new development in a market. It means having a clear strategy, and following it through with investment and persistence. It is about anticipating future needs, meeting them quicker and better than competition, and building strong customer relationships.

### *What Offensive Marketing is not*

Here are some definitions to consider, serious and not so serious:

- **Marketing is a sophisticated form of selling, done by graduates**. This is what many consumers and non-business journalists think marketing is. They believe that marketing manipulates and exploits consumers, and pushes prices up. 'Added value' means adding more frills and doubling the price.

  Marketing is not 'selling' though selling is part of the marketing approach. To borrow a phrase, 'Selling is making people want what you've got, while marketing is selling people what they want.'[3] When people, and especially politicians, say, 'We must improve the marketing of our products,' they are confusing marketing with selling, and usually attempting to gloss over a weak customer proposition.

- **Marketing is advertising, sales promotion, selling, PR, direct mail, market research**. This is a definition rarely spoken but often followed by half-baked marketers, whose most frequent haunts are the financial services and energy industries. Their employers think they are 'embracing' marketing by hiring people with a marketing title, but in reality they merely bolt on a series of marketing services to a financial or operations approach to business.

- **Marketing is what the Marketing Department does**. In many companies, that is the view of other departments, such as Operations or Finance.

  This too is a narrow definition of marketing, for which marketing people must take some responsibility. Ironically, most marketers are poor communicators about Marketing.

- **Marketing is the four 'P's – Product, Price, Place and Promotion**. This is also sometimes referred to as the 'marketing mix', and has the virtue of simplicity and clarity. 'Place' is widely viewed as distribution channels, while 'Promotion' usually includes selling and advertising as well as sales promotion.

  This definition at least recognizes that marketing is done outside the Marketing Department, but its weaknesses are that it describes marketing activities rather than the marketing approach, and does not mention 'profit'.

- **The purpose of marketing is to meet consumer needs at a profit**. The best definition yet, often used in textbooks, but unfortunately based on a sophisticated misconception.

  It fails to recognize that there may be a very real conflict between meeting consumer needs and making a profit. Every company has to do both in order to survive, but how should it strike a balance between the two? Does it aim to maximize profit, or, like many fine companies, make a 'fair' profit? Companies constantly face business choices between converting surpluses into profits or into extra consumer value, and marketers are usually best placed to advise on the right balance.

  'Meeting consumer needs *at a profit*' is therefore too vague a definition, because it ignores profit *levels*.

## Why is 'marketing' so difficult to define?

'What do you do for a living?' is a question people in Finance, Sales, Operations and even Human Resources can answer with ease at social gatherings – not so marketing people. Two minutes of superficial conversation tail away in glazed non-comprehension. This absence of a simple explanation may be one of the reasons why the marketing approach is so widely misunderstood, and often wrongly applied, not least by marketing people.

Marketing is difficult to define and explain because it is both an approach to business practised by every employee and the name of a specific department, full of people with Marketing titles. There is constant confusion between **marketing** and **marketers**. 'Marketing' is no more the exclusive role of marketers than profit is the exclusive responsibility of the Finance Department. People easily understand their financial role in helping to make profits. Yet they find it more difficult to grasp that they are also marketers, especially if they have no direct customer contact.

This is partly because the marketing approach is diverse and often intangible in a way that money (Finance Department) or people (Human Resources) are not; and partly because marketing people have either been too keen to appropriate credit for marketing success, or failed to evangelize the important role every employee can play in driving the marketing approach.

## We need a new word for 'marketing'

So, is marketing the marketing approach to business or the Marketing Department, or is it both? Today the word is used colloquially to describe both, which is very confusing for everyone.

*Finance has got its language right.* 'Finance' describes the internal department. 'Profits' describes the financial approach to business. 'Marketing' seems a reasonable word for the internal department. But we need a totally new word to describe the marketing approach (Table 3).

**Table 3. Finance has got its language right.**

| Internal department | Approach to business |
| --- | --- |
| Finance | Profits |
| Marketing | ? |

The best answer so far comes from one of my colleagues at Oxford Corporate Consultants – 'Effective Customer Value Management'. This is something which everyone, irrespective of their internal function, could accept as his or her responsibility. 'Customer', of course, covers external customers who buy products or services, and internal customers, who receive services from colleagues. 'Value' connotes the need to provide a superior mix of quality and price. And 'Management' is the process which results in customer value. The only thing missing from the definition is profitability – intrinsic, of course, to the marketing approach. This is strongly implied in the word 'Effective', which suggests efficient and profitable delivery of customer value.

**If you have better suggestions for a new phrase or word to describe the marketing approach, please mail it to Penguin for my attention.**

## Offensive Marketing Defined

Offensive Marketing involves
every employee in building
superior customer value very efficiently
for above-average profits

There are three key elements in this definition – not just customer focus, and profit orientation, but also cross-departmental commitment to both.

This is the *business* definition of Offensive Marketing. A separate definition for the not-for-profit or public sector is given in a later section. It does not seem possible to cover both effectively in a single definition.

'**. . . involves every employee . . .**' Every employee is a marketer . . . whether he or she knows it or not. And if you are in the Marketing Department, it is your job to tell everyone and to recognize their contribution.

Every employee's job should be specified and evaluated on only two axes:

- Contribution to consistently superior customer value.
- Contribution to above-average profits.

What other reason is there for being in business?

Here are a couple of examples from people who never meet the customer.

- First, the **marketing-orientated shift manager in a factory**. She is 28, has an HNC in electrical engineering and works shifts 9 days on, 4 days off. The chart in Table 4 compares her company's factory (A) with that of her main competitor (B). Company A has no market-  ing people, is more profitable and gaining market share. Company B has a Marketing Department and is losing market share. Two questions for you:

  - Which company would you prefer to work for?
  - Can company B be an Offensive Marketer?

The answer to the latter is 'Not for some time'. Company B would still be an Inoffensive Marketer if its Marketing Department included Bill Gates with Einstein thrown in.

**Table 4.  A tale of two factories.**

| Company A | Company B (Competitor) |
|---|---|
| ● Buys 10% cheaper than competition via world-wide sourcing | ● Efficient people with clear, though narrow objectives |
| ● Well informed re consumer needs | ● Little market knowledge |
| ● Runs 168 hours per week, 3 shifts | ● Ten 8-hour shifts, lots of overtime |
| ● Excellent at process engineering | ● Machinery and process totally undifferentiated |
| ● Buying, sales, engineering on new product development team | ● Does not leverage scale buying advantages |
| ● Labour cost per tonne one half that of competitor's best plant | ● No knowledge of competitive machinery, speeds, labour rates |
| ● Few lines, long runs | ● Many low-volume lines (SKUs) |

Production people in a manufacturing company or operations people in a service company are among the most important Offensive Marketers. They control the cost, quality, consistency and delivery of the customer proposition, whether it is frozen foods, insurance or consumer durables. Inefficient, high-cost operators can never be Offensive Marketers, because they cannot deliver superior consumer value at competitive profit margins.

● The second example is a **marketing-orientated accountant** in the Finance Department of an international airline. He provides accurate and timely data to all his internal customers, at reducing cost. He sticks his neck out, and forecasts future costs as well as comparing with competitors on a wide range of measures. This paragon is also working on a special project with Marketing, Sales and Operations to establish for the first time profitability by First Class, Business Class and Economy, and by type of customer (Business and Leisure).

These are examples of Offensive Marketing. The employee is *involved*. He or she understands the company vision and strategies, and knows how to help implement them. You do not need to have 'Marketing' in your title to be an Offensive Marketer.

'. . . **building** . . .' Offensive Marketers are builders, not downsizers or asset strippers. Of course they strive for efficiency and low-cost operation, so as to form a platform for superior consumer value. This, and the ability to identify growing segments and to transform markets by anticipating the future, also enables them to *build* revenue growth.

In recent years, many Western companies have pursued downsizing as a strategy, lost market share, and, for those employees retaining their jobs, become miserable places to overwork in. They get locked in a cage of reducing cost and investment, squeezing out a precarious, non-sustainable profit growth.

'. . . **superior customer value** . . .' This is achieved when *customers* recognize that you are offering a combination of quality, price and service which is superior to your competitor's proposition. The ways in which superior value can be delivered are numerous – higher quality/ same price or same quality/lower price are just two of many possible gradations.

Superior customer value is difficult both to achieve and to sustain. It must be real rather than imagined, and based on objective customer measurement. Many companies say their products or services are superior, but if they have no hard evidence to prove it, they are probably deceiving themselves and undermining their future in the process.

Sustaining superior value requires consistently improving performance, since every innovation is eventually successfully copied and competition is constantly moving on. Superiority should first be developed against direct competitors and then against all-comers. Customer experiences in other categories can affect your own by raising expectations. For example, speed of service at McDonald's makes customers impatient about queuing at supermarket checkouts. Faster copiers make fax machines seem very slow.

There is a virtuous circle between delivering superior customer value and profit levels: the reward for consistently superior value is high customer loyalty, and retention. Based on studies by Bain and Company, 'the companies with the highest retention rates also earn the best profits'.[4]

Everyone in business has customers. They may be colleagues inside your company, to whom you are providing a service. They may be external customers or consumers who buy your products. Whoever they are, one thing is definite. *They* are the judges of whether you are delivering superior value, and their view on this topic is the only one that matters.

'. . . **very efficiently** . . .'   This phrase has a number of very specific meanings within the definition of Offensive Marketing. First, it means that companies need to match their strengths to the best opportunities in the market-place. Companies achieving an efficient match will have happy customers and happy shareholders. Secondly, it requires companies to be low-cost operators, with high productivity and relentless checking of whether each cost adds to customer value. Japanese companies like Toyota, Canon and Olympus are very skilful in this area, through target costing and value engineering.[5] If a company is a high-cost operator in relation to competitors, how can it possibly deliver superior value profitably?

'. . . **for above average profits** . . .'   'Above average' means better than industry norms on a range of profit measures such as return on sales (ROS), return on capital employed (ROCE) and economic value added (EVA), all of which will be reviewed in Chapter 2.

Profit is the reward earned by companies for building superior customer value very efficiently. As John Young, former CEO of Hewlett Packard, said, 'Yes, profit is a cornerstone of what we do – but it has never been the *point* in and of itself. The point, in fact, is to *win*, and winning is judged in the eyes of the consumer and by doing something you can be proud of.'[6]

Offensive Marketing is chiefly focused on generating *long-term* profit growth. If a company consistently invests in relevant new products or services, controls risk by rigorous testing of alternatives and keeps an iron hand on cost, it is likely to deliver constantly improving customer value and to enjoy both short-term and long-term profit growth.

## Offensive Marketing Defined for the Not-For-Profit Sector

> Offensive Marketing involves every employee in building superior customer experiences very efficiently in the most cost effective way

You will notice that this definition has much in common with the 'for business' definition of Offensive Marketing. It involves every employee; seeks superior customer satisfaction, though in terms of experience rather than value, since price is not a factor; stresses efficiency; and focuses on cost-effectiveness rather than profit.

While this book does not deal specifically with the not-for-profit or public sector, many of the approaches, processes and tools contained within it are applicable to these sectors. For charities, both definitions of Offensive Marketing may be relevant – the 'not for profit' one for fundraising, and the 'business' one for commercial activities like retailing and mail order.

## Short-term Pressures Facing Offensive Marketers in Business

You may observe that most companies have short-term profit problems, and feel that the definition of Offensive Marketing does not address the constant tension between the short term and the long term. A question many marketing people in business ask with feeling goes something like this:

> **We hear what you say about Offensive Marketing, and we would love our company, Amalgamated Leisure (AL), to adopt it. But what can we do when they say it's not affordable? Despite our protests, the company under invests in plant, new products and new services. It has cut advertising, and our leisure attractions badly need refurbishment. Prices have been increased and we are losing customers. Our revenue is flat, but AL has increased profits by cutting more costs. We spend sixty hours a week running to stand still. Short-term profits are grossly overstated, since they contain no element of future investment.**

> **So what is the answer?** In practice, AL has no future with its current strategies. In time it will deservedly get a new owner or a new Chief Executive. This will provide an opportunity for a major profits write-down or a big reorganization charge, which will give AL the funds and breathing space to convert to Offensive Marketing . . . if it has the good sense to do so.

### *Offensive Marketers must hit short-term and long-term targets*

While Offensive Marketing is a long-term approach, which can take years to develop fully, the reality is that marketers have to hit short-term objectives in order to be around to enjoy the fruits of their long-term efforts.

Managing directors are unlikely to be impressed by Marketers, who, having missed profit budgets two years running, point to the brilliance of their new five-year plan. If the Managing Director is polite in these circumstances, and this is equally unlikely, he will stress that his only interest is in next year's budget, because he knows that if it is not hit, neither of you will be there in two years, never mind five.

In the short term, Offensive Marketers need to be strong tactically and very good executors. There are many steps they can take to leverage short-term profits without mortgaging the future, and some of these are covered in Chapter 2 (page 92). For the long term, they require vision and strategic skills. Marketers have to run the short term and long term concurrently, working with both hands at the same time. This is why both strategy and execution are strongly emphasized in this book.

Clearly, marketers have to recognize conflicts and trade-offs between the short and long term. This section will illustrate the dilemma faced by Offensive Marketers in pursuing long-term change, and the need for patience.

The lead-times necessary to change internal attitudes and radically improve consumer value are at least two years and often longer. It is certainly not feasible within a fiscal year, and will usually reduce profits during this period, since investment will precede the revenue benefit. That is why Offensive Marketers also need to be skilled in turning up the profit meter in the short term, in order to compensate.

Table 5 illustrates by example the difference between an Offensive Marketing company and an Inoffensive Marketer in the same industry. Taking a moral tone, we will call them the Virtuous plc and the Dissembler plc.

On the face of it, both companies are making similar operating profits of 14%. However, the *quality* of their profits is very different. Virtuous plc has a higher gross profit margin because its superior proposition enables it to command a premium price in the market-place. It is *investing* 23% of its sales revenue in future development – in advertising, R & D and capital investment. This is clearly no guarantee of future success unless the money is wisely spent, but Virtuous plc has a superior proposition, launches successful new products, has a good innovation pipeline and sound future prospects.

What about Dissembler plc, a competitor in the same industry making identical profit margins? As you can see, Dissembler is spending weakly on the future – its investment as a percentage of sales is a miserable 5% of revenue. It has unsustainable profit margins, which disguise a grisly future: a bare new product cupboard, a weakening consumer franchise and inability to finance effective R & D, plant upgrade or advertising programmes.

**Table 5. Example: quality of profits comparison.**[7]

| % | Virtuous plc (%) | Dissembler plc (%) |
|---|---|---|
| Sales revenue | 100 | 100 |
| Cost of goods sold | 43 | 61 |
| Gross profit margin | 57 | 39 |
| Advertising | 11 | 3 |
| R & D | 5 | – |
| Capital investment | 7 | 2 |
| Investment ratio | 23 | 5 |
| Operating expenses | 20 | 20 |
| Operating profit | 14 | 14 |
| Key trends→ | • Past 5-year revenue growth 10% p.a.<br>• Heavy advertising investment in new, improved products<br>• Premium-priced products, new plant, so low cost of goods sold | • Flat revenue, declining volume<br>• No recent product innovation. Little advertising<br>• Discounted pricing, so high cost of goods sold |

The table illustrates that profit viewed in isolation is a misleading measure. **For the Offensive Marketer, a more relevant measure is profit and investment as a percent of sales**. Investment is defined as 'anything with a payback longer than one year'. This covers advertising, R & D, capital investment, training, strategic market research and most direct marketing (but not sales promotion, which should pay back quickly). These are the costs which many companies cut to inflate short-term profits.

Let's take one final look at Virtuous plc and Dissembler plc's profit profile before moving on. For Offensive Marketers, current-year profits will include large investment losses for new products recently launched or still in the pipeline. In other words, profits from established products will exceed total company profits (Table 6). This second perspective on Dissembler confirms that it is severely under-investing in its business, and probably faces big trouble ahead. By contrast, Virtuous's investment in tomorrow should enable it to sustain or improve on its 14% operating profit.

**Table 6.  The make-up of 14 per cent operating profits.**

| Factor | Virtuous plc (%) | Dissembler plc (%) |
|---|---|---|
| Profit on existing products over 3 years old | 21 | 15 |
| Losses on products recently launched or in development | (7) | (1) |
| Total operating profits | 14 | 14 |

How can Dissembler convert into a virtuous cycle? It can start by buying this book, which outlines how this can be done. However, the path will be hard and long, and it is certain that Dissembler will have to raise investment and cut profit margins. How should you react if Dissembler offers you a highly paid job? Only consider it if there is new management with the time and credibility to pursue a genuine investment strategy.

Having defined Offensive Marketing, here is a recap:

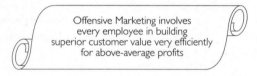

Offensive Marketing involves
every employee in building
superior customer value very efficiently
for above-average profits

I know definitions are tiresome, but this one is the lynch-pin of Offensive Marketing and the core of the remainder of the book. You've bought the book, so you may as well remember it.

## How Well Does Microsoft Meet the Offensive Marketing Definition?[8]

In the past, Microsoft has been an Offensive Marketer, although it has never employed many people with a marketing title. Now let's check Microsoft against the Offensive Marketing definition.

'. . . involves every employee . . .'    Microsoft employees appear to be heavily involved. They are often driven people and know in broad terms what the company is trying to achieve – speed, leadership, superiority. Although Microsoft is strong technically, it is customer driven. However, its style is often confrontational – what Bill Gates called 'high bandwidth communication' – and internal communications are less than perfect.

'. . . **superior customer value** . . .' Microsoft's main strength has been its ability to anticipate and act upon the future now, and to constantly drive for product improvement, as summed up by three quotations:

> '**In our industry a disproportionate amount of economic value occurs in the early stages of a product's life . . . so there is real *value* to speed.**'
> – Louis Gerstner, Chairman of IBM

> '**One of the real keys was . . . we were always a year or two ahead of where demand was really going to be . . . and we were generally guessing right.**'
> – Microsoft employee

> '**With few exceptions, they've never shipped a good product in its first version. But they never give up, and eventually get it right.**'
> – Microsoft competitor

'. . . **above-average profit**.' There has never been any doubt about Microsoft's performance on this score. While profit margins in PC hardware are paper-thin, Microsoft software achieves 25% net profit, and over 20% return on total assets.

## Will Microsoft remain an Offensive Marketer?

The answer is probably 'Yes', but this is by no means certain. Whether it will be so successful as an Offensive Marketer of the future is open to question. In the past, Microsoft has been fortunate in its market, which has boomed world-wide, and in its dominance of computer operating systems, which will become less important over time. Furthermore, growth of PCs is now slowing, and quality of software is high, so that customers do not feel obliged to rush out and buy the latest upgrade.

Microsoft's success as an Offensive Marketer of the future depends heavily on its ability to understand the interface between computers, TVs and telecommunications, and to select the right points to attack it. If they get this right, their technical skills, people, competitiveness and sense of urgency will drive them to new wins. If not, they may struggle.

I have been advised by more than one respected voice to remove Microsoft from this chapter, and understand the reasons for the viewpoint. Nike might be a safer choice as an exemplar of Offensive Marketing, but I will take the risk, and stay with Microsoft. As you read this in 2000, you will know whether I got it right.

**Figure 2.**

Like Microsoft, the Offensive Marketer anticipates, confronts issues frankly, decides, invests and takes risks. S/he does not compromise, side-step, temporize or shelve issues. The British disease of deferral drives us to our home ground . . . backs against the wall.

## Why isn't Everyone an Offensive Marketer?

Since Offensive Marketing is a 'best practice' approach to marketing, by definition few companies will fully achieve it. What is more surprising is that so few companies even attempt to climb the heights of Offensive Marketing.

Theodore Levitt's comment is still disturbingly relevant:

**'When it comes to the marketing concept today, a solid stone wall often seems to separate word and deed. In spite of the best intentions and energetic efforts of many highly able people, the effective implementation of the marketing concept has generally eluded them.'**[9]

The practice of Offensive Marketing remains the exception rather than the rule. Why?

1. **Most companies lack a distinctive vision or strategy**. The typical company rushes along from year to year in frenzied activity, without a clear vision of the future, and lacking distinctive or superior propositions. It will cut costs, undertake 'initiatives' and housekeep efficiently. It will avoid undue risks or major investments, keep a close eye on competitors so that it can remain in step and over reward its top executives. All may be well in a normal year. But in times of major change or faced by radically new competition, this company will stumble badly, looking vainly for someone else to copy.

2. **Short-termism**. This is a well-known disorder, especially in the UK and USA, though less so in Germany or Japan. Companies are run on a fiscal year, rather than a three- to five-year basis, for the benefit of pension funds and institutions ('shareholders'). They pay more attention to security analysts than to customers. Any expenditure with a payback of over one year will be regarded with suspicion, even hostility.

3. **Lack of understanding of the Offensive Marketing approach**. Companies either fail to grasp the importance of making customer relationships and satisfaction their central justification, or are unable to determine how to do this profitably.

4. **Lack of character**. Many companies understand the basics of the Offensive Marketing approach, but do not have the qualities of courage, determination, persistence and risk-taking necessary to apply it. Offensive Marketing is less a matter of intelligence and ability – since most companies have plenty of both – than of attitudes, strategy and teamwork. It is a set of shared values, grounded in a commitment to superior consumer benefits and low-cost operation.

5. **Misguided Marketing Departments**. Conventional marketing has often become a victim of its own success. The acceptance of the Marketing Department has multiplied its coordination role and created floods of paper. The day-to-day pressure is so great there is no time left to innovate. In many companies the Marketing Department, far from acting as the touchstone to innovation and enterprise, has itself become a bureaucracy, spewing paper, acting as a passive coordinator.

We will return to this theme later in the chapter.

## Has Marketing Failed?

This question is increasingly being asked, especially by Financial Directors, and even by Managing Directors.

It sometimes hangs over discussions about long-term investments, such as R & D, advertising, new-product investment, customer service improvements or long-term warranties, all of which tend to be associated with marketing. While few would disagree with the theory of the marketing approach, many would question the cost and efficiency with which it has been implemented.

Arguments used by a Finance Director might include the following:

1. ' **"Marketing" is not giving us a clear view of the future.** We spend a lot of money on consumer research, but it seems to tell us little about the future. Consumers can't articulate their future needs or priorities, especially if they know less than we do about tomorrow's technology and the vistas it will open. I'm concerned that the glut of information we have about the past is clogging our entrepreneurial arteries.' (Yes, some enlightened Finance Directors think like this.)

2. '**We're constantly being surprised and outflanked by our competitors.** They seem to be getting to market quicker with new products, and we spend our time running to catch up. We have a big new-product development programme, but the failure rate of new products is still incredibly high, and we even go national with new programmes which haven't been fully tested. We're always on the back foot.'

3. '**I am not convinced that marketing-orientated companies are necessarily the most profitable.** Some of the most profitable companies in recent years have been built up via acquisitions, deals, low operating costs and speed of reaction. There is nothing special about their products or services, but the companies are run by entrepreneurs.'

4. '**We spend a vast amount on advertising, but I question the means used to evaluate it.** Marketers, aided by their advertising agencies, always say we are underspending, but can't even justify the present level of expenditure.'

5. '**I notice that the fast-moving consumer goods companies which originated marketing seem to have lost the initiative to retailers.** Many of them appear to be struggling in mature markets with undistinctive brands and some are producing low-margin private label products for retailers just to survive. What on earth can they teach us?'

**What do you think of these arguments and which are most effective? Are they fair?** Table 7 shows an objective top-line response.

**Table 7.**

| Question | Response |
| --- | --- |
| 1. 'Marketing is not giving us a clear view of the future.' | This is a matter for the Board, following the marketing approach.<br>Your points about research and data-glut are well made. |
| 2. 'We're constantly being surprised and outflanked by our competitors.' | This is because you are following not leading.<br>However, your point about the high failure rate of new products is a powerful indictment of 'marketers'. |
| 3. 'I am not convinced that marketing-orientated companies are necessarily the most profitable.' | An increasing body of academic research, and the PIMS (profit impact of marketing strategy) studies suggest that companies with a strong customer orientation achieve above-average profit margins and growth in the long term. |
| 4. 'We spend a vast amount on advertising, but I question the means used to evaluate it.' | Tools to evaluate advertising have improved greatly in recent years.<br>It sounds as if your company is not using them. |
| 5. 'I notice that the fast-moving consumer goods companies which originated marketing seem to have lost the initiative to retailers.' | They tend to be in mature markets like food or household goods.<br>The originators of marketing – companies like Procter & Gamble, Unilever, Colgate, Kellogg's, SmithKline Beecham, Mars, Nestlé and Heinz continue to do well.<br>Many of their followers in food and household goods are struggling. |

Perhaps the most decisive sign that 'marketing works' is the speed with which the marketing approach has spread to almost every industry, from financial services to leisure, from automobiles to copiers, from airlines to accountancy, from stately homes to metal piping.

Few people today would argue with a business model that focuses on two major linked objectives – minimizing cost and maximizing customer value. Many of the apparent criticisms of marketing, as you will already have observed, are in fact implied criticisms of marketers or Marketing Departments.

## Have Marketers Failed Marketing?

**A critical view.** Table 8 gives a chart from a presentation to a blue-chip company with a long-established Marketing Department.

---
### Table 8.  Brand management is often poorly practised.

- Too much personnel turnover, too little experience
- Inability to justify spending and resist cuts
- Rooted in Marketing Departments, limited knowledge of finance or manufacturing
- Inferior people-management skills v. Sales and Manufacturing
- Housekeeping or firefighting
- Interface on international brands between local and global still creaks
- Superficial business analysis and consumer understanding, implemented with amateur project management skills
---

At this presentation no one walked out. Nobody complained. There were few questions at the end and much agreement.

**A balanced view.** Table 9 evaluates the past performance of marketers by a Managing Director, drafted in the form of a simplified personnel appraisal form.

---
### Table 9.  Marketing Department: appraisal form.

Name: *Marketing Department*
Appraised by: *Managing Director*

**Key Strengths:**
1. Contribution to consumer-driven long term business strategy.
2. Effective coordination of business activities on brand basis, across departments.
3. Intelligent, highly motivated people who work hard.
4. Runs communications function reasonably well, though has difficulty justifying expenditure levels.
5. Does good job in identifying existing consumer needs, monitoring competitive position and developing improvement plans.
6. Department role well accepted across the company.

**Key Weaknesses**
1. Limited knowledge of and interest in operations or technology.
2. Planning, forecasting and project management skills below standard.
3. Performance on new product development disappointing, with low output of genuine innovations, high failure rate.
4. Business analysis and financial skills insufficient.
5. Inability to spot new opportunities early, or to correctly anticipate change – spends too much time catching up.
6. Fails to evangelize the marketing approach across the company.
7. Lacks the data to win arguments within the Board about long-term investment and does not fight hard enough.
---

## So, are Marketing Departments necessary?

Looking at this appraisal form, which some may consider generous to marketers, you may wonder whether Marketing Departments are needed. Religions can flower without churches, or even, as the Quakers have shown, without priests. Marks & Spencer, a strong exponent of superior customer value and high profit margins, has succeeded for a hundred years without a Marketing Department (although it has a Marketing Services Department). Mercedes, with a distinctive and premium-priced product range, and good margins by car industry standards, only started its Marketing Department three years ago. Many Japanese companies manage successfully without specialist marketers, but any marketer would point out that their profit margins are often in low single figures, and their record in building shareholder value is poor, in recent years.

There are only a limited number of Western companies successfully applying the marketing approach without the help of a Marketing Department, and few are disbanded. There are sound reasons for having one, and here are the main ones:

1. **Double perspective**. Marketing Department is the only one with a clear view of external customer needs and internal company skills. The ability to understand and match these is critical to business success (Figure 3).

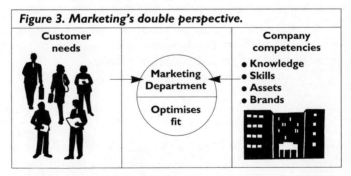

**Figure 3. Marketing's double perspective.**

Customer needs → Marketing Department / Optimises fit ← Company competencies
- Knowledge
- Skills
- Assets
- Brands

   Finance and Human Resource Departments have a bird's-eye view of the internal workings of a company, but little knowledge of customers and their needs, so their perspective is one-dimensional.

2. **Strategy and planning input**. Successful company strategies start by defining future market and customer needs. They then target those needs which their particular competencies enable them to meet in a superior way. Marketing people are well placed to set and lead this strategic agenda, because of their familiarity with market needs, their ability to forecast

future trends and their objective knowledge of company competencies.

3. **Market and segment prioritization**. Marketers can advise which markets and market segments have most future attraction, which should be dropped, and how resources should be allocated across markets and brands.

4. **Coordination and long-term project management**. Most major improvements and innovations involve wide cross-departmental cooperation, and frequently include many external agencies. The Marketing Department can coordinate proactively, using business planning processes, especially on multi-country or global projects.

5. **Category and brand management**. Someone needs to develop, plan and monitor the day-to-day business, with eyes fixed on the customer. Depending on the type of business, this will include tasks like sales forecasting, customer service, support programmes, results monitoring, analysing competitive activity and so on.

6. **Expertise**. Marketing people should possess specialized competencies, such as:

   ● Ability to anticipate future customer needs, through knowledge of market and technology trends
   ● Skill in value analysing use of resources – for example, evaluating the customer value of the various elements in a product or service and relating each of these to their cost.
   ● Business analysis and strategy development.
   ● Management and motivation of people, over whom they have no line authority.
   ● Skill in identifying opportunities and allocating resources to areas of best return.

In summary, then, the Marketing Department has a potentially very important and unique role. However, marketers spend the vast majority of their time on day-to-day operations and (often unwillingly) neglect longer-term issues such as strategy development and innovation. They also change jobs much too often. If Marketing Departments are to meet their potential in future, these issues must be tackled head-on.

## The Future is Even More Offensive Marketing

Offensive Marketing is a set of attitudes, principles and processes which release the potential of the marketing approach to transform businesses.

It is designed to make your competitors followers. Offensive Marketing is not a formula, a fad or an academic theory. It is a demanding and practical approach to business, which requires courage, persistence and determination. That is the reason why it is practised by only a minority of companies.

There are five elements in the Offensive Marketing approach, and these form the structure of this book. They are Profitable, Offensive, Integrated, Strategic and Effectively Executed, summarized by the mnemonic POISE (Table 10).

| **Table 10. Offensive Marketing: Poise** | |
| --- | --- |
| **P:** Profitable | ● Proper balance between firm's needs for profit and customer's need for value |
| **O:** Offensive | ● Must lead market, take risks and make competitors followers |
| **I:** Integrated | ● Marketing approach must permeate whole company |
| **S:** Strategic | ● Probing analysis leading to a winning strategy |
| **E:** Effectively Executed | ● Strong and disciplined execution on a daily basis |

## POISE spelt slowly

Let us take a look at the individual ingredients of Offensive Marketing in broad terms:

**Profitable**: The object of marketing is not just to increase market share or to provide good value for consumers, but to increase profit. Offensive Marketers will encounter conflicts between giving consumers what they want and running the company efficiently. One of their skills is to reach the right balance between these sometimes opposing elements.

**Offensive:** An offensive approach calls for an attitude of mind which decides independently what is best for a company, rather than waiting for competition to make the first move.

**Integrated:** Where marketing is integrated, it permeates the whole company. It challenges all employees to relate their work to the needs of the market-place and to balance it against the firm's profit needs.

**Strategic:** Winning strategies are rarely developed without intensive analysis and careful consideration of alternatives. A business operated on a day-to-day basis, with no long-term marketing purpose, is more likely to be a follower than a leader.

**Effectively Executed:** No amount of intelligent approach work is of any use without effective execution. Effective execution is not just a matter of good implementation by marketing people. It is also vitally dependent on the relationship between marketing and other departments, and on how far common strategies and objectives exist.

## How Marketers Can Spearhead Offensive Marketing

To be effective in future, and to respond purposefully to justified criticism, Marketing Departments and marketers will need to change radically in the next few years. Best-practice marketers are already moving forward on five fronts.

### 1. Structure

In mature Marketing Departments, line marketing people frequently spend 80–90 per cent of their time on short-term tactical activity. In new ones, they often have a service role, focusing on marketing activities. The result is that marketers often fail to lead the development of corporate strategy, a role they are ideally qualified to spearhead because of their double perspective. The vacuum is often filled by Finance people, inadequately, because they only have a single perspective.

**Table 11. Typical time allocation in a mature Marketing Department.**

| Development | Housekeeping | |
|---|---|---|
| ● Strategy development | ● Sales promotion | ● Internal |
| ● Innovative market | ● Routine advertising | communications |
| research | ● Routine market | ● Distributor |
| ● New product | research | marketing |
| development | ● Pricing/discounts | ● Routine analysis |
| ● Value improvement | ● Sales forecasting | ● Budgeting |
| ● Channel strategy | ● Range extension | ● Writing briefs |
| ● Relationship | ● Monitoring results | ● Administration |
| Marketing | | |
| ● External | | |
| communication        **20%** | | **80%** |

Source: Oxford Corporate Consultants Client Surveys

To remedy this, marketers need to do two things. First, restructure Marketing Departments so that the most gifted line marketers have time to think about strategy and win the future. In particular, contract back inessential administration to other departments wherever possible – one marketer's comment is indicative, 'I think often in my organization, marketing is a "skip".'[10]

Secondly, marketers need to transform their relationships with other departments, whose efforts are critical to the success of Offensive Marketing. It is remarkable how inward-looking marketers can be. They spend vast amounts of time attending seminars on how to get the best out of their advertising agencies, but give little thought to the much more important issue of how to get the best out of other departments, like Finance, Sales and Operations. This merits more attention and will be fully addressed in Chapter 4 on integration. Above all, marketers need to spend more time talking to customers and consumers (Table 12).

**Table 12.  Time allocation by contact point.**

| Contact point | | % of time |
|---|---|---|
| External agencies | *Advertising, direct marketing, packaging, research, sales promotion* | 26% |
| Others within Marketing Department | *Colleagues up, down, across* | 26% |
| On own in office | *Analysis, planning, coordination, administration* | 25% |
| Other departments (Sales, Operations, etc.) | *Routine 18% strategic 2%* | 20% |
| With customers or consumers | | 3% |

*Source:* author's estimate.

The need within Marketing Departments to separate development from housekeeping has become obvious. One way to achieve this is by having Brand Equity Managers, with overall responsibility for business performance but primary focus on managing the six development drivers capable of dramatically improving competitive position (Table 13).

---

**Table 13.  The six marketing development drivers.**

1.  Deep understanding of consumer needs and habits, and awareness of likely future changes in markets and technology.
2.  Strategy and portfolio management, setting tomorrow's agenda for the whole company
3.  Product and service development
4.  Prioritizing and monitoring investment in plant, service improvements and consumer relationships
5.  Marketing value analysis – looking at every product or service cost and relating it to consumer benefit
6.  Actively managing the Marketing approach across departments, and identifying key company competencies to be exploited.

---

Housekeeping – important tasks like sales forecasting, distributor or trade Marketing, sales promotion, direct marketing and routine communication – can be handled by specialists in a central service department, working closely with Brand Equity Managers. Figure 4 shows how this approach to marketing organization could work in a hotel company, using Marketing Equity people to manage the six key development drivers.

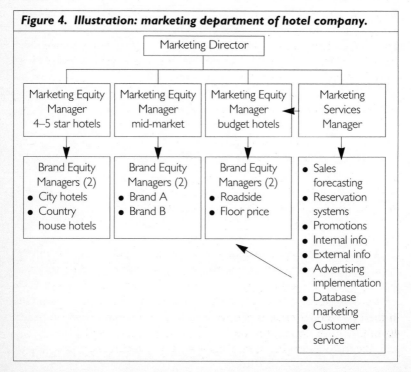

**Figure 4.  Illustration: marketing department of hotel company.**

In recent years, Marketing Services have been downsized or dispensed with altogether. The result has been to overload line marketing executives so that only the short term gets done. There is a need to increase the number of service specialists to enable the Brand Equity Managers to develop the future, the task they are best qualified to do. People in Marketing Services have two potential career paths – becoming long-term specialists or moving to brand equity management.

While in some companies this would lead to an increase in the number of marketing people, in others the new structure would generate greater efficiency from existing people, by allocating them to areas best suited to their skills, by adopting more disciplined process management (see (4) below) and by leveraging information more effectively through IT.

## 2. Relationship Marketing

One of the biggest future opportunities for marketers is leadership in further developing Relationship Marketing.

In the days before most readers of this book were born, local shop-keepers relied strongly on it. Their product range, brands stocked and pricing were usually similar to competitors, and Relationship Marketing was the key differentiator. This involved understanding the specific needs of each customer, and meeting them exactly. For instance, Mrs Jones liked her bacon streaky and thinly cut, and enjoyed a good chat, especially about her dogs. She wasn't very price conscious, wanted to buy the best and was usually responsive to suggestions for additional purchases. By contrast, Mrs Brown always shopped with a list, was very price conscious, interested in bargains and had no time for 'idle chat'.

Today, as a frequent international flier arriving at a check-in desk, you may (or may not) be told that as usual you have been booked a non-smoker aisle seat, a vegetarian meal, are in line for an upgrade from Business Class to First Class, and may be interested in a frequent flier 'spouse' offer to Rome next month. In this case, the airline has used your database derived from past requests and purchase habits to offer you an individualized travel experience.

Relationship Marketing represents a future opportunity not just to Marketers of high ticket items like cars, credit cards and financial services, but also to fast-moving consumer goods marketers. Why else does Procter & Gamble have a consumer database of 44 million households in the USA (and 7 million plus in the UK), with Kraft a close second at 40 million? Of course, the quality of these databases will vary widely, and, like many emerging areas, Relationship Marketing is prone to hype.

However, a number of important factors will continue to drive its growth:

**Falling costs of IT.** In the past few years, cost of holding and developing consumer databases has dived, and will continue to do so. Telecom costs are also declining, though not nearly so steeply.

**Feasibility of building high-quality databases.** Companies can build their own through mailings, questionnaires and promotions, buy them in from specialist operators, or, as usually happens, do both. Some of these databases contain quite detailed information, like type and age of car, size and neighbourhood of house, pets owned, frequency and location of holidays, and so on. In the USA, Donnelly's complete database includes 87 million of the 95 million households in the country, and many of these have answered seventy questions.[11]

**Growing sophistication of consumers.** As every marketer knows, today's consumers are very much in the driving seat. They have strong bargaining power, often buy in markets with surplus capacity, and can become overwhelmed with an excess of choice. Consumers have also learned the lessons of the recession years, seek superior value, and want to be treated as individuals, not as anonymous numbers or mass-market fodder.

**Response by marketers to consumer trends.** Modern Relationship Marketing views customers as potential long-term income streams, not as 'one-off' selling opportunities. Marketers of fast-moving consumer goods have always recognized this instinctively. They know that the cost of generating a single sale is uneconomic, and that the success of any brand depends on its ability to achieve repeat purchase. However, by heavily price promoting parity products, thereby investing in large numbers of price-driven brand switchers, they have often failed to translate this logic into reality.

Some of the new marketers, in categories like eating out, retailing, software, telecom and insurance, have led the way in Relationship Marketing. They have developed high-quality databases, containing information on demographics, life stage, lifestyle and past purchases, and used these to build relationships. First Direct Bank is one of the best practitioners. Many Relationship Marketers also use loyalty cards and clubs to both provide incentives and gain further information.

A further reason why Relationship Marketing appeals to companies is the opportunity it gives to make direct contact with the customer, and so remove reliance on intermediaries. This is fundamentally changing distribution channel marketing.

**Improved measurement of customer economics**. Two valuable tools in Relationship Marketing are long-term customer profit and share of customer.

Long-term customer profit involves calculating how long you are likely to retain a particular customer, estimating value of purchases less cost of retention over that period, and adding on a bonus for customer referrals. These calculations are sometimes referred to as lifetime customer value (LCV). Knowing LCV can guide you on how much to spend on customer retention, and how much on gaining new customers.

Various studies have demonstrated not only the obvious point that existing customers are more profitable than new ones, but also that companies tend to underinvest in existing customers. One of the best studies shows that, across a number of markets, *a 5% increase in annual customer retention can increase total company operating profits by over 50%*.[12] It illustrates that existing loyal customers are by far the most valuable because they:

- Involve no business acquisition cost.
- Buy a broader range of products due to familiarity with the company's total product line.
- Cost less to service, through understanding the company's business system and using it efficiently.
- Recommend products to other customers.

*The One to One Future*[13] claims that most businesses lose 25% of their customers annually, **and yet most companies spend *six times* as much on generating new customers as on retaining existing ones**. I'm tempted to repeat that. Think about it carefully.

Assuming you avoid this trap, and achieve a high customer retention rate, 'share of customer' is another valuable measure to consider. It should supplement 'share of market', not replace it. 'Share of customer' indicates the depth of commitment each customer has to you, and charts your opportunity to increase revenue among existing customers.

'Share of customer is the brand's market share of the individual.'[14] To take a simple example, heavy credit card users in the USA carry 6.2 cards: **what is your share of total credit card spending among these heavy users, and is it increasing or decreasing?** Clearly, it is important to define the competitive framework. For instance, in the above example, should you include short-term borrowing from banks in your 'share of customer'?

'Share of customer', especially among heavy users, is also an important measure in fast-moving consumer goods. Together with loyalty, it indicates the level of commitment to your brand, when compared with competitors, on a trend basis. Brands with low loyalty scores and poor share of customer will decline, even though supported by a steadily increasing series of price reductions, which may even speed up their journey to oblivion.

**Ability to develop tailored products and services economically**. Although the move by manufacturers to mass customization has been greatly exaggerated, techniques to tailor products efficiently on a low-volume basis are certainly improving. This is particularly apparent in the car industry, where each basic model has scores of options. Stoves, a cooker manufacturer, offers consumers in Germany a wide menu of alternatives, allows them to construct their own cooker and aims to deliver within two weeks. Cost of a tailored version is about 10% more than an 'off-the-shelf' cooker.[15]

However, this trend should be viewed with caution. Set against the growing *capability* to customize products is the reality that high-volume manufacture of a limited range of items should always be more efficient. Recognizing the consumer desire for better value, and the trade-off between price and choice, many leading manufacturers are deliberately cutting unnecessary choice, in setting up low-cost pan-European manufacturing sites. One has a ten-year plan to reduce its number of product varieties in Europe from 2000 to 200, in its quest to improve consumer value, by driving down price in real terms.

Services are usually much easier to tailor economically to the needs of groups or individuals, especially as IT costs decline.

**Fragmentation of media**. The increasing cost of mass media, especially TV, makes it affordable and effective only for larger brands. How to market secondary brands efficiently has become a big issue for marketers. Relationship Marketing has a part to play in the solution. At the same time, media is becoming more customized with the growth of specialist TV channels and magazines, so offering further opportunities for tightly targeted Relationship Marketing.

This brief review of Relationship Marketing is designed to highlight its importance as a spearhead and opportunity for Offensive Marketers in the future. It influences every aspect of marketing, but especially strategy, integration, allocation of resources, segmentation, branding, communication and channels.

## 3. Competency development

At present, some marketers lack the necessary skills to be effective in today's environment, and these deficiencies will become cruelly exposed in future.

Tomorrow's marketer needs to be:

- Knowledgeable about the essentials of operations, the supply chain and channel management
- Able to understand the key technologies of the business
- Literate in finance and IT
- Skilful in project planning and management
- A first-class business analyst, using data creatively to develop succinct action plans
- A skilful manager and motivator of the scores of people, inside and outside the company, who help implement the marketing approach
- Expert in opportunity identification, market research, advertising strategy and evaluation, direct marketing, customer service, etc.

This inventory of required skills is much broader than today's typical specification of a marketer. If marketers are truly to help realize the full potential of the marketing approach, more will have formal marketing qualifications, and be drawn from technical and financial as well as arts backgrounds. Yesterday's profile of the marketer with an arts degree, a cavalier lack of interest in technology and operations and weak project management skills, will become irrelevant tomorrow.

Table 14 summarizes today's and tomorrow's required Marketing Department competencies. There will be a move from marketing management to corporate business management, as the table demonstrates.

**Table 14. Marketers' competencies.**

| Today: | Tomorrow: |
|---|---|
| • Business analysis<br>• Innovation<br>• Project management<br>• Coordination<br>• IT skills<br>• Strategic skills<br>• Cost management<br>• Consumer understanding<br>• Marketing techniques | • Today's, plus<br>○ Financial skills<br>○ Technology knowledge<br>○ Database marketing<br>○ Cross-department leadership<br>○ Operations know-how<br>○ Corporate strategy<br>○ Alliances and acquisitions |
| **Marketing management** | **Corporate business management** |

Marketers will need to develop both today's and tomorrow's skills. These skills should be put in context. For instance, in Finance or Operations, marketers will not be expected to build new costing or inventory control systems, since these are specialized skills. But they will be expected to understand the basic principles, so that they can ask intelligent questions and specify their needs. Despite this qualification, you may still argue that this list of marketers' competencies looks like a list for general management. This is no coincidence – tomorrow's marketers will become increasingly well equipped for general management.

## 4. Marketing process management

For many years, people in Operations and Selling, and, to some degree, Finance, have followed process management. Their activities have been divided into a series of processes, which are clearly understood and can be equally accurately evaluated.

For example, Operations people may be assessed on number of transactions, or units produced, quality, timeliness, customer service levels and cost. Sales people are measured by revenue, cost of sales, quality of relationships and, in the case of a field sales force, interviews, orders per day, distribution, service levels and so on.

All these activities are evaluated quantitatively, either fully or in part. Performance can be compared with objectives and previous year, across other business units or countries, or even benchmarked against external companies. And most of these selling or operations activities are executed in a disciplined way, following prescribed sequences, which have been developed and refined over the years.

Outside a handful of companies marketers seem to have escaped much of this. Ask a McDonald's Manager what he plans to do tomorrow and he will tell you precisely what he expects to accomplish – perhaps £4,600 revenue, with four full-time and six part-time staff, at a cost of X, in fourteen trading hours. Ask any marketing people what they plan to do tomorrow, and the answers will understandably vary widely, a mishmash of meetings, phone calls, writing and paper pushing.

And how will they do it? Do they have an agreed 'best way' of doing things, like the McDonald's Manager, with his procedure book? Probably not. Even within companies, they often approach the processes of new product development, advertising evaluation, opportunity identification and a whole host of tasks in different ways, if indeed they use formal process management at all.

And how do marketers evaluate their business performance? Market share? 'Yes, our market share has declined, but we were heavily out-advertised by competition, and anyway our profits have grown this year because we cut spending and increased prices.' Innovation? This is hard to measure, and lead-times are long, while marketing people change jobs or assignments frequently. Quality of advertising? 'Well, our advertising awareness shot up this year. No, sales didn't increase . . . we're not sure why.'

Marketers have managed to avoid many of the rigours of accountability and the disciplines of process management, because their activities are diverse, often hard to predict, and difficult to measure. Disciplines have sometimes been resisted because they 'stifle creativity'. Marketers tend to be very articulate people, and some would rather operate on the qualitative high ground of intuition and judgement than on the plebeian territory of boring quantitative evaluation.

This is all going to change, and rapidly. Marketing is becoming more scientific, more accountable and more process driven. The best marketers are leading the way, and Managing Directors, with Financial Directors at their side, will insist that this change takes place.

Table 15 summarizes key changes in marketing management style.

**Table 15. Future changes in marketing management style.**

|  | Yesterday | Today | Tomorrow |
|---|---|---|---|
| **Style** | Seat of pants | Marketing planning | Strategic process management |
| **Accountability** | Low | Medium | High |
| **Measurability** | Low | Medium | High |
| **Orientation** | Focus on Marketing Dept and agencies | Cross-departmental coordination | Cross-departmental management |

The majority of this book – Chapters 5 to 15 – is concerned with developing winning strategies and executing them. It will treat these topics creatively yet scientifically, covering principles then processes.

## 5. Priorities

Changes in marketing structures, competencies required and a more disciplined process-driven management style will all provide Marketers with the opportunity to make a quantum leap in effectiveness. They will also lead to new priorities (Table 16).

**Table 16.  Future priorities for Marketing Departments.**

| Priorities | How |
|---|---|
| Corporate strategy business development | ● New structures<br>● New competencies<br>● Cross-departmental focus |
| Broaden competencies | ● Widen personnel selection criteria<br>● Build technical, IT, financial skills among marketers<br>● Rotate people across departments |
| Evangelize Marketing approach across company | ● Regular market reports in readable form for all departments<br>● Invite other Managers to sales meetings, away days<br>● Enhance motivating skills of marketers |
| Strengthen Marketing's leadership role | ● Finance and Operations Managers to make regular field visits<br>● Marketers to identify and exploit companies' key skills |
| More outward-facing Marketing Departments | ● Marketing people to spend more time with customers and Operations people<br>● Marketers to give others full credit for marketing successes |

Above all, marketers need to encourage everyone in the company to talk to customers, as do the Japanese: 'The Japanese have long considered marketing a business for everyone in the company, not a professional pursuit of some specialists, and Japanese engineers, designers and top managers have a tradition of participating in sales efforts, marketing research and service calls.'[16]

## A Portrait of Five Marketing Misfits

As a contrast to the route best-practice Offensive Marketers are taking towards the future, we will examine a number of different attitudes towards the marketing approach, which prejudice both the understanding of its real nature and its effective application. Five have been picked out for demonstration purposes. The first, 'Markeaucrats', are not necessarily bad at all. Every organization needs some of them. They are only bad if they are in a leadership position or if you have too many of them. By contrast, the four other types are a bad influence and represent a barrier to Offensive Marketing.

## Markeaucrats

Markeaucrats are the most difficult to spot. They are a cross between genuine marketers and bureaucrats. Here, in Table 17, is how they differ from marketers (please read across).

**Table 17.**

| Marketers | Markeaucrats |
|---|---|
| Pursue profitable growth | Maximize present |
| Flair, vision | Pedestrian |
| Innovate | Consolidate |
| Cross departmental | Functional |
| Strong at process | Efficient |

**Too few**          **Too many**

Markeaucrats are not fools, and are often very competent. They do not step out of line in the boardroom, and may be admired by board colleagues for their prudence and profit orientation. Markeaucrats are keen on compromise, very focused on short-term results, and dislike risk or radical change. Finance Directors nod approvingly in their direction, with words like 'very sound'. To be called 'sound' is the biggest insult any marketer can receive.

## The new Luddites

Once you have traced the traditional history of Marketing, and acknowledged its emergence from an era of production orientation, where capacity rather than the consumer's need dictated the market, it is not too big a step to regard Production as in some undefined way opposed to marketing.

This sets the stage for the new Luddites, who view production as an outdated and inferior form of activity. They refer to 'production orientated' companies with a curl of the lip, and assume that the Operations Department must always behave as a docile servant of the marketing group to prevent a return to the dark ages of business.

This attitude is responsible for the bickering and lack of cooperation that is so often a feature of the relationship between Operations and Marketing Departments. The posture of the new Luddite is, of course, totally unrealistic, because marketing depends on good Operations for its effectiveness. Superb advertising, customer service and product planning will be of no avail if the product or service is high cost or inferior. What is more, close cooperation between Marketing and Operations can turn up excellent profit improvements through reductions in cost.

### The egotistical employees

Employee egotism starts right from the top, with Chief Executives who are more interested in inflating their status and bonuses than in building a strong future for their companies. They are quite prepared to fleece consumers, mortgage their company's future and dismiss competent people, if this advances their own financial position.

Here are some other examples that will be easily spotted by those with an observant eye:

1. Research and Development (R & D) scientists are particularly prone to this disorder. Being people of outstanding intellect, they naturally tend to be most interested in work that is technically challenging, irrespective of its likely commerical pay-off. To counter this, marketers have to take the lead in directing R & D effort to projects with profit potential.
2. Copywriters at advertising agencies can also be difficult to motivate along Offensive Marketing lines. Some care more about creative awards than sales graphs, although they usually disguise this when talking to clients.
3. Internal bureaucrats who are more interested in following procedures than in meeting customer needs. These people can be damaging enough within the confines of a company, but when let loose on customers, as in a service business, they can be disastrous.

### The milker

Milkers are executives who think they will only spend a short time – perhaps a year or so – in their present job. They may be rolling General Managers with an international company, or Brand Managers who move quickly from job to job. The technique is to cut every cost in sight, including advertising spending, so that a vastly improved profit can be piled up over a short period. The degree to which the milker has mortgaged the company's or the brand's longer-term prospects is not apparent at the time, and when revenue or profits turn down a year later, somebody else is in the hot seat to take the blame for yet another marketing failure.

### The galloping midget

Almost invariably male, twenty-five years old and with four years' experience in marketing. Marketing is the only part of the business that matters and every department exists just to provide a service to it. Time is the only thing standing between the galloping midget and the Managing Directorship and it won't be long now.

## Sustainability of Offensive Marketing

While it will be difficult and challenging for Dissembler plc to become an Offensive Marketer, Virtuous plc and Microsoft will not remain Offensive Marketers for ever.

Companies which have failed to adopt Offensive Marketing include most banks, petroleum companies, insurers, department stores, utilities and railways, and many automobile companies.

However, it is certainly easier to remain an Offensive Marketer than to become one, because every Offensive Marketer carries forward the momentum of accumulated past investment, successful risk-taking and purposeful strategies.

The primary traps for Offensive Marketers are misreading of future needs and complacency. IBM fell victim to both:

**IBM's first major setback was the failure of its PC in the late 1970s, and while it continued to generate annual net profits of $5 billion to $6 billion through the 1980s, it lost momentum.**

**In 1991–3, IBM lost $16 billion, but in 1990 when net profit was $6 billion, the Annual Report sighted no hurricanes on the horizon. Here are some quotations from it:**

- **'The future of large computers is one of continued healthy growth.'**
- **'Our strategy is straightforward and consistent:**
  - **to provide customers with the best solutions**
  - **to strengthen the competitiveness of our products and services**
  - **to improve our efficiency.'**
- **'We are offering the strongest line-up of products and services in our history.'**

**Few annual reports of any description contain as many references to 'customers' as IBM's in 1990 before the earthquake struck.**

Some years later, Louis Gerstner, IBM's current Chairman, observed:

'At the heart of the turmoil is one simple fact: IBM failed to keep pace with significant change in the industry.

'We have been too bureaucratic and too preoccupied with our view of the world. We have been too slow getting things to market.'

Within a few short years IBM moved from bluest of blue chips to virtual basket case. For years it had hired the cream of the graduate crop. The company had a powerful internal culture, which drove performance but not change. Its R & D Department boasted a number of Nobel prize winners, and virtually invented the computer industry, but became preoccupied with technology rather than superior consumer value. IBM had vast resources, but misread the future, underinvesting in software and PCs. It was let down by poor marketing. However, IBM may well become an Offensive Marketer under Gerstner.

Some companies have successfully sustained Offensive Marketing, based on the definition earlier in the chapter, for many years, such as those in Table 18.

| Table 18. Long-term Offensive Marketers. | |
|---|---|
| Coca-Cola | Canon |
| Marks & Spencer | Johnson & Johnson |
| BMW | SmithKline Beecham |
| Procter & Gamble | 3M |
| McKinsey | Unilever |
| British Airways | Walt Disney |

While many Japanese companies, such as Honda, Sony, Fujitsu and Toyota, do excellently in generating superior consumer experiences, their low margins and inconsistent profit record in recent years exclude them from the above list.

### Checking a company's score for Offensive Marketing

If Offensive Marketing is as practical a concept as has been claimed, it should be possible to set up criteria by which the Offensive Marketing rating of a firm can be judged. Like any comparison between firms, the result will inevitably be biased and subjective due to differences in definition and market situations. The battery of Offensive Marketing yardsticks which has been constructed will not escape these criticisms, but they contain sufficient objectivity to be useful (Table 19).

| Table 19. Criteria for rating a business on Offensive Marketing. | | |
|---|---|---|
| | **Max. score** | **Your score** |
| Strong and differentiated customer proposition | 15 | |
| Ability to anticipate and act on future trends quickly | 8 | |
| Success in launching profitable new products/services which add incremental sales | 7 | |
| New markets successfully entered in past ten years | 7 | |
| Strong customer focus of total company, including operations, distribution and finance | 15 | |
| Strong profit focus of whole company, including Marketing and Sales | 10 | |
| Clear long-term strategy led by Marketing | 8 | |
| Commitment to constant improvement in quality and value for money | 10 | |
| More efficient/lower-cost operator than competitors | 12 | |
| Level of investment compared with competitors (facilities, databases, technology, advertising, R & D, people development) | 8 | |
| **Total** | **100** | |

At the 1997 Marketing Society Masterclass, 32 of those attending formally ranked their companies on these criteria. Average score was 61% and ranged from 31% to 82%. Any company scoring less than 60% should be classified as vulnerable. Urgent corrective action will be needed to secure its future.

## Does Your Company Apply the Offensive Marketing Approach?

Table 20 summarizes the key strategies and style of Procter & Gamble, a strong Offensive Marketer.

You may find it instructive to complete this table for your own company, prime competitors or, if you are studying, companies you have encountered. It should take no more than fifteen minutes to do, because answers are usually clear-cut. An Offensive Marketer will have a distinctive or superior approach to most of these topics.

**Table 20. Does your company have a consistent culture, set of processes, way of doing things?**

|  | **Procter & Gamble** | **Your company (please complete)** |
|---|---|---|
| **Products and Services** | ● Must be superior as evidenced by consumer tests and ranking <br> ● Sustainable advantage and value | ● |
| **Change** | ● Anticipate, pre-empt. Go first, don't wait <br> ● Pre-test change thoroughly | ● |
| **Support** | ● Outspend competition on media <br> ● Achieve wide distribution and trial for new products <br> ● Build long-term consumer relationships <br> ● Cut back on retailer promotion | ● |
| **Pricing** | ● Premium, but must be justified by superior performance | ● |
| **Operation** | ● High quality, lowest cost <br> ● Multi-country scale economies | ● |
| **R & D** | ● Heavy spend <br> ● Focus on new, pre-emptive technology | ● |
| **Customers** | ● High service levels <br> ● Partnership for joint efficiency <br> ● Hard-nosed negotiators | ● |
| **Style** | ● Global <br> ● Very competitive, very determined <br> ● Long-term approach <br> ● Seek leadership in all markets | ● |

# FLOW-CHART SUMMARY OF CHAPTER 1

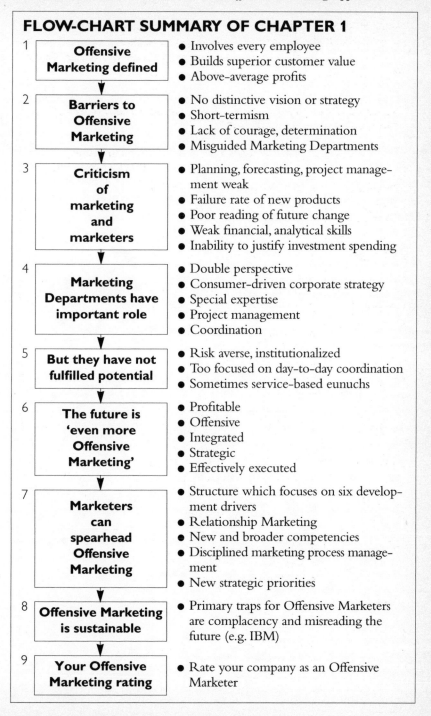

**1 Offensive Marketing defined**
- Involves every employee
- Builds superior customer value
- Above-average profits

**2 Barriers to Offensive Marketing**
- No distinctive vision or strategy
- Short-termism
- Lack of courage, determination
- Misguided Marketing Departments

**3 Criticism of marketing and marketers**
- Planning, forecasting, project management weak
- Failure rate of new products
- Poor reading of future change
- Weak financial, analytical skills
- Inability to justify investment spending

**4 Marketing Departments have important role**
- Double perspective
- Consumer-driven corporate strategy
- Special expertise
- Project management
- Coordination

**5 But they have not fulfilled potential**
- Risk averse, institutionalized
- Too focused on day-to-day coordination
- Sometimes service-based eunuchs

**6 The future is 'even more Offensive Marketing'**
- Profitable
- Offensive
- Integrated
- Strategic
- Effectively executed

**7 Marketers can spearhead Offensive Marketing**
- Structure which focuses on six development drivers
- Relationship Marketing
- New and broader competencies
- Disciplined marketing process management
- New strategic priorities

**8 Offensive Marketing is sustainable**
- Primary traps for Offensive Marketers are complacency and misreading the future (e.g. IBM)

**9 Your Offensive Marketing rating**
- Rate your company as an Offensive Marketer

# PART ONE:
## PROFITABLE

## 2. How Offensive Marketing Builds Above-average Profits

## Chapter Summary

> **Table 21.**
>
> | **P:** Profitable | ● *Proper balance between firm's needs for profit and customer's need for value* |
> |---|---|
> | **O:** Offensive | ● *Must lead market, take risks and make competitors followers* |
> | **I:** Integrated | ● *Marketing approach must permeate whole company* |
> | **S:** Strategic | ● *Probing analysis leading to a winning strategy* |
> | **E:** Effectively Executed | ● *Strong and disciplined execution on a daily basis* |

This chapter will cover the 'P' of POISE – P for Profitable. As you now know, Offensive Marketing achieves the proper balance between the firm's needs for profits and the customer's need for value.

You saw in the previous chapter that meeting consumer needs at a profit is too simplistic a definition of marketing. It fails to emphasize both the tension between consumer benefits and profits and the way in which they can work together. Profit is the reward companies earn for delivering superior customer value very efficiently. It cannot be viewed in isolation.

The chapter is divided into three sections, each addressing a separate issue affecting profitability within POISE.

**The first section** describes and challenges the financial view of profit, and outlines how Offensive Marketers should campaign to change the rules. Eventually they will win.

The key principles of financial reporting were established over fifty years ago, and pre-date the Marketing approach.

> **'This venerable financial accounting model is still being used by information age companies as they attempt to build internal assets and competencies.'**[1]

Company reports in the UK and USA fail to give a true and fair picture of a company's position, because there is no requirement to disclose intangible investments like advertising, R & D, training, innovation and customer relationships. It is ridiculous that companies can cut spending on such intangibles, and then report artificially inflated short-term profits, while stripping the long-term value of their customer equity. Ironically, the purpose of such exercises is usually to increase a company's stock market valuation. While the work of the UK Accounting Standards Board looks constructive, it still has a long way to go.

**The second section** explains how Offensive Marketers can build above-average long-term profits. This involves matching company and brand strengths to the best opportunities in the market-place and maximizes profitability, because assets are invested in areas of best return. Effective matching creates the maximum surplus, which can be allocated to superior consumer value and above-average profits. This matching has been called the Marketing Alignment Process (MAP), and guides companies in selecting the right markets for them to compete in. The four-step process of MAP is described.

**The third section** outlines how Offensive Marketers can leverage short-term profits responsibly, without mortgaging the future. A full checklist is provided. It is often necessary to generate extra short-term profit to finance the cost of additional long-term investment.

## Section 1: How Offensive Marketers Should Change the Rules

The marketer's view of accountants can be summed up in the following story:

> **An intrepid marketer, returning from a visit to launch a new product on the Planet Venus, had to make a forced landing on return to Earth. She found herself in a large field. To her relief, a well-dressed man walked towards her.**
>
> **'Can you please tell me where this is?'**
>
> **'Certainly. This is a field. It is surrounded by hedges and has a gate, which I have just closed.'**
>
> **'Yes, I know that. But where am I?'**
>
> **'You are in a field planted with grass. It belongs to a farmer called Mr Smith.'**
>
> **Suddenly the marketer had an inspiration and cried, 'I know what you do. You're an accountant.'**
>
> **The accountant looked at her in amazement. 'How did you know that?'**
>
> **'Because what you have told me is completely accurate – but totally useless.'**

If the accountant had continued the dialogue, he might have defended his function as being to provide a true and fair picture at a given moment.

### How the Financial and Marketing views on profit conflict

Marketing and Financial people often clash in their views on costs and profits.

Finance Directors tend to regard Marketing Departments with suspicion. They see them as havens for big spenders with low accountability. Marketing Departments in turn get very frustrated by the short-term approach of their companies, when cuts are made to spending on advertising, research, new plant and new product development as soon as the going gets tough. Marketers prefer to think longer term but find their plans continually thwarted by short-term profit demands.

Why does this happen? What can be done about it? This section of the chapter reviews the differences in the Financial and Marketing views of profit. It outlines how marketers in the UK and USA can change the rules of financial reporting, and the way they are applied, to give longer-term strategies the chance to succeed.

The key principles of financial reporting were established in the first half of this century, pre-dating the marketing approach to business. UK and US financial reports fail to give a true and fair picture of a company's potential because there is no requirement to disclose intangible investments like advertising, market research or R & D. These can take two to five years to pay back, yet strongly influence future success. Equally there is no process for identifying level of investment on new products, processes or services.

This outdated model of financial reporting chokes innovation and long-term investment. It favours Milkers – or those who sell the family silver, fire the staff and move on to a larger mansion. As Baruch Lev, Professor of Accounting at New York University, says, 'The generally accepted accounting principles . . . don't allow for some of the prime drivers of corporate success – investments in intangible assets such as know-how, patents, brands and customer loyalty.'[2]

In Japan and Germany, the accounting rules do permit building reserves and a degree of smoothing which enhances a longer-term approach. Companies also take a longer view in those countries. However, neither system offers a panacea, and Japanese companies in particular have failed to build shareholder value over the past seven years.

While financial reporting in the UK and USA needs to change, there is, within existing accounting rules, considerable flexibility to decide whether to take profits this year or next. Unfortunately many Managing and Financial Directors tend to utilize this flexibility negatively to maximize short-term profits.

Marketers should seek to change the rules on profits by pushing for greater disclosure of a company's customer position, intangible investment for the future, and innovation. They should also press Managing and Financial Directors to use their creativity to take a cautious view of this year's profits, so that offensive long-term strategies can be consistently pursued, and given the time they need to succeed. The way ahead will then be clear for Offensive Marketing, a more benefical approach for both customers and shareholders.

### The financial view of profit

Accounts are drawn up objectively by Finance Departments, using well-established accounting principles and checked by external auditors. The results look authoritative, precise and logical. Financial accounts reveal some of what has happened in the past. They do not tell you why, or reveal a great deal about tomorrow's prospects. However, they do provide a useful short-term scorecard.

The main financial ratios are summarized below:

**Table 22. Main headings in financial scorecard.**

| Ratio | Basis | What ratio measures |
|---|---|---|
| Sales growth | % revenue growth year to year | Customer response |
| Return on sales (ROS) | Operating profit as % of revenue | Skill in adding value |
| Return on capital employed (ROCE) | Operating profit as % of fixed and current assets less current liabilities (see *below*) | Efficiency of capital utilization |

**Sales growth** is a result of changes in the size of your markets and of your share in them. Your market share is determined by the relative customer value your products or services offer, their level of accessibility and consumer awareness.

**Return on Sales (ROS)** reflects the *cost* per unit of delivering customer value, accessibility and awareness, compared with its *price*. You may achieve excellent customer value through underpricing, and therefore fail to make a profit. As Dr Kazuo Inamori, Chairman of Kyocera and one of Japan's most successful business people, wrote: 'Maximizing profit while fully satisfying our customers' needs and desires – this is the essence of business.'[3]

**Return on capital employed (ROCE)** shows how effectively management is using capital. From a financial viewpoint there are four main elements in capital (Table 23).

**Table 23.  The financial view: four main elements of capital.**

| Description | Balance | Elements |
|---|---|---|
| (a)  Fixed assets | + | Land, buildings, equipment, vehicles |
| (b)  Investments | + | Cash and securities |
| (c)  Current assets | + | |
|  ● Stocks | | Raw materials, work in progress, finished stock |
|  ● Debtors | | People who owe the business money |
| (d)  Current liabilities | – | Money owed to suppliers, banks or other lenders |
| a + b + c – d | = | Capital employed |

As everyone in business knows, considerable judgement is necessary to arrive at these seemingly authoritative ratios. Many of the measures are frequently manipulated by honest companies, in order to project a favourable picture within the accepted bounds of 'true and fair'.[4] Examples are shown in Table 24.

**Table 24. How to cook financial accounts.**

| Measure | Cook-ability | Main Cooking Methods |
|---|---|---|
| Sales revenue | Medium | • Year-end promotion to inflate distributor inventories<br>• New product launch at year end; claim initial sales as revenue, defer support costs until next year<br>• Year-end sales on 'sale or return'. Take returns as loss next year |
| Fixed assets | Low | • Limited opportunities to vary depreciation |
| Cash | Nil | • No room for manoeuvre |
| Debtors | Medium | • Judgement on bad debts can be optimistic or pessimistic. Critical in banking |
| Stocks | High | • Classify slow-moving, possibly redundant stock as saleable<br>• Overstate net realizable value, or understate value to create future profit reserves. A rich cooking method |
| Current liabilities | Medium | • Build reserves for possible legal liabilities. A useful device.<br>• Overstate future tax liabilities |
| Operating expenses | Medium | • Judgement on redemption rates of promotion schemes, guarantees, warranties. Over- or under-estimate<br>• Invoice expenses supporting this year's sales in following year<br>• Apply favourable judgement on allocation of costs between years<br>• For international companies, allocation of central costs or royalty payments by country in order to minimize tax |
| Exceptional items | High | • Taken below 'operating profit' line, often for restructuring or major redundancies<br>• Opportunity to write down the kitchen sink and include loosely related costs which might normally be debited above the operating profit line |
| Other | High | • Take optimistic or pessimistic view on foreign exchange rates |

The word 'cooking' is never used in financial circles. Preferred terms are 'judgement' or 'creativity'. Terry Smith's *Accounting for Growth* provides a much more extensive analysis of how the financial view of profit is frequently manipulated, legally. This book is not suggesting that companies should systematically 'cook' their books, but merely demonstrating how easily this can be done.

This outline is based on the UK and USA. Outside these countries there is much greater opportunity to build reserves on a quite legal basis. In Germany and Japan, for instance, it is acceptable to use good years to build reserves and to even out the bumps in bad years. 'As a result of additional tax depreciation and the strict adherence to the historic cost principle for asset valuations, it is possible for significant hidden reserves to exist in a German company's balance sheet,' as the following example shows:[5]

> **'Deutsche Bank is the first German financial institution to adopt International Accounting Standards (IAS). In doing so, it revealed its formerly hidden reserves, of DM 20.8 billion, used to smooth out fluctuations in earnings. These reserves consisted of excluded real estate holdings, securities booked at below market value, and possible over-provisioning for bad debt.**
>
> **'In IAS terms, this meant that Deutsche Bank had understated its capital employed and therefore overstated its ROCE.'[6]**

In Japan, 'the practice of income smoothing is considered acceptable, if it will bring stabilization and enhance long-term success for the business'. The Japanese Federation of Economic Organization sees 'Capital Accumulation through forms of reserve accounting and income smoothing as beneficial . . . to the nation.'[7] Dr Kazuo Inamori strongly believes in the value of building reserves:

> **'The most fundamental fact about any economy is that it operates on a cycle. The bull and the bear are facts of life, and preparing for bad times during the good is the most basic rule of management . . . in my opinion, the term "management" should refer to managing – building a reserve during good times so a recession won't leave us crying for help.'[8]**

The difference in treatment of reserves is influenced by tax legislation but also reflects the longer-term approach of German and Japanese businesses, compared with US and UK companies, which often maximize the present.

For Offensive Marketers, the largest reserve does not appear anywhere in the accounts. This is investment in customer understanding and relationships, brand and new product development, and competency building. None of these are reflected in the **financial view of profit**, which is one of its weaknesses. Offensive Marketers can also apply a degree of smoothing, by applying pessimistic judgements to key accounting issues in good years and optimistic judgements in poorer ones. This option is not available to *in*offensive marketers, who rarely have a good year and regularly present accounting treatments at the outer limits of optimism, so that next year becomes a Mount Everest to climb.

## What's wrong with the financial view of profit?

The financial view gives a partial, short-term picture of past financial performance, and very limited guidance on the future. We saw in Chapter 1 how IBM in 1990 published figures and words in its annual report which in effect said, '*All is well, and all shall be well*', then toppled from a \$6 billion profit to a \$3 billion loss the following year.

In addition, the financial view provides few insights on the *quality* of company earnings. It does not differentiate between Company A, which has mortgaged its future and struggles to declare £100 million in profits; and Company B, whose £100 million profits include a large helping of future investment. To use a car analogy, Company A is leaking oil as it rattles along at full speed, while Company B is effortlessly cruising in third gear, with plenty of power (and probably understated profit) in reserve. While both have declared £100 million, the quality of that profit is chalk and cheese. Chapter 1 demonstrated this in the comparison between Virtuous plc and Dissembler plc, both making an ostensibly similar profit on sales of 14%, but each with very different future prospects.

From the standpoint of marketing and marketing people, the financial report, while accurate and precise, often fails to give a true and fair picture of a company's health. In striving to be prudent and conservative, it can be seriously misleading. The vast majority of Western accounting principles and conventions were developed long before the word 'marketing' was invented, and have not adjusted to the marketing approach to business. Their principal weaknesses are illustrated in Table 25.

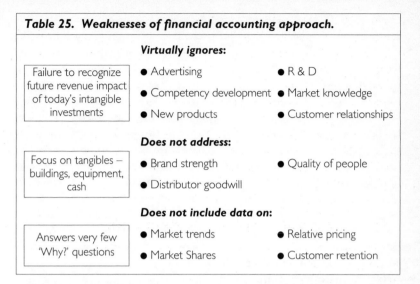

**Table 25.  Weaknesses of financial accounting approach.**

| | |
|---|---|
| Failure to recognize future revenue impact of today's intangible investments | **Virtually ignores:**<br>● Advertising   ● R & D<br>● Competency development   ● Market knowledge<br>● New products   ● Customer relationships |
| Focus on tangibles – buildings, equipment, cash | **Does not address:**<br>● Brand strength   ● Quality of people<br>● Distributor goodwill |
| Answers very few 'Why?' questions | **Does not include data on:**<br>● Market trends   ● Relative pricing<br>● Market Shares   ● Customer retention |

With the exception of tangibles – plant, property, etc. – the financial view fails to take into account the future value of investments with a payback beyond this fiscal year (Table 26).

**Table 26.  Payback of intangible investments.**

| Activity: | Typical payback period (years) |
|---|---|
| Advertising for first time | 1–2 |
| Major increase in advertising | 1–3 |
| New brand – consumer goods | 4–6 |
| Basic or applied R & D | 3–10 |
| Basic market research | 1–3 |
| Competency development, Culture change | 2–5 |
| Training | 1–2 |
| Marketing R & D | 2–5 |
| New customer acquisition | 0–3 |

**Advertising**. New or significantly increased advertising spending takes time to work, and rarely pays back in profit terms in less than one year.

**New brands**. In fast-moving consumer goods, new brand payback is five years if you are lucky – i.e. initial investment costs in R & D, plant, advertising and launch promotion are only recouped by matching profits in Year 5. For new consumer healthcare brands, payback can be seven years, for pharmaceuticals, even longer. Financial services is one of the few markets where a new product may pay back quickly.

**Basic R & D**. Standard accounting practice now allows R & D spending on specific development projects – such as a new product or process for next year – to be carried forward as an expense into next year. Investment in pure or applied research cannot be carried forward.

**Basic market research**. This covers fundamental research into consumer attitudes or habits, or new products or services.

**Competency development, culture change, training**. These are fundamental to any business, but especially those where people are a major part of the product – travel, leisure, hospitality, for instance. Development costs can be high, and impact time lengthy.

**Marketing R & D** covers activity to understand, test and capitalize on changes in consumer attitudes, technology, services and communications in the next two to ten years. For example, Procter & Gamble is spending heavily on taking a lead in new communications with an expensive testing programme on interactive media, virtual shopping and the Internet, which will not pay back for many years.

**New customer acquisition**. Time-scale and cost will vary by market. In consumer goods, new customers can be acquired (but not necessarily retained) quickly and cheaply. In business-to-business markets, both time-scale and cost can be substantial.

*So, does it really matter* that conventional financial reporting fails to recognize important intangible investments, where cost has to be taken this year but benefit will occur some years hence? It certainly does, because it actively penalizes many important investments, which are the lifeblood of any company's future (Table 27).

---

**Table 27.  Why the weaknesses of financial accounting matter . . .**

- Critical investment spending areas not reported
- Short-term approach encouraged
- Key long-term investments can be delayed or avoided without penalty
- 'Milkers' can follow 'builders' and gear up 'profits' by cutting any 'payback' investments

---

Kaplan and Norton's comments in *The Balanced Scorecard*[9] are right on target:

**'Unfortunately many organizations espouse strategies about customer relationships, core competencies, and organizational capabilities while motivating and measuring performance only with financial measures . . . in the short term, the financial accounting model reports . . . spending cutbacks as increases in reported income, even**

**when the reductions have cannibalized a company's stock of assets, and its capabilities for creating future economic value.'**

## How Offensive Marketers should change the financial view

The outdated US/UK model of financial reporting is limiting innovation, enterprise and intangible investment; and favouring cost-cutters, milkers and downsizers, who can complete a successful smash-and-grab bonus raid in two years, with a so-called 'turnaround'.

Offensive Marketers have to work within the current system, but should strive to change it. This will probably take at least twenty years, but should eventually succeed.

There are signs of change, such as the discussion on valuation of brands and databases, which are part of the much bigger issue described above. Annual reports are becoming clearer and more informative, often providing selective figures on market trends, shares and new products. Short-term downsizing now scores fewer points in the city than profitable growth. And some leading companies now focus on building shareholder value.[10] This is the present value of estimated future cash flows, which includes the benefits of new product investment. These trends favour the Offensive Marketing approach to profit. However, they do not go nearly far enough, and much more radical change is necessary.

Clearly, certain constraints have to be recognized. The effect of today's intangible investment in advertising or R & D cannot be quantified in sales tomorrow . . . *but that does not prevent it being reported.* Investors can form their own judgement, and companies reducing today's profits with intangible investments for tomorrow are more likely to get a future payoff, than those who do not invest at all.

Another constraint is confidentiality. No company wants to publish its new product development programme, its future launch timetables or its process engineering and customer service secrets. Yet this issue has been exaggerated. Many company reports contain quite detailed outlines of future strategy. In their briefings to security analysts, companies provide vast amounts of information valuable to competitors and will answer almost any question with unusual frankness. Indeed, most Chief Executives understand and address the needs of analysts and investors much more readily than those of customers.

So what is the Offensive Marketing agenda for company reporting, and the treatment of investment, profit and competitive position? Most of the existing information in US/UK accounts is useful, and should be retained, though its length could be cut in half. The following subsection outlines the Offensive Marketing approach to changing the rules on profits.

## The Offensive Marketing view of profit

To provide a true and fair picture of a company, investors need to be given better information to answer the two key questions: 'Why?' and 'What are future prospects?' These should focus on three areas critical to Offensive Marketing (Figure 5).

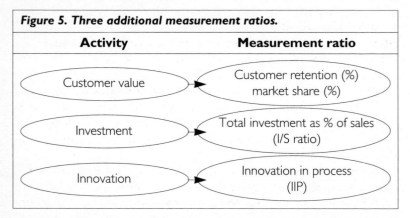

**Figure 5. Three additional measurement ratios.**

| Activity | Measurement ratio |
|---|---|
| Customer value | Customer retention (%) market share (%) |
| Investment | Total investment as % of sales (I/S ratio) |
| Innovation | Innovation in process (IIP) |

Table 28 lists the specifics of each measurement ratio which should appear in all annual reports:

**Table 28. Specifics of three key measurement areas for reporting.**

| Activity | Measurement data |
|---|---|
| Customer value | ● Total market trend (revenue and volume)<br>● Market share (revenue and volume)<br>● Relative price v. market average<br>● Customer loyalty and retention (%) |
| Investment | ● New plant<br>● Advertising<br>● Customer databases<br>● Market research<br>● Training/people development<br>● R & D  } Each as % of revenue |
| Innovation | ● Products or services launched in past 5 years as % of sales<br>● Profits split by products over and under 5 years old<br>● List of innovations in progress |

You can already hear the chorus of objections by those 'sound' people opposed to change. 'Naïve! Impractical! Manipulable!':

**Many companies don't know their market sizes or market shares**. It's about time they found out. Would you want to invest in them?

**Some companies compete in scores of markets and countries across the world**. Companies like Nestlé, Daimler–Benz or General Electric could state their shares by market and by major world region. This would certainly make their annual reports more informative. If possible, a 'share of customer' measure should also be included.

**Companies in the same markets might define them in different ways**. Of course. This is permissible as long as the definition is clear and consistent over time. Companies will always select the most favourable slant.

**Why is the investment as a percent of sales ratio (I/S) relevant**? Because the investment spending elements reduce this year's profits, while providing the engine for future growth. Gillette calls them the 'growth drivers', and is committed to at least increase them as fast as sales revenue.

**Advertising levels will vary by year, depending on new product launches**. True. This can be related to innovation activity.

**Companies may inflate their innovation ratios by including only marginally improved products as innovations**. Yes. As we saw earlier, existing financial accounts can be legally manipulated. Cheating companies will soon be ridiculed by analysts.

**What are innovations in progress (IIP)**? These would include test markets, or test countries. If Disney is making a big drive with theme parks in Asia Pacific, and has opened two in Thailand and South Korea, investors need to know progress. IIP could also include new customer service initiatives, new products, competency development programmes or customer relationship initiatives. Companies would have some discretion, and investors would look for sensible, original and relevant activity.

## The Offensive Marketers annual report summary 2021

Here, in Table 29, is what an annual report summary might cover in the year 2021.

**Table 29.  Universal Leisure Company 2021.**

**Description of business: Competes in casinos, hotels, entertainment complexes, in UK, USA, Japan**

| Customer value | Casinos | Hotels | Entertainment | Total |
|---|---|---|---|---|
| Market size (£bn)<br>Market share (%) | 140<br>10 | 300<br>2 | 60<br>5 | 500<br>4.6 |
| Net revenue (£bn) | 14 | 6 | 3 | 23 |
| Relative price indexed to market average | 105 | 125 | (80) | 107 |
| **Customer retention** | | | | |
| % of last year's customers buying this year | 65 | 70 | 35 | 65 |
| **Profitability** | | | | |
| Operating profit (£bn)<br>ROS (%)<br>ROCE (%) | 3.5<br>25<br>20 | 0.9<br>15<br>15 | 0.3<br>10<br>10 | 4.7<br>20<br>17 |
| **Investment (% of Sales)** | | | | |
| New assets, refurbishment, equipment | 5 | 5 | (15.0) | 6.3 |
| Advertising<br>Market research<br>Training, development<br>R & D | 2<br>0.3<br>1.0<br>0.5 | 2<br>0.9<br>1.0<br>0.4 | 4<br>1.5<br>1.5<br>4.0 | 2.3<br>0.6<br>1.1<br>0.9 |
| Investment to sales ratio (% of Sales) | 8.8 | 9.3 | (26.0) | 11.2 |
| **Innovation** | | | | |
| Products, services launched in past 5 years, as % of sales | 10 | 15 | (40) | 15 |
| New outlets past 5 years, as % of sales | 25 | 10 | 20 | 20 |
| % of operating profits from products, services, outlets under 5 years old | 20 | 5 | (30) | 10 |
| Innovations in progress (see *separate list*) | – | – | – | – |

Notes:
1. Innovations in progress would be listed inside the annual report, not in the Summary.
2. Summary would also contain breakdown by UK, USA, Japan.

**What does this 2021 report summary tell you?** It gives a reasonably clear picture of the company's competitive position, and its future prospects, if compared with the previous year's report. But trend comparison, not provided above for reasons of space, will be critical in judging:

- Market growth by business type and country.
- Market share and relative pricing trends. **The company is discounting prices in the entertainment business. Have they deteriorated in the past *two* years, or are there signs of pick-up?**
- Trends in customer retention, and comparisons with industry averages. For instance, 35% repeat business may be good for a leisure entertainment complex, and 70% poor for a chain of business hotels.
- Trends in investment spending and innovation.

The 2021 report tells you many useful things omitted by today's financially driven reports, and enables you to draw additional conclusions. For example, it is clear that the relatively poor profits in Universal Leisure's entertainment division are influenced by heavy investment as a percent of sales (I/S ratio of 26%, double the company average), and a high level of innovation including the development of the Virtual Reality Rides and the Epi-Centre. A look at the 'Innovations in Progress' report should indicate how effective this investment has been.

The next two sections will cover how marketers can best work within the existing financial rules to maximize long-term profitability, while also successfully meeting the necessary demands for short-term profits, in a responsible way.

## Section 2: How Offensive Marketers Build Above-average Long-term Profits

The previous section covered how Offensive Marketers can and should change the future rules on profits. The rest of this chapter outlines how to tackle the hard commercial realities that marketers face every day in balancing consumers' needs for benefits against their company's need for profits.

Changes in the economic landscape have dramatically altered this balance in the past few decades. The classical model of marketing, developed in the 1960s, concentrated on meeting consumer needs profitably, but paid little attention to the efficient exploitation of companies' strengths, in the form of assets and competencies. Assets are defined in this chapter as **things** – property, brands, factories and cash; competencies as **skills** – created by people, often by exploiting assets. Technology and new product development skills are examples.

The modern model of marketing tightly matches a company's assets and competencies to the best opportunities in the market-place. This involves very precise selection of markets, segments, channels and customers. The aim of Offensive Marketers is to focus effort on areas where assets and competencies can be *fully* exploited. This enables them to concentrate resources on attractive markets where they have real skills, thereby delivering superior customer value, and above-average profits . . . the essence of Offensive Marketing.

## The old model of marketing – classical

In the UK, the 'classical' model was developed in the heyday of fast-moving consumer goods (FMCG) Marketing, the 1960s, when markets were growing, the seller had the advantage and advertising was cheap. In this environment, assets did not have to be squeezed, mistakes could be tolerated and expanding markets could be re-segmented quite easily. Marketing Departments were starting up, flexing their muscles and stimulating companies to look outwards to the consumer.

Table 30 illustrates how the marketing environment has changed:

**Table 30.  The changed marketing environment (read across).**

| Factors | 1960s | 2000 |
|---|---|---|
| Availability of goods and services | Too few | Too many |
| Market trends | Growing | Flat |
| Market structure | Limited segmentation | Fragmented |
| Distribution channels | Passive | Strong |
| Advertising media | Little choice | Wide choice |
| Advertising cost | Low | High |
| Cost pressures | Limited | High |
| Competition | Medium | High |
| Consumers | Accepting | Demanding |

If the 1960s was the key formative decade for marketing in the UK, it was the 1950s in the USA; and the 1970s for Continental Europe. During this period, before the first major oil crisis of 1973, many of the fundamental principles of marketing were established, largely by American-owned international FMCG companies.

The whole emphasis was on satisfying consumer needs – effective utilization of internal assets and competencies was an 'also-ran'. While companies wished to be profitable, few understood the importance of matching internal skills to market opportunities as the best way to *maximize* profits. Indeed, many companies expanded into markets where they lacked any distinctive competency, and were therefore unable to add superior value profitably. One result was the 'Back to Basics' movement in the 1980s and 1990s, when companies sold off activities where they could not win, to concentrate on their core businesses.

The typical classical definition of Marketing, deriving from the 1960s, has already been referred to: '**The role of marketing is to satisfy consumer needs profitably.**' The approach was market-led, demanding: '**What do customers want, and how can we satisfy their needs profitably?**' It did not strive to maximize profitability by matching superior skills to the best opportunities, or recognize the frequent conflict between the company's need for profits and the consumer's need for benefits. In those days, marketing's role in balancing and aligning was not appreciated. The old world of classical marketing is no longer relevant to today's business conditions. A new model is needed.

### The new model – asset- and competency-based marketing

A new model was put forward in the late 1970s,[11] and summarized in the second edition of *Offensive Marketing* as **asset–based marketing**. This was later described by Alan Wolfe as follows:

> '**Asset-based marketing is a supplement to, not a substitute for, customer-orientation.**
>
> '**Alongside the search to identify customers and understand their needs should run an examination of the assets of the company and ways to use them more effectively in the market-place.**'[12]

Based on the work of Gary Hamel and P. K. Prahalad in the 1990s on Core Competencies,[13] the asset-led approach can now be extended to asset- and competency-based marketing, to establish a new model.

Table 31 shows how the approach to marketing has evolved over forty years.

| **Table 31.  The evolution of marketing.** | | |
|---|---|---|
| **Market-based** | **Market- and asset-based** | **Market-, asset- and competency-based** |
| 1960          1970 | 1980 | 1990          2000 |

In the 1960s too little attention was paid to cost, and there was over-investment in marketing, often in sectors where the company concerned had limited competence. In the 1980s and 1990s the pendulum had swung too far in the opposite direction. There has been too much emphasis on squeezing assets, an unwillingness to take risks and a corroding short-term orientation. Hopefully the new model for the 2000s will be correctly applied, to achieve the best balance between market needs, assets and competencies. This is the key to maximizing profitability and delighting customers:

- **Offensive Marketing builds above-average profits by relating a company's exploitable assets and competencies to future customer opportunities.**

Figure 6 illustrates the role of marketing. On the left-hand side are the assets and competencies of the firm – people, equipment, cash, skills and, most notable of all, brands. These generate cost. On the right-hand side is the market-place. This generates revenue.

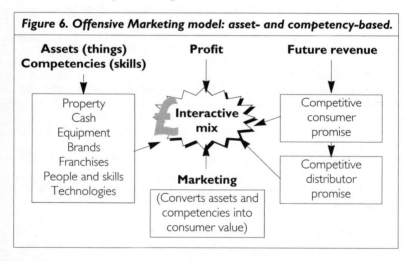

**Figure 6. Offensive Marketing model: asset- and competency-based.**

The job of marketing is to achieve the best mix – by converting company assets and competencies into consumer value. In this process, two things happen at once. The market-place is being probed for opportunities. The company's assets and competencies are being refined and exploited. And marketing is there to achieve an ideal fusion between assets, competencies and markets.

There is continuing interaction between them. An Offensive Marketer will be constantly asking, 'How can we use our assets and competencies to successfully enter new markets?' For instance, a hotel

company might feel its skills in property planning and direct marketing were sufficient to successfully move into casinos, especially if it
hired people with licensing and security skills.

Figure 7 shows the two-way interaction between assets and competencies on the one hand, and market opportunities on the other.

**Figure 7. Interaction between assets: competencies and market
opportunities.**

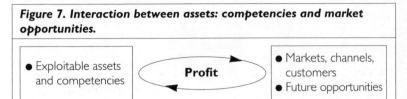

## Marketing alignment achieves the right balance

Marketing alignment is the process which matches
markets, channels and customers with assets and
competencies, to build above-average profits. It is
the task of the Marketing Department to recommend the right fit to the Board. No one in the
company is better placed to do this, since only the
Marketing Department has the knowledge both of external customer
needs and internal competencies – the double perspective described in
Chapter 1 (page 37).

The process directs you to areas which are right for *you*. They may be
wrong for other people. The maxim, 'One person's meat is another
person's poison,' applies.

For example, First Leisure is a highly effective competitor in discos,
night-clubs and leisure attractions. While it also sells food at these estab-
lishments, it would never dream of becoming a food processor, since its
competencies are in leisure, not in food manufacturing.

## Exploitable assets and competencies defined

What is an exploitable asset or competency? How do they differ? Does
it matter? Are some unexploitable? And what is a *core* competency?
This section will discuss these and other questions, as a basis for building the Marketing Alignment Process (MAP) described in the next
section. The MAP approach is critical to achieving above-average
profits.

First, **assets are things** (Figure 8).

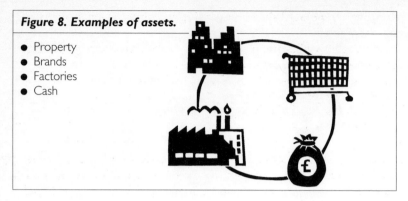

**Figure 8. Examples of assets.**

- Property
- Brands
- Factories
- Cash

This is a marketing definition of assets. It differs fundamentally from the financial definition, which generally only includes tangible assets like property, inventory, money due and money retained. Occasionally a company's financial balance sheet of assets will also include brands.

Secondly, **competencies are skills**, created by people, often by exploiting assets (Figure 9).

Examples are new product development, brand positioning, cost management or new technology. While a brand is an existing asset, a successful brand extension programme will involve the application of competencies.

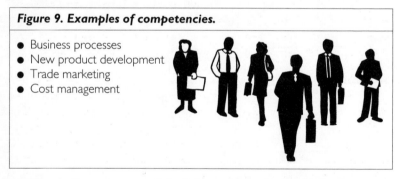

**Figure 9. Examples of competencies.**

- Business processes
- New product development
- Trade marketing
- Cost management

How well assets are exploited depends on the level of competency applied to them. Two companies may have identical customer databases, but one may be much more skilful than the other in exploiting this asset to build customer relationships. The same goes for property, or any other kind of asset. For instance, an energy company might close down a high-cost power station and have no use for it. But a leisure company could transform that same disused asset into a highly profitable entertainment complex. This is something which the power station owners lack the competency to do.

**Competencies add value to assets**. Every asset is potentially exploitable.

Here in Table 32 is a quick test for you. Are these assets or competencies, both or neither?

| Table 32.   Assets or competencies? |
| --- |
| ● Unilever ice-cream distribution in Europe?<br>● Disney's staff training and motivation? |

As you will have concluded, Unilever's ice-cream distribution system, involving vast numbers of company-owned freezers in impulse outlets all over Europe, is a massive asset. If Mars owned this, it would have a very much larger share of the world ice-cream market. Clearly Disney's staff training and motivation skills is a competency, created by people. It enables the company to maximize the return on its very expensive outdoor assets.

Is it important to differentiate between assets and competencies? Yes, because competencies represent the means to obtain the best return from assets. Assets always have a value today. They can often be satisfactorily quantified, even in the case of intangible assets like brands or databases. In the future they may rise or fall in value, depending on the effectiveness of the competencies applied to them.

Today's assets reflect yesterday's competencies. Tomorrow's assets will be determined by today's competencies. What assets and competencies have in common is that both are potential company strengths and both can be exploited well or badly.

A **core competency** is the gold standard. **It is a bundle of related skills, leading to a key consumer benefit, and competitively unique**.[14] So, on-time delivery is a key consumer benefit of Federal Express. The core competency which drives this is logistics management for package tracking, comprising a bundle of related skills such as bar-code technology and wireless communications. Table 33 illustrates core competencies for Federal Express.

| Table 33.   Examples of core competencies: Federal Express.[15] | | | |
| --- | --- | --- | --- |
| **Key benefit** | **Core competencies to deliver benefits** | **Bundle of skills comprising core competencies.** | |
| On-time delivery | Logistics management for package tracking | Bar-code technology<br>Network management | Wireless communications |

## The five-step Marketing Alignment Process (MAP)

As already described, MAP implements the Offensive Marketing approach by matching markets, channels and customers with assets and competencies, to help achieve above-average profits. The phrase 'help achieve' has been used deliberately, because MAP will only deliver above-average profits if the other elements of the definition of Offensive Marketing are met; namely, involvement of every employee, building superior consumer value and a high level of efficiency.

There is a linkage between all these elements. The MAP drives consumer value and efficiency, as well as profits, by linking a company's strengths to areas of best fit. This section will outline how to apply the Marketing Alignment Process, in order to build above-average profits, and provide some examples.

There are five MAP steps, which are summarized below. They will be covered individually on a topline basis. Further details can be found in other chapters, and will be fully referenced, as shown in Table 34.

**Table 34. The Marketing Alignment Process (MAP©).**

| Step | Process | Guidelines |
|------|---------|-----------|
| 1 | Identify exploitable assets | ● Use check-list (Exhibit 1) |
| 2 | Identify exploitable competencies | ● Use check-list (Exhibit 2)<br>● Seek core competencies |
| 3 | Rank attractiveness of priority business areas | ● Focus on markets, channels, customers<br>● Look at the future |
| 4 | Match Steps 1–3 | ● Combine assets and competencies effectively, and aim for best fit with markets, etc. |
| 5 | Identify assets and competencies to be strengthened | ● Strengthen by internal development, acquisition of people or businesses |

## STEP 1:  IDENTIFY EXPLOITABLE ASSETS

To build up a list of company assets, marketing people need to review other departments thoroughly and objectively, through discussion and analysis. *Exploitable* assets are areas where you can become stronger than competition.

The process of involving other departments in building an inventory of assets and competencies which can be exploited in the market-place not only makes everyone in the company more customer orientated, but also gives marketers a leadership role in developing corporate strategies. A check-list of the main types of company asset is contained in **Exhibit 1**, at the end of this chapter (page 102).

Table 35 contains some examples of exploitable assets which can be exploitable in their own right. For example, Coca-Cola and McDonald's have assets of world-wide distribution. Disney has a whole stable of famous cartoon personalities, Sony has a global brand name which stands for quality, and Mars has superb modern production equipment including unique processes. These assets would be a valuable source of competitive advantage even to companies with quite weak skills or competency to exploit them. For example, Alitalia or Iberia would be delighted to own British Airways' Heathrow landing slots. However, they would be unlikely to exploit them as well as BA, due to lesser competencies.

**Table 35. Examples of exploitable assets.**

| Company | Exploitable assets |
| --- | --- |
| British Airways | Heathrow landing slots |
| Kraft USA | Database of 40 million households |
| McDonald's | 10-year Disney partnership |
| Mercedes | Strong brand image and franchise |
| Motorola | Numerous technology agreements |

Most value can be achieved from strong assets, combined with exploitable competencies and linked to consumer needs. Take J. D. Wetherspoon, the pub company, for instance.

**J. D. Wetherspoon has a core competency in creating an accessible and friendly pub atmosphere through application of skills in design and layout, staff selection and training. The result is pubs with large windows so that you can look in from the outside; comfortable, modern and informal layout inside; no smoking and friendly staff. The pubs are accessible to all ages, safe and non-sexist. They contrast with the average smoky, macho, male-dominated town-centre boozer.**

**Wetherspoon has applied its core competency to well-located but under-exploited town-centre assets – often previously cinemas, post offices, banks or private houses – and exploited them by conversion to more profitable use.**

Another example of exploiting assets through competencies is the acquisition of Rowntree by Nestlé:

**Nestlé paid a high price for Rowntree on acquisition. The appeal of Rowntree was its brand assets, both chocolate and sugar based. Geographically, Rowntree competed primarily in Northern Europe and the old Commonwealth.**

**One of Nestlé's core competencies is in global marketing – the skills to achieve world-wide distribution, to tailor brands to markets, and to build global franchises. It was able to exploit the Rowntree brand assets more effectively by applying these core competencies, in, for instance, Latin America and Asia Pacific. Nestlé dominates the grocery trade in Brazil, but Rowntree brands were unknown there. Rowntree was worth more to Nestlé than to any other bidder, due to Nestlé's core competencies, which enabled it to develop the Rowntree brands.**

## STEP 2: IDENTIFY EXPLOITABLE COMPETENCIES

Exploitable competencies are those where you have or can build an edge over competitors. As a marketer, you should meet with other department heads to list the competencies which really matter in building superior customer experiences, and rank your company on each one. This will both identify a list of exploitable competencies and point to important skill areas which need to be improved to match or beat competition in future. Lists will differ by company, department and market, and **Exhibit 2** at the end of this chapter (page 103) provides a check-list of competencies for Marketing, Selling and Operations.

Here, in Table 36, are some examples of exploitable competencies.

**Table 36. *Examples of exploitable competencies.***

| Company | Exploitable competency |
|---|---|
| Walt Disney | Customer service |
| Nike | Brand positioning |
| Procter & Gamble | Global brand development |
| Toyota | Process engineering |
| Marks & Spencer | Supplier management |
| Citizen Watch | Cost management |

## STEP 3:  RANK ATTRACTIVENESS OF PRIORITY BUSINESS AREAS

This step involves reviewing the attractiveness of markets, channels and customer groups, current or future. This ranking will subsequently enable you in **Step 4** to match attractiveness with your exploitable assets and competencies. Clearly, the ideal is to identify highly attractive markets which fit your exploitable strengths, but such pleasant outcomes rarely occur in practice. The fact that a market is attractive does not mean that you are well qualified to compete in it. The ultimate object of this exercise is to focus effort in markets and channels which are *best for you*, but it is first necessary to rank them objectively.

The best way to do this is by **quantified portfolio analysis**, which is explained in detail in Chapter 7 (pages 256–61). We need to take a top-line look at this now. For the purpose of illustration, market rather than channel or customer attractiveness will be reviewed, but the same technique can be applied to all three.

Quantified portfolio analysis of markets involves developing a list of assessment criteria, weighting them by importance and scoring markets and segments against them. The advantage of this system is that it enables all markets to be compared on common criteria, while the need to develop quantified scores enhances objectivity. The system also allows markets to be scored across business units within countries, and across countries.

Selection criteria and their weighting will vary by market. However, nine criteria are usually critical to assessing any market as illustrated in Table 37.

| Table 37.  Criteria for assessing a market. | |
|---|---|
| 1. Market size (£ revenue)<br>2. Market growth (real revenue growth)<br>3. Market profitability . . . in total, for all competitors<br>4. Real pricing trends<br>5. Competitive intensity | 6. Future risk exposure . . . to government regulation, health scares, etc.<br>7. Opportunity to differentiate.<br>8. Segmentation<br>9. Distributor or retail structure. |

For particular markets, it may be appropriate to add other criteria. For instance, in sectors where property is important, such as retailing, site availability can be critical – you may have a wonderful new multiplex cinema concept, but if all the prime retail leisure-park sites are fully taken for the next five years, you will have nowhere to go and will be unable to compete.

You will probably find it worth while to construct a written guide on how to quantify and score each criterion. **Exhibit 3** provides an example of this (page 104) and Table 38 applies the approach to the frozen-foods market:

**Table 38. Market attractiveness scoresheet: maximum weighting of nine key criteria.**

| Criteria | Frozen foods |
| --- | :---: |
| 1. Market size | 8 |
| 2. Market growth | 15 |
| 3. Market profitability | 20 |
| 4. Real pricing trends[16] | 10 |
| 5. Competitive intensity | 10 |
| 6. Future risk exposure | 6 |
| 7. Opportunity to differentiate | 10 |
| 8. Segmentation | 9 |
| 9. Retail structure | 12 |
| 10. TOTAL | 100% |

Having determined the maximum weighting of key criteria, you can then score individual markets against them. For example, in frozen foods there are over sixty product segments, such as peas, pizza and Chinese meals. If you were a frozen-foods Marketer, you would need to decide in which of these segments to compete.

No one, not even Birds Eye, the market leader, competes in every product segment, and most frozen-foods companies are involved in less than ten, so how do you rank each segment against the maximum score?

Again it is useful to construct a scoring guide-sheet. This would help you decide, for instance, whether to give a particular segment the maximum score of 15 for market growth or a much lower one. Would an annual volume growth rate of 5% qualify for the maximum, or is that too low? It all depends which market you are in: 5% annual volume growth is exciting in a mature sector like processed food, but profoundly depressing in computer software. **Exhibit 4** (page 106) gives you an example of a scoring guide-sheet for frozen foods, and Table 39 applies it to two product sectors – green beans and pizza.

You can see from the table that frozen green beans is a mature, relatively unattractive market, where it is difficult to achieve differentiation. It scores a lowly 34%. Frozen pizza is reasonably attractive, with solid future prospects, even though there is intense competition, and spare industry capacity to hold down future prices. Its score is a respectable 60%.

**Table 39.** **Frozen foods market attractiveness score sheet: green beans and pizza.**

| Criterion | Max. score (%) | Green beans | Pizza |
|---|---|---|---|
| Market size (£m) | 8 | 2 | 8 |
| Market growth prospects (% annual real change) | 15 | 4 | 12 |
| Market profitability (% ROCE pre tax) | 20 | 5 | 12 |
| Real pricing trends (%) | 10 | 4 | 5 |
| Competitive intensity | 10 | 5 | 4 |
| Future risk exposure | 6 | 5 | 5 |
| Opportunity to differentiate | 10 | 3 | 6 |
| Segmentation | 9 | 3 | 5 |
| Retail structure | 12 | 3 | 3 |
| TOTAL | 100 | 34 | 60 |

**What is the practical application of this quantified approach?** For a company already in frozen foods, it would provide guidance on which of the sixty-plus product segments to prioritize for future investment and dominance. For a company considering entry, it would highlight the more and less attractive segments. For instance, you would be unlikely to enter the frozen green beans market, unless so many companies planned to exit that you could dominate it in future. The approach could also be applied to adjacent markets like canned or fresh vegetables, or chilled pizzas, and across countries.

## STEP 4:  MATCH ASSETS AND COMPETENCIES TO FUTURE MARKET, CHANNEL, CUSTOMER OPPORTUNITIES

This step involves matching and aligning **Steps 1 to 3**, to identify *where* it will be most effective for you to compete in future. This prioritization will maximize your opportunity to deliver superior value and make above-average profits.

The three sets of data you have already developed consist of exploitable assets, exploitable competencies and the relative attractiveness of various areas of the market-place to which these can be applied. You are therefore ready to implement the Marketing Alignment Process (MAP). This will be illustrated by prioritizing markets, although it can equally easily be applied to types of channel or customer.

The portfolio analysis below has two axes – **strength of assets and competencies**, derived from **Steps 1 and 2**, and **relative market**

**attractiveness**, covered in **Step 3**. It provides guidance on investment priorities, and will help you focus activity on market segments where you can deliver superior value and above-average profits. It will direct you away from markets which are either intrinsically unattractive, or attractive but wrong for you. Figure 10 outlines the investment action underlying a MAP analysis:

**Figure 10. MAP analysis.**

Strength of assets and competencies

|  | | High | Medium | Low |
|---|---|---|---|---|
| Market attractiveness | High | Invest heavily | Invest, strengthen competencies | Exit or acquire competencies |
| | Medium | Invest | Redefine strategy | Exit or acquire |
| | Low | Maximize profits or transform market | Maximize profits or exit | Exit |

If a market is intrinsically unattractive, yet one in which you have strong assets and competencies (as in the bottom left box in the figure), the first question is whether you can transform it into an attractive market. Yamaha did this with the home piano and organ market by developing a convenient and easy-to-use product, appealing to people who were not trained instrumentalists. If you do not think that the application of your competencies can achieve this kind of transformation, you should cut costs and maximize profitability. (See bottom middle box.)

The other side of the coin is that a market may be highly attractive objectively, but fail to match your assets and competencies. In this case, you have to judge whether it is practical to radically improve them, either by internal development, or by acquisition. (See top right box.)

Marketing alignment can be applied to total markets or to sub-segments, to companies or brands, to existing markets or potential future ones. The reward for doing so effectively will be above-average profit growth.

Let's look at a few illustrations of strong and weak marketing alignment. A strong example in markets is Greenalls:

Some years ago, Greenalls was a regional brewer, publican and hotel owner, operating mainly in the North-west. Reviewing its business, Greenalls decided that the future for brewing beer was unattractive, with unexciting prospects. It may also have decided that its competencies in brewing were also limited – those who drank Greenalls beer may agree.

Greenalls therefore decided to exit brewing, a bold move at the time, and concentrate on pub retailing and three- to five-star hotels. It acquired Devenish and Boddingtons pubs, developed the de Vere hotel chain, invested heavily in pub brands such as Miller's Kitchen, and prioritized the growing discount-priced hotel sector. The marketing realignment process proved successful, and Greenalls' market capitalization has grown dramatically.

A company which has not successfully aligned its business is McDonald's in the USA. While its international business, which accounts for around 50% of global sales and profits, is booming, mainly through geographical expansion, McDonald's American business is lagging.

Over the past decade, McDonald's has attempted a number of new category entries in the USA, including pizzas, low-calorie foods and children's leisure complexes. McPizzas were on test for years, and the leisure complexes were sold to rivals 'Discovery Zone', owned by Viacom. Low-fat McLean, a beef and seaweed burger, failed.

More recently, McDonald's has tried to widen its customer franchise from kids and families to adults, using the Arch Deluxe burger as a spearhead. This took two years to develop, a period during which fifty-two different types of mustard were tried out.[17]

While the adult fast-food market is certainly attractive, it fails to align with McDonald's assets and competencies – their products, store environment and noisy family environment just don't fit.

Two other examples of marketing misalignment come from two normally outstanding marketers, Sony and Procter & Gamble.

In late 1989, Sony entered the American movie and TV film business by acquiring Columbia Pictures Entertainment Inc. for $3.4 billion.[18] The initiative appears to have been driven more by Sony's vision of the future than by a tight alignment of strengths and opportunities. The reason given for buying Columbia was 'that to develop our hardware business in the future, it is necessary to augment our music software with image-based software'.[19] Presumably the latter is films.

Sony lacked two of the key competencies to enter the American movies category – English-language and entertainment skills – and obviously aimed to pick them up via acquisition. After five years, results remain disappointing. In 1995 Sony wrote off $3 billion in goodwill in its Pictures Division as well as recording $562 million in losses, and in 1996, its picture revenue was no higher than it had been in 1992.

*

Procter & Gamble entered the fragrance market by acquisition, and has already exited the mass-market segment. P&G's many competencies are based on technology, strong logic, rigorous analysis and ability to market high-volume brands. The company is most at home in markets like detergents and paper, where technology is important and everything can be objectively measured. It is much less comfortable in 'touchy feely' areas involving emotion and intuition.

As one commentator observed: 'This is a company that knows how to sell help in a package, not hope in a bottle.'[20] The fragrance market is objectively quite attractive, but it is wrong for P&G.

Finally, a classic example of successful marketing alignment was the Bic entry to the razor market with a disposable product:

Bic had a strong world-wide position in low-price ballpoint pens, under the leadership of Baron Bich. One of its major assets was ability to manufacture small plastic items, in very high volume, at low cost per unit and to good quality standards.

Bic was keen to diversify into new consumer markets,

where it could innovate by exploiting its competencies in plastics technology. Its investigation of a number of consumer categories led it to the wet-shaver market, dominated by Gillette, which was at the time trading up customers to increasingly elaborate and expensive products. Bic introduced the low-price disposable razor, sold in multi-packs, mainly through supermarkets.

Gillette was predictably slow to react since it faced a painful choice. Successful Gillette entry with plastic disposables would trade down the value of the whole market. Inaction would result in share loss. Gillette did eventually introduce a successful plastic disposable product, but too late to prevent the establishment of Bic as a strong competitor in many countries.

However, in recent years Gillette has successfully rebuilt both its position and the sector for premium razors.

## STEP 5: IDENTIFY ASSETS AND COMPETENCIES TO BE STRENGTHENED

The final step in MAP is to review your company's assets and competencies for the future.

While conducting **Steps 1 to 4**, you may have identified attractive markets, channels, customer groups or other opportunities which could not be exploited because your company lacked the competencies to do so. A decision would therefore need to be made whether to develop or acquire the necessary competencies.

Equally, your review of assets and competencies may have revealed critical weaknesses which need to be put right. These may require changes in structure, personnel or training and development programmes.

While **Step 5** is the final one in MAP, the process should be a continuous one, as the internal and external business environment changes to reveal new opportunities, and the balance in marketing alignment shifts.

However, the Marketing Alignment Process only gives you the *opportunity* to build above-average profitability. In order to attain it, you need to exploit that opportunity by developing winning strategies – 'S'– and by executing effectively – 'E' – with the right attitudes (Table 40). These areas are covered in later chapters.

| Table 40. Key elements of Offensive Marketing. | |
|---|---|
| ✓  **P:** Profitable | ● Proper balance between firm's needs for profit and customer's need for value |
| **O:** Offensive | ● Must lead market, take risks and make competitors followers |
| **I:** Integrated | ● Marketing approach must permeate whole company |
| → **S:** Strategic | ● Probing analysis leading to a winning strategy  ← |
| → **E:** Effectively Executed | ● Strong and disciplined execution on a daily basis  ← |

'P' is the reward for 'O–I–S–E'.

## Section 3: Leveraging Short-term Profits Responsibly

The Marketing Alignment Process is primarily designed to maximize medium- and long-term profitability. It is less relevant to the short-term marketing pressure cooker.

How do Offensive Marketers respond if they find themselves in a position where they have to gear up profits sharply in the next six to twelve months? The first question to ask is how you got into this not unfamiliar situation. Is it because you have just joined a company with a few short-term problems but ambitious future investment plans? Is it a 'one-off' situation that occurs infrequently in your company? Or is it an annual event, due to a lack of clear strategy and future commit- ment? If it is the latter, you should certainly be looking around. In the meantime, you have to solve the short-term problem. The Offensive Marketer will find a solution which does not mortgage the longer- term future of the business.

Most marketing people will find they receive at least one hospital pass during their career. Here is a not untypical example:

**Sales and market share of a particular shampoo brand are declining. Consequently advertising has been cut and the brand is being heavily outspent by major competitors, who have just launched better-quality products. The new- product development cupboard at your company is bare. The brand has been spending heavily on sales promotion, especially couponing. Neither its advertising nor its promotion seem particularly effective. It therefore faces further cuts in spending budget, and is under pressure to increase price in order to hit budget. Some major**

**accounts are threatening to delist. Senior management has just decided that you are the ideal person to sort things out quickly and hit budget . . . What do you do in this pressure–cooker situation?**

Your task is to increase profit in the short term, without damaging your brand's long-term prospects, while building a strong recovery position one or two years hence. Easy, isn't it? With your right hand, you fix the short term, and with your left you build for the future. Both hands will work in unison. In Table 41 is a check–list of responsible short–term profit improvement opportunities for you to consider. These are things which will pay back immediately, or in months.

**Table 41.  Check-list of short-term profit improvement opportunities for shampoo Marketer.**

| Opportunity areas | Issues |
|---|---|
| Product and packaging quality | ● Is it currently meeting specification? <br> ● Can costs be cut without affecting performance? <br> ● Can quality be significantly improved without adding much to cost? |
| Sales promotion | ● Have past results been deeply analysed? <br> ● What type of promotion works best or worst in your market? <br> ● Is promotion clearly targeted by consumer group, trial v. loyalty, trade channel and account? |
| Advertising | ● Is it working? Has it been pre-tested? <br> ● Is strategy clear, and is strategy being effectively executed? <br> ● Can buying efficiency be improved? <br> ● What is the right spend level for the short or long term? <br> ● How imaginative is your use of communications and media? |
| Product Development | ● Has R & D got any potential line extensions which would add incremental business? <br> ● Can any be developed quickly? <br> ● What is happening in shampoo in other countries? |
| Pricing | ● Develop a price elasticity model, using regression analysis and modelling techniques. |
| Distribution channels | ● Develop a medium-term recovery plan. Present retailers with your short-term action, to hold listings and space for the next year. |

| Opportunity areas | Issues |
|---|---|
| Customer service | ● Can quality be improved?<br>● Can service areas be extended? |
| Product range | ● Are there too many marginal small sizes, which may prove unprofitable on an activity costing basis? If so, trim the range. |
| Other company departments | ● How do you motivate them to give your brand a new chance? How quickly do you tell them about your new plans? |

In the very short term, the most fruitful areas to leverage for fast profit improvement are usually sales promotion, product quality and consumer value, including pricing. Changes in advertising, customer service and direct marketing normally take longer to develop and to show up on the bottom line.

So what did the pressure-cooker marketer in the shampoo example do? Here's what he had to say:

**'The brand had been under-invested in the past, and was in serious decline. Its big plus was its distinctiveness, but this had not been fully exploited. Fortunately I had worked on this brand in other smaller countries, so came to this new job with some clear ideas.**

**'The first problem was quality, which was rather variable. This was fixed in a few weeks and we merchandised the improvement strongly to the trade. I then looked at areas where we were spending large amounts of money, frankly rather ineffectively. The advertising was off-strategy, so I quickly switched to the strategy and execution which had proved most successful in smaller countries. The change was achieved in three months, and started to work right away.**

**'On the promotion side, the strategy had rightly been to build customer loyalty, but it was not being executed because most of the spending was on smaller sizes. We changed this to focus on larger sizes, and ran fewer, more exciting promotions. We also cut out couponing, which builds trial not loyalty. Unlike the UK, there were not many tailor-made promotions for individual retail accounts in this country, so we developed a menu of eight**

or so tailor-made propositions, which did not disrupt manufacturing. We offered each account a choice of promotions, as long as they placed firm orders twelve weeks ahead. This wasn't rocket science, but it built profitable promotion volume, and pleased retailers.

'Our major medium-term initiative was a distinctive premium-priced line extension, which was linked to our core brand strategy, and positioned to generate incremental business. We advertised it and it has proved very profitable.

'Two years after entering the pressure cooker, I am glad to see brand share rising again and profits 45% up. But I wouldn't like to do it again tomorrow.'[21]

This Offensive Marketer skilfully avoided falling into some of the common traps which beset marketers under pressure:

- Despite internal encouragement, he did not raise prices. For a declining brand, with a quality problem, this would have been a bad move in the medium term, even though it looked a profitable option on a six-month timescale.
- While he improved quality to parity with competition, he did not use this as the basis for a pseudo 'relaunch', all sound and fury but no substance.
- He was able to resist pressure to cut advertising further, by adopting a sharper strategy and proven new execution. In fact, he increased advertising spend and financed this by eliminating promotions on smaller sizes and couponing.
- He spent less on sales promotion, but radically improved effectiveness.
- Most importantly of all, he worked with both hands, on the short and medium term. In Year 1, his new approach to sales promotion was the main lever to hit budget. But he also spent time in Year 1 on product and advertising quality, and on the winning line extension, all of which gave the brand momentum in Year 2.
- He did not in any area reduce consumer value, even though he was searching intently for cost savings. On the contrary, his strategy was to build consumer value cost effectively.

[For a suitable fee, the author may be willing to pass on the name of this Offensive Marketer to interested head hunters.]

The check-list (Table 41, page 93) is the best trigger for developing initiatives to leverage short-term profits responsibly, and you will doubtless be able to extend it in ways relevant to your own business.

The remainder of this chapter covers three areas for leveraging short-term profits, but they are merely three of the many outlined on the check-list. Most will also have a positive effect on long-term profits. Their short-term appeal is that they can have a rapid effect on revenue at limited additional cost, and create a profit surplus *this* fiscal year. None of the methods for cooking accounts, summarized in Table 24 (page 66), has been included, but they are available if you are desperate (it sometimes happens to all of us) and need a short-term breathing space before your long-term initiatives bear fruit.

Here are three illustrations of short-term leverage areas, with some tools and examples:

**1. Value Engineering (VE).** This is also sometimes called Marketing Value Analysis. The Japanese are the experts on VE, and Robin Cooper's book, *When Lean Enterprises Collide*, is well worth reading.[22] The key questions VE addresses are: 'What is the customer value of each part of every product or service and how does this relate to its cost?' and 'How can we translate cost into greater customer value?' VE is at the heart of Offensive Marketing, constantly balancing the changing ratios of cost and value, for the benefit of both customers and producers.

It is most effective when applied at the product or service design stage, because as much as 90% of a product's costs are designed in, and these costs 'can't be avoided without redesigning the product – once a product is designed, the majority of its costs are fixed'.[23]

However, VE is also relevant on existing products or services, as a means to leverage short-term profits. Critical to effective VE is an intimate understanding of the key elements of consumer value in a product or service. Marketers need to map out the total customer experience, break it down into value elements and judge the relative importance of each one.

For an airline, the total customer experience starts with thinking about booking the journey, and ends at the final destination. It therefore includes booking, travel to airport, reservations, waiting, security, boarding, flight, arrival experience and so on.

The whole value engineering process needs to be done on a cross-departmental basis, involving people from Finance, Operations, Engineering, probably led by marketers.

Once a value breakdown has been completed, the cost of each element needs to be established, probably using activity-based costing.

You then relate the two, and search for areas of high cost/low value (action-cut cost), or low cost/high value (action-invest for more revenue).

Figure 11 gives a notional example of an insurance product, where the figures are invented, for illustration only. Insurance companies sell insurance, but customers buy confidence – confidence that the insurer will treat them fairly in all circumstances. In the diagram, the left-hand bar represents the key elements which contribute to value – in this case, confidence versus price. Confidence is built by clarity of proposition, customer service and claims response. The right-hand bar breaks these down into cost. The two bars are then compared. So price is related to underwriting, clarity of proposition to cost of communication and so on. What low-cost, high-value elements can you spot in the diagram, and what action would you take?

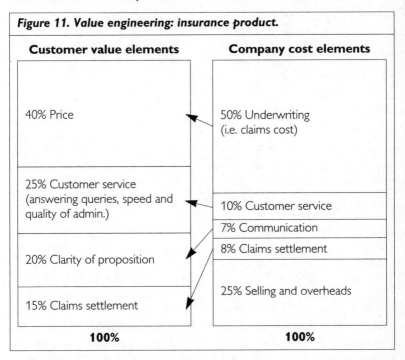

**Figure 11. Value engineering: insurance product.**

| Customer value elements | Company cost elements |
|---|---|
| 40% Price | 50% Underwriting (i.e. claims cost) |
| 25% Customer service (answering queries, speed and quality of admin.) | 10% Customer service |
| | 7% Communication |
| 20% Clarity of proposition | 8% Claims settlement |
| 15% Claims settlement | 25% Selling and overheads |
| **100%** | **100%** |

Bearing in mind that the quality of service at many insurance companies is weak, the sort of VE questions this chart will raise in your mind may include:

- Should we significantly raise spending on customer service, and fund this cost from extra revenue or even a price increase?

- What customer value is our claims settlement generating, and what is our percent customer retention level among those claiming versus those not claiming?
- Can we break down the cost and value of selling and overheads more precisely?

Another useful tool is the value engineering box (Figure 12). This is simple but effective. Key action should be taken in the 'Invest' box, where you have identified low costs which create high value; and in the 'Cut' box (low value, high cost), which calls you to get your knife out.

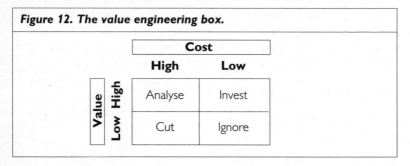

**Figure 12. The value engineering box.**

**2. Product or Service Range**. Most companies offer consumers too wide a product range. This can create confusion, add unnecessary cost, generate service or out-of-stock problems and reduce value delivered. Very often they proliferate ranges because their core products fail to offer superior consumer value. They desperately broaden the range in an attempt to shore up revenue. The fact that customers have individual needs should not obscure the reality that almost everyone wants superior value. Most diners would still prefer a set menu choice of six attractive dishes to an à la carte mêlée of a hundred choices costing 25% more.

Simple recognition of this can generate significant short-term profit savings, and marketers should lead the search for opportunities to trim ranges. In early 1996, IBM in the USA offered customers 3.4 thousand unique PC configurations, but the 1997 goal is to cut this to 200.[24] Mabuchi Motor, the world's largest producer of small electric motors for CD players, serves 70% of its customers with just twenty different models.

Here is an example from Playtex:

**Playtex in the UK had a range of seventy-five lingerie products. It noticed that the French company, with a higher market share, had only fifty products.**

The Marketing Department analysed the UK range. It was large because it had just grown, rather than because it was a properly-thought-out system, designed to cover the main sectors of the market. Many products overlapped. Some had quite limited distribution and store exposure. The costing system did not reflect the real dis-economies of running low-volume brands, which often involved unique raw materials, disproportionate write-offs of old stock, short runs and high inventory levels.

A market test was therefore set up in the UK, reducing product range from seventy-five to fifty-three. Because this did a great deal for production efficiencies and inventory costs, profits could be held even if revenue fell by 8%. In practice, in both the test and later national expansion, sales increased by 10% because the better selling products were more visible in stores and got greater sales force attention. Profits rose by 25%. The approach was extended to the USA.

**3. Asset Utilization.** What is the present level of utilization? Has the company got its price/utilization sums right? Can higher-value products be developed for use on existing plant? Can new services be launched using existing people? Are there any modified products or services that could be launched using existing facilities?

Kellogg's had a problem. The percentage brand share of Kellogg's Cornflakes was declining over the long term. The company had spare manufacturing capacity for cornflakes, but a firm policy of not producing for stores' private labels.

Kellogg's solved this problem by launching Kellogg's Crunchy Nut Cornflakes, priced at a heavy premium to the customer. It gained a 2–3% market share, mainly incremental to other Kellogg's brands.

Kellogg's exploited existing assets of brand name, flake technology, sales force and plant, but with a separate advertising positioning which attracted new consumers at high margins.

Similar questions can be asked about other assets, such as brands or customers. How can we incrementally extend our brands?[25] Are there any new usages for our products or services? How effectively are we using our customer databases, and how can we raise our level of customer retention? What other products or services do our customers need?

Returning to the opening paragraph of this section, every marketer should have the skills to leverage short-term profits without mortgaging the future. But, if you find yourself having to do this year after year, while starved of the investment necessary to build the long term, it is time to move on.

# FLOW-CHART SUMMARY OF CHAPTER 2

## *Section 1:* How Offensive Marketers Should Change the Rules

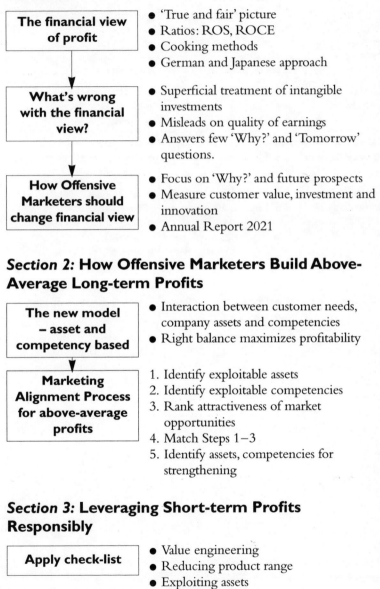

**The financial view of profit**

- 'True and fair' picture
- Ratios: ROS, ROCE
- Cooking methods
- German and Japanese approach

**What's wrong with the financial view?**

- Superficial treatment of intangible investments
- Misleads on quality of earnings
- Answers few 'Why?' and 'Tomorrow' questions.

**How Offensive Marketers should change financial view**

- Focus on 'Why?' and future prospects
- Measure customer value, investment and innovation
- Annual Report 2021

## *Section 2:* How Offensive Marketers Build Above-Average Long-term Profits

**The new model – asset and competency based**

- Interaction between customer needs, company assets and competencies
- Right balance maximizes profitability

**Marketing Alignment Process for above-average profits**

1. Identify exploitable assets
2. Identify exploitable competencies
3. Rank attractiveness of market opportunities
4. Match Steps 1–3
5. Identify assets, competencies for strengthening

## *Section 3:* Leveraging Short-term Profits Responsibly

**Apply check-list**

- Value engineering
- Reducing product range
- Exploiting assets
- Other check-list areas

**Check-list of Types of Company Asset.**                      **Exhibit 1**

| Working capital | ● Amount<br>● Availability | ● Location<br>● Credit lines |
|---|---|---|
| **Operations**<br>(plant, processes,<br>IT systems) | ● Relative modernity<br>● Exclusive elements<br>● Flexibility | ● Economies of scale<br>● Capacity utilization |
| **Property** | ● Type<br>● Location | ● Extendability<br>● Quality |
| **Customer<br>franchises** | ● Brand names<br>● Brand franchises<br>● Databases | ● Customer relationships<br>● Unique products/services<br>● Patents |
| **Sales/distribution<br>service network** | ● Size<br>● Quality | ● Coverage<br>● Relations with external<br>distributors |
| **Scale<br>advantages** | ● Market share<br>● Relative and absolute<br>media weight<br>● Purchases/leverage | ● Geographical/international<br>coverage<br>● Sales/distribution/service<br>(above)<br>● Specialist skills due to<br>scale (e.g. market research) |
| **Third-party<br>relationships** | ● Suppliers<br>● Financial institutions<br>● Joint ventures | ● Third-party agreements<br>(e.g. technology or brand<br>exploitation) |

**Check-list of Main Type of Skill or Competency.**   **Exhibit 2**

| | | |
|---|---|---|
| **Marketing** | • New product development<br>• Business analysis<br>• Unique market research techniques<br>• Planning skills<br>• Database management<br>• Category management<br>• Brand extension<br>• Brand equity measurement | • Advertising development<br>• Customer service<br>• Customer relationships<br>• Customer targeting<br>• Marketing process<br>• Spending efficiency<br>• Testing<br>• Design |
| **Selling** | • Account management<br>• Relationship development<br>• Supply-chain management<br>• Customer service<br>• Motivation and control<br>• Building partnerships<br>• Planning | • Merchandising<br>• New account development<br>• Space management<br>• Presentation skills<br>• Negotiation<br>• Pricing and promotion<br>• Trade marketing |
| **Operations** (plant, processes, IT systems) | • Industrial relations<br>• Motivation and control<br>• Process engineering<br>• Inventory control<br>• Productivity improvement<br>• Cost management<br>• Planning<br>• New facility development<br>• Health and safety<br>• Management training and development | • Flexibility<br>• Speed of response<br>• Total quality management<br>• Purchasing<br>• Capacity utilization<br>• Payment systems<br>• Commercialization of new products or services<br>• Property skills<br>• Method of supplier management<br>• Global operation |

**Ranking Market Attractiveness – Guidelines
for Determining Weighting of Criteria.**

**Exhibit 3**

## Nine Criteria for Assessing Attractiveness of Different Sectors

| | |
|---|---|
| **1. Market size** | Clearly, the larger the market, the higher the score. Markets should be evaluated in £ value, not units. A market may be growing in volume, but declining in average price per unit – as in microchips, computers and many consumer durables. Volume is therefore less relevant than value. |
| **2. Market growth** | Real-value growth, after inflation, is the primary measure. Exposure of markets to economic cycles (e.g. hotels), fashion (e.g. clothing) or climate (e.g. drinks, ice-cream) should also be considered. |
| **3. Market profitability** | This would cover total market profitability, not just your own company's. Estimates can usually be developed via competitor intelligence, published accounts and your own forecasts of competitor profitability. |
| **4. Real pricing trends** | This is self-explanatory, for the total market. You should have a view as to how far real-price changes are caused by genuine price movements, and how far by changes in product mix (e.g. fast growth in volume in premium-priced sectors can increase the real value of the total market, even though there have been no price increases). |
| **5. Competitive intensity** | This normally comprises 3 elements – competitive structure, quality of competitors and their commitment level. Views vary in the business world on what is an attractive competitive structure. Is it more attractive to compete against 4 large companies each with a share of 15%, or with 2 market leaders, holding 40% and 20% market shares? One could argue that the first structure is least attractive, because all 4 companies will be spending heavily to achieve leadership, probably calculating that there is only room for 2 or 3 major companies in the longer term. In the case of the 2 leaders with 40% and 20% shares, a clear pecking order has been established. This could be the more attractive market to an outsider, since both competitors may have become complacent.   In general, the ideal competitive structure from the viewpoint of a new market entrant is: <br> ● lots of smaller brands, companies, none dominant <br> ● medium to low calibre of company |

|  | ● limited long-term commitment to the market by existing competitors<br>This ideal unfortunately is rarely encountered today. |
|---|---|
| **6. Future risk exposure** | This market criterion would embrace issues like future regulatory changes (e.g. as in healthcare or drinks), government intervention (e.g. privatization or competition exposure policy), new legislation at local or EC level, future product availability (e.g. fish, fine art for auction houses), etc. |
| **7. Opportunity to dfferentiate** | How far is the market a commodity one, driven by price? Is it highly segmented, with fast-growing 'hot spots'? Is competition based on added value and differentiation, or on price? The latter is clearly less attractive. |
| **8. Segmentation** | In general, the more segments a market has, the more attractive to innovative Marketers. |
| **9. Distributor or retail** | What is the relative bargaining power of suppliers and distributors? What is the trend? What are distributor profit levels and trends? How well do they serve suppliers and consumers? What is channel structure and trend? What are the opportunities for dealing direct with consumers?<br>The most attractive structure for suppliers is one in which distributors are diffused and lack bargaining power; serve customers efficiently at low cost; do not market their own private label brands; and are responsive to supplier innovation.<br>Unfortunately, this ideal does not exist. |

**Scoring Guidesheet For Deciding how to Score each Product Sector within Frozen Foods**

**Exhibit 4**

### Frozen Foods Market Attractiveness: Scoring Guide Sheet

| Criterion: | Max. score (%) | Scoring guide | | | |
|---|---|---|---|---|---|
| | | Excellent | Good | Fair | Poor |
| Market size (£m) | 8 | 100+ | 70–99 | 40–69 | >40 |
| Market growth prospects (% annual real change) | 15 | 5+ | 2–4 | 0–1 | Minus |
| Market profitability (% ROCE pre-tax) | 20 | 20+ | 15–19 | 10–14 | >10 |
| Real pricing trends (%) | 10 | 3% pa | 1–2% | Flat | Minus |
| Competitive intensity | 10 | Low | Average | High | V. high |
| Future risk exposure | 6 | Low | Average | High | V. high |
| Opportunity to differentiate | 10 | V. high | High | Moderate | Low |
| Segmentation | 9 | Much | Some | Little | None |
| Retail structure | 12 | Fragmented | Spread | Focused | Concentrated |
| Total | 100 | | | | |

Using this scoring sheet, relative market attractiveness of frozen food market segments can be scored, against the maximum score for each of the nine agreed criteria. For example, frozen green beans only score 4 out of 15 for market growth prospects, because they have been flat for years, and the future looks unexciting. Their total score is only 34%, compared with a more encouraging 60% for pizza – see text, page 87.

PART TWO:
**OFFENSIVE**

# 3. Offensive Vision and Attitudes

## Chapter Summary

Offensive Marketing is a total package, in which each element of P-O-I-S-E supports the others (Table 42).

| Table 42. | |
|---|---|
| **P:** Profitable | ● *Proper balance between firm's needs for profit and customer's need for value* |
| **O:** Offensive | ● *Must lead market, take risks and make competitors followers* |
| **I:** Integrated | ● *Marketing approach must permeate whole company* |
| **S:** Strategic | ● *Probing analysis leading to a winning strategy* |
| **E:** Effectively Executed | ● *Strong and disciplined execution on a daily basis* |

Offensive attitudes, 'O', have a strong influence on I-S-E, and are described in this chapter. They stimulate 'I' for 'Integrated' by establishing a customer-centred vision and a focus on superior value which everyone can understand. They provide an environment for effective investment and long-term outlook, in which 'S' for 'Strategic' can flourish. And, with their emphasis on innovation, persistent attack and speed of response, they are crucial to 'E' for 'Effectively executed'.

Offensive attitudes are like the seven spokes of a wheel. Each spoke is connected, and together they will lead to dynamic performance:

**Vision** should be realistic, relevant, easy to communicate and capable of motivating or even inspiring employees.

**Value** is an attitude which insists on giving customers a superior combination of benefit and price. This requires not only strong marketing sense, but also a relentless drive to reduce costs and improve efficiencies.

**Innovation** needs to be pursued on two fronts – the daily trickle of ideas and improvements, and the ambitious projects. Success in innovation requires an attitude by senior management which encourages, recognizes and rewards innovative efforts, and a structure that supports this.

**Long-term** outlook is one of the most visible tests of senior management's resource and determination. Short-term expedients can weaken a company's vision and value, and reduce employees' confidence in the Board's commitment to its stated goals.

**Investment** is essential to renew and develop all assets and competencies but it must be effectively directed.

**Persistent attack** involves an overall attacking frame of mind, even though on certain fronts a company may be temporarily defending. A general attitude of attack motivates employees, places pressure on competition and creates internal drive for improved performance.

**Speed** is a test of a business's fitness. It is important to develop the capability to respond quickly to changes in the business environment or in customer needs.

The Board, aided and abetted by marketers, should aim to build Offensive attitudes across the whole company.

## Why Offensive Attitudes Are Important

How do your competitors regard your company?

· **Is it seen as formidable, offensive to the extent that existing competitors are apprehensive, and would-be competitors carefully avoid any direct attacks? Or is it viewed as an easy win, a source of future revenue gains by competitors in predatory mode? Does it set the agenda for the industry, or follow the leader?**

And how do your colleagues enjoy working there?

**Do they arrive expectant every Monday morning and depart tired but fulfilled on Friday evening? Is there direction, progress, teamwork and fun, *or is life an endless treadmill of lengthy meetings, deferred decisions and unpleasant internal politics?* Are you trudging wearily behind competitors, vainly trying to catch up, or are you setting the pace from the front?**

Table 43 will help you to rate companies you know for offensive attitudes.

The survivor attitude – in football parlance, playing for a goalless draw – demotivates people and impairs performance. It is evident that superior results may be drawn from average material, or that very able people can produce poor results. One of the keys to performance is attitude, and this in turn is moulded by the leadership, motivation and working environment provided by senior management. Attitudes are, therefore, one of the keystones of the Offensive Marketing approach, the 'O' of POISE (Table 42).

**Table 43. Quick guide to Offensive attitudes.**

| Criterion | Offensive Marketer | Survivor | Your Company |
|---|---|---|---|
| Vision | Real | Hot air | |
| Top management | Leads | Controls | |
| Customer value | Superior | Parity | |
| Innovation | Built-in | Spasmodic | |
| Outlook | Long-term | Fiscal year | |
| Investment | Consistent | Variable | |
| Strategy | Attack | Survive | |
| Decision-making | Fast | Labyrinthine | |
| Teamwork | Excellent | Weak | |
| Discussion | Leads to action | Goes on and on | |
| Tone | Positive | Defensive | |

### The right attitudes must start at the top

Some of the topics covered in this chapter are outside the normal scope of a book on marketing. But this book is not about Marketing Departments or marketing activities, it is about the marketing approach. **Whether or not a company adopts Offensive Marketing is decided by the board of directors, not by marketing people**. Boards following the offensive approach have to make hard decisions about attitude to quality, investment, costs and the consumer. In difficult times, with the familiar pressures to cut back on advertising, R & D, product quality, service levels and capital investment, what is needed is willpower and courage as well as toughness. Marketing people should always aim to influence the Board, and energetically lead the execution of the marketing approach.

Offensive attitudes are a set of shared values and approaches, grounded in a daily commitment to customers and to low-cost operation. They give companies cohesion and momentum, and employees pride and a sense of mission.

These attitudes underpinning Offensive Marketing are not to be confused with 'aggressive' marketing. One sometimes sees headlines in the marketing press announcing that Company X is launching an 'aggressive' marketing campaign. The article is usually decorated with a photograph of the perpetrator, quite likely to be a galloping midget. It will describe how money is being thrown at a problem by cutting prices, launching a huge promotion or trebling advertising spending. The informed reader can often recognize the desperate throw of an ill-prepared marketer following a leader too late, or attempting to disguise a product's lack of competitive edge by making a lot of noise. Offensive Marketers will certainly be competitive, but they are also thoughtful, imaginative and forward thinking.

## The Seven Spokes of the Offensive Approach

While a bicycle wheel with seven spokes would be offensive to a cyclist, the analogy is useful for communicating the seven attitudes which comprise the offensive approach as it illustrates the links between all seven elements. Vision moves the wheel, value is driven by innovation, innovation depends on long-term outlook and investment; and each of the elements connects with the centre, to build a core of offensive attitudes (see Figure 13).

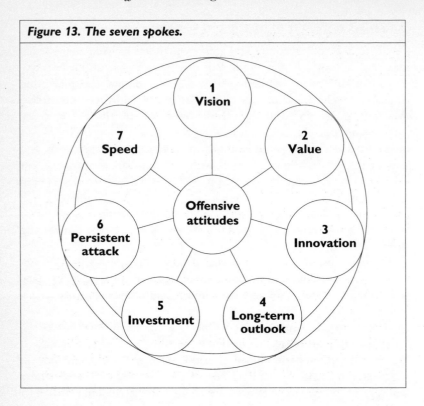

**Figure 13. The seven spokes.**

The remainder of this chapter will cover these seven elements individually, and will focus particularly on vision, which sets the wheel moving, activates the other spokes and sets the stage for the 'S' in 'POISE' – *Strategy* (Chapter 7, below).

## SPOKE NO. 1:  VISION AND PURPOSE

To succeed in the long term, businesses need a vision of how they will change and improve in the future. This vision gives the business vitality and motivates those who work in it. In reality, the word 'vision' is too large to describe many of the rather humdrum aspirations which have powered successful businesses for decades.

Clear vision is built on ability to anticipate and judge the future. This is covered further in Chapter 6.

A successful vision will usually meet six requirements, and this section will measure a number of visions against these (Table 44).

**Table 44. Vision: six requirements for success.**

| Requirement | Comment |
|---|---|
| 1. Provides future direction | ● See Chapter 6 – anticipating the future |
| 2. Expresses a consumer benefit | ● Successful visions look outwards |
| 3. Realistic | ● Believable to customers and employees |
| 4. Motivating | ● Vision must motivate and inspire employees |
| 5. Fully communicated | ● To all levels and functions inside company |
| 6. Consistently followed and measured | ● Avoid temptation to compromise when the going gets tough |

Bill Gates's vision or corporate mission for Microsoft was, 'A computer on every desk and in every home.' This met all six key requirements.[1] The Johnson & Johnson credo is similarly effective:

**'We believe our first responsibility is to the doctors, nurses, patients and to the mothers and all others who use our products and services. In meeting their needs, everything we do must be of high quality. We must constantly strive to reduce our costs in order to maintain reasonable prices.'[2]**

**This credo was written by R.W. Johnson Jr in 1943, and, subject to some slight revision in wording, has remained constant. Jim Burke, CEO of Johnson & Johnson through the 1980s, estimated that he 'spent 40% of his time communicating the credo throughout the company.'[3]**

A clear business vision will look into the future and allow a business to prepare for change ahead of its competitors. Many businesses develop competent forecasts of the future environment, but fail to confront the implications of it.

**1. Provides future direction.** Reflecting on the challenges facing a company like General Electric, CEO Jack Welch stated that the first step is for the company to 'define its destiny in broad but clear terms. You need . . . something big but clear and understandable.' Here's General Electric's vision statement:

'**We will become number one or two in every market we serve and revolutionize this company to have the speed and agility of a small enterprise.**'[4]

General Electric has already made strong progress in implementing this vision.[5]

The Annhauser Busch vision is also well drawn, but perhaps too general:

'**Through all of our products, services and relationships, we find ways to add enjoyment to life.**'

This vision has led Annhauser Busch to its goals for the twenty-first century, which are to achieve a 50% share of the US beer market, to establish a dominant position in beer internationally, and to be the quality leader in other businesses, such as theme parks.

**2. Expresses a consumer benefit**. Corporate visions deal with the future through the eyes of the consumer. Corporate objectives turn these into shareholder value. The Chrysler statement of purpose is a good example of a consumer-driven future vision:

'**Our purpose is to produce cars and trucks that people will want to buy, will enjoy driving, and will want to buy again.**'

By contrast, the Abbey National purpose is generic, and lacks either vision or customer empathy:

'**Our purpose is to create above-average growth in share-holder value by providing outstanding service to our customers.**'

**3. Is realistic.** Future vision should be imaginative yet achievable, stretching yet within grasp. This requires more than elegantly crafted statements. It calls for robust strategies, based on thorough identification of future opportunities.

AT&T's vision of 'universal togetherness'[6] is ambitious, though, to date, their ability to implement it is questionable. The company has identified a number of opportunities to give reality to this future direction, such as:

- Further developing global wireless services, forecast to treble in value in the next decade.
- Strengthening position in local phone markets where AT&T has only a 15% share.

- Making on-line services more accessible to a wider audience.
- Growing in electronic communications such as on-line shopping and electronic payment.

Daimler-Benz's vision some years ago proved unrealistic:

**Daimler-Benz pursued a vision to move from transportation group to integrated technology group. It acquired a number of companies, and at one stage produced planes, cars, refrigerators, nuclear power stations and typewriters. The assumption was that common technologies could be exploited across different businesses within the group. This did not work in practice, and the expression 'integrated technology concern' has now become something of a bad joke within the company.[7] The future direction was revised and Daimler-Benz regards itself once more as a transportation group, making automobiles, trains and aircraft.**

Even this may prove too wide a definition.

**4. Is motivating.** Creating future vision is 'as much about the creation of meaning for employees as it is about the establishment of direction . . . and the scoreboard of top management − shareholder returns − is likely to exact very little emotional pull on middle to lower level employees'.[8]

Canon's future vision is motivating as well as customer based:

**'Guided by the Company's Kyosei philosophy − living and working together for the common good . . . we bring more pleasant working conditions to the office, a better quality of life to individuals, and greater productivity to industry through innovation in cameras, business machines, and optical products.'**

The future vision of Fujitsu has similar qualities:

**'Fujitsu makes tomorrow's dreams come true today, with total computer and telecom systems, based on leading edge electronic devices.'**

By contrast, the future vision of CIBA, part of Novartis, the Swiss pharmaceutical company, is neither clear, motivating nor customer based:

**'We strive to achieve sustainable growth by balancing our economic, social and environmental responsibilities.**

**Empowered employees and a flexible organization support our commitment to excellence.'**

Only a committee could be satisfied with such a statement.

**5. Must be fully communicated.** If the future vision is clear and motivating, it will be easier to communicate and more readily accepted. Running a Workshop among blue-collar or sales people to communicate the CIBA future vision could be boring. However, communicating the strategic purpose of Kwikfit, '*Our aim is to get customers back on the road speedily and to do this in a way that achieves 100% customer delight*'; or Marks & Spencer: '*Top quality, outstanding value products and first class service*' would be straightforward.

Visions need to be simple, and easily understood. Communication has to be constant, both up, down and across the organization, as illustrated below:

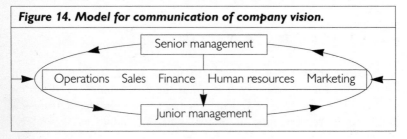

**Figure 14. Model for communication of company vision.**

**6. Must be consistently followed and measured.** Do people in back offices and plants understand, believe and act upon the company's strategic vision? Is it part of their everyday life, followed day in and day out? And, most importantly of all, does senior management conduct the business in good times and bad in ways which are seen to 'hold the dream'? If not, the future vision will rapidly lose credibility, and soon be viewed as empty rhetoric.

Many Boards and Chief Executives spend vast amounts of time designing corporate visions, sell them heavily to employees, and then promptly take decisions which undermine the vision. **A vision centred around world-class technology is unconvincing if the company concerned makes heavy cuts in its R & D budget under the guise of 'focus' or 'efficiency'.**

If the vision statement is clear and believed in by senior management, it will be measurable. GE could and did measure whether it was number one or two in any market; if it was not, and saw no potential for becoming number one or two, it would exit the market. Equally, it could measure speed to market with new products, just as Kwikfit measures customer service, and Marks & Spencer measures quality plus value.

The CIBA and AT&T visions, though, are difficult to measure, because they are too vague.

## SPOKE NO. 2: VALUE

Value is a changing ratio which relates benefits to price. It can be expressed as a **brand value equation**. This enables you to separate the three elements of brand value and to assess the relative contribution they make (Figure 15).

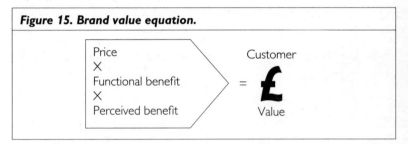

**Figure 15. Brand value equation.**

Price
×
Functional benefit
×
Perceived benefit

= £

Customer

Value

**Functional benefit** is the *objective* performance of a product or service, shorn of its imagery, i.e. the naked body. *For example, statistics collected by motoring organizations show that the Lexus is an extremely reliable car.*

**Perceived benefit** is based on the consumer's *perception* of branded products or services, i.e. the fully clothed version. *For example, most whisky drinkers have difficulty in differentiating between various products on a blind tasting basis. Yet they will pay high premiums for certain brands because the presentation and heritage create a strong perceived benefit.*

The difference between objective performance and perceived benefit is often described as the brand image.

All the elements of the brand value equation are relative, in comparison with competition, as the examples in Table 45 show.

**Table 45. Example of elements in brand value equation.**

| Brand category | Value elements (benefits/price) |
|---|---|
| Discount retailer | Parity products/lower price |
| Premium whisky | High perceived benefit/higher price |
| Wood preservation | Superior result/higher price |

The brand value equation is a useful rule of thumb, and applicable to any product or service. However, sound judgement is necessary to evaluate benefit. A suggested process to use is given in Table 46.

| Table 46. Brand value equation. | |
|---|---|
| *Price:* | Identify the category or market segment in which you compete. Take your average price, relate it to the market average, and index it. For instance, as a discount grocery retailer, your price may be 10% below the market average. This is a value advantage, and your index is 110. Not every calculation is so straightforward. Promotion prices may muddy the water – they should be taken into account. Or price comparisons may be complex, as in the case of a mortgage, where you have options of variable or fixed rates, and repayment or endowment systems. This is why good judgement based on detailed facts and market knowledge is essential. |
| *Functional benefit:* | This is feasible to establish for most products, from fast-moving consumer goods to consumer durables, where they can be blind-tested, shorn of product imagery. It is more difficult for service products, but realistic if comparative performance figures are used. For example, punctuality in consumer transport, and speed of service in retailing or fast food, are key performance indicators. In business-to-business markets, functional benefits can often be evaluated through technical testing. |
| *Perceived benefit:* | This is the most difficult of the 3 value elements to assess. Johnny Walker or Ballantines whisky are much more expensive than local brands, and the price premium is due mainly to superior imagery. How can this be quantified? The best method is to use customer attitude scores based on consumer research. Customer loyalty or retention levels are also useful indicators of relative perceived benefits. |

As with most marketing tools, the brand value equation is a judgemental process rather than a formula to be blindly applied. You cannot say, for example, that a 60:40 blind-test win on a consumer product justifies a 50% or even a 15% price premium. You can be sure, however, that it will sustain a higher price. The exact level will depend on the market, competition, the brand's starting-point, its capacity situation and future aspirations. The brand value equation is a good example of the direction in which marketing is moving. It is an inexact process which adds discipline to decision-making but requires deep understanding of customers and markets. The quantification is tempered and refined by informed judgement. That is why it needs to be done by knowledgeable marketing people, not by accountants.

Table 47 quantifies the process outlined in Table 46. The precision of the figures should not mislead you into thinking that the brand value equation is an exact process, which is why the final column 'Relative customer value' is expressed in words rather than figures. Please note that in the 'Relative price' column, the lower the price, the higher the index score.

**Table 47. Quantification of brand value equation.**

| Brand category | Functional benefit | Perceived benefit | Relative price | Relative customer value |
|---|---|---|---|---|
| Discount retailer | 95 | 90 | 110 | Average |
| Spirit brand | 100 | 300 | 67 | High |
| Wood preservation | 105 | 125 | 50 | Low |

**The discount retailer** is offering average consumer value. Its products are identical to those sold by other retailers, but functional benefit is lower due to restricted range and spartan ambience. Perceived benefit is low, but price is 10% below non-discounters, to compensate for this.

**The spirit brand** is an international one, marketed in Russia, the world's largest vodka market, dominated by local brands. Its functional quality is average, but heritage and image are extremely strong. Although it is priced well above local brands, it is offering superior value because it has such a high perceived benefit.

**The wood preservation brand** has a major value problem. Its treatment process is slightly better than competition, the company has a perception of superior reliability. However, this does not justify its massive 100% price premium.

Most products or services at best offer parity benefits at parity prices, and therefore fail to deliver superior value. Companies or brands in this position are unlikely to survive in the long term, since customers will have no particular reason to seek out their products or services. That is why a powerful commitment to value, by every employee every day, is 'Spoke No. 2' of offensive attitudes.

Achieving this standard is difficult, especially in service businesses. For instance, two of the most important factors affecting customer choice of pubs are welcome and atmosphere. Are customers greeted with a smile, served quickly and made to feel comfortable in a hospitable environment? Or are they ignored as the landlord chats with regulars, and eventually served in an offhand way? All this depends on the landlord, on his motivation, his selection and training of staff . . . and how he feels at this particular moment. A fragile thread on which to build superior value, yet a critical one.

The brand value equation can be applied to individual product or service brands, and to umbrella or corporate brands.

What are the main indicators of value? The market regularly provides clues, hints or even screaming headlines about each company's value offering. Here are some things to look at and questions to ask:

1. **What is the sales trend of existing products in existing accounts?** Sales figures are the mirror of a product's value.

2. **What is the level and trend of market share?** Again look at existing products in existing accounts. Declining product value can be obscured by gains from new distribution, line extensions or inventory building.

3. **How do your products or services perform when objectively assessed by your customers against direct competition?**

4. **Can your products sustain a price premium?** If not, how can you pretend they are better?

5. **How loyal are your customers in relation to competitors?** What is your level of repeat business? What is your percent annual retention level of customers? What are future intentions to purchase?

6. **What proportion of the customer's category purchases are of your brand?** For example, if you are a building society, what percent of each customer's total savings do you have, and how does this compare with competition? In other words, what is your share of customer, and how is this trending?

The gold standard in value is to provide a superior product or service and be a low-cost operator. This results in both satisfied customers and high profits. Customers' value requirements continually increase, and tomorrow they will expect your products and services to improve in quality and reduce in price. Does *everyone* in the company understand this, and know how s/he can help build superior value? Above all else, value is an attitude, an attitude of really caring about delivering customer value, at every opportunity, day in, day out, whatever the circumstances.

## SPOKE NO. 3: INNOVATION

The offensive attitude to innovation is the determination to lead rather than follow. 'Innovation' is a word often used to describe high-profile breakthroughs – like the American mini-van sector, which Chrysler innovated, the green energy tyre, or many new drugs. In this book it is used more broadly, to embrace any improvement in customer value or in cost of operation, the two arms of Offensive Marketing. Therefore, while the Japanese are not always innovative in R & D terms, they continually innovate in production and engineering techniques. This has enabled them to market better products at lower cost.

Innovation is most effective when viewed as a continuing process, applied to every area of the business. It is much easier to translate a bundle of individually minor developments into a major step forward than to seek and find the breakthrough innovation.

There are two main types of innovation – 'big bang' and 'drip feed'. 'Big bang' innovations usually involve heavy investment, high risk of failure and long lead-times, and have a transforming impact when successful. They are often driven by technology or by creative exploitation of distribution channels, as the successful examples in Table 48 show.

**Table 48.  Examples of successful 'big bang' innovations.**

| Example | Key driver | |
| --- | --- | --- |
| | **Technology** | **Distribution channels** |
| Boeing 777 | ✓ | |
| Chrysler mini-van | ✓ | |
| M&S chilled ready meals | ✓ | ✓ |
| Canon copier | ✓ | ✓ |
| Dell computers | | ✓ |
| First Direct Bank | | ✓ |
| Michelin's Green Energy tyre | ✓ | |
| Gillette Sensor | ✓ | |

The cost of 'big bang' innovations is high and ability to predict success low, especially where new technology is the key driver.

One of the most successful 'big bang' innovations was Marks & Spencer chilled ready meals:

The UK is still the only country in the world with a well-developed chilled ready meals business. This market was pioneered by Marks & Spencer. Requirements for success were innovative product development, and a supply chain which ensured that very short-life products were delivered and sold quickly. M&S chose its suppliers carefully, and worked jointly with them on product development and supply chain.

The result was a unique, premium-priced product range, which could either be frozen for later consumption or eaten on the same day. UK supermarket retailers were attracted to this market, but it took them many years to become effective competitors, since they had to build up a supplier base and invest in chilled distribution. M&S has retained a strong consumer franchise in chilled foods, and earns high margins.

Outside the UK, there have been many unsuccessful chilled ready meals ventures by other retailers. They have failed mainly because of weak retail distribution systems, which resulted in poor product experiences for consumers.

M&S has long since moved from 'big bang' to 'drip feed' innovation in chilled foods, as the market has matured. While 'big bang' innovation typically involves a small number of people in R & D, Marketing, Sales, Distribution and Finance, 'drip feed' innovation is the province of every employee and affects every business activity, large or small. Table 49 illustrates this difference.

**Table 49. Key drivers: big bang versus drip feed innovation.**

| Big Bang | Drip Feed | |
|---|---|---|
| ● Technology | ● Process engineering | ● Service development |
| ● Distribution channels | ● Training and competency | ● Information systems |
| | ● Marketing value analysis | ● Re-segmentation of markets |
| | ● Customer relationships | |
| | ● Product development | ● Brand development |
| | | ● Brand positioning |

'Drip feed' innovation is evolutionary, not revolutionary. It gains by small increments on a daily basis, but these mount up quickly over time, and rarely carry major risk (Figure 16).

**Figure 16.**

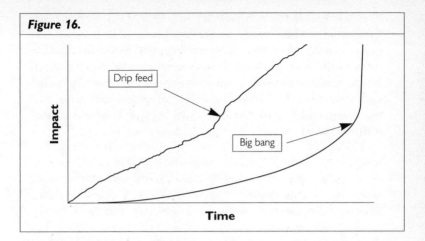

Companies which are good at steady and continuous 'drip feed' innovation succeed by creating an attitude of mind, which is always questioning, 'How can we do this better, less expensively or differently?' They include those listed in Table 50.

| Table 50. Effective drip feed innovators. | |
|---|---|
| ● Olympus | ● JCB |
| ● Komatsu | ● Nissan |
| ● BMW | ● Compaq |
| ● 3M | ● Toyota |

**3M occasionally achieves a big-bang success, as with Post-it Notes, but relies on a continuous drip feed of innovation in every area of the business, especially on new products. As their annual report says: 'Innovative products remain our engine for sustained, profitable growth.'[9]**

**3M aims to meet two broad innovation objectives – 7% of annual revenue in new products launched this year, and 30% in products introduced in the last four years. It usually achieves these objectives.**

**In doing this, it draws on *thirty* core technologies, activated by over 8,000 scientists and technologists (who account for about 10% of the total workforce). They work with colleagues in Marketing, Manufacturing and other disciplines, to discover unique solutions to customer needs and to bring new products to market faster. Many**

of these create new markets and change the basis of competition. The process is fuelled by extensive customer research, and heavy R & D spending, at 7% of sales.

Over the years, the day-to-day drip feed has swollen into a torrent of new initiatives, from non-rusting soap pads and film to make laptop computers brighter, to microstructured abrasives for finishing jet engine blades, to filters which reduce dust and odours inside cars.

It pays both to pursue the daily drip-feed innovation and to invest in the potential big bang, which can radically expand customer franchise if successful. The balance struck between the two depends on the kind of category a company is in. So how does a company create an atmosphere where innovation thrives?

The daily drip-feed innovation is primarily a question of frame of mind, which depends on senior management example and emphasis. The big-bang type is more difficult because it involves risks both for individual employees and for businesses. To ensure that people will stick their necks out and champion new ideas, large companies need the right structure and a supportive attitude to risk-takers.

Company senior management usually feels a lot more comfortable with drip-feed than with big-bang innovation, as the classic Xerox computer example demonstrates.

The early history of the personal computer revolution was Altair in 1975, Apple 2 1977, IBM PC 1981, and Apple Mac 1984. The Apple Mac, designed by a team with an average age of 21, was the first modern computer, with an easy to use screen – graphical interface. Yet as early as 1973, Xerox, in Palo Alto, California, had developed the mouse, a printer, networking which linked *a hundred* Alto computers, and graphical interface.

Apparently, Xerox senior management in New York lacked a clear vision of the office of the future. While they had the foresight to invest heavily in computer innovation, they did not know what to do with the Alto when shown it.

In 1982, Steve Jobs of Apple asked for and was given a demonstration of the Xerox Alto. According to a Xerox researcher, 'The Apple team understood more about the Alto after one and a half hours – its technology and potential – than Xerox management in New York understood after two years of presentations.'

Steve Jobs quickly hired *a hundred* engineers to copy and improve upon the Xerox approach. His vision for the Apple Mac was that it should be 'insanely great'. No design issue was too small, and it was never too late to get it right. The Apple Mac was launched at a premium price in late 1984. In the view of some, Xerox could have owned the computer industry in the 1990s – they had both the technology and resources to do so.[10]

The lesson of the Alto example is that both senior management and marketers need to understand technology and have a vision of the future. To succeed as innovators, **businesses** should be driven by technology and fear – strange bedfellows – and **individuals** by hope and excitement. *Fortune* magazine polled a large sample of American business school professors, consultants and security analysts, and developed a list of 'Eight Masters of Innovation'.[11] It then interviewed these companies to discover what made them successful innovators, and concluded that:

1. The driving forces were commitment to new technology and fear of being outpaced by competitors.
2. The most effective structure was lean, decentralized units, where engineers, marketers and finance experts were thrown together in tight groups.
3. Top management needs access to raw data rather than bowdlerized digests censored by middle management.
4. There has to be clear direction to channel and prioritize the flood of ideas.
5. It is better to start small with new innovations so as to control the risk. Put your toe into the water, check back with the consumer and then slide your ankle in. Don't jump in at the deep end with a large splash, because you may never reappear.

The driving forces of technology and fear, however, have to be converted into profitable new developments by individuals. This is where the hope and excitement come in. Assuming that they have the right organizational structure, businesses wishing to be innovative have to encourage, recognize and reward risk-takers. How well a company does this can often be answered by asking three questions (Figure 17).

**Figure 17.**

The author conducted this exercise in a large multi-billion-pound organization with the following results:

**Company X made two major innovations in the past ten years, both of which generated big revenue gains. One was a new approach to market segmentation, picked up from observation of overseas practice. The other was new pricing positioning. In both cases, the critical skill was not generating the idea, but driving it through the organization and overcoming initial scepticism.**

**Most people had no difficulty in identifying the three individuals responsible for the two breakthrough approaches. Of these three, one retired in middle management, another has been passed over for promotion for the second time, and the third is now the equivalent of Ambassador to Outer Mongolia.**

Finally, it is still true that necessity is the mother of invention, and, if the right offensive attitudes are present, innovation can spring from disaster:

**A new Managing Director took over at Playtex France. Playtex was one of three or four companies, all with market shares between 6% and 9% vying for leadership of the lingerie market. In each of the previous three years there had been a different market leader.**

Unfortunately, the Playtex workforce then went on strike, and the company rapidly ran out of product to sell. The Managing Director still had a large sales force and asked himself, 'How can I use this sales force effectively when there is no product to deliver?' His answer was to concentrate all sales-force effort on new accounts, promising delivery in six to eight weeks' time, when he thought the strike would be settled. He developed a rather sophisticated system of commando selling, in which each person worked on another's territory, as part of a commando group consisting of four people under a Manager, all staying in the same hotel. This system succeeded and, with refinements, was later used by Playtex all over the world.

Aided by two outstanding Sales Managers and a resourceful Production Director, the MD managed to move Playtex market share from 8% to 15% and increased sales by 85% in one year. Market share subsequently grew to 24% and this leadership position in France was retained for many years.

Like many other offensive attitudes, successful innovation owes as much to will-power and persistence as to imagination.

## SPOKE NO. 4: LONG-TERM OUTLOOK

The importance and value of a long-term outlook was covered in Chapter 2. Short-term performance pressures have become intense, and a year is now a long time in the life of a company. Many of the most important business initiatives take three to five years to payback, and their value cannot be assessed in a single year. That is why many companies now structure their management bonus systems on a longer-term basis.

Some time ago, Marks & Spencer had a 'bad' half-year in which profits only grew modestly. Security analysts were almost· unanimous in suggesting that Marks & Spencer had lost its touch and perhaps its way. Six months later M&S had produced half-yearly profits up by 22% and the financial press was full of articles saying the company was back on track. But how much really changed over that half-year period in the life of a hundred-year-old company?

One year also seems to be the maximum time-span most pension funds and investment groups will consider, because they themselves are subject to the pressures of short-term performance tables. A company Chairman may well hold forth to his colleagues in the morning about the short-sightedness of the stock market, then go to an afternoon meeting of pension fund trustees and express dissatisfaction with their investment results over the past six months.

The effect of these short-term pressures is to:

1. Encourage milkers to silently leach away long-term assets for short-term profits. They can cut advertising, R & D and investment, and drive prices up unreasonably.
2. Force a focus on tactics rather than long-term strategy.
3. Shift priority from product-led innovations, using design and technology, to skilful use of short-term marketing tools, to sustain products lacking any long-term competitive edge.[12]
4. Discourage investments which require a long-term view and can be justified only on this basis.

Faced with this present reality, how can a company foster a long-term outlook? Among the array of less than perfect answers, here are some of the better ones:

- Remove the revolving door from the offices of Managing Directors, especially in subsidiary companies belonging to international groups. This would help stop the operation being run solely to further the short-term career aspirations of the incumbent.
- Fully exploit the possibilities of asset- and competency-led marketing (see Chapter 2).
- Ensure that you are a low-cost operator so as to survive, or win, a price war should one occur.
- Persuade senior management to follow a highly conservative accounting policy. Over-reserve in the good years, to keep grain for lean years, as outlined in Chapter 2. There is a great deal of judgement exercised in accounting and it can be used in your favour without cheating.
- Accumulate a bank of fully tested ideas, so that you can draw a few more out at a time of crisis.
- Manage the expectations of Wall Street and the City on a very conservative base, sell your long-term vision clearly, and avoid surprises.
- Be prepared to make heavy investment if it is essential to your long-term health, even though it may result in temporary profit shortfalls.

## SPOKE NO. 5: INVESTMENT

This has already been discussed in Chapter 2, and the concept of profit and investment (P & I) was explained. The level of a company's investment is the best measure of its commitment to a long-term outlook. Investment obviously needs to be directed to the right opportunities, and, as Hamel and Prahalad point out, resourcefulness is more important than resources.[13] For instance, Kodak spent heavily and consistently on R & D, at about 5% of sales, for many years, but results were disappointing. And some healthcare companies have spent hundreds of millions of pounds on research yet failed to develop a single blockbuster drug.

## SPOKE NO 6: PERSISTENT ATTACK

A great deal has been made of the analogies between marketing and military strategies. They are often described under the heading 'Marketing Warfare'.

Some of these analogies are useful. Clausewitz, the nineteenth-century German general, would be surprised to discover that his book, *On War*, has become one of the most quoted texts in marketing. Because no war is ever won through persistent defence, an essential element of the offensive approach is persistent attack. This does not mean that a company should be attacking on all fronts all the time, since this would be impractical and unprofitable. At any moment a company is likely to be attacking on some fronts, defending on others, and perhaps retreating or exiting from non-strategic areas where the prospects for success look dim.

What is meant by 'persistent attack' is that the overall focus of a company's activity should be to attack and win. Any defensive effort is therefore part of a long-term plan which will culminate in a fresh attack. Field Marshal Montgomery always viewed defence as a temporary situation, part of an overall plan which would result in attack when the time and place were right.

There are several advantages for a company in encouraging an attacking frame of mind:

- Increased motivation; great satisfaction can be achieved by attacking and winning. Most people are prepared to hold a defensive position for some time, but to do so for years without any offensive sorties is discouraging.
- Planned attack keeps competitors under pressure, forcing them to react and reducing their ability to frame sound long-term plans.

- Since no company likes to lose a battle, a tradition of attacking creates internal pressures to remain competitive in product performance and cost. Persistent attack makes most sense when allied to the other six spokes of the wheel, especially value and innovation.

Companies following the offensive approach respond to setbacks by counter-attack, and have the will to fight back even from disasters:

**Procter & Gamble decided to enter the tampon market in the late 1960s and by the mid 1970s successfully test marketed a unique and superior tampon called Rely. As Rely moved to new areas in the USA in the late 1970s, it was still achieving percentage market shares in the low 20s, even though Playtex and Tampax had by then improved their products.**

**Disaster struck in the early 1980s, when cases of alleged toxic shock began to appear, and Rely became the focus of product liability suits. Procter & Gamble withdrew Rely and took a $75 million write-off in 1981.**

**Having exited from tampons, Procter & Gamble opened a new front in the feminine protection market by launching Always, a thin and more absorbent towel. Aiming for a 20% share, Always achieved 17% in year one in the USA, equivalent to sales of $125 million. It was expanded world-wide in the 1990s, and has been highly successful.**

There are times when companies dedicated to persistent attack will withdraw from certain markets and concentrate their attack on other more promising ones. Such issues are covered in Chapter 7, 'Developing Winning Strategies'. This is a necessary part of concentrating limited resources in areas of best return.

However, the attitude of persistent attack needs to be placed in the context of the increasing trend towards simultaneous competition and cooperation between companies. For example, food companies may manufacture products for retailers to sell under their private label, which compete with their own proprietary brands. Electronics companies may simultaneously cooperate with a competitor in a joint R & D programme, have a joint venture with another competitor in Japan, and yet compete with both in the USA. For example, Motorola has significant global alliances with IBM, Philips, Siemens, BT and Toshiba, among others.[14] As alliances proliferate, it is important to know where you are competing and to retain your attacking edge.

## SPOKE NO. 7: SPEED

Speed, either as an innovator or a fast responder, is a test of a company's fitness and is becoming increasingly important as a source of competitive advantage. An Offensive Marketer will respond quickly to changes in customer needs or in the business environment, and will counter-attack competitive thrusts. Slow response usually indicates a problem in organizational structure or attitudes.

**Toyota has cut its lead-time between clay model approval and car in showroom from twenty-seven months to eighteen months for most new products. Major time savings have been made in the translation of clay models into parts specifications through computer simulation, and in prototype changes by cutting out minor design changes at later stages. Completely new vehicles obviously take longer to develop than model changes.[15]**

At one time it was fairly accurate to describe the big company as a supertanker, where the swing of the wheel only produced a slight reaction five miles later. The small business was characterized as the cruiser, manoeuvring quickly around the supertankers. This was probably true years ago.

Many of the more effective large companies are seeking and gaining the advantages of bigness and smallness. For them, a more accurate analogy is a fleet of cruisers serviced by a battleship. 3M regards itself not as a $X billion company, but as over a hundred individual profit centres around the world. Johnson & Johnson has a similar approach of devolution to operating companies of five hundred or less people.

For international companies, there are two issues of speed. The first is **project start to launch in first country**. The second is speed from **first country to global exploitation**. Leading consumer goods companies like Procter & Gamble or Unilever expect to get non-food brands from Country 1 to Country 30 in a couple of years at most. The days when you could launch Pampers in the USA in 1961, start rolling out internationally in the late 1970s, and complete in the 1980s are long gone. In the computer industry, new product development lead-time, from start to launch, was 18–24 months in the late 1980s, but 9–12 months today. Windows 95 was launched simultaneously world-wide. The challenge is to move fast and market the right product to a high quality from Day 1.

However, it is not enough to be a fast innovator. You need to be a fast responder as well, since companies can be ambushed. When this happens, you must quickly answer three questions (Table 51).

| **Table 51. Ambush response drill.** |
| :--- |
| 1. Is this just a skirmish, or is it a serious threat to our business? |
| 2. Should we respond very fast with a proposition? |
| 3. Or should we take more time and respond with a superior offer, in terms of product, service and value? |

The answer will depend on the seriousness of the threat, the type of business you are in, and the difference in timing between 2 and 3. You could always follow 2 now, and 3 later, but that may diminish your impact and divide your focus.

When Nabisco was ambushed by Procter & Gamble and PepsiCo in the American cookie market, it decided to take the threat very seriously and opted for No. 3:

> **For decades Nabisco had ruled the roost in the US cookie and cracker market, with a share of over 40%. Two very formidable new competitors entered this market, with distinctive ranges of cookies. PepsiCo's Frito-Lay Division, brand leader in snack foods, and backed by a 12,000-strong sales force, launched Grandma's Cookies, a high-moisture product well geared to Frito-Lay's skills in selling short-life merchandise. Then, shortly afterwards, Procter & Gamble introduced a similar type of cookie, crisp on the outside and chewy on the inside, with a long life and supposedly protected by patent.**
>
> **It was not clear at this time whether soft cookies would become a smallish niche sector or whether, despite premium pricing, they would establish a strong position. The question was irrelevant to Nabisco, who knew that if they allowed either Procter & Gamble or PepsiCo to gain even a foothold in the cookie market, there would be big trouble ahead.**
>
> **So Nabisco regarded the threat as a head-on attack, and although taken completely by surprise, responded fast and offensively. Within six months, they launched a soft cookie range, exploited their brand and distribution strength, and challenged Procter & Gamble's patent. After a sustained battle royal, they saw both Procter & Gamble and PepsiCo 'off their patch'.**

## Rate Your Company for Offensive Attitudes (Table 52)

| Table 52. Criteria for rating a business on offensive attitudes. | Max. score | Your score |
|---|---|---|
| Clear, realistic and motivating vision of the future, understood and accepted by most employees | 15 | |
| A strong commitment to providing superior value to customers, backed by low-cost operations | 20 | |
| Strong emphasis on innovation throughout the business, both daily trickle and big bang, in the right balance for the industry. Stress on technology, support, recognition and reward for successful innovators. Structure where innovation can flourish | 15 | |
| Ability to achieve required short-term results, but strong focus on long-term objectives | 10 | |
| Commitment to continued investment in all assets and competencies, like brands, people, skills, technology, new products and equipment, even when faced by strong short-term pressures | 15 | |
| Overall focus on attacking competition, but at carefully chosen times and places | 15 | |
| Fast good-quality response to new opportunities or competitive threats | 10 | |
| **Total** | 100 | |

### Example of Offensive attitudes

A good example of Offensive attitudes can be seen in Field Marshal Montgomery's speech to his officers on 13 August 1942, one day after taking command of the Eighth Army in North Africa. His situation was analogous to that of a new Chief Executive or Marketing Director in a company losing market share, and with cynical, demoralized management.

Eighth Army officers (management) were sceptical about Montgomery's (Chief Executive's) chance of success. He did not have 'sand in his shoes' (i.e. knew nothing about the business), and probably had no idea of how Rommel had transformed operations in the desert (in business parlance – out of date).[16] Furthermore he had been sent from England (head office) and was the fourth commander within a year ('Not another one'). The officers were depressed by the succession of defeat and failure.

In this example, the analogy between warfare and marketing is close. Montgomery's speech comprised five of the seven spokes of offensive attitudes:

- *Vision* — We are going to fight and win. This is how.
- *Persistent attack* — We will stop all preparations for retreat and adopt an attacking attitude. In the meantime we can successfully repel any enemy attacks.
- *Long-term outlook* — We will attack when we are ready and not before.
- *Investment* — 300–400 Sherman tanks are being unloaded at Suez now. We will create a reserve corps, which we will train out of line.
- *Speed* — We should be ready to attack in two weeks.

Montgomery did not refer to **value**, since this is a commercial rather than a military concept. But he had a lot to say about his management style and values. Nor was there anything **innovative** in his speech, although the idea of an open address to his top sixty officers (managers) one day after assuming his new job was in itself innovative in those days. (How many new Chief Executives could do this convincingly?)

Here are some excerpts from Montgomery's historic speech. His notes were lost, but fortunately some inspired person took it down in shorthand:

'I want first of all to introduce myself to you. You do not know me. I do not know you. But we have got to work together; therefore we must understand each other and we must have confidence in each other. I have only been here a few hours. But apart from what I have seen and heard since I arrived, I am prepared to say, here and now, that I have confidence in you. We will then work together as a team; and together we will gain the confidence of this great Army and go forward to final victory in Africa.

'I believe that one of the first duties of a commander is to create what I call "atmosphere", and in that atmosphere his staff, subordinate commanders, and troops will live and work and fight.

'I do not like the general atmosphere I find here. It is an atmosphere of doubt, of looking back to select the next place to which to withdraw, of loss of confidence in our ability to defeat Rommel, of desperate defence measures by reserves in preparing positions in Cairo and the Delta.

'All that must cease.

'Let us have a new atmosphere.

'The defence of Egypt lies here at Alamein and on the Ruweisat Ridge. What is the use of digging trenches in the Delta? It is quite useless; if we lose this position we lose Egypt; all the fighting troops now in the Delta must come here at once, and will. *Here* we will stand and fight; there will be no further withdrawal. I have ordered that all plans and instructions dealing with further withdrawal are to be burnt, and at once. We will stand and fight *here.*

'If we can't stay here alive, then let us stay here dead.

'I want to impress on everyone that the bad times are over. Fresh Divisions from the UK are now arriving in Egypt, together with ample reinforcements for our present Divisions. We have 300 to 400 Sherman new tanks coming and these are actually being unloaded at Suez *now.*[17] Our mandate from the Prime Minister is to destroy the Axis forces in North Africa; I have seen it, written on half a sheet of notepaper. And it will be done. If anyone here thinks it can't be done, let him go at once; I don't want any doubters in this party. It can be done, and it will be done; beyond any possibility of doubt.

'Now I understand that Rommel is expected to attack at any moment. Excellent. Let him attack. I would sooner it didn't come for a week, just give me time to sort things out. If we have two weeks to prepare we will be sitting pretty; Rommel can attack as soon as he likes after that, and I hope he does.

'Meanwhile, we ourselves will start to plan a great offensive; it will be the beginning of a campaign which will hit Rommel and his Army for six right out of Africa.

'But first we must create a reserve Corps, mobile and strong in armour, which we will train out of the line . . . a British Panzer Corps; it will consist of two armoured Divisions and one motorized Division; I gave orders yesterday for it to begin to form, back in the Delta.

'I have no intention of launching our great attack until we are completely ready; there will be pressure from many quarters to attack soon; *I will not attack until we are ready, and you can rest assured on that point.*

'Meanwhile, if Rommel attacks while we are preparing, let him do so with pleasure; we will merely continue with our own preparations and *we* will attack when *we* are ready, and not before.

'I want to tell you that I always work on the Chief of Staff system. I have nominated Brigadier de Guingand as Chief of Staff

Eighth Army. I will issue orders through him. Whatever he says will be taken as coming from me and will be acted on *at once*. I understand there has been a great deal of "belly-aching" out here. By "belly-aching" I mean inventing poor reasons for *not* doing what one has been told to do.

'All this is to stop at once.

'I will tolerate no belly-aching.

'If anyone objects to doing what he is told, then he can get out of it; and at once. I want that made very clear right down through the Eighth Army.

'What I have done is to get over to you the "atmosphere" in which we will now work and fight; you must see that atmosphere permeates right down through the Eighth Army to the most junior private soldier. All the soldiers must know what is wanted; when they see it coming to pass there will be a surge of confidence throughout the Army.

'I ask you to give me your confidence and to have faith that what I have said will come to pass . . . The great point to remember is that we are going to finish with this chap Rommel once and for all. It will be quite easy. There is no doubt about it.'[18]

# FLOW-CHART SUMMARY OF CHAPTER 3

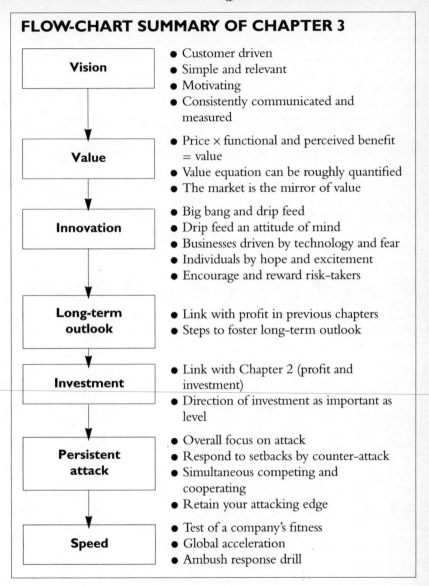

**Vision**

- Customer driven
- Simple and relevant
- Motivating
- Consistently communicated and measured

**Value**

- Price × functional and perceived benefit = value
- Value equation can be roughly quantified
- The market is the mirror of value

**Innovation**

- Big bang and drip feed
- Drip feed an attitude of mind
- Businesses driven by technology and fear
- Individuals by hope and excitement
- Encourage and reward risk-takers

**Long-term outlook**

- Link with profit in previous chapters
- Steps to foster long-term outlook

**Investment**

- Link with Chapter 2 (profit and investment)
- Direction of investment as important as level

**Persistent attack**

- Overall focus on attack
- Respond to setbacks by counter-attack
- Simultaneous competing and cooperating
- Retain your attacking edge

**Speed**

- Test of a company's fitness
- Global acceleration
- Ambush response drill

# PART THREE:
# INTEGRATED

## 4. The Integrated Marketing Approach

### Chapter Summary

We have now covered the Profitable and Offensive part of POISE. This chapter will deal with 'INTEGRATED'; the 'I' of POISE (Table 53).

| Table 53. | |
|---|---|
| **P:** Profitable | ● Proper balance between firm's needs for profit and customer's need for value |
| **O:** Offensive | ● Must lead market, take risks and make competitors followers |
| → **I:** Integrated ← | ● Marketing approach must permeate whole company |
| **S:** Strategic | ● Probing analysis leading to a winning strategy |
| **E:** Effectively Executed | ● Strong and disciplined execution on a daily basis |

Offensive Marketing is an approach to business affecting everyone. It is *not* a specialist discipline practised by a single department. Everyone should be thinking hard about both customers and profits.

Integration should be spearheaded, and monitored by the Board. Its foundations are superior customer value and profit growth, delivered by all departments, and permeated by the seven spokes of Offensive Attitudes (see Chapter 3). Companies failing to build these foundations will never become Integrated Marketers, however nice they are to customers, however well trained their front-line staff.

The starting-point and propellant for Integrated Marketing is the corporate strategy. This should be developed with open dialogue between departments, led by Marketing. The result will be a market- and customer-driven strategy with cross-departmental responsibilities and implementation.

Developing an integrated corporate strategy is only the start. Many businesses talk about integration at length and in positive terms, then do little about it. This is because it is difficult to put into action successfully. **So how can integration be made an everyday reality?** By ensuring that all employees identify their internal and external customers, and truly understand their needs; and by converting these needs into customer-driven, competitive and cost-conscious job objectives, monitored via personal appraisals, and rewarded, where appropriate, with bonuses.

There are six main barriers to Integrated Marketing: distance from customers; action conflicting with words; lack of Board consensus; internal politics; worship of technology; and tubular bells structure.

The Marketing Department can play an important role in integration, but needs to raise its game in a number of areas in future.

Among practical tools for achieving Integrated Marketing are: cross-departmental career routes; meeting customers in person; open and honest communication, especially by senior management; widely spread bonus schemes; single-site locations; business unit and category management.

## The Principles of Integrated Marketing

**'Integrated Marketing' means that every part of the business combines to deliver superior customer value at minimum cost.** This is the driving force of Offensive Marketing, and consistent with the definition of Chapter 1 (page 23). Unfortunately 'Integrated Marketing' has been used in recent years, especially in the USA, to describe a much narrower approach – that of integrating the increasingly diverse range of marketing communications, such as broadcast and narrowcast advertising, relationship marketing, sponsorship, event promotions and PR.

Integrated Marketing[1] will be used in its original broader sense.

Howard Morgens, past Chairman of Procter & Gamble, put the case for Integrated Marketing succinctly many years ago:

> **'There is no such thing as marketing skill by itself. For a company to be good at marketing, it must be good at everything else from R & D to manufacturing, from quality controls to financial controls.'[2]**

Marketing is an approach to business rather than a specialist discipline. It is no more the exclusive responsibility of the Marketing Department than profitability is the sole charge of the Finance Department.

Unlike the more specialized roles of Production, Buying, Selling and R & D, Marketing is everyone's business. The marketing approach challenges everyone to relate their work to the needs of the market-place and to balance it against the firm's own profit needs.

For example, in a marketing-orientated vehicle company, the plant manager will ensure that quality standards evaluate those things in the product which matter most to the consumer. S/he will also strive to develop new techniques of flexible mass production, in order to give customers the combination of low cost and wide model choice which they seek. Finance department will clearly identify the needs of their internal and external customers, and satisfy these, cost-effectively, on time. Within the company, the Marketing Department should lead and catalyse the application of the marketing approach.

Figure 18 – 'Two faces' – illustrates the outward and inward facing roles.

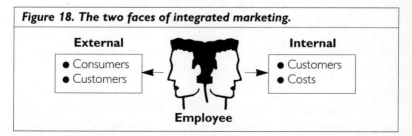

**Figure 18. The two faces of integrated marketing.**

**External**
- Consumers
- Customers

**Internal**
- Customers
- Costs

**Employee**

To be effective, Integrated Marketing requires the full belief and support of top management. The Marketing Department on its own could no more apply it to a company than a football club manager could win a match without a team.

Integrated Marketing is one of the strengths of the Japanese. They have a reputation for being slow decision-makers and quick implementers, because by the time the decision is made everyone is behind it and moving in the same direction. As Kotler says of Japanese firms: 'Marketing decisions are the product or consequence of the inputs of not just marketing people but of other functional units as well.'[3]

Merchant bankers recommending acquisitions are very fond of saying that two plus two equals more than four. Where the marketing approach flows through the bloodstream of a company, the impact of the whole is much greater than the sum of the individual parts. Where marketing is strapped on to the body corporate like a wooden leg, the reverse is true.

Talleyrand said, 'War is much too serious a thing to be left to military men.' Equally, marketing is much too serious a thing to be left to Marketing Departments.

## Integrating company vision and attitudes

Integration should be spearheaded and monitored by the Board, using its Marketing Department as integrators and evangelists. This means that the seven spokes of offensive attitudes need to be applied by everyone in the company. The 'O' and 'I' of POISE work closely together, again demonstrating that POISE is a total marketing system, not something you pick and choose from (Table 54).

| **Table 54.** | |
|---|---|
| **P:** *Profitable* | ● *Proper balance between firm's needs for profit and customer's need for value* |
| **O:** *Offensive* | ● *Must lead market, take risks and make competitors followers* |
| **I:** *Integrated* | ● *Marketing approach must permeate whole company* |
| **S:** *Strategic* | ● *Probing analysis leading to a winning strategy* |
| **E:** *Effectively Executed* | ● *Strong and disciplined execution on a daily basis* |

The result will be a clear vision of the future, drive for innovation and value, and well-understood offensive attitudes instinctively applied.

This provides the framework for the effective implementation of Integrated Marketing.

Unless this framework is established, even the most determined effort will fail. In the financial services business in particular, 'Integrated Marketing' has often been misinterpreted as 'being nice to customers'. It does not matter how well trained your front-line staff are, how effectively they segment their customers, or how concerned they are to meet customer needs, if the proposition they are offering is not good value. The inevitable outcome will be loss or demotivation of well-trained staff.

The Integrated Marketing firmament illustration in Figure 19 shows how the right environment can be developed.

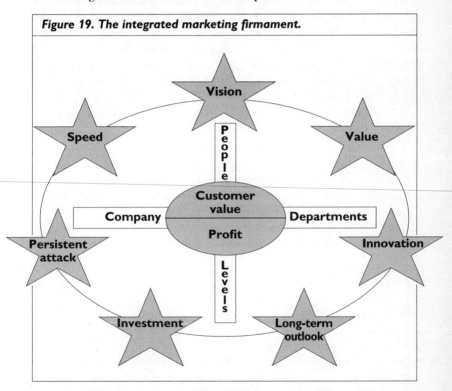

**Figure 19. The integrated marketing firmament.**

At the centre are the twin objectives of Offensive Marketing – superior customer value and above-average profits. The company axis of management levels and departments is focused on this centre. The structure is simultaneously horizontal and vertical. Everyone is concentrating on customer satisfaction and low-cost operation. Surrounding the company axis, and permeating it, are the seven elements of offensive attitudes.

Companies lacking offensive attitudes, or a communicating and action-orientated culture, have no hope of becoming Integrated Marketers. They will never reach this goal through management exhortations, policy statements or other such exhalations of hot air. The main barriers to Integrated Marketing are reviewed later in this chapter.

### Developing a corporate strategy for Integrated Marketing

Almost every company these days has a long-term strategy. All too often the strategies are tactical, and the plans focus on financial numbers, giving no clues on how they will be fairly earned from customers. Corporate strategy will be covered briefly at this stage of the book, because it is a process in which marketers should be heavily involved. It is a means to achieving clear vision, Marketing Alignment (see MAP, Chapter 2, page 82) and Integration. Chapter 6 – 'Developing a Distinctive View of the Future' – also alludes to corporate strategy.

A good corporate strategy will contain ambitious objectives, and support them through the Marketing Firmament (see Figure 19 above).

Time-scale of corporate strategies and plans will differ by industry, influenced by development lead-times – for instance, in pharmaceuticals it typically takes ten years to move a promising chemical compound from discovery to commercial exploitation. Typical corporate strategy time-scales by industry are shown in Table 55.

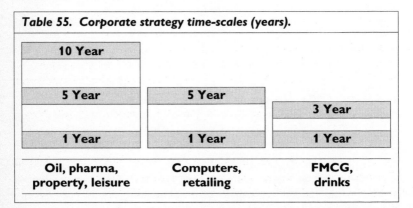

**Table 55. Corporate strategy time-scales (years).**

| 10 Year | | |
| 5 Year | 5 Year | |
| | | 3 Year |
| 1 Year | 1 Year | 1 Year |
| Oil, pharma, property, leisure | Computers, retailing | FMCG, drinks |

Ten year plans tend to be broad and companies using them will also have more detailed three or five year plans. Long-term and medium-term plans provide the foundation for one year budgets. The shaded blocks in Table 55 indicate the number of long-term and short-term plans likely to be completed by the industry. An oil company may therefore have a 10–5–1 year planning cycle, or a food processor just a 3–1 plan.

Ten things which an Offensive Marketer would like to see in a 3–5 year corporate strategy are outlined in Table 56, and covered in detail in Exhibit 1 (page 175). These can provide the foundation for Integrated Marketing.

---

**Table 56.  Key elements in aligned and integrated five-year corporate strategy.**

1. Future market vision
2. Future priorities
3. Company vision
4. Target market position
5. Target financial returns
6. Future investment
7. Key supporting strategies
8. Key plans and milestones
9. Testing programme
10. Summary of departmental responsibilities

---

You will notice that this integrated corporate strategy is very different from the conventional one, which sets a series of revenue, cost and profit objectives, and then splits responsibilities in a departmental way. The conventional approach involves a build-up of budgets and plans by Operations, Sales, Marketing, Finance and other functions.

In contrast, the five-year plan in Table 56 is developed *across* departments, *centred on future needs of markets, customers and consumers*. Only at Stage 10 does the corporate strategy split into department responsibilities – Stages 1 to 9 cover all departments, with open communication. This dialogue is led by marketers, with their unique knowledge of markets, costs and internal competencies. Table 57 demonstrates the difference between a conventional, department-based corporate strategy, and an integrated one:

**Table 57.  Yesterday's and tomorrow's approach to corporate strategy.**

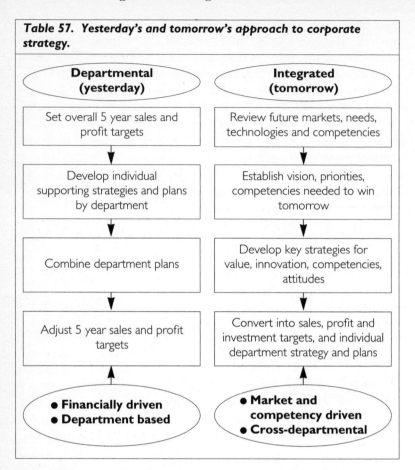

| Departmental (yesterday) | Integrated (tomorrow) |
| --- | --- |
| Set overall 5 year sales and profit targets | Review future markets, needs, technologies and competencies |
| Develop individual supporting strategies and plans by department | Establish vision, priorities, competencies needed to win tomorrow |
| Combine department plans | Develop key strategies for value, innovation, competencies, attitudes |
| Adjust 5 year sales and profit targets | Convert into sales, profit and investment targets, and individual department strategy and plans |
| ● **Financially driven**<br>● **Department based** | ● **Market and competency driven**<br>● **Cross-departmental** |

## Implementing Integrated Marketing via the Corporate Strategy

As you know, Integrated Marketing is designed to achieve the twin objectives of Offensive Marketing – superior customer value and above-average profits. It follows logically therefore that everyone in a business should be judged on three criteria only:

- **Contribution to superior customer value**. Innovation, customer relationships and investment are key drivers.
- **Contribution to superior long-term profit growth**. Cost reduction, productivity and value engineering are key drivers.
- **Inter- and cross–departmental teamwork**.

To illustrate this point, Figure 20 has two ways of describing the job of an aircraft maintenance worker. One of these is conventional, the other an Integrated Marketing description. You will have no difficulty in spotting which is which.

**Figure 20. Two possible descriptions of an aircraft maintenance worker's job.**

| Ensure all aircraft meet full engineering specifications, within agreed budget | **or** | Ensure that airline has a perfect safety record and the best punctuality record of any airline, at minimum cost |
|---|---|---|

Which is the more motivating description? There is nothing inaccurate about the description on the left, but it is inwards looking. By contrast, the one on the right looks outwards *and* inwards. It considers customers, competition and cost.

There are five key tools for implementing an integrated corporate strategy, to ensure that everyone thinks like, and is appraised as, a Marketer. They are covered individually below in Table 58.

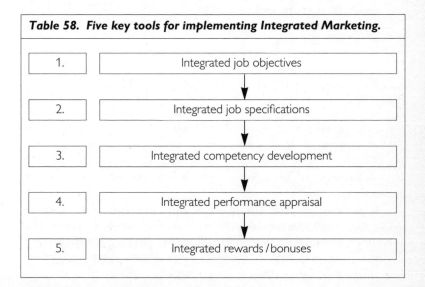

**Table 58.  Five key tools for implementing Integrated Marketing.**

| | |
|---|---|
| 1. | Integrated job objectives |
| 2. | Integrated job specifications |
| 3. | Integrated competency development |
| 4. | Integrated performance appraisal |
| 5. | Integrated rewards / bonuses |

## 1. Integrated job objectives

We will track these tools through the eyes of two imaginary Marketers, Chris Baskerville and Gill Smith. Neither has a marketing title or belongs to a Marketing Department. Chris is a thirty-two-year-old Plant Manager for a bathroom products group, and Gill a thirty-year-old IT Manager at a medium-sized building society, the Utopian.

**Chris Baskerville**'s responsibility as Plant Manager is production and dispatch of the mid-priced Park Lane range. Primary customers are

 housebuilders, and consumers aged 45–65 refurbishing their houses. Distribution channels are builders' merchants like Jewsons or Plumb, and bathroom retailers. Chris has a product range of 8K items, and has already discovered that one of the industry's principal problems is weak customer service.

He became Plant Manager two months ago, and is about to write his job objectives for next year. He looks at his predecessor's objectives (Table 59).

---

**Table 59.  Park Lane: yesterday's job objectives. (These are simplified for brevity's sake.)**

1. Produce budgeted volume of £27.5m, equivalent to 110K units
2. Control spending within budgeted figure of £12.4m or 45% of sales
3. Manage capital expenditure of £1.5m, with 4 year payback
4. Reduce labour turnover from 20% to 15%
5. Develop, with Marketing and R & D, improved processes for new product development

---

You will have already spotted what is wrong with these job objectives, and so did Chris. They are totally inward looking. Chris rightly saw his first task as sorting out who his internal and external customers were. Having done that, he asked them what they wanted. He talked to Sales, Marketing, R & D and Finance Departments, and visited a number of housebuilders, retailers and builders' merchants. This enabled him to draft a new set of job objectives, which he circulated to other departments for comment (Table 60).

These objectives will clearly need to be supported by a detailed action plan, with quarterly milestones. How do Chris's objectives differ from those of his predecessor? You will notice there are fewer numbers. These will be specified in his plans. In any case, Chris sees hitting budgeted cost and output as an assumption, not an objective. The

**Table 60. Chris Baskerville – Park Lane: tomorrow's job objectives.**

### Customer definition and needs

| External customers | Needs |
| --- | --- |
| ● Customers – distributors or retailers | ● Range and service |
| ● Consumers – all end users | ● Value |

| Internal customers | Needs |
| --- | --- |
| ● Sales Dept | ● quality, service, cost. |
| ● Marketing Dept | ● innovation, quality, product development |
| ● Finance Dept | ● data, efficiency, output, budgeting |

**Objectives**
1. Meet the quality, timing and service needs of all external customers, on a superior basis to competitors at lowest possible cost.
2. Raise customer service levels from 80% to 92% in next 18 months.
3. Develop innovative processes, work practices, and competencies, designed to enhance (1) above.
4. Contribute to new technology, and launch new products on time, faster than competition.
5. Manage, motivate and develop all employees to industry best practice in planning, operations, inventory control and cost. Cut number of lines from 8K to 5K, working with Marketing Department.

main differences are that 'Tomorrow's Job Objectives' are both inward and outward looking. They focus on customers, consumers, competitors and cost . . . on meeting needs better than competitors. The only one of these 'c's referred to in 'Yesterday's Objectives' (Table 59) was, predictably, cost.

In reality, Chris Baskerville's customer network is quite complex and requires considerable skill to manage and balance. You will also have spotted that he aims to raise customer service levels to 92%, from 80%, the industry average. He feels that anything less than 90% is unacceptable in any industry, but the cost of moving as high as 95% would involve carrying uneconomic levels of inventory. His plan to radically cut the number of lines produced from 8K to 5K will certainly help him improve service levels, and he has already discussed with the Marketing Department how best to do this.

 **Gill Smith** is going through a similar process as IT Manager of the Utopian Building Society, which is in the middle of a major downsizing programme. In Table 61, very briefly, are her old job objectives.

---

**Table 61.  Gill Smith: Utopian Building Society: yesterday's job objectives.**

1. Reduce cost budget from £3.0m to £2.5m through automation.
2. Maintain current levels of service and reliability.
3. Upgrade computer capacity in 20 branches at a capital cost of £0.4m.
4. Develop software to handle new range of general insurance products, for September launch

---

**Table 62.  Gill Smith: Utopian Building Society: tomorrow's job objectives.**

| Customer definition and needs | |
| --- | --- |
| **External customers** | **Needs** |
| ● All existing Utopian consumers | ● Clear, accurate and timely information |
| **Internal customers** | **Needs** |
| ● Branch staff, Telesales, operators, Utopian commercial management | ● Customer profiles, history, current holdings |

**Objectives**
1. Since Marketing Dept moving to life stage market segmentation, add life stage data to all consumer profiles.
2. Review competitor practice on IT, and improve upon it.
3. Integrate building society and direct marketing customer information bases, so that consumers can be managed consistently *across* trade channels.
4. Develop system for targeting best prospects for new range of general insurance products.
5. Review future IT needs of Utopian commercial management. Set up training and development plan.

Using her new format, Gill has developed a different set of objectives (Table 62).

Gill's previous job objectives were, like Chris Baskerville's, internally focused and cost not customer driven. Their purpose was to do broadly the same things, more efficiently at less cost. Her new objectives do this too, but also meet customer needs better. The emphasis is concentrated on improving customer experiences, at minimum cost.

The illustration in Figure 21 graphically illustrates the difference between integrated and functional management

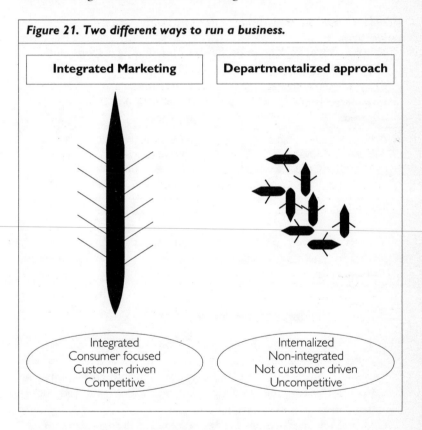

**Figure 21. Two different ways to run a business.**

**Integrated Marketing**

**Departmentalized approach**

Integrated
Consumer focused
Customer driven
Competitive

Internalized
Non-integrated
Not customer driven
Uncompetitive

Rowing is a good analogy for Integrated Marketing, since it involves an IN:OUT process, training, discipline and, above all, team-work.

## 2. Integrated job specifications

Job objectives describe desired results over a specified period, usually one to five years.

Job specifications outline responsibilities, levels of authority, skills required and reporting points. They should be developed using the principles summarized in Table 60 and Table 62, above. While job specifications will inevitably be descriptive, responsibilities should centre on customers and costs. For example, there is a right and wrong way for Chris Baskerville to describe his purchasing responsibilities (Table 63).

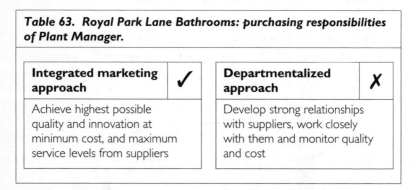

**Table 63. Royal Park Lane Bathrooms: purchasing responsibilities of Plant Manager.**

| Integrated marketing approach ✓ | Departmentalized approach ✗ |
|---|---|
| Achieve highest possible quality and innovation at minimum cost, and maximum service levels from suppliers | Develop strong relationships with suppliers, work closely with them and monitor quality and cost |

Job specifications should not change often, but need to be regularly reviewed, in line with changes in customer needs, and competitor performance.

## 3. Integrated competency development

This is the third of the five key tools for implementing Integrated Marketing. Chapter 2 described how companies can develop skills relevant to key consumer benefits, and convert them into core competencies. A company's corporate strategy will describe these skills and outline how they can be developed further.

Competency development needs to be looked at across departments, and fed into job objectives and specifications. For example, the Utopian Building Society wants to develop a core competency in Relationship Marketing, backed by powerful IT. This clearly affects Gill Smith, and is included in her new job objectives (Table 62). People in Marketing, Branch Management, Finance and Direct Sales will *also* have objectives relevant to Relationship Marketing.

## 4. Integrated performance appraisal

Performance appraisal will monitor how far people are meeting their objectives. This means everyone will be evaluated on their contribution to superior customer value and profitability, the twin cornerstones of Offensive Marketing.

## 5. Integrated rewards and bonuses

These would be paid to all levels, based on the achievement of agreed objectives. This would further enhance the move to Integrated Marketing, as this example shows:

> **When former Boeing executive, Gordon Bethune, became Chief Executive of Continental Airlines, the company had suffered years of losses, downsizing, wage cuts and reorganizations. He found demoralized employees bickering as planes departed half full and arrived late.**
>
> **To persuade travellers that Continental would become a different airline, he decided he had first to convince its own employees. So he told all departments that they would be measured together on what mattered to customers most – punctuality.**
>
> **Every department was required to approve the new timetable. Bethune promised that for each month Continental was in the top half of the Federal Government's on-time ranking, every employee would equally share half the savings of $6m. This was what it had cost Continental each month to book delayed or stranded passengers on to other airlines.**
>
> **By the second month of the offer, Continental had moved from last to first in the punctuality league table, and business passengers began returning. Share price rose ninefold in eighteen months. As a Continental baggage handler said: 'Getting the plane off the gate isn't my job or your job. We act like it's everybody's job.'⁴**

The Continental example contrasts with ill-conceived incentive schemes which reward senior management hugely, and provide lean pickings for the vast majority of employees who provide the thrust of Offensive Marketing.

## Barriers to Integrated Marketing

If Integrated Marketing is such a good idea, you would expect companies to be lining up to practise the art. It is strange that so few do it successfully. Here is an example of disintegration in one of the largest companies in the USA, which has since made and sustained a superb recovery:

> **When Lee Iacocca joined Chrysler, he soon concluded that 'all Chrysler's problems really boiled down to the same thing . . . there was no team, only a collection of independent players'.**
>
> **He discovered weaknesses in financial planning and projecting. 'Even the most rudimentary questions were impossible for them to answer.'**
>
> **Equally serious, the factories were producing to schedules not related to customer or dealer demand, with the result that there were massive inventories and monthly 'fire' sales, to reduce excess stocks.**
>
> **The system worked like this: 'At regular intervals the Manufacturing Division would tell the Sales Division how many and what types of vehicle they were going to produce. Then it would be up to Sales Division to sell them . . . to dealers . . . It had nothing to do with a customer ordering what he wanted on the car, or a dealer ordering what the customer was likely to ask for.'[5]**
>
> **Iacocca soon put things right, but wondered how this could happen after thirty years of scientific management.**

There are many reasons why companies do not follow the Integrated Marketing approach, and we shall look at six of the most common.

**The first is also the most obvious.** Businesses which are not close to the customer have not taken the first step on the road to Offensive Marketing, and are therefore in no position to achieve an integrated approach. Many of these industries have suffered historically from a lack of competition and now find themselves in a tougher deregulated environment – telecommunications, transport, public utilities and banks in Europe, for example. Most are slow to change. For instance, take banks, still largely run by 'bankers':

> **Few major UK retail banks apply Integrated Marketing. They talk a great deal about 'Marketing' and customers, but in most cases still have a set of bolt-on activities like**

advertising, direct mail, new services and market research. Despite recent improvements, in no sense could one say that major banks are customer-led.

Compare banks with retailers. In grocery retailing, there are many differentiated customer propositions to choose from. Sainsbury offers a broad range of branded and own-label products of good quality at competitive prices. Aldi has a narrow range of brands at very low prices. Marks & Spencer markets a limited selection of high-quality foods at premium prices.

Outside grocery, the picture is similar, with many effective retailers offering a range of different consumer propositions.

It is a shock to come back to banks. Each of the majors has over 1,500 outlets, clustered together on the same high streets, offering similar services at similar prices to the mass market, in bland surroundings.

Banks have been slow to move out of town, or to more convenient locations. Business hours seem designed to minimize customer visits and make access almost impossible for many blue-collar workers who cannot get away during lunch-hours. Saturday-morning opening was a grudging and patchy defensive response to building societies.

The major barrier to Integrated Marketing in banks is top management, the unrestructured old-style 'bankers'. They are not prepared to initiate the massive changes in organization and attitude necessary to make banks effective financial service Marketers. Instead, they fiddle at the fringes with 'customer initiatives' and self-indulgent advertising. They are still basically technology and operations led rather than marketing orientated.

By contrast, Sam Walton, founder of WalMart, the world's largest retailer, summed up the integrated approach succinctly:

'We put the customer ahead of everything else . . . if you're not serving the customer, or supporting the folks who do, then we don't need you.'[6]

A second barrier to Integrated Marketing is top management's failure to implement their verbal commitment to improvements. They say one thing, then do another, or, in American parlance, 'try and play both ends of the street' – as in this disguised real life example:

> The Board was reasonably committed to the idea of improving product quality and some members, including the Chairman, advocated this strongly to employees. At the same time it was pushing hard on cost reduction, with impressive success. However, the pressure for short-term profits made it impossible to invest sufficiently in measures to improve quality. Indeed, some cost cuts affected quality, and those responsible for it became discouraged at the gap between top management's statements and actions.

**A third barrier is lack of consensus on important matters of strategy at Board level.** This can prove a decisive barrier to integration, since it spawns disruption and division – what Field Marshal Montgomery described as 'poor atmosphere'. However, it may prove to be only a temporary barrier if the disagreements are resolved, as in this real case:

> The Marketing Director was keen to enter a new market sector, even though this would involve mastering new technology, heavy investment on capital equipment and a new brand. The minimum payback period would be four years, but the potential benefits of success would be high.
>
> The Financial and Production Directors presented a well-argued paper to the Board resisting this move. They pointed out that while the company's products were well accepted by consumers and efficiently manufactured, there was considerable spare production capacity. Why could not the Marketing Department think more practically and develop exciting new products using existing capacity? They were proposing an asset-based marketing approach.
>
> (You will recognize the conflict between market-led and asset-led marketing, and so did the Managing Director.) The Managing Director let things drift for a few months, perhaps deliberately, and then pushed the Marketing Department down the asset-led route, although allowing a test of the new brand. Subsequently Marketing succeeded in developing profitable new products using existing capacity, which was fortunate, since the new brand failed.

The fourth barrier is where a company has a clear marketing-led strategy, but integration is undermined by demarcation disputes or personal rivalries. The following example, also from the author's experience, will ring a bell with many who have worked in multinational companies:

The Managing Director of this UK subsidiary reported to the International President in New York. His UK Manufacturing Director reported on paper directly to him but had a strong link with Vice President, Worldwide Operations, also located in New York. Both American-based executives were of equal status, and pursued a strong but muted rivalry.

The UK Sales and Marketing team had been strengthened and made some good moves. As a result, volume of orders improved by 35 per cent over a twelve-month period. Unfortunately, the factories could not meet this sales requirement, partly because sales forecasting was a bit weak, but mainly because manufacturing never seemed to be able to achieve planned production levels – 'a sustained record of failure,' as the Sales Director acidly observed. Furthermore, management in New York showed a marked reluctance to commit to any large increase in capacity, in case the UK business gains proved only temporary.

Short or late delivery to customers became the norm. Although the UK Managing Director spent three days a month personally chairing all production planning and sales forecasting meetings, he had little leverage over his Manufacturing Director, who was reporting back to his boss in the USA. Production blamed Sales and Marketing for poor sales forecasting. Marketing blamed Production for failure to hit promised production schedules and inability to increase capacity.

The situation was exacerbated by the 'contribution' of staff groups and task forces flown over from the USA and in no time there were two companies – Sales/Marketing/Finance on the one hand, Production on the other. What should have been a marketing-led volume and profit breakthrough by a highly capable team deteriorated into backbiting and customer dissatisfaction.

**The fifth barrier to Integrated Marketing can be technology**. In rapidly expanding markets like telecommunications or software, where technology is changing fast, it may be pursued for its own sake, rather than as a way to serve the customer better. As Lou Gerstner, Chairman of IBM, said soon after taking over, 'The information revolution will happen, but only when the industry stops worshipping technology for its own sake, and starts focusing on real value for its customers.' Because a technology breakthrough can have a transforming effect on a business, there is a temptation, especially in high-tech sectors, to neglect the study of consumer needs. When such markets mature, and technology changes slow down, companies which had treated marketing as a sales service function pay the penalty, as their products and services become un-distinctive commodities, vulnerable to price attack. This has already happened in computer hardware and many consumer durable products.

**The sixth and final barrier is the tubular bells effect**, where each department reports upwards with little contact between them, only meeting at Chief Executive level. Interdepartmental discord rarely occurs openly, since there is insufficient contact to make it heard. But when it does occur, it clangs up and down the tubes, since no one at a lower level has the authority to create harmony. As for the customer and the consumer, they are left on the sidelines by such internally focused companies (Figure 21).

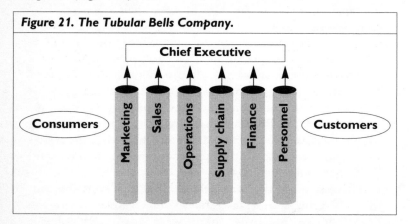

*Figure 21. The Tubular Bells Company.*

Western Marketing Departments can be as guilty as any in creating a tubular bells situation, unlike the Japanese: 'The professionalism incul-cated by Western individualism creates a barrier when it comes to marketing, since it leads to internal organization barriers that go against the "everything-is-Marketing" notion.'[7]

## The Marketing Department's Role in Achieving Integration

There is no perfect analogy to illuminate the working of the Marketing Department. Opponents of the Offensive Marketing approach might suggest that the octopus – with eight suckered arms around a mouth – provides a close likeness. But probably the best analogy is the one which relates the Marketing Department to the orchestral conductor. This is flattering to marketing, because the conductor's leadership position on the rostrum may give a glamour and status out of all proportion to his or her authority or contribution.

What the marketing person and the conductor have in common is a programme whose execution depends on the combined efforts of a number of specialists. In the case of the conductor, these are instrumentalists; for marketers, they are copywriters, engineers, operations people, accountants, sales people and researchers.

Neither the symphony orchestra nor the marketing plan will succeed unless specialists clearly understand their own role and how it relates to others. Equally, the failure of specialists to perform effectively can sabotage the whole programme, whether they are oboists who miss an entry or operations managers who miss an agreed deadline. It follows that, like the conductor, marketers must know their overall objectives, and brief, motivate and coordinate their specialists in order to achieve these in an integrated way.

People in Marketing Departments therefore depend heavily on colleagues in other departments, over whom they have no direct authority. To be a successful marketing executive, you really need to know how to motivate people.

You will occupy many roles, as decision-maker, recommender, coordinator, specifier, influencer, adviser, evaluator and leader. In each situation, you have to know what role to play and how to play it with flair. Table 64 illustrates the multifaceted roles of marketing executives, although exact roles will vary from company to company:

**Table 64. Multifaceted roles of a marketing executive.**

| Role: | Main areas of activity: | |
|---|---|---|
| Decision maker | ● Advertising<br>● Database Marketing | ● Market research<br>● Sales promotion |
| Recommender | ● Pricing<br>● Budget | ● Marketing plans<br>● Key initiatives |
| Coordinator | ● Project management<br>● New products | ● Promotions<br>● Product management |
| Specifier | ● Product or service development<br>● Packaging or product design | ● External agencies |
| Influencer | ● Trade customers<br>● Capital investment<br>● Operations capacity | ● Cost reduction<br>● Sales forecasts |
| Adviser | ● Board | ● Colleagues |
| Evaluator | ● Future vision<br>● Business analysis | ● Competitor analysis |
| Leader | ● Corporate strategy and plans<br>● Marketing strategies | ● Innovation |

It would be easy to add to the list of activities, and it is no wonder that typical marketing executives have too little time for their strategic role as leader.

To be more effective as integrators in future, marketing executives will have to raise their game dramatically in six areas:

1. **Strong involvement in developing the corporate strategy and plan**. This has already been covered. Marketers are best placed to lead the process. Their frequent failure to do so is more often due to lack of time and priority than to any Machiavellian plotting by Finance Department.

2. **Upgrading people skills**. Table 64 indicates the sophisticated abilities in people management required by marketing executives. Unfortunately, the relatively arcane skill of managing and motivating people across departments is given little emphasis in either marketing training or personnel appraisals. Add to this that marketing people tend to be less naturally skilful in managing people than their colleagues in Sales and Operations, and you have a significant problem. The result is weaknesses in both cross-departmental integration and project management.

3. **Broadening knowledge base**. This need was covered in Chapter 1. Tomorrow's marketing executives will need to develop much deeper knowledge of technology, finance and operations, in order to reach the right strategic decisions, and to work more effectively across departments.
4. **Resuming the role of innovators and entrepreneurs.** This is the most important task of the Marketing Department, but is increasingly neglected as the volume of routine tasks multiplies.
5. **Developing a cross-departmental style**. Marketers have a responsibility to keep everyone in the company fully informed about the market-place, by word of mouth, newsletters, presentations, and informally, giving recognition to others for successes (difficult though this may be for some).

    For example, a Brand Manager may have an Away Day in a hotel, to review market developments and future plans. Rather than just invite his or her brand group, the advertising agency, and a market researcher he could develop an **Extended Brand Group**, comprising the main people in R & D, Operations, Finance and Sales involved with the brand. This might double the number of people at the Away Day from say six to twelve, but would broaden the quality of discussion, and greatly extend commitment to the brand. The Brand Manager might also e-mail a monthly newsletter to the **Extended Brand Group**, with market updates, success stories, future issues and recognition of appropriate members of the group.
6. **Staying in marketing jobs longer**. Fast rotation of marketing people through jobs is a long-standing and perennial problem. Few marketing people hold the same job within a company for more than two years, and if they do, they become restless and worried. This quite unnecessary brevity of tenure, which does not apply in any other department, is damaging both to Marketing Departments, and to their contribution to Integrated Marketing. If this problem continues, it will pose a big threat to their future effectiveness, and perhaps even their long-term existence.

### How marketers can overcome barriers to integration

Rather than provide a tedious check-list of things to do, here is a fictional example of integration in which *you* are the star of the show.

**You have just been appointed Marketing Director of a company which is a leader in DIY products. Sales volume this year will be £120 million and profit before tax is pro-**

jected at £10.5 million. You head up a Marketing Department twenty-five strong, consisting of product management and marketing services, and start work next Monday.

The head-hunter said that the company had good products but was losing market share. There was concern at the plateau in profits over the past few years.

The Managing Director, in his mid-fifties, came from a manufacturing background, was rather cautious, quite keen on the idea of marketing, but not totally sure about its scope. The most powerful person on the board was the Sales Director, who operated through flair rather than numbers. Manufacturing was quite efficiently run, and the Finance Director, due to retire in two years' time, was quiet and somewhat old-fashioned. The Marketing Department contained a mix of long-serving employees from the sales force, and much younger imports from Gillette and Unilever.

You asked the Managing Director what he expected of you. He said he wanted a more professional Marketing Department, and a resumption of profitable growth.

Three months later you take stock of the situation. It is not quite what you had been led to expect. The Managing Director is supportive and has the right instincts about investment and quality. The Sales Director is very shrewd but a short-term thinker and too close to the trade. The Marketing Department is spending most of its time on maintenance activity, much of it as a service to the Sales Department. There is also a culture clash between the old-timers, who are long on experience and short on skills, and the newcomers, who are the reverse.

The real find is the number two in the Finance Department, who, before you arrived, was already developing a sophisticated system of net profit by individual product and major retail account. Julian started it on his own initiative, and had, with the cooperation of the Production and Sales Directors, managed to get work-study engineers out with Sales people and truck drivers. This gave him a basis for allocating selling and distribution costs by product and account, but until you arrived, no one had been too interested. You are very interested indeed.

At this point your main conclusions are:

- I have a good relationship with the Managing Director. As an engineer, he likes facts, numbers and analysis, which suits me. I notice he is uneasy with the Sales Director.

- Marketing Department has too narrow a role and is divided against itself.
- Sales Department is too dominant. It is writing the sales forecasts, which are of poor quality. Trade discounts are based on trade pressure. Extra services and deals are given to retailers to achieve more short-term volume.
- R & D Department has good people, but is working on too many projects, and product briefs keep changing. A lot of the projects are housekeeping or minor cost savings.
- Manufacturing is efficient, but the department feels that there are too many products, sizes and package types, and is worried by the poor sales forecasting.
- Product quality is variable and Total Quality Management (TQM) reports to the Production Director.
- The company's products do not justify their premium price and have not kept up with competitive improvements. Consequently, customer loyalty is low and declining. This is confirmed by past research, but no one has faced up to the implications.

About this time, a new five-year plan needs to be written and sent to group HQ. Previously this had been coordinated by the Finance Department. It was regarded as a chore, and consisted mainly of five-year sales and profit forecasts, with no strategies or commentaries.

The Financial Director is quite happy to let you put the plan together this year, working with his number two. Although there are some mutterings, especially from the Sales Director, along the lines of, 'When is this character going to do some marketing?' you don't feel too bad, because you started to plan two major consumer promotions soon after your arrival, have begun to develop a customer relationship programme, and also put in hand some short-term product improvements via the R & D Department. These will be coming on stream soon, and meanwhile you get to work on the new five-year plan, armed with the priceless new profit analyses.

You arrange a series of meetings with other department heads, to produce Integrated Marketing strategies.

You get Julian, your new ally in the Finance Department, to accompany you to all the meetings and your first stop is the Production Director.

This meeting goes well. You say that, based on Julian's product profitability analysis, there are a number of products which you wish to withdraw. Furthermore, your long-term plan is to cut the product range by one third and concentrate resources on five or six leading products which can be built up into 'power' brands.

The Production Director says that in that case he would like to change his manufacturing strategy, and reorganize the two factories so that one does high-volume inflexible runs on 'power' brands and the other is more of a 'boutique' – highly flexible and capable of handling short runs efficiently. You agree to set up an informal meeting with buffet supper, on the first Thursday of each month after work, between the top six people in Production, R & D and Marketing. The topic of the first meeting will be product quality and your people will be presenting results of recent consumer blind tests between your main products and competitors.

The meeting with the Director of R & D goes according to plan. You agree to reduce the number of projects and concentrate your effort on some with short-term pay-offs, others involving technological challenges with large potential but higher risk.

The final meeting, with the Sales Director, has some surprises. He has already seen the major-account profitability analysis, and has decided to give each of his key account managers net contribution rather than revenue targets. What is more, he asks you for help in developing a revised discount structure, and starts to think about varying levels of account service related to account need and profitability.

Two years later, things are going well, even though the competition has made some effective changes which you did not anticipate. A profit of £15 million looks achievable (almost 50% higher than when you arrived):

- Quality has improved, and is evaluated objectively against competition on a regular basis.
- Marketing Department has taken over responsibility for sales forecasting and this has greatly improved.
- The product range has been reduced and the manufacturing director has reorganized the two factories.

**Large savings have been made in manufacturing, distribution and inventory holdings.**

● **You have reorganized the Marketing Department, brought in two people from the Production Department, one from Sales and two from outside, and redeployed twelve others elsewhere.**

● **The new national account profitability system is working well, and all major accounts are profitable.**

● **A club for heavy users, supported by a databased customer relationship programme, looks promising.**

● **A number of product improvements have been made, and prospects in R & D for a new technology-based block-buster look good.**

● **You have, of course, radically improved the quality of advertising, sales promotion, marketing planning and packaging.**

**Finally, six months later, profits hit £17 million, the Managing Director retires and the Sales Director is promoted to take his place. It's time to look around.**

## Practical Tools for Achieving Integrated Marketing

Reaching the sublime state of Integrated Marketing is mainly a matter of vision, structure, strategy and attitude, led by the Board. However, on a tactical level, certain practical tools can be helpful:

1. **Move people across departments**. This is common in Japan, uncommon in Europe and the USA, where people change companies more often. Cross-departmental moves can be short or long term. Some successful Marketers have a production background and engineering qualifications. The role of Sales and Marketing Departments is converging as channels become more complex and customers more powerful. Switching people across departments is enlarging for individuals and productive for companies, because it breaks down barriers.

2. **Meet customers and consumers in person**. There are many ways to do this time-efficiently. A day with a field sales person, or a couple of hours listening in to tele-sales calls, is always highly educational, whether you are a Plant Manager, a warehouseman or a credit clerk. Historically, the assumption has been that 'meeting customers' is something management does (or fails to do). If you believe that everyone is a marketer, it follows that everyone should spend at least one day a year

with customers or consumers. Board members and people in the Marketing Department should have customer contact at least once a month. At present, very few meet this standard, and can always find pressing reasons for remaining cloistered in their offices.

The idea of customer days, where everyone in head office gets out in the field and serves customers, is a good one, in retailing or service businesses.

3. **Communicate openly and honestly.** This is a sound every-day principle, and modern technology has made it more feasible:

**Many larger companies are setting up their own TV channels, where executives can report progress or outline future plans at given times to either a section of people or the whole company.**

**The Halifax has its own TV channel, with an interactive question and answer facility. An assistant at a branch can ask the Chief Executive an unrehearsed question and expect an immediate straight answer. Some of the questions are tough and direct, which is as it should be.**

However, open communication is not dependent on modern technology, as this real-life example illustrates (though the name has been changed):

**James Carter was the thirty-three-year-old Chief Executive of a profitable food company with sales of over £30 million. He had joined eleven years earlier, having graduated with a first-class degree in engineering. At that time, sales were £1 million.**

**The products were manufactured in Yorkshire and sold nationally, mainly to small outlets, by about 170 van sales people, from fourteen depots.**

**Every year, James would tour all fourteen depots, with his Marketing Director (also a Cambridge engineering graduate, with first-class honours). They would meet all the van sales people in a pub near each depot in the evening. A private room would be booked, and free food and drink provided. James would arrive in his Rolls-Royce, have a couple of pints with the Sales team, give a half-hour update on company progress and plans, and then spend an hour or two answering questions. These would come fast and furious; sometimes friendly, sometimes hostile; usually tactical,**

**about prices, deliveries, bonuses, salaries; and always answered fully and directly, often forcefully.**

**In addition to this annual tour, James visited a number of depots every few weeks. The effect on morale and commitment to the company was impressive – if you spent a day in the field and mentioned James Carter, the van sales person would talk about him like a friend.**

**This food company was sold to a large international company for £15 million. By then James owned over 50% of the shares. He retired to the Channel Islands, aged thirty-four.**

4. **Spread bonuses fairly and widely**. Payments of disproportionately high bonuses to senior executives in the UK have replaced the old-style executive dining-room as a divisive factor in companies. Such policies assume that a few strategic decisions and deals, made by senior management, are the decisive factors in business success. Not so. While strategies are important, attitudes, teamwork and effective implementation are most critical in ensuring long-term success. The Continental Airlines example, in the previous section (page 157), involved bonuses spread across departments and levels, not just focused on a few star performers.

5. **Locate all departments on the same site**. If you have Marketing, Sales and Finance located at head office in London, with production operations in Wales and Scotland, you will probably be running three different companies, with limited integration between them. Integration across departments works best on single sites, preferably centred on operations. This is not always possible, but the breakdown of companies into dedicated business units is making it more feasible. Proximity to Operations enables Marketing Department to understand and integrate internal competencies better . . . and there are more typical consumers of most products in Manchester or Bradford than in central London.

6. **Organize large companies into smaller business units, or categories**. Wherever possible, break down big companies into Business Units, with their own Operations, Selling, Finance and Marketing. A minimum size of perhaps £40–50 million is often needed, in order to achieve the necessary economies of operations and manufacturing, and to justify the overheads of separate Sales and Finance Departments. This minimum will differ widely by industry, and would obviously be much higher for vehicles or durables. Business Units work best with their own dedicated operations, where they control all their costs, like autonomous companies.

The big advantages of business units are speed of decision making, teamwork, commitment and integration. All the senior managers tend to understand the business well, and will see a lot of each other. This removes barriers between departments and cuts bureaucracy.

A typical business unit structure is shown below in Table 65, for a pub retailing company.

**Table 65.**

| Head Office |
| • Managing Director   • Legal |
| • Finance Director    • Personnel |

*Business units*

| American restaurants | Pizzas | Brewing | Town centre pubs | Family pubs |

An alternative devolved structure, favoured by international consumer goods companies, is **category management**. The principle is similar to that of Business Units, with the exception that category management is limited to Marketing and possibly Sales, often on a multi-country basis, while Production and R & D may report directly to European management. A simplified health and beauty aids example is illustrated in Figure 23.

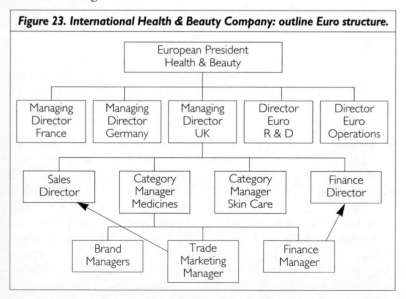

**Figure 23. International Health & Beauty Company: outline Euro structure.**

Any organization chart involving category management tends to run to at least one page and to contain both straight and dotted lines. However, category management does go some way towards devolvement, and aids Marketing Integration both locally and across countries. For example, the UK medicines Category Manager will be in frequent touch with her counterparts in France and Germany, since they will share common R & D programmes, and, to some extent, both operations and brands. And she will have a direct reporting line to the European Category Director for medicines, who is based in Brussels.

## Test Your Company for Total Marketing Integration (Table 66)

| Topic: | Maximum | Your company |
|---|---|---|
| **Table 66. Total Marketing Integration score sheet.** | | |
| | **Score:** | |
| Does the Board understand and stress the total Marketing approach? | 15 | |
| Is there a corporate strategy with convincing vision, priorities and strategies? | 10 | |
| Was this developed on a genuine cross-departmental basis? | 10 | |
| Are there agreed strategies for quality, value, innovation, competencies and attitudes? | 10 | |
| Are these understood and acted upon by every department? | 10 | |
| Is the Marketing department active as integrator and evangelist? | 8 | |
| Has every employee identified his/her customers, and really understood their needs? | 10 | |
| Are job objectives and specifications customer driven, consumer focused and competitive? | 10 | |
| Are job objectives, appraisals and rewards fully aligned? | 10 | |
| Are key integration tools being used? | 7 | |
| **TOTAL** | **100** | |

# FLOW-CHART SUMMARY OF CHAPTER 4

| | |
|---|---|
| **The integrated approach** | ● Everyone is a marketer, with internal and external customers |
| **Integrating company vision and attitudes** | ● Specified, led by Board<br>● Integrated by Marketing Department<br>● Linked to 7 offensive attitudes<br>● The total marketing firmament |
| **Developing a corporate strategy for Integrated Marketing** | ● Strategy must be corporate, covering all departments<br>● Should be driven by customers, markets and competencies |
| **Implementing an Integrated Marketing approach via corporate strategy** | ● Identify internal and external customers . . . and their needs<br>● Implement in integrated, competitive and customer-driven way<br>● Use job objectives, performance appraisal and rewards as key tools. |
| **Barriers to the Integrated Marketing approach** | ● Not close to customers<br>● Action conflicts with words<br>● Lack of board consensus<br>● Internal politics<br>● Worship of technology<br>● Tubular bells structure |
| **Marketing Department's role in integration** | ● Involvement in corporate strategy<br>● Upgrading people skills<br>● Broadening knowledge base<br>● Innovation<br>● Cross-department style<br>● Cutting job rotation |
| **Practical tools for achieving the Integrated Marketing approach** | ● Move people across departments<br>● Meet customers in person<br>● Open, honest communication<br>● Fair, widely spread bonuses<br>● Single-site locations<br>● Business unit and category management |
| **Test your company for total Marketing Integration** | ● Test your company, or one you know |

**Key elements in aligned and integrated five-year corporate strategy.**

Exhibit 1

| Key elements | Issues to be addressed |
|---|---|
| 1. Future market vision | ● Consumer needs in 5 years' time<br>● Balance of stakeholder priorities<br>● Key technology changes<br>● Competitor development<br>● Distributor needs<br>● Alternate and preferred scenarios<br>● Employee and shareholder needs |
| 2. Future priorities | ● Markets, customers, consumers and technologies to be served in 5 years' time<br>● Areas for entry and exit<br>● Acquisitions, disposals<br>● Relative priorities |
| 3. Company vision | ● Summary statement and rationale<br>● Fit with market vision and future priorities (above) |
| 4. Target market position | ● Overall revenue and share by market, category, trade channel, brand and major account – now and in 5 years' time |
| 5. Target financial returns | ● Return on sales overall<br>● By trade channel<br>● By market<br>● By category<br>● ROCE<br>● Cash flow |
| 6. Future investment | ● Advertising<br>● Market research<br>● R & D<br>● Technology<br>● Capital expenditure<br>● Competency development |
| 7. Key supporting strategies | ● Customer value<br>● Speed of response<br>● Innovation<br>● Competency and skill development<br>● Relative cost position |
| 8. Key plans and milestones | ● Convert strategies in (7) into plans, with annual or quarterly milestones |
| 9. Testing programme | ● This would be designed to build a bank of fully tested Marketing and Sales operations, and service ideas requiring significant investment when expanded |
| 10. Summary of departmental responsibilities | ● Individual departmental action responsibilities<br>● Cross-departmental activities |

# PART FOUR:
# **STRATEGIC**

## PART FOUR: **STRATEGIC**

| Table 67. | | |
|---|---|---|
| **P:** Profitable | ● | Proper balance between firm's needs for profit and customer's need for value |
| **O:** Offensive | ● | Must lead market, take risks and make competitors followers |
| **I:** Integrated | ● | Marketing approach must permeate whole company |
| **S:** Strategic | ● | Probing analysis leading to a winning strategy |
| **E:** Effectively Executed | ● | Strong and disciplined execution on a daily basis |

The next four chapters cover the 'S' of POISE – **Strategic**.

- **Chapter 5: Offensive Business Analysis** lays a firm foundation on which to build future strategies.
- **Chapter 6: Developing a Distinctive View of the Future** looks ahead and links business analysis with strategy (Chapter 7). This chapter describes how to use the six drivers of future change in order to anticipate the future.

If you do a first-class job in areas described by Chapters 5 and 6, you will unlock enough secrets of the past and future for your strategies almost to write themselves. Strategy, none the less, does deserve its own chapter:

- **Chapter 7: Developing Winning Strategies** is the one. It describes the various types of competitive advantages and strategies, how to pick the right strategy to win, and how to prevent strategic wear-out.
- **Chapter 8: Offensive Marketing Planning** is the end of the strategic section. It outlines a seven-step process for converting winning strategies into profitable plans, which deliver superior customer value.

# 5. .Offensive Business Analysis

## Chapter Summary

Objectives describe desired destination, strategies set out the routes chosen for achieving the objectives, and plans constitute the vehicle for getting to the destination along the chosen route.

Winning strategies are a necessity for any business which is to succeed in the long term. They are rarely developed in a flash of inspiration, more often evolving over time as a result of trial and error, plus rigorous business analysis.

The groundwork for strategy is prepared in five steps – the business environment, internal examination, competitor analysis, identification of key factors for success (KFS) and SWOT analysis.

**The three wheels of the business environment (Step 1)** are direct, indirect and macro. A European airline is used as an example.

**The internal examination (Step 2)** is a model which enables you to ask candid questions about your own company or brand – its past performance, attitudes, strategy and quality of execution. Where are you leading or following? Where are you winning or losing? Are you in the right markets or sectors? Which strategies are working and which are not? Are any showing signs of wearing out?

**Competitive analysis (Step 3A)** covers what you need to know about your competitors, and how to acquire that knowledge.

**Competitive analysis drill (Step 3B)** puts that knowledge to use. It involves answering seven questions about your competitors.

**Key factors for success (Step 4)** identify the performance areas in which you must match or beat competition in order to succeed. They enable you to judge your fitness in existing markets and chances in new ones, and to pinpoint priority areas for building competitive advantages.

**The SWOT analysis (Step 5)** translates the four previous steps into a format which provides the basis for developing competitive advantages. It is the connecting link between business analysis and strategy development.

All this is hard work and requires as much native grit as native wit. It has only one purpose – action, in the form of strategy development. If you thoroughly prepare the strategic groundwork by really understanding consumers, customers, competitors and costs, winning strategies are likely to emerge. The usual penalty for superficial preparation is 'me too' strategies which buckle under the pressures of the market-place.

## The Three Stages of Battle

Effective action is usually preceded by logical steps, which may be elaborately documented or followed intuitively. They are the objective, the strategy and the plan:

1. **Objectives** describe destinations ('Where are we going?'). They are usually stated in terms of revenue and profit, and should be quantifiable and measurable.
2. **Strategies** set out the route which has been chosen, or the means for achieving the objective ('How do we get there?'). Often a number of alternative strategies are evaluated before a final one is chosen.
3. **Plans** constitute the vehicle for getting to the destination along the chosen route ('What's the plan for getting there?'). They form the detailed execution of the strategy.

This threefold sequence provides a rational framework for decision-making directed towards a consistent end, and can be applied to chess as much as to battle and business: 'Chess is a . . . game in which drifting from move to move is sure to lead to disaster. It is vitally important to form a plan of campaign.'[1]

The process of making a journey also provides a simple but useful analogy. Let us suppose that you have the good fortune to be travelling to Puerto Rico, for whatever reason.

The **objective** of the journey is to get from your home to Puerto Rico. There are various alternative **strategies** for achieving this objective. You could fly there from Heathrow via Miami or New York. Or you could take a plane to Caracas and on to Puerto Rico. If you had plenty of time, it might be possible to sail by liner to New York and fly to Puerto Rico. Your preferred strategy will be selected from these alternatives based on criteria like time available, convenience of schedules, desire for stop-overs, cost, etc.

Having determined your strategy, the next step is the **plan**. This will include detailed arrangements for getting from your home to Heathrow, packing baggage, getting your ticket, method of payment and so on.

To return to the battle analogy, BMW's recovery effort in Germany provides a classic example of the three stages:

**BMW was on the verge of bankruptcy. It was producing motor cycles for a dwindling market, and making a poor return on its bubble cars and six-cylinder saloons. A take-over bid by Daimler-Benz, the makers of Mercedes, was**

**narrowly avoided, and the group was rescued by a Bavarian investment group.**

**Paul G. Hahnemann, Opel's top wholesale distributor, was appointed Chief Executive. His first objective was obviously to get BMW back on an even keel, where it was sufficiently profitable to survive in the long term. Having got there, he would then move to a more ambitious objective of challenging Mercedes for leadership of the market for high-quality executive cars.**

**He was convinced that there was an unexploited market for a sporty saloon car, which Mercedes was not tapping. As he pointed out, 'If you were a sporty driver and German, there was no car for you. The Mercedes is big, black and ponderous. It's for parking, not driving.'**

**Consequently, he evolved a strategy for producing a range of high-quality cars with better performance and a more sporty image than any other saloon. This strategy has remained broadly unchanged since. But the plans for executing it have evolved and been refined.**

**The successful rebirth of BMW is now a matter of history. The company sells over 1.1 million cars a year and has annual revenue above £20 billion.**

This sequential approach sounds quite elementary. Yet it is surprising how often executives lapse into detailed discussions of plans and ideas before they have agreed objectives or strategies.

### Aren't strategies rather academic?

Although few people question the necessity for objectives and plans for action, some people are sceptical about the value of strategies. Since the remainder of this chapter will appear irrelevant to anyone strongly entrenched in that camp, we shall briefly examine the case for using strategies.

The suggestion that strategies are too academic derives from the conviction that any discussion not related to immediate action is theoretical and of no value. Strategies are academic in the sense that their development stems from a close analysis of all relevant facts and the conclusions drawn from them. There was nothing academic about the results achieved by Johnson & Johnson, Merck and Boeing, three companies whose success is enhanced by careful preparation of the strategies for every major initiative, from new products to new markets or new countries.

A good strategy will give clear direction as to general approach, but allow some variety in execution. For example, a company's product strategy may be to achieve and maintain performance and styling superiority over all brands in the same price bracket. The detailed ways in which this can be executed are infinite and offer great flexibility. But there would be no flexibility to market a parity performance product. In that sense strategy does limit freedom of manoeuvre, but that is its objective, since in this case product performance is an issue on which no compromise is to be allowed.

The criticism that strategies are too time-consuming is based on the need for discussion with a large number of people in many departments. But such criticism is misplaced. Strategies are fundamental to Integrated Marketing. Wide-ranging discussion across departments is essential to achieve an integrated approach, since understanding needs debate. The very fact that strategies create controversy is a sound reason for giving them priority. It is much better to resolve disagreements early than to paper them over and risk slowing down action programmes. A marketing strategy discussed only within the Marketing Department is a pointless exercise.

A strategy serves as a basis of agreement for all parties on the goals towards which effort is to be directed, and helps ensure coordinated action. If there is no agreed strategy, the action taken may reflect varying assumptions as to how the objective is to be achieved, and pursue a zigzag course.

A strategy also forces management to be selective and ruthlessly to prune the less vital goals of the business. The clear identification of non-priorities can often be a troublesome process. Therefore, if a strategy has been painful to determine, it is likely to be a good one.

Those who still oppose strategy will, however, be encouraged by the fact that many of the world's greatest discoveries, such as penicillin and the law of gravity, were only found by accident. Any budding Flemings or Newtons therefore may safely ignore this section, and will be amused at the way 'strategic' has become a buzz word, applied as a prefix to almost any activity in the business vocabulary. So we have not only strategic planning, strategic management and strategic consultants, but also strategic merchandising, strategic purchasing and, of course, strategic marketing. If the wider use of the word connotes a broader acceptance that strategies should precede plans, it is to be welcomed.

## Requirements for Effective Analysis

One of the best-known books for young barristers, on the art of cross-examination, points out that native grit is even more important than native wit. In other words, thorough preparation matters more than the occasional brilliant insight, and, in any case, the two usually go together.

The same applies to the development of strategy. Strategy development is hard work and most successful when preceded by rigorous business analysis, where every relevant fact and number is cross-examined in a disciplined sequence. Table 68 summarizes the benefits of disciplined business analysis.

**Table 68.  The benefits of disciplined business analysis.**

| Benefits of doing | Penalties for not doing |
|---|---|
| ● Understanding of business<br>● Control of business<br>● Quick/correct tactical decisions<br>● Basis for clear strategy<br>● Put pressure on competition<br>● Spot opportunities early | ● Lots of undigested data<br>● Always firefighting<br>● Inconsistent tactical decisions<br>● Reaction 'strategy'<br>● Always taking pressure<br>● Late with innovations |
| ↓ | ↓ |
| Leader | Follower |

Effective analysis is comparable to a manufacturing process. It selects the relevant raw data, converts it into knowledge and finally into understanding, which is the end product of analysis. As in the case of manufacturing, quality of raw materials and care in processing are essential for a good result.

Business analysis is a continuous, though sequential process, as illustrated in Figure 24.

We are living in the days of data glut. Marketers flounder beneath the torrent of paper which rolls in like the tide every morning. To turn the tide in your favour, you need to ensure that the routine paperwork – sales, profit by product and account, market analysis, service levels and so on – arrives on your desk in usable form, not as unsifted computer printouts. The main producers of routine paper – Finance, Sales, Administration and the Marketing Department itself – will tend to be production orientated unless the recipients of this routine paper make it known exactly what they want as customers.

Finally, effective analysis has only one purpose: action. Sometimes analysis becomes an end in itself, leading forever to further analysis.

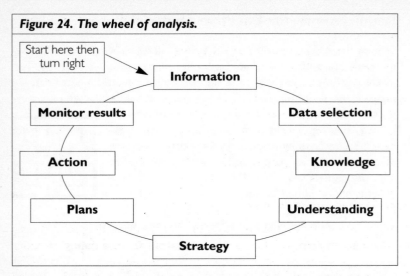

**Figure 24. The wheel of analysis.**

Start here then turn right

- Information
- Data selection
- Knowledge
- Understanding
- Strategy
- Plans
- Action
- Monitor results

This is called 'analysis paralysis'. Or it can result in the DTs – delaying tactics – where the recipient of the analysis continually asks for further data, thus disguising fear of risk and decision-taking.

There are six requirements for effective analysis, as shown in Table 69.

**Table 69.  Six requirements for effective analysis.**

1.  Right data
2.  Systematic approach
3.  Focused approach
4.  Thorough and probing
5.  Must lead to action and avoid DTs
6.  Continuous improvement

## 1.  Right data

Data needs to be organized in a user-friendly and ready-to-use way. Modern IT systems have the potential to achieve this, but often fail to do so. In most companies, IT systems are set up by Finance Department, but designed for control rather than enlightenment. Providing actionable management information tends to be a secondary consideration.

Marketers need to take a strong line on this, and insist that they are provided with quality sales and profit data by distribution channel, category, brand and major account. They also need to think very carefully about who to target in data-based customer relationship programmes, what type of information they need by customer and how the data will be used. These are important building blocks for decisions on resource allocation.

Unfortunately, in many companies they don't exist, and in others the information quality is weak and arbitrary. *Hands up the passenger transport company which has believable cost and profit breakdowns by type of fare and customer.* It is not easy to develop, but should be available. *And hands up the financial services company which has cost and profit breakdowns by customer type* **across** *products and distribution channels.* A minority of direct operations might raise a couple of fingers, but the vast majority of financial service Marketers remain embarrassed by the question.

## 2. Systematic approach

Yes, there's plenty of data out there. Too much in fact, and probably only 10% is relevant to us. This consists of 'must have' data in any category, and selected data necessary to develop strategies and plans. Let us review these separately. 'Must have' data is summarized in Table 70. You cannot run any business efficiently as a marketer unless you have most of this data.

| Table 70.  'Must have' data check-list for Marketers. | |
|---|---|
| **Market data** | **Internal data** |
| ● Market size and trend<br>● Key segments<br>● Key channels, size and trend<br>● Key account analyses<br>● Brand shares by market, channel, customer<br>● Customer demographics and loyalty<br>● Customer usage, attitudes, retention<br>● Competitor shares<br>● Brand shares by region<br>● Marketing spend by brand<br>● Channel and account margins<br>● Size of product ranges<br>● New product success/failure | ● Overall sales, costs, profits<br>● Sales, profit breakdowns by market segment, channel, brand, account and customer type<br>● Marketing spend overall and by activity<br>● Summary of direct marketing data<br>● Volume sensitivity analyses, e.g. effect of +20% and −20% in sales, on your profits<br>● Brand histories<br>● Price movements and elasticity<br>● Customer relationship monitors |

'Must have' data almost always needs to be supplemented by additional facts specific to your situation. It is required to unlock opportunities and to guide on priorities. For example, if you are in the pub business you will want sales and profits by pub type, and return on investment. If you are managing partner of a large legal firm, you will look for profit by partner; revenue and profit by market segment such as corporate tax, litigation, mergers and acquisitions, insolvency and trusts; and split between personal, corporate and government business.

## 3. Focused approach

A common error is to analyse every piece of available data, build up a massive business review, and then say to yourself: 'What action can we take based on this review?' Unfortunately the answer often is 'Not much.' This head-banging approach has a number of drawbacks. First, it is laborious. Secondly, so much energy is put into the analysis that little is left for strategy and action. Thirdly, and most frustrating of all, the analysis may uncover few opportunities for action.

The 'focused approach' is quite different. It is quicker and much more rewarding. Before you start any analysis, write down a list of possible hypotheses for action. You then work out the data needed to prove or disprove all these hypotheses. To begin with, your list of hypotheses will be quite long, perhaps ten or fifteen. You will find that some of these can be quickly screened out, but as the analysis proceeds you are likely to develop new hypotheses to add to the original list. Your aim will be to finish the analysis with three or five hypotheses for new initiatives still intact. These will form the basis for a revised set of strategies and plans. The 'focused approach' is illustrated in Table 71.

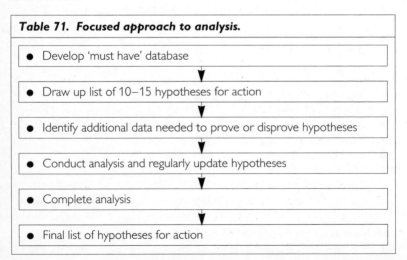

**Table 71. Focused approach to analysis.**

- Develop 'must have' database
- Draw up list of 10–15 hypotheses for action
- Identify additional data needed to prove or disprove hypotheses
- Conduct analysis and regularly update hypotheses
- Complete analysis
- Final list of hypotheses for action

Table 72 gives a list of possible hypotheses
you might draw up if you were Marketing
Director of a leading Far East airline. For the
sake of brevity, only four will be listed, though in practice you would
aim to start with a lot more.

**Table 72. Possible 'starting' list of hypotheses for Far East airline.**

| Hypotheses | Data needed to prove/disprove |
|---|---|
| 1. We need a European partner | • Estimated additional revenue through code sharing with Euro partner<br>• Review of possible partners |
| 2. We should upgrade our economy-class product | • Review sales and profits of own economy class<br>• Compare proposition with competitors<br>• Analyse differences by route length, purpose of travel |
| 3. We may need to start or buy a discount airline | • Range of likely sales and economics<br>• Review research on competitor discount airlines<br>• Analyse comparative prices, occupancy levels |
| 4. We should increase our customer relationship activity | • Analyse past results by frequency of travel and class<br>• Review competitor activity – database size, quality; segmentation method; club and loyalty propositions; strategy, spend |

The 'focused approach' enables you to concentrate on data which
may be actionable, and avoid wasting time on dead-end analysis.

### 4. Thorough and probing

By limiting the amount of data reviewed, you will be able to consider it
in more depth. The real answer to many issues is buried two or three
levels down, and not visible to the inexperienced eye. You need to
patiently peel off each layer of onion skin until you get to the core,
asking questions like:

- How good is the quality of this data?
- Is it consistent with my own experience or with common sense?
- Is it consistent with other information from different sources? If
  not, what are the reasons for the differences?
- Does external market, consumer panel or customer data con-
  form with internal sales data? If not, why not?

Thorough analysis is like peeling an onion (Figure 25).

**Figure 25.**

Procter & Gamble is the gold standard in this area – they wrestle every problem to the ground and never stop probing.

### 5. Must lead to action and avoid the DTs

This is fully covered in the previous sections. There are people who are very good at analysis, but have great difficulty in decision-making or action. Corporate planning departments used to be full of them. They tend to analyse into infinity, as an end in itself, unaware that they are using delaying tactics (DTs) to avoid the frightening prospect of taking a decision.

### 6. Continuous improvement

Good on-line IT systems enable effective analysis to be treated as a continuous process, rather than something done once or twice a year. Continuous updating makes analysis more actionable, and reduces the work-load peak during the five-year plan and budgeting season.

## The Five-step Process for Strategic Analysis

In the context of this section the word 'strategic' is justified, because we are looking at the analysis needed to develop a marketing strategy. While there are many ways of approaching this, Offensive Marketers usually adopt a five-step sequence, as in Figure 26.

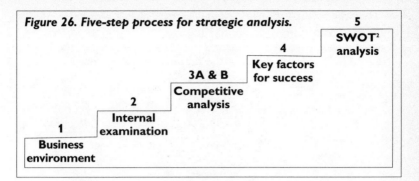

**Figure 26. Five-step process for strategic analysis.**

1. The analysis of the **business environment** involves looking at the direct, indirect and macro factors affecting your business now and in the future.
2. The **internal examination** is a medical check of your business, involving a great deal more probing than the typical executive check-up.
3. The **competitive analysis** defines your competitors, evaluates what they are doing well and badly now, and how they are likely to change in the future.
4. **Key factors for success** lists the things that really matter in your markets and identifies the priority areas for building competitive advantages.
5. The **SWOT analysis**, to use the awful abbreviation for which there appears to be no better substitute, pulls together the whole exercise, and involves a listing of your Strengths and Weaknesses, plus the Opportunities and Threats facing you.

In applying this five-step process, the person doing the analysis should bear in mind the need for focus, outlined above in the six 'Requirements for Effective Analysis'. This five-step process helps to emphasize areas of analysis likely to be actionable, but you need to be quite selective in using the check-lists, depending on your own circumstances.

We shall now briefly examine each of these five steps in turn.

## STEP 1:   THE THREE WHEELS OF THE BUSINESS ENVIRONMENT

Figure 27 divides the business environment into three wheels, representing the macro, indirect and direct factors affecting your business. Macro is on the outside, since the effect of macro factors is usually less immedi-

ate than direct ones like price changes or product improvements by
your major competitor.

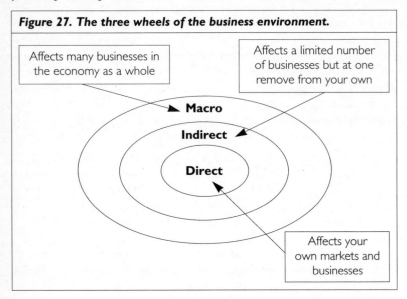

**Figure 27. The three wheels of the business environment.**

Figure 28 illustrates some of the factors in each wheel – Exhibit 1
(page 217) contains a more detailed check-list.

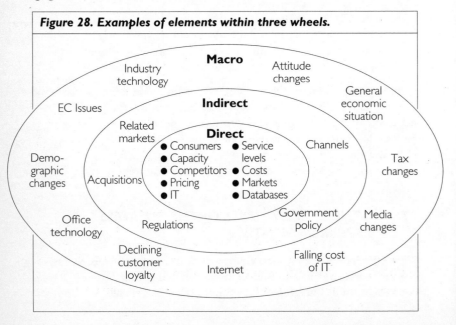

**Figure 28. Examples of elements within three wheels.**

The elements covered by the macro and direct wheels are straight-forward. The indirect wheel requires further explanation. It includes businesses which intrude on the edge of your territory, though they are not direct competitors. For instance, trains and cars are indirect competitors to airlines on short-distance journeys. It also covers related markets which are not competitive, but whose success greatly affects your own. For example, sales of agricultural equipment are heavily affected by the profitability of farming. Equally, changing fashions in outerwear influence the styles of lingerie women require.

Table 73 lists some 'indirect businesses'. The business on the left is 'related' to the one on the right.

| Table 73.  Related markets and their effects. | | |
|---|:---:|---|
| **Driver** | | **Beneficiary** |
| Washing machines | → | Cleaning products |
| Outerwear | → | Lingerie |
| Home freezers | → | Frozen foods |
| Computer hardware | → | Computer software |
| Retail outlets | → | Manufacturers |
| Heavy industry | → | Rail freight |
| Cars | → | Petrol |
| Engineering plant | → | Machine tools |
| Farming | → | Farm equipment |

The European airlines example in Figure 27 illustrates the operation of the three wheels in a rather different business environment. The indirect wheel often has more impact on future industry profitability than the macro one. For example, in Figure 27 two of the most important factors are future airline alliances and government competition policies.

Use the three wheels as a stimulus for thinking about the shape of your markets in three to five years' time. What are the key drivers for change? What effect will they have? Every business should have its vision of the future, and a view on the alternative scenarios. Chapter 6, 'Developing a Distinctive View of the Future', addresses these questions in more detail.

The firm lines surrounding each circle are misleading in their air of certainty. Indirect factors often leak into or even crash through the direct circle, and the placement of factors within circles often changes. For instance, in Figure 29 one could argue that 'Falling IT costs' and 'Declining customer loyalty', both in the macro circle, represent an opportunity for enhanced Relationship Marketing within the direct circle.

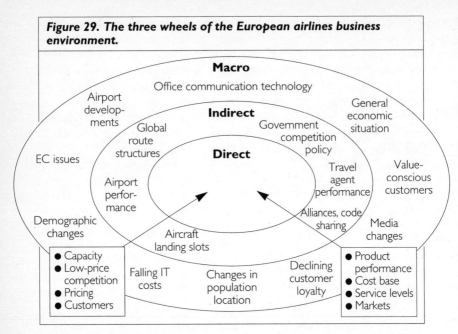

**Figure 29. The three wheels of the European airlines business environment.**

There is some linkage between circles and action timescale. So direct factors are more likely to have a short-term impact on sales and profits than macro ones, which tend to be long term. However, the linkage is not close and can change rapidly.

Figure 30 gives you an opportunity to fill in how macro, indirect or direct factors affect your own business.

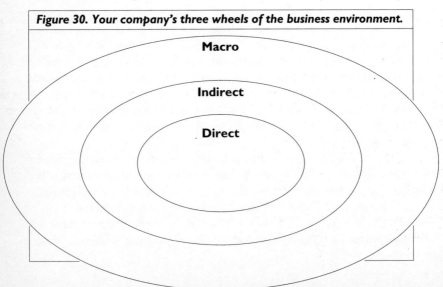

**Figure 30. Your company's three wheels of the business environment.**

See Figure 31 for a brief recap of where you are now.

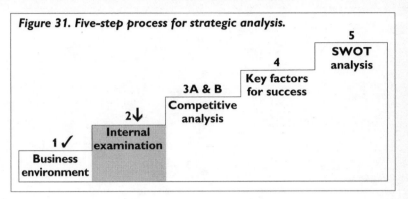

**Figure 31. Five-step process for strategic analysis.**

## STEP 2: THE INTERNAL EXAMINATION

Like a health check, the internal examination should be formally carried out once a year. The best time to do it is a couple of months before the annual update of the five-year plan, which itself should precede the budget for the following year.

The crux of the internal examination is the factual analysis of your business, which leads to knowledge and understanding. You are then able to ask a number of candid questions about past performance, attitudes, strategy and quality of execution. The answers to these questions provide new insights into the strengths and weaknesses of your products or services.

The factual analysis of your business enables you to look at the past year's events in perspective. It is also one of the strongest tools you have for ensuring that the marketing approach permeates the whole business, since, as part of the internal examination, you will also be reviewing selling, operations and financial factors which affect your overall competitive position. In conducting the analysis, you are therefore assuming the mantle of overall Business Director, even though your title happens to be a marketing one.

Figure 32 illustrates the sequence of this combination of analysis plus question and answer. The internal examination is divided into five audit areas – knowledge, performance, attitudes, strategy and execution. It audits the key elements of the Offensive Marketing approach.

Let's take a quick look at each of the stages of the internal examination in Figure 32.

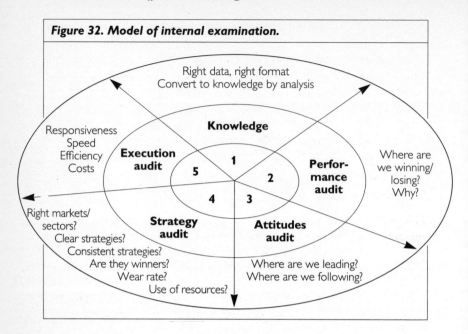

**Figure 32. Model of internal examination.**

## 1. Knowledge

This stage will involve a lot of number crunching, thinking and discussions with colleagues and customers. It will probably absorb two thirds to three quarters of the total time you spend on the internal examination. The objective of this stage is to convert facts and knowledge into understanding, through the medium of analysis. The six requirements for effective analysis summarized in Table 69 should provide a useful guide in collecting the right information – which is likely to be a bundle of facts, opinions and hypotheses – and using it in the right way.

This first stage in the process is very important, since it provides the basis for making judgements in the next four stages. It certainly makes sense to look ahead to the questions you and others will be asking during Stages 2 to 5, to ensure that the basis of knowledge and understanding accumulated in Stage 1 can provide the framework for future judgements.

## 2. Performance audit

Where are we winning? Where are we losing? And why? During this stage, as in most of the others, you will probably be focusing on markets, channels, consumers, customers, products, innovation and profits.

For example, you may find that you are winning with a stream of successful new products, but not making the most of them because you are losing on distribution and customer service. Alternatively, your short-term profit performance may look like a winning hand, but you know you are losing long term with a bare innovation cupboard and declining customer loyalty.

The questions and answers generated by the performance audit will help you identify future opportunities and areas for improvement. They will also point the way to issues for Stage 4, the 'Strategy audit'.

### 3. Attitudes audit

This will provide some important pointers as to how far you are pursuing the Offensive Marketing approach. The overriding question is whether you are leading the market or following your competitors.

The flow-chart summary of Chapter 3 – 'Offensive Vision and Attitudes' – constitutes a useful check-list (page 139), especially the sections on value, innovation, investment and persistent attack. How do some of the more recent entrants to your company feel about it? Is it a fun place to work in? Is it making progress and moving forward? Does it seem to know where it is going? Customers are also worth listening to on such topics.

### 4. Strategy audit

Building on the previous three stages, you will now want to consider some fundamental questions. Are our main strategies working or not? Which are working best and least well? Are they gaining momentum or wearing out? Are they consistent or are they being changed needlessly? Most important of all, have they been properly thought through?

You will probably at this point already be developing ideas for improving your strategies, and this topic is covered in Chapter 7.

### 5. Execution audit

Companies should aim to win on quality of strategy as well as quality of execution. This is not always possible, and excellent execution can often transform an average strategy into a winning formula.

This stage concentrates on a few key execution elements such as responsiveness – both to customer needs and to competitor initiatives – speed, efficiency and relative cost position. The areas to focus on will obviously depend on your type of business and the key factors for success in it – clearly, speed to market with new products is much more important in software than in cheese.

A detailed framework for the internal examination is given in Exhibit 2 (page 219), and the next section provides five examples.

## Five Examples of Internal Examination

This section will illustrate the internal examination with five examples:

1. Sales trend audit
2. Industry capacity analysis
3. Competitive position audit
4. Innovation audit
5. Customer relationship audit

### 1. Sales trend audit

You are shortly taking over a leading aspirin brand in the German healthcare market. It is sold primarily through the pharmacy and drug discounter channels. Your new boss, who has been the Category Manager for two years, tells you it is doing really well, with volume 10% up in the latest year, even though the market is flat. At your request,  your brand assistant has completed an analysis, identifying sources of growth by type of account, product types . . . and comparing your sales with your brand share. What do you conclude from this (Table 74), and how do you feel about next year's budget, which you have to deliver?

Table 74. Healthcare brand: analysis of sources of growth.

| Outlet audit (Cases '000) | Last year | This year | Next year's budget |
|---|---|---|---|
| Existing outlets | 500 | 450 | – |
| New accounts | – | 90 | – |
| New channel | 20 | 32 | – |
| TOTAL SALES | 520 | 572 | 630 |
| **Product audit (Cases '000)** | | | |
| Existing products | 520 | 510 | 530 |
| Line extension | – | 62 | 100 |
| TOTAL SALES | 520 | 572 | 630 |
| **Brand share (%)** | **16.5** | **17.0** | **19.3** |

Clearly all the growth has come from new accounts, and a line extension. To shed some light on these figures, you spent a day in Munich visiting pharmacists, including recently opened accounts. You formed the impression that trade stocks of your brand were heavy, thanks to a year-end deal promotion, and that the line extension launched two months ago was not selling out.

Yes, you have just received a hospital pass, positioned by your predecessor and, *much worse*, your new boss, as a try-scoring opportunity.

As you can see from the table, sales grew by 10%, but brand share by only 3% in a static market. The 7% difference represents inventory building by the trade. Next year, pharmacists are likely to cut back on inventory. And there is anecdotal confirmation that the new line extension is not selling out. Budgeted growth next year from 62K cases to 100K cases looks ambitious. Indeed, next year's budget as planned is quite unrealistic – you would do well to hold volume, never mind increase it by 10%.

The obvious lesson – never take total sales figures at face value. They should be broken down and analysed by causal factor. *What can you do about this situation?* Ensure that your Category Manager's boss gets to see Table 74 early in your tenure as Brand Manager. Then get to work on some asset- and competency-based marketing – see section on 'Leveraging Short-term Profits Responsibly' (Chapter 2, page 92).

## 2. Industry capacity analysis

This is easier to illustrate in a manufacturing than a service business, though it is equally relevant to both, as an indicator of future price trends. Table 75 refers to the beer industry in a European country.

**Table 75. Example of industry capacity analysis (barrels '000).**

|  | 2 years ago | | 2 years hence | |
|---|---|---|---|---|
|  | Max. | In use | Max. | In use |
| Competitor A | 1.5 | 1.2 | 1.5 | 0.7 |
| Competitor B | 1.0 | 0.8 | 1.0 | 0.6 |
| Competitor C | 1.0 | 1.0 | 1.5 | 1.3 |
| New Competitor 1 | – | – | 0.5 | 0.2 |
| New Competitor 2 | – | – | 0.5 | 0.3 |
| Total capacity | 3.5 | 3.0 | 5.0 | 3.1 |
| % Utilization |  | 86% |  | 62% |

*What do you conclude from this chart?*

This is a typical picture of a market which has grown fast historically, attracted new competitors and extra capacity, then matured to nil growth. The two new competitors started to build new capacity eighteen months ago, and will soon be in production. The future outlook is one of intense price competition, since future industry production is much greater than the market requires. Only Competitor C, whose main brand is very distinctive, is set to do well.

### 3. Competitive position audit

This one of the most useful audits. Technique is to list the main consumer or customer needs in your market, score them in order of importance, then rank your brand or company performance on each need. The basis for building the hierarchy of customer needs is a combination of research, knowledge and judgement. The example in Table 76 is for a medium-sized Leicester accounting firm, ranked against Arthur Andersen, which is considered to be industry best practice.

**Table 76. Accounting firm: example of competitive position versus client needs.**

| Hierarchy of client needs [10 = very important, 1 = not important] | | Competitive position v. Andersen |
|---|---|---|
| Reliable | 10 | Same |
| Meets deadlines | 8 | Same |
| Quick response to queries | 7 | Better |
| Innovative | 6 | Poorer |
| International coverage | 3 | Poorer |
| Involvement of senior partner | 5 | Better |
| Understands my business | 7 | Better |
| Understands locality | 5 | Better |
| Gives good business advice | 6 | Same |
| Competitive pricing | 7 | Better |
| High-calibre people | 9 | Same |

On the three most important criteria – reliability, meeting deadlines and calibre of people – both firms are ranked the same. The Leicester firm does less well on international coverage, but this is not of great importance to clients. It is also poorer on innovation, and this is quite important.

The Leicester firm scores better than Andersen on local business understanding and partner involvement. This is because Andersen is likely to allocate its best people to larger international companies not based in Leicester. The Leicester strategy will therefore be to push these advantages hard, and innovate more.

## 4. Innovation audit

There are two aspects to consider on innovation. The first is output – the number of your innovations which reach the market. The second is success rate. You may have a high percentage success rate, but if your total output is low, your innovation performance is not satisfactory.

Innovation, of course, covers every aspect of a business. In the illustration in Table 77, focus will be on product and service innovation, two of the more important areas.

| Table 77.  Product and service innovation audit. | | |
|---|---|---|
| **Innovation criteria** | **3 years ago** | **This year** |
| Number of significant innovations in past 5 years | 10 | 7 |
| Number successful | 3 | 4 |
| % success rate | 30% | 57% |
| % total sales in products/services launched in past 5 years | 15% | 25% |
| % incremental sales | 10% | 12% |
| Average annual sales per new product/service (£m) | 5.5 | 12.0 |
| Incremental payback per new product/service (years) | 3 | 4 |

You can draw a number of conclusions from this table, on an absolute and trend basis:

- While new product and service output is down, from 10 to 7, in the past five years, success rate is much better (57%), and sales per new item higher (£12 million per year).
- However, there has been a large increase in cannibalization of existing products by new ones. While 25% of this year's sales are in new products launched in the past five years – a commendable figure – only 12% of these sales are incremental. In other words, half of the new-product sales have been taken from existing company products, indicating poor targeting. As a result, payback on new products has worsened.

- Key action to take is to improve understanding of market segmentation, and to target new products at segments where the company is relatively weak, so that new revenue is mainly incremental.

## 5. Customer relationship audit

The issue is to identify the kind of information you need in order to build a customer-relationship marketing strategy. The purpose of this example is to briefly illustrate how stage 1 – 'Knowledge' – can be applied, using a fictional example. *You* are in a starring role. Here are some background facts:

**You have just resigned from your job as Marketing Manager with an international credit card company, and joined your brother as partner in the car distributor business he built up, Amazing Performance (AP).**

**He started in a small way selling second-hand cars after leaving school early, twenty years ago, and now owns three distributorships in the East Midlands. He is much wealthier than you are, despite your BA.**

**AP's business is reasonably successful with sales of £12 million annually, net profits of £0.5 million. Its core is sale and servicing of new executive cars. Price range is £10,000 to £40,000, with a median price of £25,000.**

**Your brother is a great personal salesman, and well-known local businessman. He is not interested in numbers or business analysis. The Service Department is run efficiently, but very impersonally, and the Finance Director is a retired Bank Manager. Main promotion events are new car launches, to which all customers are invited, and alcoholic links with the local rugby club, which AP sponsors heavily. There is no information on number of customers, lifetime customer value, customer retention level or customer profitability.**

**You are knowledgeable about Relationship Marketing, and are expected to build growth and profitability by applying it. Your brother is prepared to give you a free hand on IT and realizes he will have to invest in customer databases.**

*So, how do you handle this situation?*

**Following the Offensive Marketing approach to business analysis, you start with two simple questions. First,**

what are the key areas of actionable knowledge to
acquire? Secondly, what information has to be accessed
in order to build this knowledge?

You will form your own views about these issues. Here
are some thoughts to add to your own.

First, actionable knowledge. Recognizing that you can't
learn everything immediately, you prioritize six key questions as a basis for building a customer relationship
marketing programme:

- How many customers do we have? Who are they and
  what do they think of the AP experience?
- Can customers be segmented into types by level of
  potential and profitability?
- What is our retention level of existing customers? Is
  this good or bad?
- What is the customer lifetime value (CLV)?
  This would estimate how many cars the average
  customer would buy from AP based on current
  retention levels; level of service income; and extra
  revenue generated by word-of-mouth referrals. On
  this basis, customer lifetime revenue and profit
  could be guesstimated. This is a useful measure
  to guide you on how much to invest in retaining
  existing customers, and acquiring new ones.
- What is the basis for targeting new customers, and
  how successful is it?
- What proportion of total advertising and promotion
  funds are being spent on existing versus new customers?

Having defined the questions to ask, you now have to
decide what information is needed to answer them,
and how to acquire it. For reasons of space, this will be
limited to three of the six questions – customer profile,
retention level and customer lifetime value.

*Customer profile.* Based on service records, it is quite easy
to establish total number of customers. There are 3,000.
To get an initial feel for them, you spend a week in the
showroom talking to them as they deliver or pick up their
cars for service; conduct phone interviews with 100; and
visit the homes of another 50 who have their cars picked
up and returned after service.

You decide that the information you want is as in Table 78.

| Table 78. AP Cars: initial data required on customers. |
| --- |
| ● Occupation: |
| ● Age: |
| ● Type of Home: |
| ● Current model: |
| ● When bought: |
| ● Two previous models bought and when: |
| ● Future model purchase intention: |
| ● Attitudes to AP: |
| ● Response to AP promotions: |
| ● Profitability: |

*How do you get this information?* **You already have data on name and address, sex, last model bought, age of model and service history. The rest of the customer data, including the very important future model purchase intention, is obtained from a questionnaire sent out with an incentive for returning it. Information on profitability is worked out with the finance director, and on response to promotions, by analysing the guest lists for recent model launch parties and rugby events.**

*Retention level.* **You have one good stroke of fortune – Service Department records go back ten years. These are analysed by individual and type of car. They indicate that AP Cars is gaining customers at a rate of 25% per year, but losing 10% per year. The average customer is buying a new car every five years, but only repeat buying an AP car 40% of the time.**

**Clearly, your next move is to call up a recent sample of those still in the area who have left AP, and find out why.**

*Customer lifetime value (CLV).* **Your customer survey showed that average age was forty, mostly male, with a life expectation of seventy-five years, and buying interval of five years, at £25,000 per purchase. Trade-in cost averaging £10,000 per car then has to be deducted.**

In this example, unlike some, CLV is straightforward to work out, allowing a 25% uplift on net new car price, for service income.

At the current level of 40% retention, CLV is only £12,500. If retention level is raised to 60%, CLV more than doubles to £27,500; and at 80%, it almost quintuples to £60,000.[3]

And none of this allows for the positive effect of referrals by satisfied customers (or the devastating effect of negative word of mouth by unhappy customers).

You immediately decide to target a 60% retention rate.

*So what happened next?* There is no space to continue, but the prospects make one's mouth water. Yes, of course you identified a massive opportunity among self-employed business people and professionals, sold cars to their spouses, raised retention levels to 65%, and financed a major IT upgrade by persuading your brother to cancel the rugby club sponsorship.

The main purpose of these examples is to illustrate how analysis should lead to conclusions and action.

With a sound knowledge base from the internal examination model in Figure 30, you can now, if you wish, use Exhibit 2 (page 219) to move round it in a clockwise direction, and pose other questions on performance, attitudes, strategy, and execution.

Step 3 is the next in the process – 'Competitive Analysis' (Figure 33).

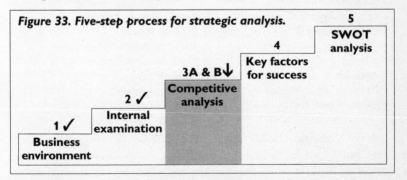

**Figure 33. Five-step process for strategic analysis.**

- 1 ✓ Business environment
- 2 ✓ Internal examination
- 3A & B ↓ Competitive analysis
- 4 Key factors for success
- 5 SWOT analysis

## STEP 3A: COMPETITIVE ANALYSIS

Why bother to analyse competitors? Some companies think it best to get on with their own plans and ignore competition. Others follow competitive moves in obsessive detail, and end up copying or reacting to competition. Offensive Marketers strive to lead and to make their competitors followers. In order to lead your competitors, you must know who they are and what they are doing, **because competition represents the standard you have to beat**.

Competition has been divided into two sections, 3A and 3B. 'Step 3A, Competitive Analysis' identifies what you need to know about competitors and how to acquire that knowledge. 'Step 3B, Competitive Analysis Drill' (see page 206) deals with how to use that knowledge. In this section, Step 3A, therefore we will stick to three questions:

1.  What do you want/need to know about your competitors?
2.  What are the main sources of information about competitors?
3.  How can you develop a good-quality system for analysing competitors?

**What you want/need to know about your competitors**. Table 79 summarizes the main things you would probably like to know about your competitors. The items on the left of the table will be known to most companies which conduct market research and remain alert.

**Table 79.  *What you need/want to know about competitors.***

| What most companies know about competitors | What most companies do not know about competitors |
| --- | --- |
| Overall sales, and profits | Size, quality of databases |
| Sales and profits by market | Relative-cost position |
| Sales revenue by brand | Customer service levels |
| Market shares by brand | Future strategies |
| Organization structure | New product or service plans |
| Distribution system | Profit by brand |
| Identity of key executives | Profit by distribution channel |
| Advertising spending | Database marketing results |
| Consumer attitudes | Sales efficiency |
| Past marketing strategies | Marketing efficiency |
| Customer retention levels | Future investment plans |

A few companies know most or all of the items in both columns, even though information on competitive cost position and profit by market or brand may be fragmentary and based on enlightened guess-work. None of this requires industrial espionage or unethical conduct. It can be generated by hard, persistent and well-organized effort on a company-wide basis, led by the Marketing Department.

**Main sources of competitor information**. There are three main data sources – recorded, observable and opportunistic.

- **Recorded data** is easily available in published form either internally or externally. Competitor annual reports are an example.
- **Observable data** has to be actively sought, and often assembled from a number of sources. Competitor pricing falls within this category.
- **Opportunistic data** requires planning and organization, because information often arrives through different departments, and needs to be coordinated. Much of this type of data is anecdotal, such as conversations with equipment suppliers or competitors at trade fairs.

Table 80 illustrates data types by major source.

**Table 80. The three main sources of competitor information.**

| Recorded | Observable | Opportunistic |
|---|---|---|
| ● Annual reports | ● Pricing | ● Suppliers |
| ● Published data | ● Distribution levels | ● Trade shows |
| ● Credit reports | ● Promotions | ● Sales people |
| ● Trade press | ● Advertising | ● Seminars |
| ● Brokers' reports | ● Planning applications | ● Social contacts |
| ● Presentations to security analysts | ● Results of tenders | ● Ex-employees |
| ● Market research | ● Patent applications | ● Distributors |
| ● Government reports | | ● Relationships |

Competitive data is like a jigsaw puzzle. Individual pieces do not usually have much value. The critical skill is both to collect most of the pieces and to assemble them into an overall picture. This also enables you to identify any missing pieces and to take the necessary steps to collect them.

Using determination and skill, you can normally find out anything you want to about a competitor, legally. Unfortunately this rarely happens since few companies seek, organize and evaluate competitive data, as the collection of negatives in Table 81 indicates.

**Table 81. Typical company practice in collecting competitor data.**

| Recorded data | ● Not analysed over time | ● Not diffused over time |
|---|---|---|
| Observable data | ● Not recorded <br> ● Not coordinated | ● Not selected or evaluated |
| Opportunistic data | ● Not actively sought | ● Not disseminated |

It is surprising that so few Western companies effectively analyse competitors (in contrast to the Japanese, who do it very well), since the consequences of weak competitive analysis can be most unpleasant, and definitely bad for the health of senior executives (Table 82).

| Table 82.   Result of poor competitive data handling. | |
| --- | --- |
| • Failure to pre-empt competitive threats | • Overload of unanalysed data |
| • Regular nasty surprises | • Emphasis on most recent events |
| • Reacting role | • Lack of mature perspective |
| | • Follower, not leader |

**How to develop a quality system of competitor analysis**. Superior competitive analysis can obviously be a source of competitive advantage. The missing element in most companies is that responsibility for evaluating competitors is widely dispersed within and across departments. The jigsaw never gets assembled and no one knows which pieces are missing. Competitor analysis can only be effective when the total Integrated Marketing approach (Chapter 4) is applied. In Table 83 are some suggestions for doing so.

**Table 83.   How to assemble the competitive jigsaw.**

1.  Select key competitors to evaluate. Focus on three or four per market at most.
2.  Apply the right resource levels to the task. It is usually worthwhile having at least one full-time analyst, to chase, coordinate and evaluate competitive data.
3.  Select and brief data collectors in each department. This would include people in Sales, Purchasing, Operations, Marketing, R & D and Finance.
4.  Insist on regular returns from data collectors.
5.  Publish regular tactical and strategic reports on competition. The tactical ones could be fortnightly and widely circulated. The strategic ones would be less frequent, perhaps quarterly, and go to senior management only.

## STEP 3B: COMPETITIVE ANALYSIS DRILL

With a sound base of competitive knowledge, the next step is to put it to use. One of the best systems for doing this, which fits the Offensive Marketing approach, is the competitive analysis drill, used by General Electric in the USA.[4] This involves answering seven questions about competitors.

## 1. Who is the competitor? Now? Five years from now?

Major competition consists of those products or services which the consumer regards as a viable alternative. It follows that the product may have different competitors in different segments of a market, as in the case of the Deutsche Rail passenger business:

> **Deutsche Rail's (DR) main competitor is the car, followed by airlines and express bus companies. The exact nature of DR's competition varies according to purpose of travel, journey distance, time of week and type of customer.**
>
> **For example, airlines are in general competitors only for longer distances. And cars are strongest at weekends, when all members of the family are free to travel to the same destination, and the cost per person is thereby reduced.**

The identity of a company's or a brand's major competition should be reviewed regularly because the situation may change. Beware: don't just keep tabs on the usual competition, but watch out for newcomers emerging from unsuspected corners.

Factors which can cause changes in competitor identity include:

- **Acquisitions**. By acquiring Capital Cities/ABC, Disney became a leading player in TV channels.
- **Deregulation**. Before deregulation, BT had one competitor. Ten years later it had 150.
- **Rapid growth in import penetration**. Japanese examples are numerous. Italy and Sweden have also become strong in consumer durables throughout Europe via Indesit, Zanussi and Electrolux.
- **Changes in the relative importance of distribution channels**. First Direct Bank and Dell both succeeded by innovating new channels.
- **Application of new technology to your markets**. Quartz technology transformed the competitive line-up in watches.
- **Major changes in base raw materials**. The change from glass to plastic in packaging.
- **Legislation**. Privatization and deregulation.

All of these factors need to be watched closely. They may cause a shift in your allocation of resources or provide new marketing opportunities.

## 2. What are the investment priorities, objectives and goals of your major competitors?

You know what your competitors have done in the past, and buried in there are many clues as to what they are likely to do in the future. As a marketing investigator, there are many pointers which will help you.

The attitudes and philosophies of your competitors deserve close study. With successful competitors, these attitudes tend to be deeply ingrained and change little, if at all. Any competitor of General Electric or Matsushita will know that their objective in any market is likely to be brand leadership, with little interest in being number two or number three for long. Many Japanese competitors are prepared to wait five or ten years before receiving a return on their investments when entering new markets.

Another pointer to competitive priorities and goals is previous success or failure. It is quite normal to continue with a successful formula and to change one which is not working. If a competitor has been psychologically scarred by a particular product category or market, you ought to know, as in this example:

**A major international company had the capability to enter the French market in its prime product category. It had a superior product and know-how, and was faced with relatively unsophisticated local competition, following a strategy of low prices, mediocre quality.**

**However, international management was not prepared even to consider entry to France. Seven or eight years earlier, this company made a very ill-advised acquisition in France, and had to fold the acquired company after two years with heavy losses. It was possible to elicit the bare facts only in private conversation, since none of the present management team wished to talk about the experience. The fact that the market had changed, and that past mistakes could be avoided in future, carried little weight.**

A further pointer to future competitive goals is direction of advertising and capital investment. Rational competitors advertise most heavily on products, services or markets which they believe have the most future potential. Knowledge of competitive capital investment, which can often be picked up from equipment suppliers or planning applications, is an invaluable guide to future competitive intentions.

A final pointer is relative cost position. We are assuming that your company has mapped out its relative cost position by major market by competitor. Since your competitors may well have conducted a similar exercise, it is logical to expect them to try hard to reduce cost in markets where they are high-cost operators. The message is: never be complacent about a lower-cost position.

## 3. How important is your specific market to each competitor and what is the level of its commitment?

The answer to this question tells you what effort each competitor is likely to make to defend or improve its position in your markets.

The factors influencing level of competitive commitment to a product or category are:

1. Percentage of company profits in this category in the UK and world-wide.
2. Whether the category is perceived as a growth area.
3. Management attitude, heritage, emotion.
4. Profit margins.

Anyone attacking Kodak in colour film, or Canon in office copiers, can expect strong retaliation. But Kodak would not react nearly so strongly in the hospital equipment market.

Table 84 shows the relative importance and commitment in the UK branded eating-out market.

**Table 84. UK eating-out market: commitment and importance by competitor.**

| Company | Importance | Commitment |
|---------|-----------|------------|
| McDonald's | High | Very high |
| Whitbread | Very high | Very high |
| Bass | Medium | Medium |

Importance is *high* to McDonald's since eating out comprises its total business and the UK is a significant market; in the USA, importance would be *very high*. For Whitbread, with Beefeaters, Brewers Fayre, TGI Friday and many family pubs, importance is *very high*, since food is its most profitable business, and the vast majority of its sales are in the UK. Bass is mainly a brewing, international hotels (Holiday Inn) and betting company, so UK eating out is relatively less important (*medium*).

## 4. What are the competitors' relative strengths and limitations?

This will become evident from your competitive analysis. When measuring your competitors it is important to use your own business as a yardstick. In what respects is each competitor better or worse than you are? Which of its strategies are working and which are not? Is it safe to assume that the former will be continued and the latter changed?

Some of the more important areas for evaluating competitors are listed in Table 85.

| Table 85. Key areas in which to evaluate competitors. | |
| --- | --- |
| ● Customer franchise<br>● Cost of operations<br>● Product quality and value<br>● Service quality and value<br>● Speed of response | ● Persistence and determination<br>● Innovation<br>● Financial position and attitudes<br>● Attitude to risk<br>● Willingness to make long-term investments |

## 5. What weaknesses make the competitors vulnerable?

Knowing these gives you a trump card. You can then attack competitors with your strongest forces at their weakest points. A list of possible weaknesses that make competitors vulnerable is given in Table 86.

| Table 86. Weaknesses which make competitors vulnerable. | |
| --- | --- |
| ● Lack of cash<br>● Low margins<br>● Poor growth<br>● High-cost operations or distribution<br>● Over-dependence on one market<br>● Over-dependence on one account<br>● Strength in falling sectors<br>● Short-term orientation<br>● People problems<br>● Inconsistency | ● Unclear priorities<br>● Low customer retention<br>● Predictability<br>● Product or service obsolescence/ weakness<br>● High market share<br>● Low market share<br>● Premium-price positioning<br>● Slow moving/bureaucratic<br>● Fiscal-year fixation<br>● Liable to be acquired |

Most of these are obvious, and we shall examine only a few.

**People problems** can make a competitor vulnerable. If a competitor is experiencing high personnel turnover or frequent management changes, it becomes an attractive target for attack.

**Low market share** is a conspicuous weakness. But a competitor with a high market share can also be in peril, despite apparent dominance. It may have become complacent. Retailers or distributors may wish to topple it, or at least encourage stronger competition. It can also be open to a price war. And, most important of all, a company with a high market share may have a limited interest in launching new products because of the risk of cannibalizing existing ones.

**Fiscal year fixation** Every company likes to hit its budget. A good time to attack a competitor with a major initiative, like a new brand launch, is the last quarter of its fiscal year. The competitor has the choice of doing nothing, and giving you a free ride for three months. Or of responding with heavy defensive spending and probably missing its annual budget, with adverse effect on both morale and careers.

### 6. What changes are competitors likely to make in their future strategies?

This question will usually answer itself if the first five questions have been thoroughly analysed. However, it is worth while at this stage estimating where competitive divisions or brands stand on the portfolio analysis of the group to which they belong. (See Chapter 7, pages 253–61 for a discussion of portfolio analysis.) Are they seen as strong investment candidates, or 'cash cows' to finance developments elsewhere?

It is always more comfortable competing against a cash cow, on which profits are being maximized, than against a 'star', on which heavy investment is richly lavished.

### 7. So what? What effects will all your competitors' strategies have on the industry, on the market and on your strategy?

This is the question which pulls together the whole process of competitive analysis described above.

### STEP 4: KEY FACTORS FOR SUCCESS

Having completed the first three steps – the three wheels of the business environment, the internal examination and the competitive analysis – we are now ready to grind on to Step 4, the key factor(s) for success (KFS).

Plotting the KFS in your markets enables you to identify how well equipped you are to enter or compete in them. You should not attempt to look at all factors for success, only the handful of most important ones – perhaps between four and five. Inability to meet these usually constitutes a barrier to entry to new markets or points to poor future prospects in existing markets.

The two main values of KFS are that they enable you to judge your fitness for existing or new markets and to identify priority areas for building competitive advantages. An edge over competitors in any of the KFS is likely to be important and exploitable.

The nature of KFS will vary widely by market. Useful questions to ask in determining KFS include:

1. **What are the largest areas of cost in this business?**
   In fast-food outlets they will be the cost of materials and labour; in cosmetics or perfumes they will probably be packaging and advertising; in railways the costs of track, signalling and trains.
2. **Looking at other companies in this business, what have been the main reasons for their success or failure?**
   Product range may be a factor. In some businesses, companies with the widest and narrowest product ranges are among the most successful, while those in between languish. In the oil or defence businesses, relations and contacts with government are a KFS. In service businesses, quality of customer service is usually a KFS.
3. **In which areas of your business is it possible to build a competitive advantage?**
   Looking at what has worked or not worked for competitors over the years will produce some answers. But there may be opportunities waiting there which have been overlooked by competitors.

Table 87 demonstrates the different KFS in the Marketing of colour film and greetings cards.

### Table 87. Key factors for success.

| Colour film | Greetings cards |
|---|---|
| Good-quality product | Ability to spot changing needs |
| Competitive price | Strong design capability |
| Wide retail distribution | Effective distribution strategy |
| Strong relationship with processors | In-store stock control/merchandising |
| Advertising support | Efficient production |
| | Efficient inventory control |

The colour film market in the UK is so dominated by Kodak that the KFS *differ* between Kodak and other competitors. The KFS in Table 87 are written from Kodak's viewpoint, and Kodak is strong on all five factors listed.

Kodak's product is good, though not superior to Fuji's. Its price is slightly higher than Fuji's, but not beyond the level justified by reputation. The relationship with independent laboratory processors is so strong that Kodak was able to persuade them to invest heavily in new equipment at their own expense, prior to the introduction of its (unsuccessful) disc camera.

From the viewpoint of Fuji, or 3M, which does most store private-label film (e.g. Boots), the KFS in the UK would be different. Because of the entrenched position of Kodak, they need to offer either a superior product or a lower price.

In the case of greetings cards, it is also clear that, to be effective, any competitor has to score well on all six factors. An effective distribution strategy is unusually important in this category, since the competing alternatives include mail order, franchised shops (e.g. Hallmark), supermarkets, stationers, variety stores, specialist card shops, newsagents and specialist wholesalers. In addition, because the product range is so wide, a sophisticated store merchandising system is essential, to ensure that space is related to sell out to consumers, by individual card and by category.

Like everything else, KFS can change. Such a change can provide a threat to existing competitors and an opportunity to new ones. For example, to compete in the frozen-food market it used to be necessary to have a large fleet of refrigerated vehicles. This gave an advantage to large manufacturers and was a barrier to entry for smaller ones. However, the move by many grocery retailers to central warehousing for frozen foods meant that a small manufacturer could get to market with only a few trucker vehicles, and with the growth of specialist hauliers, even this could be contracted out.

Equally, companies can change the nature of KFS by innovation, as Canon did in copiers for small offices and home use. Before Canon's creation of this market, a KFS in copiers was a well-organized sales-service force to call regularly on offices, and dealers. Canon's pc machines were largely self-maintaining, due to use of cartridges and replaceable parts, therefore reducing the importance of this KFS. Consequently, Canon was able to sell its personal copiers through the new distribution channels of office product retailers and mail order, thereby side-stepping the high fixed costs of a large sales and service force.

## Step 5: SWOT Analysis

This familiar technique is the final step in the strategic groundwork. It translates the four previous steps into a format which provides the basis for developing winning strategies (Figure 34).

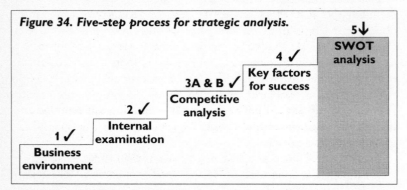

*Figure 34. Five-step process for strategic analysis.*

The SWOT analysis (see Table 88) is a summary of your strengths and weaknesses, and of the opportunities and threats facing you. It can be applied to brands, markets, channels, divisions or companies, and has three main functions: planning, offensive and defensive.

*Table 88.  Three main functions of SWOT analysis.*

| Function | Result and value |
|---|---|
| Planning | Connecting link between business analysis and strategy development |
| Offensive | Use your *strengths* to attack *competitive weaknesses.* Identify and exploit best opportunities |
| Defensive | Highlights threats. Basis for heading off most important threats or preparing counter attack |

The quality of a SWOT analysis will obviously depend on the thoroughness of the four steps preceding it, and its practical usefulness can be enhanced by following a few simple rules:

1. Keep it brief, perhaps two to three pages at most.
2. Relate the statement of strengths and weaknesses primarily to the KFS identified in Step 4 (page 211). This will ensure that you concentrate on the important strengths.
3. Strengths and weaknesses should, wherever possible, be stated in competitive terms. You are looking for *exploitable* strengths,

areas in which you are stronger than the competition. It is reassuring to be 'good' at something, but it is more effective to be 'better'.

Below is a wrong and a right positioning of a strength. The wrong positioning is a bland statement.

*Wrong:*  ✗ Over the years, Britain has won almost seventy Nobel prizes for sciences.

*Right:*  ✓ Over the years, Britain has won more Nobel prizes for sciences per capita of population than any other country . . . and over ten times more than Japan.[5]

4. Statements should be specific, without limiting opportunities. Consider the wrong and right expressions of the Bic strength below:

   *Wrong:*  ✗ Bic manufactures plastic ball-point pens to higher quality standards and lower cost than any competitors.

   *Right:*  ✓ Bic is the world's best manufacturer of high-quality small plastic objects at low cost.

   The right statement opens up the possibility for Bic of using its strength in markets other than ball-point pens. Indeed, Bic decided to use this strength as a means to challenge Gillette by creating the market for disposable plastic razors. The wrong statement limits Bic to exploiting its skills in the ball-point pen market only, and is therefore too confining. It is too specific.

5. The SWOT analysis should not just be confined to marketing issues, but cover the whole company operation. For example, relevant topics could include technological opportunities and risks, the company's relative cost position versus competitors, comparative service levels, attitudes to investment and risk, degree of marketing orientation and core competencies.

6. Be objective, both about your own company and about competitors. The SWOT analysis is an important strategic tool, not a device for making senior management feel good.

7. Objective analysis of competitors is also difficult. In general, companies tend to overrate the strengths of large competitors and underrate those of smaller ones.

Having completed the strategic grind, we now need to develop a clear vision of the future, which is the subject of Chapter 6. When that is established we will be fully prepared to develop winning strategies (Chapter 7).

# FLOW-CHART SUMMARY OF CHAPTER 5

| | |
|---|---|
| **The three stages of battle** | ● Objectives<br>● Strategies<br>● Plans |
| **Requirements for effective analysis** | ● Right data<br>● Systematic approach<br>● Focused approach<br>● Thorough and probing<br>● Actionable<br>● Continuous improvement |
| **Five-step process for strategic analysis** | ● Business environment<br>● Internal examination<br>● Competitive analysis<br>● Key factors for success<br>● SWOT analysis |
| **Step 1: Three wheels of business environment** | ● Macro factors<br>● Indirect factors<br>● Direct factors |
| **Step 2: Internal examination audit** | ● Knowledge<br>● Performance<br>● Attitudes<br>● Strategy<br>● Execution<br>● 5 examples |
| **Step 3A: Competitive analysis** | ● Knowledge needed and sources<br>● Competitor analysis system |
| **Step 3B: Competitive analysis** | ● Seven-step drill |
| **Step 4: Key factors for success (KFS)** | ● Identify largest cost areas<br>● Learn from successes, failures of others<br>● Look for areas to build advantage |
| **Step 5: SWOT analysis** | ● Planning, offensive and defensive functions<br>● SWOT should be related to KFS<br>● Need to be stated competitively |

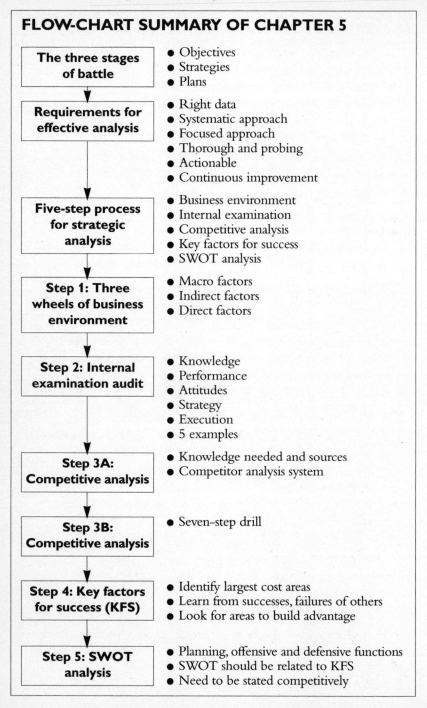

---

**Selective Check-list: The Outside Business Environment**   **Exhibit 1**

## 1. Macro factors (longer-term: 3–5 years)

*General economic:*
- Price inflation
- Cost inflation (eg energy, commodities, labour)
- Unemployment
- Consumer spending
- Exchange rate
- Interest rates
- EC issues

*Attitudinal:*
- Consumer attitudes
- Employee attitudes
- Distributor attitudes
- Industrial-relations climate

*Competitive thrusts:*
- Within own industry
- Outside own industry
- UK
- Other western countries
- Newly industrialized countries (NICs)

*Management attitudes:*
- Acquisitions
- New products
- Organization structure
- Growth
- Investment
- Marketing
- Quality
- Risk

*Technological developments:*
- Home technology
- Office technology
- Operations technology
- Distribution and supply
- Speed of technological change

*Regional:*
- Population changes
- Unemployment
- Consumer attitudes

*Demographic:*
- Age profile, size of household unit, etc.
- Life changes and style

*Long term advertising trends:*
- Proliferation and diffusion
- Cost
- Technology
- Consumer impact

*Transportation/distribution:*
- Speed and cost
- Regulation and restrictions

## 2. Indirect factors (mid-term and indirect)

*Performance of related products/services:*
- Growth trend of related products/services
- Changes in type of related products/services

*Developments in related markets:*
- Technology
- Performance improvements
- Past or upcoming changes in regulations
- Relative price changes
- Changes in presenation/packaging
- Changes in fashion

*Distribution channels:*
- New channels
- Changes in relative importance of existing channels
- Changes in distributor strategy
- Changes in concentration/bargaining power

*Government policies:*
- Regulation vs de-regulation
- Direct vs indirect tax
- Competition policy
- Attitude towards international companies
- Attitude towards business

## 3. Direct factors (shorter term: 1–2 years)

*Consumers*
- Total market and segment trends
- Factors driving market
- Changes in product performance needs
- Changes in service needs and expectations
- Attitudes to value for money
- Attitudes to price/quality alternatives
- Attitudes to new products/innovation

*Buyers/distribution channels:*
- Changes in strategies, needs, structure, criteria for purchase
- Effect of new entrants or acquisitions among buyers
- Attitudes to price/quality/service alternatives
- Attitudes to new products/innovations
- Use of IT and new techology

*Bought-in products/services:*
- Policy on contracting out
- Raw material and energy price trends and availability
- Transportation price trends
- Short term advertising cost trends
- Quality/performance levels

*Government policy:*
- Changes in tax (eg higher national insurance for higher-paid employees)
- Changes in VAT
- New regulations (eg NHS drugs, de-regulation policies)

*Technology:*
- UK or worldwide

*Competitors:*
- Capacity situation
- Performance levels (products and services)
- Pricing changes
- New products/acquisitions
- Cost structure/competitiveness
- Marketing strategies
- Investment levels
- New competitors
- Technology and IT

**Exhibit 2**

*Framework for Annual Brand/Company Health-check*

## 1. The Market

*Market performance overall:*
- Value
- Volume
- Real value

*Market performance by segment (see Chapter 9):*
- Physical product type
- Geographic area
- Demographics and life style
- Types of usage
- Consumer benefit area
- Pricing levels or bands
- Type of payment
- Level of loyalty
- Heavy users
- Characteristics of related products
- Branded vs private label

*Factors driving the market and individual segments:*
- Consumer habits
- Trends in related markets
- Changes in distribution channels
- Distributor attitudes
- Innovation and technology
- Advertising and marketing spending levels
- Pricing
- New entrants to market

## 2. The Company or Product/Service

*Sales trends (real value):*
- Overall
- By market segment
- By trade channel
- Existing and new accounts
- Existing and new products/line extentions
- Type of customer (eg loyal)

*Market-share trends:*
- Volume and value shares (brands)
- Relative market position (brands)
- Share mix (brands)
- Share of customers and trends

*Trade distribution and space trends:*
- By channel and major account
- Sales per account stocking
- Account gains/losses
- Partnerships – efficient consumer response (ECR)

*Pricing:*
- Overall real value per unit
- Changes in mix
- Trend in relative price vs competition
- Volume vs price-elasticity graph
- Inflation recovery index

*Buyers/distributors/retailers:*
- Percentage of sales by top ten accounts
- Trends in sales and share
- Discount trends
- Relative bargaining power

*Operations:*
- Relative quality
- Real-cost trends per unit
- Process differentiation
- Industry capacity utilization
- Brand/company capacity utilization

*Customer Relationship Audit:*
- Relative customer acceptance
- Trial/loyalty levels
- Awareness/image trends
- Customer retention levels
- Customer service trends
- Customer gains, losses

*Innovation Audit:*
- New developments
- New distribution channels
- New market segmentation
- New technology
- Innovation output
- Innovation success rate
- Brand franchise development

*Profit analysis:*
- By product
- By customer type (eg loyal or heavy user)
- By trade channel and major account

### 3. Allocation of Resources Audit – Questions to ask

*Product and service quality:*
- Relative product and service quality?
- Economic effect of 10%, 20%, 30% improvement
- Relative effectiveness of spend on extra quality vs reduction in price vs increase in advertising?
- Consumer test plans and results?

*Consumer focus:*
- Spending on existing vs new customers
- Payback on new customers
- Effect of spending on retention levels
- Effect of quality on retention levels

*Gross profit:*
- What is the mix by growth and declining products or services?
- Is there an active value analysis programme?
- What are the results?
- Contact between Marketing and Operations?

*Advertising:*
- Is the consumer promise right?
- Does the execution work?
- How do you know?
- Choice of media?
- Percentage of market spending?
- Allocation of funds vs opportunities?
- Management of outside agencies?
- Consistency of promise across media?

*Sales promotion:*
- Is it offensive rather than defensive?
- Is there a proper system of promotion analysis?
- Do we know profitability by type of promotion?
- Right mix between consumer and distributor spend?

# 6. **Developing a Distinctive View of the Future**

## Chapter Summary

This chapter is the second one under Strategic, the 'S' of POISE:

| Table 89. | |
|---|---|
| **P:** Profitable | ● *Proper balance between firm's needs for profit and customer's need for value* |
| **O:** Offensive | ● *Must lead market, take risks and make competitors followers* |
| **I:** Integrated | ● *Marketing approach must permeate whole company* |
| **S:** Strategic | ● *Probing analysis leading to a winning strategy* |
| **E:** Effectively Executed | ● *Strong and disciplined execution on a daily basis* |

You have already established the factual framework for strategy development in Offensive Business Analysis. Before using this to construct your strategy, you first need to peer into the future, so that your strategy is equipped to weather tomorrow's challenges. That is the purpose of this chapter.

Developing a distinctive view of the future enables Offensive Marketers to shape their strategies and exploit opportunities ahead of competitors.

Successful anticipation of future changes is a critical Marketing skill. Anticipation differs from forecasting. Its purpose is to confront tomorrow's issues today. Unfortunately, many companies rush into strategies without first establishing a vision and future direction.

Marketing Departments are best equipped to lead the development of future thinking on a cross-departmental basis, and the ideal internal tool to achieve this is the **long-term plan**. The failure of Marketers to control and direct long-term plans is one reason for their declining influence on Boards.

There are six key factors driving future change, and each needs to be fully understood by Marketers leading the development of future vision (Table 90).

| **Table 90.  Six key factors driving future change.** |
|---|
| 1.  Customer needs<br>2.  Channels<br>3.  Technology<br>4.  Regulation<br>5.  Costs<br>6.  Competition |

The factors can be applied to any kind of business, whether consumer or business-to-business, whether product or service.

A number of offensive principles for future thinking are set out in this chapter:

- Build a real perspective from the past, based on deep understanding.
- Determine how the impact of each of the six key drivers will change in future.
- Develop scenarios to assign future probabilities over time.
- Use imagination to change the rules – like Swatch.
- Get familiar with latest selling formats and technology tests relevant to your business.
- Challenge today's price/performance assumptions . . . into the future.

## Is It Realistic to Anticipate the Future?

The answer is, 'Yes.' The purpose of anticipating the future is not to forecast it exactly, since all forecasts will inevitably be wrong. The purpose is to understand the possibilities, so that you can build strategies which last, and exploit opportunities ahead of competitors. The process involves analysis, reflection and insight, leading to opportunities, scenarios and issues.
Looking forward enables you to confront tomorrow's issues now, to take action today to exploit opportunities, to test hypotheses at low cost or to head off threats early. In this way you will become a leader rather than a follower.

Anticipating the future is exciting and difficult. Key variables include chance of technical success, speed of change, cost levels, competitor initiatives and convergences between markets. Not even Microsoft's Bill Gates knows how the future convergence between software, entertainment, computers and telecommunications is going to work out. But at least he and others can guess sensibly what kind of a race it is going to be, the qualities the winner needs and who the main runners are likely to be. They don't know how long the race will last, how high the jumps or the exact competencies of each horse and rider. They do know that those failing to address the future technology and consumer issues at a deep level will certainly lose.

## Anticipating the Future Deserves Priority, but Rarely Gets It

Anticipating the future and planning to exploit it now is a fundamental task of marketing and marketing people. It is an essential exercise to map out the framework for strategies and plans aimed at future success.

All too often, though, companies leapfrog straight from analysis to strategy, omitting the vital step of **future vision**. Companies which fall into this trap usually write strategies to meet yesterday's rather than tomorrow's conditions. Such strategies are unlikely to last long, and very likely to be changed frequently, thereby losing effectiveness.

Even when the task is tackled, it tends to be the victim of lip-service. How many boring presentations have you been to which aspire to foretell the future, but do so as in Table 91.

**Table 91.  Associated Industries plc: view of the future** (read across).

| Factor | Future view | |
|---|---|---|
| Markets | ● Flat, no volume growth <br> ● Pricing pressures | ● Greater segmentation |
| Consumers | ● Desire higher quality, lower price <br> ● Drive for value | ● Increasing sophistication <br> ● Demographic changes, especially ageing |
| Competitors | ● All lowering cost bases <br> ● Increasing industry capacity | ● New Far Eastern entrants |
| Distribution channels | ● Fragmenting <br> ● Distributors and retailers concentrating and combining | ● Distributor bargaining power growing <br> ● Growth in distributors own brands |
| Communications | ● Increasing cost of TV <br> ● Growth of new TV channels <br> ● Fragmentation of media | ● Narrowcast, specialized media <br> ● Infomercials, Internet, interactivity <br> ● Growth in number of external agencies to manage. |

Such a view of the future is virtually worthless, but could easily pass muster in many corporate plans. Everything in Table 91 is sound, so what is wrong with it? First, views of the future should not be 'sound'. They should be exciting and stimulate animated discussion. Secondly, they should be distinctive. Table 91 could be applied to almost any company or industry. Thirdly, they should be actionable, triggering innovative thinking on future strategies and opportunities.

There is a painful contrast between the few Offensive Marketers who surge into the future with powerful headlights at full beam, and the majority who creep forward peering in the rear-view mirror. Many companies have an overwhelming desire to move to implementation without first establishing vision, and future direction. They focus on housekeeping rather than house-building.[1] Figure 35 illustrates the yawning gap between importance and time spent on the future versus the present.

Having a distinctive view of the future does not guarantee business success. The view may prove to be misguided. Competitors may have a similar vision and get there first, as happened when Matsushita beat Sony to the post on VCRs. The cost of the vision may be too high (e.g.

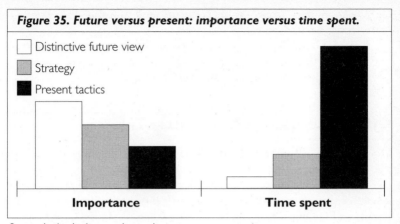

**Figure 35. Future versus present: importance versus time spent.**

- ☐ Distinctive future view
- ▨ Strategy
- ■ Present tactics

Importance      Time spent

*Source:* Author's views and experience

the Concorde aircraft), or the profitability too low (e.g. many low-priced 'people's airlines'). Or the company may develop the technology to support the vision, but lack the marketing skills to exploit it (e.g. Xerox's Palo Alto computer centre, referred to in Chapter 3, page 126).

However, a deeply considered view of the future makes business success much more likely, as the growth of Motorola from early days shows:

**Motorola is world No. 1 in pagers, two-way radios, and cellular phones. Sales are over $30bn.**

**The core of the company was built on car radios in the 1930s. The founder, Paul Galvin, had a small radio business, in trouble after the Wall Street crash. He became interested in the potential of car radios. At the time, they were expensive, with installation costs sometimes over 20% of the price of the total car, and they suffered from interference.**

**Galvin believed there was a potentially large market for reasonably priced radios which gave good reception, and were easy to work and install. He challenged his employees to develop one, and had a prototype installed in his Studebaker car in time for the Radio Manufacturers' Show. Unable to afford a booth, he demonstrated the radio from his car, parked at the entrance to the show. Based on favourable response, he launched the radio at half the price of customized models under the new Motorola trademark. Later Galvin decided to enter the police radio business and his statement about it is classic:**

**'There was a need and I could see it was a market nobody owned.'**

**Paul Galvin's success was driven by a carefully tested vision of the future, based on business analysis and knowledge of customers, costs and technology.**[2]

## Offensive Marketers Lead Future Thinking

Developing a distinctive view of the future is the responsibility of the Board. But it cannot be built by a few people sitting behind closed doors in a boardroom, and requires the best thinking of the whole organization, from technologists to process engineers, from sales people to IT managers. Marketing Departments are best placed to manage the process, and to gain commitment to the results. They can do this by organizing data analysis, by managing interaction across departments, by interviewing and by coordinating.

The best medium for focusing on the future is the **long-term plan**, which is usually updated annually. Possible steps and timetable are outlined in Table 92, for a company with a calendar-based fiscal year.

| | | |
|---|---|---|
| *Table 92.* | **Board programme for anticipating the future, led by Marketing Department.** | |
| **March** | Agree outline process with Board | • Marketing Department recommendation to Board following consultation with other departments |
| **April** | Collect data | • Analyse past results, draw lessons<br>• Marketing Department summarizes trends in channels, consumers, markets, competitors<br>• Relevant departments outline future costs, technology, regulation, using format developed by Marketing Department |
| **May** | Review data | • Summarize into 10-page booklet<br>• Distribute to all departments<br>• Organize cross-department discussion and brainstorming sessions, including outsiders, led by trained facilitator |
| **June** | Board away weekend | • Interactive sessions led by Marketing Director<br>• Outline strategic intent, list of opportunities |

| | | |
|---|---|---|
| **July** | Convert into priorities. Write up plan | ● Review outline in workshops with people across departments<br>● Finalize strategic intent, opportunity list, test plan and milestones |
| **August** | Feed into next year's budget plan | ● Next year's budget to derive from and align with long-term view |

One of the reasons why many Marketing Departments are losing influence is that they repeatedly fail to grasp the opportunity to lead companies into the future by taking ownership of the long-term planning process, which is often rushed and handled superficially under pressure. Exhibit 1, chapter 4 (page 175) suggests a format for an integrated five- year plan, driven by future vision.

In Figure 36 are two alternative responses by a Marketing Director to a request from his boss for a five-year plan.

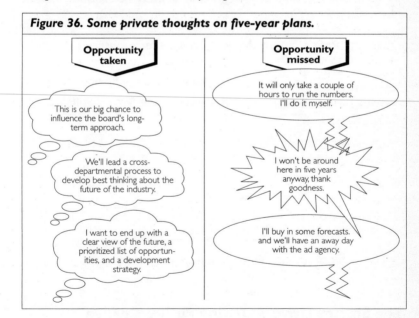

**Figure 36. Some private thoughts on five-year plans.**

It is easy for people in mature industries like food to say that there is little likelihood of major change in the future, just because there are limited opportunities for product innovation. However, the frequency of 'food scares' that fundamentally alter consumer perceptions disproves this complacent view.

There are six major factors driving future change, which need to be closely studied and understood, as follows:

| Table 93. Six key factors driving future change. |
|---|
| 1. **Customer needs** |
| 2. **Channels** |
| 3. **Technology** |
| 4. **Regulation** |
| 5. **Costs** |
| 6. **Competition** |

The need to anticipate the future is most obvious in industries experiencing rapid changes in technology (e.g. electronics) or regulation (e.g. financial services). It is less obvious but equally important in low-technology industries. Table 94 takes the six key factors driving future change and relates them to two very different UK industries – office equipment and milk. While consumer needs in milk are changing slowly, and there is little new technology, industry deregulation and the move from doorstep to supermarkets is creating rapid change.

**Table 94.  Rate of future change by change factor: office equipment versus milk.**

| Six factors driving future change | Rate of change by industry | |
|---|---|---|
| | Office equipment | Milk |
| 1. Customer needs | Rapid | Slow |
| 2. Channels | Slow | Rapid |
| 3. Technology | Rapid | Slow |
| 4. Regulation | Slow | Rapid |
| 5. Costs | Rapid | Rapid |
| 6. Competition | Medium | Medium |

The six factors driving future vision are reviewed in the next section.

## The Six Key Drivers Driving Future Change

Future vision examines today's rules and figures out how to change them in your favour for tomorrow. Of the six drivers, 'customer' will be covered in more detail than the others, since this is the most important.

## 1. Customers

Table 95 gives a brief check-list of consumer opportunity areas, which will be developed in more detail below (some of these will be further expanded in Chapter 9, 'Offensive Segmentation'). Because of the importance of this check-list, it is retained here in the text rather than relegated to an exhibit at the end of the chapter.

**Table 95. Customer future opportunity check-list.**

| Area of opportunity | Questions to ask: |
|---|---|
| *Basic needs* | ● How could these change in future?<br>● If prices were halved, what would happen?<br>● What could upgrade expectations?<br>● How well are basic needs being met?<br>● What are barriers to meeting basic needs better?<br>● What are main areas of dissatisfaction?<br>● What added value features are sought?<br>● Which types of people are least well served?<br>● Which specialist needs are unmet?<br>● What is the trade-off between needs? |
| *Demographics* | ● How well is each demographic or industry group served?<br>● What new demographic groupings can be developed, e.g. single parents, extended families?<br>● What is the future trend? |
| *Life stages* | ● What are they? How are they changing?<br>● How well is each life stage served by the industry? |
| *Habits and usage* | ● Where and when is the product used and not used?<br>● Why isn't it used all the time?<br>● What is in-home versus out-of-home usage?<br>● Which usages are growing or declining? Why?<br>● How does usage differ by demographic group? |
| *Attitudes* | ● What is the customer attitude towards the industry and specific products or brands?<br>● How will attitudes to environmental and safety issues develop?<br>● How is this likely to change in future?<br>● What industry changes are necessary to improve attitudes? |

**Basic needs**. These always exist, and change slowly. Consumers are often unaware of future needs, either because the products which meet them do not yet exist or because they are too expensive. As a Marketer with future vision, you should concentrate on defining basic needs, and ignore the fact that technology is at present unable to meet them affordably. Take the car, for example:

> **Today's customer is generally satisfied, and cars are marketed on the basis of styling, safety, image, performance and reliability.**
>
> **The car in use, however, has major areas of weakness for the consumer. Traffic congestion, aggressive behaviour, unpredictable journey times and parking problems make driving a less and less attractive experience. Most important of all, the car is a very expensive and, in some ways, an inconvenient product.**
>
> **Purchase and operation are costly, and few products lose value more quickly. To use the product, you have to stop for refuelling, which is extremely inconvenient . . .**
>
> **Therefore a permanently powered, low-cost method of personal transportation will continue to be a basic unfulfilled need, threatening the future of both the oil industry and the internal combustion engine.**

Basic needs develop over time. As each is successfully met, another emerges. Table 96 illustrates the development of needs in the hair shampoo market.

**Table 96. Development of basic needs in hair shampoo.**

- Shiny, healthy
- Shampoo and conditioner
- Frequent use, naturals
- Anti-dandruff treatment
- Colour treated, permed, damaged hair
- Hair types – oily, regular, dry
- Cleaning

1950                                                                 2000

In shampoos, basic needs are now quite complex. Pioneering new brands have used technology and skilful marketing to create new benefits – Head and Shoulders for anti-dandruff; Timotei for frequent use; Wash n' Go for 2 in 1 shampoo and conditioner; and Pantene Pro 5, Organics, for shining and healthy hair. There is certainly another stage beyond shining/healthy hair. What is it likely to be and can you get there first?

A new shampoo brand launched today on a platform of superior cleaning would fail, because the consumer has moved beyond this basic need. Equally, Pantene Pro 5 would have failed in 1950, since the basic need it now meets was not well enough developed then – it would have been a brand before its time.

**Demographics**. These should be categorized on both a common-sense and imaginative basis. Conventional demographic analysis is useful. Everyone knows that older people and one-person households are growing in importance. Some groups have special needs or are badly served. For example, until recently older people were overcharged for motor insurance, and non-smokers for life assurance.

Beyond this, more imaginative demographic groupings can be defined and tracked. Figure 37 is a chart from a presentation on the future of the

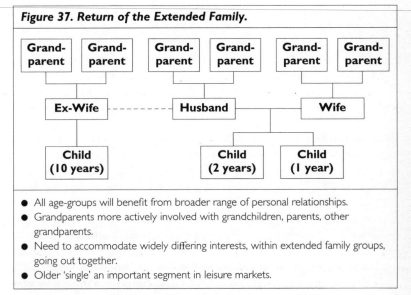

**Figure 37. Return of the Extended Family.**

- All age-groups will benefit from broader range of personal relationships.
- Grandparents more actively involved with grandchildren, parents, other grandparents.
- Need to accommodate widely differing interests, within extended family groups, going out together.
- Older 'single' an important segment in leisure markets.

*Source:* Oxford Corporate Consultants.

leisure market which reorganizes conventional demographics into interesting new patterns, presaging the return of the extended family.

In the 1980s the motor industry missed the opportunity to develop mid-price sports cars targeted at affluent male over-50s, nostalgic for the days of their youth, when they couldn't afford a sports car. The booming market in vintage sports cars should have alerted manufacturers to this opportunity.

It was first recognized by the Japanese and belatedly fully catered for in the 1990s. MG, Jaguar, Mercedes and BMW had ignored it for over twenty years. Equally, car manufacturers have consistently under-marketed to women in relation to their importance and potential.

In the USA, Motorola has developed targeted Marketing programmes for its cellular phones and pagers among African-Americans, who have a higher ownership of pagers than whites and represent a segment with high future potential.

**Life stages**. Everyone has life stages, often more than Shakespeare's seven. A life stage is a set of occupational and family circumstances which affects attitudes and habits. It revolves around work, marital status, children, parents, income level, balance between work and leisure and so on.

A modern interpretation of Shakespeare's seven stages would be child, teen, young, partnered, married with children, empty nesters and elderly singles. Each of these could easily be subdivided – for instance, needs of children vary greatly by age-group.

Identifying the life-stage model most relevant to your market, and projecting it forward, will help you identify future changes in consumer needs. Two quite obvious future trends are growth in number of elderly people, and reduced government ability to finance health care. Consequently self-medication, over-the-counter medicines and retirement homes all have strong growth prospects.

**Habits and usage**. The Sony Walkman is often instanced as an intuitive invention, which could not have been identified by research. It is quite true that twenty years ago a direct question to a consumer such as, 'Would you be interested in buying a product that enables you to listen to high-quality taped music in private as you sit or walk?' would have produced a mystified response. The consumer had managed to live without this product, had difficulty in visualizing it and felt no pressing need.

However, a more circumstantial approach to habits and usage would have revealed a future need for the Sony Walkman. Consider these facts:

- The fixed location of taped music centres meant that they could only be listened to at home, and therefore at limited times.
- People had become used to listening to radios outside the home, in cars and, to the frequent annoyance of others, out of doors.
- Most popular music was listened to by young people, who are more flexible in changing habits.
- People have private preferences in music and often like to listen on their own.
- They often have boring periods in their day when they can't read or talk, but could listen.

Just as in a murder investigation, the direct question will bring a denial, so in visioning the future, a set of logical presumptions, circumstantially woven together, can produce new answers. One of the most useful questions to ask about future habits and usage is, 'Why don't they use our type of product all the time?' Applying this question to cleaning teeth led to the successful development of dental gum. Most people spend less than five minutes a day cleaning their teeth. Why? Because they have to use a brush and paste in a bathroom at home. Delivery of oral health through chewing gum enables people to clean their teeth after snacks or meals, or throughout the day, as a supplement to regular brushing.

**Attitudes**. In detergents, the number of product variants has quadrupled in the past decade. Consumers are thoroughly confused by the plethora of powders, concentrates, liquids, bios, non bios, colour cleaners, refills, in a bewildering range of sizes. But they want a more sophisticated solution than an 'all-in-one' brand. The first manufacturer or retailer to come up with a product range that really meets consumer needs will score heavily.

Some industries, such as energy, utilities or financial services, are scarred by consumer cynicism, providing an opportunity for trusted branders from other industries to enter the market in future.

## 2. Channels

In many industries, distribution channels will change faster than consumer needs over the next ten years. A company with competencies only in yesterday's channels will gradually lose access to the consumer. Equally, development of new channels can be integral to entering new markets, as Dell demonstrated through the direct marketing channel with computers, Canon through office retailers with personal copiers.

There are two key questions to ask about the future of distribution channels. First, '**What will future consumer needs be and how well are existing channels likely to serve these?**' A simple grid can be used. Take clothing, for example, a market whose channels only serve consumers moderately well. While Marks & Spencer would score well, most other channels do not, and this is a market ripe for channel change (Table 97).

**Table 97. Clothing: channel effectiveness in meeting future consumer needs.**

| Consumer needs | Relative channel ranking | | |
| --- | --- | --- | --- |
| | Department stores | Specialists | Direct mail |
| Convenience | ✓ | ✓✓ | ✓✓ |
| Product range | ✓✓ | ✓ | ✓✓✓ |
| Accessibility | ✓ | ✓✓ | ✓✓ |
| Quality | ✓✓✓ | ✓✓ | ✓ |
| Customer service | ✓ | ✓✓ | ✓✓ |
| After-sales service | ✓ | ✓ | ✓ |
| Price | ✓ | ✓ | ✓✓ |
| Product in stock | ✓✓ | ✓✓ | ✓✓ |

Key: ✓✓✓ = Very good, ✓✓ = Good, ✓ = Weak

The grid can be completed by applying numerical rankings to each need, and then scoring each channel against it. Or it can be an informal prompt. The result gauges future channel strength, and, together with historical trends, can be used to evaluate the prospects of each channel.

For example, in the USA, grocery retailers are losing share of total food to restaurants and fast food, since eating out offers fully prepared food with high service levels at reasonable prices. The inconvenience of shopping and home preparation of food increasingly justify the premium of eating out.

The second question to ask about the future of your channels is: '**Looking at trends in other industries, what alternative channels might emerge in future?**' Also ask yourself questions like: 'Could petrol be delivered weekly to storage tanks at offices?' or, 'Frozen food is often delivered to the home in Germany via telesales – why not in the UK?' As usual, some of the questions will be quickly dismissed, others, however, will prove fruitful.

In Table 98 is a simple check-list of channel types for consumer goods. Business to business markets will have different channels.

| **Table 98. Basic check-list of channel types.** | |
| --- | --- |
| ☐ High Street retailers | ☐ Direct marketing via telesales |
| ☐ Out-of-town retailers | ☐ Party plan home selling |
| ☐ Leisure parks | ☐ Home delivery |
| ☐ Direct from manufacturer | ☐ Shopping malls |
| ☐ Mail order | ☐ Wholesale |

Some markets, like soft drinks, have a wide range of channels which serve the consumer well. Their channels will change slowly. Others serve their consumers poorly and are liable to change rapidly in future. For example, if you were thinking of taking up sailing, as a complete novice, where would you buy a boat? How do you get advice as a first-time buyer? How do you get exposure to a reasonable range? Since you probably do not have time to visit the London or Southampton boat shows, the answers are likely to be unsatisfactory. This is a market waiting for channel innovation.

Offensive Channel Marketing is covered in detail in Chapter 15.

## 3. Technology

The importance of technology to shaping the future is obvious. That is why marketing people must have a grasp of major technologies and a view, based on discussion with experts, as to how each might develop. The most important future technologies are those with the potential to meet basic consumer needs better, as this statement by David Packard, joint founder of Hewlett Packard, indicates:

> **'To warrant serious pursuit, an idea must be both practical and useful. Out of those ideas that are practical, a smaller number are useful. To be useful, an invention must not only fill a need, it must be an economical and efficient solution to that need.'**[3]

3M is another company with a fine record of using technology for the benefit of customers:

> **3M is a world leader in adhesive, imaging and non-woven products. It draws on thirty core technologies to market products to consumer, office supply and health-care markets.**

**3M has many leading share positions, but aims to build new markets. It has 'created many markets by developing products people didn't realize they needed'.**[4]

**Examples are Scotchgard™ fabric protector, reflective sheeting for highway signs, and seals which can withstand extreme temperatures in auto or power plants. For the auto industry, 3M has developed sealants which can replace rivets, are quicker to apply and lower cost.**

**Many of 3M's products meet obvious consumer needs by developing new technology, like the Scotch Brite™ non-rusting soap pad, or the O-Cell-O™ Stayfresh™ sponge, which kills odour-causing germs. '3M products continue to change the basis of competition . . . by innovation.'**

It is not enough to be familiar with the implications of technology in your own market. Technology in related or converging markets is also relevant – telecom companies need to understand the technologies of computing, broadcasting, electronics and entertainment, as well as telephone and cellular communications.

And technology in unrelated markets – such as home shopping, interactive media, virtual reality training and personal communications – is likely to affect the future of most businesses in the future, because it will fundamentally influence consumer habits.

### 4. Regulation

New legislation, deregulation, privatization, voluntary codes, can all shape your future business environment and competitive position.

Possible future change can be evaluated by talking to industry experts, civil servants and regulators; by identifying the probable, the possible and the unlikely; and by setting up lobbying objectives and plans to achieve change in your favour.

As the marketing person leading the long-term planning process, you can specify the data needs, get qualified people in other departments to collect it, and jointly draw conclusions about the future.

### 5. Cost, pricing and profit

What drives these, and how are they likely to change in the next five to ten years? What are your main cost elements today, and how will they be different tomorrow? How are they affected by volume? What degree of cost reduction is necessary to radically increase demand? At what point is most profit made in your industry, and how is this likely to change?

Let's take an example from the personal computer (PC) industry in the 1990s, and imagine that we are a PC manufacturer in 1990, looking to the future. We would be looking forward to continued rapid revenue growth, and expect this to more than compensate for a slight drop in percentage profit margins.

What *actually* happened to PC manufacturers in 1990–95? Yes, sales doubled from $44 billion to $90 billion. But net profit plummeted from $3.5 billion to $1.3 billion, as Table 99 shows.

| **Table 99. World PC manufacturer revenue and net income, 1990–95.** | | |
|---|---|---|
|  | **1990** | **1995** |
| Revenue ($bn) | 44.0 | 90.0 |
| Net profit ($bn) | 3.5 | 1.3 |
| % Profit margin (%) | 8.0 | 1.4 |

*Source:* McKinsey database, Annual Reports

So where did all the profit go to? In 1990–95, in the PC industry, there was a massive transfer of profit from PC manufacturers, such as IBM, Compaq and Apple, to microprocessors, notably Intel, and operating system providers like Microsoft. By 1995, microprocessors accounted for only 13% of PC industry revenue, but 61% of industry profits, as in Figure 38.

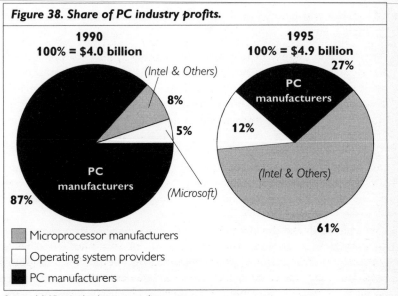

**Figure 38. Share of PC industry profits.**

*Source:* McKinsey database; annual reports

This example illustrates that sources of industry profitability can change dramatically even over a five-year period. It is important to know where profit is being generated in your industry today, as a basis for estimating future change.

Over a longer period, there has also been a fundamental change in the way industry profits are divided between manufacturers and retailers. Manufacturers used to be more profitable than retailers, while today the reverse is true, as retailers have increased their relative bargaining power and moved closer to consumers.

### 6. Competition

Competitive analysis is covered in the previous chapter. By their activities, competitors also shape the future of your industry and the expectations of consumers. They, like you, will be developing plans to improve products, reduce cost, increase productivity and enter new market sectors. They represent a constantly improving standard. This means that to improve your long-term market position significantly, you have to beat your competitors' customer offer five years hence, an issue covered by the next section.

## Future Standards Always Rise

'Today's competitive differentiators become tomorrow's price of market entry.'[5]

The haircare example in Table 96 above illustrated how consumer needs develop over time, stimulated by competition and innovation. Product or service elements which differentiated specific competitors yesterday are rapidly copied today. They become the norm, or minimum requirement to compete in a market, and no longer provide a source of competitive advantage.

To win tomorrow, you have to not only do the basics well but also offer added-value products or services *on top*. As in Olympic high jumping, the qualifying and winning heights are always rising. Today's 'compete and win' propositions often merely add up to a 'compete' position tomorrow (Figure 39).

Applying this to the airline market for business travellers, the position in ten years' time could look as in Figure 40.

 The best competitors, like BA and Singapore Airlines, all offer competent staff, punctuality, safety and so on. These are necessary to compete, and

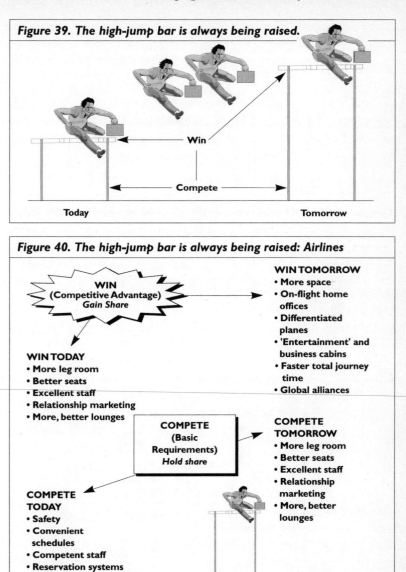

**Figure 39. The high-jump bar is always being raised.**

Win

Compete

Today

Tomorrow

**Figure 40. The high-jump bar is always being raised: Airlines**

**WIN**
**(Competitive Advantage)**
*Gain Share*

**WIN TOMORROW**
• More space
• On-flight home offices
• Differentiated planes
• 'Entertainment' and business cabins
• Faster total journey time
• Global alliances

**WIN TODAY**
• More leg room
• Better seats
• Excellent staff
• Relationship marketing
• More, better lounges

**COMPETE**
**(Basic Requirements)**
*Hold share*

**COMPETE TOMORROW**
• More leg room
• Better seats
• Excellent staff
• Relationship marketing
• More, better lounges

**COMPETE TODAY**
• Safety
• Convenient schedules
• Competent staff
• Reservation systems
• Punctuality

2008

1998

*plus*
**COMPETE YESTERDAY**
• Safety
• Convenient schedules
• Competent staff
• Reservation systems
• Punctuality

failure to achieve them results in loss of market share. To build market share tomorrow, airlines will need to offer excellent rather than competent service, more leg room, better entertainment and so on. Today's 'share builders' rapidly become tomorrow's competitive norm.

## Offensive Approach to Developing a Powerful View of the Future

This section will outline a number of offensive marketing principles for applying the six key drivers of future vision.

### 1. Get a real perspective and deep understanding of the past

Put yourself ten years back in time. Based on knowledge then, what would you have expected today to be like? How would your vision of the future ten years ago differ from the reality today? Which of the six key drivers of future vision has been most important? What was the extent of change over the ten–year period? What were the big surprises and how could they have been anticipated?

Take the UK market for beer as an example (Table 100).

**Table 100. 1998 UK beer market: expectations versus reality on six key drivers.**

| Key drivers | Expected 10 years ago | Reality today |
|---|---|---|
| 1. Consumers | ● Volume decline<br>● Low alcohol will grow fast | ● _Volume stable_<br>● _Premium-priced bottled lager well up_ |
| 2. Channels | ● Independents squeezed out<br>● Growth in supermarkets, more drinking at home | ● _Independents buoyant_<br>● As expected<br>● _Cross-Channel trade_ |
| 3. Technology | ● Better taste for low alcohol and low calories | ● _Draught beer in cans_ |
| 4. Regulation | ● Major change following MMC enquiry | ● _Brewery ties loosened_<br>● _Longer opening hours_<br>● Smaller outlets sold off to independents |
| 5. Costs | ● Continued tax increases<br>● Cost in line with inflation | ● Overhead costs up, due to spare capacity |
| 6. Competition | ● Continued rationalization and concentration | ● _More than expected, leaving Bass plus Scottish & Newcastle dominant as brewers._ |

The bigger surprises versus expectation ten years ago are underlined in the table. **Which ones could have been reasonably anticipated?**

## 2. Determine how the impact of each of the six key drivers will change in the future

One of the worst ways to anticipate the future is to extrapolate past trends mathematically, either with or without regression analysis. Instead, carefully evaluate the factors driving past change, and forecast their likely impact in the future. Is past consumer spending growth due to an increase in number of people purchasing, trading up to higher-value products or services, or higher frequency of use? Has it been influenced by new-product innovation, total market pricing or levels of advertising? How will these change in the next five years?

This is the 'plus five' technique – developing a deep understanding of the past, and applying the lessons to the future, five years hence.

The rapid growth of computer software has been influenced by the increase in penetration of personal computers (now slowing) and significant performance improvement with each new wave of software (now levelling). So, unless dramatic new usages can be developed, future growth of computer software is likely to be much reduced.

If you had forecast trends in frozen foods from the mid 1980s based on a straight extrapolation of the past, you would have anticipated a buoyant future, impressed by a decade of consistent real growth. In fact, this market became ex-growth quite suddenly, in 1985. Why? Because, in the past, growth had been driven by the increase in ownership of chest freezers. Ownership, however, had moved close to saturation by 1985, there was a move to smaller upright freezers, and chilled foods – a more convenient format – were growing rapidly. A look behind the headline figures would have given you a better measure of the future.

## 3. Assign probabilities over time

This approach is particularly useful in markets where regulation or technology are changing rapidly. Often it is reasonably straightforward to decide *whether* something is likely to happen, and much more difficult to determine *when*.

A good process is to list key change factors, and to label them definite, probable, possible or unlikely, over three, five, and ten year time spans.

Table 101 illustrates this approach from the viewpoint of a major TV contractor.

**Table 101.  Future scenarios in TV media: probabilities versus time.**

| Change factors | 1–3 years | 4–5 years | 6–10 years |
|---|---|---|---|
| Cable TV over 20% of total TV viewing hours | Unlikely | Unlikely | Probable |
| Fully interactive TV used by over 15% of homes | Unlikely | Possible | Probable |
| TV used broadly for grocery shopping | Unlikely | Possible | Possible |
| Major proliferation in number of TV channels | Definite | Definite | Definite |
| Integrated TV, phone and PC in over 20% of homes | Unlikely | Unlikely | Probable |
| Video libraries (on demand) broadly available | Unlikely | Probable | Definite |

Simple scenario options like these can stimulate discussion across departments and among experts, to enable you, the marketing person, to draw conclusions about probability and time.

## 4.  Use imagination to change the rules

Swatch is a good example of this:

**Ernst Thomke was headhunted from Beecham Pharmaceuticals, to become Managing Director of ETA, a leading Swiss group making mechanical watches. ETA was operating at the top end of the market, which was shrinking.**

**The company badly needed to build volume by also competing in lower-price sectors dominated by quartz watches, which ETA did not make.**

**Thomke decided to avoid the Japanese middle ground and to target the low-price sector. He set his team a target retail price of $25 per watch, which, in view of high trade mark-ups and other costs, meant a production cost of about $5 per unit. Quality was to be high, with maximum standardization, and variation only allowed to the case appearance, dial, hands and strap.**

**This specification was achieved, using innovations involving seven patents. The watch was marketed like fashionwear to eighteen- to thirty-year-olds. Fun, excitement, fashion and design were the core of the proposition, which was heavily supported with high-impact advertising and promotion. Distribution included fashion**

stores, sports outlets, gift boutiques and shop-in-shops within department stores.

Swatch transformed and greatly expanded both the world and the Swiss watch industry by developing a differentiated view of the future.[6]

Swatch exploited five of the six key drivers affecting future vision (Table 102).

**Table 102. Swatch use of six key drivers.**

| Key drivers | New view of future by Swatch |
|---|---|
| Consumers | ● Market watches as exciting, low-cost fashion items to the under 30s |
| Channels | ● Select unconventional channels consistent with the consumer image |
| Technology | ● Apply new technology, such as welding face cover to case, to achieve targeted consumer value |
| Costs | ● Drive down cost through technology, standardization, high volume, and very low labour content |
| Competition | ● Need to change the rules in order to compete successfully with low-priced competitors in high-labour-cost country |

One driver – 'Regulation' – was not relevant in this case.

## 5. Familiarize yourself with latest selling formats and technology tests

- If you market through retailers or distributors, visit the most recently opened stores or any test formats. These represent tomorrow's norm.
- Visit or check on any tests of new technology which could affect your consumers or channels tomorrow. Video on demand, videophones, smart cards, virtual reality shopping, interactive TV and new telecom developments are examples.
- Review relevant overseas innovations.

## 6. Challenge price/performance assumptions

'JVC engineers saw the possibility of home video recording in a $50,000 Ampex machine . . . Canon set itself the goal of producing a copier for $1,000' when Xerox cost thousands.[7]

In some markets, private label retailer brands offer similar quality to brand leaders at half the price by using a lower-cost business system. And discount airlines can sometimes undercut the prices of their full service competitors by 100% or more.

## Rank Your Company for Future Vision (Table 103).

| Table 103.  Your company's ranking for future vision. | Max. score | Your score |
|---|---|---|
| Strong Board involvement in anticipating the future | 15 | |
| Robust and forward-looking 5 year plan process | 9 | |
| 5-10-year plan process led by Marketing | 10 | |
| Strong cross-departmental involvement in developing future vision | 10 | |
| Imaginative annual update of future vision of markets | 8 | |
| Most people in company have clear and informed view of future | 10 | |
| Six change drivers carefully reviewed | 15 | |
| Company understands future of own and related technologies | 11 | |
| Strong and relevant database used to anticipate future | 12 | |
| TOTAL | 100 | |

# FLOW-CHART SUMMARY OF CHAPTER 6

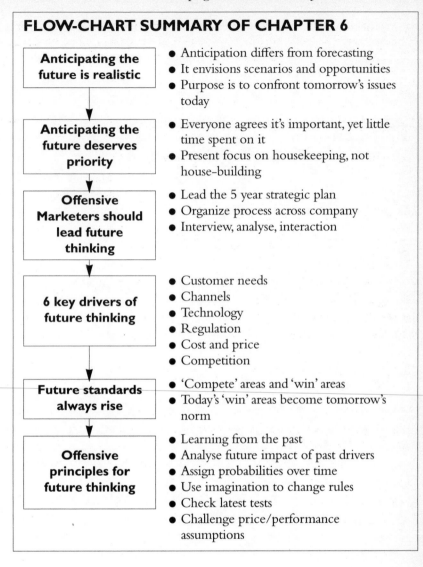

| | |
|---|---|
| **Anticipating the future is realistic** | • Anticipation differs from forecasting<br>• It envisions scenarios and opportunities<br>• Purpose is to confront tomorrow's issues today |
| **Anticipating the future deserves priority** | • Everyone agrees it's important, yet little time spent on it<br>• Present focus on housekeeping, not house-building |
| **Offensive Marketers should lead future thinking** | • Lead the 5 year strategic plan<br>• Organize process across company<br>• Interview, analyse, interaction |
| **6 key drivers of future thinking** | • Customer needs<br>• Channels<br>• Technology<br>• Regulation<br>• Cost and price<br>• Competition |
| **Future standards always rise** | • 'Compete' areas and 'win' areas<br>• Today's 'win' areas become tomorrow's norm |
| **Offensive principles for future thinking** | • Learning from the past<br>• Analyse future impact of past drivers<br>• Assign probabilities over time<br>• Use imagination to change rules<br>• Check latest tests<br>• Challenge price/performance assumptions |

## Reader Competition

### 100 Bottles of
# *Moët & Chandon*
# *Champagne*
### to be won

Having got this far in the book, you have qualified to enter the *Even More Offensive Marketing* competition.

Please tick the appropriate box to answer the questions below:

1. What is your occupation?

   College student ☐

   MBA student ☐

   Practising Marketer ☐

   Marketing services or agency executive ☐

   Other (please specify) _____ ☐

2. Please write down your age and sex.   *Age:* ☐ *Sex:* ☐

3. How many books on business have you read in the last year? ☐

4. Did you buy or read Hugh Davidson's previous book, *Offensive Marketing*?   *Yes:* ☐ *No:* ☐

Now, attach a 100–200 word case example of *Even More Offensive Marketing* either from your own experience or from published sources, and fill in your name and address below. Then mail this sheet, plus your 100–200 word case example, to: Department Hugh/Marketing, Penguin Press Marketing, 27 Wrights Lane, London W8 5TZ. All qualifying entries will be included in a random draw, to be made on 25 September 1998. Closing date for entries is 30 August 1998.

Name: _____ Title (if applicable): _____

Company (if applicable): _____

Address: _____

_____

_____

Telephone: _____

Name of shop where bought: _____

Address: _____

# 7. Developing Winning Strategies

'Supreme excellence consists in breaking the enemy's resistance without fighting. Thus the highest form of generalship is to baulk the enemy's plans. The next best is to prevent the junction of the enemy's forces. The next in order is to attack the enemy in the field. The worst policy of all is to besiege walled cities' – Sun Tsu

## Chapter Summary

| Table 104. | |
|---|---|
| **P:** Profitable | ● Proper balance between firm's needs for profit and customer's need for value |
| **O:** Offensive | ● Must lead market, take risks and make competitors followers |
| **I:** Integrated | ● Marketing approach must permeate whole company |
| **S:** Strategic | ● Probing analysis leading to a winning strategy |
| **E:** Effectively Executed | ● Strong and disciplined execution on a daily basis |

This chapter is the third out of four in the strategy section; the 'S' of POISE. It translates the findings from the two previous chapters – on business analysis and anticipating the future – into winning strategies which are robust and forward looking.

Offensive strategy involves the development of competitive advantages, and the application of these to build winning strategies. Key strategic decisions involve concentrating resources into areas of best return, and selecting the most effective points to attack. The ideal strategy concentrates your strongest resources against your competitors' most weakly defended areas.

The chapter covers five main ways to develop winning strategies:

1. **Using portfolio analysis to build strategic priorities**. Portfolio analysis is a device for determining strategic resource

allocation by market, channel, customer, business unit or brand. Different types of portfolio analysis are reviewed, compared and illustrated.

2.  **How to develop competitive advantage**. This is the ability to do something better than your competitors. It is often based on the exploitation of assets and competencies, covered in Chapter 2 above. A range of competitive advantages is described. At least one is necessary in order to build a winning strategy.

3.  **Turning competitive advantages into winning strategies**. Companies or brands have a wide repertoire of strategies to choose from. The repertoire includes head-on, flanking, niche, guerrilla, range, regional concentration, diplomacy, or encirclement.

4.  **Selecting the right strategy for your company or brand**. Head-on strategy is reserved for companies with large purses and strong stomachs. Otherwise, all strategies in the repertoire can be used by most companies. The right strategy for yours will be influenced by its size, resources, assets and competencies, by the opportunities available, and by competitors' weaknesses.

5.  **How to spot and avoid strategic wear-out**. Winning strategies are as vulnerable to life cycles as products. They will wear out unless thy are nurtured, updated and modified in response to changing market needs and new competitive moves.

I recognize that the section on Quantified Portfolio Analysis (pp. 253–61) is pretty heavy going but believe its importance, as a business tool, will repay the extra reading effort.

## Defining Vision, Corporate Objectives and Values

A number of words are used by writers and business people to describe future strategic direction. They include vision, values, mission, objectives, among others. Vision has already been fully covered in Chapter 3. This brief opening section will clarify how these expressions differ and how they are related.

**Vision** has a similar meaning to **mission**. Both imply a strong measure of foresight, imagination and vocation. Their role is to provide clear signposts to the future, and a motivating horizon for employees to fix their sights on. If you have clear signposts, developing winning strategies to get there becomes easier and more relevant. And if you can point to inspiring horizons, people will work much harder to reach them.

**Corporate objectives** are usually more specific and mundane than visions. They translate visions into quantitative goals, such as revenue, profits or earnings per share.

**Values** describe the beliefs, personality and style companies aim to cultivate in pursuing their visions and corporate objectives. Here is an example of values:

The Body Shop has a distinctive set of values, described as:

- **Different: human rights campaigning, fair trading, no animal testing**
- **Informative: education of staff and customers**
- **Sensitive: community projects around the world**
- **Alternatives: source materials from indigenous people where possible**
- **Straightforward**
- **Committed: issues, values**
- **Good value: refill service, minimal packaging**
- **Responsible: energy efficient, minimize waste.**

Body Shop's values are in contrast to the collection of clichés and platitudes many companies wheel out.

## Setting *Stretching* Corporate Objectives

Corporate objectives convert vision into measurable goals. These are usually financial. The example below, from 3 M, is unusual in adding an innovation goal to three profit-based objectives:

The long-term financial goals of 3 M are:

- Earnings, per share growth of at least 10% year
- Return on stockholders' equity of 20% to 25%
- Return on capital of at least 27%
- At least 30% of sales in any one year derived from products introduced within the four previous years

Key strategies for achieving these objectives will be innovation, customer satisfaction, internal expansion and productivity improvement.

There is an undoubted psychological element in setting targets, as athletes have often shown. The long-standing barrier of the four-minute mile was eventually broken by Roger Bannister, but his feat was rapidly emulated by many others, suggesting that the barrier was as much psychological as physical. Lord Forte, a very successful businessman, put it well some time ago:

'It is amazing if one sets a target, how easily one hits that target. Unfortunately, I have learnt this at a very late age: I wish I had known it consciously before, instead of only subconsciously. If a manager says that this is the objective in two years' time, and we want to reach that turnover or make that profit, it is quite amazing how one does it – given the possibility, of course. You must not say, we are going to jump 8 feet, because that is out of the question. You'll break your neck. But what is the record – 6 feet 7 inches? Try and jump that. And when you've succeeded, put it up another ¼ inch. The art of reaching business targets is not to aim at the impossible, but to aim at the championship level – which you already know to be possible.'[1]

Objective-setting is a good measure of a company's success in using Offensive Marketing techniques.

## Offensive Strategy

The purpose of Offensive Marketing is to win. Everyone would like to find a fast-growing market with high margins and little competition. Few are so fortunate. The most important question for marketing people is this: **'Why should customers buy our products or**

**services rather than our competitors', now and in the future?'**
Unless the answer is clear, convincing and backed by unambiguous
evidence, you do not have a winning strategy.

As the Koran says: 'If you don't know where you're going, any road
will take you there.' Offensive strategy is all about setting priorities. It
involves:

- Selecting the most effective point at which to attack. The classic
  military offensive concentrates the attacker's strongest weapons
  on the enemy's weakest lines of defence. Marketing follows similar principles, and the most successful attacks are pinpointed on
  targeted segments, against selected competitors.
- Concentrating business resources into the areas of best return.
  This usually calls for the movement of resources (Operations,
  people, Advertising, R & D) from areas of low return into areas
  of high return.
- Developing competitive advantages, so that your planned attack
  at a selected point is effective.

Offensive business analysis, covered in Chapter 5, is essential for all
three of these moves, and portfolio analysis, which is dealt with in the
next section, is useful in clarifying the first two.

## Using Portfolio Analysis to Build Strategic Priorities

Portfolio analysis is a useful graphic device for examining the competitive position of products, services or businesses, and for conducting a
similar exercise on competitors. It is too crude to use in isolation, but
can be helpful in focusing the more extensive analysis described in
Chapter 5 (pages 189–215), or in triggering detailed strategic
discussion. The structure of the portfolio also forces executives to set
priorities and make choices. Portfolio analysis is most often used to
determine resource allocation.

Portfolio analysis has developed from the original Boston Consulting
Group matrix of 'Stars, Cows, Children and Dogs', through the second-
generation McKinsey/GE market attractiveness and competitive pluses
model, to the third generation of quantified portfolio analysis.

All three are valuable tools in building strategic priorities. They will
be examined in turn, and their advantages, disadvantages and applications summarized.

## 1. The Boston Consulting Group (BCG) matrix

BCG invented portfolio analysis, and its original model is still useful. The BCG matrix relates relative market share (RMS) to market growth. If you have a 40% market share and your nearest competitor 20%, your RMS is 2.0. Likewise, your competitor's RMS is 0.5.

A product with a high RMS in a growing market is a 'Star', while a minor product in a falling market is a 'Dog'. In between, you have 'Cash Cows', with high market shares in mature markets, and 'Problem Children', which have low shares in fast-growing markets.

Figure 41 summarizes the BCG matrix.

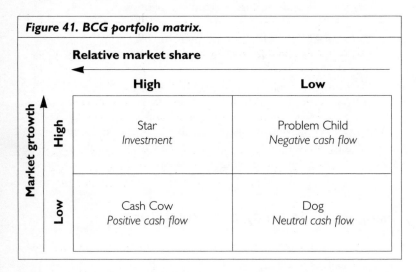

**Figure 41. BCG portfolio matrix.**

In allocating development resources like advertising, R & D and capex, the theory is that you funnel the vast majority into 'Stars', and some into 'Problem Children' in the hope that they can be turned into 'Stars'. You starve the 'Cows' and 'Dogs'. The principle is that 'Cows' finance the investment costs of 'Stars'. The 'Problem Child' is a temporary box – sooner or later you have to decide whether to promote it to 'Star' or relegate it to 'Dog'.[2]

**Evaluation:**
**Pro:**

1. The BCG matrix is simple and elegant. As a graphic device, it is fun to use, and propels decision making.
2. It remains a useful quick guide to resource allocation by country, market or brand, and for your own company or competitors.

**Con:**

1. Most companies, markets and brands are 'Dogs'. Booz Allen & Hamilton estimated that, based on traditional portfolio analysis, 72% of business units in US industry were 'Dogs', 15% 'Cash Cows', 10% Problem Children and only 3% 'Stars'. This is not surprising when you consider that most markets in the West are mature, and only a small minority of companies or brands are market leaders. This restricts the value of the BCG matrix, since most brands and markets tend to sit around the mid point to bottom right of the total square.

2. A fast-growing market is not necessarily an attractive one. Growth markets attract new entrants, and if capacity exceeds demand, the market may become low margin and therefore unattractive. Furthermore, growth markets often run into long-term problems. No market keeps on growing for ever, and there is always the risk that companies will gear up capacity two or three years ahead for growth which shudders to a halt.

3. High relative market share is only one measure of the strength of a brand or company. For instance, General Motors has for decades been market leader in the US automobile market, with a high RMS. This conceals many weaknesses. Compared with Chrysler, GM is a high-cost operator; is weak in the two fastest growing market sectors – people carriers and household trucks; and it has a very fragmented range, with overlap between brands.

## 2. The McKinsey/General Electric matrix

This overcomes a number of the disadvantages of the BCG model. **Market attractiveness** replaces **market growth**, and includes a broad range of measures. The same applies to **competitive pluses** replacing **relative market share** which is only one of the measures used. Figure 42 illustrates some of the elements comprising market attractiveness and competitive pluses; and how the McKinsey/GE matrix can be applied to some UK retailers.

For example, Dixons is a 'Star', because it has many competitive pluses, and competes in relatively attractive markets. Saxone, by contrast, is a lacklustre competitor in the crowded and mature market for shoes. It is a 'Dog'.

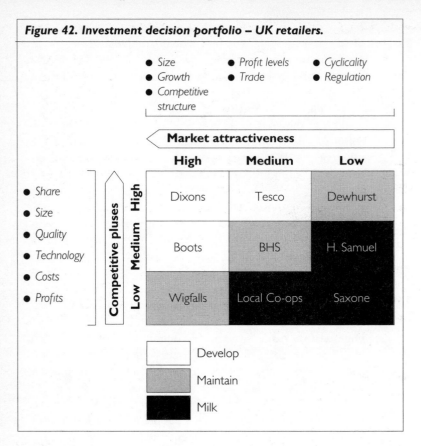

Figure 42. Investment decision portfolio – UK retailers.

### Evaluation:

**Pro:** The McKinsey/GE Matrix is a valuable development of the BCG portfolio analysis. Its broader range of measures generates more insights, and forces the user to think deeply.

**Con:**
1. It gives too little emphasis to competencies in competitive pluses.
2. The allocation within boxes may be subjective and unquantified.

## 3. Quantified Portfolio Analysis (QPA)

QPA© works on similar principles to the McKinsey/GE matrix, but on a more quantified basis. It has two axes – market attractiveness and relative strength – and consists of a quantified process which is outlined below, in brief. Both axes consist of a number of criteria, which are given a maximum weighted score based on relative importance. A scoring guide helps quantify scores for companies or brands being assessed. The resulting output is a percentage score for each company or brand on both axes of the portfolio. This increases objectivity and accuracy, and allows for comparability across markets or countries.

This section will describe how QPA can be used to prioritize *brands*. For brevity, the frozen foods market, illustrated in Chapter 2, has again been used, but this time for brand rather than market-sector prioritization.

The nine criteria for assessing market attractiveness of frozen foods from Chapter 2, page 86, are repeated in Table 105.

**Table 105. Market attractiveness scoresheet: weighting of nine key criteria.**

| Criteria | Frozen foods |
|---|---|
| 1.  Market size | 8 |
| 2.  Market growth | 15 |
| 3.  Market profitability | 20 |
| 4.  Real pricing trends[3] | 10 |
| 5.  Competitive intensity | 10 |
| 6.  Future risk exposure | 6 |
| 7.  Opportunity to differentiate | 10 |
| 8.  Segmentation | 9 |
| 9.  Retail structure | 12 |
| Total | 100% |

Guidance on how to apply these criteria to individual frozen food market sectors was given in Chapter 2 (pages 86–7). Frozen green beans scored low at 34% for market attractiveness, and frozen pizza did better at 60%.

The approach to market attractiveness in the brand example below will remain constant. What will change is the other axis. For **market** prioritization, as in Chapter 2, the other axis covered strength of assets and competencies. However, for **brand** prioritization, the other axis analyses relative brand strength.

The two portfolio analyses in Figures 43 and 44 show the similarities and differences in axes used for market segment portfolio (as in Chapter 2) and brand portfolio analysis (illustrated in this section). In the case of the latter, brand prioritization is based on a combination of market attractiveness and brand strength. So, the ideal is a strong brand in an attractive market.

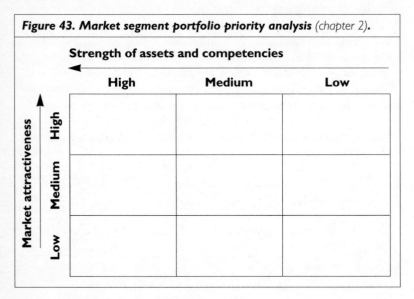

**Figure 43. Market segment portfolio priority analysis** (chapter 2).

**Figure 44. Brand portfolio priority analysis** (this chapter).

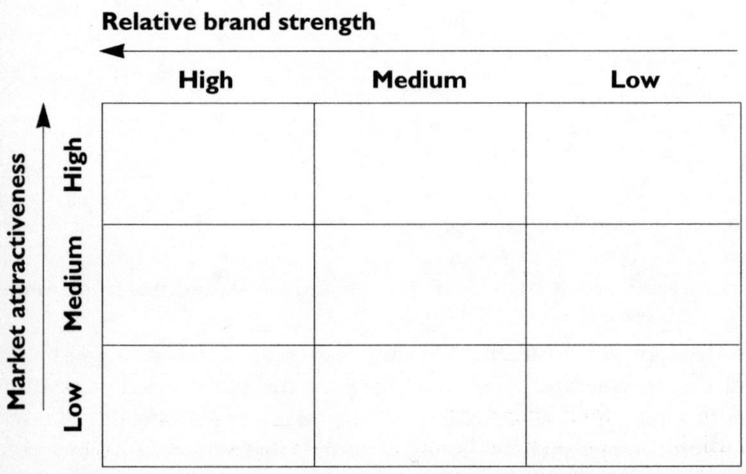

In each portfolio analysis, market attractiveness is the common factor. For market segment priority, the strengths of the whole company or business unit are relevant, while for brand priority, it is the strength of individual brands that matters. In all portfolios, the best place to be is top left, the worst place is bottom right.

Birds Eye frozen foods will be used to illustrate a brand-range portfolio analysis, applying relative brand strength criteria. Birds Eye happens to be an umbrella brand, with a number of sub brands and products. The brand portfolio analysis could equally well be used to prioritize a number of individual brands like Crunchie, Snickers, Kit Kat, etc.

**How do you go about this exercise with Birds Eye?**

First, evaluate each frozen food market sector relevant to Birds Eye. You already know that green beans is an unattractive market sector, scoring only 34%, but have to cover many other sectors.

Secondly, score each Birds Eye brand for relative brand strength. You need to decide the criteria to use in judging brand strength, and how to weight them. These will vary by type of brand. In Table 106 is an example of a possible scoresheet for ranking Birds Eye brands, using eleven criteria, totalling a maximum score of 100%.

**Table 106. Relative brand strength criteria weighting: BIRDS EYE.**

| Criteria | Weighting |
|---|---|
| 1.  Brand profitability | 12 |
| 2.  Relative consumer value | 15 |
| 3.  Relative brand share and trend | 9 |
| 4.  Market sector position | 7 |
| 5.  Sales level and trend | 7 |
| 6.  Differentiation | 12 |
| 7.  Distribution and trade strength | 7 |
| 8.  Innovation record | 6 |
| 9.  Future potential (plans, extendability) | 10 |
| 10.  Awareness and loyalty | 7 |
| 11.  Investment support (advertising, R & D, etc.) | 8 |
| TOTAL MAXIMUM SCORE | 100% |

You would then determine measures to use in scoring each individual Birds Eye product or brand on each criterion, and a system for doing this is detailed in Exhibit 1 (page 289).

Once all Birds Eye markets and brands were scored, a brand-range portfolio could be constructed, and it might look as in Figure 45.

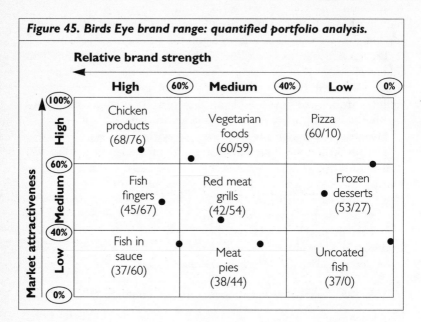

Figure 45. Birds Eye brand range: quantified portfolio analysis.

This is how the portfolio analysis has been constructed:

- Chicken products is an attractive sector (scored at 68%), and the Birds Eye brand within it is very strong (score 76%). This combination of strength in market sector and brand adds up to a powerful position for Birds Eye, justifying placement in the prime top left box.
- At the other extreme – bottom right – is uncoated fish. This is an unattractive commodity market (score 37%), with low margins for suppliers, dominated by private label. Birds Eye has chosen not to compete in this market segment (score 0%).

This portfolio analysis can be used as a guide to resource allocation and strategic priority. Chicken products clearly merit high priority. Vegetarian foods and fish fingers also deserve investment, while meat pies and frozen desserts do not, for Birds Eye.

Portfolio analysis facilitates decision making and helps pin-point issues. For example, on red meat grills, the brand is reasonably strong but the market unattractive. Is it practical to make the market more attractive in future, and therefore justify investment?

### Evaluation of quantified portfolio analysis (QPA):

**Pro:**

1. Requirement to quantify adds additional objectivity, but many elements remain subjective.
2. Because it is process driven, and clearly defined, QPA can be used for cross-country and cross-market comparisons.

**Cons:**

1. More time consuming than BCG and McKinsey/General Electric matrices.
2. Requires judgements by experienced line managers in order to be fully effective, and unlike BCG, cannot be constructed by analysts.

### Overall evaluation of portfolio analysis:

Portfolio analysis is a useful tool to guide strategic investment priorities by market, business unit, channel or brand. A considerable amount of offensive analysis is necessary to get good results and simplistic application is dangerous. Some of the choices are subjective, and objectivity can be greatly increased by setting up a quantified process, using a common scoring system across markets and countries.

## Develop Competitive Advantages

Competitive advantage is achieved whenever you do something better than competitors. If that something is important to consumers, or if a number of small advantages can be combined, you have an **exploitable** competitive advantage. One or more competitive advantages are usually necessary in order to develop a **winning** strategy, and this in turn should enable your company to achieve above average growth and profits in its industry. Competitive advantages are the concrete expression of exploitable assets and competencies.

**Why is competitive advantage worth having?** It enables you to develop winning strategies and puts you in the driving seat, placing pressure on competition. It's much more fun to lead than follow.

There are six key elements in developing competitive advantage. Five have already been covered, and the sixth will be reviewed in the next section.

**Table 107.  Key elements in developing competitive advantages.**

| Element | Chapter | Status |
|---|---|---|
| 1. Offensive vision and attitudes | 3 | ✓ |
| 2. Integrated marketing approach | 4 | ✓ |
| 3. Offensive analysis | 5 | ✓ |
| 4. Anticipating the future | 6 | ✓ |
| 5. Portfolio analysis | 2 & 7 | ✓ |
| 6. Familiarity with types of competitive advantage | 7 | Next |

## Types of Competitive Advantage

There are many types of competitive advantage. The main ones are listed in Table 108, and then covered individually:

**Table 108.  Main types of competitive advantage.**

| | |
|---|---|
| 1.  Superior product or service | 6.  Superior assets |
| 2.  Perceived advantage | 7.  Scale advantages |
| 3.  Global skills | 8.  Attitude advantages |
| 4.  Low-cost operator | 9.  Legal advantages |
| 5.  Superior competencies | 10.  Superior relationships |

### 1.  Superior product or service

A superior product or service benefit is based on reality not perception. Such benefits are real, provable in fact, and recognized by consumers. Proof can be established by consumer and technical testing for products, and by performance levels and consumer attitudes for services. Routes to superior benefits include those in Table 109.

**Table 109.  Examples of routes to superior benefits.**

| Product | | Service | |
|---|---|---|---|
| ● Better end-result | ● Ease of use | ● Speed | ● After-sales service |
| ● Superior design | ● Speed of use | ● Quality | ● Personalized service |
| ● Longer lasting | ● Reliability | ● Flexibility | ● Responsiveness |
| ● More features | | ● Reliability | |

Having a better product or service is one of the most powerful competitive advantages. Self-deception in this area is, however, rife. Many companies assume their products or services are better, even though they have no supporting evidence. Others · succeed in establishing proven technical advantages, which are either not apparent or not important to their customers or consumers.

Boeing offers real service superiority to its customers:

**Boeing has field representatives in fifty-six countries, who provide training, engineering and spare parts support to 500 airlines around the world. It has a 600,000 square foot Customer Training Centre in Seattle, which trains 6,000 pilots a year.**

**Boeing now offers airlines next-day shipment on routine spare parts orders, many times faster than the industry standard of 20–30 days.**

In Table 110 are some other examples of product or service benefits.

**Table 110. Brands offering superior performance benefits** (read across).

| Brands | Superior performance areas |
| --- | --- |
| Honda engines | Reliability |
| Schroder Unit Trusts | Investment results |
| Disneyland | Quality of service |
| First Direct Bank | Service and value |
| Marks & Spencer | Innovative chilled foods |
| Polaroid | Speed of result |
| Mercedes | High resale value |

## 2. Perceived advantage

The superior benefits just covered can be physically proved by demonstration, by objective evaluation or by blind product tests among consumers. Perceived advantage, by contrast, is in the mind of the consumer – a result of a product's imagery and personality. The auction of Jackie Kennedy's possessions is an example of perceived value. Proceeds were over eight times Sotheby's estimate, and President Kennedy's rocking chair fetched £265,000, over a hundred times the estimate. The buyer did not purchase a rocking chair but an image, a perceived association with a famous man.

Perceived advantages are usually built through advertising and presentation. They are seen most often in products associated with social occasions or visible consumption. Examples are clothes, cosmetics, soft drinks, alcoholic drinks, sporting goods or cigarettes. Marlboro, with its cowboy image, has powered its way to almost 30% of the US market. The brand is well marketed, but there is no reason to believe Marlboro cigarettes are objectively superior to other premium brands in consumer acceptance.

Coca-Cola is an example of a brand whose image and heritage are sufficiently strong to overcome apparent product weaknesses:

**For some years before the launch of New Coke, Pepsi-Cola was preferred in blind tests to market leader Coca-Cola by American consumers.**

**Then Coca-Cola introduced New Coke, which had been preferred to original Coke in scores of blind-taste tests. However, consumer reaction to New Coke was so mixed that the original formulation, renamed Coca-Cola Classic, was reintroduced as a sister brand six weeks later. Subsequently it heavily outsold New Coke. So we have the paradoxical situation of Coca-Cola Classic outselling the same product to which it lost on blind test. This confirms what was obvious to many – that the advantages of Coca-Cola lay in its image and history, not in the product.**

Perceived advantage can also be developed through design, heritage, or styling. That is why a Porsche Carrera Coupé costs 86% more than a TVR Griffith, even though the latter has faster acceleration – described by *What Car?* as having 'more muscle than the Pontypridd front row, wicked looks, slingshot acceleration . . .' (Table 111).

| Table 111. Car comparisons. | | | |
|---|---|---|---|
| **Car model** | **Price (£)** | **Max. speed** | **Acceleration (0–60 in seconds)** |
| TVR Griffith 5.0 | 34,595 | 167 | 4.1 |
| Porsche Carrera 4 Coupé | 64,305 | 168 | 5.3 |

While it could be argued that the Porsche is better engineered, more reliable and has outstanding resale value, the main reason why customers pay high prices is perceived image advantage.

Equally, natural medicines generate strong loyalty among some consumers, especially in Germany, even though their performance in clinical tests is generally unimpressive.

Table 112 outlines types of perceived advantage, with examples.

| Table 112. **Examples of types of perceived advantage** (read across). | |
| --- | --- |
| **Types of advantage** | **Examples** |
| Design | ● Fashionwear |
| Advertising-generated image | ● Marlboro cigarettes |
| Association | ● Personalities, early adopters, authority figures |
| Place of sale | ● Limited availability<br>● Use of exclusive outlets |
| High price | ● Luxury goods |
| Exclusivity | ● Coutts, Dunhill, Cartier |
| Health | ● Bottled water, herbal remedies |

This table is more relevant to products than to services. It is difficult to achieve a perceived service advantage. If the advantage is not real, the service reputation will rapidly dissipate, even through a single incident.

Here is an interesting situation. Take a whisky which only breaks even in blind test against competitors. It has, however, a heritage going back to 1650, and is perceived as superior by customers who pay premium prices for it. So, the brand has a perceived advantage, based on its heritage. Does it also have an actual advantage, based on the fact of its long ancestry, even though the product itself is only at parity?

### 3. Global skills

The competitive advantage includes global distribution; ability to produce and market effectively on a multi-country basis; skills at entering new countries; and structures which achieve global efficiencies in R & D, manufacturing and marketing, while meeting local needs and providing a motivating work environment.

Coca-Cola, with a world-wide soft drinks share of over 40%, is widely distributed in most countries of the world, and, together with companies like McDonald's or Mars, is also very skilful at successfully entering new countries. 'The number of customers we can actively reach out to with our products climbed from less than 2.2 bn in 1984 to more than 5.2 bn now . . . there is virtually no place on earth where the people do not both know and like Coca-Cola.'[4] Coca-Cola's global skills provide a formidable challenge to local competitors.

### 4. Low-cost operator

This is not a matter of 'We work lousy, but we work cheap', and it goes beyond low-cost production. A low-cost operator (LCO) strives to achieve lower costs than its competitors for similar products or services, on all elements built into the final delivered entity. This requires low costs not only in operations but also in selling, distribution, administration, IT and even marketing. The LCO is striving for a cost advantage to provide a winning strategy of superior value.

Marketers can play an important part in achieving LCO, by cutting out unnecessary products, forecasting sales accurately, using common raw materials wherever possible and relating cost to customer value.

There are many ways to develop competitive advantage through low-cost operation. Here, in Table 113, are some of them.

**Table 113. Examples of competitive advantage through low-cost operation.**

| Routes to LCO competitive advantage | Examples |
|---|---|
| High productivity | ● Sales per square foot in retailing<br>● Capacity utilization in plants, hotels, planes<br>● Concentration of synchronized factories, suppliers – e.g. Toyota City |
| Low overheads | ● 'Small is beautiful'<br>● Effective capital investment<br>● Eliminate costs which do not benefit customer |
| Low-cost selling | ● Focus on smaller number of larger customers<br>● High productivity<br>● Effective use of IT |
| Limited product range | ● Aldi sells small grocery range in high volume, buys cheaply and discounts pricing |

The virtuous marketer cuts out unnecessary cost, and invests the savings in advertising, R & D, capex or better customer value, in order to sustain profitable growth.

Some companies achieve low-cost operation by exploiting a number of advantages:

**The Equitable Life, the oldest mutual life assurance company in the world, founded in 1762, is a low-cost operator compared with most life companies. As a mutual company, it has no shareholders to pay dividends to, and all profits are ultimately channelled back to its customers (i.e. policyholders). In addition, the Equitable does not pay commission to Agents or Brokers, and generates new business through advertising and recommendations by financial journalists and policyholders.**

**The Equitable's low-cost position assists it in achieving good performance on pensions, and this in turn produces new business. The strategy is circular. As long as the Equitable continues at or near the top of the performance tables, its low-cost structure can be sustained.**

### 5. Superior competencies

Development of superior competencies is fully covered in Chapter 2. As was observed there, superior competencies usually take a long time to build and are important competitive advantages, since they are difficult and time-consuming to copy.

You might argue, with some justification, that all the competitive advantages listed here are examples of effective exploitation of assets and competencies.

For instance, IKEA, the home furnishing retailer, has a competitive advantage in purchasing, enabling it to offer consumers high quality at low prices. This advantage is based on superior competencies in 'product design and engineering, in warehousing, and in purchasing raw materials and packaging at the most favourable prices'.[5]

Building superior competencies is not a matter of saying: 'Let's do more training.' The process needs a firm foundation of consumer understanding, skills in IT or technology, clear strategic direction and offensive attitudes. (See Exhibit 2, Chapter 2 (page 103), for check-list of competencies.)

### 6. Superior assets

These may consist of property, cash or brands, which can be leveraged to achieve competitive advantage. (See Exhibit 1, Chapter 2, page 102, for a check-list.)

## 7. Scale advantages

Size can be a source of competitive advantage (or the reverse if it produces complacency or bureaucracy). In almost any business, size can generate a financial advantage with the use of advertising. One million pounds' worth of advertising will result in a given impact whether your company is large or small. If your revenue is £100 million, £1 million of advertising is equivalent to 1 per cent of sales, whereas if it is only £10 million, the same advertising effort accounts for 10 per cent of sales.

This principle applies to the costs of selling. To cover a particular account universe, you need a certain number of sales people. If Company A has a sales force twice as big as its nearest competitor, but a market share three times greater, its sales force cost ratio will still be lower. It therefore has a larger resource at less relative cost.

Scale advantages can also operate strongly in manufacturing and service operations. If you are a large retailer, property developers or investment groups are much more likely to contact you first about hot development prospects, and you will get an early bite at new retail or leisure parks.

The competitive advantages of scale largely explain why market leaders usually achieve much higher profit margins than the second or third contenders, and why market leadership is often an important objective for Offensive Marketers.[6]

## 8. Attitude advantages

Any of the attitudes described in Chapter 3, 'Offensive Vision and Attitudes', can constitute an important competitive advantage.

## 9. Legal advantages

Patents, copyrights, sole distributorships or protected positions can provide competitive advantages. Patents are particularly important in the pharmaceutical and electronics industries.

## 10. Superior relationships

These may be with customers, influencers or decision makers. They can range from relationships with distributors, partners or government ministers, to civil servants, suppliers or institutional investors.

For a company in the international fine art business, like Christie's or Sotheby's, strong relationships with a limited number of major collectors are an essential requirement in order to win the really big Sales, and strong relationships with major museums and dealers are necessary to realize good prices at such Sales. And, of course, the two are connected, because you will not gain access to fine collections unless you have a good reputation for successful Sales.

On a more pedestrian level, your local Prontaprint may have established many strong customer relationships merely by remembering people's names, giving them a good welcome, superior service and fair pricing.

Increasingly, relationships are being managed on a remote but individual level through databases, and between total organizations, such as supplier and retailer, or companies working together on joint brand development or technology projects. For example, Sainsbury is cooperating with the Royal Bank of Scotland on banking, while Nestlé and Disney have a long-term sales promotion agreement.

## Which Types of Competitive Advantage Matter Most?

Are all types of competitive advantage equally important? Can they be ranked? Are some hotter than others? And how do they relate?

The answers to these questions are not straightforward. Relative importance of each type of competitive advantage will vary by market. For instance, superior actual performance is very important both in services and in product markets where end users can objectively evaluate real performance (e.g. machine tools or detergents). By contrast, in markets where imagery is critical, and social display a key purchase motivator, perceived advantage is often what matters most, and marketers in fragrances, soft drinks, spirits, cigarettes and luxury goods know this well. Why do people continue to buy French wines, when a New World wine of equivalent quality can be bought at a much lower price?

In relative terms, types of competitive advantage which are growing in importance include:

- low-cost operation to satisfy increasingly value conscious consumers;
- superior competencies, which can create many types of competitive advantage, and are difficult to copy in the short term;
- superior relationships, a potential advantage, which is benefiting from growth both in the understanding of the economic value generated by customer loyalty, and in cooperative partnerships between companies.

By contrast, competitive advantage based on superior *actual* product performance appears to be reducing in importance, as the capability of others to copy quickly improves. And in a world of growing deregulation, where expanding countries take a different view of patent protection, legal advantages will decline in significance.

Many types of competitive advantage are related. Asset or competency exploitation underlies most of them. Actual or perceived product superiority builds brand share, and drives scale, attitudes and relationships favourably.

If a single type of competitive advantage had to be chosen as most important, it would be superior product or service quality in the eyes of target customers, and on aspects most important to them. This is a predictable view for a marketer to take, but it is supported by Buzzell and Gale,[7] based on their PIMS (Profit Impact of Marketing Strategies) findings. Analysis among thousands of businesses of relative product quality, relative cost, market-share levels and trends, and return on investment, yielded these conclusions:

**'In the long run, the most important single factor affecting a business unit's performance is the quality of its products and services relative to competitors:**

- **In the short term, quality yields increased profits via premium prices.**
- **In the longer term, superior and/or improving relative quality is the most effective way for a business to grow. Quality leads to both market expansion and gains in market share . . .**

**On average, businesses with superior quality products have costs about equal to those of their leading competitors.'**

## What Is Your Competitive Status?

Table 114 shows the five levels of competitive advantage. The objective of any company should be to move up to one of the top two levels. Those in the two bottom levels will struggle to survive in the long term unless they step up. **Which level is your company on?**

Most companies inhabit levels 3 and 4, and probably generate most of the 'Dogs' identified in Booz Allen and Hamilton's portfolio analysis of American business units (see page 255). Competitive advantages need

**Table 114. Five levels of competitive advantage.**

| Level | Competitive status | Examples |
|---|---|---|
| 1 | One or more large advantages | ● Honda |
| 2 | A number of smaller advantages adding up to a large one | ● McDonald's (internationally, though less in USA) |
| 3 | Advantages present, not fully exploited | ● General Motors |
| 4 | No significant competitive advantages | ● Most companies |
| 5 | Competitive disadvantages | ● British Gas<br>● Co-op Grocery |

to be sustained, and can easily be lost through changes in customer needs, new technology or competitor initiatives.

1. **One or more large advantages**. Coca-Cola, Disney, Toyota, Procter & Gamble, Hewlett-Packard and Honda are among companies in this enviable position. Honda's large advantages lie in core competencies 'in engine design and manufacture which are leveraged into competitive advantage across the focused range of products that Honda manufactures and sells; motorcycles, cars and power products like lawnmowers and small boat engines'.[8]

2. **A number of smaller advantages adding up to a large one**. Many companies claim this status unsustainably. You may indeed have a number of smaller competitive advantages, but if their effect is dispersed, they will not add up to a large one. In the case of McDonald's internationally, the claim is sustainable. Their advantages in site selection, staff training, advertising, store design, lighting, supplier management and globalization, generate consistently strong consumer experiences. This has been achieved despite a relatively pedestrian product offer, and a modest record of recent innovation both within and outside fast foods.

3. **Advantages present, but not fully exploited**. General Motors is still clear market leader in the US vehicle market, but its share is declining, and its costs are much higher than the number three company, Chrysler, which has higher profit margins.

4. **No significant competitive advantages**. Most companies fall into this category. They often lack either distinctiveness or

competitive edge. You can prove this for yourself by counting up the number of distinctive products or services you have experienced in the past year. Out of the tens of thousands available, you may have difficulty in reaching double figures.

5. **Competitive disadvantages**. Companies in this category usually only survive in the long term if they enjoy monopoly positions, protection from competition or compensating competitive advantages.

British Gas has two major competitive disadvantages – its brand image, and exposure to unattractive long-term gas supply agreements. However, it does have the potential to exploit its advantage of scale.

Co-op Grocery has one major competitive **advantage** in not having to make profits, and being able to pay out surpluses to customers in the form of dividends. This advantage is insufficient to compensate for competitive disadvantages in scale, structure and management. However, the potential for Co-op Grocery is demonstrated by the Co-op's positive performance in banking and funerals.

## Turning Competitive Advantages into Winning Strategies

Having completed the strategic groundwork and developed your competitive advantages, you are now in a position to carve out a winning strategy. Any company has at its disposal a wide range of possible offensive strategies. The eight main ones are summarized in Table 115 and reviewed in turn.

| *Table 115. Strategies for exploiting competitive advantages.* | |
|---|---|
| 1. Head on | 5. Regional concentration |
| 2. Flanking | 6. Product range |
| 3. Encirclement | 7. Guerrilla |
| 4. Niche | 8. Diplomacy |

### 1. Head on

This strategy involves a direct frontal attack to drive back or overwhelm a competitor. To apply a head-on strategy successfully, a company needs strong products and heavy marketing support, since existing competitors are likely to counterattack in order to maintain their position.

A head-on strategy is most appropriate for a large, well-financed company, prepared to fight a long battle of attrition. As in warfare, head-on attacks in business rarely produce quick breakthroughs. Companies like Procter & Gamble, Coca-Cola, Glaxo-Wellcome and Microsoft have successfully used the head-on approach. It is also a favourite among Japanese companies, especially in their home market.

To succeed with a head-on strategy, you need a strong proposition and lots of staying power, requirements which Marriott met with its Courtyard mid-priced hotel chain:

> **Until the early 1980s, Marriott only operated in the pre-mium end of the US hotel market, with 350-room full-service units. At that point, Marriott judged that future growth potential in the premium sector was limited, and decided to enter the mid-price segment, which represent-ed 45% of all US hotel rooms.**
>
> **It spent five years researching, testing and refining a winning proposition, having ascertained that its main competitors – Holiday Inn, Ramada Inn and Howard Johnson – received only moderate consumer ratings, because they operated older, franchised locations to inconsistent standards.**
>
> **'Courtyard by Marriott' was launched. Each unit had 150 rooms, and resembled a garden apartment complex. Service was limited, security tight but understated. Rooms had large free-standing desks, king-size beds and a separate sitting area, with a couch. They were larger than competitors and cost less.**
>
> **Courtyard, a frontal attack on competitors, was rolled through the USA and internationally. Competitors reacted by renovating mid-priced units, cutting room rates and, in the case of Holiday Inn, by launching Holiday Inn Express. The quality of Courtyard's planning, however, enabled it to succeed long term in the mid-priced hotel sector, against entrenched competition.[9]**

Retailers frequently pursue a head-on strategy when launching their own-label brands – a typical approach is to meet or beat quality of brand leader at a lower price. Head-on attacks are also habitual in markets where technology or product models change frequently, as in cars, computer hardware or new over-the-counter medicines (e.g. Tagamet, Zantac and Pepsid in the US).

## 2. Flanking

This strategy involves attacking a competitor on a flank which is weakly defended. The competitor may lack skills in this sector, regard it as a low priority or be committed to a 'milking' strategy. In any event, a flanking attack is likely to draw a much weaker response than a head-on offensive, because the defender may not feel directly threatened, at least in the short term.

Flanking strategy follows the classic approach of attacking the competitor's weakest point with your strongest weapon. It needs to be followed through at pace, because the threat posed by the flanker becomes clearer over time and can eventually lead to a strong competitive response.

In general, more companies use flanking than head-on strategy, and flanking tends to be lower risk with a higher probability of success. This appears to apply in both business and in war. In an analysis of 280 campaigns from the Greek Wars to the First World War, Liddell Hart concluded that in only six (2.1%) did a head-on assault produce decisive results.[10]

The classic flanking moves in business tend to involve price (high or low), neglected segments or product innovation. Bic flanked Gillette in razors by innovating the low-priced disposable sector. Knorr and Batchelor flanked Heinz canned soups in the UK, by introducing low-price packet soups after Heinz had seen off an earlier head-on attack by Campbell's. In each case the 'fortress' was slow to react, aware that strong reaction would accelerate the growth of a new lower-margin sector.

Another flanking approach is to change the rules of competition through innovating in products, technology or distribution channels.

At one time IBM was a walled city, immune to assault, and had successfully withstood many head-on attacks against its mainframe com-

puters. It was flanked by PCs. These targeted more flexible, empowered client individuals outside Central DP Departments, and eventually offered network capability. Equally, Canon changed the rules in copiers and flanked the previously dominant Xerox (Table 116).

**Table 116. Copiers: the Canon flanking move** *(read across)*.

| Competitive focus | Xerox | Canon |
| --- | --- | --- |
| Customer target | Large businesses | Small businesses |
| Distribution channel | Direct selling via field force | Office retailers |
| Service needs | Direct call | Replaceable cartridge |

The need for a large field sales force to sell and service copiers gave Xerox a sustainable barrier to entry, especially to smaller businesses which were expensive to call on. Canon removed this barrier by developing the replaceable cartridge, which could be bought from office retailers, and eliminated the need for a service call. It used a flanking strategy, facilitated by technology, to change the rules of competition.

A flanking attack by a competitor should not be ignored just because it increases the total market and leaves your sales unaffected. It is likely to reduce your **share** of the market and may later turn into a head-on attack.

## 3. Encirclement

Encirclement occurs when a brand or company is surrounded by a hostile competitor, attacking it from a number of points. This is a difficult strategy to mount in competitive markets, and easiest to sustain in mature low-technology sectors, where new technology provides little basis for a break-out by the encircled company or brand.

A sophisticated example of this strategy is the encirclement of Persil (Lever) by Ariel, Bold, Daz and Fairy (P & G) in the UK detergents market, as Figure 46 illustrates.

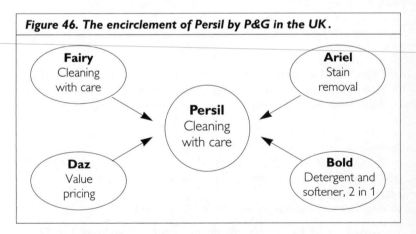

**Figure 46. The encirclement of Persil by P&G in the UK.**

**Persil was the long-term brand leader in fabric cleaners, although it has now been overtaken by Ariel. The UK fabric cleaning market is heavily segmented, but the two largest sectors are stain removal, and cleaning with care. It is difficult to operate in both sectors with a single brand, since a positioning of heavy-duty stain removal is not consistent with care to fabrics in the consumer's mind.**

Ariel led the P & G encirclement with a single-minded heavy stain-removal strategy. It was supported by Fairy Detergent, attacking Persil head-on with cleaning and care. Daz focused on the CD demographic groups with discounted pricing and targeted advertising. And Bold attacked from another angle, with a combined detergent and fabric conditioner, offering cleaning, care and convenience.

Lever, a very effective marketer, attempted two breakout strategies. One was to launch Radion as a head-on competitor to Ariel. The other was to try to broaden Persil's proposition to cover stain removal through introducing Persil Power. Neither initiative succeeded.

## 4. Niche

Niche markets are too small or specialized to attract large competitors. They are small harbours which the supertankers cannot enter.

Factors which can make niche markets uninteresting to large competitors include the need to acquire specialized skills or the lack of volume against which to amortize high overheads.

Morgan Cars is a niche marketer. It caters for a customer seeking the nostalgia of a hard-riding pre-war sports car, as described by *What Car?* when it awarded Morgan a four-star rating:

'The ride's as hard as a rock, comfort and space minimal, noise levels deafeningly high, and overall the sports car has about as much refinement as a tractor. Wonderful!'[11]

This is not a specification with much appeal to Ford or General Motors, and yet the current wait for delivery of a new Morgan is six years.[12] Morgan cars lack broad appeal, but they have great attraction for a small group of people prepared to pay a considerable price in order to own a Morgan.

Another niche marketer is W. Jordan (Cereals) Ltd.

Jordan's had been a small family milling business for 125 years until, in the early 1980s, it pioneered the UK markets for cereal bars and granola breakfast cereals. It has since found itself in direct competition with the likes of Quaker, Weetabix, General Mills, United Biscuits and Mars. That it has survived in the face of such opposition is confirmed by the countless 'enquiries' it has received from prospective purchasers in recent years.

**The Jordan family have long been advocates of the merits of wholefoods, and their granola and cereal bar products are therefore high in whole grains, seeds, nuts and fruit; low in sugar and other bulking agents, and totally devoid of artificial additives. These products were also among the first in the UK to carry nutritional labelling, and initially they were sold only through health-food stores – still an important distribution channel.**

**This approach is not without its drawbacks, in that high product specifications necessitate higher prices, and the absence of preservatives shortens shelf life. In addition, the taste and texture of the finished product are not universal in their appeal.**

**Jordan's larger competitors seek to develop brands with much greater volume potential. Thus they must compromise the strict canons of the wholefood movement in order to achieve broader consumer appeal.**

Like Morgan cars, Jordan's is aiming at a limited audience with a distinctive product and benefit.

Almost without exception, niche products are premium-priced, to compensate the marketer for lack of scale in production and distribution. In addition, they usually command above-average profit margins.

A niche strategy can lead in a number of directions. The niche may be an end in itself, as in the case of Morgan or Jordan's, or it may be a means to establish a toehold in a larger market. The Japanese often use a niche strategy as an entry point and subsequently expand across the larger market to which the niche is a small opening. In motor cycles the original niche was 50cc 'toys'; in cars it was small vehicles; and in TV sets it was miniaturized portables.

Table 117 illustrates variations of the niche strategy.

**Table 117. Niche strategy variations.**

| Long-term niche operators | Niche as entry point only |
| --- | --- |
| Baxter's soups | Honda 50cc bikes |
| Hyperion CDs | Toyota small cars |
| Virago books | Panasonic TV sets |
| Harrods | Virgin PEP |
| Drambuie | Halifax Bank |
| Harley-Davidson | Volvo |
| Ferrari | Kellogg's |
| Body Shop | Coca-Cola |
| Ben & Jerry ice-cream | Snapple |

**When does a niche become a mass market?** Some niches grow steadily over time and convert into mass markets when they attract competition attacking the original niche product or company.

Kellogg's and Coca-Cola both started life as niche brands. Kellogg's was originally a health product called Sanitas Corn Flakes. Coca-Cola was invented by a pharmacist and initially sold as a semi-medical product.

Premium beers used to be niche and are gradually becoming mass market. Volvo started off as a niche product, appealing to the minority of customers who wanted a safe, functional, long-lasting car, and who were not particularly interested in styling or performance. It has since broadened its appeal, with improvements in styling and performance.

A niche can rapidly convert into a mass market, where prices fall as volume grows and the early niche marketers are confronted by mass marketers with large resources. Three of the main circumstances driving conversion are:

- Market growth. A niche market may grow in size to the point where it becomes attractive to mass marketers.
- Acquisition of a niche company by a larger business, with brand development skills and a commitment to build volume.
- Entry to a niche market by a major industry player. This tends to attract other mass-market competitors, who move quickly to avoid being 'left out'.

An example which includes all three circumstances is health drinks, which, after two decades as a niche, moved rapidly to mass-market status in the mid 1990s.

**Snapple pioneered the health drinks market. It was founded in 1972 as Unadulterated Food Products Inc. and only hired its first full-time sales person in 1979. The founders' formula was 'to deliver a true health drink at a premium price to health-concerned consumers at stores they visit often'. Over the years, new flavours were launched, including the very successful iced tea, using 'hot fill' bottling of freshly brewed tea. Distribution was also greatly extended.**

**Market growth was rapid from a modest base. However, the entry of Coca-Cola with Fruitopia, and the acquisition of Snapple by Quaker in the mid 1990s, quickly moved health drinks from niche to centre stage in soft drinks.[13] Quaker overpaid for Snapple ($1.4bn in late 1994), did not manage the brand well, and resold it to Triarc Companies in 1997 for only $300m.[14]**

Anyone can find niches, and they are discovered by deep understanding of how markets segment. The secret is to ensure that a niche is the right size – large enough to be profitable, but not sufficiently large to attract the supertankers, at least not in the early days when you are establishing a position. Some niche marketers are small companies. Others are large but have developed the knack of operating with many small-volume products. Two of the most skilful exponents of niche marketing – American Home Products and Reckitt & Colman – are major companies.

It is easy to deceive yourself that your No. 4 brand is a niche leader, when in reality it's a weak 'Me 4' mass-market brand. **How can you tell?** Your shampoo may be market leader among red-haired musicians in Glasgow, but is this a real market segment?

A genuine niche product or service will be clearly differentiated from mass-market competitors, deliberately targeted at a specific minority group of consumers, and premium priced. Table 118 will enable you to check whether your supposed niche product is a 'me too' in disguise.

**Table 118. When is a 'niche product' a 'me too', in disguise?**

| Niche requirement | Qualifying questions |
|---|---|
| Distinctive benefit | ● How is your product/service different? <br> ● Does customer recognize this? |
| Narrow appeal | ● Does proposition appeal strongly to a defined target group? |
| Premium price | ● What is price v. mass-market brands? |
| Recognized consumer segment | ● Is niche segment real and recognized by consumers, or is it a figment of the marketing imagination? |

The same product may be mass market in one country and niche in another. For example, Gauloise and Gitane cigarettes are brand leaders in France, but have narrow appeal in many other countries.

## 5. Regional concentration

The principle behind this strategy is that it is better to be a large fish in a small pond than the reverse. In addition to local market knowledge, regional concentration can give a marketer the advantages of brand leadership in miniature, allied to a speed of reaction and market responsiveness unavailable to a national or international operator. The German beer market is a good example of successful regional concentration by local producers.

Like a niche strategy, regional concentration can be used as an entry point to a market. Walkers Crisps started in the UK as a regional brand in the Midlands and has gradually expanded to become national market leader, although this was an accident of history rather than a planned strategy. Regional concentration can also be used as a permanent strategy, and many companies have decided to focus only in large home markets, like Germany, USA or Japan, or in a limited number of countries.

Regional concentration remains a viable strategy, especially in large countries, or groups of countries, for companies with genuine local strengths, and in markets where speed or service levels are important. There are many successful local companies in beer, wines and spirits, chilled foods, utilities, retailing and banking, but few in industries like pharmaceuticals, paper, entertainment, computers or consumer durables, where global reach, R & D and economies of scale are important.

As consumer tastes and markets converge, and global companies continue to strengthen their position, regional concentration will become a less attractive strategy in future.

## 6. Product range

Product proliferation through offering a very wide product range is sometimes described as a 'saturation' strategy. The principle is that you offer retailers or distributors every conceivable product type and option, absorb a high proportion of stock and display space, and thereby limit opportunities for competitors. The privately owned Seiko Corporation of Tokyo is one of the most skilful practitioners of this strategy, with its world-wide range of over 2,000 watches under the Lorus, Pulsar and Seiko brands. Individual countries select their own ranges from the world-wide catalogue.

There are obvious dangers in a strategy of product proliferation. It may create major manufacturing diseconomies, and is vulnerable to a focused attack by a supplier with a narrow range.

The Mars Group's strategy is the opposite of Seiko. Mars believes in a very limited range of 'power brands', strongly advertised and very efficiently produced in high volume.

Establishing the right product-range strategy, which achieves the best balance between meeting the needs of target customers and achieving efficient low-cost operation, is often a complex question. It was frequently given too little priority in the past by Western companies, partly because it is not something for which any one department has prime responsibility. In practice, it should be a prime area for leadership by marketing people.

Product-range strategy does appear to be more of a preoccupation among leading Japanese companies. It is very well covered in Robin Cooper's book, *When Lean Enterprises Collide*, a study of management systems inside twenty Japanese companies, including Olympus, Nissan, Citizen and Komatsu.[15] Some of the issues he identified as relevant to developing a product range strategy include:

- **Market segmentation**. In constructing a range strategy, it is essential to have a clear understanding of how the total market segments, and what the product or service needs of each segment are. This enables a company to cover all segments in which it wishes to compete with a comprehensive range involving minimum overlap.

  For instance, in its Walkman range, Sony had five playback models, including two cheaper ones to create a mass market and two specialist ones – water resistant for sports enthusiasts and auto-repeat for foreign-language students. Cooper summed up the basic dilemma facing Sony, 'Too many models would cause production and distribution costs to be too high. Too few models' would result in 'too many sales . . . lost to competition'.[16]

- **Blocking competition**. 'By designing a full product line, a firm gives its customers minimum reasons to look at competitive offerings and virtually eliminates niche competition.'[17]

- **Trading up customers**. Many companies prefer to compete in a number of price segments, so that they can trade up customers over time and retain long-term relationships with them.

- **Building competencies**. One of the reasons why Olympus follows a full-line strategy is its desire to filter down the high-end technology developed for more expensive products into higher-quality products at the lower end of the market.

As described elsewhere in this book, many Western companies, like Procter & Gamble and IBM, while recognizing the importance of customization and relationship marketing, are at the same time reducing proliferation of product varieties, in order to save cost and improve delivery of customer value.

### 7. Guerrilla strategy

The best book on this topic is by Che Guevara,[18] who defines the main elements in guerrilla strategy as:

- Defeat of the enemy as the final objective.
- Use of surprise.
- Tactical flexibility.
- Concentration of attacks on ground favourable to the guerrilla.

The analogy with business is inexact, since the business guerrilla does not aim to defeat its large competitors overall and is quite satisfied to win small skirmishes. However, the three other elements mentioned by Guevara have some application to the small business competing with larger operators.

Typical guerrilla tactics involve attacking a competitor's weak product, its status with a specific retailer or distributor outlet, or a small geographical area. Whereas guerrilla tactics are usually employed by small companies because they require speed of reaction and flexibility, they are sometimes used by larger operators in the form of 'fighting brands'. These are a means either to use up spare capacity, or to put pressure on competitors in market sectors important to **them**, but where **you** have a low market share. Fighting brands are usually floor priced, and can be used tactically in the short term as well as strategically in the longer term.

Smaller companies, following Che Guevara's advice, often use surprise and tactical flexibility as weapons against large competitors. Here are some examples:

**Virgin has consistently competed against large international businesses, whether in music, airlines or financial services. Among the unconventional weapons Virgin uses are:**

- **Legal action, or the threat of it. Virgin rarely goes to court, but when it does, it usually wins. Legal initiatives serve both as a deterrent to competitors and as a source of favourable editorial and consumer awareness, on ground favourable to Virgin. Big companies tend to be ill at ease when defending themselves against allegedly illegal tactics directed at a smaller competitor.**
- **Event marketing. Activities like the transatlantic speed record for ships, and round-the-world ballooning, not only generate millions of pounds' worth of low-cost publicity, but also foster Virgin's image as adventurous and fun.**
- **Issue advertising in the national press, on topics affecting Virgin, like airline competition policy, spawn wide media publicity and become news stories in their own right.**

**Local Texan diaper maker, Drypers, competed with Procter & Gamble's market leading Pampers and Luvs in the US, and used a low-price strategy in its home town Houston. P & G flooded the market with $2 coupons. Drypers countered with its own $2 'converter coupons', which stated that the $2 P & G coupon could be used to buy Drypers. Retailers accepted these converter coupons for the purchase of Drypers and many unwittingly sent them to P & G for redemption payment.**[19]

It is difficult for small companies to successfully sustain a guerrilla strategy over the long term. They are likely to either become much larger, or, after some tactical successes, to sell out to a bigger competitor, like Minnetonka, which for years taunted Procter & Gamble and Colgate through innovation in liquid soap and toothpaste, and was eventually acquired by Johnson Wax.

## 8. Diplomacy

A strategy of diplomacy covers any form of external development, such as acquisitions, joint ventures, licensing or cooperation with third parties. However, arrangements which fall short of acquisition are gaining in popularity, especially as offensive strategies in overseas markets. Their value is to fill gaps in knowledge or skills of each of the parties or to pool compatible resources.

Diplomacy is a way of winning a war with-  out firing a shot. It is probably the fastest-growing type of strategy, driven by convergence between markets, external industry benchmark-ing, globalization and the high cost of developing new technology.

The result is that companies are cooperating with other businesses in some countries and markets, competing in others.

**'Like nineteenth-century diplomats, Europe's media moguls draw and redraw borders and alliances. Powerful players wake up to find themselves excluded from key consortia formed in secret talks. Others end up in conflicting alliances, where friends in one market are foes in another. And some see old allies turn into unexpected competitors.'**[20]

The skills required both to compete and cooperate are very different from those needed to lead a head-on attack, just as the competencies which bring success to soldiers, diplomats and politicians vary widely.

Companies which supply both branded and private label products compete and cooperate on a daily basis with their distributors, which, in many cases, have strong brand names themselves.

Table 119 summarizes a number of situations involving a strategy of diplomacy.

**Table 119.  Some examples of business diplomacy.**

| Type of initiative | Example |
|---|---|
| Licensing technology | Komatsu licensed technology from competitors of Caterpillar as part of its vision of becoming World No. 1. |
| Distribution | When Glaxo launched Zantac in USA, Hoffman La Roche, which had a 700-person field force with spare capacity, agreed to team up with the smaller Glaxo force to distribute Zantac. |
| Shared competencies | General Mills, with skills in breakfast cereal marketing and product development in USA, joined up with Nestlé, which had a strong European presence, to form Cereal Partners. |
| Long-term technical development | Ford and General Motors are working together to develop an electric car. |
| New market knowledge | Many computer, telecom and entertainment companies are cooperating on developments where their skills converge. Companies often develop partners to launch in foreign countries they do not know well. |
| Co-branding | Safeway/Abbey National, Mercedes/Swatch. |

An increasing number of companies are establishing local or global alliances, especially in high-tech industries, communications and entertainment. Motorola, for example, has global alliances with IBM, Philips, Siemens, BT and Toshiba.

## Picking the Right Strategy to Win

In selecting the right strategy, it is important to be aware of the repertoire available, to consider alternatives and to make clear choices. All of the strategies outlined above are possibilities for any size of company, except the head-on strategy, which is recommended only for large and very seasoned companies.

The main factors affecting your choice of strategy will be size and resources, strengths, competitive weaknesses and market opportunities. A careful consideration of these will enable you to select a winning strategy and avoid the lethargic middle of the road favoured by less successful companies.

In most markets, there is room for a brand leader, a differentiated No. 2, a low-price product and niche brands. If your company or brand is a 'me too' No. 3 or No. 4, you do not have a strategy and will not survive for long unless you develop one.

## Spotting Strategic Wear-out

Winning strategies need to be nurtured, updated and modified to meet changing consumer needs and competitive challenges; otherwise they will soon wear out and become losers.

Companies with previously winning strategies, such as Polaroid and Avon, lost their touch. In the case of Polaroid, slow growth in amateur photography and improved product performance from non-instant competitors blunted the edge it had enjoyed. Avon was slow to respond to the challenge to its distribution system posed by the growing number of part-time jobs available to women and the falling number staying at home during the day.

Factors which contribute to strategic wear-out include those in Table 120.

---

**Table 120.  Reasons for strategic wear-out.**

1. **Changes in customer requirements**
2. **Changes in distribution systems**
3. **Innovations by competitors**
4. **Poor control of company costs**
5. **Lack of consistent investment**
6. **Ill-advised changes to a successful strategy (a speciality of galloping midgets)**

---

Of the six reasons for strategic wear-out listed above, two relate to market changes, one to competition and three to internal factors – in other words, 'own goal' situations. There does not appear to be any research on the relative importance of these reasons or why they occur, and the commentary below is therefore based on personal experience:

1. **Changes in customer requirements**. While these have speeded up, they still tend to occur gradually over a number of years. A company keeping close to its customers should therefore be able to update and refine the execution of its strategies to match changing circumstances. Reasons for not doing so include complacency created by past success, and unwillingness to tinker with a successful strategy.

2. **Changes in distribution systems**. These also usually evolve slowly. However, they are often more difficult for companies to respond to than changes in consumer needs, since companies tend to be loyal to existing customers, are loath to upset them by participating in new channels, and may lack the competency to do so.

3. **Innovations by competitors**. This is always a significant threat, both from existing and from new competitors.

4. **Poor control of company costs**. This can smother a strong strategy through weak execution, which reduces customer value.

5. **Lack of consistent investment.** Even strong strategies will wither over time if they are not well supported by product or service investment, by renewed plant and by spending on customer communication and support.

6. **Ill-advised change to a successful strategy.** This can happen for a variety of reasons. The company may be acquired and its new owners, almost as a reflex action, may decide to stride out in new directions. New management may be hired from outside, and react similarly. Strange as it may seem, some companies just get tired of long-standing strategies, successful though they may have been, and seek change for its own sake. Sometimes the strategy becomes poorly executed, and successive groups of managers may forget or never learn its original intent, not surprisingly misapplying it.

    If a long-standing strategy is up for change, it is essential first to understand its history correctly, then evaluate whether the strategy or the recent execution of it is at fault; and finally, to thoroughly test the replacement strategy against the original one before dropping it.

## Rate the Strength of Your Company or Brand Strategy (Table 121)

| Table 121.   Criteria for ranking your company or brand strategy. | | |
|---|---|---|
| **Criteria:** | **Max. score** | **Your score** |
| ● Does your strategy call for superiority in at least one area of high importance to customers? | 10 | |
| ● Is this superiority consistently achieved? | 12 | |
| ● Is your strategy underpinned by at least one significant competitive advantage, or a robust collection of smaller ones, or neither? | 8 | |
| ● Is your strategy viewed by customers as differentiated? | 12 | |
| ● Has it been consistently followed through? | 8 | |
| ● Are the basics of the strategy well understood by senior management? | 8 | |
| ● Are they understood and applied by all employees? | 8 | |
| ● Is the strategy strengthening, weakening or standing still? | 12 | |
| ● Is the company investing enough to ensure the strategy is sustainable? | 12 | |
| ● Is it regularly updated in execution, in line with changing customer needs? | 10 | |
| Total | 100 | |

Eastman Kodak, Sears Roebuck, General Motors, IBM, Apple and American Express are among yesterday's stars, who were slow to change the strategies that had brought past success. When companies are enjoying the benefits of winning strategies or growing markets, they tend to assume they will continue for ever. The truth is they never do.

**How do you prevent strategic wear-out**? By following the offensive marketing approach, and every aspect of POISE.

# FLOW-CHART SUMMARY OF CHAPTER 7

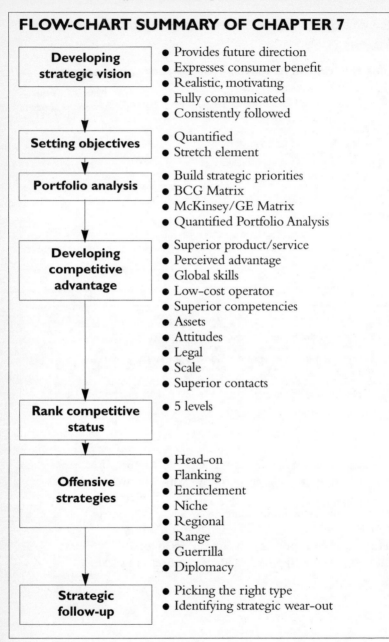

**Developing strategic vision**
- Provides future direction
- Expresses consumer benefit
- Realistic, motivating
- Fully communicated
- Consistently followed

**Setting objectives**
- Quantified
- Stretch element

**Portfolio analysis**
- Build strategic priorities
- BCG Matrix
- McKinsey/GE Matrix
- Quantified Portfolio Analysis

**Developing competitive advantage**
- Superior product/service
- Perceived advantage
- Global skills
- Low-cost operator
- Superior competencies
- Assets
- Attitudes
- Legal
- Scale
- Superior contacts

**Rank competitive status**
- 5 levels

**Offensive strategies**
- Head-on
- Flanking
- Encirclement
- Niche
- Regional
- Range
- Guerrilla
- Diplomacy

**Strategic follow-up**
- Picking the right type
- Identifying strategic wear-out

**Measures Used for Ranking of Birds Eye Brand Range**

**Exhibit 1**

### Table A.  Measures for ranking brand strength – Birds Eye.

| Criteria | Max. score | Measure |
|---|---|---|
| Brand profitability | 12 | • % and absolute profit<br>• Trend, outlook |
| Relative consumer value | 15 | • Relative consumer acceptance versus relative price. Trend and outlook |
| Relative brand share and trend | 9 | • Absolute brand share and trend<br>• Relative brand share |
| Market sector position | 7 | • Brand position in growing versus flat or declining sectors |
| Sales level and trend | 7 | • Absolute sales level<br>• Trend in volume and revenue |
| Differentiation | 12 | • Points of real and perceived difference<br>• Importance to consumer |
| Distribution and trade strength | 7 | • Distribution level and trend<br>• Visibility |
| Innovation record | 6 | • New product output and success rate |
| Future potential | 10 | • Extendibility of brand<br>• Pipeline of new products |
| Awareness and loyalty | 7 | • % spontaneous brand awareness<br>• Repeat purchase levels |
| Investment support | 8 | • Advertising, R & D, capex spend and quality versus competition |
| TOTAL MAXIMUM SCORE | 100 | |

Based on the measures in this table, you can construct a scoring guide sheet for your brands. This will ensure that consistent criteria are used in scoring Birds Eye brands across market sectors and countries. Some criteria, like 'Future potential', involve subjective judgement. Others, such as share, sales or profitability, can be quantitatively measured.

Here is an example of how one of the more subjective criteria – future potential – could be scored:

290 Even More Offensive Marketing

**Table B. Example of brand strength scoring guide sheet.**

| Criteria | Max. score | Scoring guide | | | |
|---|---|---|---|---|---|
| | | **Excellent** 8–10 | **Good** 5–7 | **Fair** 1–4 | **Poor** 0 |
| **Future potential** | **10** | ● Extendibility successfully tested<br>● Proven pipeline of new products | ● Probable extendibility<br>● Untested new product pipeline | ● Limited extendibility<br>● Some new products being developed | ● Brand fully extended<br>● Bare new-products cupboard |

# 8. Offensive Marketing Planning

## Chapter Summary

This is the last chapter in the section covering the 'S' of P-O-I-S-E – 'Strategic'.

**Table 122.**

| | | |
|---|---|---|
| **P:** Profitable | ● | *Proper balance between firm's needs for profit and customer's need for value* |
| **O:** Offensive | ● | *Must lead market, take risks and make competitors followers* |
| **I:** Integrated | ● | *Marketing approach must permeate whole company* |
| **S:** Strategic | ● | *Probing analysis leading to a winning strategy* |
| **E:** Effectively Executed | ● | *Strong and disciplined execution on a daily basis* |

→ ←

It pulls together material from previous chapters, especially on offensive business analysis and offensive strategies. There are cross-references to other chapters, placing marketing planning in its full context.

The bulletin board at the beginning of this book says that it is written for competitive people who are serious about strengthening their marketing skills. This chapter will definitely test your commitment. Marketing planning is a complex topic and a certain amount of detail is essential to communicate it effectively. It is also highly practical, which is why almost half this chapter is devoted to a complete marketing plan for a fictional UK brand – Rasputin Vodka.

The objectives of marketing planning are to learn from the past, anticipate the future, identify opportunities, develop winning strategies and turn these into excellent plans.

Common faults in marketing planning are lack of integration with other company plans such as Sales and Operations, overemphasis on analysis, resulting in drowning by numbers, and lack of effective action. Offensive Marketing planning is designed to achieve balance between analysis and creativity, between thoughtfulness and practicality.

As marketing becomes more international, so the integration of country or brand marketing plans to the rest of the organization grow in complexity. A brand plan on Pampers in the UK, for example, would need to be integrated with the European Paper Category Marketing Plan and with the UK country marketing plan, and aligned with Sales, Supply Chain and Operations plans.

Other key issues to be decided on marketing plans are time-scale (which combination of 1, 3, 5, 10 years), level of detail, people involved, responsibilities and roles of different management levels, and process to be used.

Offensive Marketing planning involves a seven-step process, which is fully explained and illustrated in this chapter:

1. **Business analysis**
2. **Future thinking**
3. **Opportunity identification**
4. **Set objectives**
5. **Build strategies**
6. **Develop plans**
7. **Monitor results**

This seven-step process is relevant not just to marketing planning, but to any kind of business plan, whether corporate, category, sales or operations.

## Good and Bad Marketing Plans

It was 8 p.m. on a Friday evening, and fourteen people were crowded into a smallish conference room in Germany. They were a mixture of Americans, Germans and English, nearing the end of their fifth consecutive day of meetings on the German marketing plans . . . and nearing the end of their tether.

The American International President, having observed that the company was market leader with 15–24% shares in UK, France and Italy, compared with only 5% in Germany, had been determined to improve this position. He had therefore generously allocated five whole days to the German meeting, compared to one day for the other major countries.

The German team was very well prepared, and spent Monday and Tuesday presenting analyses of the market following a detailed specification set by head office in Chicago. These and many other hypotheses for past failure were discussed at length on Wednesday to Friday.

Now, at last, at 8 p.m. Friday, the German team presented their marketing plan for the following year. Discussion finished at 11 p.m., because the American team had a Saturday-morning flight from Frankfurt to Chicago. Everyone had done a very hard week's work, everyone without exception was exhausted, but nothing had been decided.

This real-life description of overkill marketing planning will be familiar to many, especially those working for American multinationals. In this example, three hours were spent on possible action, forty-seven on business analysis. In reality, there were only two key issues to be resolved:

- Whether a major investment in developing a special range of products tailored to the particular needs of the German market should be made.
- The other was related – how to improve quality of distribution, since, while the company's products were quite widely available, they tended to be stocked by the smaller outlets in any given city or town.

Unfortunately, these two key issues received little attention, since the five-day meeting diverted into a welter of detail.

Table 123 outlines some of the characteristics of good and bad marketing plans.

**Table 123. Good and bad marketing plans** (read across).

| Good marketing plans | Bad marketing plans |
|---|---|
| ● Brief and concise | → Cure insomnia |
| ● Relevant analysis | → Endless analysis |
| ● Majority of effort in opportunity identification, strategy development, action | → 90% of effort in business review, general discussion |
| ● Focus on competitive advantage | → Focus on completing complex formats |
| ● Cross-departmental involvement | → Planning in marketing silo |
| ● Plans in constant use | → Plans lie undisturbed for a year |
| ● Strategic and actionable | → Highly tactical, short term |
| ● Updated regularly | → Ignored until next plan |
| ● Monitored constantly | → Not monitored |
| ● Motivating | → Demotivating |

In marketing planning, effort is needed to get the right balance between rigorous analysis and creativity. Too often, completion of the formats required by the plan is so time-consuming that marketers get quickly submerged by the weight of paper and have little energy left to devote to strategy and innovation. At the other extreme, creative plans built on superficial analysis may prove misdirected. Offensive Marketing planning is designed to achieve balance and competitive advantage, using a process which is time-efficient and practical.

## Where Do Marketing Plans Fit?

Marketing plans cover different levels, depending on the structure of the company.

For an international company competing in a range of market categories, marketing plans will need to derive from the corporate marketing plan, and link into total country plans, as well as world-wide plans for the category (Figure 47).

For a single-country company, with a number of separate business units, the situation will be simpler, with business unit marketing plans

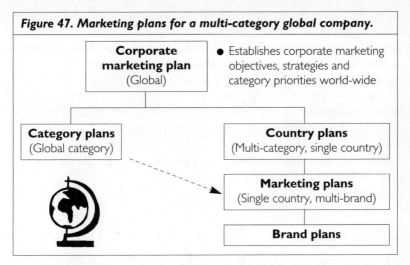

Figure 47. Marketing plans for a multi-category global company.

linking in to the total business unit plan and the corporate marketing plan as Figure 48 shows:

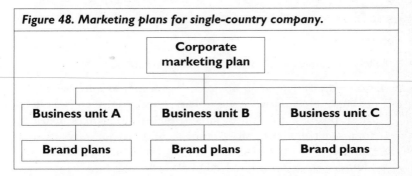

Figure 48. Marketing plans for single-country company.

Every marketing plan, whatever the level, must be aligned to a total business plan **above**, and Sales, Operations and Financial plans **across** (Figure 49).

Figure 49. Link of marketing plans above and across.

In any business, alignment of the marketing plan to other internal plans above and across is essential to avoid duplication of effort and to ensure consistency across departments. This provides yet another opportunity for marketers to spread the marketing gospel, making the whole company customer-driven.

Unfortunately, marketing plans are often developed in isolation from Sales and Operations, and then thrown 'over the wall' to them at a late stage. This leads to narrow strategies and weak execution (Figure 50).

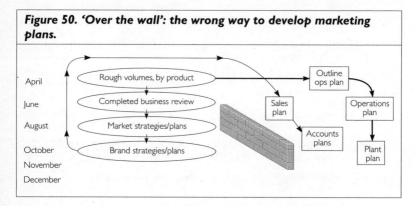

**Figure 50. 'Over the wall': the wrong way to develop marketing plans.**

Likely outcomes of this marketing wall game are that:

- Account plans are never completed, or if they are, link weakly to brand plans. **How many plans have you seen where total revenue for all brands (marketing) differs from total revenue for all channels and major accounts (sales)?**
- Unnecessary cost will be added to plans, because there has been no discussion between Marketing and Operations about alternatives. Quite often, two different marketing plans may be equally effective, but one will enable Operations to use its capacity much more efficiently than the other. In addition, the more notice Operations has about new products or services, about peaks and troughs in volume, the more effectively it will be able to manage change.
- Interaction between brands and trade channels is not properly thought through. Increasingly, brand offerings need to be tailored to the specific requirements of *different* channels, and at the same time communicate a consistent proposition across *all* channels. For instance, a mortgage product may be sold through retail branches, directly by phone, and offered by independent

financial consultants. The way the product is positioned may differ by channel, but needs to be credible to the consumer who visits a branch one day, gets a direct telesales contact two days later and sees a financial consultant the following week.

- The quality of the marketing plans will be sub-optimal, since the views of Sales and Operations people will be heard too late in the process. They almost always have valuable thinking to contribute, and can review plans from a wide variety of perspectives.

Clearly, the wall must be removed and replaced by a lively interaction between Marketing, Sales and Operations, informally, and formally in workshop sessions. This is expanded upon in later parts of this chapter, and Figure 51 provides a summary, which contrasts with Figure 50 above.

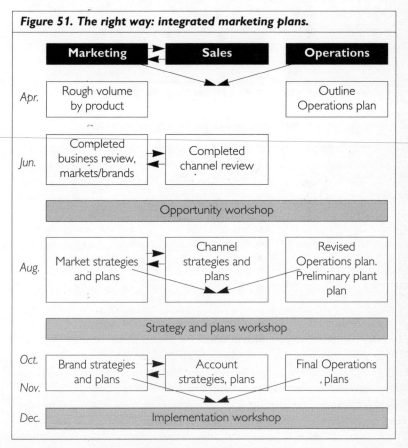

**Figure 51. The right way: integrated marketing plans.**

| | Marketing | Sales | Operations |
|---|---|---|---|
| Apr. | Rough volume by product | | Outline Operations plan |
| Jun. | Completed business review, markets/brands | Completed channel review | |
| | Opportunity workshop | | |
| Aug. | Market strategies and plans | Channel strategies and plans | Revised Operations plan. Preliminary plant plan |
| | Strategy and plans workshop | | |
| Oct. Nov. | Brand strategies and plans | Account strategies, plans | Final Operations , plans |
| Dec. | Implementation workshop | | |

The *integrated* approach to marketing planning takes no longer than the 'over the wall' method, but results not only in much stronger strategies but also in dramatically superior implementation. After all, the vast majority of marketing implementation is handled by Sales and Operations people. If they understand the purpose of the plans and have actively contributed to their development, they will obviously feel more committed to success.

## Other Key Issues in Marketing Planning

Marketing planning is a challenging process with which many companies have difficulty. In addition to the crucial question of integration covered above, there are a number of other key issues which need to be resolved before embarking on the marketing planning process.

**What time scales should be used?** Most companies have one and three or five year plans. Some, in industries like pharmaceuticals, where product development lead items are very long, also have a ten year plan. Some of the options appear in Table 124.

**Table 124. Some time-scale options for plans (years).** *(Read across chart.)*

| | | |
|---|---|---|
| 10 → | 5 → | 1 |
| 10 → | 3 → | 1 |
| | 5 → | 1 |
| | 3 → | 1 |
| • Visionary<br>• Market selection/<br>  priorities<br>• Internal v. acquisition | • Key objectives<br>• Major strategies<br>• Allocation of<br>  resources<br>• Test and<br>  development plans | • Fiscal year budget<br>• Quarterly milestones<br>• Development plans |
| **Very broad** | **Specific strategies and plans** | **Detailed implementation** |

Each plan and the accompanying process is different. The ten-year or very long-term plan will probably be driven by people at the centre of the company, and cover issues such as future market priorities, technology, brand and product development, and acquisitions. This very long-term plan, once completed, provides the context for the medium-term (three to five year) plan, which is much more specific and focuses primarily on strategies, targets and plans.

The one year plan, or budget, stems from these and deals with detailed implementation. It applies the strategies previously agreed as part of the medium-term plan.

The rest of this chapter deals mainly with the one year marketing plan, written in the context of a medium-term three year plan, which it is assumed has already been completed.

Every company will have a one-year plan. There are advantages in having a 10-3-1 planning system, even if you are not in a long lead-time industry, because:

- The ability to look forward ten years is liberating, encourages future vision and stimulates long-term thinking.
- Although the choice for the medium-term plan is usually between three and five years, three is appropriate for most companies. It is far enough away to allow for ambitious development, but close enough to provide urgency. For many, the speed of change is such that five years is too long a period for medium-term planning.

10-3-1 plans should be updated annually, and each aligned with the sensible cycle for calendar year planning as shown in Table 125.

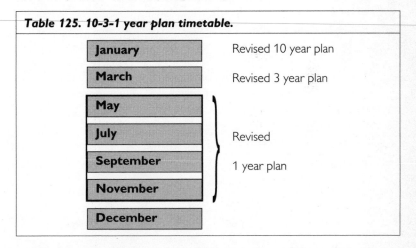

**Table 125. 10-3-1 year plan timetable.**

|  |  |
|---|---|
| January | Revised 10 year plan |
| March | Revised 3 year plan |
| May | |
| July | Revised |
| September | 1 year plan |
| November | |
| December | |

**How much detail is needed?** Be concise and focused. Avoid too much detail in commentary, and relegate it to exhibits. If a plan is too long, it will be neither read nor understood by anyone except the writer. More importantly, it will end up in a file, not as a working document. As a guideline, a one-year plan for a major market or major brand should not exceed ten pages, excluding exhibits. This requires both selection and compression.

Level of detail will also be influenced by resources available. A two-person marketing group in Malaysia will go into much less detail than a hundred-person team in the USA. By far the most time-consuming part of any Marketing plan is the business analysis section. Chapter 5, pages 184–8, outlines the requirements for effective analysis. Productivity can be maximized by building up analyses continuously over the year, rather than trying to handle the whole analysis process within a single month; and by *focusing* analysis on particular hypotheses for action, and using it as a basis for proving or disproving them. The worst error is to try and analyse every available piece of data.

**Who should be involved in marketing planning?** The marketing plan is the primary responsibility of the Marketing Department, especially Marketing Managers and Brand Managers. However, they need to work closely with people in Sales and Operations, providing brief and clear summaries at various stages of the process and involving them in workshops.

 Establishment of an extended brand group on a continuous basis can also provide a valuable framework for cross-departmental communication. The extended brand group consists of anyone having a significant effect on the success of a brand, whether in Sales, Operations, Finance, Human Resources or external companies. The group should not be too large and members would also be selected on the basis of skills and competencies. Table 126 illustrates possible composition of an extended brand group.

| Table 126.  **Extended brand group – possible composition.** | | |
|---|---|---|
| **Core brand group** | **Extended brand group** | |
| Brand Manager | Brand Manager | Sales Account Manager |
| Assistant Brand | Assistant Brand Manager | Financial analyst |
| Manager | Ad agency executive | Market Research Manager |
| | Ad agency creative | R & D Manager |
| | Operations Manager | Direct marketing agency |
| | Supply Chain Manager | IT Manager |

The extended brand group can be invited to meet for half-day workshops at two or three points of the marketing planning cycle, and perhaps for an away-day review in the close season. Such workshops, however, are no substitute for thorough analysis. To make workshops effective, marketing people need to prepare carefully and to pre-circulate high-quality summaries of key data.

The brand group would also communicate with members of the extended brand group through the year via e-mail, quarterly progress newsletters and informally.

**Should the marketing planning process be up or down?** The answer is up, down and across. In practice, certain issues, like corporate financial objectives and overall strategies, have to be decided at a high level and fed down. Equally, in a global company, various strategic guidelines may need to be established centrally or regionally. For example, it would be uneconomic to develop different Ford car bodies for each country, or tailored advertising in every country for a global hair-care brand. Within such top-down strategic requirements, there should be considerable scope for adaptation and innovation by market, brand, channel and country, on a bottom to middle-up basis.

3M is a company which believes in flexible, self-reliant business units, but follows four key strategies world-wide, which influence marketing thinking (Table 127).

---

**Table 127.  3M: four key corporate strategies.**[1]

1. Innovative products. At least 30% of today's sales to be from products launched in past four years.
2. Superior customer satisfaction. Aim to be the *preferred* supplier in every market.
3. International expansion.
4. Productivity improvement, as measured by real-sales growth per employee.

---

# Objectives of Annual Marketing Planning

Marketing planning is a demanding and time-consuming process. **Why do it? And is it worth the time?**

These questions can be tested by considering how a company could operate without marketing plans. This must certainly be feasible, since, until a few decades ago, marketing planning did not exist. The likely style of a company not using marketing planning is top down, where autocratic leaders determine strategies, or 'seat of the pants', where tactics overwhelm any attempts at strategic thinking.

Marketing planning enables managers at least once a year to think deeply about their business – both to consider the past and to look into the future. The process also demands answers to difficult questions which might otherwise be ignored.

In this context, marketing planning can be said to have six major objectives, against which the total process should be carefully evaluated (Table 128).

| Table 128.  Six main objectives of marketing planning. | |
|---|---|
| 1.  To learn from the past<br>2.  To anticipate the future<br>3.  To spot and prioritize relevant opportunities<br>4.  To develop winning strategies | 5.  To allocate resources to best advantage<br>6   To blueprint excellent implementation |

## The Seven Key Steps in any Business Plan

These seven steps are intrinsic to the Offensive Marketing approach, and relevant to any business plan, for any level, whether global or local, corporate or business unit, and for any function such as Marketing, Sales or Operations. It is difficult to see how any of the seven steps could be omitted without affecting plan quality.

The next three sections will review these seven steps, then apply them to a brand marketing plan for Rasputin Vodka.

Much of the ground comprising the seven steps has been covered in previous chapters and these are referenced in Table 129.

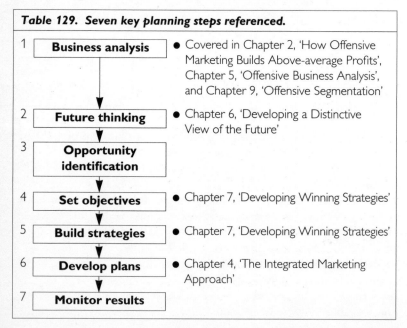

**Table 129.  Seven key planning steps referenced.**

1  **Business analysis** — ● Covered in Chapter 2, 'How Offensive Marketing Builds Above-average Profits', Chapter 5, 'Offensive Business Analysis', and Chapter 9, 'Offensive Segmentation'

2  **Future thinking** — ● Chapter 6, 'Developing a Distinctive View of the Future'

3  **Opportunity identification**

4  **Set objectives** — ● Chapter 7, 'Developing Winning Strategies'

5  **Build strategies** — ● Chapter 7, 'Developing Winning Strategies'

6  **Develop plans** — ● Chapter 4, 'The Integrated Marketing Approach'

7  **Monitor results**

## Application of the Seven Key Steps to Marketing Planning

These are summarized in the master table (Table 130), which lists the seven steps, the topics covered by each one and key tools to use. While this looks pretty heavy, it is the crux of marketing planning and well worth looking at closely.

| **Table 130. Master table: 7 key steps in marketing planning.** | | |
|---|---|---|
| **Step** | **Topics covered:** | **Key tools to use:** |
| **1. Business analysis** | ● Business environment<br>● Markets<br>● Channels<br>● Own business<br>● Competition<br>● Technology<br>● Competencies | ● *3 wheels of business environment*<br>● *Internal examination*<br>● *Competitive analysis*<br>● *Key factors for success (KFS)*<br>● *SWOT analysis*<br>● *Segmentation*<br>● *Portfolio analysis* |
| **2. Future thinking** | ● Anticipating the future<br>● Reviewing scenarios<br>● Establishing strategic direction<br>● Developing future thinking | ● *6 key drivers of future thinking*<br>● *Probability analysis*<br>● *7 spokes of offensive attitudes* |
| **3. Opportunity identification** | ● Identify main opportunity areas<br>● Generate opportunity long-list<br>● Screen and test opportunities<br>● Prioritized opportunity list | ● *Outcome of Steps 1 and 2*<br>● *Extended brand groups*<br>● *Idea-generation techniques*<br>● *Concept testing* |
| **4. Set objectives** | ● Market development<br>● Market share<br>● Revenue<br>● Investment<br>● Innovation<br>● Profits | ● *Corporate strategy and plan*<br>● *Outcome of Steps 1 to 3* |

| Step | Topics covered: | Key tools to use: |
|---|---|---|
| **5. Build strategies** | ● Overall marketing sub-strategies<br>➤ Product/service<br>➤ Pricing/value<br>➤ Communication<br>➤ Distribution<br>➤ Brand development<br>➤ Sales promotion<br>➤ Internal marketing<br>➤ Profitability | ● *Brand portfolio analysis*<br>● *Types of competitive advantage*<br>● *Types of offensive strategy*<br>● *Strategic wear-out monitor*<br>● *Extended brand groups* |
| **6. Develop plans** | ● Plans to support strategies<br>● Development projects<br>● Quarterly milestones<br>● Method of evaluation | ● *Extended brand groups*<br>● *Monthly activity summary* |
| **7. Monitor results** | ● Monitoring methods<br>● Monitoring timetable | ● *Quarterly review formats* |

## Step 1: BUSINESS ANALYSIS

This analyses the past, and draws lessons for future application, using the approaches covered in Chapter 5, 'Offensive Business Analysis'. Other key tools are segmentation (Chapter 9), which can be used to sub-divide markets and channels; and portfolio analysis.

There should be a separate list of conclusions for each of the seven main topics to be covered within business analysis.

## Step 2: FUTURE THINKING

This step peers into the future, recognizing that it will be very different from the past.

Step 2 is most relevant at a corporate level, since a company's chosen vision and values will guide its approach in all countries, markets and channels. However, Step 2 also deserves consideration at market, country and brand level, since future vision for individual markets should be consistent with the corporate one.

### Step 3: OPPORTUNITY IDENTIFICATION

The main output from this step will be a prioritized list of relevant opportunities.

Opportunity identification is covered in more detail in Chapter 11, pages 449–53.

The overall topics to be addressed during this step are:

- **Identifying main opportunity areas**. There is no point in developing great ideas which prove irrelevant because the company lacks the competencies to exploit them. Therefore the target areas for idea generation need to be staked out early. These will include key competencies, market or channel segments already prioritized in Step 1, and target consumer groups.
- **Generation of ideas relevant to opportunity areas**. Ideas will flow through via the previous steps, use of idea generation techniques such as brainstorming, and meetings of the extended brand group. The largest tranche of ideas may well come from the business analysis in Step 1, since the very nature of this step is to develop a long list of hypotheses, and to prioritize or refine them through analysis.
- **Screening and concept testing**. An opportunity screening method needs to be established. Based on this, a short-list of relevant opportunities can be drawn up, for consumer or customer concept testing, using short statements on card to describe each concept.
- **Prioritized opportunity list**. This will comprise those ideas which have survived screening, and come through the concept testing with flying colours. These are the opportunities to develop further.

### Step 4: SET OBJECTIVES

Objectives need to be established for each of the six topics in the master table above, on a basis consistent with the corporate, country and business unit objectives.

### Step 5: BUILD STRATEGIES

These will consist of a statement of overall marketing strategies, designed to meet the objectives, and a set of supporting sub-strategies, each covering topics like product/service or price/value.

Relevant tools are quantified portfolio analysis for establishing brand investment priorities, and the many types of competitive advantage and offensive strategies described in Chapter 7.

The varied perspective of the extended brand group will also be useful at this point.

### Step 6: DEVELOP PLANS

This step converts the strategies into offensive action plans, which can be monitored and measured. These plans should comprise short-term activity, spanning the fiscal year, and longer-term development projects which may take years to come to fruition. It can be worthwhile to look ahead eighteen months by quarter, and to set quarterly milestones for evaluating progress on development projects.

Another key element in plans is a testing programme, which involves trying out new approaches to products, services, pricing or communication, on a limited basis, at modest cost and low risk. This is marketing R & D – the lifeblood of the future.

Every Marketing Department needs a full cupboard of successfully tested approaches, which can be expanded with confidence in the years ahead.

### Step 7: MONITOR RESULTS

This is a simple step to execute, but often neglected, due to time pressures. The marketing plan should specify the proposed method of evaluation, when it will be applied, and by whom.

## Application of the Seven Key Steps to Brand Planning

The process of the seven key steps applies equally to brand planning as to market or indeed channel planning. However, there are a number of extra tools to use at the business analysis step which apply specifically to **brands**. This section will outline these additional Step 1 tools (Table 131).

---

**Table 131. Key brand analysis tools.**

| | |
|---|---|
| ● **Brand history** | ● **Brand positioning statement** |
| ● **Brand conversion model** | ● **Brand scorecard** |
| ● **IDQV** | ● **Loyalty check** |

**Brand history**. This encapsulates the key learning, which is preserved through generations of managers. It briefly covers, in two pages or less, the main brand events over the past ten years, things like major changes in product, service, packaging, proposition, sizing, range, together with results of major tests, and share history for all major brands. Exceptional factors like product recalls, short-term supply or quality problems would also be included in the brand history. And major external events such as competitor brand launches or relaunches, exceptional seasonality (e.g. very hot summers for beer), deregulation, unusual changes in tax, would also be noted and dated. A pricing history should be completed as an exhibit.

A brand history provides an accurate record of past events affecting a brand, so that historical sales and profit changes can be better understood by those running the brand today. Marketing people change jobs frequently within and across companies, and much valuable information can be lost without brand histories. They do, of course, need to be regularly updated.

**Brand conversion model.** This is a simple and quick way to check a brand's health, and its top-line strengths and weaknesses. It uses three measures among your target customers to assess priority areas for developing the brand's business. Recent data on all three measures should be available from your own consumer research.

You have a number of choices in defining each of these measures, and the only rule is to use the same definition consistently:

- **Awareness**. Spontaneous awareness, where customers are asked by researchers to 'name any brand of household paint' they can think of without any prompting, is the most demanding measure, and the one used here.

  An alternative is 'prompted' awareness, where customers are shown a list of household paint brands, and asked which ones they have heard of. Obviously 'prompted' awareness scores are always much higher than 'spontaneous'.

- **Trial**. The question is how far back you go. Does a single trial ten years ago count? Should you take 'Ever used' as your measure, or a shorter time-scale, such as 'Past year', for which the customer's memory may be reasonable. Much will depend on your product category, and frequency of purchase. In Table 132 we have used one year.

- **Regular purchase and loyalty**. Again, regular purchase can be defined in a variety of ways. The definition used here is 'at least 50% of category purchases in your brand'. So, if you were managing Club biscuits, a person buying Club three of the last five times she purchased any chocolate biscuit countline, would qualify as a 'regular'.

Table 132 gives an example of the brand conversion model. **What do you conclude from it?**

**Table 132. Example of brand conversion model: soft drink – Brand A.**

| The 3 measures | % target customers | Conversion ratio (%) | Measures strength of: |
|---|---|---|---|
| (a)  Spontaneous awareness | 15 | – | *Ad quality and spend* |
| (b)  Tried in past year | 10 | 67 | *Brand proposition* |
| (c)  Regular purchase (b)÷(c) | 2 | 20 | *Value delivery* |

It shows that:

● Spontaneous awareness for your brand is 15% of your target customers.
● Ten per cent have tried the brand in the past year, so your conversion rate from awareness to trial is 67% (10÷15).
● Two per cent are regularly using your brand, so conversion rate from trial to regular usage is only 20% (10÷2).

In this example, your conversion from brand awareness to trial is very high at 67%, indicating that you have a strong **brand proposition** – the brand advertising, availability and appearance are all working well. However, your conversion from trial to regular purchase is terrible at 20%, pointing to weak product performance. Action would be to stop all spending until you have radically improved the product.

The brand conversion model is most relevant to consumer goods bought at least three times a year. Individual brands can be compared with other company brands or competitors, as in Table 133, using analysis to determine future action. Brand A is the same brand as in the previous table. **What do you conclude from Table 133, and do you agree with the action suggested?**

**Table 133. Further examples of actionable brand conversion models.**

| The 3 measures | Brand A | Brand B | Brand C |
|---|---|---|---|
| Spontaneous awareness | 15% | 4% | 10% |
| % Awareness to trial | 67% | 75% | 33% |
| % Trial to regular usage | 20% | 66% | 50% |
| Action suggested: | ● Stop advertising ● Improve product quality | ● Increase advertising spend | ● Improve advertising quality |

Brand B has enormous appeal to those aware of it, but its potential is stunted by low awareness, because it is being starved of advertising.

**IDQV**. This stands for **impact**, **differentiation**, **quality** and **value**. IDQV is a valuable brand planning tool, developed by Novaction SA, an innovative research company best known for market modelling and simulations. Novaction established IDQV as the four key factors affecting brand success, based on the evaluation of 5,000 case studies involving 30,000 brands. Table 134 and the subsequent explanation are derived from Novaction's pioneering work.

**Table 134. Summary of IDQV.**

| Measure | Elements | Measurement data |
|---|---|---|
| Impact | Spontaneous brand awareness x brand availability | ● Brand distribution level ● Advertising research |
| Differentiation | Actual or perceived *difference* v. competitors as viewed by consumers | ● Product, service testing ● Market research |
| Quality | Product or service *performance* v. competitors | ● Product, service comparisons among customers |
| Value | Relative product or service quality related to price | ● Conversion from trial to regular usage ● Brand loyalty levels |

IDQV can be applied to products or services, and consumers or customers. It is also relevant to business-to-business markets.

Like the brand conversion model, IDQV can be used to check brand strengths and weaknesses. This may be based on broad judgement and guesswork, or on extensive market research. IDQV is a quick-check method and not a substitute for the more detailed brand strength score-card outlined later in this section.

- **Impact** covers the questions, 'Have I heard of this brand and can I get it easily?' If spontaneous awareness is 20%, and weighted brand distribution 70%, impact is 14% (20% × 70%).
- **Differentiation. 'Do consumers or customers view this brand as different or distinctive from competitors in performance, design, characteristics, image or service levels? Or is it another "Me Too"?'** The differentiation may be in the consumer's mind, rather than an objective fact, therefore perceived not actual.
- **Quality.** The question here is whether the brand is viewed by consumers as better than competition. A brand may be differentiated but not better, or vice versa. These are two different measures.
- **Value.** Value is an equation relating quality to price (Figure 52). If a product has parity in quality, but is 10% lower priced than competitors, it offers superior value. If it is 10% better in quality, but 50% more expensive, its value is inferior.

**Figure 52.**

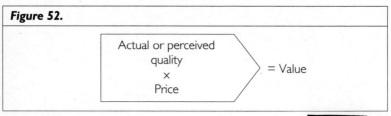

$$\frac{\text{Actual or perceived quality}}{\text{Price}} = \text{Value}$$

IDQV can be quickly quantified, using judge-ment, and available facts. **What would you con-clude from Table 135?**

**Table 135. Example of IDQV scoring – computer software brand.**

|  | Maximum score | Your brand | Competitor brand |
|---|---|---|---|
| Impact | 35 | 15 | 25 |
| Differentiation | 20 | 20 | 5 |
| Quality | 25 | 15 | 20 |
| Value | 20 | 10 | 10 |
| Brand strength | 100 | 60 | 60 |

Your brand is highly differentiated, but little known and only of average quality. Action needed is to improve quality, then strengthen awareness and availability. Your competitor brand is a much bigger seller, of good quality, premium priced, well known and widely available. But lack of differentiation makes it vulnerable to attack.

**Brand Positioning Statement (BPS).** This is a one-page summary of the key elements which make up your brand proposition and personality. It is another way of testing your brand strength. The BPS should be reviewed at least annually at the beginning of the business analysis step in brand planning, and modified if necessary as part of Step 6 – Develop brand plans.

The BPS has a number of components (Table 136).

**Table 136.  Elements in Brand Positioning Statement (BPS).**

| Elements | Issues |
| --- | --- |
| 1.  Brand name | *What name do customers or consumers use?* |
| 2.  Market description | *How would customers describe this?* |
| 3.  Target audience | *Who are we selling to?* |
| 4.  Brand discriminator | *What benefits (rational or emotional) does the brand deliver best?* |
| 5.  Core consumer proposition | *Emotional and functional* |
| 6.  Brand differentiators | *How is the brand different?* |
| 7.  Brand personality | *Image and associations* |

The BPS should never exceed one page in length, and needs to be succinctly expressed. It answers or fails to answer the question: **'Why should customers buy this brand in preference to competitors?'** The example in Table 137 demonstrates this.

**Table 137.  Brand positioning statement: IKEA.**[2]

| Elements | Issues |
| --- | --- |
| 1.  Brand name | *IKEA* |
| 2.  Market description | *Home furnishings* |
| 3.  Target audience | *Under 45 years old, families with children* |
| 4.  Brand discriminator | *Good quality and superior value* |
| 5.  Core consumer proposition | *High-quality, well-designed products at low and affordable prices* |
| 6.  Brand differentiators | *Size of store, design style, layout, service levels* |
| 7.  Brand personality | *Swedish, classless, environmentally concerned, sophisticated, ethical* |

**Brand strength scorecard.** This is a more elaborate way of evaluating a brand's strengths and weaknesses than the quick-check in IDQV, involving the use of the quantified portfolio analysis. An example of how to construct a brand scorecard for Birds Eye was given on page 259 of Chapter 7.

**Customer loyalty check.** This is the final additional tool to use in brand planning, at an early stage in the process. The importance of customer loyalty as a basis for profitable growth is increasingly recognized.[3]

As part of your brand business analysis, you need to evaluate your brand's level of consumer or customer loyalty, overall and relative to competition; who your loyal customers are: what they are worth to you in profits on an annual and lifetime basis; how much you have been spending on them; and where the best opportunities for attracting more loyal customers lie. The loyalty check provides a tool to do this (Table 138).

---

**Table 138. Brand loyalty check: key questions to ask.**

- What is your brand's level of repeat purchase?
- How does this compare with the industry average?
- What is the annual and lifetime value of a loyal customer, in revenue and profits?
- How are you allocating marketing spending between loyal, and new or transitory customers?
- What is the profile of your loyal customers? How do you recruit more?
- How well are you rewarding loyal customers?
- What opportunities can you give loyal customers to buy more, or to recommend you to others?

---

In the USA, average customer repurchase rates in the car industry are a miserable 30–40%. Yet Lexus achieves 63%, partly because it deliberately targeted Mercedes and Cadillac buyers, who were more difficult to switch, but easier to hold than younger, more fashion-conscious buyers of Jaguars and BMW.

After decades of price promoting to get new consumers, in common with the rest of the US grocery industry, Procter & Gamble decided to cut down promotion and use the savings to reduce prices. This was a way to reward loyal customers, and to avoid wasting resources on temporarily attracting new users, with a low loyalty attitude. Despite strong initial resistance from retailers, who were addicted to price promotion, the new P & G strategy proved successful with consumers, and generated large manufacturing savings by removing the peaks and troughs of promotions.

To guide you on the economics of direct marketing, you need to know the average and lifetime value of your loyal customers. This requires a clear understanding of the brand conversion cycle above – cost per trier, percent conversion from trial to regular purchase, annual profit value per regular purchaser, and likely loyalty period. Some consumers may only be loyal to a brand for weeks, but many *Radio Times* 'loyals' have bought weekly for over ten years, and some Mercedes 'loyals' have stayed with the brand for decades.

The annual profit value of a regular user of Ariel is about £15, while a three to four times a week pub visitor can be worth over £200 per year in profit to the landlord. A heavy night-club user in London or Las Vegas can generate over £1 million per year in annual profits, and a leading Cadillac dealer calculated that the lifetime value of an average Cadillac buyer was $332K.[4]

Why are these statistics important? Because they can guide you on the economics of how much to invest to retain a loyal customer, and how to allocate resources between existing customers and potential new ones. Although the profit value of a brand heavy user in detergents is modest, sophisticated marketers like Procter & Gamble and Lever Brothers can still justify heavy investment in direct marketing.

A clear perspective and strategy on loyal versus new customers is an important issue to resolve in brand planning.

The next two sections will demonstrate a brand marketing plan in action, by using a fictional vodka brand called Rasputin. It applies the seven-step marketing planning process just described, and demonstrates how to use a number of analysis tools outlined in this and in previous chapters.

## Background to Rasputin Vodka Marketing Plan

*(This is a fictional example, for illustration only)*

### Company background – Petrograd plc

1. Petrograd plc is a UK-based company, started by three ex-employees of Grand Met in 1985, and financed mainly by 3I. The core of the business is the Nicolai II brand, with a 200-year-old heritage of association with the Russian royal family. Petrograd plc started a joint venture with the Nicolai Company in 1989, and acquired it in 1990. The Rasputin brand was launched in 1991, and is No. 2 brand in the UK.

2. Current-year revenue is £260 million, operating profit £30 million, and ROCE only 12%. Profit margins are below industry averages since the company is still in a heavy capital and marketing investment phase.

3. Petrograd plc is a specialist vodka company, and its major markets are the UK, Eastern Europe and South-East Asia. In Russia, it uses independent distributors, but in the UK and South-East Asia, its products are distributed by United Distillers, world leaders in whisky and gin.

4. There are two vodka plants. Nicolai II is produced outside Moscow, Rasputin near Bristol.

5. Nicolai II is premium-priced, trading on heritage, tradition and quality, targeted at the 30–50-year-old AB drinker. Rasputin is lower priced, though not a discount brand, and aimed at 18–40-year-old CD drinkers. Its image is trendy and light-hearted. Nicolai II is sold in many countries. Rasputin is only in the UK so far.

6. Petrograd plc is a young and dynamic company, and most employees are aged under thirty-five. Its future vision is to associate vodka and its own brands with fun and excitement, and to become the world No. 2 vodka company by 2005, No. 1 by 2020. Its values are innovation, closeness to customers, speed, responsible use of alcohol and environmental awareness.

7. Primary competitors are Turgenev, Finale, store private label and, especially in Russia, local brands.

## Your task

The Rasputin Brand Manager left six months ago, and you joined three months ago from Coca-Cola, where you were assistant Brand Manager on Sprite. Your task is simple – **turn round Rasputin** – and you have just started work on next year's brand Marketing plan. You are using the Offensive Brand Planning process. Because the plan must not exceed ten pages of A4 text, you will be following all seven steps, but only using tools relevant to your needs.

## Preliminary list of hypotheses

As described in Chapter 5 ('Offensive Business Analysis'), it is essential to focus your data search, and to concentrate analysis on a limited number of areas likely to lead to action rather than turning over every stone on the beach. The way to do this is to make a list of possible hypotheses for action before you start your brand marketing plan process, and to use the process to prove or disprove each hypothesis. As you progress, the list of hypotheses can be updated, with some falling by the wayside and new ones appearing. This should enable you to finish up with four or five hypotheses which have survived rigorous analysis, and provide the basis for radical new action.

Table 139 consists of your first raw list of hypotheses after three months on the job at Rasputin.

| Hypotheses | Data analysis needed |
|---|---|
| **Table 139. Rasputin vodka – hypotheses prior to starting the marketing plan.** | |
| 1. Packaging is important, but Rasputin bottle and label is unappealing | ● Review competitor packaging in spirits <br> ● Look at soft drinks <br> ● Brief pack designer |
| 2. Around half vodka usage is by women. Are their needs properly served? Is there an opportunity for a Rasputin line extension for women? | ● Analyse female vodka consumption habits – time, place, mixer usage, long v. short drinks, low v. high alcohol level, occasion, volume per capita, etc. v. males |
| 3. Petrograd plc does not understand why people drink vodka, and how the market segments by benefit area | ● Search existing and published research <br> ● Talk to experts in the industry by phone <br> ● Decide whether to commission segmentation study, with Nicolai II |
| 4. Youth event marketing is underused in this market | ● Phone Coke friends. Talk Levi, Nike <br> ● Identify low-cost, high-profile sport for sponsorship <br> ● Develop events with Yates Wine Lodge, Rank Nightclubs, etc. |
| 5. The whole vodka market is underadvertised v. soft drinks | ● Analyse ad spend by competitor brand in spirits <br> ● Review ad tracking studies <br> ● Top line study on economics of advertising <br> ● Talk to Millward Brown |
| 6. Rasputin has succeeded mainly due to brash, loud, humorous and quirky positioning, with lower price a much less important factor | ● Analyse Rasputin price elasticity and response to advertising <br> ● Model effect of higher advertising financed by price increases when new bottle launched |

| Hypotheses | Data analysis needed |
| --- | --- |
| 7. Music can be a winner in vodka market with youth. Can Rasputin dominate this area? | ● Check competitor use of music in advertising, clubs, promotions<br>● Explore solus opportunities and links with soft drink mixer brands |
| 8. Most vodka advertising is too sophisticated and consists of 'one off' ads, not campaigns | ● Analyse competitor advertising impact |
| 9. Rasputin, with single-minded focus on CD young consumers, can be positioned to trade as differentiated No. 2. Build up distribution to parity with Turgenev, and block out smaller brands | ● Talk to key customers, having done some consumer concept testing<br>● Analyse Rasputin and competitor distribution by channel and key customer |
| 10. The display and publicity value of Rasputin personality has been underplayed | ● Check past Rasputin activity and evaluate<br>● Talk to trade<br>● Estimate cost/benefit |
| 11. Company values of responsible drinking and environmental concern not fully applied on Rasputin | ● Check Rasputin and competitor activities and reputation in these areas<br>● Identify opportunities for improvement. |

This early list of hypotheses will guide you on Step 1 of the brand planning process, 'Business Analysis', and give you a flying start on Step 3, 'Opportunity Identification'. Inevitably, though, some of the content of the business analysis section will be basic map-reading background, not related to your list of hypotheses.

The next section illustrates the seven-step marketing planning process on Rasputin vodka. Those experienced in the spirits market will quickly spot that the author has never worked in this sector, and any suggestions for improvement will be welcomed.

The vodka market has been selected for illustration because it is likely to be relevant and interesting to readers of this book.

# Rasputin Vodka Marketing Plan

## STEP 1 – BUSINESS ANALYSIS

As usual with marketing plans, most of the time and gruntwork are absorbed by the business analysis, but this is the foundation on which strategies and plans will be built.

### (a) Brand history (launch year 1991) (Table 140)

| Year | Sales revenue £ m | Market share (%) | Media spend £ m | Profits (£ m) | Comments |
|------|-------------------|------------------|-----------------|---------------|----------|
| 1991 | 9.5 | 2.5 | 2.5 | (2.5) | Quality problems |
| 1994 | 23.2 | 8.3 | 2.0 | (1.0) | |
| 1995 | 27.6 | 9.6 | 2.0 | 1.0 | Citron launch |
| 1996 | 31.0 | 10.5 | 1.5 | 3.0 | New package |
| 1997 | 29.5 | 9.5 | 1.0 | 4.0 | New advertising |

Note: Rasputin sales revenue excludes duty, VAT and trade margin.

### (b) Three wheels of business environment – vodka (Figure 53)

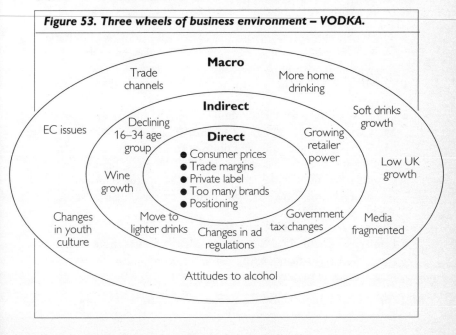

Figure 53. Three wheels of business environment – VODKA.

Macro

Indirect

Direct

Trade channels

More home drinking

EC issues

Declining 16–34 age group

Soft drinks growth

- Consumer prices
- Trade margins
- Private label
- Too many brands
- Positioning

Growing retailer power

Low UK growth

Wine growth

Changes in youth culture

Move to lighter drinks

Changes in ad regulations

Government tax changes

Media fragmented

Attitudes to alcohol

## (c) Total market trends (Table 141)

**Table 141.  Total market trends.**

|  | 3 years ago | Last year | 1997 | Next year | 3 years hence |
|---|---|---|---|---|---|
| Total vodka market (m litres)[5] | 38.1 | 40.0 | 41.0 | 41.5 | 42.5 |
| % of all spirits | 17.5 | 17.1 | 17.4 | 17.5 | 17.7 |
| Rasputin market share (%) | 8.3 | 10.5 | 9.5 | 10.3 | 11.5 |
| Rasputin revenue (£ m) | 23.2 | 31.0 | 29.5 | 33.5 | 39.7 |
| Rasputin media (£ m) | 2.0 | 1.5 | 1.0 | 2.1 | 2.5 |

*Key conclusions:*

1. Slight volume growth in vodka.
2. Rasputin share loss this year due to reduced media, loss of Safeway distribution.
3. Share gain next year due to new Bass listing, new bottle, increased media with new campaign and event marketing.

## (d) Key market segments

The conventional segmentations which seem to matter in vodka are region, demographics, price and usage level, and these need to be shown in exhibits. Main conclusions are:

- The vodka user is young with the 16–34 age-group accounting for 67% of revenue (versus 36% for whisky)[6], skewed to the CD social group, and as likely to be female as male.
- Consumption levels in Scotland are over three times the national average.
- Price is segmented by alcoholic strength and brand type. Most vodka is 37% ABV, but Turgenev Blue Label is 45% ABV. Main price points are premium (Turgenev Blue Label), mainstream brands, secondary brands, discount brands and private label, in that descending order. Rasputin is priced at secondary-brand level. The premium sector is small at under 5% of value.
- Heavy users are mainly in the 16–34 age-group.
- Primary usage method is mixing with carbonates, fruit juices, mixers and, in Scotland, with beer and lager as a chaser. Vodka is seen as suitable for any occasion.

More distinctive approaches to segmentation need to be developed.

## (e) Key channel segmentations (Table 142)

| Outlet type | % volume | Trend |
|---|---|---|
| Grocery multiples | 18 | Growth |
| Multiple off licences | 7 | New store formats |
| Retail independents | 10 | Decline |
| Pubs/clubs | 52 | Fewer customer visits |
| Hotels, restaurants, etc. | 13 | Flat |
| TOTAL | 100% | |

Source: A. C. Nielsen

- Trend by grocery multiples to stock only Turgener and private label.
- Certain pubs and nightclubs have a trend and pace-setting image among the young.

## (f) Rasputin Vodka – competitive position, overall and by segment

Rasputin is clear No. 2 brand, ahead of Finale, but far behind Turgenev (45% market share). Rasputin's position has weakened in the past year after steady growth since launch.

By segment, Rasputin has above-average strength among C1C2 males, and 16–34-year-olds. It is weak in Scotland and the north, strong in London and the south-east, weak among heavy users and women.

## (g) Rasputin Brand Conversion Model (among 16–34 age-group) (Table 143)

| | Rasputin (%) | | Major competitor (%) | |
|---|---|---|---|---|
| | % Target group | Conversion ratio | % Target group | Conversion ratio |
| Spontaneous awareness | 25 | – | 80 | – |
| Awareness to trial | 9 | 36 | 30 | 38 |
| Trial to regular usage | 3 | 33 | 15 | 50 |
| Action: | ● *Improve advertising* ● *Strengthen brand proposition* | | | |

**Conclusions:**
1. Only 9% of target group has tried Rasputin in the past year, and only 3% are regular users. Rasputin's conversion rates are weak.
2. Spontaneous awareness of 25% is good, considering the brand's newness. This indicates the brand has achieved impact. However, weak translation of awareness to trial (36%) suggests a weak selling message, and poor conversion from trial to regular usage (33%) indicates softness in the brand proposition. Awareness to trial conversion among women is very low.

## (h) Rasputin IDQV (among 16–34 age-group) (Table 144)

| Measure: | Maximum score | Rasputin | Competitor |
|---|---|---|---|
| Impact | 35 | 18 | 32 |
| Differentiation | 30 | 17 | 17 |
| Quality | 15 | 10 | 12 |
| Value | 20 | 16 | 14 |
| Brand strength | 100 | 61 | 75 |

**Conclusions:**
1. Rasputin's lowish impact is due partly to awareness level, partly to limited distribution, especially in pubs.
2. Major competitor is not strongly differentiated and Rasputin has an opportunity to score here.
3. Rasputin has an excellent product, which wins on consumer blind test, but its packaging and image are inferior to competition, which reduces its quality score. It scores well on value because it is lower priced.

## (i) Rasputin Brand Positioning Statement (BPS) (Table 145)

| Brand Name | Rasputin |
|---|---|
| Market description | Vodka |
| Target audience | C1C2D class males, aged 16–40 |
| Brand discriminator | Brash, 'in your face' style |
| Core consumer proposition | Stylish and designed for youth |
| Brand differentiators | Product quality, bottle shape and colour |
| Brand personality | Young, light-hearted, humorous, brash irreverent |

*One-line summary:*
*Rasputin is the modern brand for successful young people who don't take life too seriously.*

**Conclusions:**
- Brand discriminator, consumer proposition, and differentiators all too general, and need strengthening in marketing plan. BPS can then be modified and improved. 16–40 age group too wide.

## (j) Brand scorecard (Table 146)

This is a more elaborate version of IDQV.

| Criteria | Maximum score | Rasputin score | Competitor score | Comment on Rasputin score |
|---|---|---|---|---|
| 1. Brand profitability | 12 | 6 | 11 | *Heavy investment* |
| 2. Relative consumer value | 8 | 6 | 5 | *See IDQV* |
| 3. Relative brand share and trend | 12 | 5 | 10 | *Declining No. 2 brand* |
| 4. Market sector position | 6 | 5 | 5 | *Strong in young, CD* |
| 5. Sales level and trend | 8 | 4 | 7 | *Declining* |
| 6. Differentiation | 10 | 6 | 6 | *See IDQV* |
| 7. Distribution and trade strength | 9 | 4 | 8 | *Weak* |
| 8. Innovation record | 6 | 3 | 4 | *Average* |
| 9. Future potential (plans, extendibility) | 9 | 6 | 5 | *Good* |
| 10. Awareness and loyalty | 6 | 3 | 5 | *See IDQV* |
| 11. Investment support (advertising, R & D, etc) | 7 | 3 | 4 | *Recent cutback* |
| 12. Heritage | 7 | 4 | 6 | *New brand* |
| TOTAL | 100 | 55 | 76 | – |

*Note:* Criteria are similar to earlier Birds Eye example on p. 259, with 'Heritage' added. Maximum scores differ from Birds Eye because markets are different.

**Comments:**

Rasputin score at 55% is reasonable for No. 2 brand, but major competitor score at 76% is very strong. Main areas on which to focus Rasputin improvement are differentiation, distribution and investment support. These will drive brand share and sales trends.

## (k)  Rasputin customer loyalty check (Table 147)

| | |
|---|---|
| Rasputin loyalty level (%)[7] | 36% |
| Industry average on loyalty (%) | 39% |
| Rasputin loyalty trend v. last year | Down |
| Profile of loyal Rasputin customers | 16–24 CD |
| Annual gross profit value of loyal Rasputin customer (£) | £35 |
| Lifetime profit value (£)[8] | £175 |
| % of total sales from Rasputin 'loyals' | 60% |
| % of total Rasputin marketing spend on 'loyals' | 30% |

**Key conclusion:**
Rasputin spending too much trying to recruit new users, not enough on holding and rewarding loyals. Database Marketing has been weakly exploited to date.

## (l)  Topline competitor review (Turgenev)

- Key strategies of major competitor are development of new vodka mixer products, and premium higher-alcohol vodkas, as line extensions.
- Major competitor strengths are strong market position, international brand advantages, innovation skills and strong long-term commitment to brand building.
- Main competitor weaknesses are lack of local flexibility, retail trade suspicion of its high share, possible complacency and probably lowish priority ranking of UK market, compared with faster growing countries.

## (m)  Key factors for success in UK vodka market

- Brand positioning.
- Differentiation.
- Level and quality of Marketing support.

## (n) Rasputin Swot analysis (brief version) (Table 148)

### Table 148. Rasputin strengths, weaknesses, opportunities and threats.

**Strengths:**
1. Superior product taste when mixed with juices or soft drinks.
2. Lowest cost of goods due to new plant, high operating efficiencies.
3. Most flexible manufacturing process, able to handle medium runs efficiently.
4. Cult brand in nightclubs, and 'Youngs' bars, like Yates.
5. Disproportionate strength among 16–34 age-group, C1C2 class.
6. Superior trade marketing skills due to skilful young accounts team.
7. Vodka specialists – Vodka is Petrograd plc's only business.
8. Indications that Rasputin name and image has potential.

**Weaknesses:**
1. Lower profit levels than competition, due to investment spending.
2. Weak among AB class, over-40 age-group.
3. Inferior product for shorter drinks like Bloody Marys.
4. Weak in Scotland.
5. Lack of long-term heritage.
6. Inconsistent advertising proposition, lack of powerful campaign message.
7. Packaging distinctive, but unattractive to some target consumers.
8. Weak standing among women, turned off by brash image.

**Opportunities:**
1. More, stronger advertising.
2. Change in media spend mix – more TV, direct mail, narrow-cast media.
3. Develop event marketing strategies, programmes, using soft drink models.
4. Test raising price, as advertising and packaging strengthened.
5. Radically strengthen packaging, while retaining differentiation.
6. Focus more single-mindedly on 18–28, C1C2 class, the key users and opinion-formers.
7. Use clear focus to establish trade position as differentiated No. 2 brand, and build distribution, space.
8. Develop joint promotions with Levi and Coca-Cola.
9. Target 'opinion forming' locations for 'Youngs' – nightclubs, selected bars, new retail and leisure parks, 'young' and trendy pubs.
10. Build up environmental credentials, via packaging, links with Greenpeace.
11. Select high-impact, high-image areas for sponsorship – e.g. bungee jumping, white water rafting – and link to event marketing.
12. Test new brand or line extension tailored to Scotland.
13. Cut spend on new customer activity, invest more on loyals.
14. Improve consumer understanding by undertaking market segmentation study.

**Threats:**
1. Higher priority to UK market by major competitor.
2. Over-35-year-old vodka drinkers may graduate to other drinks.
3. New taxes by government.
4. Fashion swing away from vodka by young people.
5. Continuing growth of store private label.
6. Loss of Rasputin key account distribution.
7. Future unwillingness by Petrograd to invest fully in Rasputin 'turnaround' programme.

## STEP 2:  FUTURE THINKING

- Rasputin UK will closely follow the overall strategy established by Petrograd plc (see page 314 above).
- Rasputin's vision in the UK is to become the leading brand among 18–28 CDs by 2005, and vodka market leader by 2020. The brand will stand for irreverent fun and excitement.
- Rasputin will be viewed by its customers as concerned and active both on environmental topics and campaigning issues, and in encouraging responsible use of alcohol among young people.

## STEP 3:  OPPORTUNITY IDENTIFICATION

This would be a half-page section prioritizing the top ten opportunities. The opportunities developed for the SWOT analysis would be used as a starting-point. Further ideas would then be developed in a workshop with the Extended Brand Group, using idea generation techniques. These would be prioritized and listed into a Top 10.

## STEP 4:  SET OBJECTIVES

**Table 149.  Rasputin objectives.**

|  | This year | Next year | 3 years hence |
|---|---|---|---|
| Total vodka market (m litres) | 41.0 | 41.5 | 42.5 |
| Rasputin market share (%) | 9.5 | 10.3 | 11.5 |
| Rasputin revenue (£ m) | 29.5 | 33.5 | 39.7 |
| Rasputin media (£ m) | 1.0 | 2.1 | 2.5 |
| Rasputin profits (£ m) | 4.0 | 4.5 | 6.0 |

*Additional objectives:*

1. Rasputin also has an innovation objective, aiming to generate 12% of revenue three years hence in products not yet launched, and to develop the most distinctive and attractive packaging of any spirits brand.
2. Rasputin has an awareness objective – to raise spontaneous brand awareness among target group from 25% now to 35% in three years' time.

## STEP 5: BUILD STRATEGIES

Key Rasputin strategies for meeting brand objectives are:

(a) **Overall**. Target the brand much more single-mindedly against 18–28-year-old C1C2 consumers, both male and female, and build on cult brand status in nightclubs, 'youngs' bars. Through a combination of powerful and distinctive advertising and media selection, and attractive eye-catching packaging, build trade distribution and consumer sales to achieve brand leadership among the target group in five years' time. Retain loyalty among this group as they grow older, and sustain dominance among 18–28-year-olds, for long-term brand leadership.

(b) **Product packaging**. Further improve upon product superiority in long drinks, and develop distinctive and preferred packaging among target group, with better environmental properties.

(c) **Pricing value**. The strategy is to narrow price differential versus the brand leader from 15% lower at present to 5% lower in three years' time, by moving price up gradually as brand proposition strengthens.

(d) **Communication**. Convince target audience that Rasputin is a warm, fun brand that makes the best long drinks and is radically different in style. Use media which generate coverage and impact, and cultivate Rasputin's irreverent and campaigning image – likely to be combination of TV, cinema, editorial, interactive and specialist youth publications. Posters will not be used, since these are dominated by major competitor. Direct marketing and original, low-cost sponsorship, plus event marketing and campaigning, will be the key elements of the communication strategy.

(e) **Distribution**. Strategy will be to achieve mass distribution in grocery multiples and off-licences by positioning Rasputin as a clearly differentiated No. 2 brand, enabling retailers to stock Turgenev, Rasputin and private label. The company's superior skills in trade marketing will be used to maximize space and visibility.

   In the 'on licence' trade, saturation distribution and high-impact merchandising will be achieved in all nightclubs, 'young' pubs and theme restaurants frequented by the target group.

(f) **Brand development.** Capitalizing on Petrograd's skills in flexible mass production, the potential for a Rasputin positioning (product, packaging, advertising) tailored to Scotland will be researched and tested. The opportunity for a proposition appealing to females in the target group will also be investigated, and tested both as a Rasputin line extension and as a new brand.

In the medium term, no work will be done on flavoured vodkas and higher-alcohol premium products, although a ready-mixed line extension may be tested.

(g) **Sales promotion** will focus on creating high in-store merchandising impact and rewarding loyal Rasputin customers, to encourage word-of-mouth recommendation and peer-group usage. Wherever possible, it will be combined with sponsorship activity, event marketing and direct marketing.

(h) **Internal Marketing.** Rasputin brand will implement Petrograd's policy of strong internal marketing by establishing an Extended Brand Group; making bi-monthly presentations to Operations; setting up an instant access IT system with updated on-line brand and market information available to every employee; and establishing cross-departmental development projects, especially on marketing value analysis.

It will also contribute material to Petrograd's interactive internal TV channel, and actively participate in the programme to rotate people between Sales, Marketing and Operations.

Petrograd employees, in all departments, will be given the opportunity for involvement in Rasputin's campaigning activities for Greenpeace and other selected causes.

(i) **Profitability.** Strategy is to achieve 15–16% profit as a percentage of sales, and 18–20% ROCE. This higher ROCE will be achieved by high capacity utilization, efficient operation and tight control of working capital. In order to invest to recover sales momentum, a lower than targeted return on sales has been approved for the next two years.

## STEP 6: DEVELOP PLANS

Plans comprise two sections – key activities next year and development plans covering one to three years. For the sake of brevity, this step will focus on illustrating the former, though longer-term plans are briefly covered under the 'profitability' heading.

## (a) Key activities next year

**Packaging**. Subject to successful technical and consumer testing, launch the new triangular bottle, with labels on all three sides, and a new transparent glass/plastic material for easy disposal, in period 8. Advantages for consumer are instant recognition, distinctiveness and environmental pluses. Advantages for retailers are lighter bottles, elimination of breakage and more efficient use of space because triangular bottles nest together on shelf.

**Pricing**. Increase price to trade by 5%, in period 8, when new bottle is launched.

**Communication**. Adopt an overall campaign strategy of 'Rasputin – radically different'. Tight targeting of 18–28-year-old C1C2 consumers. Key steps to be developed with advertising, direct marketing, media and sales promotions agency are:

- Agreement to integrated communications strategy, covering all areas.
- Translation of this integrated strategy into broadcast, narrowcast advertising, direct marketing, sponsorship, campaigning, event marketing and other sales promotion.
- Initial development of high-impact broadcast campaign, achieving top quartile scores for on-strategy, persuasion and brand name recall on pre-testing.
- Translation of this into other media and activities.

Plan is to hold back all media spend until period 8, when a four-month continuous campaign will be run from September to Christmas.

On sponsorship, Rasputin will research possibilities among current loyal consumers, checking their interest areas, personalities and musicians most admired and causes supported. Based on this, Rasputin will commit to vigorous support of one major charity (e.g. Greenpeace, Friends of the Earth, League against Cruel Sports), and one competitive activity (e.g. bungee jumping, white water rafting). Also emerging from this research will be the Rasputin Musician of the Year and Rasputin Most Admired (outrageous?) Personality of the Year. These events will be extensively publicized, and winners used to endorse Rasputin in advertising.

**Distribution**. The Rasputin relaunch plan of new packaging and communications will be presented to major multiples in period 2, and the rest of the trade in period 4 to 5. Aim will be to raise weighted distribution from 45% currently to 60% by year end, and 70% by end of next year. Visibility and space will be increased by space management and efficient consumer response (ECR) programmes, and through exciting displays developed for each trade class, except grocery multiples (where they won't be accepted). Special display and music packages will be developed for nightclubs and trendy 'youngs' bars, visited by opinion-formers. Much higher priority will be given to pubs visited by younger people.

**Database marketing**. Rasputin's currently weak database will be radically increased and updated, working closely with the Nicolai II brand group. Means for achieving this are being developed, but aim is to achieve direct coverage of 50% of 18–28-year-old vodka users and 40% of all vodka users by end of next year; increasing to 80% and 65% by the end of the following year.

Options will include sharing lists with companies or brands with similar profiles (e.g. lager, jeans or soft drinks companies), exploiting lifestyle databases like National Shoppers Survey, use of retailer, pub or nightclub lists, and development of own list through sales promotion. Significant funds have been allocated to direct marketing for the future, including geodemographic activity.

**Brand development**. See below, under development activities.

**Market research**. A major market and trade channel segmentation study will be undertaken in period 1, results available period 3. Objectives are to identify a distinctive new needs or benefits-based approach to market segmentation; to link market and channel segments for more effective trade marketing; to identify potential for a brand or line extension targeted at women; to check different usage and mixer habits, especially in Scotland; and to refine understanding of differences in needs by demographic group, plus strengths and weaknesses of the Rasputin brand.

**Sales promotion**. Joint promotions will be run with Coca-Cola and Levi 501. Promotions will link in to Rasputin's Musician of the Year, Personality of the Year and sponsored activities.

**Internal marketing**. Extended Brand Group has already been established, with half-day workshops scheduled for periods 1, 3 and 5, focusing on the period 8 relaunch. Rasputin Brand will publish a two-page informal newsletter monthly to all employees, focusing on business progress, future plans and campaigning activities. The instant-access IT system available to every employee will be in place for all company brands by period 6. The cross-departmental marketing value analysis group has already met, and set a £500K targeted cost saving for Rasputin next year.

**Profitability**. Gross margin will be increased from XX to XXX next year due to higher capacity utilization, savings on the new bottle, price increase of 5% in period 8 and £500K targeted savings from value analysis.

**Table 150. Development projects over one year: summary.**

| Project | Cost £K | Key milestones |
|---|---|---|
| 1. Improved taste for long drinks | 85 | Month 6 – product test<br>Month 15 – in production |
| 2. New mixer vodka | 200 | Month 10 – product test<br>Month 15 – test market<br>Month 24 – national |
| 3. Female targeted product ⎫<br>4. Product for Scotland ⎭ | 100<br>90 | Month 3 – research available<br>Month 8 – product test<br>Month 12 – final test<br>Month 18 – national |

**Table 151. Milestone summary (next six quarters).**

| Qtr | Product/pack | Advertising | Pricing | Promotion |
|---|---|---|---|---|
| 1 | | Clubs and pubs | | Coca-Cola Bungee Jump |
| 2 | | Speciality youth media | | Levi 501 Musician of the Year |
| 3 | New pack | New campaign | +5% | Relaunch Direct Marketing |
| 4 | | ▼ | | Rasputin Personality of the Year |
| 5 | Taste | | | Greenpeace Direct Marketing |
| 6 | Female product | ▼ | + 5% | |

**Table 152. Investment spending summary.**

| Spend area | Cost £K next year | Resulting additional gross profit £K | |
|---|---|---|---|
| | | Next year | Year after next |
| R & D | 475 | – | 3,000 |
| Capital expenditure | 400 | 200 | 200 |
| Broadcast media | 1,225 | 1,000 | 1,200 |
| Narrowcast media | 300 | 200 | 250 |
| Direct marketing | 400 | 250 | 250 |
| Sponsorship | 200 | – | – |
| Campaigning | 200 | – | – |
| Internal marketing | 50 | – | – |
| Market research | 250 | – | – |
| TOTAL | 3,500 | 1,650 | 4,900 |

**Comments:**

1. R & D gross profit of £3000K is from new products.
2. Additional gross profit on media spend higher the year after next, due to late start of advertising next year (September) and carryover effect into following full year.
3. Additional gross profit from other areas too speculative to quantify.
4. Sales promotion spend is not included above, and all activity will pay out immediately.

## STEP 7: MONITOR RESULTS

**Table 153. Monitor results.**

| Key activity | How to monitor | When | By whom |
|---|---|---|---|
| Media | Share, tracking, econometrics | Period 12 | Brand Manager |
| Direct Marketing | Cost per response, and conversion rate v. annual profit value | Periods 6 and 12 | Brand Manager |
| Period 8 brand relaunch | Awareness, market share, distribution, sales, profits | Period 12 | Brand Manager |
| Sponsorship | Involvement and coverage | Periods 3 and 8 | Assistant Brand Manager |

| Key activity | How to monitor | When | By whom |
|---|---|---|---|
| Campaigning | Involvement and coverage | Periods 3 and 8 | Assistant Brand Manager |
| Internal Marketing | Cross-departmental involvement | Periods 3, 8, 12 | Human Resource Director |
| Market research | Action taken | Period 6 | Marketing Director |
| Development projects | Monthly review | Monthly | Marketing Director |
| Budget performance | Monthly sales, profits | Monthly | Brand Manager |

## Closing Comments on Marketing Planning

Key points to note about this practical example of a brand marketing plan are:

- The initial list of hypotheses, regularly updated, helps you focus on action at an early stage, and makes the business analysis quicker and more effective.
- By the time you have completed the business and SWOT analyses, you should have a reasonably clear idea as to how you will develop winning strategies. If not, your business analysis has been too superficial.
- Output of SWOT analysis should highlight at least 50% of future opportunities. Aim to double these during opportunity identification process.
- Your level of ambition on objectives will be influenced both by future vision, and quality of the list of prioritized opportunities.
- If you have winning strategies, strong plans should emerge.
- A comprehensive and effective brand plan should not exceed ten pages. Of this, at least four to five pages should be devoted to strategies and plans – the action part of the document. Details should be relegated to exhibits. My excuse for the fourteen-page length of the Rasputin vodka marketing plan is that these pages are smaller than A4.

Marketing and brand plans are important blueprint documents for a company and deserve close scrutiny *across* departments. Copies of the brand plan should be sent to the Marketing Director, Sales Director, Extended Brand Group and Category Director at least two weeks prior to a half or full day meeting to review, improve and approve the plan.

# FLOW-CHART SUMMARY OF CHAPTER 8

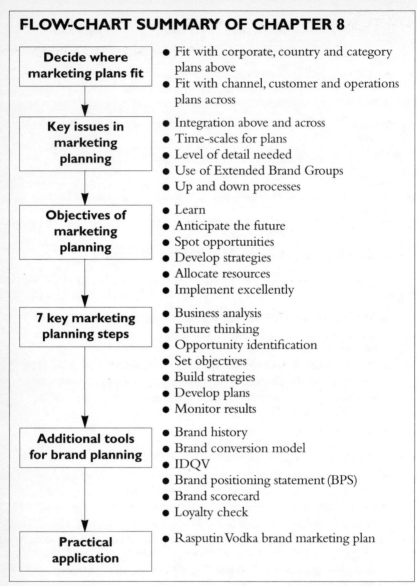

| | |
|---|---|
| **Decide where marketing plans fit** | • Fit with corporate, country and category plans above<br>• Fit with channel, customer and operations plans across |
| **Key issues in marketing planning** | • Integration above and across<br>• Time-scales for plans<br>• Level of detail needed<br>• Use of Extended Brand Groups<br>• Up and down processes |
| **Objectives of marketing planning** | • Learn<br>• Anticipate the future<br>• Spot opportunities<br>• Develop strategies<br>• Allocate resources<br>• Implement excellently |
| **7 key marketing planning steps** | • Business analysis<br>• Future thinking<br>• Opportunity identification<br>• Set objectives<br>• Build strategies<br>• Develop plans<br>• Monitor results |
| **Additional tools for brand planning** | • Brand history<br>• Brand conversion model<br>• IDQV<br>• Brand positioning statement (BPS)<br>• Brand scorecard<br>• Loyalty check |
| **Practical application** | • Rasputin Vodka brand marketing plan |

# EXECUTION

## Summary of Chapters 9–15

The final seven chapters will cover the 'E' of P-O-I-S-E, – *Effective Execution.*

**Table 154.**

| | |
|---|---|
| **P:** *Profitable* | ● *Proper balance between firm's needs for profit and customer's need for value* |
| **O:** *Offensive* | ● *Must lead market, take risks and make competitors followers* |
| **I:** *Integrated* | ● *Marketing approach must permeate whole company* |
| **S:** *Strategic* | ● *Probing analysis leading to a winning strategy* |
| **E:** *Effectively Executed* | ● *Strong and disciplined execution on a daily basis* |

A potentially winning strategy can be made to look mediocre by weak execution. And a parity strategy can become very competitive through outstanding implementation.

The seven areas covered are all essential to effective execution of winning strategies. They are:

- **Chapter 9: Offensive Segmentation**. This chapter describes segmentation and outlines a five-step process for applying it. Segmentation strategy should be developed on a cross-departmental basis, not in a hole in the corner of the marketing department.
- **Chapter 10: Offensive Brand Development.** Existing brands are a valuable asset for most companies, and need to be fully exploited. New brands are necessary to exploit opportunities not accessible to existing ones.
- **Chapter 11: Offensive New Product and Service Development.** Innovative, superior and distinctive products and services are often the most powerful fuel for driving brands forward, and for achieving sustainable competitive advantage.
- **Chapter 12: Offensive Communication** is the means to persuade and convince consumers and buyers of the advantages of brands, products and services, whether established or new. It has itself entered a phase of rapid change, where strength of core advertising proposition, selection from the growing choice of media, and ability to tailor messages to different audiences all need to be well handled.
- **Chapter 13: Offensive Market Research** provides an essential intelligence system to help identify opportunities, screen and develop them and monitor Offensive Marketing performance.
- **Chapter 14: Offensive Pricing,** together with quality and brand positioning, determines consumer value. And superior value is the most compelling reason to buy. For reasons of space, sales promotion is not addressed in a separate chapter, but there are a number of good specialist books on this topic.
- **Chapter 15: Offensive Channel Marketing**. In many industries, distribution channels are changing faster than consumers. Understanding and exploiting channels often with tailored propositions, sometimes with different brands, is an increasingly important part of Offensive Marketing.

# 9. Offensive Segmentation

## Chapter Summary

Segmentation involves subdividing markets, channels or customers into groups with different needs, and meeting these needs more precisely with a targeted proposition.

Markets are becoming increasingly more segmented as techniques of flexible mass production make it possible to meet a range of needs economically, and specialized media targets consumer groups more tightly. But the driving force behind segmentation is the growing desire of consumers for individualized products and services at reasonable prices.

Companies have to balance the benefits of segmentation against the pitfalls of fragmentation, where consumers are offered too wide a range of similar propositions. This can result in consumer confusion, and unproductive extra costs.

Offensive segmentation is forward looking and uses future vision. It aims to develop a distinctive and practical approach to segmentation. However, the topic is potentially so complex that it can lead to madness. The purpose is to be simple but not simplistic.

There is a **five-step process** for developing segmentation strategies, on a cross-departmental team basis:

1. **Identify what to segment.** Markets, channels, customers and products or services can all be segmented. It is important at the outset clearly to define the entity you plan to segment, and to delineate its boundaries.
2. **Establish a master matrix.** This will help you to see the wood for the trees. It will consist of three or four important segments, within which consumer or customer needs differ widely.
3. **Develop alternate types of segment.** In doing this, consider the eight main types of consumer and customer segmentation. They are physical characteristics, geographical area, demographics, usage, benefit areas, price and payment method, behavioural and characteristics of related products.

   Using existing market information, and adding to it with any new segmentation research needed, develop a long-list of potential market segments. Wherever possible, estimate their size, likely future trend and rough profitability.

4. **Evaluate segment attractiveness.** Establish criteria for evaluating the attractiveness of segments and their fit with your assets and competencies. Use the quantified portfolio analysis (see *Chapters 2 and 7*) to do this, and produce a short-list of priority segments.

5. **Finalize segment strategies and priorities.** Determine strategy on degree of sector specialization, and prioritize your final short-list of segments, being realistic about the level of total resources likely to be available to exploit them.

## Principles of Market Segmentation

Segmentation involves subdividing markets, channels or customers into groups with different needs, to deliver tailored propositions which meet these needs more precisely.

Segmentation is most often applied to **markets**, but it is equally relevant to **distribution channels** or **customers**. Because similar principles apply to segmenting all three, this chapter will concentrate on **markets**.

The word 'market' is used to describe total revenue spent on broadly similar products or services. So the 'market' for dog products in the UK is worth about £800 million at retail selling prices. Everyone knows what a dog product is. Having a total market figure is useful to manufacturers and retailers, and enables them to read their market share.

However, every market can be divided into scores of segments. It is easy to identify some of those frequently used by dog-food marketers, such as:

- **Product types**. Moist, semi-moist, dry, mixers, treats, biscuits, individual pieces in gravy, plus dog accessories such as dog collars.
- **Product varieties.** Tripe, chicken, turkey, beef heart and so on.
- **Packaging types**. Cans, bags, boxes, with differing opening devices.
- **Dog type**. Large or small.
- **Demographics**. Rural or urban, age, income level, with and without children.
- **High-value users**. Heavy users, breeders, vets.
- **Attitudes of pet ownership**. Attitudes vary widely. A pet may be treated as a human companion by an elderly lady, as a fashion accessory by a country-house owner, as an educational toy by parents with young children.

It is evident that the possible segments are almost endless, though not as many as the 5 million dog owners in the UK. In one study, Clancy and Shulman broke down a market 8,515 ways.[1] You could further analyse the dog-product market by breed or age of dog. However, the frustrating thing about the vast majority of these breakdowns is that most sub-markets have rather similar needs – it is unlikely, for example, that dog-food needs will differ much between Alsatians, Labradors, or red setters.

A **sub-market** only becomes a segment if its members have significantly different needs from the average. That is why very few sub-markets turn out to be segments. Genuine segments are of high interest to marketers, especially if they are newly discovered, since products or services tailored to their particular needs will deliver superior customer experiences.

There is usually a trade-off between the opportunities provided by segmentation and the economics of mass production. Companies targeting a number of segments will usually have higher costs per product or brand than those with mass-market products. To justify this, they need to achieve higher prices for their segmented offers.

Ford pioneered mass production in 1908, 'the concept of a static car model at the lowest price'.[2] General Motors and, specifically, Alfred Sloan, invented systematic market segmentation:

> **In the early 1920s, Ford's volume share of the American car market was a massive 60%, achieved with the low-priced Model T, and the high-priced Lincoln. General Motors with only 12% had nine models and seven brands, but did not compete in the low-price sector dominated by Ford.**
>
> **By the mid 1920s, General Motors had divided the total market into a number of price segments, and established five price/quality sectors, each covered by a brand (Figure 54).**

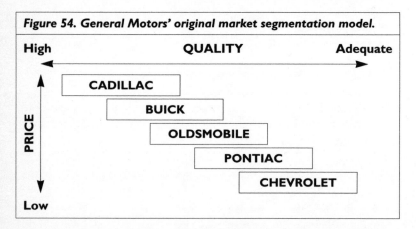

*Figure 54. General Motors' original market segmentation model.*

> **General Motors cars were usually positioned towards the top of each price segment, so as to compete on quality with lower-priced cars, and on price with cars in the segment above. General Motors' objective was both to compete in a targeted way across the whole market and to trade consumers up the GM brand range, in stages,**

over a lifetime. By the 1930s, General Motors' market share had grown to over 40% and its price/quality approach to market segmentation continued for many decades.[3]

Unfortunately, GM failed to sustain the differentiation of this early segmentation model. Chevrolet lost its clear identity, while Buick, Oldsmobile and Pontiac were pushed into the centre of the market, with similar price bands. The launch of the distinctive low-price Saturn range came much too late, and many opportunities were missed. 'With the exception of Saturn and Cadillac, they are all back in the middle, trying to be everything to everyone.'[4]

Over the past century, there has been a trend from customization, through mass production, towards micro-segmentation and, perhaps eventually, back to customization.

**Table 155. Market characteristics and drivers: 1900–2020.**

| Period | Market characteristics | Production characteristics | Consumer power | Type of media |
|--------|-----------------------|---------------------------|----------------|---------------|
| 1900 | Customized | Customized | Low | Print |
| 1920 | Mass | Mass production | Medium | Print |
| 1970 | Segmented | Diversified mass production | Medium | TV, print |
| 2000 | Micro segments | Flexible production | High | Targeted |
| 2020 | Mass customization | Individualized production | Very high | Highly targeted, and interactive |

As Table 155 shows, there are three important factors driving markets towards greater segmentation:

● *Production characteristics.*
● *Consumer power.*
● *Media development.*

In some industries, flexible manufacturing techniques can produce diverse ranges very economically. Consumers have increased their bargaining power in a world full of spare capacity, and can insist on more individualized products and services. Media has become very targeted and particular interest groups can now be reached easily through specialist TV channels or magazines.

Segmentation is also being driven by two other factors not included in Table 155:

- The trend towards global marketing and multi-country production – **a segment may be small in a single country, but if it can be tapped in half a dozen, from a single production site, it can be met economically on a scale equating to local mass production**.
- The desire of companies to trade up average unit price paid by consumers or customers – **many markets today are static in volume, but revenue can be built by identifying and exploiting higher priced product segments**.

## What are the Practical Applications of Market Segmentation?

There are three distinct applications – segment prioritization, discovering new segments to exploit and gaining incremental business through understanding of market segments. Successfully applied, segmentation can build both sales and profits, and is a potential source of major competitive advantage.

### 1. Segment prioritization

This follows similar principles to market prioritization, covered in Chapter 2 (pages 84–8). Just as companies select markets on which to focus, so they need to decide *which* segments within each market to compete in. They may wish to compete in every conceivable sector, as Honda does in the Japanese motor-cycle market. However, they are more likely to be selective and to only compete strongly in attractive segments which fit their skills. So, Harley-Davidson concentrates single-mindedly on large, expensive, high-performance motor cycles.

If you don't carefully segment a market, decide which to be in and which not to be in, and tailor exact propositions to each segment, you will probably end up 'in the middle', offering a generalized product or service which fails to meet the needs of any segment. Such untargeted products are usually forced to compete on price, to counter their limited appeal.

### 2. Identifying new market segments

The opportunity to discover new market segments is always exciting to marketing people. Success can open the door to new products, often at premium prices, and incremental sales. Starbuck's coffee in the USA tapped this potential when it targeted the sophisticated consumer:

> **Starbuck's Coffee Company is a chain of coffee shops which opened in Seattle in 1971. In the past five years, revenue has increased from $65 million to $700 million, and the number of outlets from 116 to 1,004.**
>
> **Per capita consumption of coffee in the USA has been falling since the mid 1960s, but in the past ten years gourmet coffee sales have grown from 10% to 20% of total sales, influenced by the success of Starbuck's.**
>
> **Starbuck's saw potential in the sophisticated consumer. This segment was defined as people who are health conscious, like to travel and identify with gourmets. It accounted for 18% of all consumers (Starbuck's 1992 prospectus).**
>
> **Starbuck's objective is to become the largest speciality coffee roaster and retailer in the USA. The sophisticated consumer was targeted with a differentiated proposition, through company-owned coffee shops which provided:**
>
> - **Superior coffee at a premium price. High-quality beans are grown at high altitude, roasted slowly and protected from air throughout production.**
> - **Stylish and elegant cafés – 'a cultured refuge from everyday hassles'.**
> - **Excellent customer service.**
>
> **The reward for identifying and developing the gourmet coffee segment is a cult brand with a loyal following – the average Starbuck's customer visits eighteen times a month, and 10 per cent do so twice a day.**[5]

Another company to identify a new segment was Fuji, the photo film company. 'Quicksnap' was the first single-use disposable camera:

> **The idea for the single-use camera originated from qualitative Fuji market research in USA, UK and Japan. It addressed the segment of consumers who were concerned about dropping or losing expensive cameras in outdoor locations.**
>
> **Fuji developed a camera which cost under $10, was pocketable, portable and disposable, and took good pictures.**

In practice, the new camera addressed a much wider segment than that originally envisaged. It could be taken anywhere without risk, and expanded the opportunity to take pictures on impulse. Ease of use also appealed to inexperienced photographers, especially teenagers and older people.

Fuji's 'Quicksnap' was a big success in Japan, and soon accounted for 20% of its film sales, mostly incremental. Unfortunately for Fuji, though, Kodak, using a crash-action new product programme, beat it to the punch in the USA, with a single-use camera called 'Funsaver', which also expanded the total film market.[6]

## 3. Understanding segments as a means of building incremental revenue and profits

Many new products cannibalize sales of existing products. They not only fail to build **incremental** business, but also weaken current products. A primary reason for this is weak understanding of market segments and how they interact.

New products should capitalize on brand strengths, but, as much as possible, target different segments from existing products, like Gillette, Starbuck's and Nivea:

Gillette's primary interest is in the higher-price 'systems' segment of the razor market, rather than disposables. This is partly because the profit on a systems cartridge refill is around three times higher than on disposables, partly because Gillette is more skilful at competing on quality and positioning rather than on price and convenience. It is represented in both market segments, with Gillette Sensor on systems razors and Gillette Good News on disposables. Following the launch of Sensor in the USA, total market volume share accounted for by disposables fell from 52% to 40% and market value accelerated.[7]

Gillette therefore used Sensor not only to build brand share, but also to develop the most attractive segment. Following the success of Sensor, Gillette then extended the brand into a new segment, with Sensor for Women. Sales, which were totally incremental, exceeded $40 million in the first six months, way above expectation.[8]

★

Starbuck's has line-extended the brand *incrementally* by targeting new distribution channels and related product categories. It has launched Starbuck's coffee ice-cream, together with Dreyers, who make and distribute to super-markets; Frappuccino low-fat coffee drink in a bottle, distributed by PepsiCo; Double Black Stout, a coffee laced with beer. Starbuck's is also test Marketing brand-ed whole roast coffee beans in supermarkets.

Not all of these initiatives will likely succeed in the long term, but due to careful selection of channel and market segments, those that do will generate *incremental* sales.[9]

★

Nivea segments the facial-products market in Germany primarily by age-group. Its market leading Nivea Visage range, with a 17% share of the $700 million category, is targeted at younger women.

A range aimed at women over 50 – Nivea Vital – com-prises night and day creams, and a regenerating concen-trate. It has built a new sector, and gained a 5% market share, mainly incremental.

Nivea is now considering a facial range aimed at 40–50-year-old women, who have different attitudes, needs and expectations, compared with the over-50s.[10]

As was shown in the previous chapter, a strong understanding of segmentation is also essential in constructing the optimum product range, which covers your target segments effectively at minimum cost and without unnecessary product or service overlap.

## Pitfalls to Avoid

### 1. Fragmentation

The distance between successful segmentation and wasteful fragmenta-tion is short. Fragmentation consists of breaking a market down into so many sub-segments that consumers become confused, retail distribution is difficult to maintain and large diseconomies of marketing and production are incurred.

Fragmentation often occurs when companies seek to repeat the results they or their competitors achieved by early segmentation. They tend to focus on very fine differences, which are frequently of little importance to any group of consumers.

Unit and investment trusts are one example – the customer has a choice of over 2,000 products, and, unsurprisingly, is thoroughly confused.

## 2.  The 'majority fallacy'

The fact that a prospective new product or service, on research, loses out to the market leader does not mean that it will be unsuccessful, as long as it is distinctive and appeals strongly to a worthwhile segment of consumers. So if two very different products are being compared, strength of preference should be checked and carefully evaluated.

For example, in a head-to-head preference test among sports-car enthusiasts, the Morgan might lose out heavily to an equivalent priced MG. Nevertheless, among those preferring the Morgan, strength of preference would probably be high, giving the car a viable following.

## Offensive Segmentation Approach

The principles of segmentation can be applied to products, services, channels, customers and consumers.

The offensive approach to segmentation has a number of characteristics.

### Forward-looking

Segmentation will affect tomorrow's allocation of resources and development priorities. In line with Chapter 6 ('Developing a Distinctive View of the Future'), any segmentation model should anticipate the likely situation three to five years hence.

### Practical

Segmentation must be actionable. The segment target should be clearly identifiable, capable of measurement and of being reached efficiently by media or sales people.

**For example, a segmentation study of business buyers categorized them into democratic, autocratic, deal-minded and pragmatic in buying style. The research revealed very different attitudes towards product quality, price and**

**service among these groups, identifying genuine segments with real exploitation potential. Unfortunately, however, it proved impossible to pin-point these different buyer types in practice, and no action was feasible or taken.**

## Distinctive

Developing distinctive segmentations requires both realism and creativity. There are no 'correct' answers, as in mathematics, and the secret of effective segmentation is to keep an open mind as to the possibilities. Most markets or channels can be segmented in a wide variety of ways, and new ways to segment will always be discovered over time. A combination of deep knowledge of consumer or customer behaviour plus a good measure of creativity is most likely to uncover distinctive approaches to segmentation.

## Manageable

It is quite easy to construct a segmentation model so complex that it confuses rather than enlightens. To avoid this, a master matrix should be established at an early stage. This aims to identify three or four important segments, where needs vary widely between consumers or customers. More detailed segmentation can then be related to the three or four major segments within the master matrix.

For example, in air travel there are numerous segmentations, but three key ones, which would feature in any master matrix – journey length, cabin class and purpose of travel (Table 156).

**Table 156. Airline travel: segmentation master matrix.**

| Key segments | Difference in requirements within segments |
| --- | --- |
| Journey length | Comfort and service levels differ by length of haul |
| Cabin class | Customer expectations differ by cabin class |
| Purpose of travel | Business and leisure travellers have different criteria and needs |

Within each key segment there are many sub-segments. For example, meal, seating and entertainment requirements may vary widely by journey length. To state the obvious, a flight from Tokyo to London would require different seat types, food, service levels and staff language skills, compared with a short-haul flight within Europe.

## Interlinked

Understanding the linkages between segments can generate new insights and reveal new sub-segments. For example, the three master matrix airline segments are closely interlinked.

By linking purpose of travel to cabin class on the London–Tokyo route, you can create sub-segments. How many can you develop from Table 157 below?

| Table 157. London–Tokyo by air: example of segmentation. |

| Travel purpose | Cabin class by purpose | European business people | Japanese business people |
|---|---|---|---|
| BUSINESS → | PREMIUM | PREMIUM | PREMIUM |
| | ECONOMY | ECONOMY | ECONOMY |
| LEISURE → | PREMIUM | **Conclusions:** | |
| | ECONOMY | 1. London–Tokyo is primarily a leisure route. | |
| | | 2. A small minority of leisure travellers buy premium class. | |
| | | 3. A majority of business travellers book economy class. | |
| | | 4. Most European business travellers fly premium class, while most Japanese business people fly economy class. | |

In this example, for the sake of clarity, we have combined first and business class into a single heading – business class.

You can see that among business travellers, Japanese and Europeans comprise distinct sub-segments: Japanese business people are much more inclined to travel economy, expect high-service levels, prefer Japanese airline staff and have different food preferences compared to Europeans. How far is it economic to offer them a distinctive customer proposition? This is the kind of issue raised by interlinking of segments. Table 158 lists possible sub-segments generated from Table 157.

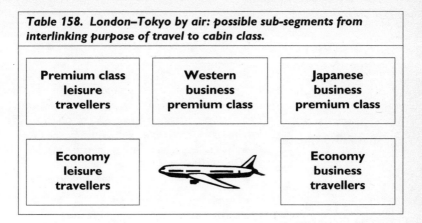

**Table 158.** *London–Tokyo by air: possible sub-segments from interlinking purpose of travel to cabin class.*

You may well ask what action can be taken from this analysis. Possibilities include:

- Develop special marketing packages for premium class leisure travellers.
- Creation of new cabin class to satisfy needs of full fare economy business travellers, who travel in economy but have different needs from leisure travellers.
- Increase proportion of Japanese cabin crew to raise service levels and language skills for Japanese travellers.
- Change mix of European versus Japanese food.

### Quantifiable

For each segment, it should be possible to estimate size, future trend, profitability and competitive structure, in order to prioritize relative importance.

## Offensive Segmentation Process

The offensive segmentation approach can be translated into a five-step process, which should result in a distinctive and creative approach to segmentation, and the identification of priority segments. These can then be exploited by brand extensions, new brands and acquisitions or alliances, while the totality can be used as a basis for reviewing and improving product and service-range strategy.

The five-step process is summarized in Table 159, and reviewed step by step through the remainder of this chapter.

**Table 159. Five-step process for offensive segmentation.**

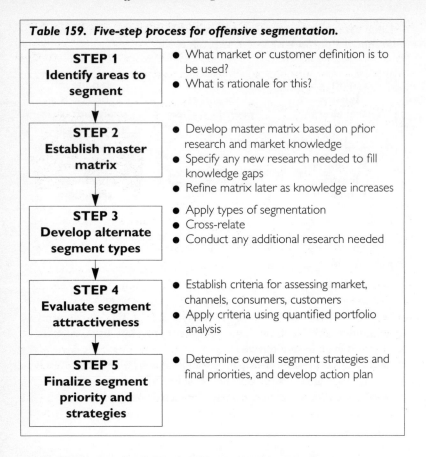

| | |
|---|---|
| **STEP 1**<br>**Identify areas to segment** | ● What market or customer definition is to be used?<br>● What is rationale for this? |
| **STEP 2**<br>**Establish master matrix** | ● Develop master matrix based on prior research and market knowledge<br>● Specify any new research needed to fill knowledge gaps<br>● Refine matrix later as knowledge increases |
| **STEP 3**<br>**Develop alternate segment types** | ● Apply types of segmentation<br>● Cross-relate<br>● Conduct any additional research needed |
| **STEP 4**<br>**Evaluate segment attractiveness** | ● Establish criteria for assessing market, channels, consumers, customers<br>● Apply criteria using quantified portfolio analysis |
| **STEP 5**<br>**Finalize segment priority and strategies** | ● Determine overall segment strategies and final priorities, and develop action plan |

## Who should be involved in the segmentation process?

It is important to execute this process on a cross-departmental basis, both to tap expertise and to gain broad commitment within the company to the results.

How a company decides to segment its markets is a very important decision, with fundamental impact on where to compete and where not to; on product range; on allocation of resources; and on R & D priorities, to name just a few implications. It therefore affects everyone in the company.

While the process should be cross-departmental, and certainly not something done in splendid professional isolation by the Marketing Department, care should be taken not to select too large a team. Every member of the segmentation team should have a specific role, responsibility and expected contribution to make.

Make-up of the ideal team will depend on the type of company, and the nature of the segmentation exercise to be undertaken. For example, a channel segmentation team in a financial services company would involve a different group of people from a customer segmentation team in a computer hardware company.

Any team is likely to include people from Marketing, Market Research, Sales, Customer Service and Finance. The reason for the presence of the first four is obvious – they are all customer facing, and will have a contribution to make to any segmentation study, whether it is directed at markets, channels or customers. A  high-calibre representative from Finance, experienced in activity costing, is also essential, to help size the segments and establish their current and future profitability.

The critical input areas in developing segmentation strategies are knowledge of consumers, customers, distributors, competitors and costs. It is likely to be worthwhile involving someone from Operations, and you should ensure that the team members from customer-facing departments really do have first-hand knowledge of customers. For instance, it is preferable to involve a tele-sales supervisor rather than her administrative boss, and a field sales person rather than an office-bound sales coordinator.

Who should lead the teams? In the case of market or customer segmentation, probably a marketing person; for channel segmentation, a sales manager.

In setting up the segment strategy team, normal team guidelines would apply:

- Team members would be selected by the team leader in consultation with department heads.
- Project objectives, monthly milestones, tasks and timetables would be agreed by team members, and signed off by their department heads.
- A process for handling the project would be agreed.
- Each team member would be given individual objectives and tasks to be monitored at each team meeting. These would be incorporated within their total job objectives, and included in the annual appraisal.
- Once the segmentation strategy was agreed by the team, it would be presented to the Board for comment and commitment to the required course of action.

How long is this process likely to take? Much longer than you think, if it is to be conducted rigorously and to high standards. At least six months if additional market research is required; three to four months if it is not.

Like every other aspect of Offensive Marketing, segmentation strategy and implementation should be continuously improved. The fact that you have just completed a massive segmentation exercise is not a reason for shelving the issue for three years until it needs updating. Segmentation methods should be reviewed at least once a year, during the annual marketing planning process and whenever there are any significant changes in market circumstances.

## STEP 1:  IDENTIFY AREAS TO SEGMENT

What definition do you use in your segmentation process? This is important to determine, because otherwise you may spend time segmenting the wrong market or customer group.

In the airline business, it is much too limiting to focus on the time spent on the plane, or even the period from airport entry to airport exit. Viewing the total journey experience from door to door is more relevant. This approach has enabled airlines to identify and satisfy new needs, like Fast Track security clearance, and arrival lounges with clean-up facilities at journey's end for business class passengers. Airlines also need to know what leisure passengers do at journey's end – are they staying with friends or relatives, constructing their own travel packages or roughing it? What are their accommodation, car rental and information needs, and how do these segment by journey length and purpose of travel? Understanding and satisfying these needs can lead to higher customer loyalty, greater differentiation for the airline and additional services.

Determining how widely or narrowly to define markets requires skilled judgement. For the purpose of segmentation, it is best to focus on markets which are direct and indirect substitutes for your own, but within your distribution channels. For instance, if you competed in frozen pizza, you would include frozen and chilled pizza in your segmentation exercise, since they are both stocked by supermarkets. You would briefly look at restaurant, fast-food pizzas and home-delivered pizza, but not segment them in detail.

Imagine yourself as Marketing Director of Coca-Cola, about to undertake a segmentation study of a major country. How would you *define* the market to segment, and where would you draw the line, among the categories in Figure 55?

**Figure 55. Coca-Cola: definition of market to segment – where to draw the line?**

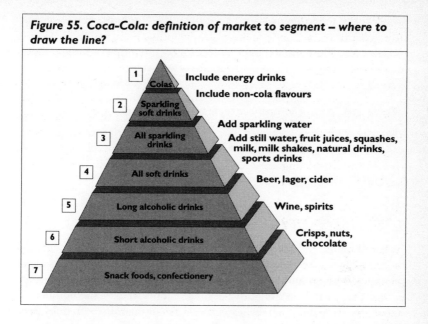

All these categories compete with Coca-Cola, some much more directly than others. For manageability it would be practical to draw the line under either level 3 or level 4. These markets would be segmented in detail. Levels 5 and 6 would be covered briefly. Snack foods and confectionery would probably not be segmented, although Coca-Cola would bear in mind their importance both as accompaniments to soft drinks and as indirect competitors for the consumer's money.

However, it would be quite feasible to take a more radical approach, and include tap water for drinking as a competitor, which Coca-Cola in fact does.

## STEP 2: ESTABLISH MASTER MATRIX

In the complex jungle of segmentation, the master matrix helps you see the wood for the trees.

Your master matrix should be relatively simple, though not simplistic. It should consist of the top three or four segments **within which consumer needs differ widely**. A segment may be very important to consumers, but if it is equally important to everyone, it provides no basis for segmentation and is therefore of little interest to a segmenter. For example, in chilled foods freshness is very important as a customer benefit, but is strongly desired by everyone, whether you divide them by age, income level, frequency of shopping, ethnic group, region or any other classification.

Table 160 illustrates a master matrix for segmenting the motor insurance market into three master segments – age, vehicle type and driving record.

**Table 160. Motor insurance: segmentation master matrix.**

| Master segments | Examples of segmentation | |
|---|---|---|
| | Grey | Young |
| Age (years) | 50–60 | 16–20 |
| Vehicle type | 5-year-old Honda | New coupé |
| Driving record | Excellent | Bad |

While there are many other ways to segment and sub-segment the motor insurance market – like purpose of use, location, medical history, number of drivers and life stage – the three in the table are key ones. It is clear that even with only three segmentation variables, the number of sub-segments which can be carved out are numerous and only two rather extreme examples have been given in the table.

Working out a master matrix is important, not only to provide clarity, but also to guide you on the information needed about customers. It will also enable you to decide whether you already have enough internal and external data, to carry out a convincing segmentation process, or whether more data is needed to fill gaps.

The master matrix can usually be constructed using existing market research and knowledge, even if you have not conducted a specific segmentation study previously. As your knowledge base builds, the master matrix can be refined and developed.

## STEP 3: DEVELOP ALTERNATE SEGMENT TYPES

You already know that segmentation is a creative process and one of the most exciting areas of marketing practice. Your aim is to develop a distinctive approach to markets, channels and customers.

While you should know how your competitors segment, it is wise to avoid adopting industry norms. Companies using similar approaches to market segmentation often crowd into previously attractive segments and rapidly make them unattractive.

In undertaking a segmentation exercise, it is useful to have a checklist of types of segmentation. This can never be exhaustive, since skilful marketers will always think of new ones. The remainder of this section provides a comprehensive check-list covering consumers, buyers or customers and channels.[11] As usual, consumers will be covered in detail, customers on a more summary basis. Channel segmentation will be reviewed later in Chapter 15.

## Types of Consumer Segmentation (within Step 3)

There are eight main types, as in Table 161.

| Table 161. Eight main types of consumer segmentation. | |
|---|---|
| 1. **Physical characteristics** | 6. **Financial factors, including pricing** |
| 2. **Geographical area** | **bands** |
| 3. **Demographics** | 7. **Consumer (buyer) behaviour** |
| 4. **Usage characteristics** | 8. **Characteristics of related products** |
| 5. **Benefit areas** | |

Each of these eight will now be reviewed in turn.

### 1. Physical characteristics

These cover anything you can see, feel or smell about a product or service. They include product, packaging, size, variety; and, in the case of services, literature, plastic cards and physical elements like cashpoints. Examples in this section will utilize two very different types of market – bathrooms and business documents. Table 162 summarizes.

| Table 162. Market segmentation: examples of physical characteristics. | | |
|---|---|---|
| **Bathrooms** | | **Business documents** |
| Size | Basin | Paper-based |
| Colour | Shower | Electronic-based |
| Shape | Toilet/bidet | Colour variants |
| Layout/design | Furniture | Document design |
| Tap types | Add-ons | |
| Bath | | |

Bathrooms have many physical characteristics, documents fewer.

### 2. Geographical area

This segmentation method is used to cover straightforward issues like region, urban/rural, and town size. The development of geodemographics has widened segmentation modes, driven by companies like CACI (Acorn) and CCN (Mosaic). Geodemographics is 'the analysis of people by where they live', or, a snappier alternative, 'locality marketing'.[12]

The main source of geodemographic data is the government census, but this may be supplemented by credit information, electoral rolls or specific market research.

At least six geodemographic neighbourhood classification systems are in use in the UK, with between forty and a hundred segmentation variables. An address's postal code attaches it to the appropriate neighbourhood classification, and this in turn can be linked to consumer data or sales-territory analyses.[13]

A customer profile for a fictional mid-price hotel chain is shown in Table 163, using four of the sixty ACORN neighbourhood classifications.

**Table 163.  Customer profile – mid-price hotel chain, using four ACORN segments.**

| Neighbourhood type | % of UK population | % hotel brand users | Mid-price hotel index |
|---|---|---|---|
| Wealthy suburbs, large detached houses | 2.6 | 7.5 | 288 |
| Villages with wealthy commuters | 3.2 | 10.0 | 313 |
| Mature, established home owning areas | 3.3 | 2.8 | 85 |
| Council areas, young families, some home owners | 3.0 | 0.4 | 13 |

In this example the level of usage of mid-price hotels is over twenty times higher in wealthy commuter villages than in council areas.

Geodemographics are valuable in providing much more precise market segmentation than conventional demographics. Their main drawback is the age of the census data on which they are based – this can be over ten years old.

## 3. Demographics

We have defined demographics very broadly, to include personal characteristics and lifestyle of consumers, as well as the conventional breakdowns. Examples are given in Table 164.

**Table 164. Examples of demographics, personal characteristics, lifestyle.**

| Demographics | Personal characteristics | Lifestyle |
|---|---|---|
| Age | Height | Make of car |
| Social class | Weight | Annual mileage |
| Income level | Clothing size | Age of car |
| Sex | Skin type | Leisure activities |
| Family status | Hair colour | Credit cards used |
| Working status | Hair type | Health/slimming |
| Education | Bust size | Ownership of durables |
| Ethnic origin | Foot size | TV programmes watched |
| Household size | Medical conditions | Holidays and travel |
| With/without children | Oral health | Money and investments |
| Type of home | Fitness level | Pets |
| Education | Hearing/eyesight | Home details |

The vast majority of this data is factual, and can be collected from a variety of sources. There are many useful government publications, including the annual *Social Trends Survey*,[14] which is a bible for Marketing people.

Lifestyle data is collected by a number of specialist companies, such as Computerized Marketing Technologies (CMT) and International Communications and Data (ICD). Each regularly mails out lifestyle questionnaires in large volumes. This data is used primarily for direct marketing to tightly identified market segments.[15]

Relevance of this type of data varies widely by industry. **Demographics** provide key segments for most businesses: quite small age differences among children are critical to toy and snack-food marketers, while in nightclubs the 16–20 age-group has different needs from the 21–25 age-group. **Personal characteristics** matter a lot in industries like haircare, clothing, medicines and footwear. And **lifestyle** can be important, although it is difficult to define, measure and target, except through databased marketing.

Another form of segmentation related to demographics is **psychographics**. This is concerned with people's attitudes and beliefs. Examples of psychographic groups are need-driven, outer-directed and inner-directed people.

Psychographics have been around since the 1960s. While advertisers have found them valuable in determining advertising positionings – for instance, targeting a headache remedy to *confident* medicine users – marketers often struggle with the difficulty of applying psychographics in practice. 'Having identified a psychographic group, it is very difficult to find its constituent members "on the ground".'[16]

## 4. Usage characteristics

The main usage sub-segments are place, purpose, time and occasion of use. The potential variety of usage segments can be most easily demonstrated by example, again using bathrooms and documents (Table 165).

**Table 165. Examples of types of usage characteristic.**

| Type of usage | Bathrooms | Documents |
|---|---|---|
| Place | In home<br>Out of home<br>(Hotels, holidays) | Large offices<br>Small offices<br>Homes<br>Multi location |
| Purpose | Relaxation<br>Hygiene | Information<br>Decision-making<br>Communication |
| Time | Morning<br>Evening | 24 hours a day |
| Occasion | Routine<br>Special event | Mainly weekday |

In documents, multi-location offices can be treated as a different segment from single locations, through use of office network systems.

A classic example of market segmentation by usage area is Kit Kat, which doubles as a piece of confectionery and as a chocolate biscuit. The four-finger large bar is positioned mainly as indulgent confectionery, for out-of-home usage, while the two-finger bar is sold in multi-packs primarily for in-home and lunch-box usage.

## 5. Benefit areas

This provides one of the most promising opportunities for distinctive segmentation. Benefit areas change over time and new ones can emerge or be discovered. For example, aspirins used to be taken mainly to combat head pain, but are now used regularly by many people as a counter to heart disease. Table 166 illustrates benefit areas in bathrooms and business documents.

**Table 166. Examples of market segmentation by benefit area.**

| Bathrooms | Documents | |
|---|---|---|
| ● Pleasure | ● Simplify information flow | ● Speed of production |
| ● Decorative | ● Organize data | ● Design and colour |
| ● Enhances house value | ● Ease of use | ● Just-in-time systems |
| ● Impresses others | ● Impact in presentation | ● Select key data |
| ● Functional | | |
| ● Relaxation | | |

Xerox focuses on three main customer benefits:

- Make documents *better* – ease of use, just-in-time, reliability, networks
- Make *better* documents – colour, design
- Work *better* with documents – simplify information flow[17]

## 6. Financial factors, including pricing bands

This consumer segmentation covers who pays, how to pay, and how much.

'Who pays', the company or the individual, is an important segmentation method in the airline business, since it fundamentally affects price elasticity. And where does the small business or self-employed person fit in? For them the dividing-line between business and personal spending can be imprecise. 'Who pays' also affects segmentation in the car market – companies were slow to grasp the growing influence of working women who bought their own cars.

'How to pay' can be a segmentation issue in retailing, or high ticket consumer products and services. Extended credit and instalment payment can be useful marketing tools.

In most markets, 'how much' or price-band segmentation is especially important. The General Motors' price-based model, illustrated in Figure 52, is a classic early example of this. **What are the main price bands in your market, and what is your competitive position in each?**

Table 167 shows a fictional example of price-band segmentation in the mail-order clothing market. Market pricing has been broken down into seven price bands, based on market research – how many bands to use, and how to bracket them, is a matter of judgement. The figures for Catalogue A and Catalogue B reflect actual sales by price band. **What do you conclude from this price segmentation table?**

**Table 167. Mail-order clothing: price band segmentation.**

| Price band (£) | Revenue by price band (%) | | |
| --- | --- | --- | --- |
| | Total mail-order market | Catalogue A | Catalogue B |
| Over £80 | 3 | 6 | 2 |
| £60–£80 | 7 | 9 | 6 |
| £50–£60 | 9 | 12 | 9 |
| £40–£50 | 15 | 13 | 16 |
| £30–£40 | 31 | 15 | 33 |
| £20–£30 | 20 | 25 | 19 |
| Under £20 | 15 | 20 | 15 |
| TOTAL | 100% | 100% | 100% |

You will have noticed that Catalogue A's performance is eccentric. It is overachieving in the two bottom and three top price bands, but doing relatively badly in two large price bands between £30 and £50. There are four possible reasons for this underperformance – too few items offered between £30 and £50, poor value of those offered, supply problems or weak on-page presentation. By learning from price-band segmentation, Catalogue A can strengthen its future product offer.

## 7. Consumer (buyer) behaviour

This method of segmentation centres around what buyers actually do rather than who they are or what they think. It is very relevant to customer relationship marketing. There are four main questions to ask:

- What is the consumer's usage status – current user, non-user, lapsed user?
- Who are the loyal consumers?
- Where are the heavy users?
- What priority should be given to existing loyal consumers versus potential new users?

All these questions are issues of segmentation.

Figure 56 is an illustrative brand usage map.

This chart should be read across. It shows that 20% of the target buyer universe is currently using your brand – current users are the base for evaluating usage level and loyalty level.

The usage level section of the chart indicates that heavy users of the category account for 60% of brand volume. Heavy usage needs to be defined. Does ten, twenty or thirty pints a week constitute heavy usage of beer?

**Figure 56. Brand segmentation – usage map.**

| Usage status | % of target buyer universe | | | | |
|---|---|---|---|---|---|
| | Current user (20%) | Recently lapsed (10%) | Long past lapsed (20%) | Never used (50%) | → 100% |

| Usage level | % of total brand revenue | | | | | | | | | |
|---|---|---|---|---|---|---|---|---|---|---|
| | Heavy users (60% of total revenue) | | | Average users (25%) | | | Light users (15%) | | | → 100% |
| **Loyalty level** | High (40%) | Med. (14%) | Low (6%) | High (15%) | Med. (7%) | Low (3%) | High (8%) | Med. (4%) | Low (3%) | → 100% |

The third level of the brand usage map covers consumer loyalty levels. The currency here is your brand's share of total category purchases made by each consumer. If s/he buys fifteen packs of toothpaste in a year, and chooses your brand ten times, your 'share of customer' is high at 67%, and this consumer would be classified as high in loyalty to your brand.

Share of customer levels have to be defined by market – if your brand is a children's breakfast cereal, a 25% share of customer might rank as 'high' loyalty, because cereals are bought on a portfolio basis from a repertoire of brands – people might have five or six in their kitchen cupboards.

You will already have absorbed the major learning about your brand from this chart, namely:

- Current user base is strong at 20%.
- Heavy users account for 60% of brand volume. This looks quite good, but is it higher or lower than for other brands?
- Sixty-three per cent of revenue is accounted for by highly loyal users, most of them (40%) in the heavy category.[18]

**So, what action could you take based on the brand usage map?**

Here are some possible action steps:

- Focus on high-loyalty heavy users (40% of your total revenue), and aim to convert medium-loyalty heavy users (14% of revenue), up to high.

- Target recently lapsed heavy users and try to bring them back into the fold. Your main problem will be to identify who they are and how to reach them.
- Identify why 50% of consumers have never used the brand. Is the reason awareness, availability, lethargy or attitude? What are the likely costs of converting this group, and what, in particular, is the rationale of heavy users for not using your brand?

An important usage segmentation issue for marketers is how best to allocate resources between existing customers and new ones. Every marketer knows that £1 spent on an existing customer is likely to produce a better return than £1 spent on new customer prospecting. This is obvious, and has already been covered in earlier chapters, since to gain a new consumer you may have to invest in awareness, access and sales resource . . . and, in the end, may fail to make a sale.

Any business, however efficient, is always losing consumers, and needs at least to replace them. Table 168 summarizes issues that have to be resolved in determining relative investment priority between the two big usage segments of existing and new consumers

**Table 168. Segment priority issues: existing versus new consumers.**

| Existing consumer | New consumer |
|---|---|
| • What is relative profitability of each type of existing consumer?<br>• How does it compare with profit on new consumers, in short-term, long-term?<br>• What are opportunities for increasing share of existing consumer's purchases in your category?<br>• What is scope for increasing total category purchases among your consumers?<br>• What new categories or products can you sell to existing consumers? | • Which are the most profitable types of new consumer?<br>• What are the key reasons for non purchase and how strong are they?<br>• What is likely cost of gaining a new consumer, what is payback period, and what is life-time value?<br>• What are your company or brand growth targets?<br>• How far will existing consumers take you? |

## 8. Characteristics of related products

This has already been covered in Chapter 5, page 191. Changes in household fashions or paints fundamentally affect colour and design of baths. Outerwear fashions strongly influence the underwear women wish to buy. And innovations in washing-machine technology or performance will impact the kind of detergents needed.

This completes the review of the eight types of **consumer** segmentation. Types of **buyer** or customer segmentation are briefly covered in Exhibit 1 at the end of this chapter. This is of particular relevance to readers operating in business-to-business markets or through buyers and distributors.

Step 3 in the six-step segmentation process – 'Develop Alternate Segment Types' – is easily the most time-consuming, and is now completed (Table 169). You will now be able to segment your markets, brands and customers into a long-list of segments and, where necessary, cross-relate these into sub-segments. In completing this process you may decide to specify extra research to fill knowledge gaps or to undertake a segmentation study.

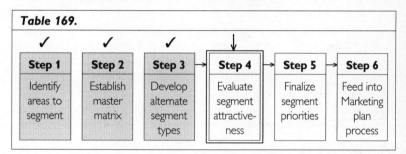

**Table 169.**

| Step 1 | Step 2 | Step 3 | Step 4 | Step 5 | Step 6 |
|--------|--------|--------|--------|--------|--------|
| Identify areas to segment | Establish master matrix | Develop alternate segment types | Evaluate segment attractive-ness | Finalize segment priorities | Feed into Marketing plan process |

## STEP 4: EVALUATE SEGMENT ATTRACTIVENESS

You now have the raw material of a long-list of possible segments to consider. You are spoilt for choice. Your next decision is to prioritize them – to decide which ones you plan to invest in and develop, which to compete strongly in and which to exit or ignore. This is where the Marketing Alignment Process (MAP) and the Quantified Portfolio Analysis (QPA) again come in useful.

Using the QPA, you will be able to construct your list of segment attractiveness criteria, develop a quantified scoring system and score each segment. The same quantified approach can be used to evaluate the fit of your assets and competencies with each segment; if your competencies are mainly in premium-price niche marketing, they will fit poorly with an attractive and large low-priced segment.

The main criteria for prioritizing segment attractiveness will always include:

- Ability to quantify the size of the segment.
- Ability to identify and reach the people in the segment.
- Segment size and future trend.

- Likely future profitability.
- Competitive structure.
- Segment fit with your assets and competencies.

The shaded triangle in the portfolio analysis in Figure 57 is the area in which you will seek to focus and invest. The ideal is highly attractive segments closely aligned to your assets and competencies. These take time and effort to find, and in practice you may have to settle for less in the short term. This will result in a portfolio chart similar to the one in the figure, where each segment fits into one of the nine boxes . . . more or less.

**Figure 57. Typical segment evaluation portfolio analysis.**

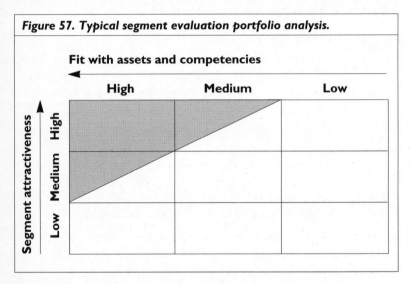

## STEP 5:  ESTABLISH FINAL SEGMENT PRIORITIES AND STRATEGIES

You now have a short-list of segments which are attractive and fit with your assets and competencies. These will be candidates for possible future investment. In practice, you may not have the resources to exploit all of them at once, so a further selection process may be necessary. Equally, you will have discovered or confirmed that a number of segments you currently compete in either look unattractive in the future or fail to fit well with the competencies you plan to develop in the years ahead. Decisions will have to be taken on whether to milk, mothball, exit or sell out of such segments.

The final prioritization stage is a good time to consider the main types of segment strategy available to you, and how well each fits with your competencies and future vision. Two of the main strategic issues in segmentation are degree of specialization and level of differentiation.

Companies have the option of competing broadly or narrowly by market, channel or country. Five of the more widely used segment strategies are those in Table 170.

## Segment Strategy (within Step 5)

### *Degree of specialization*

---

**Table 170. Alternate levels of segment specialization.**

- Single market segment
- Single channel segment
- Multi market segment
- Product segment focus across many markets
- Full market coverage

---

These alternative degrees of segment specialization can be illustrated by reference to the car and engine market (Table 171).

---

**Table 171. Segment specialization in automobile and engines market.**

| | |
|---|---|
| **Porsche** | ● Single market segment, high-priced sports cars |
| **Daewoo** | ● Single channel segment, direct to consumer |
| **Mercedes** | ● Multi-market segment, mid- to top-priced cars, mini vans, etc. |
| **Honda** | ● Product segment focus across many markets. Petrol engines in cars, motor cycles, lawnmowers, boats |
| **Ford** | ● Full market coverage, competes in all market segments |

---

Figure 58 is a portfolio analysis blank on degree of segment specialization. Where does your company or brand fit on this, and how many boxes are covered?

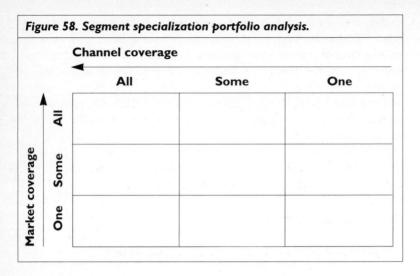

**Figure 58. Segment specialization portfolio analysis.**

## Level of differentiation

Market segment theory distinguishes between a **mass** strategy, where one product covers a very large market, and **differentiated** strategy, where a number of products are targeted at specific segments. The model T Ford is usually given as an example of 'mass strategy' and petrol is a modern market also following this approach, with little differentiation. Toys and watches are examples of markets following a differentiated segment strategy.

'Mass' strategy usually involves high volume, low prices, and 'me-too' product or service design. The basis of competition will probably be price, and to succeed you need to be a low-cost operator. This type of strategy is falling out of favour, due to low margins, vulnerability to price attack, consumer desire for variety and the development of flexible mass production.

Table 172 gives examples of mass and differentiated consumer segments.

**Table 172. Consumer markets: examples of mass and differentiated approach to segmentation.**

| Mass (limited differentiation) | Differentiated |
|---|---|
| ● Cheddar cheese | ● Bottled water |
| ● Petrol | ● Skincare products |
| ● Milk | ● Toys |
| ● Vegetables | ● Magazines |
| ● Car rental | ● Sports trainers |
| ● Motor insurance | ● Confectionery |

Two of the most interesting contrasts are petrol and bottled water. Petrol has been very poorly marketed to consumers as a mass undifferentiated commodity for decades, and the entry of effective low-cost operators like Tesco and Sainsbury has placed enormous pricing pressure on the petrol majors. Bottled water, on the other hand, has been skilfully marketed: the various brands are differentiated, have distinctive image and packaging, and command a price many hundred times that of tap water.

Even relatively 'mass' markets also have segments. You can buy four grades of ordinary frozen peas, various sizes like petit pois, flavours like minted or peas mixed with rice, peas frozen within two and a half hours of picking (Birds Eye Garden Peas) and so on.

## Final Segment Prioritization (within Step 5)

Having determined your strategies on degree of segment prioritization and level of differentiation, you are ready to prioritize the short-list of segments you have developed. Segmentation needs to be done in a descending hierarchy. The Marketing Director would be responsible for recommending the company's overall segmentation approach and the priority to be given to alternative markets in consultation with other Board members. Marketing Managers would break markets and customers down into segments, and the Sales Director would segment channels and major accounts, in consultation with other departments, as in Figure 59.

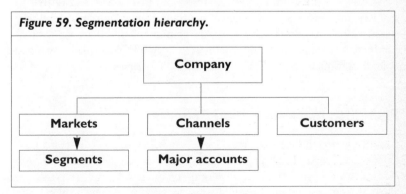

**Figure 59. Segmentation hierarchy.**

A fictional segmentation priority portfolio for a company applying a multi-market but not full coverage approach to over-the-counter medicines could be as in Figure 60.

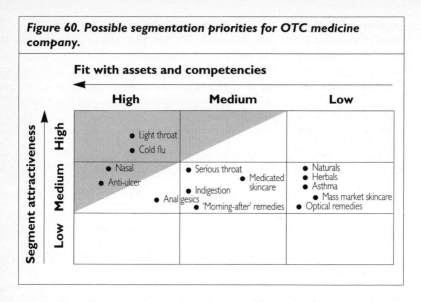

**Figure 60. Possible segmentation priorities for OTC medicine company.**

This particular company is likely to prioritize allocation of capital expenditure, R & D and Marketing funds on light throat, cold/flu, nasal, serious throat and anti-ulcer markets. It will need to consider carefully how much priority analgesics, and medicated skincare deserve, and what can be afforded in the context of other higher priority demands on resources.

Specific markets like light throat or cold/flu would then be re-segmented, and focused segment priorities determined within them.

Finally, channels would be segmented and prioritized, and related to priority markets. For example, in many European countries, grocery supermarkets and drug discounters are primary channels for light throat products – lozenges, medicated confectionery and such like – whereas cold/flu products are sold mainly through pharmacies.

## Feed into Marketing Plan Process

Once segments have been prioritized, detailed strategies and plans have to be developed. High-priority segments can be exploited through extension of existing brands, development of new brands, acquisitions, alliances and new country entry. Decisions need to be taken on how to allocate development resources – R & D, advertising, promotion and capex – between high-priority segments, where you plan to increase market share, and mid-priority segments, where the objective is to hold market share. And plans to maximize profits, exit or sell brands in low-priority sectors have to be worked out and executed.

## Check Your Score for Offensive Segmentation

Here in Table 173 is your opportunity to evaluate how good a job your company, or one you know, is doing on segmentation.

| Table 173. Check your score for offensive segmentation. | 'Yes' score: | Your company's score |
|---|---|---|
| ● Do you have a clear definition of your total market? | 5 | |
| ● Do you understand how segments differ from sub-markets? | 5 | |
| ● Have you developed a simple master matrix, covering the most important 3 or 4 segments? | 8 | |
| ● Do you know the size, trend and profitability of your master segments? | 8 | |
| ● Using the 8 main types of segmentation, have you identified and sized all relevant segments in the market? | 10 | |
| ● Is your method of segmentation different from that of competitors? | 8 | |
| ● Have you identified and exploited any new segments in last 5 years? | 8 | |
| ● Have you prioritized segments for attractiveness? | 12 | |
| ● Do you implement a clear investment strategy for each priority segment? | 10 | |
| ● In past 5 years what % of your new product revenue has been incremental? | 10 | |
| ● Do you segment distribution channels as well as markets? | 8 | |
| ● Does your 5 or 3 year corporate strategy have an impressive section on segmentation, and is it implemented? | 8 | |
| TOTAL | 100 | |

# FLOW-CHART SUMMARY OF CHAPTER 9

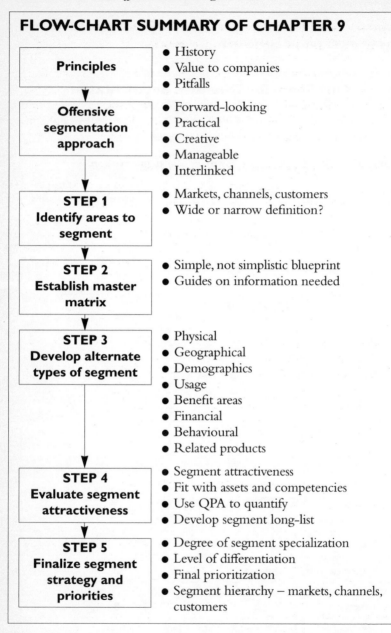

| | |
|---|---|
| **Principles** | • History<br>• Value to companies<br>• Pitfalls |
| **Offensive segmentation approach** | • Forward-looking<br>• Practical<br>• Creative<br>• Manageable<br>• Interlinked |
| **STEP 1 Identify areas to segment** | • Markets, channels, customers<br>• Wide or narrow definition? |
| **STEP 2 Establish master matrix** | • Simple, not simplistic blueprint<br>• Guides on information needed |
| **STEP 3 Develop alternate types of segment** | • Physical<br>• Geographical<br>• Demographics<br>• Usage<br>• Benefit areas<br>• Financial<br>• Behavioural<br>• Related products |
| **STEP 4 Evaluate segment attractiveness** | • Segment attractiveness<br>• Fit with assets and competencies<br>• Use QPA to quantify<br>• Develop segment long-list |
| **STEP 5 Finalize segment strategy and priorities** | • Degree of segment specialization<br>• Level of differentiation<br>• Final prioritization<br>• Segment hierarchy – markets, channels, customers |

## Buyer or Customer Segmentation

**Exhibit 1**

Any market is likely to have marketers who sell, customers who buy and consumers who use the product or service. Customers are usually buyers with specialist knowledge, working to agreed specifications and purchasing in high volume. Table A gives examples of three different types of customer – airlines, retailers and manufacturers:

**Table A. Examples of marketers, buyers, users.**

| Marketer (develops and sells) | Buyer (buys for external or internal consumers) | User (uses product or service) |
|---|---|---|
| Boeing | World airlines (e.g. BA) | Pilots, engineers, cabin staff, passengers |
| Nestlé | Retailers or wholesalers (e.g. Sainsbury) | Mass-market consumers |
| SKF Bearings | Corporate purchasing managers (e.g. GEC) | Production Managers, machine operators |

Users may be external and paying, or internal and company employees. For example, pilots and airline cabin staff are as much consumers or users of planes as the paying passengers. If cabin staff are dissatisfied with safety, ease of internal movement and location of galleys, their morale and efficiency will be affected and the paying consumer will suffer.

The eight types of **consumer** segmentation outlined in the text (page 353 onwards) also apply to **buyers**, but have different subsegments, as in Table B.

**Table B. Eight main types of buyer segmentation.**

| 8 main segment types | Applications/sub-segments |
|---|---|
| 1. Physical characteristics | As for consumers, but specification based for buyers. Includes design, size, colour, material. |
| 2. Geographical area | As for consumers. Includes regions, and countries. May be sales territory based. |
| 3. Demographics | ● Customer size<br>● Sales trend<br>● Industry type, seasonality, stability, profitability |
| 4. Usage characteristics | As for consumers – place, purpose, time and occasion of use. |

| 8 main segment types | Applications/sub-segments |
|---|---|
| 5. Benefit areas | As for consumers. Examples are speed, safety, reliability, economy in use, flexibility, longevity, service levels, after sales service, training packages, warranties, guarantees and technical service. |
| 6. Financial factors | As for consumers – who pays, how to pay, and how much. This covers terms, discounts, credit, advertising or promotion support, instalments and pricing levels. |
| 7. Buyer behaviour | As for consumers. Existing, lapsed or new customers? Loyal v. promiscuous? Attitudes to price v. quality and service. |
| 8. Characteristics of related products | • Bearings have to be related to machines in which they will be used. (SKF)<br>• Planes have to be related to runways, and airport space, storage. (Boeing) |

As an illustration, these eight segment types will be applied on judgement to Boeing world-wide in Table C.

**Table C. Application to Boeing of eight main types of customer segmentation.**

| 8 main segment types | Application to Boeing | |
|---|---|---|
| 1. Physical characteristics | • Design<br>• Capacity | • Configuration<br>• Size |
| 2. Geographical area | • World-wide | • Country and local priorities |
| 3. Demographics | • Customer size<br>• Future growth plans. | • Current plane inventory |
| 4. Usage characteristics | • Customer route structure<br>• Haul lengths | • Business/leisure passenger mix<br>• Customer logistical skills |
| 5. Benefit areas | • Fuel consumption<br>• Reliability, safety, ease of operation<br>• Flexibility in use and configuration (e.g. rapid seat changes)<br>• Resale value | • Speed of delivery<br>• Level of tailoring needed by customer<br>• Passenger capacity<br>• Appeal to cabin staff<br>• After sales service<br>• Training packages |

| 8 main segment types | Application to Boeing |
|---|---|
| 6. Financial factors | ● Price levels          ● Trade-in or swap deals<br>● Payment method and timing |
| 7. Buyer behaviour | ● Balance between large existing customers in West, and fast-growing new customers in East, especially China |
| 8. Characteristics of related products | ● Airport facilities – runways, maintenance, space<br>● Air-traffic control systems<br>● Future fuel outlook. |

Business-to-business marketers face many of the same segmentation issues as consumer marketers, such as:

● How many market sectors should we aim to cover, and with what products?
● Which geographical segments should we prioritize?
● Which types of customer do we target?
● Which benefit areas do we concentrate on delivering best? How far do we tailor benefits to niche requirements, and what are the economic effects of this?
● What are the alternate price levels and payment systems, how do they segment and which provide the best mix between cost and buyer or consumer benefit?
● What type of buyer should we target?
● How may changes in characteristics of related products affect future segmentation?

# 10. Offensive Brand Development

## Chapter Summary

'Offensive Brand Development' is the second chapter under 'E' for **Effective Execution**.

| Table 174. | |
|---|---|
| **P:** Profitable | ● Proper balance between firm's needs for profit and customer's need for value |
| **O:** Offensive | ● Must lead market, take risks and make competitors followers |
| **I:** Integrated | ● Marketing approach must permeate whole company |
| **S:** Strategic | ● Probing analysis leading to a winning strategy |
| **E:** Effectively Executed | ● Strong and disciplined execution on a daily basis |

It is related closely to the earlier chapter on 'Offensive Marketing Planning' (Chapter 8). As you know, this outlined a seven-step Marketing process, described a number of brand planning tools and provided an illustration of a total brand marketing plan for a fictional Rasputin vodka brand.

This latest chapter will cover brand development in more detail, and examine how companies can fully utilize their existing and new brand resources to achieve growth objectives profitably. It aims to answer important questions like:

- What is your branding strategy? Is it a single master brand (like Honda), favoured by the Japanese; or a series of self-standing brands (like Ariel or Twix), preferred by P & G and Mars?
- How far can existing brands be extended?
- What are the main types of brand business system?
- How do you define 'power' brands, and how do you select and develop them?
- What are the fifteen offensive brand development tools?
- Why are so many traditional brands declining?
- How do you deliver consistent brand propositions to different stakeholders, like consumers, buyers, employees and investors?

The chapter begins with twelve conclusions about brand development, such as:

- Why brands die.
- How strong brands are distinctive business systems, not just names.
- Why masterbranding as a strategy is gaining ground.
- Requirements for success in brand development.
- When to launch new brands.
- Implications of the trend to global branding.

Guidelines for successfully extending brands are then described.

This is followed by a section summarizing **Offensive Brand Development tools.** Some of these, like the brand conversion model and the brand scorecard, have been described already in previous chapters. Others, like the Brand Iceberg and brand development worksheet are outlined in this chapter for the first time.

The chapter finishes with a **seven-step process for brand development**, using an imaginary soft drinks company, the Riviera Soda Fountain Co., as an example.

## Twelve Conclusions about Brand Development and Offensive Principles

### 1. A brand's value lies inside the consumer's mind

A 'brand' is shorthand for a collection of attributes which strongly influence purchase.

Brands enable **consumers** to identify products or services which promise specific benefits. They arouse expectations about quality, price, purpose and performance.

A perfume in an expensive-looking bottle branded 'Chanel No. 5' will command a high price. If it was cheaply packaged, consumers would become confused. The reality would fail to meet their expectations about the brand, and, rather than thinking 'What a bargain!' they would probably decide not to buy. Equally, while Chanel No. 5 is a strong brand name for an expensive perfume, it would arouse the wrong expectations for a household cleaning product.

Brands enable **marketers** to build extra value into products or services and to differentiate them from competitors. Well-known brand names are a company's most valuable assets. They represent the accumulation of years of favourable consumer experiences and heavy investment in advertising, presentation and quality.

However, many so-called brands are no more than labels attached to 'me-too' products. To qualify as a brand rather than a label, a product or service must own a place in the consumer's mind, and Table 175 shows how this can be acquired.

---

**Table 175. Criteria for brands rather than labels.**

- Significant brand-name awareness
- Reasonable availability to target group
- Consistently delivered consumer benefit
- Clear consumer understanding of benefits associated with the brand

---

Now, let's move up a notch. How do strong brands differ from ordinary brands (Table 176)? Additional criteria have to be met. How does your brand rate?

---

**Table 176. Additional criteria to qualify as STRONG brand.**

- High brand awareness
- Wide availability to target group
- Superior and distinctive product or service proposition
- Continuously improving proposition

---

In Table 177 are some examples of strong and weak brands.

**Table 177.  Examples of strong and weak brands.**

| Strong | | Weak | |
|---|---|---|---|
| Coca-Cola, Levi's, Canon, BMW, Lego, Disney, Gillette, Nike | *Superior propositions delivering strong profit growth* | Most financial services, utility and petrol brands. | *Names bolted on to 'me-too' propositions* |

A brand name's value lies inside the customer's mind. Its mechanism can be compared to a continuous production line. The company feeds in raw materials of product or service performance, pricing, advertising and so on. The customer reacts to and processes these into attitudes and image. The final result is a mental inventory. Then the process begins again, as illustrated in the brand continuum in Figure 61. It can therefore be seen that a brand image is dynamic not static; it will strengthen or weaken in line with the company inputs.

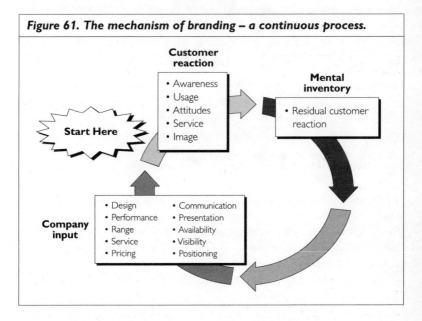

**Figure 61. The mechanism of branding – a continuous process.**

## 2.  Brands are business systems, not just names

Branding goes well beyond names and symbols. These are just the tip of the Branding Iceberg, the visible one sixth. What really matters is the five sixths below the waterline. Strong branding is the result of successful business strategy. It is not a matter of manipulating advertising, name and presentation. Is your brand just a name, or is it shorthand for a distinctive business proposition?

Figure 62 illustrates the Branding Iceberg for a chilled food brand. What you can see is above the waterline – things like brand names, symbols, presentation and advertising. What you can't see are the assets and competencies which will drive the brand. Things like low-cost operation, high quality, strong R & D, integrated marketing and so on.

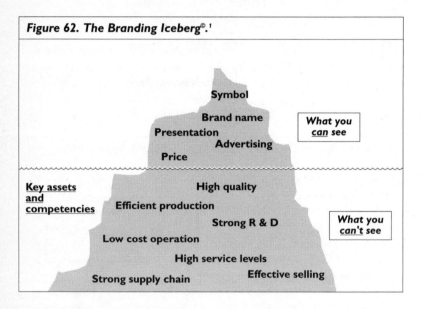

**Figure 62. The Branding Iceberg©.[1]**

The exact elements of the Branding Iceberg will differ by market, although most of those in the table would be included. For instance, 'Presentation' would be **packaging** for consumer goods companies, **store fascias and interiors** for retailers, and **branch offices, people and literature** for mortgages.

You will have noticed that elements below the waterline are company-related competencies or assets, while those above the waterline refer to a specific brand. This is because the business system driving most brands below the waterline is company wide and will often cover a number of brands.

In constructing a Branding Iceberg, you should only include below the waterline elements which are different or superior, as in Figure 63 for Equitable Life.

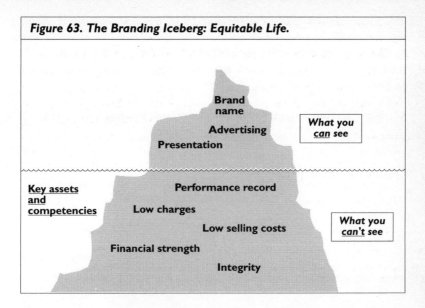

**Figure 63. The Branding Iceberg: Equitable Life.**

Brand name
Advertising
Presentation

*What you **can** see*

Key assets and competencies
Performance record
Low charges
Low selling costs
Financial strength
Integrity

*What you **can't** see*

Equitable Life, founded in 1762, is a strong financial services brand, driven by a superior business system. It is a low-cost operator because it deals direct with customers through a relatively small sales force, and is a mutual, thereby handing on all profits to customers. Low-cost operation helps Equitable achieve superior rankings in the league tables for pension performance. Its unintrusive selling approach and below-average charges build the reputation for integrity.

The Branding Iceberg highlights that the strength of many brands derives more from powerful underlying business systems than from advertising or promotion.

### 3. There are four main types of brand business system

A number of alternative business systems are now available to branders, and choices can be made. When branding started, this was not the case, since it was a means to distinguish the goods of one producer from another. Branding and production were inextricably linked.

Now they are increasingly separating. Manufacturing, distribution, selling or even R & D may all be contracted out, with branders concentrating on selected core competencies. Table 178 demonstrates the four main types of brand business systems. The right-hand column, 'Brand development', is the critical one, since this function tends to generate most profit and the first three types of brander are usually the most profitable.

**Table 178.  Four main types of brand business system.**

| Type of Brander | Retailing | Finance | Production | Distri-bution | Product develop-ment | Brand develop-ment |
|---|---|---|---|---|---|---|
| 1. Franchisers or branding co's (Nike, AA, McDonald's) | ▓ |  | ▓ |  |  | ▓ |
| 2. Own-brand retailers (M&S) |  |  | ▓ | ▓ |  |  |
| 3. Branded manufacturers (Kelloggs) | ▓ |  |  |  |  |  |
| 4. Private-label manufacturers (Courtaulds) | ▓ |  |  | ▓ | ▓ | ▓ |

Functions:  ☐ **Handled by brander**
▓ **Contracted out**

The four main types of **brand business system** outlined in this table are:

- **Franchisers and branding companies.** A branding company like Nike defines its competencies as design, R & D, brand development and supplier management. It therefore contracts out production and distribution. Franchisers like McDonald's or Benetton have similar business systems, although they retain at least partial control over retailing, which may be franchised or company controlled.

    The franchisee is the other side of the franchise coin. Franchisees are usually operators, with limited influence over brand system design or brand development, but have a critical effect on the quality of brand implementation.

- **Own-brand retailers**. Some retailers, like Marks & Spencer, market all products under their own brand. Others, like Burton, offer a mix of own brand and leading national brands. Production, and sometimes distribution, is contracted out to manufacturers or third parties, while product development is often shared.
- **Branded manufacturers** like Kelloggs and Hewlett Packard, who produce solely for the brands they own, sometimes contract out distribution.
- **Private-label manufacturers**. Companies like Northern Foods or Courtaulds specialize in producing for retailer owned brands like Marks & Spencer. They control neither branding nor retailing, and their bargaining power and margin are primarily dependent on product development skills, low-cost operation and customer service. Other private-label manufacturers also produce for the brands they themselves own – for example, United Biscuits is both the leading biscuit producer for private-label retailers and, under McVities, the leading brand (though recipes differ.)

As indicated above, most profit in these business systems accrues to the company which controls brand development since this provides the opportunity for differentiation. Franchisers are usually more profitable than franchisees, branding companies generate higher margins than their suppliers, and manufacturer branders are generally more profitable than those supplying private label.

Companies may vary their branding systems by type of business and by country, depending on the local environment and their own competitive position. Determining which branding system(s) to use is an important strategic decision.

The separation between branding and production is spreading rapidly into service industries.

### 4. There are many different approaches to brand naming

There are two major types of brand name – **masterbrands** and **individual brands**. Ford is a masterbrand, Twix is an individual brand.

- **Masterbrands** are a single name and proposition used to cover many different product areas. The Japanese favour masterbrands with names like Sony, Canon, Honda and Hitachi. They may be used on their own, backed by a description of category as in Hitachi TV. They may be accompanied by an individual brand, such as Ford (masterbrand) Mondeo (individual brand), or by a number, like BMW 320. Or masterbrands may be used at a secondary level to endorse an individual brand, as with Nestlé's Kit Kat or Lever's Persil. Table 179 describes variants of masterbrands.

**Table 179. Masterbrand variants.**

| Types | Examples |
|---|---|
| Masterbrand plus generic category description | Barclays Bank, Hitachi TV |
| Masterbrand plus number | BMW 320, Nikon AF220 |
| Masterbrand plus individual brand | Ford Mondeo, Halifax Liquid Gold |
| Individual brand, masterbrand endorsement | Nestlé Kit Kat, Lever Persil |

How would you categorize your own brands, and which box would you put these brand combinations into – American Express Gold Card, Mars Bar? Is Gold Card a category descriptor or is it an individual brand? Is Mars Bar an individual confectionery brand, or has it, with expansion into other categories, like ice-cream and milk drinks, become a masterbrand? These are the kind of issues which need to be thought out as part of brand-name strategy.

● **Individual brands** usually comprise one product type in one market, and include different models, sizes, product/service options and packaging formats. Examples are Lexus or Twix.

**Table 180. Lucozade: transition from individual to masterbrand.**

| 1970 | 2000 |
|---|---|
| **Lucozade (Individual brand)** (one flavour, in glass bottle) | **Lucozade (Masterbrand)** → **Lucozade Sports**, **Lucozade Energy**, **Lucozade NRG** |

The dividing line between masterbrands and individual brands is not always easy to define. Increasingly, individual brands are being extended into a wider range of categories, and emerging as masterbrands. Lucozade, which started life as a specialist brand to help make sick children well, has graduated into a sports and energy soft-drinks masterbrand (Table 180).

● **The brand name continuum**. Brands may vary from 100% masterbrand to 100% individual brand, with many gradations in between. For example, with McDonald's 'Big Mac', the master-brand McDonald's is the most important element influencing consumer purchase, whereas with Nestlé's Kit Kat, the individual brand name, Kit Kat, matters most to consumers.

The continuum in Table 181 illustrates different degrees of importance between the master and individual brand.

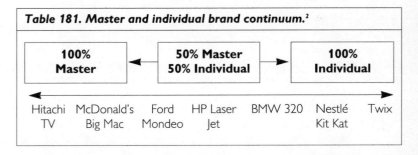

**Table 181. Master and individual brand continuum.**[2]

|  |  |  |
|---|---|---|
| **100% Master** | ◄— **50% Master 50% Individual** —► | **100% Individual** |

◄─────────────────────────────────────►
Hitachi   McDonald's   Ford   HP Laser   BMW 320   Nestlé   Twix
TV           Big Mac    Mondeo    Jet                      Kit Kat

## 5. Masterbranding as a strategy is gaining ground

The arguments for and against masterbrands and individual brands are well known. The 100% masterbrand (also referred to as an 'umbrella' brand) can generate high volume and critical mass by spanning a wide range of markets; it uses advertising support efficiently because of its size, can be extended into new categories at limited risk, and is both a flag and a motivator for employees.

The main potential drawback of masterbrands is overextension. If they try to be all things to all people, they end up meaning nothing to anyone. Any night on TV you can see meandering image ads for mas-terbrands which are the ultimate in bland brands. A second theoretical drawback to masterbranding is that it can spread the effects of adverse publicity from any product within the umbrella. However, this increas-ingly applies to individual brands today, when press and media quickly penetrate to the company behind them.

Proponents of individual branding, like P & G, Mars, PepsiCo,

Coca-Cola and Philip Morris, justify their strategy by saying that it creates clear and distinctive identities. Their brands are seen as experts in their chosen areas of expertise, and usually command premium prices.

Table 182 summarizes the advantages and disadvantages of 100% masterbranding, at the same time expressing the position of 100% individual brands in reverse.

**Table 182.  Masterbrands: summary of advantages and disadvantages.**

| Advantages | Disadvantages |
|---|---|
| ● Offer scale across many categories<br>● Use scale to finance large advertising spend<br>● Scale and product range increase efficiency of customer relationship marketing<br>● Strong basis for employee commitment<br>● Platform for alliances with other masterbrands<br>● New products can be launched with limited spending | ● More difficult to achieve distinct brand identity<br>● Quality of products and services within masterbrand may vary<br>● Tempting, and easy, to overextend<br>● Impact of bad publicity on any item affects total masterbrand |

Why do some companies favour masterbrands, others individual brands? Practice varies by industry and by country. What can be learned from this?

Within the car industry, General Motors has always favoured individual brands; BMW, Mercedes and Jaguar follow the masterbrand approach; Volkswagen and Ford use both. Within confectionery, Nestlé and Mars are mainly individual branders, while Cadbury employs both – Cadbury umbrella branding for chocolate bars, individual branding for filled countlines and sweets.

What about country practice? The Japanese generally favour masterbranding. They have many, such as Toyota, Canon, Sharp, NEC, Nintendo, Toshiba, Fuji, Honda and Casio to name but a few. Admittedly, in some cases, sub-brand names support or even supplant the masterbrand in the case of Walkman and Lexus, while Matsushita has a stable of strong individual brands such as Panasonic and Quasar. But the predominant impact is from the umbrella name. Johansson and Nonaka in *Relentless – The Japanese Way of Marketing* identified a number of reasons for this:[3]

● Japanese companies use corporate branding to demonstrate that they guarantee and stand behind all their products. 'Most

Japanese communications conspicuously display the corporate name and logo.'[4]

- Umbrella branding reflects Japanese emphasis on the group and the company rather than the individual. 'The corporation's identity and the identity of the individual employee merge, a positive motivational effect.'[5]

In addition, the Japanese are presumably aware of the advantages of umbrella branding in generating efficiencies in advertising spending and customer-relationship programmes. Furthermore, few Japanese companies use brand management, a system which tends to favour and sustain individual branding.

However, companies which pursue individual branding often have good reasons for doing so:

- First, if they already own strong individual brands, it makes sense to develop and expand them. As you saw in the Lucozade example in Table 180, some individual brands are even graduating to masterbrand status, spearheading a range of products.
- Secondly, individual brands may be a long-established part of the company culture, which brings with it strong competencies in managing them successfully.
- When expanded globally, the scale of individual brands can be greater than many umbrella brands. For instance, some, like Marlboro, Coca-Cola, Pampers and Heineken, have sales of over £1 billion, as has Ariel in Europe alone.

So what does the future hold? While many individual brands will remain strong, and companies will continue to combine umbrella and individual branding, the umbrella system is likely to gain most in the future.

Here are some reasons for this view:

**(a) Continued growth in service industries will benefit umbrella branding.** In most developed countries, service industries – retailing, finance, hospitality, telecoms, computers and entertainment – will increase their share of gross national product, whereas manufacturing is expected to decline. Most service companies use umbrella branding, partly because they came later to marketing, partly because the consumer benefits they offer are more transferable across categories. Service companies like M & S or Sainsbury, which establish strong credentials among consumers for quality, value and integrity, can stretch these into new categories like finance or petrol retailing. It is more difficult for manufacturer brands to spread into new categories, even with heavy advertising investment, because they get more typecast by consumers. Heinz could not move its brand into confectionery, nor Cadbury's into baked beans.

**(b) The future structure and economics of advertising favour umbrella branders.** The cost of mass advertising has grown to a point where only larger individual brands can afford it, and, in future, communication will become more diffuse as specialized media channels develop. This favours umbrella branders, who have the ability to spend heavily on advertising while limiting it to a fairly low percent of sales. Umbrella branders may also find it more economic to launch new products than individual branders.

**(c) Umbrella branding is in tune with the move to integrated marketing.** People like to work for a large brand which their friends have heard of and enjoy seeing the advertising. Of course, people at Nestlé Rowntree in York are also proud to be associated with Kit Kat, but very few individual brands are of this size. As the message that 'everyone is a marketer' spreads, the umbrella brand will become increasingly valuable as a motivating force, to be marketed both to external customers and to employees internally.

**(d) Customer relationship marketing is growing, and benefits most from umbrella branding.** Umbrella brands can run databased marketing programmes and customer clubs across their whole product range. This is cost-effective, because overhead costs are spread across a broader volume base, and there are opportunities to cross-sell.

Compare this to the situation on a Unilever or P & G brand. It may be economic to run customer relationship programmes on large brands like Persil or Pampers. But it is almost certainly uneconomic to do so on small brands alone. The most efficient approach would be to use a group of brands, possibly across divisions, on a themed basis. Facts like these have led individual brand companies to give more priority to their often latent corporate brand umbrellas – Lever Brothers and Nestlé are examples. They can see the opportunity to use corporate names both to endorse individual brands and to enhance the credibility of multi-brand initiatives.

**(e) Distributor or retailer brands are gaining share in most markets in most countries.** Most are masterbrands. They are well developed in the West in categories like grocery, clothing, DIY and consumer durables. In the future, they appear likely to grow in all countries, especially developing ones, where retailer concentration is lower, and in many markets. Distributor or retailer brands tend to use the masterbrand approach, and very effectively too – Marks & Spencer, Sainsbury, Tesco and Migros are examples.

**(f) There is likely to be a major culling of smaller brands in the next few years, and individual brands will suffer most from this process.** At present, there are too many brands in relation to consumer needs, retailer space and company ability to promote. They become more vulnerable to elimination as retailers strive to improve return on space, companies seek greater operational efficiency and advertising costs escalate.

Most of the smaller brands tend to be individual brands rather than masterbrands.

While umbrella branding seems likely to gain ground in future, progress will be gradual rather than sudden and will vary widely by company and country. There will continue to be a very important place for well-marketed individual brands.

### 6. Brands have different stakeholders with different needs, which have to be met

Brand names are vehicles for communicating distinctive propositions to a company's stakeholders. Who are the stakeholders?

Most companies have five types of stakeholder – shareholders, customers or buyers, consumers or users, employees and suppliers. All stakeholders have an economic influence on the company. Clear and distinctive brand propositions change stakeholders' attitudes in your favour. Brand names and stakeholders need to be closely aligned, in order to achieve effective total communication, as illustrated in Figure 64.

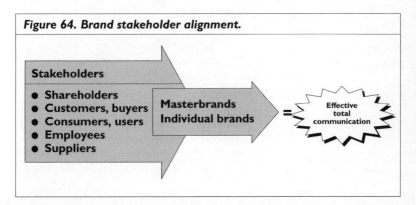

**Figure 64. Brand stakeholder alignment.**

**Stakeholders**

- Shareholders
- Customers, buyers
- Consumers, users
- Employees
- Suppliers

Masterbrands
Individual brands

= Effective total communication

Each brand stakeholder has different needs, and these are likely to be managed by a variety of departments within a company, which can cause inconsistent brand communication. Table 183 illustrates this issue for a car company.

**Table 183. Car company: stakeholder needs and internal contact points.**

|  | Shareholders | Dealers | Consumers | Employees | Suppliers |
|---|---|---|---|---|---|
| **Needs** → | ● Security<br>● Performance | ● Meets specification<br>● Margin<br>● Superior value | ● Superior value<br>● Good service | ● Security<br>● Motivation<br>● Reward | ● Fair dealing<br>● Confidence |
| **Internal contact point** → | ● Finance Dept<br>● Board | ● Sales Dept | ● Customer Relations Department<br>● Dealers | ● Managers | ● All Depts, especially Operations |

Stakeholder needs may be met by a single brand or by a number of brands. The challenge for companies is to develop core brand propositions, tailor them to meet different stakeholder needs and manage the process consistently across a range of different departments. This is by no means easy, and rarely done well if at all.

The chart in Table 184 demonstrates how Orange might tackle the issues, applying the values supporting its brand proposition. For

**Table 184. Example of potential Brand Stakeholder Alignment©: ORANGE** (read across)

| Orange brand proposition | Shareholders | Consumers | Employees |
|---|---|---|---|
| Innovation | Innovative | Superior technology | Innovative attitudes |
| Simplicity | Clear communicator to City | Easy to understand | Good internal communication |
| Integrity | Honest with City | Customer value | Fairness |
| Optimism | Upbeat; realistic | Image | Motivation and excitement |
| Authority | Believable | Knowledgeable expert | High competencies |

simplicity, only shareholders, consumers and employees have been covered. You will see how each of the brand values can be effectively delivered, with variations in emphasis to meet differing needs of the three different stakeholders.

For example, the company's skill in innovation would need to be communicated clearly to all three stakeholders, but positioned differently to each to meet their specific needs. **Shareholders** would expect Orange to lead the industry in new products and services, both today and tomorrow; **consumers** expect their products and services to be better and different; **employees** would expect Orange to encourage and reward innovation internally.

Only companies applying the 'Integrated Marketing Approach' (Chapter 4) can hope to successfully achieve Brand Stakeholder Alignment (BSA). If they do not they risk both failure to meet stakeholders' needs and delivery of a confusing and inconsistent message across stakeholders. This will apply particularly when, as sometimes happens, stakeholders occupy more than one role (e.g. employee shareholders, or shareholder consumers).

A key issue for branders is to determine a branding strategy by stakeholder type. Will one masterbrand be used for all stakeholders? Or different masterbrands? Or a combination of masterbrands and individual brands? Table 185 indicates how Ford approaches this issue.

**Table 185.  Choice of branding by stakeholder type.**

| Stakeholder | Ford |
|---|---|
| Shareholder | Ford Motor Co. |
| Customers, dealers | Ford Division (e.g. cars, trucks) |
| Consumers | Ford plus brand |
| Employees | Ford Division, country |
| Suppliers | Ford Division, country |

## 7. The requirements for success in a new brand are easy to state, difficult to achieve

To succeed, a new brand needs to achieve awareness among the target audience, and trial purchase. It must also deliver superior value, to generate repeat purchase and a long-term profit stream. This is quite simple to state. Table 186 is equally applicable to business-to-business markets, consumer services or fast-moving consumer goods.

**Table 186. Requirements for success in new brand.**

| Requirement | | Means to achieve |
|---|---|---|
| 1. Superior consumer or user value | → | Strong proposition at competitive price |
| 2. Relevant distinctiveness | → | Product/service design and development |
| 3. Low-cost operation | → | Every department consumer and cost driven |
| 4. Marketing and sales support | → | Sufficient quality and amount to achieve awareness and trial |
| 5. Superior buyer value | → | Convincing and profitable sales proposition |
| 6. Acceptable economics | → | Reasonable payback and good level on-going profit margin |

It all sounds so straightforward and easy, yet everyone knows that new brands involve high risk and usually fail. Why is this?

Each of the six requirements is in practice quite challenging in competitive markets. There are, indeed, many pitfalls snaring the path to new-brand success, even for gnarled and wary marketers (Table 187).

**Table 187. Pitfalls to new brand success.**

- New brand *is* distinctive or better, but in performance areas unimportant to the consumer or user.
- Level and quality of marketing support is insufficient to gain consumer awareness or stimulate trial.
- Superior new brand value is not sustained. Competition quickly improves products or services and/or cuts prices heavily.
- New brand beats revenue targets, but heavily cannibalizes sales of other company brands – incremental revenue low.
- Low-cost operation is not achieved in practice, and margins therefore insufficient or price too high.

Failure rate of new brands is much higher than for new products using an existing brand name. This is because the cost of gaining consumer awareness and trial, and therefore the revenue necessary to achieve acceptable profits, is much greater for new brands.

Consequently new brand names should be launched very selectively, where some or all of the conditions in Table 188 apply.

**Table 188.  Circumstances to use new brand name.**

- No existing company masterbrands or individual brands can be stretched far enough to capitalize on new opportunity.
- The new brand is capable of achieving the six requirements for success (see Table 186, on page 388).
- Opportunity is a sustainable breakthrough whose potential can only be exploited fully with a new brand.
- The proposition and economics of the new brand have been thoroughly pre-tested.

## 8. There is no practical reason why brands should die, but they frequently do

The next chapter, on 'Offensive Product and Service Development', covers the **product life cycle**, and the main reasons for new-product failure. Many of these also apply to new-brand failures.

However, there is no brand life cycle to correspond with the product life cycle. In most markets, and especially in high-tech ones, products have to be continuously improved – no one today would buy a Model T Ford to drive to work or a 1970 IBM computer product as big as a haystack – but brands can be sustained.

In theory, there is no reason why brands should not last for ever. In practice, though, most brands are not yet even seventy-seven years old, the span of a normal lifetime. Alcoholic drinks are the most venerable, with brands like Chartreuse and Haig tracing a history back for hundreds of years. Most but not all high-tech brands are post-war. Fast-moving consumer goods are somewhere in the middle – an analysis of the Top 100 grocery brands shows that 38% were launched before 1950, accounting for 42% of Top 100 brand value (Figure 65).

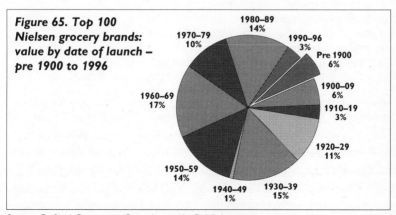

**Figure 65. Top 100 Nielsen grocery brands: value by date of launch – pre 1900 to 1996**

- 1980–89 14%
- 1970–79 10%
- 1990–96 3%
- Pre 1900 6%
- 1900–09 6%
- 1910–19 3%
- 1920–29 11%
- 1930–39 15%
- 1940–49 1%
- 1950–59 14%
- 1960–69 17%

*Source:* Oxford Corporate Consultants, A. C. Nielsen

The oldest grocery Top 100 brand is Schweppes Mixers (soda introduced in 1798), but the average age is only forty-eight years, compared with over a hundred years for the Top 100 short-drink brands. It remains to be seen whether today's leading brands will last for centuries, like Chartreuse. But it is certainly true that many well-established brands have died in recent decades, and that the process will continue. Figure 66 illustrates a few dead brands in the UK.

**Figure 66. Famous brands which have died.**

Today's strong brands should last for decades. However, most companies have too many brands and too few strong ones. Scores of established brands have died or are in their death-throes. **Why?** Table 189 lists some of the reasons.

**Table 189.  Why brands die.**

- **Growing brand competition**
- **Deliberate execution**
- **Acquisition followed by rationalization**
- **Weak marketing**
- **Weak quality or high-cost production**

**Growing competition**. Existing brands are extending, new brands are entering UK markets, especially from overseas, and, most of all, retailer private-label brands are growing in most categories, whether grocery, drinks, white goods or DIY. These forces exert great pressure on weaker brands.

**Deliberate execution.** There have been many deliberate brand executions, especially in the car industry, and MG had a narrow escape. The main reason is that companies have too large a range of brands in relation to their available advertising or selling resources, and therefore have to discontinue smaller brands in order to concentrate on those with most potential. Secondly, global rationalization drives branding change – that is why the best-selling Ford Cortina brand was withdrawn, why Mars changed the name of Marathon to Snickers.

**Acquisitions** often create brand-name duplication. When Burroughs and Sperry were acquired, both names were dropped and replaced by Unisys. The Rowntree name has largely been replaced by Nestlé.

**Weak marketing** can also kill brands. So can **inferior quality** or **high-cost production**. But the main reason for the death of brands is lack of a distinctive business proposition. Weak brands may once have had this, but lost it. Or they may always have been 'me-toos' and proceeded on their inevitable way to the graveyard.

## 9. In many Western markets, leading brands now fail to achieve real sales growth

If you were Brand Manager of a major grocery brand, and forecast a real decline in sales in your five-year plan, you would probably be forced to raise your projection and heavily castigated in the process. While you would not score too many points with management for either innovation or Offensive Marketing, realism could be on your side.

It is becoming more difficult in the West to increase real volume even on major brands. Many markets in the USA and Europe are static or declining in overall volume, increasingly penetrated by retailer private label, and even subject to new entrants. Allowing for the increase in retailer brand share, the size of the market for branded manufacturer goods is often falling steadily.

This is apparent in grocery, one of the better-documented markets in the UK, where, between 1989 and 1995, seven of the Top 10 grocery brands experienced real decline (Table 190).

| Table 190.  Nielsen top UK grocery brands in 1989: 1989–95 real trend.[6] | | | |
|---|---|---|---|
| Real annual sales trend (grocery) 1989–95 | | | |
| **Brand** | **%** | **Brand** | **%** |
| Coca-Cola | +7% | Nescafé | – |
| Ariel | –1% | Chum | –4% |
| Flora | +1% | PG Tips | –5% |
| Persil | –4% | Andrex | –3% |
| Heinz Beans | –3% | Whiskas | –4% |

*Source:* Nielsen, Check Out, Oxford Corporate Consultants

Of the Top 50 Nielsen grocery brands in 1989, only twenty achieved real growth over the same period. Twelve fell by 5% annually in real terms, and six grew by at least 5%. These six outstanding performers, which averaged 9% per annum real growth, were Coca-Cola, Walkers, Robinsons, Ribena, PepsiCola and Lenor. Congratulations to all who managed these brands, four of which were launched over sixty years ago. This does not imply that the remainder are poorly marketed – these are tough times, and it could be argued that even holding volume in mature, saturated markets, with strong own-label competition, is impressive.

For example, the three Heinz brands – beans, soups and ketchup – with an average age of ninety-eight years, held real revenue in 1996, while Anchor butter, and Cadbury's Dairy Milk, introduced over ninety years ago, gained.

The moral for brand developers is that brand size and power alone do not guarantee future growth. In mature markets, the natural momentum for leading brands is real decline. Brands like Walkers, Tango, Pampers and Felix, which have achieved dramatic real growth, have had to innovate, invest and implement effectively in order to earn it.

### 10. In attempting to gain real growth, brands are adding many new items to their ranges, often ill-advisedly

Caught in a dilemma between the high cost of launching new brands and the need for growth, many branders have indulged in unproductive 'brand churn'.[7] They add a host of marginal new-product varieties to existing brands, but fail to achieve significant incremental volume. The result is lower sales per product, added operational costs and consumer confusion from too much choice.

For instance, taking eighteen out of the Top 30 brands in the well-researched grocery sector as an example, the number of products or varieties on offer to the consumer increased by a factor of more than three between 1982 and 1994. This proliferation of products would be more understandable if the brands concerned were growing rapidly, but, as you have seen, most major grocery brands are struggling to hold real volume. In practice, then, volume per individual variant, a key measure of operational efficiency, has in many cases fallen by over 50%.

'Brand churn' has become a significant business problem, often created by marketers. Principles for tackling such 'mis-extension' are covered below.

## 11. Effective brand extension has become a critical Marketing skill

Brand extension is the process of strengthening and broadening a brand's franchise through repositioning, performance improvements or the launch of new products and services.

Marketers often ask questions like, 'How far can this brand be stretched?' or, 'When will the elastic snap?' Such questions reveal a wrong approach. They imply that brands are things to be exploited, for short-term advantage, rather than developed imaginatively over the longer term. Is your company a brand exploiter or a brand developer? Table 191 will help you to assess this.

**Table 191. Attitudes of brand exploiters versus brand developers** *(read across).*

| Brand exploiters' attitudes | Brand developers' attitudes |
|---|---|
| ● Avoid any spending with payback longer than one year | ● Balance short-term profit needs with investment for long-term development |
| ● Do not be 'pedantic' about the purity of the brand's core proposition | ● Really understand and nurture the core of your brand proposition<br>● Strengthen and develop this core over time |
| ● Be 'entrepreneurial' and extend the brand as widely as possible | ● Launch new products which both build and extend this core |
| ● Raid the core advertising budget to support new line extensions | ● Give new products or services additional support. Don't raid the core budget |
| ● Introduce sub-brands, with support in Year 1 only | ● Always gain *incremental* volume |
| ● Create continual 'brand news', through new launches and cut back on communication of core proposition | ● Build operational efficiency with brand extensions |

Why is brand exploitation so favoured? Because it appears to offer short cuts, quick boosts to profitability and lots of activity. This is attractive to marketers who do not expect to work on a brand for more than two years, and to companies striving for short-term profit gains. The Gucci brand was exploited when it was extended across hundreds of categories, often with products such as plastic and canvas handbags which did not meet the core proposition of top-end luxury

– a situation since decisively corrected by Gucci's present owners. The Cadillac brand was exploited when used on the 'Cadillac Cimarron', actually a Chevrolet Cavalier with leather seats and some luxury appointments. It failed, but not before hurting the Cadillac image.[8]

### 12. There is a strong trend towards global brand development, tailored to local conditions

This is a major topic in its own right and will only be covered briefly here.

The level of global branding appears to be overestimated in the largely anecdotal literature on the subject. There are many large local brands, especially in the USA, Japan and Germany. For instance, only forty-eight out of the top hundred advertised mega-brands in the USA in 1994 were international brands. Among the fifty-two largely American brands were Tylenol, a pain reliever owned by Johnson & Johnson with sales of over $800 million; Hershey, market leader in confectionery; Sears stores; and MCI Telecommunications. Between them, these brands spent over $500 million on advertising.

Further evidence that the trend to global branding has been exaggerated comes from a study of six key globalizers (Colgate, Kraft, Nestlé, P & G, Quaker and Unilever) by Boze & Patton. Of 1,792 brands studied, only 4% were 'global' – defined as sold in thirty-four or more countries. As many as 65% were marketed in three countries or less, and only five brands – Colgate, Lipton, Maggi, Nescafé and Palmolive – were sold in all sixty-seven countries studied.[9]

However, there is no doubt that the trend towards global branding is increasing, driven by pressures on costs, the demonstrable success of many international brands and convergence in desired consumer benefits across countries.

Table 192 lists markets where brands are largely global, and those which remain primarily local. What do you think are the reasons for this?

**Table 192. Examples of markets where brands are mainly global versus local.**

| Largely global branding | | Largely local branding | |
|---|---|---|---|
| **Markets** | **Brand example** | **Markets** | **Brand example** |
| Petrol | *Shell* | Holidays | *Thomsons* |
| Luxury products | *Hermes* | Retailing | *Wal-Mart* |
| Credit cards | *Visa* | Frozen foods | *Dr Oetker* |
| Skincare | *Oil of Ulay* | OTC medicines | *Tylenol* |
| Cars | *Toyota* | Hot beverages | *Folgers Coffee* |
| Computers | *Compaq* | Insurance | *Prudential* |

| Markets | Brand example | Markets | Brand example |
|---------|---------------|---------|---------------|
| Software | *Microsoft* | Retail banks | *Barclays* |
| Soft drinks | *Coca-Cola* | Utilities | *Thames Water* |
| Entertainment | *Disney* | Transport | *Deutsche Rail* |
| Brown goods | *Sony* | Local telecom | *BT* |
| Documents | *Xerox* | Cheese | *Sainsbury* |
| Aircraft | *Boeing* | Furniture | *DFS* |
| Earth movers | *Caterpillar* | Jewellery | *Samuel* |
| Sportswear | *Nike* | Gambling/bingo | *Coral/Gala* |

While global branding is often explained in consumer terms as a way of meeting benefits like softness and style, which can transcend national boundaries, its main driver is business economics. In industries where origination costs like R & D and advertising development are high and can be handled centrally or regionally, the international brander will gain advantage by spreading these costs against revenue from many countries. Equally, the global operator can achieve lower running costs through large plants serving many countries, plus economies in bulk purchasing of raw materials, packaging, IT systems and advertising. However, these advantages can only be gained if a reasonable level of homogeneity in product or service content is feasible across countries.

Table 193 lists some of the characteristics which determine whether an industry is likely to be global or local. An industry with global potential will exhibit many but by no means all of these.

**Table 193. Characteristics favouring international branding.**

| | |
|---|---|
| **High origination costs** | ● High R & D as percentage of sales (e.g. pharmaceuticals)<br>● High advertising as percentage of sales (e.g. cosmetics, fashion)<br>● Processes and systems training important and developed centrally (e.g. McDonald's) |
| **High running costs** | ● High capital costs (e.g. paper, steel, cars)<br>● Economies of scale (e.g. cars)<br>● Process engineering skills important (e.g. Mars) |
| **Consumer factors** | ● Some homogeneity in required benefits and usage habits across countries (e.g. VCRs, computers)<br>● Fashion and styling important (e.g. Levi)<br>● International culture (films, music, Coke) |
| **Other factors** | ● Lack of anti-competitive local regulation<br>● Tactical flexibility not a key factor for success<br>● Industry has companies with international outlook |

Processed food is likely to remain a mainly local industry, because R & D and advertising costs are a modest percentage of sales; only limited economies of scale are available; and local tastes vary widely. This is despite the fact that the industry has a number of skilful international marketers such as Unilever, Nestlé, H. J. Heinz, Kraft and BSN, most of whose business consists of local brands or products.

International branders do not hold all the cards. Their structures tend to be complex, and higher cost, unable to match the lean local competitor in either speed of reaction or employee motivation. While they have been quite successful in accelerating speed of new-product development and in involving local management more in international strategy, many of their processes remain cumbersome and demotivating to employees on the front line (Table 194).

**Table 194.  Problem areas for international branders.**

| Problem | Attempted solutions |
|---|---|
| Local country needs vary | *Review economics of varying product or service offer by country, balancing extra cost v. likely benefits* |
| Local management demotivated by lack of involvement in marketing strategy – 'just executors' | *Involve local managers in global teams and establish local centres of excellence* |
| Lack of flexibility, slow response rate | *Move to smaller local business units, and empowerment on tactical issues* |

Most of the issues in international branding involve trade-offs between additional revenue available from meeting local needs more exactly, and additional cost of doing so: between the economies of scale, on the one hand, and local speed, flexibility, motivation on the other.

'International branding' is in fact a misnomer for this topic. The benefits of international marketing are driven by common consumer positioning and economies of scale, not by common brand names. While it is ideal to have one single brand name world-wide, common positionings which generate the required economies of scale can be marketed under different brand names.

For example, Procter & Gamble's 2-in-1 hair care brand is called 'Wash and Go' in Europe, 'Rejoice' or 'Rejoy' in the Far East and 'Pert Plus' in the USA. Aquafresh toothpaste, SmithKline Beecham's global brand, uses the Odol name in Germany, because Odol is a classic brand over a hundred years old, associated with oral health.

This completes the twelve conclusions about brand development and the outline of offensive principles. The next section will cover guidelines for effective brand extension (Table 195).

**Table 195.**

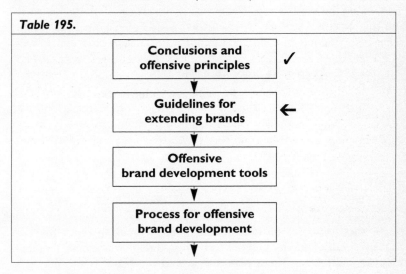

## Guidelines for Extending Existing Brands[10]

### 1. Really understand how your markets and channels segment

This understanding will enable you to target your brand extensions to build incremental volume rather than cannibalizing your existing business. If, for example, your total market share is 40%, and you decide to launch a new product into a market segment where your share is only 5%, you have a good chance of generating much incremental new business.

Superior understanding of segmentation will enable you to build rather than fragment brands. In general, any new product should add more than your fair share, through clear targeting. If your brand has a 40% share and you launch a new product, you can normally expect to take 40% from yourself and 60% from competitors. However, with effective targeting you should do better than this, and aim to gain at least 80% from competition. (Chapter 9 tells you how to achieve this result.)

### 2. Clearly identify the core of your brand proposition

This will be included in your Brand Positioning Statement – see Chapter 8, page 311. The core of a brand consists of the elements consumers most associate with it and constitutes the primary reason for purchase. A brand core can be ascertained through consumer and customer research, backed by judgement.

Among the possible core elements, it is usually most effective to focus on one or two. Here are some choices. Which of the attributes in the table following represent the most important core element of each brand?

| Table 196. Alternative brand core elements. | | | |
|---|---|---|---|
| | **Possible core elements** | | |
| **Brand** | **1** | **2** | **3** |
| Ribena | Blackcurrant | Great taste | Health benefits |
| Mercedes | High performance | High resale value | Superior engineering |
| Gucci | Fashionable | Leather | Exclusive |
| First Direct | Via telephone | Convenient | Superior service |

In each case, the most important core element is under (3). For Ribena, health benefits are core, as is great taste. Blackcurrant, although the original flavour, is not core, and indeed the brand is available in a range of flavours, each delivering the two core benefits. The core of Mercedes is superior engineering, and this, together with very limited design changes in new models, builds the other core element of high resale value. High performance, in terms of acceleration, is not core to Mercedes, since many less expensive cars outperform it.

Exclusivity, backed by high quality, is core to Gucci. That is why the brand languished when it was applied to humdrum products and sold through mass-market outlets. Since re-establishment of its core proposition, which involved cutting product range from 20,000 to 5,000, raising quality and tightly selecting outlets, the brand has regained momentum.

Convenience and superior service are the core of First Direct Bank. Telephone delivery of the product is non core.

The brand inner core, outer core and 'no-go' areas will be reviewed later in this chapter under the 'Brand Circle' (page 406).

### 3. Strengthen and develop the brand core over time

Brand development needs to be planned over at least a five-year time scale. Companies readily accept the necessity to plan their capital expenditure five to ten years ahead, but are strangely reluctant to apply the same thinking to brands. How many five-year brand development plans have you seen?

Capital equipment has only a five- to twenty-year lifespan, while most major brands have been around for at least forty years, and should last another forty. Companies not producing five-year development plans fail to accept the logic of the oft-quoted phrase, 'Brands are our most important asset'.

The centrepiece of a five-year brand plan is future objectives, and desired brand positioning five years hence. From this, plans to broaden or narrow positioning, to enhance brand distinctiveness, to improve products or services, to enter new market or channel segments, to capitalize on new usage occasions or to enter new countries, can be developed. Figure 67 shows a five-year brand opportunity tree, with examples.

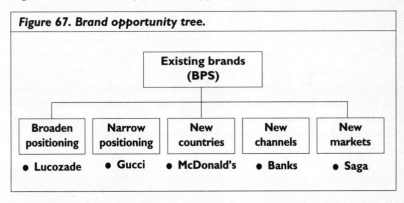

**Figure 67. Brand opportunity tree.**

Broadening positioning over time is a popular five-year strategy, since, if successfully done, it promises substantial extra volume at strong margins. Lucozade is a classic example of this (Table 197).

**Table 197. Lucozade: long-term broadening of positioning.**

| Period | Positioning | Key initiatives |
|--------|-------------|-----------------|
| 1980 | Convalescent drink for children | Flavours |
| | | Light version |
| | | Cans |
| 1985 | Energy and refreshment | Carbonated |
| | | Sports pouch |
| | | Sports drink |
| 1995 | Energy and sports | NRG, Isotonic |

Lucozade sales grew five-fold in 1985–95, and its positioning broadened from 'helps sick children recover' to broad-appeal sports and energy drink.

**Halifax** has widened its positioning from building society to broad-range financial services company covering mortgages, banking, insurance, pensions and investment.

It is less common for brands to narrow down their positioning, but this is sensible if there has been overextension. Gucci is an illustration of this. So is Xerox. Xerox moved its brand into brokerage, investment banking and insurance (e.g. Xerox Life). It has now withdrawn from these ill-conceived brand extensions and sold the businesses, returning to its core as 'the document company'.

Many American brands, such as **McDonald's**, find additional sales hard to get in the USA, and their five-year brand development plans focus heavily on geographical growth.

**Ginsters** has built its brand around convenience and motorway outlets, and many banks are developing their brands through direct channels. Both **M & S** and **Saga** have moved into financial services markets.

Brand development needs to be planned over time on a gradualist basis, which is why five years is the minimum planning time-scale needed. Lucozade could not have developed from a drink for sick children into a performance sports drink in one move. It had to mount the steps in between, on the **Brand Extension Staircase** (Figure 68).

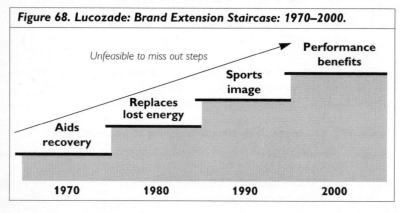

**Figure 68. Lucozade: Brand Extension Staircase: 1970–2000.**

### 4. All line extensions must support the core proposition and add something more

If the core proposition is high quality and premium priced, a brand-line extension which is average quality and low priced will erode the core proposition.

In the case of Lucozade, each line extension offered the core proposition of 'replaces lost energy'. Each also added something on top, like flavour variety, packaging for out-of-home usage, extra energy and so on.

By contrast, the Persil brand was extended inconsistently, especially when the ill-fated Persil Power was launched (Table 198).

**Table 198. Persil: inconsistent brand development in past.**

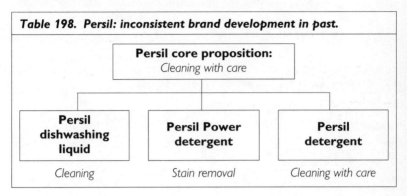

In this example, Persil had three sub-brands, only one of which communicated the core proposition of cleaning with care. Inconsistent or conflicting sub-brand messages weaken a brand's core proposition.

## 5. Brand line extensions must add significant incremental sales

One of the most common mistakes in brand development is to add lots of new items, usually called 'line extensions', which draw their sales mainly from your existing products. Ways to avoid this and generate largely incremental sales have already been covered and are summarized in Table 199.

**Table 199. How to build incremental sales with new items.**

- Target segments, either market, channel, demographic or usage, where your existing share is below average.
- Ensure the new item meets a new need.
- Give the new items incremental marketing support, to maximize incremental sales.
- Continue to support existing brand items strongly when you launch new ones, to focus pressure on competitors.
- Plan now for additional initiatives on existing and new items over the next twelve months.

Some companies have guidelines on the minimum level of incremental brand sales a new item must generate. As a rule of thumb, if the new item does not add at least 10% incremental sales revenue, it is probably not worth the effort or cost.

### 6. Build operational efficiencies into line extensions

Wherever possible, use existing capital equipment, facilities, raw materials and assets in developing new items, so as to maximize gross profit margins. This is common-sense asset-based marketing.

## Offensive Brand Development Tools

This section will outline a number of tools, which are useful aids in both brand planning (Chapter 8) and in offensive brand development (this chapter). Ten have already been described, mainly in this chapter and the previous one. They will be mentioned and referenced. The other five are headlined in Table 200 and will be explained below.

**Table 200.  Fifteen offensive brand development tools.**

| Tools | Covered | Chap. | Reference | Pages |
|---|---|---|---|---|
| Brand continuum | ✓ | **10** | Table 181 | p. 381 |
| Branding Iceberg | ✓ | **10** | Figure 62 | p. 376 |
| Brand Stakeholder Alignment | ✓ | **10** | Figure 64 | p. 385 |
| Brand opportunity tree | ✓ | **10** | Figure 67 | p. 399 |
| Market segmentation | ✓ | 9 | | |
| Brand conversion model | ✓ | 8 | | p. 307 |
| IDQV | ✓ | 8 | | p. 309 |
| Brand positioning statement | ✓ | 8 | | p. 311 |
| Quantified portfolio analysis | ✓ | 7 | | p. 256 |
| Brand scorecard | ✓ | 7 | | p. 259 |
| | | | | |
| Power brand definition | ✗ | | | – |
| Brand staircase | ✗ | | | – |
| 1-minute test | ✗ | | | |
| Brand circle | ✗ | | | |
| Brand development work sheet | ✗ | | | |

## 1. Power brands

These are important brands, with growth potential, which merit significant future investment. How do you identify them?

On a quantified portfolio analysis, you would expect them to be in or near the top left box, with high brand strength in reasonably attractive markets. Such brands would also score well on the impact-differentiation-quality-value (IDQV)[11] test, and on the brand conversion model. To qualify for the 'power' label, a brand should meet most of the characteristics in Table 201, although these will obviously differ by market and company.

| Table 201. Ideal characteristics of power brands. |
|---|
| • Significant volume<br>• Compete in segment(s) strategically important to company<br>• Distinctive or superior proposition<br>• Sustainable proposition<br>• Responsive to marketing support<br>• At least average operating profit<br>• Requirements for success match company competencies<br>• Demonstrated growth potential<br>• Identified opportunities for extension<br>• Multi-country position, or potential to achieve it<br>• Delivers good value |

The same brand may be classified as 'power' in one company, but not in another. For a large health-care company, a mature brand with sales of only £4 million could be unexciting, but for a small company with total sales of only £10 million, it would almost certainly be treated as a power brand and given a lot of resource.

Classifying brands into 'power', 'secondary' and 'other' is a useful shorthand means of allocating brand development resources – R & D, advertising, promotion and capital expenditure. Power brands should always receive a much higher share of company development spending than their share of company sales or profits, as Table 202 shows.

**Table 202. Example of power brand allocation of development spending, within a company range of brands.**

| Brand type | % of company revenue | % of development spending | % of company operating profit |
|---|---|---|---|
| Power | 65 | 85 | 60 |
| Secondary | 25 | 15 | 25 |
| Other | 10 | – | 15 |
| Total | 100 | 100 | 100 |

## 2. Brand Staircase

This was briefly shown above, in Figure 68 (page 400), in relation to Lucozade. The Brand Staircase is a graphical way to illustrate where your brand has come from and where it is going. It can be very simple, as in the Lucozade example, or more complex, covering various aspects of performance such as product, service and value. Undue complexity defeats the objects of this tool. It is best to focus just on propositions and segments.

The imaginary example in Figure 69 uses the Leopardstown Insurance Company, which insures high-value (over £100K) house contents through independent financial advisors (IFA). Its proposition to its 45–65 year old high-income customers is lower price and better service, due to specialization. The figure indicates how this core proposition can be developed over the next five years.

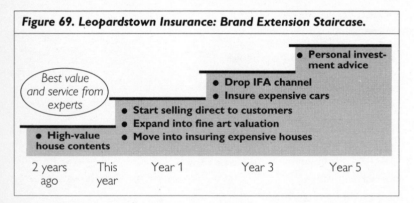

**Figure 69. Leopardstown Insurance: Brand Extension Staircase.**

Best value and service from experts

- Personal invest- ment advice
- Drop IFA channel
- Insure expensive cars
- **Start selling direct to customers**
- **Expand into fine art valuation**
- **High-value house contents**
- **Move into insuring expensive houses**

2 years ago | This year | Year 1 | Year 3 | Year 5

Leopardstown's brand development direction is to retain the proposition 'Best value and service from experts', to extend its product range into other services for high net-worth individuals, and to move gradually away from the independent financial advisor (IFA) channel into direct selling. The Brand Staircase provides a useful summary of future direction and options in a single chart.

## 3. One-minute test[12]

This is a simple method for making an early check of a brand's position and potential. The technique is to get people to list anything that comes to mind about a brand, 'Starting now . . . and you've got sixty seconds exactly.' It can be used with colleagues in the office, in Sales, in Operations, or with customers and buyers, either individually or in groups. The urgency provided by the sixty-second time-limit ensures a spontaneous response, and is also time-efficient. When you have got a couple of dozen responses, organize the output under headings. This is clearly not a consumer research technique, but a quick and rough guide. Table 203 is an example using After Eight chocolate, which Nestlé Rowntree is starting to develop further, with an assortment box.

| Table 203. After Eight: results of one-minute test. | |
|---|---|
| (a) **Physical product** | Thin crispy dark chocolate squares with soft mint filling |
| (b) **Presentation** | Dark green box, rococo gold leaf clock, small paper sleeves for mints |
| (c) **Target consumer** | Adults. 30 years plus. Mainly women. BC social class. |
| (d) **Usage occasion** | Special but not that special. Evening not day time. Useful 'thank you' gift. |
| (e) **Image** | An affordable luxury. Used to be aspirational, glamorous: less so now. |
| (f) **Development opportunities**<br>● Product/packaging | ● Liqueur fillings, e.g. crême de menthe, chartreuse<br>● Thin wafer version with different flavours<br>● Ice-cream dessert – thin individual slices<br>● Clock-face formation – like Terry's chocolate orange<br>● After Eight Gold – premium quality version<br>● Crispy Mint version |
| ● Image | ● Restore glamour, excitement |
| ● Usage occasion | ● Impulse version, for out-of-home use, bought for personal consumption – e.g. 3-decker crisp chocolate bars |

## 4. Brand circle

This tool visually represents the properties of a brand, and consists of four circles. In the middle is the inner core. This comprises the brand's intrinsic qualities (see page 398 above for how to identify the core of your brand proposition). The outer core consists of optional attributes, which can be used to stretch the associations of the brand name but are not essential to its future. The inner and outer core represent the brand as it is today. Extension areas cover possible directions for moving forward in future, consistent with the inner core. 'No-go' areas are to be avoided, since any move into them would erode the inner core.

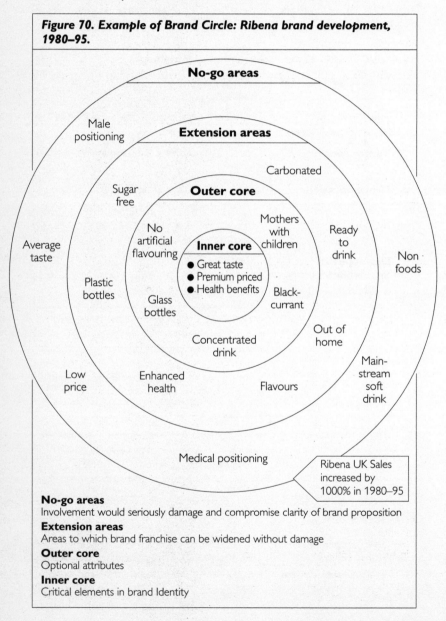

**Figure 70. Example of Brand Circle: Ribena brand development, 1980–95.**

**No-go areas**
Involvement would seriously damage and compromise clarity of brand proposition
**Extension areas**
Areas to which brand franchise can be widened without damage
**Outer core**
Optional attributes
**Inner core**
Critical elements in brand Identity

The Brand Circle can be completed from your consumer knowledge and the results of any ideas sessions on brand extension opportunities. Figure 70 illustrates how Ribena was extended from a blackcurrant concentrate in a glass bottle, into a broad-range drink with a variety of flavours, packaging, usage occasions and product types. The inner and outer cores describe the brand as it was in 1980, and extension areas summarize the initiatives taken to expand its consumer franchise in 1980–95. This was well-managed brand development, retaining the integrity of the inner core and achieving a ten-fold sales increase over fifteen years.

## 5. Brand development work sheet

This is a check-list, to guide you on priorities for brand improvement. It sets out the main levers of brand development (which obviously differ by industry), rates your relative position versus competitors on each lever, and has columns for improvement priorities and steps. In general, improvement activity should be concentrated on the more important levers, where your position is parity with or inferior to competition. Table 204 illustrates a brand improvement worksheet for a clothing retailer, marketing exclusively under its own brand and targeting ABC women aged 25–45.

### Table 204. Brand improvement work sheet: clothing retailer.

| Key levers | Relative position | Improvement | |
|---|---|---|---|
| | | Priority | Step |
| Design | Weak | X | New design |
| Colour selection | Same | | |
| Quality and comfort | Better | | |
| Customer service | Same | | |
| Differentiation | Weak | X | More testing |
| Range | Same | | |
| Value | Better | | |
| Pricing | Same | X | Raise selectively |
| In-store presentation | Better | | |
| Innovation | Same | | |
| In-stock performance | Weak | X | New system |

This retailer has a quality product providing good value and supported by superior in-store presentation. However, the products lack design flair, are not strongly differentiated, and customer goodwill has been lost through out of stocks. The four priority areas for improvement are backed by action steps. Price will be raised selectively on new more stylish dresses and skirts, when they are introduced, and the stock control system will be radically overhauled.

## Process for Offensive Brand Development

This section will outline a seven-step process for brand development, utilizing the principles and tools already covered by this chapter. It will indicate which of the brand development tools can be used at each step of the process. The next section will apply the process through an imaginary Southern European soft-drinks business. In the interests of brevity, tools will not be illustrated in this drinks example, since they have already been demonstrated above.

The seven-step process starts with brand stakeholders and finishes with detailed brand input to meet long-term objectives. It is not essential to follow all seven steps, and you may, for example, start at Step 3, omitting the first two steps on Brand Stakeholder Alignment, if these are not relevant to you.

The offensive brand development process is strategic and long term. It is about thinking and future direction, not about numbers or tactics. The process therefore needs to involve quite senior levels of management – certainly the Marketing Director, probably the Managing Director, although most of the work will be done at a lower level. Time-scale covered should be at least three to five years, and output from this process can be fed into the three- or five-year plan at a strategic level.

The flow chart in Table 205 summarizes the process, and indicates relevant tools.

**Table 205. *Seven-step offensive brand development process.***

| Process: | Optional tools to use: |
|---|---|
| 1. **Define, prioritize brand stakeholders** | ● Brand Stakeholder Alignment (BSA) |
| 2. **Identify stakeholder needs, check alignment** | ● BSA<br>● Segmentation |
| 3. **Define 5 year objectives by segment** | ● Segmentation |
| 4. **Categorize brands by type (e.g. 'Power')** | ● Quantified portfolio analysis<br>● Brand continuum<br>● Brand scorecards<br>● Power brand definition<br>● Brand positioning statement |
| 5. **Determine core and extendibility of brands** | ● Brand development worksheet<br>● Brand circle<br>● 1-minute test<br>● Brand Staircase<br>● Brand Iceberg<br>● Brand opportunity tree<br>● Brand conversion model<br>● IDQV |
| 6. **Identify gap v. strategic objectives** | |
| 7. **New brands, acquisitions, licences** | ● Same tools as for Step 5 |

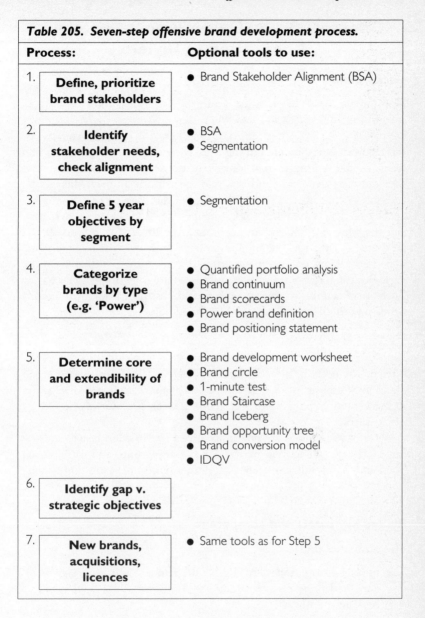

# Offensive Brand Development Process – Application to Riviera

## Background

You joined the Riviera Soda Fountain Company three years ago, straight from INSEAD, and have been Brand Manager on Med Fizz for the past year. A new American Managing Director, Jean Laporte, has just arrived from Levi-Strauss, and the Marketing Director has resigned. Jean wants to take a fundamental look at brand development opportunities over the next five years, and you have been made Project Manager, in addition to your normal responsibilities on Med Fizz.

The Riviera Soda Fountain Company (RSFC) is based in St Tropez, and has sales of £350 million, operating profits of £40 million. It is a long-established company, and has grown rapidly over the past ten years, since being acquired by a management buy-in team and floated on the Paris Bourse. Riviera operates mainly in Southern Europe. France is its largest market, followed by Spain, Italy and North Africa. Distribution is handled both direct and through franchised bottlers.

## Riviera segments

Riviera competes in the cola market, where it is a differentiated No. 3 brand in Southern Europe, in lemon and orange carbonated drinks, and in fruit-based carbonated drinks. It has a weak position in the energy drinks market.

Most of its products are premium priced by 10%, and heavily advertised. Riviera's strength is in the 15–30 age-group, and BC1 social class, and its brands are seen as stylish, southern French and aspirational.

## Riviera key assets and competencies

The main ones are:

- Strong distribution network in all channels, but especially in bars, mid-price restaurants, due to long-established bottler and trade relationships.
- Good R & D, and superior skills in flavour delivery.
- Very high product quality, with most brands winning blind tests.
- Excellent understanding of Southern European consumers, with brand positioning and advertising tailored to their aspirations and lifestyle.

- Young, energetic management, with little hierarchy and fast decision making

## Riviera brands

The company name is the Riviera Soda Fountain Company, changed from the Riviera Company five years ago. This brand is marketed to key stakeholders such as the financial community, bottlers, trade customers, employees and others.

The individual brand line-up is summarized in Table 206.

| Table 206.  Brand line-up. | | | |
|---|---|---|---|
| **Brand** | **Target customer** | **Product type** | **Brand core** |
| Koala Cola | 15–35 BC | Cola range | Makes friends |
| Med Fizz | 25–45 C | Citron flavours | Refreshing |
| Ice N Lemon | 15–35 BC | Fruit carbonate | Thirst quencher |
| St Tropez | 20–40 BC | Energy drink | Performance |

All brands, except Med Fizz, which is mid-priced, are supported by the Riviera masterbrand at a secondary level, e.g. 'Riviera Koala Cola'. Riviera stands for cosmopolitan, stylish, relaxed and premium price.

Koala Cola, symbolized in advertising by a cola-drinking Koala bear, who makes friends with everyone he meets, is by far the company's largest brand, with sales of £150 million.

The Riviera brand map looks as in Figure 71.

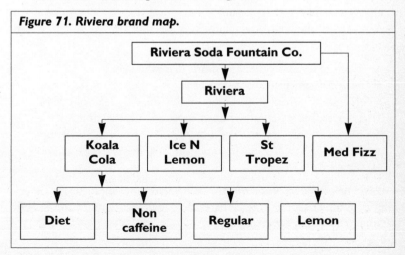

**Figure 71. Riviera brand map.**

# Riviera: The Seven-step Process

## STEP 1.  DEFINE, PRIORITIZE BRAND STAKEHOLDERS

Riviera's main stakeholders are, in order of priority:

(a)  Consumers
(b)  Employees
(c)  Customers and bottlers
(d)  Shareholders
(e)  Suppliers

## STEP 2.  IDENTIFY STAKEHOLDER NEEDS, AND CHECK ALIGNMENT

The different needs of stakeholders have to be identified, and met, by the brand proposition, as in the Orange example in Table 184 (page 386). The proposition has to be consistent across stakeholders, but tailored to the specific needs of each one. The values of Riviera as exemplified in its brands are stylish, relaxed and South European.

Most of Riviera's stakeholders are aged 25–40 and of BC social class, so in demographic terms the brand is well aligned.

## STEP 3.  DEFINE FIVE-YEAR OBJECTIVES BY SEGMENT

This needs to be done for a variety of segments, such as market, demographics, price point and channel.

Following analysis, opportunity identification and discussion with Jean, you have obtained Board agreement to future development, which involves the following key initiatives:

● Enter the bottled water and sports drinks markets.
● Enter the mid-priced cola market.
● Strengthen Riviera's position in the 25–40 year old C1C2 demographic segment, which is forecast to grow rapidly.
● Exit the energy drinks market by selling or swapping St Tropez.
● Sell or discontinue most minor brands, in order to improve operational efficiency.

At your presentation to the Board, you set out development objectives by product segment, price band, demographic segment and benefit areas (e.g. refreshment versus energy).

## STEP 4. CATEGORIZE BRAND BY TYPE

You have established a set of criteria for power brands, secondary brands and others, and summarized the strategic implications of this in a chart for the board (Table 207).

**Table 207. Strategic implications of brand categorization.**

| Brand category | Development strategy | Allocation of resource strategy |
|---|---|---|
| Power | Gain share | Invest at level ahead of present market share |
| Secondary | Hold share | Invest in line with market share |
| Non-development | Maximize profit | Cut cost, minimum support |
| Other | Sell or exit | Cut cost, no support |

Applying the brand-category criteria, you classify your brands as in Table 208.

**Table 208. Riviera: brand classification.**

| Brand category | Classification | 5-year direction (£m) | | |
|---|---|---|---|---|
| | | Sales | Investment | Profits |
| Koala Cola | Power | 270 | 47 | 28 |
| Ice N Lemon | Secondary | 100 | 15 | 15 |
| Med Fizz | Secondary | 80 | 10 | 9 |
| St Tropez | Sell | – | – | – |
| New | To be decided | 110 | 33 | 8 |
| Others | Sell or exit | 40 | – | 10 |
| Total | – | 600 | 105 | 70 |

These figures are no more than an initial 'sighting shot', to provide a feel for orders of magnitude and rough priorities, since you have not yet formally established the extendibility of each brand. But you do know that Jean wishes to increase sales from £350 million now to £600 million in five years' time, while retaining margins. And your first look suggests that not only will Koala Cola have to be strongly developed, but that heavy investment in at least one new brand will be needed. You are quite sure that Koala Cola has the size and potential to justify its ranking as a power brand, and are keeping an open mind as to whether Ice N Lemon or Med Fizz can be promoted to power brand later. This will depend on the view taken on their extendibility, and whether this fits with the segments the company wishes to develop.

## STEP 5. DETERMINE CORE AND EXTENDIBILITY OF BRANDS

You execute this step by reviewing all recent research, and using the relevant brand development tools. In particular, you want to decide whether any of your three major brands can be extended into the three new segments the board has in principle agreed to enter – bottled water, sports drinks and mid-priced cola. Table 209 gives a very brief summary of your conclusions on the three major brands, for each of which you have completed Brand Circles.

**Table 209. Core and extendibility of major brands.**

| Brand | Core proposition | Differentiating factors | Extendibility |
|---|---|---|---|
| Koala Cola | Friendliness<br>Warmth<br>Premium priced | Koala bear<br>Square bottle | Possibly sports drinks<br>Not mid-priced segments<br>Not non-cola<br>Other 'social' products |
| Med Fizz | Refreshing<br>Mid priced | Med lifestyle<br>Light-blue bottle | Possibly mid-priced cola<br>Possibly sports drinks<br>Not water |
| Ice N Lemon | Fast and lasting thirst relief<br>Premium priced | Tangy taste<br>Slice of lemon symbol<br>Cool style | Water, with lemon<br>Sports drink |

## STEP 6. IDENTIFY GAP VERSUS STRATEGIC OBJECTIVES

All three of your major brands are possibilities for a sports drink, with Koala Cola the least likely candidate. You decide to develop and check out a number of possible propositions for a sports drink, testing the preferred one under Ice N Lemon, Med Fizz and a couple of new brand names. You hope Ice N Lemon will win, since you would prefer to market a premium-priced entry, and have hopes that it will become a power brand, with particular strength in Spain and Italy.

Ice N Lemon is your only possible existing brand candidate for the water market. You will consumer-test various concepts, with Ice N

Lemon and alternative brand names, one of which is Riviera Marina. The Ice N Lemon water concept will feature the well-established slice of lemon in an iceblock, and the product will be water with a tang of lemon or orange and lemon. Positioning will be thirst quenching and cool style.

You will also be researching the effect of Ice N Lemon bottled water on the existing fruit-based product. Will a water entry have an adverse effect on the taste image of the existing product? If so, you would have to abandon thoughts of extending into the water market.

Med Fizz is a mid-priced lemon and orange drink, marketed on a Mediterranean lifestyle basis. Can it be extended to cola, or will the normal rule apply that cola and non-cola don't mix? Your guess is that Med Fizz will not extend into mid-priced cola, and that you will need to launch a new brand to succeed in this sector. In view of the high cost of launching a new brand, however, you may do some research on Med Fizz as a cola, just to check out your judgement.

Your thinking about the transferability of Koala, with the friendly bear image, to other 'social' products, opens up the possibility of licensing the brand to a snacks or clothing producer. This is worth investigating. You certainly do not wish to make the product, because others could do it better. Whether or not you want to distribute it will depend on how far the distribution channels of snacks and informal clothing are similar to your own.

You now have a significant consumer research programme to undertake, and this will guide you on the final step.

Based on the preliminary 'sighting shot' you made in Step 4, your guess was that new brands would have to contribute about £110 million of the £600 million sales revenue target five years hence. You now guesstimate that this may be on the high side, and that existing brands are more extendible than you thought before undertaking Step 5.

## STEP 7.  NEW BRANDS ACQUISITIONS, LICENCES

You think it likely that you will need a new brand to tackle the mid-price cola market. Since there is no likely acquisition or licensing candidate, this new brand will have to be developed internally on a green-field basis.

You are quite optimistic that Riviera can enter the sports drinks and water markets by extending existing brands. Your view on this depends on the outcome of some imaginative new concept research already in progress. Your expected final line-up, to be resolved when research results come in, is shown in Table 210.

**Table 210. Brand development process: expected final strategic options.**

| Task | Options and action |
|---|---|
| Develop Koala brand | Investigate non-drink licensing or contract options |
| Enter water market | Test out concepts, using Ice N Lemon v. new brand names. Check out image effect on existing Ice N Lemon brand |
| Enter sports market | Test out concepts, using Med Fizz and Ice N Lemon brands, plus new brand options |
| Sell St Tropez | Companies, to whom it is worth most, to be identified. Approach with dazzling presentation on St Tropez, then request sealed bids |
| Strengthen Riviera in 25–40 C1C2 segment | Focus effort via Koala Cola. Also ask for plans on Ice N Lemon, and include in any new brands plans |

It looks as if you will be able to develop a robust brand development plan to meet corporate objectives. Certainly worth the effort, even though it's taken you sixteen hours a day for the last three months, including weekends and bank holidays, to get there. Oh, by the way, share on your brand, Med Fizz, is heavily down in the last quarter. You'd better hurry up and fix it.

## FLOW-CHART SUMMARY OF CHAPTER 10

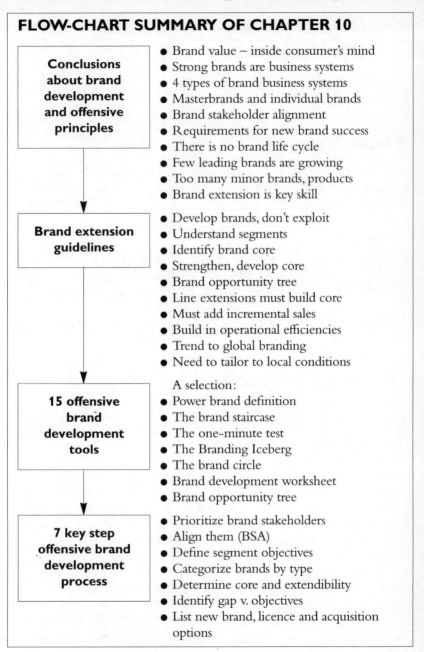

**Conclusions about brand development and offensive principles**

- Brand value – inside consumer's mind
- Strong brands are business systems
- 4 types of brand business systems
- Masterbrands and individual brands
- Brand stakeholder alignment
- Requirements for new brand success
- There is no brand life cycle
- Few leading brands are growing
- Too many minor brands, products
- Brand extension is key skill

**Brand extension guidelines**

- Develop brands, don't exploit
- Understand segments
- Identify brand core
- Strengthen, develop core
- Brand opportunity tree
- Line extensions must build core
- Must add incremental sales
- Build in operational efficiencies
- Trend to global branding
- Need to tailor to local conditions

**15 offensive brand development tools**

A selection:
- Power brand definition
- The brand staircase
- The one-minute test
- The Branding Iceberg
- The brand circle
- Brand development worksheet
- Brand opportunity tree

**7 key step offensive brand development process**

- Prioritize brand stakeholders
- Align them (BSA)
- Define segment objectives
- Categorize brands by type
- Determine core and extendibility
- Identify gap v. objectives
- List new brand, licence and acquisition options

# 11. Offensive New Product and Service Development

## Chapter Summary

This chapter outlines the key principles of New Product and Service Development (NPSD), another important topic within the 'E' of POISE, Effective Execution.

| Table 211 | |
|---|---|
| **P:** Profitable | ● Proper balance between firm's needs for profit and customer's need for value |
| **O:** Offensive | ● Must lead market, take risks and make competitors followers |
| **I:** Integrated | ● Marketing approach must permeate whole company |
| **S:** Strategic | ● Probing analysis leading to a winning strategy |
| → **E:** Effectively Executed | ● Strong and disciplined execution on a daily basis ← |

Previous chapters have already covered topics which form the foundation of success in NPSD – things like prioritizing segments and brands to develop, adopting an integrated approach to marketing and using rigorous analytical and planning processes. The present chapter will build further on these foundations, and cover the main activities of NPSD – opportunity identification, idea generation, screening, testing and launching.

NPSD is the keystone of Offensive Marketing. Nothing is more important than having superior and distinctive products and services, constantly improving them and building a core competency in developing new ones. Together with efficient low-cost operation, it is a winning combination. However, while every company would support this mantra, few do enough to act on it, and many lack any objective measure of consumer product or service performance versus competition.

It is important to believe that superior product or service benefits can always be developed, however difficult the category. A check-list of improvement benefits is provided in this chapter.

However, between 79% and 97% of new products fail, dependent on the industry. Main reasons for failure are discussed in this chapter.

Four important issues affecting new product and service success are analysed. They are:

- How to establish total NPSD resource needed.
- How to organize NPSD.
- How to allocate R & D resource, and prioritize projects.
- How to evaluate corporate NPSD performance.

A seven-step NPSD process, applicable to most businesses, completes the chapter. The seven steps are:

1. Opportunity identification.
2. Initial idea screening.
3. Developing technical briefs.
4. Building products, services.
5. Developing and validating support elements.
6. Agreeing final plan.
7. Launching in test market or nationally.

## The Foundation of New Product and Service Development

Some people think that lots of bright ideas are the key to success in New Product and Service Development. Articles are replete with the many techniques for idea generation, such as attribute listing, synectics, dissatisfaction studies and brainstorming. No wonder so many new products fail.

Good ideas are, of course, important. However, unless they are built on a solid foundation – effective structure, well-allocated resource and strong process – they will wither and die. Figure 70 demonstrates the rock on which the more visible and glamorous aspects of New Product and Service Development activities need to be built.

Much of the foundation has already been covered in previous chapters, and this one will focus mainly on internal organization for New Product and Service Development (NPSD), level and

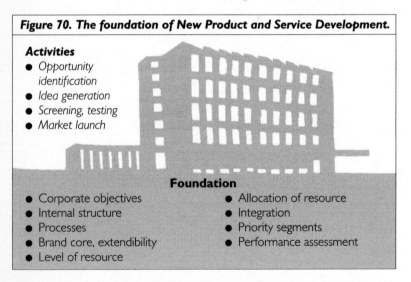

**Figure 70. The foundation of New Product and Service Development.**

**Activities**
- *Opportunity identification*
- *Idea generation*
- *Screening, testing*
- *Market launch*

**Foundation**
- Corporate objectives
- Internal structure
- Processes
- Brand core, extendibility
- Level of resource
- Allocation of resource
- Integration
- Priority segments
- Performance assessment

**Table 212. New Product and Service Development.**

| Coverage | Foundations | Activities |
|---|---|---|
| Previous chapters | • Corporate objectives<br>• Priority segments for focus<br>• Integration<br>• Priority brands for focus<br>• Brand core, extendibility<br>• Areas for new brand development | • Opportunity identification (1) |

| Coverage | Foundations | Activities |
|---|---|---|
| This chapter | ● Internal NPSD structure<br>● Level of resource<br>● Allocation of resource<br>● Evaluating NPSD effort<br>● NPSD processes | ● Opportunity identification (2)<br>● Idea generation<br>● Screening<br>● Testing<br>● Launch |

allocation of resources, evaluation and best-practice process. Opportunity identification and idea generation will, of course, also be covered. Table 212 summarizes aspects of NPSD foundations already reviewed, and those to be dealt with now.

Previous chapters provide much of the foundation on which this one is built, and cover the following topics.

## Corporate objectives

Five-year revenue and profit needed from NPSD. Setting stretching corporate objectives is described in Chapter 7 (page 251). Once you have established the desired total revenue and profit by year over the next five years, calculate your expectations as they are now, and estimate the gap. This is called gap analysis. The gap represents revenue and profits to be generated from new and improved products (or distribution channels) in the next few years. Figure 72 illustrates a **profit gap**

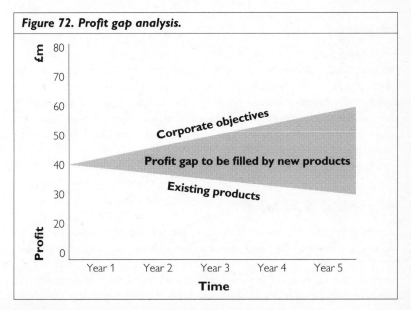

**Figure 72. Profit gap analysis.**

**analysis** – a **revenue gap analysis** can also be constructed using similar principles.

In this table, corporate objective is to increase profits from £40 million to £60 million in the next five years. Contribution of existing products, assuming no innovation at all, will lapse from £40 million profits today to only £30 million in five years' time. This is a fast moving market, and £30 million or half the profits in five years' time therefore need to come from new products.

This task is not as tough as it looks.

In practice, you will already have a number of new products, and line extensions planned, tested and ready to launch. Improvements to existing products and plans for new distribution channels may also be in train. Most of these new initiatives will utilize existing brands, but some may require new ones.

### Priority segments for focus

New product ideas should be generated in areas relevant to the future business strategy. To develop and launch ideas in unattractive segments where your company lacks competencies is asking for trouble. The Marketing Alignment Process (Chapter 2) aligns markets and competencies, and market segmentation (Chapter 9) forms the basis for prioritizing market and channel segments.

### Integration

NPSD should be led by the Marketing Department, but more than any other operational activity it is a team task. Strong integration between Marketing, R & D, Operations, Sales, Finance and IT is essential. R & D and Manufacturing for new products, and IT plus Operations for new services, are the cornerstones. Finance is also of special importance in accurately predicting future costs – no easy task, and one which unfortunately is often poorly handled.

Chapter 4 describes the Integrated Marketing approach.

### Priority brands for focus

In the previous chapter, on 'Offensive Brand Development', you have already established the core and extension areas for each brand. You know the existing and new market and channel segments that you wish to prioritize in future. New product or service ideas can therefore be efficiently allocated to existing or new brands.

### Opportunity identification

This is a continuous process, and not a one-off activity pursued intensively only when annual or five-year plans are being prepared. Some opportunities will already have been developed during Offensive Business Analysis (Chapter 5), including the SWOT analysis. Relevance of this is assured by relating it to key factors for success (KFS) in your market.

Chapter 8, 'Offensive Marketing Planning', which includes the Rasputin Vodka example, demonstrates how to build opportunity hypotheses at the beginning of the marketing plan process, using facts and analysis to prove or disprove them, and constantly updating and refining them. At the end of this process your Top 10 opportunities would be listed and prioritized.

### NPSD strategy

This would be summarized in a couple of paragraphs in marketing and brand development plans – see Chapter 8, pages 326 and 329. It would only be a skeleton, and require detailed elaboration as part of NPSD.

*

You have already built a reasonably firm basis for effective NPSD. This chapter will develop these foundations further, elaborate on opportunity identification, and suggest a process for handling NPSD, which concentrates on the main **activities** like screening, testing and launching.

The remainder of the chapter is divided into four main sections:

● Key principles of NPSD.
● Issues to resolve.
● Why most new products and services fail.
● A seven-step process for implementing NPSD.

## Key Principles of New Product and Service Development

### 1. NPSD and innovation are the keystone of Offensive Marketing

How does NPSD fit within the five elements of P-O-I-S-E: Profitable, Offensive, Integrated, Strategic and Effectively Executed?

Any company which has clear future objectives and vision, successfully identifies the segments and brands to focus them on, and implements through innovation and low-cost operation, is likely to be highly successful in NPSD.

Effective NPSD is essential to continually deliver 'superior customer experiences', as in the definition of Offensive Marketing. Unless your prices are below average, this means generating and sustaining product or service superiority compared with competition. Many companies deceive themselves on this score. They assume that their products or services are better, and may consider it heresy to suggest otherwise. Such assumptions are dangerous. It is essential to prove, and prove again beyond dispute, through objective product and service testing with target customers, that your offering is better than the competition. And this superiority must be more than technical, 'proven' in the laboratory. It must be acknowledged by consumers and customers. Techniques for doing this, such as consumer blind-product testing and objective customer service surveys, are covered in Chapter 13 – 'Offensive Market Research'.

Product and service development is the single most important corporate activity. Every company believes that top product quality is essential, but few actually do something about this belief. Here are two relevant statements on this subject:

**'It is difficult, if not impossible, to find anyone who doubts the prime importance of product appeal. The need for top product quality is a universally acknowledged truism among companies. However, the fact remains that there are vast differences in the extent to which individual companies actually do something about this belief. It is also a fact that the largest profits generally go to those businesses which most devotedly follow a policy of insisting on a competitive advantage, no matter how small, for every product or service they market.'**[1]

★

 **'There is a mythical corporation known as Lip Service Inc. It does not manufacture pomades for chapped lips. Instead it manufactures executives who say, "We're determined to mount an aggressive acquisition program" and "Our company is dedicated to being in the forefront of key breakthroughs in the all important field of new products."**

'Of course, all the key people thrusting forward and breaking through at Lip Service are only expected to talk about these things, not to do them. New product development and marketing, especially, is the "motherhood" of management. You never read a president's letter to stock-holders that says, "New products could cost this company its shirt, and we're going to steer clear of them." Just the opposite. New productry is a synonym for success and executives desperate to appear "modern" make it the order of their day.

'The doing, not the talking, is a traumatic experience for any company.'[2]

Product or service superiority can be achieved and sustained in any category, even one regarded as a price-driven commodity. You do not need to be dramatically ahead. In most markets a 5% or 10% difference will win if it is in a performance area important to the consumer or customer, and communicated strongly. Grocery retailers have gained long-term market share by exploiting quite small differences consistently. Marketers of bottled water have flourished by creating strong images and differentiated positioning.

Differentiation in so-called commodity markets can also be created by surrounding them with superior services. Take burgers, for example. It is debatable whether McDonald's has a better product than its competitors. However, its back-up services of convenience, speed and friendliness add value to a rather pedestrian product and combine to produce a strong customer proposition.

By contrast, major oil companies, together with insurance companies, have been among the weakest consumer marketers. In contrast to the bottled-water brands, their NPSD record has been poor, and, predictably, they now face years of torrid competition from low-cost operators like grocery superstores. Castrol is the exception and its reward is a 34% share of the UK retail lubricants market:

The major petrol companies in the UK (and elsewhere) have had little success in building distinctive consumer benefits into their petrol or oil products. They have tended to regard them as commodities, and, with tied distribution, different brands of petrol rarely compete head-on. 'Oil companies . . . have been slow to manage their brands and, as a result, petrol has been perceived as a homogeneous commodity with

nothing to differentiate one company's product from another.'[3]

In the motor-oil market, with the exception of Mobil 1, they have also shown limited initiative. The only two brands to build up distinctive consumer positions were independents – Duckhams and Castrol. Prior to acquisition by BP, Duckhams innovated multi-grade oil, developed a distinctive product colour and aimed at the motoring enthusiast, but has not been strongly supported in recent years. Castrol, owned by Burmah Castrol, has a strong branded position world-wide, despite its lack of tied outlets, thanks to a high performance image well supported by distinctive advertising.

Nor have the majors performed strongly as service marketers or as retailers. Quality of service on British forecourts compares poorly with the USA. The petrol majors were slow to exploit the opportunity of high-traffic sites as retail outlets, and now in some of the better forecourt convenience stores sales of groceries exceed sales of petrol.

## 2. The product life cycle can kill brands or sustain them – the choice is yours

There is a product life cycle. There is no brand life cycle. As observed in the previous chapter, a 1970 IBM computer and a Model T Ford are antique products and belong in a museum. Yet IBM, and Ford, despite a few ups and downs, continue as strong brands, sustained by a succession of new products.

The product life cycle is a truncated version of the seven ages of man and consists of growth, maturity, saturation and decline.

According to this concept, sales volume peaks soon after maturity, but is sustained during saturation by product or service improvements, line extensions and so on. Profits are meagre during the early stages, when heavy investment has to be made. But they are maintained even during decline, as additional operating efficiencies are achieved and marketing support reduces. In the end, though, the product – like man – dies. The Booz Allen chart given in Figure 73 illustrates this process.

The product life cycle is not an accurate representation of marketplace reality, and is more an indication of what can happen to companies which neglect NPSD.

In practice, well-marketed brands defeat the product life cycle by

**Figure 73. Product life cycle.**[4]

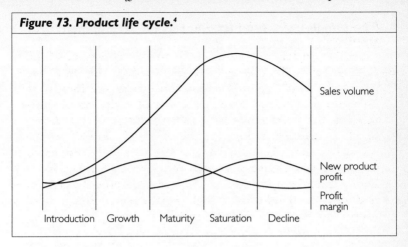

Sales volume

New product
profit

Profit
margin

Introduction  Growth  Maturity  Saturation  Decline

continually renewing and extending their product ranges. Consequently, some products within a brand portfolio may be at a late stage of the product life cycle, while others will be in the introductory or growth stage. This is particularly apparent in the car market. A major manufacturer may have four basic bodies or products, of which one may be new and thriving, another a tired seven-year-old, and the remaining two in mid life.

Computers, software, consumer durables and many business-to-business products have quite short life cycles. They need to be reinvigorated regularly with new products, and improvements to existing ones.

Other markets, like food, alcoholic spirits and many services, change more slowly. However, even in these categories, continuous improvement is now becoming the norm. Individual innovations may often be quite small, but over the years they can drive cumulative change and more efficient use of resources.

Coca-Cola Classic is among the least changed of products over time – indeed, the formula is claimed to be a closely guarded secret, known to few, and unchanged this century. Yet the product continues to grow through broader distribution, new country entry, packaging innovation and imaginative marketing support. And the broader Coca-Cola brand has also been expanded through sub-brands, like the very successful Diet Coke.

Coca-Cola Classic, however, is an exception. In most markets, quality and innovation are propelling rapid product change, and this is increasing, as competition intensifies and consumers become more demanding. The product life cycle is alive and well. It ruthlessly kills products and services which ignore it.

## 3. The principles of product and service development are similar, but applications differ

New product development is self-explanatory. Here are some examples of new service developments.

| Table 213. Examples of new service developments. |
|---|
| ● New design and layout for restaurant chain |
| ● 'Home arranger' for mortgage lender |
| ● Fast-track airline check-in for business class |
| ● Loyalty card for pub chain |
| ● Call-waiting service for telephones |
| ● Customer service desks for retailer |
| ● Itemized billing for doorstep milk |

It will be apparent from these examples that service developments are centred either on physical improvements (e.g. refurbishment of pubs) or on innovations driven by people and IT systems (e.g. loyalty cards for pub chain).

Obviously people – their objectives, attitudes, skills and training – are an important element of any service proposition. By contrast, consumers of products are unlikely to ever meet the people who develop, make, market or sell them. This leads to important differences between product and service development in lead-times, cost and risk.

Because product development involves R & D and conversion to mass production, lead-times can be quite long, from a year for a food product, to two to five years for a new car, and seven to ten years for a new drug. Development cost and therefore risk is also high.

This whole area merits more research, and the table in Figure 74 outlines broad magnitudes of cost, risk and time-scale for a new household product and a new financial service.

Clearly, order of magnitude will vary by type of innovation, even within categories. A new frozen pizza topping may only take weeks to develop and launch, whereas a new global haircare brand, based on new technology, could cost over £300 million, including Year 1 launch, and involve over five years' development. Equally, for an airline, new uniforms for cabin crew would involve much less effort and risk than a new class of travel. Figure 74 covers only significant developments, supported by advertising.

While cost, risk, time-scale and relative role of R & D, and IT, differ widely between new product and new service development, the same principles, and process, are broadly applicable to both.

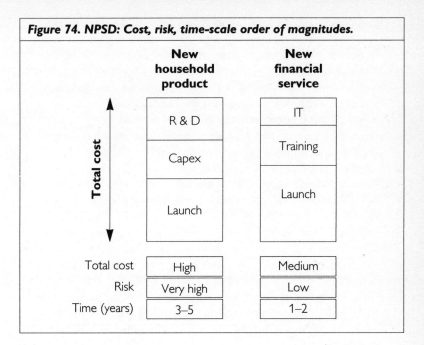

Figure 74. NPSD: Cost, risk, time-scale order of magnitudes.

| | New household product | New financial service |
|---|---|---|
| Total cost | High | Medium |
| Risk | Very high | Low |
| Time (years) | 3–5 | 1–2 |

## 4. Testing to reduce risk is an essential part of successful NPSD

Market research and testing are the main ways to reduce the risk of NPSD, and to increase the chance of success. Testing can range from informal trials with key customers to a full-scale launch of a new global brand in a smallish 'lead' country like Taiwan or the Netherlands.

There are four main stages of formal testing:

- **Concept testing.** This is quick and low cost. At its simplest, it involves summarizing new product or service propositions in a few lines, individually on a white card, and getting consumers or customers to rank them. Concept testing is fully covered later under 'Offensive Market Research' (Chapter 13). It can be conducted with individuals or in groups, with either simple or elaborate props. Major purpose is to screen out weak ideas, and to find ways to strengthen promising ones.
- **Testing individual stimuli.** Purpose of this stage is to test all the individual elements in your new product or service proposition individually, before combining them at the next stage. Every significant element in the proposition may be individually

tested and ranked versus competition. This would cover product (e.g. new airline menu), packaging, advertising (e.g. rough print layout or TV ad), direct marketing literature, new credit card layout and so on.

Once you are satisfied with the performance of each individual element, you can then test the totality.

- **Test of total proposition**. In some industries, this can be done with one or two leading customers, or by direct contact with a small number of heavy users, early adopters or industry experts.

In consumer goods and services, simulated test markets (STM) are often used for this purpose. Among the leading STM brands are Novaction's 'Designor', Research International's 'Microtest' and Burke's 'Bases 2'. Techniques vary, and clients can tailor them to their needs. However, most incorporate a consumer test of the new product or service versus the leading competitor; a test of advertising impact, relevance and persuasion; a simulated shopping situation where consumers are given a certain amount to spend on a display of products which includes the test brand and its competitors; and a volume forecast for the new product.

The volume forecast is built up partly from data obtained during the test, partly from estimates made by the client. The test situation generates product preference, response to advertising and purchase intent. The client is responsible for providing an estimate of retailer distribution of the new product, a Year 1 marketing spending plan and likely competitor response. All this input goes into a 'black box', and provides the basis for estimates of the new product's prospects.

From this description, you would be fully justified in assuming that this 'black box' technique could not possibly forecast likely future volume at all accurately. Surprisingly, though, accuracy is quite impressive, within 10–15% of subsequent marketplace results, when the final test plan has been faithfully followed.

What is more, the STM techniques can answer 'What if?' questions satisfactorily, like: **'What will happen to my volume and market share if I double advertising and raise my price by 10%?'** or, **'If I increase product acceptance by 20%, and hold price, what will happen to my volume?'**

The main limitations of STMs is that they do not measure retailer acceptance or reaction, therefore do not truly represent real life market conditions, including competitor reaction.

- **Market test of full proposition**. This involves launching the whole new proposition commercially in the market-place, with retailers or distributors and, of course, competitors. Location can vary from a handful of stores to a small country like Denmark or Taiwan used as a test market for a whole region such as Europe or South-East Asia.

The main disadvantages of full market tests are cost and time. And, unlike simulated test markets, which are conducted confidentially, market tests reveal your hand to the competition.

Table 214 summarizes the four stages of testing.

| *Table 214.* **The four stages of NPSD testing.** | | | | |
|---|---|---|---|---|
| **Stage and purpose** | | **Types of test** | **Cost** | **Time (months)** |
| 1. *Concept testing*<br>● Test strength of proposition at low cost | ▼ | ● Alternative new product or service ideas, succinctly summarized in words, or using pictures and samples, rated by customers | Low | 1–2 |
| 2. *Testing individual physical stimuli*<br>● Check strength of *individual* elements of marketing mix | ▼ | ● Consumer product tests<br>● Clay model tests (cars)<br>● New restaurant layout test<br>● Test of advertisement (rough)<br>● Packaging tests<br>● Test literature for finance product | Mid | 2–3 |
| 3. *Confidential test of total proposition*<br>● 'Laboratory' test of total plan (e.g. simulated test market) | ▼ | ● Consumer response to product service, packaging, price, advertising, resulting in sales forecast<br>● Test of total proposition with selected heavy users, major customers, early adopters | Mid | 2 |
| 4. *Market test of total proposition*<br>● Launch into a real market-place | ▼ | ● Test in panel of stores or with one single chain<br>● Limited area test, e.g. Tyne-Tees, Tele-Luxemburg<br>● 'Lead country' launch, e.g. Taiwan<br>● 1- or 2-unit test for new retail or motel concept | High | 3 to 12 |

Cost increases with each stage. While the research cost of a simulated test market might only be £30K to £40K, a full-scale test market in a UK TV area could cost up to £1 million, once the expense of manufacturing start-up, low-volume production and the origination of packaging and advertising have been taken into account.

The four stages of testing are not obligatory. Whether you undertake the full treatment will depend on the importance of the project, cost and risk involved, and predicted speed of competitor response. Stages 1 to 3 would usually be advisable for any significant new product. Stage 4 would probably only be undertaken if a company felt the proposition was protectable in the medium term due to technology, distinctive competencies or the need to invest major future capital.

**Why test at all?** Testing enables you to discard potential failures at each of the four stages; to translate good ideas into excellent ones through constant interaction with the consumer or customer; to try out alternative propositions, prices and marketing support levels; and to forecast sales more accurately so that the launch is handled efficiently.

There can often be a trade-off between testing and speed to market. While this needs to be seriously considered, the advantages of timely and effective testing are frequently overwhelming. Lack of testing is as often attributable to poor planning as to considered assessment of possible competitive reaction.

## 5. Superior product or service benefits can always be developed

**Figure 75.**

No, we don't aim for product superiority because we have tied distribution

Our trouble is we're in a commodity market – all that matters is price

In certain markets – for instance, some industrial goods, cars and consumer durables – it is easy to see how, with skilful marketing and R & D, superior products can be developed. But, in many others, superior product benefits are hard to come by.

One can either accept the difficulties as insoluble (and the remarks with which this section opened take that line) or follow a basic belief that product superiority can always be developed. There is more hope in the latter, and it usually pays off, especially if a systematic approach, using check-lists, is employed.

Table 215 provides a check-list of product and service improvement benefits.

| **Table 215. Inventory of product and service improvement benefits.** | |
| --- | --- |
| **Category** | **Benefits** |
| Convenience | ● Speed, ease of use, flexibility, accessibility, lower frequency of use, ease of disposal, saving of time or space |
| Personal service attributes | ● Friendly, reliable, trusted, helpful, knowledgeable, practical, efficient, welcoming, enthusiastic, responsive |
| Subjective physical characteristics | ● Softness, taste, texture, comfort, smell, exclusivity, fashion, reliability, safety, versatility, design, prestige, exclusivity, clarity, purity, ambience. |
| Objective physical characteristics | ● Space, access, speed, absorbency, shock-resistance, protective finish, cleaning, waterproof, fireproof, environmentally safe, strength, longevity, fit, flexibility, effectiveness, acceleration, colour, no side effects, range, choice, availability, visibility, insulation |
| Physical dimensions | ● Thickness, size, shape, design, layout, miniaturization |

This list of benefits covers many categories, although the same word may be used in different senses. For example, 'safety' in an airline means that you don't crash; in a bank it assumes the bank doesn't crash; for furniture it means 'solid and fireproof'. 'Reliability' is a benefit in most markets. In computers or cars, it means, **'doesn't go wrong'**; for planes and trains, it is **'arrives on time'**; for financial services, it relates to **size and safety**.

It is surprising how relatively small the total number of benefits is. Prove this yourself by listing all the main customer or consumer benefits in your market, and checking how many do not appear in Table 215.

## 6. Believe that small differences matter – the 5% factor

Even apparently minor differences in product or service performance, which may be spurned by a company's management as being unimportant, can be significant to the consumer, especially in product categories with high purchase frequency. When so many markets are oversupplied with almost identical offerings, being 5% better in the mind of the consumer can be a winning margin, especially in service businesses. The difference between 98% reliability and 93% is very significant.

## 7. Products are pathways to consumer benefits

A technical success may be of no interest to the consumer. Irradiation of food at low and safe levels lengthens product life, but is likely to stumble on the emotional resistance of consumers. Technical performance is certainly important, since every consumer wants a product to fulfil its purpose well, but it should not be viewed in isolation. Consumers are emotional as well as logical beings.

A product which is regarded by scientists as being at technical parity with its competition may nevertheless be regarded by consumers as superior for non-technical reasons: most people prefer brown eggs to white ones, even though they taste the same.

Consumers are also influenced by the derivation of a product. Faced by two products which are technically identical, they are likely to prefer the one containing the most natural materials or with strong environmental credentials.

## Why Most New Products and Services Fail

While estimates vary widely both overall and by market type, there is strong evidence that most new advertised products, and many new services, fail.

Clancy and Shulman estimate failure rate of new packaged goods at 80%, and believe it is similar in financial services.[5] Cooper and Kleinschmidt estimate that 75% of new products fail at launch.[6]

Clear definitions in NPSD are essential. **What is success?** One criterion is the manufacturer's view of success, but this is likely to be unduly favourable. Table 216 gives an objective definition of 'success' for advertised new consumer products and new brands in consumer packaged goods in the UK.

**Table 216. Definition of success: new consumer goods products, brands.**

| Criteria | New products, existing brands | New brands |
|---|---|---|
| Market share | Significant incremental market share increase | Sustainable level of brand share |
| Stability | Gain sustained over at least 3 years | Growing share after 3 years |
| Payback | 1–2 years | 3–5 years |
| Operating profit | 7–12% | 8–15% |

If this table appears bland, that is no accident. Even within the limited field of consumer packaged goods, it is difficult to generalize about new products. Year 1 sales of £25 million might be considered a failure for a new heavily advertised mass-market confectionery brand, while £10 million would be excellent for a new medicine or skincare brand. This is because the latter have higher margins, and, once launched successfully, are more sustainable.

One of the most comprehensive studies of new product failure was conducted across eighty-four grocery product classes over a ten-year period in the UK and USA, using demanding but reasonable criteria of minimum sales levels, and indicated a 3% new product success rate.[7] **Fifty-eight of the eighty-four categories did not have a single new product success in the ten-year period**.

The very high failure rate of new products tends to be taken for granted by marketing people as a fact of life. However, it is a serious indictment of marketing performance, and an important reason why the credibility and influence of Marketing Departments is in decline. High product-failure rate is not an immutable law of nature, and certain companies like 3M, Procter & Gamble, Unilever and Gillette have quite high success rates, bucking the general trend.

What are the main reasons for the lamentably high failure rates of new products? Most lie in the foundation of NPSD – companies bolt new product activities on to a quicksand foundation of inadequate commitment, structure and priority.

There follow some of the more specific reasons for new product and service failure.

## 1. Lack of company commitment

This brings us back to Lip Service Inc., where rhetoric is more important than investment. The trouble with new products, from the viewpoint of many boards, is that they are expensive, will probably lose money this fiscal year and are quite likely to fail. This rather unattractive financial and bonus scenario accounts for lukewarm senior management attitudes, even though it is recognized that new products and services are usually the only route to real growth.

Such limited commitment is often apparent in unwillingness to set corporate new product targets, inadequate allocation of resources and weak integration.

To succeed in the battle for internal resources, new products need positive discrimination in their favour. 'New Products' may have a manager, but is rarely a function. For most people in a company, it is a by-product, to be fitted in when their main tasks allow.

**What is commitment?** It is a conviction by senior management, following thorough analysis, that a new project can be successfully accomplished, together with the willingness to pursue it without reservation and the determination to ride out obstacles when they occur.

Commitment to new products and services is unfortunately rare. More common is half-hearted attachment, allied to plans to bale out if the going gets tough. Management continually looks over its shoulder, asking, 'Should we really be entering this business?' The willingness to consider getting out is too high. This usually results in compromise, retreat and failure.

Commitment is a combination of business logic and gut feeling, but it is the latter which sees companies through in hard times, when things are looking sour. Over thirty years ago, Procter & Gamble committed itself to entering the paper market, but success was very slow in coming, and involved many setbacks:

> **Procter & Gamble investigated the market for consumer paper products (toilet and facial tissues) and liked what it saw. The market had reached a good size, was expanding fast and offered sufficient margins to permit heavy advertising and promotion spending.**
>
> **What is more, the criteria by which consumers judged the performance of paper products – notably softness, absorbency and wet strength – could be assessed objectively, just like the whiteness result of a washing powder.**
>
> **There were only two snags – Procter & Gamble knew nothing about paper technology, and the two entrenched competitors, Scott Paper and Kimberley Clark (Kleenex), were well-managed companies.**

**Procter & Gamble bought a small regional paper firm called the Charmin Company, and used that as a base for learning about the business. It spent some years developing a better tissue. Eventually, a method of adding perfume was worked out and on consumer blind test Procter & Gamble's perfumed product beat the competition by 2 : 1.**

**A test market was opened, supported by heavy advertising and full-size free samples delivered to consumers' homes. The brand quickly gained a high share. However, when the launch activity was over, market share plummeted. The perfume had novelty appeal, but when this wore off, consumers went back to their regular brand.**

**Procter & Gamble did not give up. Senior management continued to feel that the company had the technical and marketing skills to succeed in paper. They were convinced that the strategy was right and that a flawed execution should not deter them.**

**More R & D work was done and eventually a product was developed with superior softness and wet strength. This was tested and launched nationally. It ultimately achieved brand leadership in toilet paper and paper tissues.**

**Subsequently Procter & Gamble entered the disposable nappy (Pampers) and feminine hygiene markets (Always), capitalizing on their competencies in paper. Global profits from paper now exceed $1.2bn, equivalent to 25% of total P & G profits.**

Japanese international marketers are also well known for their willingness to soldier on through adversity, in pursuit of an opportunity they feel is within their grasp, and this is one of the key reasons for their successful new products record. When Seizi Kato, later Chairman of Toyota, spent over ten years trying to establish the company in America, he at one time recommended throwing in the towel, but Tokyo refused to do so. In Seisi Kato's words:

'**The reality was that the first ten years of Toyota's export efforts to the USA had been nothing but a series of humiliations and frustrations, with little to sustain us but a burning ambition to realize this dream of dreams . . .**

**we had kept on trying, determined that we would take two steps forward for every step backwards.'**[8]

Nineteen years after their first disastrous entry to the US market, Toyota became the leading imported car. As Robert Heller observes, **'Persistence can turn a losing cause into a victory, provided that the essential resources are available'**[9] – and provided that the initial judgement was right.

### 2. Lack of balance between enthusiasm and objectivity

People involved in a new products operating team must be concurrently enthusiastic yet realistic. And senior management should be committed to new products, yet objective in assessing proposals put forward for approval. These contrasting requirements are difficult to balance effectively.

### 3. Conflict between speed and quality

Speed between starting and completing NPSD projects is increasing every year. Companies are getting faster to market in the first country, and either launching globally in one move, as with the latest version of Microsoft Windows, or expanding to a few dozen other countries within a year or so.

Companies are therefore under pressure to increase speed, both to pre-empt competition and to save cost; in general, the longer an NPSD project takes, the higher the fixed overhead cost of R & D and origination.

Because many new products and services involve discovery, uncertainty and unpredictable competitor activity, unreal speed may affect the quality of a project, contributing to its failure. This risk is intensified if NPSD budgets are also cut to achieve short-term corporate profit targets.

### 4. Lack of rigorous process

Does your company have an NPSD process? Is it flawed, or not properly observed? If so, you are not unusual. Superficial business analysis, weak project management, changes in the NPSD team, poorly planned consumer research, lack of cross-departmental co-operation and failure to conduct proper testing before launch are often responsible for new product failure.

## 5. Product or service does not deliver sufficient extra value

Unless a new offering is distinctive or achieves a superior mix of performance and price, it is unlikely to either succeed or be sustainable.

## 6. Underestimated costs

Future costs are often difficult to estimate, and it is tempting to take a 'best circumstance' view of them. Consequently, new product costs are often well above estimate, and since cost overruns are not a relevant justification for increasing prices, profits prove disappointing.

Areas where costs seem to be most often underestimated are development, conversion of prototypes to mass production and marketing launch, where too little allowance is made for competitor reaction. It is preferable to be realistic rather than 'best circumstance' in outlook, and essential to have the support of high-quality financial people, skilled in future costing.

# Key Issues to Resolve on NPSD

This section will cover four key issues which need to be resolved before establishing a NPSD process. They are as in Table 217.

| Table 217. Four key issues on NPSD. |
| --- |
| 1. How to establish total NPSD resource needed |
| 2. How to organize NPSD |
| 3. How to allocate R & D resource |
| 4. How to evaluate NPSD performance |

None of these issues have simple or generally accepted answers.

## 1. How to establish total NPSD resource needed

The first thing to determine is how to define NPSD resource. This goes well beyond R & D spending, much of which is spent on cost-reduction and process engineering projects unrelated to NPSD. A sensible definition of NPSD resource would be any cost primarily associated with NPSD origination or launch, across every department. Primary NPSD cost areas would be R & D, IT, Operations, Sales and Marketing, and among the largest items would be those in Table 218.

**Table 218. Main NPSD cost areas for products and services.**

| Function | NPSD cost areas | |
| --- | --- | --- |
| | **Products** | **Services** |
| Marketing development | ● Personnel<br>● Market research<br>● External agencies<br>● Packaging development<br>● Other origination costs | ● As for products, but presentation development rather than packaging |
| Marketing launch | ● Advertising<br>● Promotion<br>● PR<br>● Event marketing<br>● Direct marketing | ● As for products. *Add*<br>● Display<br>● Marketing literature<br>● Staff training |
| R & D | ● Technology research<br>● Development and testing<br>● Translation to plant | ● Much of R & D is IT and technology based |
| Sales | ● Sales department resource<br>● Planning<br>● Retail testing, incentive and advertising costs | ● Sales department resource<br>● Planning, staff training<br>● Trade literature and incentives (if distributor involved) |
| IT | ● Incorporate new product on data systems | ● New on-line data<br>● Management, control systems |
| Operations | ● Fit product on to existing lines, modify or build extra plant | ● Adjust operations to new product |

The next step is to use this definition to estimate NPSD spend over the past three to five years. Spend can then be broken down both by cost area, as in the table above, and by type of activity, such as product improvements, new products or services, line extensions, or totally new brands. What is the overall trend in recent years, both in absolute terms and as a percent of sales? Which activities have been least, and most, effective? What benefit and value is each cost area providing, and how can these be improved? How effectively are NPSD funds being spent compared with competition?

A straightforward piece of offensive business analysis like this will provide a powerful perspective on how effective your NPSD spending is, how it can be improved, and strong clues as to what future resource should be allocated. In practice, it is rarely carried out, because responsibility for NPSD is so widely spread across departments. Does your company even have a figure for total NPSD spend? Most do not.

Having analysed the past, how should future NPSD resource levels be established? Five methods are in use, similar in principle to the approach for setting advertising budgets, as follows:

(a) **Historical approach.** This method will use history as a base and adjust up or down from this base for the future. Its weakness is that historical spend levels may have been wrong.

(b) **Residual approach.** This system, if it can be called such, is to leave the decision on NPSD spend until the end of the budget process, and to allocate 'what we can afford' after profit requirements and all other costs have been allocated. The result is almost always too low an allocation.

(c) **Match competition.** Approach is to estimate what competitors are spending in absolute terms and as a percent of sales, and to relate your own spend to this. The method may not be relevant, since competitors may have more or less ambitious NPSD needs than your company, and may be pursuing them more or less effectively. Furthermore, it is both speculative and defensive.

(d) **Percent of sales.** This is an important measure, especially trended over time and broken down by type of activity or cost. It is best to use **NPSD spend as percent of new product sales** as the measure. Relating NPSD spend to **total** sales is less useful, because in any one year total sales consist mainly of unchanged products, which do not benefit from NPSD spend.

However, NPSD spend as percent of new product sales is more useful as a measure than as a system of allocation.

(e) **Task approach.** This is by far the best method. To be effective, though, it requires offensive business analysis of past NPSD spend (see above), gap analysis to establish future revenue and profits needed from new products, and a breakdown of the gap figure by major type of project. These pieces of information will enable you to establish the task, and to estimate future NPSD resource needed, on a basis strong enough to resist any rational attempts to cut.

## 2. How to organize NPSD

This question is often asked in too narrow a context – that of the Marketing Department. As such, the issue is a hoary old chestnut.

Should NPSD be an additional task of existing Marketing Line Managers, or the sole purpose of a dedicated new products group? The drawbacks of both are well known. Managers of existing brands tend to be so busy running them that they have no time for NPSD even on a rainy Friday afternoon. A new products group may lack feel for the hurly-burly of the market-place, and run into 'not invented here' attitudes when they hand over new products to existing line management to run.

This narrow question is becoming less relevant, as new development projects become increasingly international and cross-departmental. Their success depends less on Marketing Department structure, more on corporate commitment, allocation of resources, clear objectives and integration. These factors will drive a type of organization appropriate to each company, and this will differ depending on its size, aspirations and culture.

It is not, therefore, meaningful to talk about 'right' or 'wrong' structures for NPSD. But it is often worth while to handle 'housekeeping' types of NPSD, where products or services are being improved or extended, differently from major new projects.

Straightforward product or service improvements, and conventional line extensions, are in general best handled by existing line management, with the involvement of an Extended Brand Group.

Significant new initiatives, involving high cost, long lead-times and unusual challenges are often most effectively managed by cross-departmental project teams. They can be part time or full time, depending on their role and on the importance of the project. Basic requirements for such a project team, which may well be led by a marketer, are to:

- Establish a project leader and team members.
- Set clear and measurable objectives for the team and for individual members, broken down by month or quarter.
- Communicate frequently, and evaluate performance against agreed milestones at least monthly.
- Appoint a member of senior management as project sponsor, to link up with the team, provide advice, remove barriers and help with internal politics.

Project teams may be local, international or a combination of the two. Video-conferences, e-mail, fax and phone remove the need for frequent meetings among project team members, who can communicate effectively even when spread across continents.

The ultimate approach to NPSD, now being considered by at least one major multinational, is to develop the three- or five-year corporate plan, identify the half-dozen future initiatives critical to its success and appoint full-time project teams to run them. Each member would be contracted to the project team for two to three years, or whatever the project length was, and heavily incentivized at project completion if objectives have been achieved. The major benefits of this approach are:

- High-priority marketing development projects get handled with the discipline and dedication of new factory builds.
- Full cross-departmental integration.
- Continuity of people in team, until project completion.
- Everyone in the project team has accelerated learning about other functions, and becomes more transferable across functions.
- Team leadership is excellent preparation for becoming a general manager.

### 3. How to allocate R & D resource

This relates primarily to product development, but similar issues apply to allocation of scarce and expensive IT resource for service development.

R & D involves risks and some inevitable waste. Only a minority of the work results in commercial applications. The setting of clear R & D priorities concentrates effort and reduces waste.

R & D allocations need to be taken at both a macro level, 'top down', and at a micro level, 'bottom up'. Macro allocations are to types of technology and activities. Strategies for these should be decided at Board level. They need to be adjusted to reality, through exposure to 'bottom up' projects developed by people close to the market-place. Table 219 summarizes this.

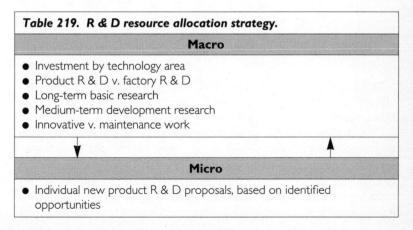

**Table 219. R & D resource allocation strategy.**

| Macro |
|---|
| • Investment by technology area |
| • Product R & D v. factory R & D |
| • Long-term basic research |
| • Medium-term development research |
| • Innovative v. maintenance work |

| Micro |
|---|
| • Individual new product R & D proposals, based on identified opportunities |

Investment by technology area is outside the scope of this book. Most companies will wish to develop superior competencies in at least one key technology area, whether R & D or IT. Technology emphasis should be directed towards the company's priority market sectors – those with future attractiveness where competencies can realistically be built.

From a marketing viewpoint, an important macro strategy issue is how much time to spend on genuinely innovative work, and how much on maintenance tasks such as making minor improvements or cost savings to existing products.

The pressure for the immediate is as strong in R & D as elsewhere, and unless a clear priority is set, short-term projects with a low potential pay-off will clamour for attention and receive it.

An R & D profile map, like the one in the next table (Table 220) is a useful aid to resource allocation strategy. It helps identify whether the deployment of a company's R & D effort by type of activity is both what it expects and what it wants.

**Table 220.  Example of R & D profile map.**

| % of spending | Type of technology | Origin of product concept | Relation to business |
|---|---|---|---|
| | Development *(technology known to company)* | Market driven *(marketing department)* | Existing products |
| | | | New products |
| | Basic *(technology new to company or new to world)* | Technology-driven *(R & D on own initiative or in response to marketing brief)* | New businesses |
| | | | New technology |

In balancing innovative projects against short-term ones, future cash-flow requirements must not be forgotten. Few businesses can afford to launch more than one block-buster new product every couple of years, and short-term/low-risk projects finance these and meet immediate profit requirements.

Once a division between genuinely new work and maintenance or replacement effort has been determined, priorities should be set for individual projects. This is a continuous process and very much a matter of judgement. Obviously, the highest priority should be given to those projects with the best profit potential, and this is affected by marketing, technical and cost variables.

The three questions that should be asked about any product development project are:

1. Assuming technical success, what is its profit potential in the market-place?
2. What is the chance of technical success?
3. How much R & D time and cost is it likely to absorb from start to completion?

The answers will obviously be quite rough, but each question should be considered and an eventual priority arrived at, based on a balance between them.

A useful device for bringing some order to these generalities is the product development priority table, illustrated in Table 221.

Scores are allocated for market potential and likelihood of technical success. Priority is set, based on these factors plus likely cost and time-scale. Four fictional projects are included in the table for the purposes of illustration.

**Table 221. Product development priority table.**

|  | Project number | | | |
|---|---|---|---|---|
|  | **1** | **2** | **3** | **4** |
| Market potential (max. 100)* | 90 | 25 | 40 | 60 |
| Percentage chance of technical success | 55 | 100 | 70 | 20 |
| Likely time-scale (years) | 5 | 0.25 | 2 | 4 |
| Estimated cost (£000)** | 950 | 30 | 60 | 400 |
| Priority Rating (A–D)*** | A | A | B | D |

\*  *The score ranges from 0–100. 0–25 is a marginal improvement in consumer benefit; 26–50 is a significant improvement; 51–100 is a major breakthrough.*
\*\*  *This column refers to R & D departmental costs.*
\*\*\*  *Priority rating A is best, D worst.*

An analysis of this table shows that Project 1, which offers a breakthrough opportunity with a reasonable chance of success, gets priority A, even though the gestation time is five years. Project 2 also gains top priority because, despite its marginal market potential, it involves no technical challenge and can be developed very quickly. Project 3 is worth pursuing too, but Project 4 would be dropped.

An orderly approach to priority-setting will reduce waste but will not eliminate it, because research is a creative rather than a mechanical process.

## 4. How to evaluate NPSD performance

### How should this be assessed? By whom? How often?

At the company level, quantitative innovation targets in annual reports are valuable because they are public and measurable. They send a strong message throughout the organization, and influence vision, values and culture. Chapter 2 suggests that all company reports should contain innovation objectives, and the Universal Leisure Company 2021 (on page 74) provides an example.

3M aims for 30% of this year's sales in products launched in the past four years; Gillette for 40% in the last five; and both regularly achieve these demanding targets.

Hewlett-Packard publishes vintage charts annually, showing the breakdown of today's sales by year of product introduction, covering each of the past four years individually, and Year 5 and beyond as a single total, as in Figure 76.[10]

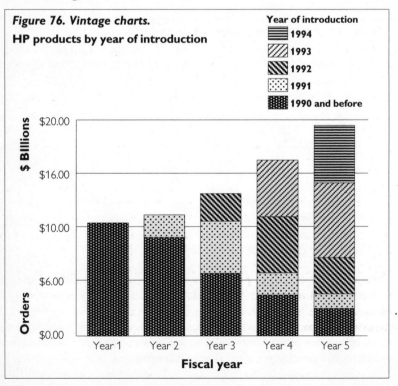

**Figure 76. Vintage charts.**
HP products by year of introduction

Year of introduction
- 1994
- 1993
- 1992
- 1991
- 1990 and before

On a more detailed level, NPSD **output** and **success rate** can be evaluated. A practical point at which to start measuring output is when a concept idea has been successfully consumer-tested.

Table 222 assumes there are four more stages after validated concept: product or service development; testing of proposition; test marketing; and launch. It summarizes output and success rate through the four stages. How good do you think this performance is for a toy manufacturer over a two-year period?

**Table 222. Toy manufacturer: new product output, success rate** (read across).

| Stage: | Output | Success | Success rate % | Cumulative % |
|---|---|---|---|---|
| Validated concept | – | 300 | – | – |
| Development | 300 | 200 | 67 | 67 |
| Proposition test | 200 | 100 | 50 | 33 |
| Test market | 30 | 15 | 50 | – |
| Launch | 70 | 40 | 57 | 13 |

Of 300 initially validated concepts, 40 or 13% have succeeded nationally. Output is therefore 300, success rate 13%. About 100 fell out at the development stage, due to either feasibility or cost. Another 100 failed to pass muster at the final proposition hurdle. A hundred reached the market-place, 30 in test, and 70 nationally without market testing.

The Board should see a new product output and success rate table at least quarterly. And all company development projects merit a monthly priority review by the Marketing Director, since priorities can change rapidly.

**Output** measures *level* of NPSD effort, while **success rate** evaluates the *effectiveness* of that effort.

## Suggested NPSD Process

No standard process can be applied in detail to every situation, since different industries and companies have different requirements. However, there is a broad sequence of activity which is best practice in most circumstances. This consists of opportunity identification, idea generation, screening and prioritizing of ideas, technical development, business-plan development, final testing and launch.

Some companies will follow the full process. If speed is of the essence, steps may be omitted or handled concurrently. Companies can move faster through processes in markets where they have vast prior experience, or on minor projects; more slowly in new sectors or when building new competencies.

The seven-step process summarized in Table 223 is structured as a general purpose design for NPSD, and can be modified to fit particular situations. It may be used for total businesses or for brands. To simplify the explanation, the process has largely been applied to a brand.

**Table 223. General purpose NPSD process – seven steps for a brand.**

| Step | Process | Key Elements |
|---|---|---|
| 1 | **Opportunity identification** | ● Identify areas for collecting ideas<br>● Establish criteria for evaluation<br>● List ideas already developed<br>● Generate new ones |
| 2 | **Initial idea screening** | ● Apply criteria and screen<br>● Write up best ideas into concepts<br>● Test out with users qualitatively |
| 3 | **Develop technical briefs** | ● Discuss with R & D and/or IT<br>● Write brief, for product or service<br>● Get approval and priority for development |
| 4 | **Develop products, services** | ● Technical development of concept<br>● Develop outline Marketing plan |
| 5 | **Develop support elements, validate** | ● Progress advertising, presentation, packaging<br>● Research overall proposition and main elements with consumers, customers<br>● This may include a simulated test market |
| 6 | **Final plan** | ● Operations, Sales, Finance involvement<br>● Marketing plan<br>● Operations plan and action, including capital investment<br>● Sales and trade or distributor marketing plan<br>● Finalize packaging, advertising, customer literature, direct marketing, PR, sales promotion, trade activity<br>● Communicate internally, train staff |
| 7 | **Launch and one step ahead (test market or national)** | ● Implement test, roll-out, or national launch plan<br>● Develop next initiatives, for Year 2, to keep one step ahead.<br>● Monitor results, prepare for Year 2 or 3 relaunch. |

Each of these steps will be reviewed individually below.

## STEP 1: OPPORTUNITY IDENTIFICATION

### Identify areas for collecting ideas

Opportunity identification and idea generation need to be focused on market segments, channels, brands and competencies already earmarked as future priorities. This ensures that good ideas with consumer appeal have a fair chance of commercial success.

This prioritization has already been covered in previous chapters, and is summarized in Table 212, on the foundations of NPSD (page 420).

It can be brought to life by preparing a one- or two-page opportunity development brief, to guide those whom you wish to generate new ideas. A suggested format for this on a brand is given in Table 224.

| Table 224.  Format for opportunity development brief (1–2 pages). ||
| --- | --- |
| 1.  Future brand objectives | *5-year sales, market share* |
| 2.  Priority market segments | *Identify existing priority segments and likely future ones for expansion* |
| 3.  Brand core proposition | *One-sentence statement* |
| 4.  Brand extendibility | *Attach copy of Brand Circle chart* |
| 5.  Distribution channel priorities | *Current priorities, future extensions* |
| 6.  Summary of current ideas under development | *One-line description, target timing* |

This is clearly a confidential document. It would be circulated, together with the latest Brand Positioning Statement, to the Extended Brand Group and Opportunity Identification Teams. A shorter and less confidential version could be used when wider internal or external groups are involved.

### Establish criteria for evaluating ideas

These need to be formally established in order to ensure consistent treatment over time, overriding changes in internal management. People submitting ideas are entitled to know how these will be assessed, and to be confident they will be treated objectively and fairly. It is usually possible and sensible to agree company-wide criteria, applicable to all businesses. An example of possible criteria is shown in Table 225.

> **Table 225.  Possible criteria for evaluating ideas.**
>
> ● Strategic relevance, *i.e. within priority areas*
> ● Exceeds minimum volume *level (will vary by market)*
> ● Volume to be mainly incremental to existing business
> ● Distinctive
> ● Fits or exploits existing company competencies
> ● Easily understandable
> ● Relevant to consumer and customer
> ● Protectable and sustainable

These criteria are ideal and few ideas will meet all of them. If desired, they can be converted into a numerical system for scoring new ideas.

### List ideas already developed

You will already have built up a sound inventory of ideas and hypotheses during Offensive Business Analysis, SWOT analysis, and by checking past marketing plans. Other ideas may also have arrived from internal or external sources, or be on file from past regimes.

### Generate new ideas

There are numerous ways to develop new product or service ideas, but it is difficult to forecast in advance which ones will produce the best results for a given company. The secret is to start by using them all and then to drop the ones which are least fruitful. And the most important single rule about new idea generation is to ensure that it is systematic and continuous, not ad hoc and spasmodic. Table 226 comprises a check-list of the main sources of ideas, with action steps on how to manage each one.

Customers, consumers and employees are often the most productive sources of new ideas:

(a) **Customers** are always a major source, since they either use the products or services themselves or are close to the user. You and your competitor have an equal opportunity to access them. They will usually respond only if they feel their ideas will be taken seriously by someone who is really listening.

(b) **Consumers** are valuable in reacting to specific ideas, and ranking them. They can also be useful when mixed in groups with creative people, engineers and R & D, especially if they are heavy users, or, in the case of industrial goods, at the leading edge.

**Table 226. Main new ideas sources and how to activate them.**

| Ideas source | How to activate |
|---|---|
| (a) Customers | ● Brief sales force on where ideas needed<br>● Train sales people in accessing, reporting new ideas from customers<br>● Establish reward and recognition system |
| (b) Consumers | ● Focus on heavy users, early adopters of new ideas<br>● Use group discussions, dissatisfaction studies<br>● Expose consumers to new concepts and ask them to rank, then develop |
| (c) Employees | ● Brief on needs<br>● Acknowledge all suggestions, reward best ones<br>● Use Extended Brand Groups or special cross-departmental project teams to develop ideas, using idea generation techniques |
| (d) External agencies and suppliers | ● Ad agencies, consultancies, suppliers are all good sources, but need to be briefed and motivated |
| (e) R & D or IT technical ideas | ● Ideas can be generated from technical hypotheses or breakthroughs as well as from consumer needs<br>● Encourage R & D and IT to come up with technical ideas even if they can see no obvious consumer application. |
| (f) Competitors | ● Develop an effective competitor analysis system (See Chapter 5, pages 203–11)<br>● Use competition as a basis for improvement |
| (g) Overseas sources | ● Data sources<br>● Personal visits |
| (h) Patents | ● Search recently registered and expiring patents |
| (i) Previous new ideas on file | ● Old ideas may have been wrongly assessed<br>● Times and markets change |

(c) **Employees**. Successful companies have established a company culture that encourages every employee to seek new ideas for improving the company's production, products and services. Toyota claims that its employees submit two million ideas annually, about thirty-five suggestions per employee, and over 85% of them are implemented. Kodak and some American firms give monetary and recognition awards to their employees who submit the best ideas during the year.[11]

## Using Idea-generation Techniques (within Step 1)

In addition to the regular flow of new ideas from a variety of sources, formal idea-generation projects are also essential. These need to be well prepared and skilfully managed. The key steps are to identify specific areas for idea generation, select a cross-departmental team, brief the team and then run an ideas session using a range of techniques.

This professional approach is much more likely to produce results than the often aimless 'away days', involving a meeting of marketing and advertising agency people away from the office in a country hotel. There is little point in a Brand Manager standing in front of a flip chart, somewhere in Middle England, and saying: 'Now let's have some new product ideas in the market for X.'

There are many techniques for generating new ideas from groups of people. The best known is the brainstorming or idea-generation group. Typical size is from three to ten people, usually from varied back-grounds. Possible members are a heavy user, a customer, a sales represen-tative, a technologist from a different product field, a marketing person, an advertising agency creative person, an engineer and a telesales or customer service person. The focus is on generating as many ideas as possible. No evaluation of quality occurs during the group session because this would inhibit the flow of creativity.

The leader of the group is usually the key to its success, and he or she needs to be well prepared.

Other group idea-generation techniques include **synectics, trigger sessions** and **attribute listing**, and some of the methods used are described in the listing below.

A number of stimulants can be used to create a flow and 'prompts' to overcome blockages or dead ends in group sessions. These include:

- **Point of entry questions** to switch the line of thought. If a group were considering a new type of car brake, the leader might ask: 'How can you stop a car that has no brakes?' or, 'Why doesn't a ship have brakes?'
- **Analogies.** These stop the brain moving along familiar lines.
- **Attribute mixing.** The group would be asked to list the elements most important in structuring a new product, such as image, ingredients or types of consumer. For the most important elements a series of attributes is developed. For example, types of consumer might include commuters, tourists, teenagers, etc. A limited number of attributes would be selected by the group and written on coloured cards. These cards could then be mixed to stimulate discussion and ideas.

- **Lateral thinking.**
- **Mood tapes.** Musical or visual images from films or TV can create a brand 'mood', and be used as a basis for ideas.
- **Role playing.** Each member of the group is asked to assume a different character, perhaps a particular type of consumer or customer. What would this character do in certain specified situations? What are his or her unmet needs? What irritates them?
- **Drawing on flip charts.** Pictures of animals, people, cars can stimulate ideas, or be used to tell a stimulating story about a product or service.
- **Customer tapes.** Short real-life excerpts from real customer experiences.

It will be evident that many imaginative idea techniques are available and others can be developed. You have a long-list of promising ideas. They now need to be pruned and screened into a strong short-list for testing.

## STEP 2: INITIAL IDEA SCREENING

Step 2 is the first stage of formal screening, although a lot of rough screening will have occurred during Step 1. Screening, however, is continuous, and should formally occur at each of the seven processes. Think of a new product idea as a suitcase on an elevator. It has to move from the basement to the penthouse on the top floor, and stop on each floor for inspection by ever more senior staff members. If on any floor it fails the inspection, it is removed from the elevator, and that is that. Another good analogy is the steeplechase – a new product has to clear a number of specified jumps, each higher than the one before.

Initial idea screening is on the ground floor and probably will be done by a Brand Manager, involving most of the following elements:

### Apply criteria and screen

Criteria will already have been established, as part of Step 1 (see Table 225, page 450). If these have been quantified, the better ideas can be scored and a pass mark set. Alternatively, simple judgement, taking the criteria as a guide, may be used.

### Write up the best ideas into concepts

This is an art in itself, and very important. It is rarely given enough priority. Good ideas can fail in consumer testing through poor conversion into concepts. Concept statements should be brief (no more than fifty words), clear, describe the proposition and express a consumer benefit. They should consist of short sentences, using everyday consumer language, not advertising jargon, and be simple to understand without further explanation. Table 227 provides an example of a concept for an improved fax machine.

---

**Table 227. Example of concept statement: new fax machine.**

'This new executive fax is very compact, sized 10" × 10", and fits easily on any desk. It sorts incoming faxes in correct order. The fax is very fast, handling 20 pages a minute and comes in a choice of four colours.'

---

This concept statement would be consumer tested against others, and ranked. It contains four benefits – compactness, sequential sorting, speed and colour. The interviewer would aim not only to understand the consumer appeal of the total proposition, but also the relative contribution of each benefit. In this way, individual concepts can be strengthened by removing weak benefits, replacing them with stronger ones taken from other concepts.

### Test out concepts with users qualitatively, in small groups

At this point, concepts are still being checked, refined and developed, probably with groups of target consumers in discussion with a trained moderator. The strongest concepts may be improved, rewritten and retested a number of times. The interviewer should go through them phrase by phrase, checking reaction to each element, and the specific wording, as well as the totality. Special groups of interviewees, such as doctors, technicians, retailers, home economists, can also be tested in addition to consumer groups.

Procter & Gamble is 'best practice' in concept development, applying typical rigour and determination to the task. One of their techniques is the **Concept Laboratory**, which works as follows:

**This is often a two- to three-day exercise, typically involving an advertising agency person, R & D group head, and Brand Manager responsible for the programme. There will be an interview room for consumer discussion groups led by a moderator, and a meeting room from which executives can view the discussions unseen.**

**The Brand Manager will have prepared a number of concepts, on white boards, for the moderator to use, and six to eight groups of consumers will have been booked**

to appear at specified times over the next two to three days.

The first consumer group will be exposed to, say, six concepts over a one-hour period by the moderator. They will discuss each one, dissect it, and rank it compared to the others.

The executives will view this activity through a one-way mirror, analyse the learning and consider paradoxes (apparent contradictions) and paradigms (ideal requirements). They will then adjust and strengthen the concepts.

These adjusted concepts would then be exposed to the next group of consumers, the results reviewed, the concepts retested and so on. The process would continue until the winning concept(s) had been identified and refined.

### Check concept winners quantitatively

Quantification is important in order to validate the relative strength of each concept, to compare it against previous norms, and to make final improvements. Concepts doing well at the qualitative stage may not reach the required standard on quantification, and be dropped.

It is worthwhile keeping a summary of quantitative concept test results for at least five years, both to avoid retesting losing concepts and to provide a bank of scores against which to rank new concepts.

### STEP 3: DEVELOP TECHNICAL BRIEFS

This is the stage at which significant development costs will start to be incurred. At Steps 1 and 2, costs have been modest. A management decision now has to be made whether to allocate scarce R & D or IT resource to developing the concept to final product or service format. As the idea moves up the cost gradient, the screening levels become more demanding.

Working with R & D and Finance, the Brand Manager would complete a development brief for the winning concept, and submit it for approval to the Marketing Manager or Director. If approved, the concept would become a development project within R & D, and its progress monitored at least monthly.

The development brief would summarize previous concept research, outline the benefits and characteristics to be built into the product or service, set a target cost and very succinctly provide a commercial justification. The brief would be one page only, and a format is outlined in Table 228.

| Table 228. Development brief for new product or service. | |
|---|---|
| **1. Brand name** | State planned name. New or existing brand |
| **2. Market** | Describe market sector, size and trend |
| **3. Consumer target** | Outline demographics and other relevant points |
| **4. Consumer benefit** | Specify benefit this project will deliver to the consumer, and how it will be different and better than competition |
| **5. Competitive advantage** | Derive from (4) above |
| **6. Research support for benefit** | Substantiate the appeal of the proposed benefit, by reference to consumer or technical research and concept testing |
| **7. Commercial opportunity** (£K) <br> *Extra revenue* <br> *Extra cost* <br> *Extra profit margin* | Year 1      Year 2      Year 3 <br> . . . . . . . .    . . . . . . . .    . . . . . . . . <br> . . . . . . . .    . . . . . . . .    . . . . . . . . <br> . . . . . . . .    . . . . . . . .    . . . . . . . . |
| **8. Development description** | Specify how product or service benefit should be achieved, and indicate target cost and pricing. |
| **9. Planned launch date** | State date of any market test and national launch |

Let's say, for example, that the project is a new financial service for high net worth individuals, offered by a bank. Overall consumer benefit might be:

**We will meet all your savings and investment needs and provide you with an experienced personal account handler who will have access to all our internal experts on your behalf.**

Specific development description to the IT and Human Resource Departments (Item 8 from Table 228) might be:

- **New software to enable all savings and investment data for high net worth individuals (HNWI) to be accessed on a single on-screen database.**
- **Integrated on-screen data for both bank branches and direct tele-sales.**

- **Internal selection and training programmes to develop high-calibre HNWI personal account handlers with broad-ranging knowledge.**

## STEP 4: DEVELOP PRODUCTS, SERVICES

You now have a potentially winning concept and a development brief. This stage is crucial in turning a promising concept into a winning product or service. The development brief must be met as specified, for both benefit and cost.

Technical development can take weeks or months. Marketing people should use this time concurrently to structure an outline business plan. This assumes the development brief will be successfully met. It will comprise outline strategies and economics. Strategies would cover the standard areas of product, presentation, customer service, advertising, pricing and trade channel. Economics would include rough revenue, market share, costs, marketing spending and profits, culminating in a profit-and-loss plan for the first three years.

At this stage, when technical development is not yet proven, it is not usually worth investing in the cost of advertising or packaging origination. You would only risk such concurrent activity if speed was of the essence, and competition either ahead or breathing down your neck.

Once technical development is complete, a product would be consumer blind-tested against competitors, and the next step would not be undertaken unless or until you had a preferred and differentiated product.

New services can be more difficult to consumer test directly against competitors. However, elements like new menu items in a restaurant or a new seat type for an airline can easily be consumer blind-tested. And the overall proposition for a new financial service can be tested by mocking up leaflets or brochures and comparing with competition, perhaps blanking out the competitive brand name.

It is important, before clearing a project for advance to Step 5, to demonstrate that it is technically feasible at the planned cost, and can deliver the competitive advantage targeted in the brief. If you are not convinced, you should rework the project or scrap it.

## STEP 5: DEVELOP SUPPORT ELEMENTS, VALIDATE

Your project has survived stepping up the first four levels and now arrived at the next. Step 5 involves validating all the individual elements in the marketing plan, and evaluating the totality of the proposition. At this level, advertising, packaging and, in the case of services, consumer presentation will be developed. These may be consumer tested individually, versus competition, and then as a totality.

Meanwhile, the marketing plan will be further developed and refined. Screen again very critically before taking the next step (Step 6).

## STEP 6: DEVELOP FINAL PLAN

Using consumer research results from Step 5, and latest costs, detailed marketing plans can now be finalized, in close consultation with Operations and Sales, who will be primarily responsible for implementation.

At this stage, a Board decision has to be taken whether to conduct a limited market test next, or whether to move immediately to national or multi-country launch.

## STEP 7: LAUNCH AND ONE STEP AHEAD

This is the final level, and is likely to involve big money. Even as the new product or service is being launched nationally, you should be planning your next moves, so that you can keep one step ahead of competition with product improvements or service upgrades in the months ahead. You may also, as part of your national launch, be testing a more offensive variant of your plan in one area, such as upweighted advertising, house-to-house product sampling, extra direct marketing activity, a wider product range or even an extra-strength product.

Although the launch is the final step in the development process, it is only the start of the life of the new product or service. The first year is the most critical period, when customers will form views. If these are unfavourable, they will be difficult and expensive to change in subsequent years. You can be almost certain that competition will react, and allowance for this needs to be built into your plan. You should have considered various competitor response scenarios before you launch, and determined how best to counter, so that you can act quickly if and when they occur. And you need to rigorously evaluate each element of your plan in the reality of the market-place, ruthlessly searching for ways to strengthen the proposition.

# FLOW-CHART SUMMARY OF CHAPTER 11

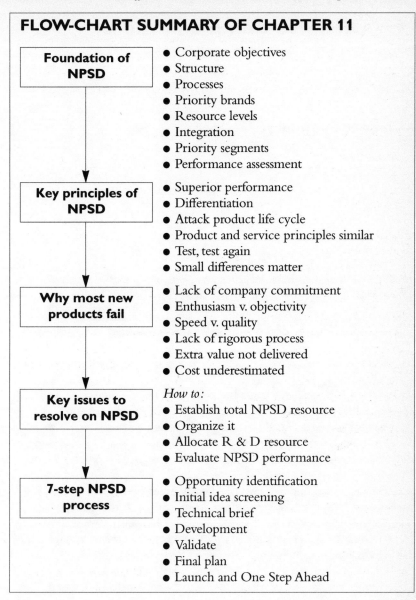

**Foundation of NPSD**
- Corporate objectives
- Structure
- Processes
- Priority brands
- Resource levels
- Integration
- Priority segments
- Performance assessment

**Key principles of NPSD**
- Superior performance
- Differentiation
- Attack product life cycle
- Product and service principles similar
- Test, test again
- Small differences matter

**Why most new products fail**
- Lack of company commitment
- Enthusiasm v. objectivity
- Speed v. quality
- Lack of rigorous process
- Extra value not delivered
- Cost underestimated

**Key issues to resolve on NPSD**
*How to:*
- Establish total NPSD resource
- Organize it
- Allocate R & D resource
- Evaluate NPSD performance

**7-step NPSD process**
- Opportunity identification
- Initial idea screening
- Technical brief
- Development
- Validate
- Final plan
- Launch and One Step Ahead

# 12. Offensive Communications

## Chapter Summary

**Table 229**

| | |
|---|---|
| **P:** Profitable | ● Proper balance between firm's needs for profit and customer's need for value |
| **O:** Offensive | ● Must lead market, take risks and make competitors followers |
| **I:** Integrated | ● Marketing approach must permeate whole company |
| **S:** Strategic | ● Probing analysis leading to a winning strategy |
| → **E:** Effectively Executed | ● Strong and disciplined execution on a daily basis ← |

This chapter focuses on communications to consumers and customers, and only incidentally refers to distributors, employees and shareholders, since these are specialized targets outside the scope of a general book on marketing.

'Communications' is a much broader word than 'Advertising', which is often used synonymously with broadcast media, especially television and press. It covers any visual or audio medium which creates brand awareness or attitude changes. Posters, sponsorship, event marketing, informercials, word-of-mouth comment, certain types of sales promotion, direct marketing and the use of sales people as influencers all qualify as 'Communications'. Indeed, one could easily extend the definition to packaging, and legal cases or news stories, both of which can achieve strong publicity – sometimes by design, often not. However, because of the importance of advertising to many marketers, it receives the primary emphasis in this chapter.

With proliferation in types of media, and ability to target audiences more precisely, choice of media has become an important decision. The old scenario, where the major brander would opt for a media schedule of peak-time TV, topped up by magazines and posters, is gone for ever. Even within TV, some American homes can receive over 500 channels, and there are specialist channels for opera, art, slimming and personal health.

Most of the important questions on communications remain

unchanged, although the answers have become more complex. The first part of this chapter covers key principles and questions like:

- How communication works.
- How communication differs from other outside purchases.
- How to manage external agencies.
- How to achieve integrated communications.
- How much to spend on communications.
- Identifying and selecting key targets.
- Determining what to say – the communications strategy.
- How to evaluate creative work.

The second part of the chapter outlines an eight-stage process for Offensive Communication Development, which builds on the key principles and translates them into action. The eight process steps described are:

1. Decide on communications objective, task and budget.
2. Develop communications strategy.
3. Establish media strategy (Steps 2 and 3 are often concurrent).
4. Develop creative work and outline media plan.
5. Evaluate creative work, approve for research.
6. Pre-test communications with target customer. Evaluate, improve.
7. Produce creative work, agree media plan. Run programme.
8. Evaluate results. Further improve. Keep **one step ahead**.

This process is relevant to most types of communication and business, although for low-budget programmes or specialist media not all the steps will be necessary.

## Key Principles

### 1. How communication works

Communication creates awareness of the existence and advantages of goods and services. It is a form of personal salesmanship designed to make consumers see a brand or organization in a more favourable light.

With a familiar brand, consumers will have formed a number of different impressions, both favourable and unfavourable, based on previous usage, recollections of past advertising, attitude to packaging and price and opinions of friends and others. Communication will add to this set of impressions by attempting to reinforce favourable attitudes and to loosen or eliminate unfavourable ones.

The devices used are information, reason and emotion. Communication interacts with all the other elements that make up the image of a brand and contribute to its performance, which is why its effect is so difficult to pin down.

The chart on the mechanism of branding from Chapter 10 on 'Offensive Brand Development' (Figure 61) is repeated below as Figure 77. It illustrates that communication is only one of the many company inputs to customers. These inputs create awareness, usage, attitudes and image, which are stored in the consumer's mental inventory. This process is continuous, with further inputs of communication, performance and

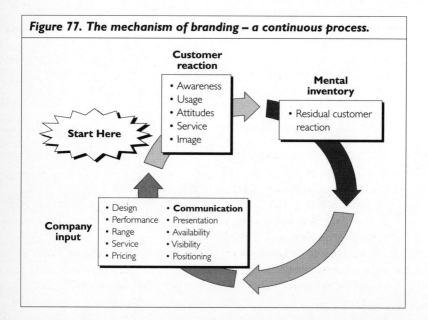

**Figure 77. The mechanism of branding – a continuous process.**

service, creating new consumer reactions. These result in modifications to the mental inventory.

Strong brands can be built up with little or no paid advertising communication, although this is exceptional. Marks & Spencer, the BBC and Virgin are examples. The first two rely on favourable product usage, generating strong word-of-mouth support. The third gained unpaid communication through media reporting, legal cases, and imaginative high-profile events.

The ideal communications scenario is to spend heavily against the right target audience, with a powerful and well-executed strategy backed by a preferred product or service which is widely available and very visible.

## 2. Why run mediocre advertising?

Advertising is expensive and carries your product name. Very good and very bad advertising both cost the same. If you insist on top quality in your products and services, why accept less from your advertising? As long as you allow plenty of time for advertising development and make it very plain to the advertising agency that you want not just good, but outstanding material, you should succeed in getting it.

Never, like the American client in the example below, run advertising just to 'be on the air':

**A distinctive new campaign was developed for a slimming product by a very famous copywriter. It was built around consumer testimonials by people who had been fat. There was a strong analogy with Alcoholics Anonymous, and the test commercials consisted of broken-down-looking women in stark, limbo-like settings, recalling how they had lost weight after 'becoming hooked' on the brand.**

**The effect was depressing. The research even more so, with a substantial proportion of consumers saying it was the worst advertising they had ever seen. However, it was decided to run the advertising on the basis that some advertising was better than none at all and that no alternative campaign was available.**

**The result was that sales continued to decline, the money was wasted and, much worse, an unattractive image was conveyed of both the consumer and the product.**

Advertising using a weak communications strategy or poor execution is unlikely to deliver value for money. Most companies have insufficient funds to finance all their communication tasks, and have to prioritize spending ruthlessly. So why waste any of these scarce resources on less than outstanding communication? Whatever the competitive pressure, it is usually best to delay spending until you have a strong communications campaign.

Only strong messages get noticed by consumers, whose attention is becoming increasingly difficult to attract.

### 3. The limitations of advertising

Advertising is not the all-powerful persuader which many of its critics imply. The average consumer in the UK is present at the showing of about 15,000 commercials every year. An advertiser spending £1 million in that period would buy less than ten of those viewings, or under 0.1 per cent of the total.

To make your £1 million investment pay, you have to establish a presence in the minds of consumers. Each person has only finite mental storage space, and, with only a 0.1 per cent share of exposure, your advertising will have to work very hard to get through. In countries like Spain and Italy, where the typical viewer is exposed to over 20,000 commercials per year, you have to work even harder.

From the viewpoint of the advertiser, the consumer's mind resembles a filing cabinet.[1] The file contains sections like 'retailers', 'banks', 'cars', 'telephones', 'beer' and so on. File contents change weekly as new messages enter and others are disposed of.

Messages are bombarding consumers from many directions. In the USA, 18 million unsolicited phone calls are made daily, equivalent to almost one per household every week.[2] On average, these households received 3,000 coupons a year,[3] and outside the home there is no let-up: 16,000 new grocery products were launched in 1992, more than one each hour.[4]

All the time the number of messages is increasing, but only a small proportion will enter the cabinet. Most individual file headings contain only a few messages, and as a new one comes in, an old one is likely to move out. Some files contain quite old material like 'the sunshine breakfast', 'Guinness is good for you' and 'the real thing', because new messages have lacked the power to dislodge them. Most individual messages are quite thin, but a few, like BT, Gillette or BMW, have more detailed entries.

While some marketers spend over £20 million per year on communications and still manage to lose market share, others, like Starbuck's Coffee (under £2 million annually on measured media in USA), Body Shop and Virgin, succeed in making very little expenditure go a long way.

## 4. How communications differ from other outside purchases

Communications are mostly purchased from outside suppliers, such as advertising, direct marketing, media, event management or PR agencies. They are intended to add value to the product after manufacture, or to the service after delivery, by increasing the consumer's perception of its value.

Communications cannot be equated with the raw materials that go into a product, even though they are purchased externally and also carry the brand name, as Table 230 shows.

**Table 230. How communications purchasing differs from raw materials purchases.**

|  | Communications | Raw materials |
| --- | --- | --- |
| Buying specification | *Broad and subjective* | *Detailed and objective* |
| Cost | *Same, irrespective of quality* | *Varies with quality* |
| Assessment of quality | *Difficult* | *Easy* |
| Correct amount to buy | *Not known* | *Exactly known* |

It might be fairer to compare advertising with the purchase of capital equipment, since advertising is generally accepted as a long-term investment. But no accountant is prepared to depreciate this year's advertising campaign over two years, never mind five, since its effect on sales cannot be precisely measured.

These analogies illustrate the uniqueness of advertising as a form of expenditure. It is an investment, but it cannot be depreciated. Its quality cannot be evaluated objectively. No one is quite sure how much or how little it is best to buy. And, most unusual of all, advertising costs the same whether it is of the highest quality or the lowest. Indeed, the same communications supplier usually delivers both high- and low-quality communications to different clients.

Communications is unusual in one other respect. It is an area of business where companies are best informed about competitor activity. Levels of competitor spending can be measured by brand, by geographical area, by type of media and message. Share of spending can be compared with share of market by company and brand. Effectiveness of competitive communications can be checked through awareness and attitude surveys or advertising tracking studies. No other area of business can be so precisely monitored. And in no other area of the business is value for money more difficult to measure.

### 5. How to manage external agencies

Every year, there are dozens of public seminars on how to manage advertising agencies, and agency-client relationships. Unfortunately, there are rarely any seminars on more critical topics, like how marketers could work more effectively with Operations and Manufacturing. Why is this? Marketers enjoy discussing how to manage agencies, as the only groups over which they have real power – inside the company they operate largely by persuasion. Galloping midgets can make their names overnight as hard men by firing agencies.

Marketers spend too much time with agencies, and too little with internal colleagues in Operations and Finance or with customers.

Some key principles on effective management of agencies are suggested (Table 231), in the hope that they will free up more time for marketers to talk to Operations people. The overriding principle is to create a climate where creativity can flourish. New ideas are fragile things and easily crushed by traditional thinking or highly elaborate approval procedures.

---

**Table 231. Key principles of managing communications agencies.**

- **Establish your requirements from each agency**
- **Agree payment basis, including performance bonus**
- **Agree levels and quality of staffing**
- **Agree annual objectives for each agency**
- **Establish agreed joint operating procedures**
- **Motivate agencies as if they were clients**
- **Evaluate performance jointly against agreed objectives**

---

**Establish your requirements from each agency.** As types of communication increase, **Integrated Marketing communications** has become a buzzword, especially in the USA. This propounds the less than revolutionary view that all forms of communication should conform to a consistent strategy and plan, and be managed as a totality rather than as a series of loosely related activities. In response to this, some advertising agencies have attempted to build a one-stop total communications shop, but few have been totally successful, because most clients still prefer to deal with a number of different specialists. Achieving an integrated communications result through such a diffused structure requires considerable client skills in project planning and management.[5]

On a single major brand, it is not unusual for a client to have agencies for advertising, media, event marketing, sponsorship, PR, sales promotion and direct marketing. Each agency needs to understand the total brand communication strategies and the contribution expected from it. The result should be a clear and consistent message to the consumer, even though fashioned by different external agencies. An analogy is the international football team, whose members spend most of their lives playing for different clubs, each with a distinctive style of play. The international coach has to convert this into a single and consistent approach.

**Agree payment basis, including performance bonus**. Payment can be a percentage of media spend, or a fee based on planned workload. The latter system is now most common, except with media agencies and some advertising agencies.[6]

Quality of agency output can vary dramatically, by client and over time, and a performance bonus system, to be paid in addition to base remuneration, has many advantages. Because client revenue and market share can be affected by many factors other than advertising, it is preferable to base a performance system on quality of communication, validated by consumer research. However, in the 1996 Marketing Forum study, less than 10% of communications agencies were paid by results, which suggests a missed opportunity.

**Agree levels and quality of staffing**. Levels should be set to do the job efficiently, with few hierarchies and avoidance of unnecessary client contact. Every client wants the best talent in the agency, and there is no reason why even a middle-ranking spender should not get it.

**Agree annual objectives for each agency**. These will differ by type of agency. Client should agree output – such as number of campaigns, quality standards and means of assessment.

**Establish agreed joint operating procedures**. Agency and client should discuss their relative roles in the communications process. Is the client primarily responsible for developing the communications strategy, and if so, what contribution are agencies expected to make? Who at the client is responsible for various types of decision? Will the Marketing Director be present at all major agency presentations, to avoid wasting agency time in making several different presentations to various levels of management? What are standard time-scales for various tasks? How quickly and on what basis will client respond to agency recommendations? How frequent will agency invoices be, and how quickly will they be paid? What data will the client give to the agency, and how will confidential information be handled?

These and other operating issues are best discussed at the outset, so that ground rules can be agreed and consistently followed.

**Motivate agencies as if they were clients**. Most agency people are clever and hard working, and want their clients to be successful. They are motivated by demanding clients who set clear objectives, evaluate agency proposals fairly and efficiently and treat them as partners. They are not motivated by clients who are inconsiderate, unprofessional or indecisive, and who think the agency's primary role is to entertain or humour them.

A good starting-point for clients is to tell the advertising agency that they value its freedom from the traditional thinking in which they are enmeshed and hope it will exploit this objectivity to develop radically new ideas. While they appreciate that innovation involves risk, they are prepared to accept this, subject to appropriate testing.

No client ever tells an agency openly that it is not enthused at the prospect of breaking new ground and quite satisfied to ring the changes on humdrum and conventional approaches. It can, though, imply this loud and clear through its reaction to new ideas.

No agency, however determined, will continue to generate radically new thinking for a client who is frightened by it. Many companies like the thought of new ideas in the abstract, but will not accept the iconoclastic approach which can make them a reality. The caption to a *New Yorker* cartoon of a Chairman addressing his Board sums this up well: 'What we need, gentlemen, is a completely new idea that has been thoroughly tested.'

Clients have to go further than giving the agency a charter to think freely. They have a part to play in bringing their knowledge of the consumer to bear on the communications task, and in approving the advertising.

**Evaluate performance jointly against agreed objectives**. Experienced clients often conduct formal joint evaluations with their agencies. They are joint because the client assesses agency performance versus agreed annual objectives, and identifies areas for improvement. And the agency does the same, equally candidly and constructively, with the client. This exercise should be conducted at Marketing Director level.

## 6. How to achieve integrated communications

Imagine yourself as Marketing Manager of a mid-sized car brand. Your communications budget is £36 million, and your mind boggles as you break it down (Table 232).

**Table 232. Mid-size car: communications budget.**

| Medium | Consumer target | Key consumer benefits | Cost £m |
|---|---|---|---|
| TV | BC1 adults aged 30–65 | *Space and reliability* | 20.0 |
| Magazines | BC1 employed women, 35–60 | *Space and reliability* | 3.0 |
| Informercials | As for TV | *Space, reliability, style* | 1.0 |
| Direct mail | Business executives | *Space, reliability, style* | 1.0 |
| Racing sponsorship | As for TV | *Space, reliability, performance* | 3.0 |
| Internet | BC1 adults, 25–35 | *Space and reliability* | 0.3 |
| Interactive Cable TV | Motoring enthusiasts | *Space, reliability, performance* | 0.8 |
| Dealer material | As for TV | *Space and reliability* | 2.0 |
| PR | Journalists, opinion formers | *Benefits tailored to individuals* | 1.3 |
| Event marketing | As for TV | *Space, reliability, style* | 3.6 |
| | | Total | 36.0 |

This communications plan involves at least ten different media, and would probably require six external agencies. **How can you meet the specific needs of each consumer target group and also communicate a consistent message?** To state the obvious, you do not want to be communicating space and reliability to car owners on broadcast TV, and dynamic performance in magazines to the same people.

The answer is to develop an overall communications plan – a more detailed version of the table above – and brief each agency on its role within this plan. It is essential to identify the consumer targets for each medium and the key benefits to be emphasized. Key benefits, such as space and reliability, should be communicated in *every* medium, but *additional* ones, like performance or style, can be offered to particular audiences as well.

By taking advantage of the privacy of direct marketing, marketers can talk to their high-profit customers in a way that is relevant to them but does not confuse the message to the broader audience.[7]

The complexity of media choice is increasing all the time, and achieving effective yet consistent communication will challenge the management skills of even the best marketers.

## 7. How much to spend on communications

**'I know that half of my advertising budget is wasted, but I'm not sure which half'** is a comment that was made many years ago and has now passed into advertising folklore.[8] Accountants particularly enjoy repeating it – some consider that the estimate of 50% waste is too low, typical of the optimism of marketers.

Setting communications budgets and assessing their effectiveness remains an approximate art, and although techniques are available for making the whole business more scientific, some have serious weaknesses. The evaluation of communications still relies heavily on the personal judgement of experienced executives. A number of different factors influence advertising effectiveness, making it difficult to evaluate (Table 233).

---

**Table 233. Ten factors influencing advertising effectiveness.**

| | |
|---|---|
| ● Absolute media weight | ● Relative product or service quality |
| ● Weight v. competition | ● Choice of media |
| ● Strength of strategy | ● Efficiency of media buying |
| ● Strength of execution | ● Campaign wear-out |
| ● Level of brand availability | ● Relative pricing |

---

Every company would give a lot to know the effect of advertising on its sales, but this can rarely be done with precision, except in the case of mail-order sales. Because advertising is only one of the numerous variables which affect sales, many of the tools for evaluating communications use intermediate measurements. The assumption is made that increases in things like brand awareness and favourable attitudes will feed through into extra sales. However, Boards are understandably unimpressed by such measures unless they can also see an increase in sales.

The most difficult types of communication to assess are in markets where a number of major brands are heavily advertised and major spending is needed to even hold share; and 'slow-burn' activity, like sponsorship or PR, whose effect is hard to separate from other communications expenditure. There is a temptation to spend most heavily on types of communication which can be precisely justified rather than those which are most effective.

The majority of companies use either arbitrary or subjective methods for deciding how much to spend on communications. The main approaches have similarities with those used to fix new product and service budgets. They are:

| Table 234.  Six main approaches for setting communications budgets. | |
|---|---|
| ● **Task** | ● **Share of market** |
| ● **Historical** | ● **Match competition** |
| ● **% of turnover** | ● **Residual** |

**The task approach.** This involves setting certain marketing objectives, deriving from the task communications has to fulfil and allocating budget accordingly. The objectives may be set in terms of revenue and profit, in which case the translation to a communications budget is necessarily rather vague. Or they may be more sophisticated and spelt out in the number of advertising messages necessary to achieve desired levels of awareness or changes in attitude. Tasks will also cover launches of new and improved products, line extensions.

The task approach can be useful if it is based on detailed analysis of past results, but should not be used in isolation from other methods.

**Historical.** This method relates next year's communications budget to spending in previous years.

**% of turnover.** This allocates a fixed percentage of a brand's sales turnover to communications. When the brand's volume grows, spending will increase, and vice versa. Although this method needs to be used with discretion, its strength is that it feeds success and starves problem areas. Its weakness is that the percentage is often determined arbitrarily – **why should it be 3% rather than 6%?**

**Share of market.** This involves estimating the amount of future advertising spending for the category and relating a brand's share of this to its target share of the market. Here is an example:

| Table 235.  Share of market. | |
|---|---|
| Estimated total market advertising spending next year | £25m |
| Target brand share | 10% |
| Planned advertising budget for brand next year (i.e. 10% of £25 million) | £2.5m |

This method is not ideal, because the figures are estimated and there is no definitive evidence on the most profitable relationship between share of category advertising and share of market sales.

**Match competition.** This is the second worst method. It is both speculative and defensive.

**Residual.** This the worst method of all, but surprisingly used by some quite sophisticated companies. The system, if it can be called such, is to leave the communications budget until last and allocate whatever is left after costs and profit requirements have been calculated.

Advertising budgets set by this method are the most likely to be cut later, because there is no clear rationale for their levels.

None of these approaches is ideal and a combination of task, percentage of turnover and share of market is most useful. However, the truth is that deep and pragmatic analysis, using a variety of data sources and tests, is more valuable than any mechanical system. Considering how much is spent on communication, and how difficult it is to determine value for money, it is surprising how little is invested on researching effectiveness – usually less than 1% of total advertising spending.

Here, in Table 236, is a suggested approach to setting brand communications budgets which combines systems and pragmatism.

---

**Table 236.  Setting brand communications budgets.**

- **Classify the brand**
- **Set the communications task**
- **Analyse past brand responsiveness**
- **Establish minimum effective spend by media type**
- **Ensure advertising quality is high**
- **Estimate theoretical budget needed using task and share of spend methods**
- **Pragmatically adjust theoretical budget by applying other criteria above**

---

**Classify the brand.** Is it a 'power brand', 'secondary' or 'other'? A brand's classification is determined by its score and position on the quantified portfolio analysis (QPA). Many of the criteria for power brands or for measuring brand strength – such as relative value, differentiation, demonstrated growth potential and future prospects – are also indications of likely response to advertising support.

As in the case of the Riviera Company (Chapter 10, Table 207, page 413), the vast majority of the communications budget should be invested in power brands, whose objective is to gain market share.

**Set the communications task**. Market share, sales, customer trial, customer loyalty, awareness, attitudes and product launches are all likely to feature in this.

**Analyse past brand responsiveness**. Here, in Table 237, are some ways in which responsiveness to past communications expenditure can be assessed.

**Table 237. Brand responsiveness overall and by media type.**

| Type of analysis | Key elements |
| --- | --- |
| 1. Profitability of sales gains v. cost | *Evaluate gain in sales or brand share during and after advertising period, compared with base period* |
| 2. Advertising tracking studies | *Use consumer research to track changes in your brand awareness, usage and image during and after advertising v. competition* |
| 3. Market testing | *Test in limited geographical area higher levels of spending, and no spending at all. Compare differences v. rest of UK* |
| 4. Anecdotal | *Talk to sales people, distributors, retailers and colleagues, and get their playback* |

Econometric analysis takes this process of evaluation further and is becoming more widely used. Its purpose is to isolate the effect of advertising from other possible influences on brand share and then, using multiple regression, model the effect of such things as:

- Price differential between analysed brand and leading competitors.
- Share of category advertising.
- Distribution levels and trends.

The model will help to identify the effect of each of these variables on brand share.

**Establish minimum effective spend by media type**. In certain media, like TV or magazines, the minimum spend level necessary to break through the threshold of consumer communication can be roughly estimated. The theory is that advertising levels below this threshold will be too low to make any impression on consumers.

A great many brands advertise at levels below this threshold and waste vast amounts of money. Why? Because in marketing there is a natural trend to diffusion rather than concentration and because any Brand Manager wants to work on an advertised brand.

Minimum spend levels for TV will vary by country and by category.

For a fast-moving consumer brand, 800 GRP (gross rating points), covering, say, 70% of target consumers eleven times a year, is 'ballpark' for threshold in the UK. This could cost at least £1.8 million, and sustain only two advertising campaigns of four weeks' duration annually.

Minimum spend levels for specialist media, or for highly targeted niche brands, would, of course, be much lower.

**Ensure advertising quality is high**. Only run outstanding advertising, proven by pretesting. This has already been covered.

**Estimate theoretical budget needed using task and share of spend methods**. This theoretical calculation should be modified by the other strategic and pragmatic criteria outlined above.

For a power brand, where the intention is to build position, the brand's share of future total market spending should exceed its present market share.

Table 238 applies these criteria to setting a TV budget for a major brand. It is best to start with a 3 year plan for perspective, and then to track back to next year's budget.

**Table 238.  Power Brand A: factors relevant to setting TV communications budget.**

| Factor | This year | Next year | 3 year plan |
|---|---|---|---|
| Brand status | Power | Power | Power |
| Brand strength score (%) (page 289) | 65 | 68 | 75 |
| Key tasks | | | |
| ● Brand share (%) | 17 | 19 | 24 |
| ● Brand awareness (%) | 26 | 30 | 35 |
| ● Attitude gains | + 3 | + 6 | + 10 |
| ● Relaunch | No | Yes | No |
| ● Launch new products (No.) | 1 | 1 | 3 |
| Min. spend level £m | 1.8 | 1.9 | 2.2 |
| Past response to spend | High | N/A | N/A |
| Quality of advertising (based on testing) | Medium | High | Very high |
| **Brand A Plan** | | | |
| Spend (£m) | 6.0 | 7.3 | 9.5 |
| % total market spend (%) | 20 | 22 | 25 |
| Market share (%) | 17 | 19 | 24 |

In this table, the brand aims to increase market share from 17% today to 24% in three years' time, and will achieve this through new products, plus a radical improvement in quality of advertising. Its share of total market spending is planned ahead of its market share, to help drive share growth. By improving quality of advertising, productivity and impact will be increased – otherwise a much higher share of spending would be necessary, both to build share and to support new products. Desired result is to increase brand strength score from 65% to 75% (based on quantified portfolio analysis).

Not surprisingly, advertising is most effective on products or services with superior performance, since customer usage experience reinforces the favourable attitudes built up by the advertising. Various special analyses by A.C. Nielsen confirm this.[9]

## 8. Identifying and selecting key targets

This is the first step in developing a communications **strategy**.

In selecting targets, the first task is to decide on relative priority between acquiring new customers and retaining or developing existing ones. For a new brand, the former would be the prime priority, but for a well-established product, existing customers would be the main target. Previous chapters have already highlighted that, for most brands, existing customers represent the best source of profitable revenue growth. To underline this point, in fast-moving consumer goods (FMCG) in the USA only a minority of customers make over 50% of their category purchases in one brand, rather than a number of brands.[10]

The second task is to identify the heavier users among your existing customers and to determine the most effective way to reach them. In most FMCG categories, around one third of households account for two thirds of brand volume, and even in widely purchased mass-market categories, like coffee, a very small number of households account for a high proportion of revenue. For instance, in the USA, Folger's is the brand leader in coffee, yet as few as 4% of US households account for half its volume. Footwear brands in the USA demonstrate even more dramatic trends. A study of eighteen brands, quoted by Garth Hallberg, show that 77% of volume was accounted for by one third of users, who **comprised only 2% of total households**.[11] Tight targeting is therefore especially important to avoid expensive wastage in media spending.

In some markets, targets include influencers, purchasers and users. **What is their relative importance? How far should special communications effort be focused on heavy users, style leaders or early adopters of trend-setting new products? If you are**

**marketing Cadillac cars, whose average owner is 65 years old, how far will you try to appeal to younger users now, or should you wait until a more appropriate new model is available?**

In service markets in particular, a company's employees are also a key communications target, even for broadcast media.

Targeting should be as specific as possible. For example, the target for the Co-operative Bank 'ethical investing' campaign was as follows:

**Table 239. Co-operative Bank communications targeting.**[12]

| Targets | Comment |
| --- | --- |
| ● Aged 25–50 years<br>● ABC1 social grades | *Highest-value consumers* |
| ● Competitor current accounts | *Focus on switching competitor customers* |
| ● Caring professions<br>● Socially concerned | *Natural affinity with bank and campaign proposition* |

Boddington's defined its target audience by attitude (Figure 78).

**'We developed a targeting hierarchy along an axis of drinking discernment:**

**'To build the credentials of Boddington's outside its heartland, we initially targeted those towards the top of the triangle, to gain acceptance first amongst those most difficult to impress. Only when credentials had been established would we gradually move to the wider audience.'**

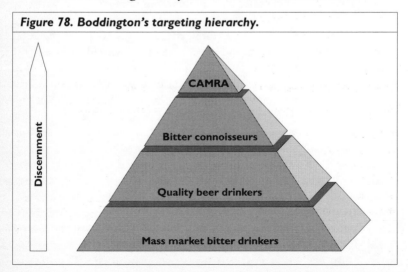

**Figure 78. Boddington's targeting hierarchy.**

Targeting often involves hard and difficult choices. The decisions involved are important, since they form the basis for creative evaluation, media planning and assessment of results.

## 9. Determining what to say – the communications strategy

The communications strategy will derive from a brand's marketing objectives and strategies. It is one of the means for achieving brand objectives.

The Brand Positioning Statement (BPS) – see Chapter 8, page 311 – is therefore the starting-point for developing the communications strategy.

A clear and distinctive communications strategy, even if only moderately executed, is more likely to increase sales than an exciting campaign with no strategy. The communications strategy should cover four main headings, and be totally consistent with the BPS.

- **Target audience** has already been covered.
- **Key consumer benefits** should be in performance areas of importance to the target audience. A major cause of weak communications is the inclusion of too many benefits. One is best, two is a challenge. Complex or unclear benefits are not absorbed by the consumer.
- **Support for benefits**. This section will cover facts which support and justify the key benefits. It can also list communication claims cleared for use by R&D and Legal Departments.
- **Tone of communication**. This will reflect the desired brand personality established in the BPS.

Table 240 summarizes these points.

| Table 240. BPS related to communications strategy. | |
|---|---|
| **Brand positioning statement** | **Communications strategy** |
| ● Brand name | |
| ● Market description | |
| ● Target audience ——————▶ | *Target audience* |
| ● Brand discriminator/benefits<br>● Core consumer proposition ——————▶ | *Key consumer benefits* |
| ● Brand differentiators ——————▶ | *Support for benefits* |
| ● Brand personality ——————▶ | *Tone of communication* |

Much TV advertising appears to lack any clear strategy. 'Too much of it is pretentious nonsense, highbrow and incomprehensible. Copywriters and art directors . . . regard advertising as entertainment – or an art form . . . we sell or else.' This is not a comment by a client: it is a statement by David Ogilvy, one of the most brilliant copywriters of all time.[13] The successful campaigns of Direct Line and Boddington's both reflected vigorous strategy development.

When Direct Line decided to advertise on TV, after years of press support, its marketing objectives were to enter the 'must get a quote from' category of insurers, to build brand awareness and increase response rate. Its communications strategy was as follows:

**Table 241.  Direct Line: TV communications strategy.**[14]

| Target audience | Sensible private motorists aged 25 +, who drive sensible cars sensibly |
|---|---|
| Key consumer benefits | Direct Line Insurance – the easy way to get the best possible motor cover at the best possible price |
| Support for benefits | DLI is convenient to use, and offers first class service – as proven by consumer research. It is owned by the Bank of Scotland and is lower priced than traditional insurers |
| Tone of communication/ personality | Interesting, humorous, down to earth |

Boddington's marketing objective was quite different – to build a strong national brand identity while sustaining its regional base in Granada. Its consumer targeting has already been reviewed above, and the communications strategy could be described succinctly (Table 242).

**Table 242.  Boddington's: communications strategy.**[15]

| Target audience | North-westerners and premium beer drinkers who are unpretentious ordinary blokes |
|---|---|
| Key consumer benefits | Boddington's is the ultimate smooth-drinking pint |
| Support for benefits | Boddington's is creamy pouring, settles out into a light clear golden colour with a tight creamy head |
| Tone of communication/ personality | Mancunian. Accessible, humorous, unpretentious |

## 10. How to evaluate creative work

Assess advertising sympathetically but ruthlessly. Here are some suggestions for how to evaluate a proposed new TV campaign. Much of this is
applicable to any type of communication, from a magazine ad to a
financial services leaflet.

The advertising agency has just completed
its first presentation. During the past two
hours you have listened to the culmination of
weeks of work. The account planner covered
the strategic background, the account director
developed it and the famous copywriter has
just sat down after persuasively outlining the
first two commercials in storyboard form.

Now they are looking at you, and awaiting a response. Your
Marketing Director is deep in thought but nods at you absent-
mindedly. **How do you evaluate a new campaign?**

**The right mental approach**. Start by putting yourself in the shoes of
your target customer and paint a mental image of him or her. What
kind of houses do your typical customers live in, what are their interests
and how do they see your product or service? It is helpful to have a
picture or montage of your target consumer on the wall in the meeting room.

**First gut reaction**. What is your instant first response to the advertising idea? Will the advertising be noticed? Will it be received and
enjoyed? Is it memorable? Is it entertaining for your consumer? Is the
idea capable of sustaining a long-term campaign, to run for years, or is
it a one-off advertisement? Always seek campaigns, not individual
advertisements.

Unless it passes these simple tests, the advertising is unlikely to work.
Do not get into a detailed evaluation of advertising which follows
strategy but is really boring.

**Stimulus and response**. Think what the consumer will take out of the
advertising, not what is being put into it. A classic example of miscom-
munication is where the airline pilot in mid-journey comes out of the
cockpit, switches off the movie everyone is watching and says, 'Don't
panic.' The response to this stimulus is the opposite of that desired –
sheer panic. So ask yourself whether the advertising is likely to have the
intended effect on the consumer.

**The pictures**. Having adopted the outlook of your consumer, take the
agency's storyboard and look through the pictures twice. Do not look at

the words at all at this stage, because, for television, the pictures ought to tell the story on their own.

When you have scanned the pictures twice, put down the story-board, close your eyes and recall the impression they have made on you in thirty words or less (consumers rarely have more than thirty words of recall for a commercial). What are the key elements you recall from the pictures?

At this stage, write your impressions down on a piece of paper. Then study it and ask yourself whether the storyboard is 'on strategy'. Your thirty-word recall should be right in line with the strategy, because otherwise the storyboard is **off strategy** and is therefore unacceptable in its present form. If you decide the board is on strategy, proceed, still ignoring the words, to debate whether it is likely to interest consumers. Here are a few checkpoints:

- Is the brand name intrinsic to the story, or will people remember the commercial but not the brand?
- Is the situation likely to be interesting to consumers? Is it one with which they can identify or not? Is it totally static or does it have a story, style, mood and effects? Are the people interesting? Is the commercial too gimmicky, exploiting the copy-writer's latest fad?
- Is the storyboard believable, or does it lack conviction?
- Is the structure of the board simple and easy to understand?
- Is this commercial different from most other ones on the air and likely to stand out, or is it another run-of-the-mill uninspired effort?
- Does the commercial strike the right tone? Is it appealing to consumers on their level or is it patronizing and esoteric?
- How well is the commercial likely to wear? Does it represent a campaign idea which can be developed and run for years, or will people quickly get tired of it?

**The words**. Now read the words − twice − in association with the pictures. Their job is simple: to supplement the pictures and to enhance their impact.

Having done that, ask yourself again whether or not this commercial is of interest to your consumer. And check that the words too are on strategy. Then look at each frame individually and check whether the words support the picture, or whether they are pulling in different directions − the words saying one thing and the picture conveying a different impression; audio and video must interlock.

**Full understanding.** At the two previous stages, you will obviously ask the agency to clarify anything about the pictures or words which is not clear. But now is the time to clarify things like:

- Whether the agency envisages a musical accompaniment or not, and if so, what type of music is planned.
- What kind of 'characters' does the agency have in mind for the people in the commercial?
- Can certain complicated optical effects be achieved in reality or not?
- Are there any examples of analogous special effects?

**Initial response to the agency.** This should cover all the above points, concentrating particularly on how far the commercial meets the strategy and how interesting and involving it is for the consumer. It should be confined to a broad evaluation and not dwell on details.

## 11. How to assess communications results

In evaluating advertising effectiveness, every marketer, and indeed every finance director, wants to know the future profit stream generated by advertising less cost. This would provide the magic but usually elusive profit number. Cost is a fact, and easy to measure. Future profit stream can be quite accurately measured in direct marketing if you work out a system for estimating the long-term revenue value of your customers.

By contrast, sponsorship and public relations are extremely difficult to assess on a profit-and-loss basis, and no convincing method has yet been developed.

Mass media can be measured satisfactorily, as the book series *Advertising Works* demonstrates.[16] However, effective measurement requires considerable effort, involving pre-planning, use of a number of assessment tools and extensive analysis. All too often this effort is not made, and marketing people are rightly accused of being insufficiently accountable.

For those who wish to make the effort, here are some suggestions.

Techniques for assessing the strength of individual advertising campaigns are more advanced than those for establishing budgets, but still far from perfect. Campaigns can be evaluated before they have been produced (pre-testing) and after the cost of production has been incurred (post-testing).

Pre-testing is a way of checking out creative approaches, comparing alternatives and fine tuning. It enables the advertiser to bounce ideas off consumers and to have a dialogue with them at low cost. There is no denying its value, but it can be a time-waster when used to test mediocre ideas or to placate stubborn copywriters. Some of the most useful pre-testing can be done at a very early stage, using verbal concepts or simple pictures.

Post-testing occurs after the advertisement has been made, the campaign is running and large amounts of money have already been spent. Some would argue that testing at this stage is too late. But for those who see advertising as a continuous and long-term investment, post-testing can check the strength of the strategy, pin-point whether the execution is effective and even provide genuine clues about the effect on sales. The main methods of evaluating advertising are summarized in Table 243.

**Table 243.** *Techniques for evaluating effectiveness of advertising campaigns.*

| Type of testing | Factors which each technique can measure: | | |
|---|---|---|---|
| *Pre-testing* | **Strength of strategy** | **Strength of execution** | **Effect on sales** |
| Group discussion | Sometimes | Yes | No |
| Awareness, recall, persuasion | Yes | Yes | No |
| Concept tests | Yes | Yes | No |
| *Post-testing* | | | |
| Recall and playback | No | Yes | No |
| Awareness/attitude tracking | Yes | Maybe | Maybe |
| TV area test markets | No | No | Yes |
| Econometric analysis | No | No | Yes |

- Recall and playback involves interviewing consumers who were watching TV at the time of the first transmission of the commercial. Their recollection of any elements is recorded and compared with norms stored in a databank consisting of hundreds of commercials. The limitation of the technique is that recall does not equate with persuasiveness.
- Awareness and attitude studies (often referred to as 'tracking studies') call for more extensive consumer interviews and enable comparisons to be made between competing brands, both before and after the start of a new advertising campaign. Studies may be repeated at regular intervals to establish trends in aware-

ness, usage and product attitudes. See Chapter 13, 'Offensive Market Research', especially Table 246.

● TV area tests consist of an advertised area and a control area. Advertisers wanting to put their toe into the water can advertise in one TV area only and compare sales trends there with the rest of the country. Alternatively, in running a national campaign, they can exclude advertising from one TV area and compare sales and market share with the rest of the country. In each case, they can start to analyse the effect of advertising on sales.

## 12. Run successful campaigns for decades

Once you have developed a clear strategy and strong execution, stick with it. Fight off marauding marketing or agency people who have become bored with it, want to try something new or wish to make a name for themselves.

By all means refine and update a winning campaign, just as you would a successful product. Do not change without cast-iron evidence, based on convincing research.

If you happen to run a famous campaign and someone wants to change or ditch it, ask these questions:

1. Do we really understand the importance of the part of the consumer's mind which we are lucky enough to occupy?
2. Is the problem the strategy, or today's execution of it? Do not change your strategy just because the execution is no good.
3. What is the motive for changing? Are people in the company bored with the same old thing? How do you know that the new approach is better than the tried and tested old one? Has its merit been thoroughly researched and tested in the market-place?

Finally, while you should never make change for change's sake, **never be satisfied with your advertising**.

Offensive Marketers continually strive to upgrade and improve the performance of their products. The same applies to advertising. The launch of a successfully tested new pool of TV commercials is not the completion of a project, but merely part of a continuous process of advertising development. It is always worth while to test alternatives and to experiment with new approaches. Even if they don't work, much can usually be learned for future application.

The task of developing better advertising is continuous and never finished.

## Eight-step Process for Offensive Communications Development

This section translates the key principles of Offensive Communications into a brief eight-step process, using a number of tools already described (Table 244).

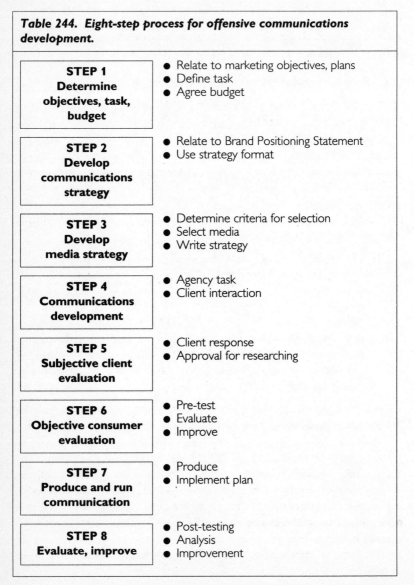

**Table 244. Eight-step process for offensive communications development.**

| | |
|---|---|
| **STEP 1**<br>**Determine objectives, task, budget** | • Relate to marketing objectives, plans<br>• Define task<br>• Agree budget |
| **STEP 2**<br>**Develop communications strategy** | • Relate to Brand Positioning Statement<br>• Use strategy format |
| **STEP 3**<br>**Develop media strategy** | • Determine criteria for selection<br>• Select media<br>• Write strategy |
| **STEP 4**<br>**Communications development** | • Agency task<br>• Client interaction |
| **STEP 5**<br>**Subjective client evaluation** | • Client response<br>• Approval for researching |
| **STEP 6**<br>**Objective consumer evaluation** | • Pre-test<br>• Evaluate<br>• Improve |
| **STEP 7**<br>**Produce and run communication** | • Produce<br>• Implement plan |
| **STEP 8**<br>**Evaluate, improve** | • Post-testing<br>• Analysis<br>• Improvement |

## STEP 1:  DETERMINE OBJECTIVES, TASK, BUDGET

- Check and reread marketing objectives, strategies and plans.
- Establish communications objectives and tasks.
- Use systems and pragmatic tools (page 474) for setting total communications budget. See Table 238.
- Work out preliminary split by type of media.
- Get internal agreement to communications budget.
- Brief all external agencies on total communications budget.
- Agree objectives, operating procedures and performance measurement with each agency.
- Agree how different agencies will communicate among themselves, and with you, for integrated communications.
- Develop initial list of product or service claims, agreed by your Legal and R & D departments.

## STEP 2:  DEVELOP COMMUNICATIONS STRATEGY

- Check and reread Brand Positioning Statement (BPS).
- Develop overall communications strategy, consistent with BPS, using format on Table 240, page 477, above. Involve agencies, legal, R & D, but, as marketer, lead the process.
- Translate overall strategy to any sub-brands, or specialist target groups, but ensure consistency of message.
- Consumer concept-test alternative strategies, and use results to strengthen strategy.
- Get communications strategies agreed internally.

## STEP 3:  DEVELOP MEDIA STRATEGY

- Handle concurrently with Step 2.
- Determine impact, coverage and frequency objectives versus target consumer.
- Review full range of potential media with agencies.
- For each medium, evaluate fit with target audience, image, impact, cost-effectiveness, fit or overlap with other media, and potential role in total media strategy.
- Write media strategy, specifying planned media mix, rationale and cost impact.
- Get media strategy agreed internally with communications strategy.

## STEP 4: COMMUNICATIONS DEVELOPMENT

- Final communications and media strategy briefing with agencies.
- Agree with each agency how creative work will be evaluated, including consumer research and market testing plans.
- Creative development by agencies, including any new claims for clearance.

## STEP 5: SUBJECTIVE CLIENT EVALUATION

- Ongoing subjective evaluation of agency proposals by client (see pages 479–81).
- Client approval to creative work, for consumer pre-testing.
- Client clears any new claims with legal or R & D.

## STEP 6: OBJECTIVE CONSUMER EVALUATION

- Pre-test storyboards or other low-cost visuals with consumers, and check scores against averages for other ads previously tested. Evaluate interest level, communication of key benefits, persuasiveness, believability and brand-name recall.
- If advertising tests strongly, proceed, making further improvements based on research. If not, go back to the drawing board.
- Final approval by client and by regulatory authorities if applicable.

## STEP 7: PRODUCE CREATIVE WORK AND RUN IT

## STEP 8: EVALUATE RESULTS, IMPROVE

- Conduct business impact evaluation – sales, share changes versus cost.
- Econometric analysis.
- Post-advertising consumer research.
- Adjust future spending plans.
- Use results of evaluation to further improve communications programme and keep one step ahead.

# FLOW-CHART SUMMARY OF CHAPTER 12

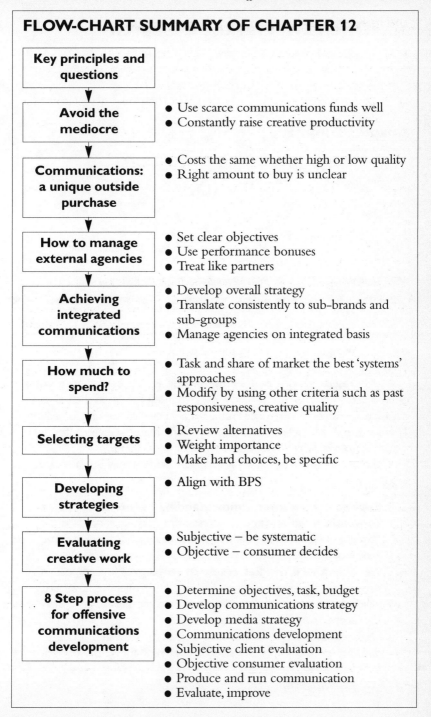

**Key principles and questions**

**Avoid the mediocre**
- Use scarce communications funds well
- Constantly raise creative productivity

**Communications: a unique outside purchase**
- Costs the same whether high or low quality
- Right amount to buy is unclear

**How to manage external agencies**
- Set clear objectives
- Use performance bonuses
- Treat like partners

**Achieving integrated communications**
- Develop overall strategy
- Translate consistently to sub-brands and sub-groups
- Manage agencies on integrated basis

**How much to spend?**
- Task and share of market the best 'systems' approaches
- Modify by using other criteria such as past responsiveness, creative quality

**Selecting targets**
- Review alternatives
- Weight importance
- Make hard choices, be specific

**Developing strategies**
- Align with BPS

**Evaluating creative work**
- Subjective – be systematic
- Objective – consumer decides

**8 Step process for offensive communications development**
- Determine objectives, task, budget
- Develop communications strategy
- Develop media strategy
- Communications development
- Subjective client evaluation
- Objective consumer evaluation
- Produce and run communication
- Evaluate, improve

# 13. Offensive Market Research

## Chapter Summary

| **Table 245.** | |
|---|---|
| **P:** Profitable | ● Proper balance between firm's needs for profit and customer's need for value |
| **O:** Offensive | ● Must lead market, take risks and make competitors followers |
| **I:** Integrated | ● Marketing approach must permeate whole company |
| **S:** Strategic | ● Probing analysis leading to a winning strategy |
| → **E:** Effectively Executed | ● Strong and disciplined execution on a daily basis ← |

New technology is changing the face of market research, and the pace of change is likely to be greater in the next ten years than in the previous thirty.

Market research is one of the most exciting aspects of marketing, but is often ill-served by marketers. Much research is left to rot on shelves as an occasional source of reference, rather than being a fulcrum for action. There is too much tactical, defensive and confirmatory research, too little that drives forward the frontiers of consumer understanding.

The main principles of Offensive Market Research may be summarized as follows:

1. **Superior consumer understanding generates major competitive advantage.** Understanding consumer needs is the cornerstone of Offensive Marketing, and market research is a prime source of this knowledge.
2. **Develop a real market research strategy.** Most companies have market research budgets, but few have offensive strategies, which spell out the role of market research and how it can generate superior consumer understanding.
3. **Use research as a torch not a crutch.** Research produces data, not decisions. It is a device for improving the quality of decisions, not a crutch to bolster weak decision makers, to 'prove' the obvious or to justify postponement of decisions.

4. **See the people behind the numbers.** Professionally conducted research and informal customer contact should be run in harness, since each has a limited value in isolation.
5. **Look for the action.** Unless research results in action, it is not worth doing.
6. **Good research requires imagination.** In order to bring out real, as opposed to surface, motivations, the interviewer has to stimulate interest, and this requires a creative approach. Marketing executives should apply more of the creativity to research which they reserve for advertising and presentation.
7. **The best information may cost nothing**. Every company possesses a great deal of processed and raw data which may be neglected or in the wrong format.
8. **Integrate all data, and keep on asking, 'Why?'** The various types of internal and external data should be integrated to provide a total picture of consumers and customers.
9. **Select excellent research companies and build partnerships.** You do this for advertising, with advertising agencies. Why not also for research companies?

## Why So Much Market Research Is Inoffensive

All is not well in the land of market research, although many of its inhabitants are prospering, and industry turnover increased 11% this year. Every marketer is familiar with the old saw: **'I know half of my advertising budget is wasted, but I'm not sure which half.'** It could be transmuted to market research as, **'I know half my market research budget is wasted, yet I also know I'm underspending.'** Too little is spent, often on the wrong type of research, and then insufficient action is taken.

A new piece of consumer research should be an exciting voyage of discovery, opening up new perspectives for innovation and improvement. Marketers should anticipate the outcome with the same sense of excitement as the result of a major sporting event. **What new perspectives will emerge, what fresh opportunities for action? Will expectations be confirmed, exceeded or completely confounded?**

Too often, though, research pursues a disappointing and predictable journey, through old and familiar scenery, creating no excitement, charting no new frontiers – the business equivalent of a scoreless draw in football. Why?

Let's take another angle. Ask the Marketing Director of even well-run companies questions like these:

- Does your company have a really deep understanding of consumer or customer needs?
- Do you have a distinctive way of segmenting your market which differs from your competitors?
- Have you got a clear idea how consumer needs in your markets will change in the next five years?

The honest answer will often be, 'No.' **Why?**
There are lots of reasons. Here are some:

### Too much tactical, too little strategic research

Tactical research which answers short-term questions, but fails to build the big picture, spreads like weeds. But strategic research, like **Market Segmentation** or **Usage and Attitude studies,** can easily be delayed until next year or the year after, because they are long-term investments in consumer understanding. Consequently, a company may spend quite heavily on tactical research yet know little about its customers.

## Poor planning

Research is often commissioned in a hurry, with insufficient thought by marketers. Objectives may be fuzzy, action standards not established in advance, and expected use of results not spelt out beforehand.

## Weak knowledge of research techniques by marketers

With the disappearance of many in-house market researchers, and the removal of great swathes of marketing middle management in the past ten years, many of today's marketers are less well trained in the basics of research. In order effectively to brief research agencies, and to evaluate their proposals, it is necessary to understand the pros and cons of different research techniques, the fundamentals of sample sizes and the realities of interviewing.

## Undifferentiated research

The purpose of investing in market research is to gain competitive advantage. Yet many companies buy the same continuous research – advertising tracking studies, consumer panels, retail audits, service monitors and such like – as their competitors do. It is true that a smart company can often exploit identical data better, especially when it's available on line. However, smart companies also differentiate standard research by integrating it with other data or setting up special analyses.

The analogy in manufacturing terms is buying in a piece of standard machinery, and using your engineering team to modify it in-house to create advantage.

## Lack of integration of new with existing research

Most marketing consultants will have had the experience of asking a new client for a list of past market research projects, and encountering a mountain of undigested reports commissioned by a range of people, conducted by a variety of research companies, and using different techniques. They discover that no one has attempted to stitch this patchwork of data into an integrated design. Each new piece of research was conducted and assessed in isolation, sometimes duplicating data already available.

This scenario is not exceptional. Indeed, it frequently occurs, fuelled by the rapid turnover of marketing people, and their preference for 'starting with a clean sheet' – a convenient way of saying they haven't got time to examine the past.

The essence of successful market research is to build a composite portrait by combining data from many sources into a convincing totality, over time. These sources may include continuous external research, one-off studies, internal sales figures, syndicated reports, customer database information and anecdotal material. They will sometimes conflict, and resolving inconsistencies between different data sets is often a valuable learning experience. Companies which view each piece of data in isolation have no hope of building this accurate portrait. In its place, they will have an unclear and misleading silhouette of their consumer.

Integrated communications are much discussed. Integrated market research is equally important.

**So what can be done to establish the sort of offensive market research programmes which best-practice companies pursue as a means to gaining competitive advantage?**

- Follow a number of offensive principles, and establish strong processes to ensure they are applied. These are covered below after a brief section on the fundamentals of market research.

## The Fundamentals of Market Research

Market research is about facts and impressions extracted from customers. It leads to better business decisions. It helps a company to keep in touch with what consumers think of its products or services and those of its competitors, and it monitors their actions in the marketplace. Of course, research is not a way of guaranteeing success, but its effective use makes success more likely.

The key questions which market research can answer quite well are:

- How do consumers evaluate our products or services against those of competitors?
- What are they looking for in this market and how far are we providing this effectively?
- How are consumer tastes changing?
- What are consumers buying from whom and why?
- How do consumers react to these new ideas we have thought up?
- What is our level of customer loyalty, retention, and why?

Market research is a complex industry. At the risk of oversimplification, it takes three forms:

1. **What consumers buy.** The word 'consumer' is used broadly, since it covers retail buyers, shoppers, fund managers and industrial purchasing agents. We are all consumers.

2. **What they know and think, and why**. The raw material for this is consumer awareness, needs, attitudes, images and reactions.
3. **How they react in a simulated situation**. What is consumer reaction to possible future marketing initiatives like new advertising, new products or new services?

Table 246 elaborates on these categories of research. This table is also a rough league order of the reliability of research. What people are buying is a fact and therefore quite easily ascertained. What they think

**Table 246. Table of main types of market research.**

| Type | Purpose | Most typical method(s) |
|------|---------|------------------------|
| *What people buy or do* | | |
| Retail audits (e.g. Nielsen) | Measure market position | Checkout scanning data |
| Consumer panels (e.g. AGB) | Measure market position, consumer activity | In-home scanners |
| Activity studies | Measure shopping trips, leisure pursuits, service levels | Telephone interviews |
| *What people think and why* | | |
| Usage and attitude studies | Profile of products/ services | Telephone or in-home |
| Market segmentation studies | Identify market sub-segments | Telephone or in-home |
| Continuing advertising/ usage studies | Trend data on awareness and attitudes | Telephone or by post |
| Opinion-former studies | Get views of opinion-formers | Personal interviews |
| Product tests | Compare products | Hall, van or in-home testing |
| Advertising studies | Measure advertising impact | Telephone |
| Buyer/distributor studies | Get buyer attitudes | Telephone or in person |
| Employee attitude studies | Measure employee attitudes | Personal interviews |
| Exploratory research | Probe consumer motivations | Small discussion groups |

| Type | Purpose | Most typical method(s) |
|------|---------|------------------------|
| **Simulated situations:** | | |
| Simulated test markets (STMs) | Test new products or services, estimate volume | Simulated retail store |
| Advertising tests | Persuasiveness of advertising · | Various |
| Concept tests | Test advertising, product, packaging or promotion ideas | Small groups with concepts, pictures or words |
| Trade-off research | Forecast consumer behaviour | Personal interviews |

about existing products or markets is also a fact, but opinions are volatile. There is both art and discipline in choosing who to interview and in making certain that interviewers are consistent.

Simulated situations are the least reliable, because they deal with the future, rather like peering into a crystal ball. The techniques used, though perhaps not the insights, are superior to those of Mystic Meg. But the interpretation of simulated research requires experience, caution and the occasional pinch of salt.

The most frequently used research types are continuous measurement monitors, usage and attitude studies, product tests and discussion groups.

**Continuous measurement monitors** take a variety of forms. All have in common continuous measurement over time at weekly, monthly, quarterly or annual intervals, so that trends can be established and evaluated.

Market measurement panels measure consumer purchases. There are two main techniques for doing this. The retail panel reads sell-out from a representative selection of stores, primarily using checkout scanning data. The consumer panel traces the same picture through a national panel of customers who record their purchases at home using an electronic device to scan the bar codes of packages.

**Advertising tracking studies** involve interviewing thousands of consumers weekly to check awareness and attitude to advertising, linked to product usage.

**Service monitors** use a similar technique to track customer satisfaction in service industries.

**Usage and attitude studies** question consumers about their habits and reactions to particular products in the market. They used to come up with rather predictable information, but the better ones today use imaginative techniques and are often combined with market segmentation analyses and concept tests.

**The product test** evaluates product appeal. Consumers are asked to rate products either in isolation against their usual product (single placement) or head to head against a competitor (paired comparison). They can be done blind, where the products are in blank packs, or on a named basis, where they are identified.

Product tests are frequently used in the food, household goods, textile and drinks industries, among others. In other categories, like automobiles, models can be constructed for consumer assessment. Services can be rated by using concept material, or even through test stores in retailing or leisure.

**Group discussions** involving, say, four to eight groups of six to nine people, are a very popular research method . . . not least because they are inexpensive and can be set up quickly. Sometimes they are used just to get a 'feel' for consumer reaction to advertising concepts or new ideas, or they may be run as a preliminary to a larger study.

Groups provide a fast hotline to the consumer and are helpful in screening hypotheses, identifying the questions to ask in a larger study and providing guidance on consumer language. However, group discussions should not be used as a basis for key decisions – these deserve the backing of quantitative research conducted on a representative sample of target consumers:

> **'The world-wide head of marketing at a leading global company attended a presentation at which one of his European executives recommended a change in consumer positioning to a Pan-European brand. He asked what research had been done to justify this change. After a certain amount of foot-shuffling, it became apparent that only three group discussions had been conducted . . . in Switzerland, hardly a mainstream market. He rejected the change: "I'm not prepared to base this company's global strategy on the opinions of 18 Swiss housewives." '**

## The Nine Principles of Offensive Market Research

### 1. *Offensive market research is a major source of competitive advantage*

If one had to nominate the single most important opportunity for competitive advantage, for most companies it would be **superior understanding** of consumers, customers, markets and employees.

 This understanding enables companies to develop distinctive and relevant products and services, to target the most attractive markets, to focus costs on areas of greatest consumer value, and to motivate employees. Of course, there is a world of difference between understanding an opportunity and actively exploiting it. But understanding is the crucial first step towards Offensive Marketing – **'involving every employee in building superior customer value very efficiently for above average profits'**.

Effective use of market research is one of the primary means to achieve this understanding – the other is to retain regular first-hand contact with customers, consumers and employees.

Yet few companies use market research effectively. Where there is an internal Market Research Department, its focus is often too narrow. It frequently defines its internal customers as members of the Marketing Department, not as every employee; it rarely builds up the totality of research results into a big and moving picture summary that the average marketer can access and understand; it may underemphasize customer and employee, as opposed to consumer, research; and it sometimes reeks of conservatism, rather than creativity and excitement.

Where there is no internal Market Research Department, responsibility for research is usually devolved to individual business units or brand groups. The result can be diffusion of activity, lack of consistency in approach and over-reliance on outside agencies.

Offensive market research has a unique capability to build lasting competitive advantage, yet few professional market researchers inside and outside companies do enough to *market* this fact. They can be insufficiently forceful in accessing top management, and in pushing their corporate customers to plan, manage and act on research in the most effective way. Many of their industry publications and deliberations are pedantic and obscure, focusing on details rather than fundamentals.[1]

Here are the titles of two recent articles from the *American Journal of Consumer Research*.[2]

'Asymmetric Decoy Effects on Lower-Quality versus Higher-Quality Brands: Meta-Analytic and Experimental Evidence'

'Liberatory Postmodernism and the Re-enchantment of Consumption'

The content of each is exactly what the titles would lead one to expect.

This situation adds up to a major opportunity for companies which take market research seriously. Research is not boring. It is one of the most exciting and powerful engines of profitable growth.

## 2. Develop a real market research strategy

Most companies have market research budgets. Few have market research strategies backed by three-year plans. Have you ever seen one? Good ones are as rare as original Bugattis.

A market research strategy will spell out how to achieve the objective of gaining superior consumer understanding as a route to major competitive advantage. This will be covered in more detail in the section on 'Process for Implementing Offensive Marketing Research' later in this chapter. Here are the sort of questions a market research strategy should aim to answer:

- **What is the role of market research in the company?** Why do we spend money on it? What benefits do we expect to gain? How can it be used to build long-term advantage?
- **Who are the main objects of our research?** Customers, consumers, employees, shareholders? Broadly, how will research effort be allocated between these stakeholder groups?
- **What is the broad priority to be given to various categories of research?** Continuous research versus one-off? Strategic versus tactical? Should there be a policy on minimum frequency of product comparison tests, or major market studies?
- **How will the company's research inventory be disseminated internally?** How can relevant information on key topics be summarized in easy to use form, and delivered on a tailored basis to all internal customers? For example, everyone in the company could be interested in total market trends, company and brand shares, and performance of new products. But the Key Account Manager on Dixons wants to know everything about Dixons, across all the company's markets;

and while the Category Manager of Sony TV sets needs top-line data on Dixons, her main interest is everything to do with a single category – TV sets.

- **How will effectiveness of research spending be monitored?** First, is the right kind of research being done – is actual spending by type in line with strategy? Secondly, is anyone really analysing it rather than giving it a few flicks of the eyeball? Where are these analyses, and do they spell out action steps? Thirdly, and most importantly, what action has actually been taken as a result of research?
- **What is our strategy for achieving differentiation in research?** What is 'best practice' in management of research, and how can we surpass it? What are the opportunities for integrating internal sales and profit data, continuous consumer measurement numbers and sell-out figures from key customers? Are we at the forefront of practice or not? What approach will be taken to innovate new approaches to research? How do we make these proprietary to us?
- **What is our external-supplier strategy?** Do we build long-term partnerships with a small number of key suppliers? If so, what advantages in cost, continuity and innovation do they provide? How do we keep our proprietary approaches confidential? If not, what is our rationale for this strategy?
- **What is the strategy for ensuring consistency of research technique?** This is relevant over time and across countries.

| Table 247. Key elements of best-practice market research strategy. | |
| --- | --- |
| ● Clear stakeholder priorities | ● Integrated |
| ● Innovative | ● Strong strategic content |
| ● Well communicated | ● Consistent |
| ● Actionable | ● Differentiated |

### 3. Use research as a torch not a crutch

Research lights the way forward, but only illuminates the areas you point it at, and never provides a complete picture. It produces data and insights, not decisions.

Research is a device for improving the quality of the information on which decisions are based. Market research is sometimes wrongly regarded by executives as a kind of 'answer machine' into which they can drop any questions or problems which bother them, in the hope that it will make judgement unnecessary. Applied in this way, research is doomed to misuse and will be stretched beyond its capabilities.

The sight of timid decision makers using research as a crutch leads some executives who view themselves as red-blooded to make statements like, 'People with a feel for their markets don't need research', or, 'most entrepreneurs have no time for research'. They are right to the extent that all business people should be close to their customers. They are wrong in implying that 'gut feel' is a substitute for good-quality research. Both are necessary, and complementary. Even marketers with a strong instinct for their customers are sometimes surprised by the results of new research. Understanding the consumer is an art which is never totally mastered. It requires constant relearning.

### 4. See the people behind the numbers

The impact of a legal case, especially one involving a jury, can be only dimly communicated in the Law Reports. Many of the incidents will have been omitted, the atmosphere of the court is absent, the appearance and manner of the participants is not described and there is no reference to the demeanour of the accused or the witnesses.

Equally, a research report can be fully appreciated only by marketers with up-to-date and first-hand knowledge of their company's customers. Marketing people are sometimes justifiably accused of being out of touch and more in tune with the executive lifestyle than with the typical consumer. It is important to get out 'where the rubber meets the road', to talk frequently to consumers and the trade, if only to gain a background feel in interpreting formal research.

Professionally conducted research and informal customer contacts should be run in harness, since each has limited value in isolation.

Senior management, especially the Managing Director and Marketing Director, also need to retain access to raw data. In large organizations, research results often reach Marketing Directors in predigested reports which have been minced, blended and filtered through layers of management. These reports will gain a much richer texture if marketers can also get their hands on occasional chunks of raw information – unedited videotapes of group discussions, computer tabulations and direct access to research fieldworkers.

For example, at one company the Managing Director spends at least one hour a month flicking through some of the previous week's orders. At another, management regularly conducts consumer checks by personally calling on homes at random to get a reaction to company products.

## 5. Look for the action

Every market raises questions that it would be interesting to research. But unless the research is likely to lead to action, it is not worth doing. Some research, such as continuous retail or consumer panels, is useful as a background to Offensive Marketing. You could live without detailed information on market size or brand share, and many smaller companies do.

However, for those able to afford it, this kind of data tells how you are performing in the market-place, how well the competition is doing, what your position is by account, service or product and geographical area. It also holds clues as to why brand shares are changing. Is your share rising because of distribution gains, extra advertising weight, pricing changes, sales promotion or all of these, and what are the relationships?

All this is quite basic, and continuous panel data is very rewarding to those who are thorough. However, because the need for continuous research is accepted without question by some companies, it can become part of the wallpaper – there, but taken for granted.

Non-continuous research – 'ad hoc', as it is inelegantly called – is carried out to answer particular questions, and this should also lead to concrete action. To ensure that research projects result in action, most companies write a formal brief, and some insist on a subsequent report from the Marketing Department, outlining action taken.

The brief for a major piece of research such as a usage and attitude study deserves at least the same degree of attention as an advertising strategy.

Once the research is completed, an internal summary and an action report, perhaps two pages long, should be written by the marketing person sponsoring it. Unfortunately, this discipline is often ignored, as in the example below:

**This major company has a large market research budget of over £2 million. Its Market Research Manager is technically excellent and has pushed forward the frontiers of knowledge with some pioneering studies. His primary interest, however, is in very sophisticated research and he has little patience with bread-and-butter projects, although some are carried out.**

**Integration between the Marketing Department and Market Research is weak. The marketing people are not knowledgeable about research, and the impetus for many projects comes from the Market Research Manager.**

**Market research briefs are sketchy, and when reports are issued, Marketing rarely, if ever, writes its own internal action memos.**

**The result of this is that too much pathfinding and too little pedestrian work is done, so that simple but important questions are left unanswered; the value derived from the research is limited, mainly because Marketing is not sufficiently disciplined to confront the action issues raised by it; and finally, because there is not a consistent approach to market research, methods and questionnaires change, and opportunities to compare different studies or to check trends over time are lost.**

## 6. Good research requires imagination

The objective of most research is to uncover consumer attitudes and feelings. Although the means of measuring these may be mechanical, the thinking behind the technique and the questioning must be imaginative. Consumers rarely analyse their real reasons for buying even major commitments like insurance policies and houses, never mind instant coffee and yoghurt.

For example, if you ask consumers a direct question about why they buy a particular brand, you are likely to get the kind of feedback shown in Table 248, which is not very nourishing.

| Table 248.  Non-actionable consumer playback. | |
| --- | --- |
| **Reason for using last brand:** | **%** |
| Always used | 20 |
| Relative used/recommended | 15 |
| Saw advertising | 10 |
| Recommended by friend/neighbour | 14 |
| Bought on special price offer | 12 |
| No particular reason | 21 |
| No answer or don't know | 8 |
| Total | 100 |

Finding out what consumers really think involves more than throwing a broadly directed question at them. In order to bring out real, as opposed to surface, motivations, the interviewer has to stimulate interest, and this requires a creative approach.

The need for imagination in research is often overlooked by marketing people, who reserve all their creativity for advertising, promotions and packaging. Research should not only be imaginative but also sympathetic, since the researcher may in the early stages be working with a product which only half solves the problem, and with consumers who have difficulty in envisaging how they would use the product.

Combining imagination with sympathy and objectivity is no easy task, and the example below features a product strong enough to survive the absence of this combination, 3M's 'Post-It' notes, now a major brand within 3M's $1bn office supplies business. It is a classic example:

**Dr Silver was working in 3M Central Laboratories to develop adhesive with maximum holding power. Instead, he discovered one that would stick but could be easily lifted off.**

**He sent out samples, but nothing happened for several years. Then a colleague, Art Fry, a keen chorister who sang in two church services every Sunday, needed markers for his hymn book. Fry knew of Silver's work, and developed a peelable hymnal marker in the 15% of R & D time 3M allowed for his own projects. He felt there was potential for the product, but he 'didn't have the words for it'.**

**The marketing people did surveys of potential customers, and results were very poor. Consumers had managed without such a product and couldn't see the need for it. Fry reasoned that people would have to use the product to discover what it was good for. So he distributed samples to colleagues and asked them to come back for more when they ran out. He recorded usage and found that it exceeded usage of Magic Tape by the same people. Magic Tape was 3M's biggest-selling office product. Meanwhile, surveys conducted by the Marketing Department continued to show that consumers had low interest in the product.**

**However, 3M began selling Post-It notes in four cities, with advertising support but no sampling. The test failed. A new test was opened in Idaho, with a heavy advertising and sampling plan. Results were sensational and the product was subsequently launched in the USA, and internationally.**

Post-It notes are still growing and the product was included in the exhibition of 'The World's 100 Best-ever Products' at the Victoria and Albert Museum, London. The lesson is clear. It was pointless to use traditional research techniques to evaluate this totally new product, as the marketing people had attempted to do. The informal research technique used by the scientist, Art Fry, was in fact the right one. The marketers totally failed to identify the importance of sampling.[3]

## 7. The best information may cost nothing

The most obvious and least expensive sources of information are often overlooked, frequently left unprocessed, or circulated to the wrong people.

A senior executive in a global company once commissioned an in-depth analysis of a major competitor, involving benchmarking, interviews with ex-employees and so on. The consultant heading this study was amazed to discover that this senior executive had not even read the competitor annual report.

For companies with field sales or merchandising forces, sales analysis can be productive – reviewing trends in daily call rates, sales per call, distribution gains and losses, and display levels. A great deal of useful anecdotal data can also be collected.

Regular analysis of internal raw data often pin-points new problems and opportunities, as the disguised example below shows:

Following two quite stable years, sales of a US kitchenware product began to fall away, and during the period from January to June they were 16% below the previous year.

The company in question had excellent internal data breakdowns, and sales were analysed by territory. It was discovered that five territories (out of 80 in the whole country) accounted for three quarters of the product's national deficit.

The five salesmen involved had massively loaded the trade on a bonus the previous December and consequently had to accept a large amount of returned product in the period from January to June. Outside these five territories, the brand was only 3% behind the previous year, and, in relation to its very limited marketing spending support, reasonably healthy.

There has been an explosion in the amount of low-priced 'off the peg' data about companies and markets. It ranges from government statistics and syndicated reports to trade journals. The variety is such that one can often initially screen the potential of a possible new market without spending more than £1,000. Much of this data is available on-line.

Opportunities for direct customer contact are also escalating and provide rich sources of data, through advice lines, discount cards, information services and complaints by phone or letter.

### 8. Integrate all data and keep on asking, 'Why?'

Data zooms in at marketers daily from every direction, and more is always available to masochists. It is easy to get snowed under. Companies need to set up efficient yet simple Marketing Information Systems, and marketers need to ration the time they spend on getting the facts they need to make decisions.

A large global company will have vast tranches of data by country and across countries. Marketing databases usually fall into four cat-

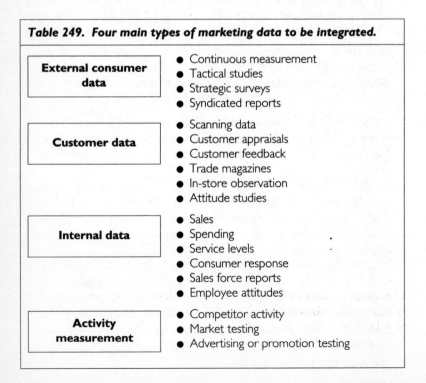

**Table 249. Four main types of marketing data to be integrated.**

| | |
|---|---|
| **External consumer data** | ● Continuous measurement<br>● Tactical studies<br>● Strategic surveys<br>● Syndicated reports |
| **Customer data** | ● Scanning data<br>● Customer appraisals<br>● Customer feedback<br>● Trade magazines<br>● In-store observation<br>● Attitude studies |
| **Internal data** | ● Sales<br>● Spending<br>● Service levels<br>● Consumer response<br>● Sales force reports<br>● Employee attitudes |
| **Activity measurement** | ● Competitor activity<br>● Market testing<br>● Advertising or promotion testing |

egories, and each needs to be integrated with the others into a logical whole (Table 249).

Large companies may find it economic to have a Marketing Information Unit, which identifies the needs of its internal customers, feeds them regular tailored reports and provides access to extended on-line data.

In many companies, marketers have to find their own way through the jungle of information, and make their own efforts to integrate it. The best ones decide what data they really need, arrange for it to be delivered to them in a simple and usable way, validate the facts by comparing information from different sources, keep on asking themselves and others '*Why?*', **then make decisions**. They have a good eye for numbers, can spot inconsistencies between different data sources, are constantly learning, and strive to get to the bottom of every important issue – they wrestle it to the ground.

Each of the four boxes in Table 249 is interrelated, and helps build up the total picture of **superior understanding**. Supposing you have just taken over a brand whose market share has declined over the past six months. **What steps do you take to understand why?** First you check the facts. Your main source of data on share is a consumer panel. **Do other relevant sources of data point to the same trend?**

| Table 250.  Share decline: first, check the facts. | |
|---|---|
| **External consumer data** | ● Check other continuous measurement data, e.g. retail audits, usage data in Ad Tracking studies |
| **Customer data** | ● Source relevant customer data<br>● Interview customers |
| **Internal data** | ● Relate internal sales data to external consumer data<br>● Check customer inventory levels |

Checking the facts involves cross-sourcing three of the four main boxes in Table 249. If the original facts appear true, then develop hypotheses as to why brand share has declined, and finally access all four boxes to check out the validity of your hypotheses.

## 9. Select excellent external research companies and build partnerships

Unlike advertising, where the best and the worst usually cost the same, outstanding research and researchers sometimes cost more, and may be worth it. Once you have found excellent research companies, it pays to build long-term partnerships, in the same way as with advertising agencies. They get to know your business well, provide consistency of approach, and should come to you first with new ideas. To ensure competitive cost, and continued freshness of thinking, it is advisable to occasionally put projects out to tender, while retaining the overall objectives of building long-term relationships.

**What should you look for in identifying excellent research agencies?** Let's take a situation where you have provided a written brief for a research study to three outside companies. Table 251 lists some criteria for selecting the best.

---

**Table 251. Main criteria for selecting research agency.**

1. Has the agency fully understood your brief?
2. Does the proposal meet the requirements of your brief?
3. Has the agency questioned aspects of your brief and improved it?
4. What is the quality of the agency people working on your business?
5. What is the likely quality of the fieldwork? How will it be checked?
6. Does the agency have imaginative approaches and techniques?
7. How practical and businesslike is the agency?
8. Has the agency considered a number of research structures, and selected the most cost effective one?
9. What is cost per interview? How competitive? If more expensive, why?
10. What other clients has the agency worked for in this research field? Check references for client satisfaction levels

---

## Process for Implementing Offensive Marketing Research

The remainder of this chapter will describe the process to implement the principles of Offensive Market Research which have just been covered. It is an eight-step process, as outlined in Table 252, treated from the viewpoint of a Marketing Director.

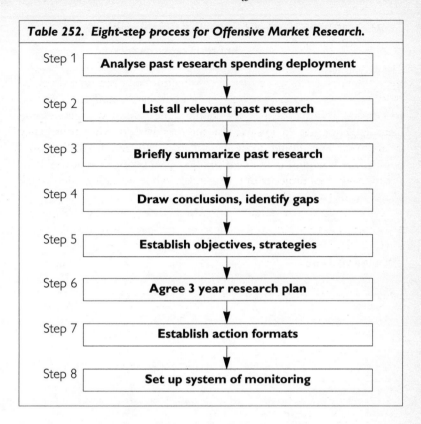

**Table 252. Eight-step process for Offensive Market Research.**

Step 1 — **Analyse past research spending deployment**

Step 2 — **List all relevant past research**

Step 3 — **Briefly summarize past research**

Step 4 — **Draw conclusions, identify gaps**

Step 5 — **Establish objectives, strategies**

Step 6 — **Agree 3 year research plan**

Step 7 — **Establish action formats**

Step 8 — **Set up system of monitoring**

## STEP 1: ANALYSE PAST RESEARCH SPENDING DEPLOYMENT

Past research spending should be broken down by type, separating continuous from ad hoc, strategic from tactical. **'Strategic'** research has lasting value and pushes forward your frontiers of understanding. Market segmentation or usage and attitude studies are an example. **'Tactical'** research is designed to answer a particular question and its contribution to knowledge is usually short term. A test of alternative varieties for a new frozen-food meal range or a comparison of two different leaflet presentations for a financial services product are an example. The main criterion for differentiating between strategic and tactical research is whether the information will have future value in twelve months' time. Table 253 gives an example of a past research analysis for an imaginary hair care company.

**Table 253. Analysis of past research: hair care company.**

| Research type | % of total research spend | | Value to company |
|---|---|---|---|
| | Last year | This year | |
| Market measurement | 35 | 47 | High |
| Advertising tracking | 15 | 20 | Medium |
| **Total continuous** | **50** | **67** | **Medium** |
| Usage and attitude | 10 | – | High |
| Market segmentation | 8 | – | High |
| Consumer usage videos | 7 | – | Very high |
| Strategic product testing | 5 | 5 | Medium |
| Quantified concept tests | 10 | 3 | High |
| **Strategic ad hoc** | **40** | **8** | **High** |
| Tactical product testing | 3 | 1 | Low |
| Advertising testing | 3 | 1 | Medium |
| Group discussions | 4 | 8 | Medium |
| Promotion tests | – | 10 | Low |
| Packaging tests | – | 5 | Medium |
| **Tactical ad hoc** | **10** | **25** | **Medium** |
| **Total** | **100%** | **100%** | **–** |
| **Research spending as % of revenue** | **1.5** | **1.0** | **–** |

**What do you conclude from this table?** Market research spending has been cut back heavily from 1.5% of total revenue to 1.0%. And the vast majority of this cut has come from strategic ad hoc research, which this year only accounted for 8% of total spend compared with 40% the year before. This may be acceptable, since you don't necessarily need to run major usage and attitude studies every year, but the size of the change does raise questions . . . and suspicion about 'milking'. It's probably worth going back another two years to analyse past spending trends further.

**Is continuous research strategic or tactical?** It can be either. The answer depends on how effectively it is used.

The final column in the table is 'Value to company'. This is your subjective view, and based on action taken, related to cost. This will help prepare your approach to future research allocation in Step 6.

The most valuable research recently carried out by this company was the consumer Usage Videos. These involved spending half-days in the homes of a hundred consumers and fifty hair salons, making videos showing exactly how women washed and treated their hair in practice. It generated a number of promising new product and packaging ideas.

## STEP 2: LIST ALL RELEVANT PAST RESEARCH

Most companies have a list of research conducted over the past five years or more. It will usually specify the title of each study, date and location, and may include sample size.

Marketing people should be familiar with every research study relevant to their brand over the past few years. When taking over a new marketing job, a good starting-point is to scan the past research list and review all studies of possible interest. They can be initially glanced at, then those of real interest speed-read and noted.

## STEP 3: BRIEFLY SUMMARIZE RELEVANT PAST RESEARCH STUDIES

Any research study which you have noted in Step 2 as relevant and useful should be briefly summarized, in fifty to a hundred words.

Table 254 is an example, for an imaginary continental European railway.

| Table 254. Example of brief summary: past market research study. | |
|---|---|
| **Title of study:** | On-train quality of service research |
| **Date of study:** | October 1995 |
| **Structure:** | 4,000 self-completion questionnaires, on train |
| **Key findings:** | Ranking of items seen as most important:<br>1. Comfort of seating     4. Cleanliness of lavatories<br>2. Reliable in timing     5. Air conditioning<br>3. Speed of journey     6. Price of ticket |
| **Comments:** | This is unconvincing. It is unbelievable that air-conditioning is more important than price. No breakdown by business and leisure travellers, and commuters. 'Certainty of finding a seat' ranked as No. 1 in other research, was not included in list of items researched. |

## STEP 4: DRAW CONCLUSIONS, IDENTIFY KNOWLEDGE GAPS

**What are your overall conclusions about this inventory of research? What are your key areas of understanding, summarized in two to three pages? Does this add up to a superior understanding of consumers, customers and other relevant stakeholders? If not, what steps do you need to take to achieve this, and what is likely cost and time scale? Are there any major knowledge gaps which need to be filled?**

You may well find conflicts between different pieces of research, and need to take a view as to which is most reliable. For example, in the continental railway example, half a dozen different studies ranking factors most important to rail customers had been carried out. They used different techniques, different types of sample, and produced different rankings. After evaluating the robustness of each piece of research and applying some common sense, you concluded that the most convincing ranking of factors was as in Table 255.

**Table 255.  Continental Rail: level of importance of journey factors by passenger type.**

| Factor | Long-distance business | Leisure | Commuter |
|---|---|---|---|
| Reliability | 2 | 4 | 3 |
| Avoiding interchange | 1 | 2 | 1 |
| Certainty of seat | 3 | 3 | 5 |
| Price | 7 | 1 | 4 |
| Speed | 5 | 5 | 7 |
| Frequency | 6 | 7 | 2 |
| Comfort of seats | 4 | 6 | 6 |

Leisure travellers and commuters pay for their own tickets, long-distance business travellers do not – thus the difference in attitude to pricing.

Two other conclusions you drew about the railway research were that:

● Almost all past research had been conducted on trains, mainly because this was inexpensive and easy to do. However, it left a massive knowledge gap – the company knew nothing about non-users.

● Only the train experience was researched. Little was known about the total travel experience – from first thinking about making a journey, to booking, to reaching the train, to arriving at final journey destination.

Both these gaping holes would need to be filled by future research.

## STEP 5:  ESTABLISH OBJECTIVES AND STRATEGIES FOR OFFENSIVE MARKET RESEARCH

Many of the questions relating to Step 5 are outlined above within 'The Nine Principles of Offensive Market Research'.

Here, in Table 256, is an example of Offensive Market Research objectives and strategies. It applies to a company with a Market Research Department, albeit a small one. However, most of the strategies are equally feasible for companies without one.

---

**Table 256.  Example of Offensive Market Research objectives and strategies.**

**Objectives:**
To disseminate throughout the company a superior understanding of present and future consumer, customer and employee needs, in order to deliver superior experiences, with very efficient use of marketing resources.

**Key strategies for achieving objectives:**
1. Focus primarily on consumers, but also cover customers and employees.
2. Gain a much deeper understanding of consumer habits, needs, attitudes and future aspirations than competitors.
3. Develop distinctive and proprietary approaches to segmenting markets, channels and customers.
4. Objectively monitor product and service performance and value, constantly identifying opportunities for improvement.
5. Develop superior techniques for new concept development, screening and test Marketing, so that future winners reach their full potential, and losers are spotted early.
6. Constantly strive to discover new research approaches, and gain exclusive use of these for the company in its major markets.
7. Objectively evaluate value for money gained by each major type of marketing spend, and identify opportunities for improvement.
8. Ensure that research data is integrated and disseminated throughout the company in usable formats, tailored to specific departments or job holders.
9. Develop superior internal competencies and processes, so that market research is well planned, implemented, and effective action taken.
10. Wherever possible, build long-term partnerships with the best research agencies.

---

Now you are ready to develop a research plan, and budget.

## STEP 6: AGREE 3 YEAR RESEARCH PLAN

The 3 year plan would execute the agreed objectives and strategies and then be translated into next year's budget. It should be quite brief, say four to five pages, and cover issues such as:

- **How much should be spent on market research, both in absolute terms and as a percentage of sales?** This is a much better question to ask than the normal one, which is: 'How little can we get away with spending on market research?'

  The principles for setting market research budgets are similar to those for setting advertising appropriations. The budget should be determined by the objectives and strategies agreed, and the activities necessary to execute these. As a rule of thumb, a consumer branded company should be spending at least 0.5% of sales on market research, with 1.0% a sensible target.

- **What are the main types of research to concentrate on in future?** Your analysis of past research, and view on value for money, at Step 1, is a useful starting-point here. What balance between continuous, strategic and tactical work should be aimed for?

  Of course, the amount of tactical research needed will depend on future marketing plans and conditions, and cannot be mandated precisely ahead. Yet all too often a total market research budget is set, tactical research requirements pour in and the strategic studies are cut to accommodate them. This is upside-down thinking. Strategic research should be set in stone, and, if necessary, tactical research cut in order to finance it.

- **How will we reach and stay at the leading edge of market research?** What promising new techniques or approaches are being tested? What contributions are our research suppliers making to this thinking? How much of the budget should be allocated to experimental research? As a rule of thumb, apply at least 5%.

- **Over the next three years, how far should research be contracted out?** Clearly objectives and strategies should be set internally, by company people. In addition, any research areas where core competencies or competitive advantage can be built up should also be handled internally. You may have developed distinctive skills in integrating internal and external data on to a single database; or in developing and testing concepts. In such a case, you would only contract out parts of this work on a secure basis.

Within this general question, you also need to decide how market research will be organized internally. Is a Market Research Manager or Marketing Services Department required? If not, how can marketing people develop the necessary skills, and how are budgets and processes to be coordinated in a consistent way?

- **What is your 3 year plan for research agencies?** Will you develop long-term partnerships, with some guarantees of minimum revenue in return for competitive pricing and a top-class team on your business? Or will you put most research out to tender? Who are your preferred suppliers? What arrangements are there for confidentiality? Will your preferred suppliers come to you first with new ideas and approaches?
- **Who are your main internal research customers, and how will you meet their needs?** How will your success in doing this be measured?
- **What are internal processes for planning and acting upon research?** How satisfactory are they, and what further improvements can be made?
- **How will the available body of company research be integrated and disseminated to your internal customers?** What is format? What is delivery system – hard copy, on-line, company TV station?
- **How will the implementation of the 3 year plan be monitored?** Quarterly milestones and review at Marketing Director level are desirable.

## STEP 7: ESTABLISH ACTION FORMATS

Consistent formats are used in best-practice companies for planning, implementation and action steps.

### Planning

A one-page plan should precede the approval of any research. The most important elements are the objectives, and anticipated practical applications. Here, in Table 257, is an uncompleted example.

---

**Table 257. Market research proposal.**

**Country:**
**Brand or category:**
**Title of study:**
**Background:** [*List any previous research done on this topic, giving dates and study titles. What was the main finding?*]
**Objectives:** [*Why is this research needed? What opportunities is it likely to generate? What problems is it designed to solve?*]
**Anticipated applications:** [*What possible action steps can be taken as a result of this research? If the research involves quantification versus competitors, action standards should be set within the proposal, to prevent 'fudging' later. For instance, in a blind test of a new product, the proposal might specify that a 60:40 win is required for a 'Go' decision.*]
**Competitive advantage:** [*What advantage is this research expected to generate? In what way is the research innovative or different?*]
**Technical issues:** [*What methodology is to be used? What is sample size? What breakouts are needed?*]
**Research company:**
**Estimated cost:**
**Timetable:** [*Planned start. Fieldwork completed. Results available.*]

---

 Here is a completed example, for the Continental Railway Company:

---

**Table 258. Market research proposal.**

**Country:** France and Germany
**Brand or category:** Long-distance Passenger Rail Travel
**Title of Study:** Long-distance Business Transport Study
**Background:** Five studies have been conducted on this topic in past three years. These are listed in an exhibit. All were conducted on-train, and did not cover non rail users.
**Objectives:** To identify how to increase share of travel among existing rail users; which non rail users to target; and how to develop the most convincing proposition to convert them.
**Anticipated applications:**
- Improve access and parking facilities at stations.
- Review usage and value of executive lounges at stations.
- Identify the most cost effective improvements to on-train service.
- Provide guidance on potential of a mid-class for business travellers.
**Competitive advantage:** This research will guide on strengthening competitive position versus car on journeys above 150 miles, and plane between 200 to 400 miles.

**Technical issues:** Regular train users to be interviewed on train. Occasionals and non train users by phone at office or at home. Sample size will be 2,000 business people, split equally by frequent rail travellers, occasional, and non-rail travellers. At least 600 of the sample will have travelled by plane four or more times in the past year. Split required by France, Germany; male, female; income, age; self-employed, small company, big company.

**Research company:** TransNational Inc.

**Estimated cost:** DM 500,000.

**Timetable:** Start fieldwork 10 April. Complete 31 May. Top-line report end June. Full report mid July.

You may attach a list of the main questions you want answered to the market research proposal – this will help the research agency in drawing up a questionnaire.

## Implementation

It is desirable to have a standard company technique for conducting recurring types of research, like product tests, usage and attitude studies, and concept tests. In this way, you can compare results of different tests over time and across countries.

## Action steps

Every piece of one-off research should be briefly summarized, and planned action specified. This summary should be written by the person responsible for carrying out the action, usually the line marketer. Some marketers feel Market Research Managers should be responsible for writing research summaries, since they are the experts.

It is essential for marketers to write these action summaries because:

- This guarantees that they read and think about the research they commissioned.
- Marketers are best placed to weigh the commercial implications of possible actions.
- Marketers should be accountable for making effective use of research they have authorized.

They are responsible for implementing the action steps they recommend.

A research summary should be about one page in length, and cover objectives of research, key findings and planned action.

## STEP 8:  SET UP MONITORING SYSTEM

This system would monitor achievement of planned market research objectives, strategies and plans; regularly review value for money being delivered by various types of research; and, most importantly, check what actions are planned as a result of each research study completed in the past quarter.

It should be presented to the Marketing Director quarterly, the Managing Director every half year, the Board annually.

# FLOW-CHART SUMMARY OF CHAPTER 13

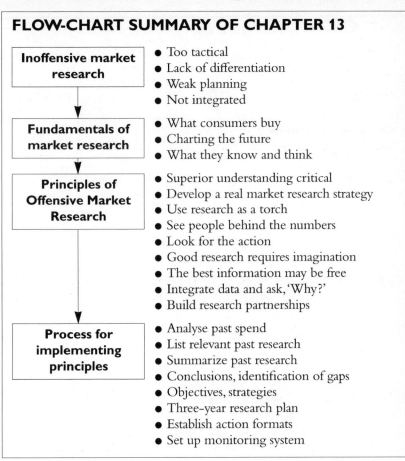

| | |
|---|---|
| **Inoffensive market research** | • Too tactical<br>• Lack of differentiation<br>• Weak planning<br>• Not integrated |
| **Fundamentals of market research** | • What consumers buy<br>• Charting the future<br>• What they know and think |
| **Principles of Offensive Market Research** | • Superior understanding critical<br>• Develop a real market research strategy<br>• Use research as a torch<br>• See people behind the numbers<br>• Look for the action<br>• Good research requires imagination<br>• The best information may be free<br>• Integrate data and ask, 'Why?'<br>• Build research partnerships |
| **Process for implementing principles** | • Analyse past spend<br>• List relevant past research<br>• Summarize past research<br>• Conclusions, identification of gaps<br>• Objectives, strategies<br>• Three-year research plan<br>• Establish action formats<br>• Set up monitoring system |

# 14. Offensive Pricing

## Chapter Summary

| Table 259. | |
|---|---|
| **P:** Profitable | ● Proper balance between firm's needs for profit and customer's need for value |
| **O:** Offensive | ● Must lead market, take risks and make competitors followers |
| **I:** Integrated | ● Marketing approach must permeate whole company |
| **S:** Strategic | ● Probing analysis leading to a winning strategy |
| **E:** Effectively Executed | ● Strong and disciplined execution on a daily basis |

Together with product or service performance, pricing is the main determinant of a brand's value to its consumers or users.

Price has no relevance in isolation. It translates products or services into **propositions** which can be valued. Value is an equation linking **relative quality** to **relative price**. This equation is detailed in a Value Map.

Offensive Pricing requires a high quality of analysis, deep understanding of external customers and internal costs, and willingness to really think through alternative pricing scenarios ahead of decision dates. To do this, Offensive Marketers need a firm grasp of the key concepts which facilitate pricing decisions. These are price elasticity, trade-off or conjoint analysis, econometrics, activity-based costing, sensitivity analysis and competitor analysis.

The eight key principles of Offensive Pricing are:

1. **Know your price dynamics.** By applying simple rules, you can quickly draw general conclusions about the price sensitivity of your markets and brands.
2. **Choose your price segments.** You should have a clear strategy as to which price segments you wish to compete in and why.
3. **Achieve clarity of pricing.** If consumers are confused by your pricing system, they are likely to think your prices are higher than they really are, and to regard your brand with suspicion.

4. **Always consider the alternatives.** Pricing is a creative process, and a variety of pricing and value options should be looked at. The Value Options Map is a useful tool.
5. **Target your price changes** by type of consumer and occasion of use.
6. **Avoid profit cannibalization when pricing new products or services.** Use new products to take profits from competition, not from yourself.
7. **Pricing should optimize your return on capacity, especially on perishable products.** Pricing decisions on limited-life products or services, like hi-tech or fashion products, passenger transport and seasonal goods, are particularly challenging.
8. **Pricing mistakes should be remedied fast.**

The chapter ends with a five-step process for implementing the principles of Offensive Pricing.

## Introduction

Advertising and design play their part in influencing the consumer, and really good presentation can have an important impact. However, for most brands the rating of product and service versus price is what matters most.

Pricing is one of the most difficult areas of marketing in which to make decisions because there are so many variables involved. The reaction of three groups has to be considered before setting or changing a price: consumers, distributors or retailers, and competitors. Their interactions are hard to read.

Pricing decisions often have to be taken quickly without testing, but usually have a major effect on profit, one way or the other. What is more, pricing is different from other elements in the marketing mix in one important respect. As Peter Doyle put it:

**'Pricing is the only element of the market mix that directly generates revenue; all the others add costs.'[1]**

Producers are not the only group to find pricing difficult. Consumers today have to work harder than ever before to understand where real value lies. Twenty years ago, they had a much easier time. There was more limited choice, products or services had a 'regular price' and this was reduced, on a disciplined basis, on short-term promotions. Now many brands are so encrusted with almost continuous promotions, first-time buyer discounts and special payment options that consumers are suspicious of even apparently good value. **Will other stores be cheaper? Will the discounts off kitchens be 75% next month, compared with 'only' 65% today? Is there a catch somewhere in this 'Sail to France for £1 offer' in the** *Radio Times*?

There are so many choices that consumers, reacting as if faced by an encyclopaedic menu in a restaurant, sometimes have difficulty ordering anything.

The result of this growing complexity is that consumers seek brands they can trust, simplicity and clarity, and honest advice.

This chapter will cover the 'Fundamentals of Offensive Pricing', outline the 'Eight Key Principles of Offensive Pricing', and convert these into action via a 'Five-step Offensive Pricing Process'. For the purpose of this chapter, sales promotion, which provides short-term improvements in customer value by cutting price or offering merchandise incentives, is regarded as a form of pricing (although clearly it also has numerous other important manifestations).

## Fundamentals of Offensive Pricing

### 1. Price is one of only two key elements in value

Price is a concrete expression of the value consumers attach to your products and services in the reality of the market-place. If you believe your product or service is superior to competition, you should either price at parity and grow market share, or at a premium and sustain share. Failure to achieve either result would be a clear indication that end-users did not share your beliefs, which would then become an expensive illusion.

Price has no relevance in isolation. Let's say the price of a car is £10,000. This information in itself is useless. You cannot convert it into a *value* judgement unless you know the age and type of car. For a new Skoda, £10,000 is very expensive. For a two-year-old BMW 328, it would be very attractive. **Price translates products or services into propositions which can be valued.**

Value is an equation (Figure 79) relating quality to price (see pages 119–22, Chapter 3 above):

### Figure 79. Price: value equation.

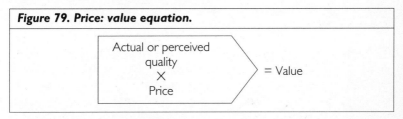

This brand equation can be detailed in a Value Map, which compares various quality/price alternatives. Quality is defined as 'the consumer judgement on product/service proposition *relative* to competition'. In the map (Figure 80), both quality and price are compared to competition. The rankings in the boxes are value rankings.

Having completed a Value Map, which establishes your value delivery today, you can use it to check the robustness of your overall strategy. If, for example, you have a share-growth strategy, but are only offering acceptable value, you are living in fairyland and need to change either your strategy or value delivery. Figure 81 summarizes the market-share implications of the Value Map.

The Value Map should be regularly updated, as your own and competitor propositions change.

The future expectation of most consumers is that quality will improve and price reduce in real terms. Offensive Marketers will respond to this desire for continuously improving value.

**Figure 80. Value map.[2]**

PRICE

| | | Higher | Parity | Lower |
|---|---|---|---|---|
| | Parity Superior | Good value | Very good | Excellent |
| | | Poor value | Acceptable | Very good |
| | Worse | Terrible value | Poor | May be acceptable |

Quality

**Figure 81. Strategic implications of Value Map.**

PRICE

| | | Higher | Parity | Lower |
|---|---|---|---|---|
| | Parity Superior | Hold or gain market share | Grow | Super growth |
| | | Decline | Hold share | Grow |
| | Worse | Exit | Decline | Hold or lose share |

Quality

## 2. Cost-plus and demand pricing

The most favoured approaches to pricing are cost-plus and demand pricing.

**Cost-plus** involves taking your costs and adding on a fixed percentage for profits. The advantages are simplicity and less price competition between companies. But the drawbacks are overwhelming for manufacturers in highly competitive markets, since 'cost-plus' does not take into account competitive reaction.

The other problem with cost-plus is that it ignores the demand curve for the brand or the category. A rise in price due to cost pressure could reduce profit if sales revenue fell heavily.

**Demand pricing** is the better method because it takes market response into account. The only justification for a price increase is that it will increase profit and, unless a company is badly strapped for cash or is deliberately milking a product or service, profits should be looked at from a long-term viewpoint.

With this method of pricing, you want to know what would happen to the sales revenue trend if prices were increased by 10% – whether it would grow or fall so heavily that a price increase would reduce profit.

If a price increase could be expected to deflate profit, it should obviously not be pursued. And if rising costs are a big problem, the solution should be found through cutting costs or increasing volume.

In essence, demand pricing ignores cost. If an increase in price looks likely to raise long-term profit, it should be considered, even though costs remain stable or decline. Whether or not you increase price in this situation depends on your market share objectives. Value rather than cost is what determines pricing.

### 3. Offensive Marketers understand the key tools which guide decision-making on pricing

**Price elasticity** is the 'ratio of sales change to price change.'[3] A brand whose volume responds sharply to price changes has high elasticity and the reverse is true. Consumers who are very price conscious have highly elastic demand – their willingness to buy is *greatly* affected by price. The table in Figure 82 illustrates price elasticity for Fairy Liquid. It is moderate at 1.6, indicating that for every 10% cut in price, sales will increase by 16%.

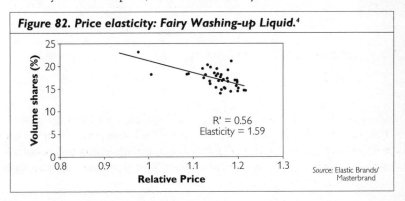

**Figure 82. Price elasticity: Fairy Washing-up Liquid.[4]**

R' = 0.56
Elasticity = 1.59

*Source:* Elastic Brands/
Masterbrand

Most studies on consumer goods suggest a price elasticity in the 1.5 to 2.5 range. So, for every 10% reduction in price, sales grow by 15–25%. Information Resources Inc. studies by CEO Fulgoni revealed a mean elasticity of −2.0. Fulgoni identified that the price effect could be greatly enhanced by advertising features and product displays. Where both were used, the average sales effect was much greater, illustrating yet again that the various elements of the marketing mix work best in combination.

Price elasticity can be established by historical analysis of market share versus price *relative* to competition. Relative price is always a more important measure than absolute price. It is usually worth while to go back at least three years, on a monthly basis, so that you have thirty-six individual observations on which to base your line of 'best fit'. This is relatively straightforward if you have sound continuing data on market share and price (although you need to take into account other factors, such as new product launches, quality changes and levels of advertising). If you do not have market-share data, you may still be able to construct a rough but useful elasticity model, using your own sales figures, allowing for any major channel inventory changes and tracking your relative price versus major competitors.

However, as anyone in the airlines or telecom industry will tell you, it is essential to work out price elasticity *by user type*. In the passenger travel industry, business customers have much lower price elasticity than leisure customers, for the obvious reason that they don't foot the bill. Table 260 is an example of price elasticity by journey purpose on a UK railway.

**Table 260.  Passenger rail: price elasticity by journey purpose.**

| Purpose | Business | Leisure | Commuter |
|---|---|---|---|
| Elasticity | 0.30 | 1.30 | 0.30 |

Price elasticity is very low for business travellers or commuters, moderate for leisure passengers. For the former, a 10% cut in price would only increase sales by 3%. In this situation, it would be profitable to increase rather than reduce price (though regulation may prevent this). For leisure travellers, a 10% cut in price would increase sales by 13%.

Elasticity may also vary by distribution channel, with Harrods lower than Aldi, and by time or occasion of use – restaurants always charge less for lunch than dinner, even though the offer is reasonably similar. As all drinkers will know, price elasticity in a pub is at its lowest near closing time – people are more interested in getting a last drink than checking the price.

**Econometrics** is a statistical technique for analysing a range of variables over time, identifying their impact on sales, and interrelationships. It is sometimes used to sort out the relative effect of changes in advertising, pricing, and sales promotion on sales. Researchers can analyse historical data on all these independent variables, and work out a 'best fit', estimating the effect of each factor on sales. Such a model can be regularly updated and used as a guide on future pricing or marketing mix decisions.

**Market research.**[5] A check by Clancy and Shulman in the USA showed that only 12% of American companies did any pricing research. A survey of 300 North American companies by McKinsey produced a similar result — only 15% of companies had done any research to 'measure or predict price elasticity' in the past year.

**So is it a waste of time to research pricing options?** It can be. Some companies still ask consumers how much they would be prepared to pay for given products or services, and then attempt to incorporate the results into price elasticity and profit models. This facile type of questioning can produce misleading answers, since consumers are being asked to predict their response to a speculative future purchase situation. Trade-off or conjoint analysis, covered below, is a much better, though more expensive, way to tackle this kind of question.

Market research can provide valuable insights on pricing, and is relatively inexpensive in relation to the likely profit improvement generated. Here are some examples:

- **Price testing** Higher or lower price levels can often be tested in panels of stores, in discrete geographical areas or, especially, in business-to-business markets, with specific groups of customers or industry types.
- **Simulated test markets (STMs).** These are covered on page 430 of Chapter 11, 'Offensive Product and Service Development'. As part of STM, the volume impact of alternative price levels can be estimated with a reasonable level of confidence.
- **Trade-off or conjoint analysis.** These are two different names for the same technique.

    'This . . . enables a researcher to evaluate many different concepts using approaches borrowed from experimental psychology.

    'Essentially, the researcher designs an experiment to test multiple factors — name, key features, key benefits, price — by showing different combinations to different people. By analysing these results, a company can capture the main effects of, say, seven factors, by exposing consumers to a relatively small set of concepts.

'In practice, this technique permits a company to evaluate thousands of potential concepts at a price comparable to a traditional test of perhaps five concepts.'[5]

Trade-off analysis is analogous to the use of circumstantial evidence in a legal case. This enables lawyers to knit together a number of different factual strands, and analyse them to draw a conclusion.

Why don't businesses test more and use powerful techniques like these? **Because their priorities are wrong.**

And perhaps Clancy and Shulman are right when they say:

'The researcher's real barrier to using conjoint analysis has often been company management. Managers don't understand the procedure and *often* don't want to understand.'

**Activity-based costing.** Every cost is an estimate, and some estimates are more accurate than others. Accountants need costs primarily for control and to meet statutory and senior management requirements. Costs for a total company, or by major department or by operations area (e.g. manufacturing plant, retail store or hotel) are therefore usually sound.

However, marketers need costs for different reasons – to take decisions on brands, channels, products and services. In general, the more costs are broken down or allocated, the less accurate they become. This applies especially to overheads like warehousing, sales forces, engineering and general management. The usual procedure of allocating these costs across brands, based on share of revenue or volume, can give a misleading picture of brand profitability. For example, large brands, especially if heavily promoted, often absorb a disproportionate amount of sales-force time. And small brands, particularly those with unique raw materials or service problems, can take up a wicked amount of Manufacturing, Operations and Supply-Chain time. Most sets of accounts conceal this reality by arbitrary cost allocation, which is why most companies have product or service ranges which are uneconomically wide.

Activity-based costing confronts this issue, and involves delving into those key activities which determine cost. It would, for example, highlight brands which take up disproportionate amounts of sales-force time, due to service or warranty problems, and establish the real cost of warehousing large versus small brands. Previously 'allocated' costs can then be adjusted to reality. Because activity-based costing involves special exercises, which can be time-consuming and expensive, it is best applied to large cost areas where allocation by brand or channel is arbitrarily estimated. Over time, a series of such exercises will enable a company to build up more accurate principles for cost allocation.

**Sensitivity analysis.** This involves working out in advance the answers to relevant 'What if?' questions on pricing, to facilitate quick and accurate decisions when the crunch comes. You are much more likely to pass a 'sudden death' exam if you have thought deeply about the issues beforehand, and the same applies to pricing.

Of these issues, the most important ones to understand are the effect of price changes of 5%, 10% and 20% on your costs and profits. It is probably reasonably straightforward for you to estimate the effect of these changes on volume. Your accountants, possibly using activity-based costing, can then calculate the cost and profit implications. Their figures will be influenced most by the ratio between fixed and variable costs, and the possible need to invest in new operational capacity in future. A simplified sensitivity analysis which estimates the effect of ± 10% in price is illustrated in Table 261.

**Table 261. Sensitivity analysis – consumer durables brand (£m).**

|  | Price now | +10% price | –10% price |
|---|---|---|---|
| Sales ('000 units) | 1,000 | 900 | 1,200 |
| Sales (£m) | 100 | 99 | 108 |
| Fixed cost of goods | 20 | 20 | 20 |
| Variable costs | 50 | 45 | 60 |
| **Gross margin (£m)** | **30** | **34** | **28** |
| Fixed operating exp. | 6 | 6 | 6 |
| Variable operating exp. | 14 | 13 | 17 |
| **Total expenses (£m)** | **20** | **19** | **23** |
| **Operating profit (£m)** | **10** | **15** | **5** |

In this example, you calculate that a 10% price increase will reduce your volume by 10% from 1,000K units to 900K. This means that your sales revenue only drops marginally from £100 million to £99 million. Your fixed costs do not change, but your variable costs fall, reflecting lower volume. The estimate of operating profit at £15 million, a 50% increase, looks good.

The 10% price cut looks much less attractive, even though it drives volume up by 20% and revenue up to £108 million. It is unattractive because variable costs rise 20%, in line with volume increases, and profits will be halved, if your estimates are right.

**Competitor analysis.** Making price changes in a competitive market is analogous to playing poker. All prices are relative, and correctly calculating competitive reaction is an important factor in successful pricing strategy. **Will your main competitors match your price change? Across their whole brand range or only part? How quickly? How consistent are they likely to be, or is a big surprise in store?**

You can make reasonable estimates of competitor reaction by studying past form. You need to understand your competitor's economics, past reactions, attitudes, management and strategy. **Is the competitor a high-cost operator, who would fear to lose a sustained price war? Where does this brand stand on the competitor's portfolio analysis – is it a priority global brand or a local one being harvested? What is the price elasticity of competitor brands? Have there been any recent management changes – is there a nutter at the helm, or a prudent long-term oarsman?**

Because pricing decisions often have to be made quickly, Offensive Marketers should use these tools to achieve a deep understanding of pricing options, so that when decision-time arrives they are well prepared to act decisively . . . and win.

## Principles of Offensive Pricing

### 1. Know the price dynamics of your markets

Even before doing any detailed analysis, you can quickly develop a feel for the price dynamics of your markets by being aware of the following:

- **Frequency of purchase** has a major influence on the sensitivity of individual products or services to price changes. Those in markets where frequency of purchase is high – like babyfoods, fast foods, petrol, bread and commuter rail – tend to be very price-sensitive.
- **Degree of necessity** affects markets rather than products within them. If a product category is very necessary to its users, changes in the prices of all products are less likely to affect its size. Cigarettes is a prime example. But discretionary markets –

like confectionery, consumer credit, clothing or cars – are more adversely affected by general price increases.

- **Unit price** is another factor. High-priced items like holidays, cars, furniture and consumer electronics tend to be subject to long deliberation and considerable price-consciousness, although status and styling may also affect the outcome.
- **Degree of comparability** also influences the price-sensitivity of brands – consumers are less price conscious about personal pensions than about grocery products, because they are more difficult to compare.
- **Degree of fashion or status** affects pricing, but sometimes in reverse; fashion, cosmetic brands or exclusive drinks may use high prices as a way of establishing quality.

The operation of these general principles is illustrated in a number of different markets by Table 262. By applying these broad principles, you can draw some general conclusions about the likely price sensitivity of certain products/services and markets in about five minutes flat. With this under your belt, you can then analyse price/volume relationships in your market.

**Table 262. Factors influencing price sensitivity by market.**

| Criteria | Mass markets | | | |
| | Babyfoods | Clothing | Motor insurance | New cars |
| --- | --- | --- | --- | --- |
| Purchase frequency | Very high | Low | Low | Low |
| Necessity | High | Medium | High | Medium |
| Unit price | Low | Medium | High | High |
| Comparability | High | Medium | Medium | Medium |
| Fashion | Low | High | Low | High |
| Effect of pricing: *on markets* | Medium | Medium | Low | High |
| *on brand* | High | Medium | High | Medium |

Two extensive studies in fast-moving goods markets provide valuable clues about price elasticity related to brand size and age.

One involved regression analysis of 500 brands over three years using continuous consumer panel data; and the other reviewed 300 brands in 50 markets, again over three years.[6]

The findings conform to common sense and may be more broadly applicable to other categories. Three of the main findings were:

- **Brand leaders are less price-sensitive than smaller brands.** This is because consumer loyalty to large brands is usually above average. As a rule of thumb, advertising is relatively more effective on large brands, whereas sales promotion is better for smaller brands.
- **New brands have above-average price elasticity.** This is no surprise. Consumers take time to form a hard view of the relative value of a new brand, and to make decisions on trial or loyalty. During the formative period, pricing and promotion can be powerful weapons.
- **Short-term price and value promotions show diminishing returns.**

## 2. Choose your price segments

Every market is segmented by price brackets. In general, stronger brands occupy the upper pricing half, while commodity products and weaker brands are in the lower half.

The bar chart in Figure 83 illustrates price segmentation for a clothing market. Note that the top-price sector accounts for only 9% of volume but 18% of value, while the bottom-price sector is almost the reverse.

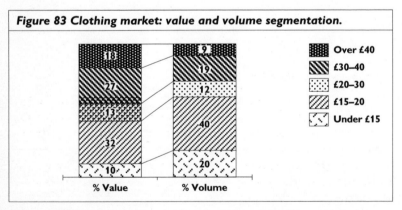

**Figure 83 Clothing market: value and volume segmentation.**

It is important to set a price sector strategy. Is your strategy, like that of Seiko Watches or Pedigree Petfoods, to compete at every price point and to blanket the market with your products? Or is it to focus on the top 20% of selected market sectors, like BMW and Nike Shoes?

Perhaps your strategy is to concentrate on the lowest price sector, like Aldi Stores, exploiting efficient low-cost operation. Or, like many Japanese global marketers and store private-label brands, you may use low price as an initial entry point, and once established, widen your coverage of price segments by moving upwards.

There are many alternative strategies for pricing. What matters is having a clear one, which has been fully thought out, rather than drifting across the price segments. Obvious considerations are:

- **Profitability**. Some price sectors are very much more profitable than others. For example, in the car market, the top 10–15% of the pricing band is quite profitable, while the bottom 20% is overcrowded and produces lean returns.
- **Fit with your company.** What price sectors best capitalize on your strengths? Are you a sophisticated marketer with strong brands and heavy R & D backing? Or does your expertise lie in low-cost operations, fast reaction and a limited range of high-volume products?

  Companies which have been successful in one price sector often have difficulty in moving into new ones. In general, though, it is easier to move up than down. Companies attempting to move down can suffocate in high overheads and wither in the absence of large marketing budgets.
- **Competitive intentions**. Watch out for the Japanese trick. When the Japanese entered the motor-cycle market with small machines, Harley-Davidson, with its 750–1000 cc superbikes, hardly noticed. Now Harley-Davidson is in a tough battle with Honda in the exalted price sector it once owned.

### 3.  Achieve clarity of pricing

If consumers do not understand your pricing system or consider it confusing or illogical, there are two likely implications. First, they will trust your brand or company less, and secondly they will probably overestimate your actual prices.

The original Marks & Spencer stores in the 1890s achieved the ultimate in pricing clarity. They were called 'penny bazaars', and featured the slogan, 'Don't ask the price, it's a penny'.[7]

British Telecom for years had a complex and confusing pricing structure, which has now been considerably simplified:

**BT's pricing structure remained largely unchanged from the 1950s to the early 1990s. Its basis was distance of call and time of day. In the UK there were twelve different call types, and more internationally.**

**Customers had a poor understanding of the system,**

although most did know that calls after 6 p.m. were cheaper. Customers were dissatisfied and confused. Most over-estimated the cost of calls, *often by a factor of two or more.*

Apart from customer dissatisfaction, BT had other powerful reasons for clarifying its price structure in the 1990s:

- Oftel had mandated BT to cut its overall prices heavily in real terms.
- Changes in technology had altered the cost of various call types, giving competitors the opportunity to reduce price on high margin call types – mainly long distance and international.
- Competition was intensifying, and, starting with new digital technology, could charge by the second, a system consumers preferred to BT's cumbersome unit approach.

Following a major customer research programme, BT established a clear new structure, based on easily remembered three-minute price points. Weekend calls were 10p for three minutes, evening calls 20p, and weekday calls 30p. BT advertised these clear price points, then moved to charging by the second, a system customers preferred.

It succeeded in increasing revenue, despite large price cuts costing £900 million per year, by stimulating the total market.

## 4. Always consider the alternatives

Pricing is often regarded as a somewhat mechanical aspect of marketing, but in fact it provides plenty of opportunity for creativity and this can pay off handsomely. For a start, price is only one part of the marketing mix, and the profitability of a change in price should be compared with all the other viable alternatives.

Suppose, for example, that a 10% increase in price was being considered and expected to bring in £1 million extra sales revenue and £400,000 additional net profit. Before recommending such an increase, it would make sense to consider whether various other possible combinations would raise profit by more than £400,000, like these:

- Increase the price by 5% and run an extra promotion.
- Hold the price and reduce advertising by £300,000.

- Raise price 15% and adopt a major product or service improvement.
- Alter payment or delivery arrangements, change the conditions of free maintenance or technical assistance, or increase guarantee/warranty periods.

A useful tool in considering the various changes in the marketing mix available to you is the Value Options Map. This contains boxes for the main change factors and enables you to consider various combinations. Three options are reviewed in Table 263. Six 'change factors' including price, are considered, and the economic effect of each option package is estimated. Option 1 looks the best of the three.

| Table 263. Value options map. | | | | | | |
|---|---|---|---|---|---|---|
| | **Key change factors** (read across) | | | | | |
| **Option** | **Product quality** | **Service quality** | **Quantity per unit** | **Price** | **Presentation** | **Advertising** |
| 1 | Improve by 15% | Add new services | No change | + 15% | Improve by 25% | Increase by 25% |
| 2 | No change | No change | No change | + 10% | No change | No change |
| 3 | Improve by 5% | Add new service | Reduce by 5% | +10% | Improve by 10% | No change |
| | **Estimated option economics** | | | | | |
| **Option** | **Full year extra sales effect £m** | | | **Full year extra profit effect £m** | | |
| 1 | + 1.6 | | | + 0.7 | | |
| 2 | + 1.0 | | | + 0.4 | | |
| 3 | + 1.2 | | | + 0.5 | | |

The Value Options Map can be completed by marketing people, using the results of previous market research and their knowledge of the market. Alternatively, the options could be modelled by a researcher. The best option, No. 1, involves a 15% price increase, accompanied by product and service improvements, supported by more advertising.

## 5. Target your price changes

Price elasticity varies by type of consumer, shopping environment and occasion of use. Loyal customers, by definition, are less price-elastic than occasional users. Someone shopping for fun in a leisure context or on holiday is likely to be less price-focused than an unsalaried housewife doing the weekly grocery shop on a tight budget.

Offensive Marketers need to have sound knowledge of the differing price elasticities of their customers, and to understand the role pricing plays in the value equation. Pricing is a means for linking supply and demand in the most advantageous way. The objective of Offensive Marketers is to get as many consumers as possible to the point where they acknowledge their brand experience as 'superior' and become regular users. Price should be targeted to reach this objective.

**Who are the best target prospects?** Those you have most chance of moving up to the 'superior brand experience' camp. Table 264 illustrates the priority for targeting price benefits by type of consumer. In this example the majority of pricing resource is targeted at occasional users, then loyal users and, finally, potentially loyal non-users. Bottom of the list are the professional switchers, and those who have tried and rejected the brand due to dissatisfaction with your proposition, since you have no chance of taking them over the superior value threshold, through price alone. With this latter group, price only becomes relevant if your basic proposition is strengthened.

**Table 264. Priority for allocation of pricing benefits.**

| Attitudes to brand product and service | Target for price benefits | High |
|---|---|---|
| Occasional users | High focus. Use price to convert to regular usage | ↑ |
| Loyal customers | Reward this group, which is the core of your business | |
| Past neutrals | Target heavy users | |
| Heard of brand, never used | Target heavy users | |
| Not heard of brand | Pricing irrelevant | |
| Hostile rejecters | Pricing irrelevant | ↓ |
| Promotion junkies | Low priority | Low |

'Promotion junkies' are consumers who tend to switch from brand to brand, depending on which offers the best deal today. In the value equation, pricing for this group is the predominant factor. In the detergent market, for instance, 16% of shoppers actively seek out price promotions, and account for 64% of promotion expenditure.[8]

**Why bother to channel price benefits to loyal customers when they have a high demand curve and low pricing elasticity?** Because loyal customers are the lifeblood of your business, and you neglect them at your peril. There is also an equity in the distribution of pricing benefits. In the long term, regular users expect to be appreciated and even rewarded for their loyalty. If they see price reductions being heavily beamed to new users, they will not be pleased – for example, long-term mortgagees are not amused to see new buyers being offered lower rates.

### 6. Avoid profit cannibalization when pricing new products

A company needs to guard against cannibalism breaking out in its midst. This may sound like a particularly nasty form of office politics, but it affects products rather than people. Profit cannibalization occurs where a marketing initiative by one product or service severely damages the profits of other products in the *same* company.

The chapters on New Product and Service Development and Market Segmentation emphasized the importance of thinking **incrementally** about new products. Incremental gains for a company will be maximized when new products are well targeted to take business from competitors, and profit per unit is above the existing average.

Mercedes followed these principles when it successfully launched the C series of mid-sized cars:

**Until the launch of the mid-size C series, Mercedes had only marketed large cars in two series, E and S.**

**For many years, BMW had prospered with its mid-size 3 series model, and Mercedes decided to enter this sector, competing against Audi, Ford, Vauxhall and Peugeot as well as BMW. Clearly there was a possible risk of trading down Mercedes buyers to the smaller car, or damaging the company's premium quality image.**

**The Mercedes C range was targeted at the high-quality end of the mid-sized car market, and priced accordingly, at a premium to BMW and Audi, and well above other competitors.**

**World-wide the C series was very successful, accounting for 40% of Mercedes car sales. More importantly, there was little trading down, and 50% of C range purchasers had never owned a Mercedes before.**

## 7. Use pricing to optimize your return on capacity, especially with perishable products

If you have a long-life product, effective management of your production capacity – one of your main assets – should not be too difficult. The key principle is to ensure that your assets and capacity are used efficiently to generate output, in the form of products, which has high value to customers. There is little point in using valuable assets to churn out undifferentiated commodity products, and this book attempts to explain how to achieve high value.

If, however, your product or service is perishable, pricing and capacity management are more challenging.

The definition of 'perishable' has broadened in recent years. Certain types of food have always been perishable, in the sense of having a limited life. Many fashion goods are equally perishable – burnt ochre may be 'the colour' in autumn, but just try selling it in January. Seasonal goods like Easter eggs or Christmas decorations are perishable – they could be kept until next year but inventory carrying costs would be high. Many consumer services are perishable: whenever a train slides out of Euston, or an aircraft takes off from Heathrow, the empty seats are as saleable as rotting strawberries – their time is past. And in other markets, prices fall so fast that time is of the essence – for instance, average prices for D-Ram electronic chips fell by over 65% in one quarter compared to the previous year in 1995. In such cases, the product is not perishable, but its value is.

The basic principles of pricing perishable products can be seen in any weekend outdoor market. Let us suppose you are running a flower stall. Your customers come to you because your products are always fresh and prices are reasonable. Demand is not always predictable and sometimes, by midday on Saturday, you still have a lot of stock, which will be unsaleable on Monday.

You can either cut the price, sell off the stock to less scrupulous merchants for sale the following week or compromise between the two. If you make a practice of cutting prices on Saturday afternoon, your Friday and Saturday morning customers may delay their purchases until then. You will be trading down customers who would otherwise have paid full price.

 This is a dilemma packaged holiday companies have been struggling with for years. They have often made the mistake of overestimating demand, committing to hotel and aircraft capacity to back it, then having to offer late-booking

discounts to use up spare capacity. Observing this, consumers hold off booking even longer next year, and you are sucked into a non-virtuous circle of increased discounting. Holiday companies have now become a lot smarter, by taking cautious views of future demand, offering early-booking discounts and merchandising the possibility that late bookers will find the cupboard bare.

Here are some guidelines for pricing perishable products:

**Use all the available demand forecasting tools**. This includes econometrics, market research and economic analysis. Having developed the best possible forecast of future demand, take a slightly conservative view. At the margin, it is much better to have run out of fully priced strawberries at 4 p.m. on Saturday evening than to be giving them away at 5.30 p.m. Marks & Spencer understands this well – look at the empty shelves for short-life baked goods in late afternoon. This phenomenon flashes two messages to consumers – 'M & S products are fresh,' and 'Shop early.'

**Understand and act upon the price elasticities of different customer types**. Railways know that students and pensioners are frequent leisure travellers and have high price elasticity. They target them by means of special travel cards, whereby they pay a small fixed fee and gain low-price travel for a year. Beefeater restaurants do the same thing with pensioners, using its Emerald Club.

**Analyse capacity utilization and use price to maximize it**. The key to pricing perishable products and services is to utilize full capacity at the highest possible price. The ideal for an airline is to take off with a full load at full prices, and no unhappy over-looked passengers left on the ground. In practice, this almost never happens, and skilful use of discounting is inevitable. Offensive airline marketers will have excellent historical analyses of load factors and prices for every flight, fast and accurate information systems providing exact booking status, and quick local decision making on pricing, following well-established guidelines.

For many marketers, capacity utilization may differ by time of day, or by season. Railways generally have high utilization in early mornings and evenings, and at night (freight), but lots of capacity in the middle of the day. This is addressed through price offers such as Saver Fares to leisure travellers in off-peak periods. Business hotels face similar issues at weekends, and retail stores have low utilization on Mondays or Tuesdays.

**Ensure your cost allocations are first class**. Correct pricing of perishable products and services requires a deep understanding of real costs, especially the true split between fixed and variable.

### 8. *If you make a mistake on pricing, admit it and remedy fast*

Anyone can make a mistake on pricing, and the important thing is to face up to it and put it right, fast. There is usually no practical reason why this cannot be done. But it is difficult to put into effect, because neither people nor companies like to admit they have made mistakes.

The irony is that mistakes do not matter too much if they are spotted and remedied quickly. This, of course, applies to every area of the business. As one executive with wide experience in acquisitions said, 'The key is to recognize a mistake early and then move quickly to cut losses.'

## Process for Offensive Pricing

A five-step process is recommended. The first two steps involve consumer and channel analysis; the next two cover cost, capacity and competitor analysis; and the final one generates objectives and strategies, built up from the analysis in the previous four steps.

Offensive Pricing requires **high-quality** analysis, and it is no coincidence that four of the five steps are analytical ones. There is no escape from serious number-crunching, and no place for sloppy thinking. Markets are cruel and unforgiving to those who get their pricing wrong or fail to deliver superior value.

The five-step process is summarized in Table 265.

**Table 265. *Five-step process for Offensive Pricing.***

| Step 1 | **Consumer or end-user analysis** | ● Price elasticity<br>● Market research<br>● Perceived product or service quality<br>● Consumer value |
|---|---|---|
| Step 2 | **Channel or distributor analysis** | ● Channel or account price strategy<br>● Channel margins, discounts<br>● Channel value delivered |
| Step 3 | **Competitor pricing analysis** | ● Elasticity<br>● Perceived performance and value<br>● Current price/value strategy<br>● Future strategy |

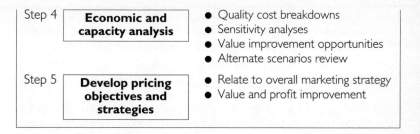

| Step 4 | **Economic and capacity analysis** | ● Quality cost breakdowns<br>● Sensitivity analyses<br>● Value improvement opportunities<br>● Alternate scenarios review |
| --- | --- | --- |
| Step 5 | **Develop pricing objectives and strategies** | ● Relate to overall marketing strategy<br>● Value and profit improvement |

## STEP 1: CONSUMER OR END-USER ANALYSIS

Start by standing back and looking at the general price dynamics of your markets and brands – see Table 262 on page 529 above. Then analyse past price promotions and volume effect of changes in your relative price versus competition, and **construct a price elasticity chart**, like the Fairy Liquid one on page 523. On your larger brands, identify the main influences on sales through econometrics – this can either be done in-house or by an outside modelling agency like MMB or Henley. Scan your existing inventory of market research for any useful information on consumer attitude to price or value in your markets.

If your products or services have a number of identifiable user types, or different user occasions, develop a view on the relative price elasticity of each one. The UK railway price elasticity chart, Table 260 on page 524, is an example. In a pub or restaurant, price elasticity is highest early in the evening, and this is the reason for price discounts on 'happy hour' drinks or 'early bird' dinners before 7 p.m.

Bigger brands and companies should consider investing in specific price and value research, like conjoint analysis.

Next, check the perceived quality of your product or service proposition versus competition. Again, review past consumer research. **Talk to customers. Is your relative quality better, parity or worse?**

You can now combine the above elements to make a **value judgement**, comparing the relative quality of your proposition with your relative price. Complete the Value Map (Figure 80 on page 522 above). Then examine the Strategic Implications Map (Figure 81 on page 522) and check the fit with your current strategy.

## STEP 2: CHANNEL OR DISTRIBUTOR ANALYSIS

Check forward to Steps 1 to 3 in the 'Process for Offensive Channel Marketing' at the end of Chapter 15 (pages 570–73).

Identify the margin, discount and consumer pricing strategies of each channel and major account. **How might these change in future? What are their margin aspirations, and how do they evaluate them – percent gross margin, sterling gross margin per linear foot, or some more sophisticated measure?** How well are your brands meeting these aspirations? **If you raise your price, how quickly will the channel or major account react, and will it attempt to raise percent margin? What value for money is the channel providing in return for the margin, discounts and services you are providing? Can this be improved to the consumer's advantage?**

## STEP 3: COMPETITOR PRICING ANALYSIS

Check back to pages 206–11 in Chapter 5 for overall 'competitive analysis drill', and relate it to pricing.

Put your major competitors through the same processes as you applied to your own brands in Step 1. Establish price elasticity, relative quality and relative value. Then analyse each competitor's past behaviour. **What is their growth, profit strategy, overall, and in this market? Are they seeking to grow share or hold on and raise profit margins? What is their cost base – have they recently reduced it, and if so, will they use the savings to improve customer value, perhaps cut price, or will they build profit margin instead?**

Next, evaluate how competitors handle price changes – who initiates or leads price changes in each market. Usually it is the brand leader, but not always – there may be an ambitious No. 2 brand which suddenly cuts price, or an eccentric No. 3 brand, which, desperate for extra profit this year, leads with a price increase. **For competitors who do not initiate price increases, what is their 'following' strategy? Do they follow immediately? Do they hold off for three months and build extra short-term volume? Or do they pretend to follow, with a list-price increase, but in reality hold their prices by promoting heavily?**

## STEP 4: ECONOMICS AND CAPACITY ANALYSIS

The importance of high-quality costs has already been emphasized. Identify the kind of cost breakdowns you need, and lay out a charted schedule of these. Explain to Finance Department why they are necessary, and how you will use the results. Check on how accurately overheads and fixed costs are allocated by brand or major account, and, where the numbers are large, insist on activity-based costing exercises.

Armed with this data, and working closely with Finance, develop a number of Sensitivity Analyses (see Table 261 on page 527), indicating profit effect of various price or value changes. Discuss it with people in Finance and seek their input. They will be impressed to meet a profit-driven marketer. They are likely to provide valuable insights.

Use the Sensitivity Analysis to consider 'What if?' questions and possible improvement opportunities. **What if we improve product quality by 10%, increase warranty from two to three years, and raise price by 5%?** The aim is to relate every cost to its consumer value. Eliminate high-cost elements which have low value to the consumer. Seek low-cost benefits with high consumer value. This is your job – making every cost your company incurs work hard on behalf of the consumer. This will enable you to use price to highlight your superior value.

## STEP 5:  DEVELOP PRICING OBJECTIVES AND STRATEGIES

This step capitalizes on the analysis done in the four previous steps, and converts them into action. A format and example for pricing objectives and strategies on a successful consumer goods brand is given in Table 266.

And no, this brand is not Müller Yogurt, nor is it Walker's Crisps. Wouldn't we all like to be sitting in the driving seat on a brand with such a powerful position? Clearly most brands hold fewer cards. It is the objective, though, of all Offensive Marketers to move their brands into strong bargaining positions.

What pricing strategy would you follow on this brand? There is clearly a case for raising price by 10% and garnering the extra £3.5 million profits. In most UK companies, such a case would be made strongly at Board level. This Brand Manager took the view that a price rise, especially so soon after the Quarter 4 increase, was off-strategy, because the brand's primary objective was to increase share while sustaining profitability. The basis for this was that the brand had the potential to achieve a dominating 30% market share in five years' time, and 15% operating profit. The Brand Manager should win her case as long as her company doesn't run into profit trouble on other fronts, and as long as the Operations Department deliver their promised cost reductions.

---

**Table 266. Format and example: pricing objectives and strategies.**

### A   FACTUAL BACKGROUND

**1. Relative price per unit versus market average, past 6 quarters**

|                      | Q1  | Q2  | Q3  | Q4  | Q5  | Latest Q6 |
|----------------------|-----|-----|-----|-----|-----|-----------|
| *Relative price index* | 110 | 108 | 108 | 112 | 115 | 115       |

**2. Relative strength of brand proposition (quote relevant market research)**

a) *Recent product blind tests*
   v. Brand X   60:40
   v. Brand Y   56:44

b) *Attitude, image studies*
   On top 6 most important consumer criteria for purchase, our brand rated 20% higher than next strongest competitor

c) *Judgement of relative brand strength versus best competitor*
   120 (Index).

**3. Recent value improvements**

● Improved product launched, Q4, with new package graphics
● Freephone consumer advice and helpline set up Q4, advertised on pack, women's magazines, Internet, and via editorial publicity

**4. Recent brand share and advertising trends**

|                           | Q1   | Q2   | Q3   | Q4   | Q5   | Latest Q6 |
|---------------------------|------|------|------|------|------|-----------|
| Value share (%)           | 18.6 | 18.8 | 17.2 | 18.4 | 19.0 | 19.3      |
| Share total ad. spend (%) | 21.0 | 16.0 | —    | 35.0 | 30.0 | 22.0      |

**5. Results of econometric analysis**

| *2 years ending* | Q1   | Q2   | Q3   | Q4   | Q5   | Latest Q6 |
|------------------|------|------|------|------|------|-----------|
| *Price elasticity* | 1.50 | 1.53 | 1.57 | 1.50 | 1.45 | 1.43      |

**6. Brief summary of competitor pricing strategies**

● Brand X has significantly reduced costs in past year, is pursuing a share growth strategy. It is unlikely to increase price this year. A reduction is possible.
● Brand Y's company is under profit pressure. Brand Y is a high-cost operator, is losing market share, and will follow any price increase we make.

**7.  Sensitivity analyses on current cost base**

| | Current position | Impact of possible price changes | | |
|---|---|---|---|---|
| | | +5% | +10% | –5% |
| Market share (%) | 19.3 | 18.7 | 18.2 | 20.9 |
| Sales (£m) | 87 | 84 | 82 | 94 |
| Operating profit (£m) | 10 | 10.9 | 12.3 | 8.5 |
| Operating profit (%) | 11.5 | 13.0 | 15.0 | 9.0 |

## B.  OVERALL MARKETING STRATEGY

Gain market share over next 3 years, by offering continuing value improvement to consumers, and spending a slightly higher % of total market advertising than our % share of market. We aim to cut operating cost base by 5% per year, mainly through improved manufacturing and supply chain efficiencies, to hold profit margin at 11.5% for next 2 years, and increase it to 14% in Year 3.

## C.  PRICING STRATEGY

Over the next year, we will continue to price at a 12% to 15% premium to the market. This will reduce to 8% to 10% in Year 2, as we play back cost savings into improved consumer value. In Year 3, we will maintain this lower premium, and apply cost savings partly to more advertising, partly to raise operating profit to 14%.

## D.  ALTERNATE SCENARIO PLANNING

1. *Market stabilizes (v. 5% volume growth currently).* Hold price, increase advertising and improve impact.
2. *Brand Y leads market with 5% price increase.* Do not follow. Focus effort on taking share from Brand Y.
3. *Brand X cuts price by 5%.* Do not follow for at least 6 months. Increase advertising and promotion. Review situation in 6 months and take final decision.

## FLOW-CHART SUMMARY OF CHAPTER 14

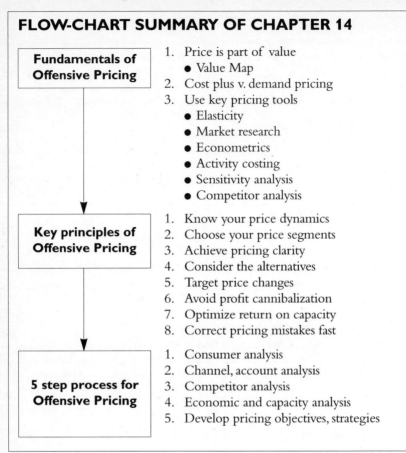

**Fundamentals of Offensive Pricing**

1. Price is part of value
   ● Value Map
2. Cost plus v. demand pricing
3. Use key pricing tools
   ● Elasticity
   ● Market research
   ● Econometrics
   ● Activity costing
   ● Sensitivity analysis
   ● Competitor analysis

**Key principles of Offensive Pricing**

1. Know your price dynamics
2. Choose your price segments
3. Achieve pricing clarity
4. Consider the alternatives
5. Target price changes
6. Avoid profit cannibalization
7. Optimize return on capacity
8. Correct pricing mistakes fast

**5 step process for Offensive Pricing**

1. Consumer analysis
2. Channel, account analysis
3. Competitor analysis
4. Economic and capacity analysis
5. Develop pricing objectives, strategies

# 15. Offensive Channel Marketing

## Chapter Summary

This is the last of the seven chapters on Offensive Execution.

| **Table 267.** | |
|---|---|
| **P:** Profitable | ● Proper balance between firm's needs for profit and customer's need for value |
| **O:** Offensive | ● Must lead market, take risks and make competitors followers |
| **I:** Integrated | ● Marketing approach must permeate whole company |
| **S:** Strategic | ● Probing analysis leading to a winning strategy |
| **E:** Effectively Executed | ● Strong and disciplined execution on a daily basis |

The main fundamentals of Offensive Channel Marketing are as follows:

1. **Channels exist to serve consumers**. Their purpose is similar to that of brands. Both exist 'to build superior customer value very efficiently for above average profits'.
2. **Channels are segmented, just like markets**. They segment to achieve differentiation and to serve different customer needs.
3. **Channels can add value to a brand's consumer proposition**, by offering image, services and point-of-sale impact.
4. **Influence over the final consumer affects allocation of industry profitability**. Both producers and retailers regard consumers as their property, and compete to influence them, since this is key to the industry division of profits.
5. **Branders have the option of owning their own marketing channels**, and are showing increasing interest in doing so.
6. **Producers and distributors compete within and across channels**. Competition is broadening . . . fast.
7. **For producers, Channel Marketing requires business-to-business marketing skills**. Marketing household brands to Tesco is more like marketing Boeings to airlines, and has little in common with mass marketing to consumers.

The key principles of Offensive Channel Marketing are:

1. **Establish clear channel requirements for your brands**. Apply six factors.
2. **Use quantified portfolio analysis (QPA) to determine channel strategies**. Treat channels like markets. QPA will help you decide channel and major customer priorities.
3. **Align channel and market strategies**. This requires a higher level of cooperation between Marketing and Sales than is customary.
4. **Find ways to increase influence over your channels**. Influence equals bargaining power in the fight for share of industry profits.
5. **Tailor your products and services to channel needs**. Channels and major accounts deserve to be treated like customers, and to receive tailored propositions.
6. **Seek to develop new channels**. These can improve your bargaining power with existing channels, and broaden your availability.

The chapter finishes with a seven-step process for implementing the fundamentals and key principles of Offensive Channel Marketing.

# The Fundamentals of Offensive Channel Marketing

## 1. The role of marketing channels

Marketing channels exist to link producers to consumers. They vary greatly in complexity and efficiency. The channel for electricity is simple and almost ideal – the producer has mass distribution and the consumer has instant availability, literally at the flick of a switch. By contrast, the channel for man-made fibres is extremely complex – the chain runs through spinners, dyers, weavers or knitters, garment manufacturers and retailers, until it finally reaches the consumer.

Marketing channels reach backwards to raw materials and forwards to the consumer, as Table 268 shows. 'Raw material' can consist of products, data or services.

**Table 268  The full range of marketing channels.**

| Raw material procurement | Raw material processing | Finished goods production | Inter-mediaries | Retailers or distributors | Consumers or users |
|---|---|---|---|---|---|

Companies have the option to handle each stage themselves or to contract it out to independent third parties. For example, a wine company may own its own vineyards, make its own bottles and corks, process and ship to distributors, and only rely on third parties at the end of the channel. By contrast, a sports-shoe brand may buy in finished product from the Far East, and deliver to wholesalers and retailers for sale to consumers. In this case, the brander focuses activity exclusively on R & D, product design and specification, quality assurance, marketing and brand development.

This chapter will not cover backwards integration, and will concentrate on channel steps from finished production to consumer. These steps account for between 15% and 40% of retail price in product and service markets.[1]

Why are channels necessary? Because the producer is usually a long distance from the consumer and because skills differ by channel type. The distance between producer and consumer is extending, as products made in the Far East by American-owned companies are sold in Europe, as service production moves from back rooms in High Street banks to low-cost central locations.

Marketing channels have five major roles as far as producers are concerned:

- **Consumer access.** The primary role of channels is to provide consumers with convenient access to products and services.
- **Presentation**. The final channel should present products and services in good condition in an appropriate environment. For example, chilled foods should be fresh, undamaged and attractively presented in temperature-controlled cabinets.
- **Endorsement.** The very fact of stocking a product or service implies a degree of endorsement by the channel. This may add lustre if the channel is a prestige one, like Tiffany's or Harrods, but have negative effects if the channel is a low-price discounter and the product a luxury one. Level of endorsement for the producer can vary, from stocking, to promoting, to using the channel brand name. The channel gives its highest level of endorsement to a producer whose goods it brands with its own name, but the producer pays a heavy price in loss of consumer influence.
- **Additional services.** Table 269 shows some examples of services that channels can add to the producer proposition.

**Table 269. Marketing channels: examples of services which add value.**

| Type of service by channel | Examples of channel services |
| --- | --- |
| Breaking bulk | Redistributing to smaller outlets |
| Customer trial | Test driving cars; trying out clothes, music, computers |
| Customer advice | Independent financial advisers; beauticians |
| Customer guarantees | Opportunity to return goods; warranties |
| Financial packages | Credit, instalment payments |
| Home delivery | Durables; household items |
| After-sales service | Copiers, cars; computer helplines |

- **Money.** Channels collect money from consumers or other channel members, take ownership of goods and services, and pay producers.

## 2. Types of marketing channel

Most products or services reach the consumer by more than one type of outlet:

- Airline tickets can be bought direct from city ticket offices, by phone from airlines, from the internal travel departments of large companies, through travel agents or at the airport.

- Consumers can purchase crisps from pubs, leisure centres, clubs, cafés, stations, vending machines, grocers, newsagents or garages.
- Clothes are available from department stores, sports shops, boutiques, mail-order firms, specialist clothing shops, market stalls and variety stores.
- Pensions can be bought direct over the phone, in-home from a sales person, from independent advisers, banks and building societies.

For the majority of markets, one type of channel is predominant, even though others of less significance may exist. The main types of channel are **direct selling, distributors, agents, franchisees, sales brokers, wholesalers and retailers** (see Figure 84).

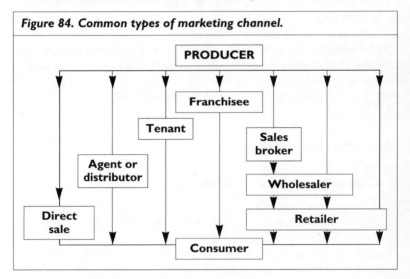

**Figure 84. Common types of marketing channel.**

In **Direct Selling**, the product is sold by the producer straight to the consumer. Life assurance, encyclopaedias and certain toiletries are sold in this way. The main direct-selling channels are phone, in-home calling, party plan and mail. Mail order remains a very important direct channel, either via agents or direct with the catalogue company.

**Distributors** usually act as the manufacturer's agent in selling its product, often on an exclusive basis. Many of the cars and petrol in the UK are sold through distributors. They normally own their premises and provide capital and labour. Manufacturers are responsible for the product and its advertising or promotion. They may also help with personnel training, technical advice or financial loans.

**Franchising** is common in soft drinks, launderettes, doorstep milk, fast food and speciality retailing, e.g. Hallmark cards and Benetton. Coca-Cola is the most famous franchiser of all. It provides specially prepared syrup to the bottlers and is responsible for developing advertising, promotion and merchandising. The bottlers dilute and carbonate the syrup and distribute it throughout their franchised area. The advantage of franchising for a company is that widespread distribution can be achieved quickly and at low cost. Many branders, such as McDonald's or Coca-Cola, have a mix of franchisees and company owned channels.

**Sales brokers** are independent sales companies which sell the products of a number of non-competing manufacturers and get a commission on sales or fee in return. Their customers are either companies too small to have their own sales force or larger ones who use brokers temporarily to meet a short-term situation like a distribution drive or the launch of a new brand. Sales brokers are common in the USA and are becoming more widely used in the UK.

The **tenant** is a feature of the licensed drink trade. Unlike the distributor, the lessees only rent their premises from the brewer. Lessees usually have limited freedom of manoeuvre in the products they can purchase.

Wholesalers, retailers and mail order are too well known to require any elaboration.

This chapter will focus mainly on the retailer, and its viewpoint will be that of the producer or supplier.

## 3. Channels exist to serve consumers

The purpose of channels is similar to that of brands. Both exist to 'build superior customer value very efficiently for above-average profits'. Producers, intermediaries and retailers all have different roles and objectives, but their primary purpose is to serve the end-user. One category which serves the consumer poorly is mobile phones:

**Mobile phone hardware is made primarily by global manufacturers like Motorola or Panasonic, and usually carries their brand names. The network will be provided by operators such as Cellnet or Vodaphone. Selling and servicing, as well as pricing, is usually carried out by local 'service providers', some of whose areas overlap. Phone accessories, like car kits or leather cases, are mostly sourced from specialist manufacturers located in the Far East.**

**No wonder consumers are defecting at a rate of over 20% a year. They are thoroughly confused, not at all sure who they are dealing with and dissatisfied with the value delivered by the total marketing channel.**

What are the fundamental needs consumers or users expect to be satisfied by marketing channels? These will vary by type of market and consumer, but are likely to include the eight factors in Table 270. Each of these can be delivered in different combinations.

| Table 270. Eight main consumer needs from marketing channels. | |
|---|---|
| Clarity | *What does the channel sell and stand for?* |
| Convenience | *Not far to travel. Good parking and opening hours* |
| Range | *Choice of relevant products and services* |
| Price | *Range of price points, payment methods. Good value* |
| Quality | *Related to price, should give value* |
| Service | *Helpful attitudes, speedy transaction time, relevant services* |
| Environment | *Easy to use, clean, fit for the purpose* |
| Image | *Fit with product or service category, and buying occasion* |

## 4. Most markets are segmented into a variety of channels, which serve customer needs differently

Retailers segment markets to meet the requirements of their target consumers, by developing propositions which combine the eight needs (see Table 271) in different ways. Compare Harrods and Aldi in the table, for instance.

| Table 271. Harrods and Aldi: eight main consumer channel needs. | | |
|---|---|---|
| | **Level of provision of needs** | |
| **Need** | **Harrods** | **Aldi** |
| Clarity | High | High |
| Convenience | Low | High |
| Range | Wide | Narrow |
| Price | High | Low |
| Quality | High | Medium |
| Service | High | Low |
| Environment | Stylish | Basic |
| Image | Stylish | Basic |

Both retailers have a clear and differentiated proposition, and offer good value to their consumers. Harrods does this through style, range, quality and service. Aldi achieves it via a narrow range, basic environment, reasonable quality and low price.

Producers exploit a range of distribution channels, both to achieve wide availability of their products or services and to reach specific target consumers. Figure 85 is an example of a relatively complex market in channel terms – bathrooms. The diagram is simplified to avoid being soporific.

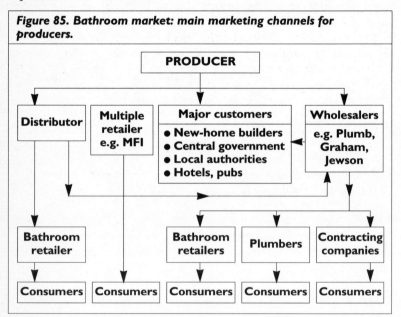

**Figure 85. Bathroom market: main marketing channels for producers.**

Consumers buy from specialist bathroom retailers, who have extensive ranges, usually sourced from distributors; from plumbers or contracting companies who are most likely to buy from a trade wholesaler like Plumb Centre; or from multiple retailers. Wholesalers often have retail shops for consumers as well as trade counters.

Major customers such as hotel chains, local education authorities or new-home builders like Wimpey may be handled by both producer and major wholesaler. The latter are likely to present a joint proposition which the producer will manufacture and the wholesaler deliver and install.

Distributors carry very wide ranges. They primarily supply bathroom retailers, but also deliver slow-moving or exotic items to wholesalers with narrower ranges.

This is an example of a slow-moving and rather inefficient marketing channel, which offers consumers wide choice but falls down on convenience and speed of delivery.

## 5. Channels can add considerable value to a brand's consumer proposition

Every retailer has the potential to offer the producer availability and visibility to the consumer. For most mass-market brands, especially those relying on impulse purchase, maximum availability is an essential element of brand building. Coca-Cola has, for decades, pursued a policy of placing its products 'within an arm's length of desire'. By the mid 1990s the number of consumers Coca-Cola 'could actively reach out to with . . . products was over 5 billion, up from 2.2 billion ten years earlier.[2] By contrast, for high-image brands like Chanel, restricted availability may be a key strategy, reinforcing exclusivity.

Some retail channels move well beyond the basic function of availability, and greatly enhance a brand's image or proposition:

- Irish theme pubs are an ideal environment for Guinness beers.
- Specialist games and computer stores, targeted at boys aged 9–16, provide the informal browsing atmosphere required, with demonstration units, spotlighting, dark fixtures and music.[3]
- Availability in fashionable nightclubs builds the image of drink products aimed at 18–30 year olds, especially at launch.

The eight main consumer needs from marketing channels, listed in Table 270, are the areas where channels can add value to brands. These areas often involve important trade-offs, like availability versus image, price versus range and price versus service levels. Producers need to make decisions on these issues in determining their channel strategy.

## 6. Influence over the final consumer affects allocation of channel profitability

Once upon a time retailers were passive channels which gratefully received goods from producers and resold them to the public. The producer was very much in control and channels played second fiddle because private labelling was undeveloped and producer brands called the tune.

The concentration of retail power, increasing trade marketing sophistication and the growth of private labelling have changed all that. The division between manufacturer and retailers is becoming blurred. Retailers like Marks & Spencer, Ikea and Dixons specify, brand and market their own products, using manufacturers as sub-contractors.

Now retailers regard the producer's 'ultimate consumer' as their own customer. They have become 'the customer's buying agent, not the producer's selling agent'.[4] In many cases they own the consumer, and are seen as the category authority. A few years ago, if you asked consumers for the best source of advice on food recipes, they would probably have named Heinz or Kraft. Today they are much more likely to nominate Tesco or Sainsbury.

The issue of 'who owns the consumer' is not an academic one, since it fundamentally affects the division of industry profitability between producers and other participants in the marketing channel. In practice, of course, no one 'owns' consumers, who are free agents. However, share of industry profitability is affected by consumer influence. **How is this influence achieved, and by whom?** Table 272 summarizes the main weapons in this battleground.

**Table 272.  How consumers are influenced and by whom.**

| Key influence areas | Main wielders of influence areas | | |
| --- | --- | --- | --- |
| | Branded producers | Retailers or distributors | Intermediaries |
| Strong branded product or service | ✓ ✓ | ✓ | |
| Brand advertising | ✓ ✓ | ✓ | |
| Direct Marketing | ✓ | ✓ ✓ | |
| Direct contact | | ✓ ✓ | |
| Availability | ✓ | ✓ ✓ | ✓ ✓ |
| Presentation | ✓ | ✓ ✓ | |
| Customer service | ✓ | ✓ ✓ | |
| Pricing | ✓ | ✓ | |

Branded producers hold two good weapons in this battle for consumer influence – strong brands and advertising. They can also market direct to customers by phone, mail or personal contact. And they can influence availability, presentation and pricing by exploiting the strength of their consumer franchise with channel owners.

However, in many industries, retailers or distributors hold more of the cards, especially if they have built their own strong brands. Intermediaries have little direct influence on the consumer, since their primary role is to provide services for producers or retailers. Consequently, their profitability is usually well below the industry average.

The primary determinant of how industry profitability is allocated is the relative brand strength of producer versus retailer or distributor.

Strong-brandèd producers, like Wrigleys, Microsoft, Nike and American Express, tend to have above-average industry margins, even though they market via strong channels, with a powerful influence over consumers. Weak branded producers struggle even to achieve availability, and usually have to pay heavily for it.

## 7. Branders have the option of owning their own marketing channels, or of using a third-party one, or both

There are at least five alternative channel ownership options open to branders, as Table 273 shows:

**Table 273. Alternative channel ownership strategies for branders.**

| Brands marketed | Ownership of Marketing channels | Examples |
|---|---|---|
| 1) All | None | Philip Morris, Mars, P & G |
| 2) All | All | M & S, Avon, Ikea |
| 3) Some | All | Tesco, Boots, B & Q, BT |
| 4) None | Some | Small retailers |
| 5) All | Some | Amex, Levi, McDonald's, Coca-Cola, Merck, Shell, Ford, Prudential |

1. **Own all brands, no channels.** This is the traditional route for branders of consumer goods.
2. **Own all brands and all channels**. M & S owns the branding of all products marketed in its stores. One of Avon's major advantages over the last hundred years has been its control of distribution.
3. **Own channels and some of brands marketed through them**. Boots controls its channels and markets a range of brands, including its own. BT is in a similar position, but has to allow other telecom brands access to its network.
4. **Own no brands and only part of channel**. This is an unattractive strategy, providing minimum influence over the consumer. Small operators usually lack the scale or resource to develop their own brands. Neither do they have much influence over their marketing channels, since they typically source from powerful wholesalers or distributors.
5. **Own brands and some marketing channels**. American Express has its own travel and exchange outlets, but relies mainly on non-owned channels in marketing its cards. Levi

Strauss has developed its own Original Levi Stores, which are the only source of Levi custom-made jeans, but these are a minority of its channels. McDonald's owns most of its stores, but franchises others; and Bass owns some of the outlets to which it markets beer brands.

The same applies to Coca-Cola, which owns some bottlers, Shell and Ford, which own petrol stations or dealers, and Merck, the pharmaceutical company, which has bought into its distribution channels in the USA.

**Which of these ownership strategies has your company pursued in the past decade, and what changes of approach are you or your competitors likely to make in the next decade?** The extended time-scale in the question is deliberate, since distribution decisions have a long-term impact.

As Peter Drucker points out:

**'Many businessmen – especially makers of industrial products – are as unaware that they use distribution channels, let alone that they depend on them, as Molière's Monsieur Jourdain was of the fact that he spoke prose.'[5]**

Distribution channels resemble the hour hand of a clock. They are always moving, but each individual movement is so small as to be almost  imperceptible. The cumulative effect over a number of years can, however, be massive. New approaches to distribution are often easier to develop than superior products, yet they can lead to equally large breakthroughs in profit.

### 8. Producers and distributors increasingly compete within and across channels

In their efforts to raise influence with the consumer and improve the presentation of their products and services, **branded producers** are increasing investment in direct consumer marketing. They are also establishing direct-selling channels with consumers, opening up telephone help and advice lines, and even investing in retail or wholesale marketing channels. Soft-drinks branders are buying back bottlers, fast-food branders taking back franchisees.

**Retailers and distributors** in turn are strengthening their consumer brand images, exploiting their own branded products and services, capitalizing on their improving consumer databases and adding new consumer services.

The result is a broadening of competition, as oversupply in provision of goods and services is joined by overcapacity in the channels which

market them. Tomorrow's competitive scenario within marketing channels will be very different from yesterday's, as Table 274 shows.

**Table 274. Changes in competitive scenario within and across channels.**

| Issue | Yesterday | Tomorrow |
|---|---|---|
| *Private label growth* | Branded producer dominates premium price sectors, private label confined to low end | Private label competes in all price sectors, increasingly targets profitable top end |
| *Cross-industry competition* | Supermarkets compete with other supermarkets | Supermarkets compete with banks, pubs, fast food, restaurants, petrol companies |
| *Branded producers' isolation from consumer* | Branded producer markets mainly via third party channels | Branded producers go direct, buy into part of distribution channels, set up consumer service lines |
| *Growth of direct marketing* | Limited use except for high ticket items | Increasing use by branded producers and retailers at all price points |

In this increasingly competitive environment, where the dividing
lines between branded producers and marketing channels are becoming
blurred, and companies are simultaneously competing and cooperating
with each other, there has been a trend towards partnerships between
producers and distributors.

These partnerships usually involve joint effort to identify cost reductions in the supply chain, and to increase efficiency of consumer presentation and promotion. In consumer goods categories, this activity is
called **efficient consumer response** (ECR). ECR can offer larger
branders the opportunity to gain competitive advantage over their
smaller rivals, as well as the chance to share the cost benefits of greater
efficiency with retailers.

However, cooperation and partnerships do not alter the abiding reality
that producers and retailers will always be in competition with each
other, to increase share of total industry profits.

### 9. For producers, Channel Marketing requires strong business-to-business marketing skills

While meeting the needs of consumers or users is always the ultimate
target of most marketers, channels guard the gate. You need to access
and motivate channels in order to reach users.

This requires two-stage marketing. And marketing to channels or retailers calls for quite different skills from marketing to consumers or users. This particularly applies when the final consumers consist of millions of people. Some companies are good at mass marketing but weak at Channel Marketing. This is apparent in the way many consumer goods marketers have been totally outmanoeuvred by their multiple-retailer channel.

Marketing to channels requires business-to-business marketing skills. Trying to interest Boots in stocking a new skincare brand is more like selling a fleet of new Boeings to Swissair, than marketing skincare products to the mass consumer.

Here is an example of some of the competencies required for Channel Marketing – you will see how similar they are to Boeing's business to business transactions with airlines:

| **Table 275. Competencies required for channel versus business-to-business marketing.** | | |
|---|---|---|
| | **Type of marketing transaction** | |
| **Competencies required by producer** | **Sale of new skincare brand to Boots (customer)** | **Sales of new Boeings to Swissair (customer)** |
| ● Clear understanding of customer strategy, needs | ✓ | ✓ |
| ● Compelling positioning of advantages of your products | ✓ | ✓ |
| ● Knowledge of competitor offer | ✓ | ✓ |
| ● Economics of your products for customer | ✓ | ✓ |
| ● Contact with key customer decision-makers | ✓ | ✓ |
| ● Ability to tailor products to customer requirements and operating systems | ✓ | ✓ |
| ● Fit of new product with existing range | ✓ | ✓ |
| ● After-sales support programme | ✓ | ✓ |

Clearly the required marketing and knowledge skills will differ between skincare brands and Boeings. In one case, a potential consumer franchise is being offered, in the other a fleet of planes. However,  it is obvious that these required skills differ radically from those called for in mass consumer marketing, which revolve around understanding millions of users rather than a small number of specialist buyers. The resourceful national account manager would feel much more at home marketing Boeing 777s than the typical consumer goods Brand Manager. Yet the latter must develop a sound understanding of Channel Marketing, and should not be surprised that this involves much new learning.

## Key Principles of Offensive Channel Marketing

### 1. Establish clear channel requirements for your brands

In selecting marketing channels for new products or services, or in reviewing channel arrangements, producers need to consider six key factors: exposure to target customers, performance requirements, influence, flexibility, producer profit and distributor needs. Each one is assessed below:

(a) **Exposure to target consumers.** From the producer's angle, the primary purpose is to make products or services available and visible to *target* consumers. A good product may fail because it is in the wrong channel or not exposed to the people most likely to buy it.

(b) **Performance requirements**. Suppliers want products to reach the consumer in high-quality condition.

   In addition, they may wish the channel to provide certain skills which are a necessary part of the sale. Insurance companies operating through insurance brokers, banks or accountants will expect a high level of know-how about their products, as well as high ethical standards.

(c) **Influence**. A supplier's influence over its channels depends upon degree of ownership, the number of links in the channel and the consumer appeal of its products or services. Large and powerful companies like BMW or Coca-Cola have a lot of influence over their independent distributors or franchisees, because their strong consumer appeal provides the channel with a large profit opportunity. At minimum, suppliers need enough bargaining power to achieve their aims of exposure to the right consumers, maintenance of product quality and profitability.

(d) **Flexibility**. Channel decisions are often long-term in effect, but even so it is desirable to retain maximum flexibility to alter channel emphasis.

(e) **Producer profit**. Offensive Marketers will seek the type and mix of distribution channel that gives them maximum revenue at minimum cost in the long term.

(f) **Channel needs**. Owners of distribution channels usually have clear marketing and profit strategies. They will not bother with products or services which fail to fit.

## 2. Use Quantified Portfolio Analysis (QPA) to determine channel strategies

It is as important to segment channels as markets. Use the five-step market segmentation process described in Chapter 9 (pages 347–67) to segment and prioritize channels.

The Quantified Portfolio Analysis approach is particularly relevant, and the criteria for assessing channel attractiveness are similar to those used for evaluating market sector attractiveness.

The type of portfolio analysis to use will already be familiar to you and is repeated in Figure 86.

As with other QPAs, you build a list of criteria representing the ideal channel and totalling 100%, then score each channel on each criterion.

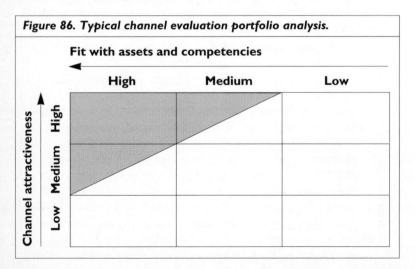

**Figure 86. Typical channel evaluation portfolio analysis.**

You do the same with your assets and competencies. To illustrate this, a leading German frozen foods brand, which does not supply private label, will be taken as an example.

For the sake of brevity, only five criteria will be used for each axis, and they will not be scored.

The five criteria this leading brand will use to evaluate channel attractiveness are:

- Size of branded frozen food market in company's main categories – fish, ready meals and desserts. 'Branded' excludes private label.
- Likely future trend by channel.
- Likely future profit margin for company.
- Quality of channel presentation and stock rotation.
- Ease of working with channel.

Five criteria for channel fit with company assets and competencies are:

- Company revenue and market share in channel.
- Channel attitude and future strategy towards brands versus private label.
- Channel attitude to major premium price brands.
- Channel interest in partnerships and ECR (Efficient Consumer Response).
- Channel willingness to stock full range of company products.

The resulting portfolio analysis looks as in Figure 87.

**Figure 87. Major German frozen foods company: channel portfolio analysis.**

| | | Fit with assets and competencies | | |
|---|---|---|---|---|
| | | **High** | **Medium** | **Low** |
| Channel attractiveness | High | Multiple A<br>Multiple B | Home delivery | |
| | Medium | | Multiple C | Freezer centres |
| | Low | Large independents | | Wholesalers |

For illustration, let's look at four of the channels:

**Multiple A.** This major account is gaining share of frozen foods, and has only a moderate interest in its own private label. Its stores are large and well run. The company already has an above-average market share in this account, an ECR partnership in place, and achieves average net profit margins from it.

**Home delivery.** This is an important channel in Germany, using catalogues, telephone ordering and weekly delivery. It is committed to premium brands, and generates above-average profits for the company. Company share of this channel is low, due to past neglect – this will change in future.

**Large independents.** The company has the biggest sales force calling direct on large independents, since it also sells chilled and ambient foods. Its share and profitability in this declining channel are both high.

**Wholesalers.** This channel is unattractive to the company and will receive low priority. Wholesalers redistribute to small independents, caterers and general stores. They tend to buy low-priced brands on deal, require special pack sizes, stock a narrow range, and generate below-average profit margins for the company.

### 3. Ensure alignment between channel and market strategies and plans

Channel and customer plans are usually developed by Sales people, market and brand plans by marketing people. It is fatal to build these plans in isolation. Sales and Marketing executives need to discuss channel and market aspirations early in the planning process, and to iron out any inconsistencies.

For instance, in the frozen foods example, let's suppose that the Marketing Department sees a big opportunity to increase sales in small, single-serve packs. As it happens, the majority of the small-pack market is sold by small independent stores, served by wholesalers. And wholesalers are the lowest channel priority for Sales Department. This kind of issue would need to be identified and resolved, before time was wasted on drawing up detailed brand plans for building small-pack business.

Integrated Marketing Planning, covering channels and markets, accounts and brands, is covered in Chapter 8 (pages 296–7), and the table repeated below as Table 276 summarizes the right way to integrate marketing plans.

**Table 276. The right way: Integrated Marketing plans.**

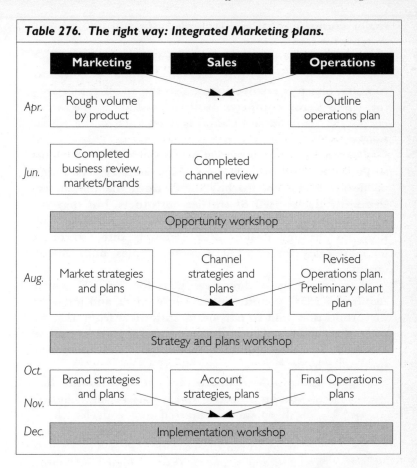

| | Marketing | Sales | Operations |
|---|---|---|---|
| Apr. | Rough volume by product | | Outline operations plan |
| Jun. | Completed business review, markets/brands | Completed channel review | |
| | *Opportunity workshop* | | |
| Aug. | Market strategies and plans | Channel strategies and plans | Revised Operations plan. Preliminary plant plan |
| | *Strategy and plans workshop* | | |
| Oct. Nov. | Brand strategies and plans | Account strategies, plans | Final Operations plans |
| Dec. | *Implementation workshop* | | |

## 4. Find ways to exercise influence over your channels

Influence translates into bargaining power, and this enables producers to achieve their marketing objectives through channels at minimum cost. The most powerful bargaining chip any producer can have is a strong franchise with the channel's customers. Improving a brand's consumer value creates a virtuous trigger, where increasing consumer strength converts into greater channel influence for the producer.

Another way to enhance your position in channels is to help build their total business, as Sharp has done in copiers through its independent dealers:

**The UK copier market is relatively flat in volume. It is segmented by size of machine, with the largest used by**

major companies for high-volume tasks and the smallest suitable for home use.

Canon is the UK market leader, followed by Xerox and Sharp. Other competitors include Toshiba, Ricoh and Minolta. Sharp is relatively strong in the small copier sector, while Xerox competes most successfully in the larger corporate segment, and Canon is strong across the whole market.

There are two main marketing channels – direct selling to end-users, and distribution via specialist dealers. Large corporate users tend to buy direct from manufacturers. Primarily dealers sell to smaller customers, but they do some business with larger companies. Sharp markets its products through dealers, Xerox mainly direct through its own sales force, while Canon pursues both major channels.

Sharp drew up a three-year plan for the UK which required a 285% volume increase in copiers, and a rise in the proportion sold to corporate customers from 15% to 26% of total sales. The ambitious volume gain would be achieved by new product innovation and increased marketing impact.

One of the problems Sharp faced in confronting this tough objective was its marketing channel. Sharp was committed to the dealer channel and for a variety of reasons did not want to sell direct (although it had a small national account team which sold hardware to corporate customers, then handed them over to dealers for servicing). However, Sharp's dealers were mainly independents, relatively unsophisticated in their business methods, and not particularly attractive to corporate customers, who felt more comfortable dealing with Canon or Xerox direct. Sharp therefore decided to develop a dealer management programme, carrying independent quality certification to high standards. This was called the Sharp Integrated Quality Standard (SIQS).

Working with a consulting firm, Business Development Unit, and a number of institutes, Sharp reviewed all standards across eight business areas, including Marketing, Sales, Finance, Human Resources, Health and Safety. From this review, it developed the Sharp IQS, which incorporated standards like ISO 9002, TQM, and MQA as well as other standards of quality, ethics, service and customer satisfaction specified by Sharp.

Sharp had seventy dealers, and many were expected to be relatively cynical about this well-meaning initiative. Sharp's first step was low key: a pilot test with three dealers. This worked well, and for the national launch, all dealers were invited to meetings in four different locations. Fifty-two showed up. After a full presentation, dealers were invited to agree to the first stage of the Sharp IQS, which was a three-day evaluation and appraisal of their business. This would be done by independent consultants (BDU), who would handle each project confidentially. The exercise was to be partly subsidized by Sharp, but the dealer would pay £1000 towards the consultancy fees of the initial audit. Forty-nine agreed, and forty moved to Stage 2 and beyond.

For the complete programme, the cost to Sharp was over £1 million, and individual dealers paid £6K–£11K. Most of the participating dealers have now gained the Sharp IQS. Sharp is close to achieving its three-year plan, with volume almost trebled in a static market, and 40% of its total revenue is now from corporate customers.

### 5. Tailor your products and services to channel needs

Many producers market to a number of distribution channels, often with different requirements. Skilful Channel Marketers identify the needs of channels for different products, packages, sizes, services and supply arrangements, and match the potential revenue benefits of providing these against the extra cost. The Channel Marketer faces similar issues to global branders, who try to balance efficiencies of standard international propositions against the need to meet specific local requirements.

Table 277 summarizes the type of issues Channel Marketers need to resolve.

**Table 277.  Key issues for Channel Marketers.**

| Strategic areas | Issues |
|---|---|
| Product or service range | ● *What type of range best fits the consumer demographics of the channel or individual store?*<br>● *How wide a range can the channel handle and merchandise?* |
| Packaging or presentation | ● *What product sizes does the channel need?*<br>● *What case configurations do intermediaries prefer?*<br>● *What information do intermediaries need to pass on to their customers?* |
| Pricing | ● *How does the channel or account pricing strategy fit with the producer's strategy?*<br>● *How can any pricing conflicts across channels be resolved?* |
| Consumer service levels | ● *What services does the channel offer to its consumers?*<br>● *How can the producer enhance these?* |
| Channel service levels | ● *Do products fit channel's handling systems and space availability?*<br>● *What frequency of delivery is needed?*<br>● *How far ahead are new products or services planned?*<br>● *How can producer and channel co-operate to maximize efficiency of supply chain and sell-out to consumer?* |
| Branding strategy | ● *What role do producer's brands play in channel's overall branding strategy, which may include private label?*<br>● *Is the channel seeking high end, niche, mass market or discount brands?* |
| Channel and category development | ● *What can producers do to build the channel, or the categories in which they compete?* |

The varied channel requirements of greetings cards illustrate some of these points. There are at least eight distinct channels, with differing needs in price, types of product, ranges and delivery systems. Table 278 demonstrates this.

**Table 278.** **Greetings cards: characteristics of differing trade channels.**

| Channel type | Average price | Main type | Range | Source of goods (main) |
|---|---|---|---|---|
| Specialist card | High | Everyday | Very wide | Direct |
| Newsagents | Medium | Everyday | Medium | Wholesale |
| Stationers | Medium | Everyday | Medium | Wholesale |
| Non-food multiples | Medium | Everyday | Medium | Direct |
| Department stores | High | Everyday | Wide | Direct |
| Grocery multiples | Low | Christmas | Narrow | Direct |
| Mail order | Low | Christmas | Medium | Catalogue |
| Other | Low | Christmas | Medium | Wholesale |

Compare the very different needs of specialist card shops and grocery multiples. Specialist card shops stock a wide range of over 2,000 cards, which sell at premium prices. They require extensive merchandising and sophisticated stock-control systems from producers.

Grocery multiples provide limited space and no ambience, have a narrow range of card types, sell mainly in multipacks at relatively low prices. They need little servicing from manufacturers and usually get central warehouse deliveries.

Channels offer outstanding opportunities for the Offensive Marketer who sets clear strategies, innovates in response to change and executes with strength and resolution. The keys to success are a deep understanding of customer and consumer needs, and skill in meeting these needs *efficiently*. It is easy, but ineffective, to respond fully to every conceivable channel need, and, in doing so, to destroy the operational economics of your business. You should always look hard for tailoring opportunities which are highly valued by channels but involve you in little extra cost.

### 6. Ensure consistent presentation of your core brand proposition across channels

Tailoring brands to channels should be done without compromising your core proposition. Consumers often shop across channels and will be confused by major inconsistencies. They will understand that they can buy your brand more cheaply in a discounter than in Harrods. But they will be puzzled if they are buying a PEP and find that the same bank has different charges when they purchase by telephone as opposed to in person at a High Street branch.

If you have a major point of difference, ensure that it is exploited through every channel. For instance, Coca-Cola's glass waistline bottle had been a distinctive icon for over half a century, but for many years was abandoned when translated to commodity plastic litre bottles for supermarkets. This error has now been corrected, with dramatic effects on Coca-Cola's grocery store sales.

## 7. Seek to develop new channels

Companies entering new markets may find that existing channels do not meet their needs. They therefore innovate their own. McDonald's and Avon have done this very successfully, and are skilled at adapting their channel approaches over time. McDonald's can now be found in converted pubs, motorway service stations, bowling alleys, ferries and airports. Avon has adapted to changes in women's working habits, and now achieves over 40% of its US revenues outside the home, mainly in offices.

Companies operating in established channels may also innovate new ones to extend their product reach, improve its presentation or reach a particular target group. The UCLA Medical Network in Los Angeles has covered all three opportunities:

> **Occupancy rates in American hospitals are low at 50% and the sector has lost patients to low-cost managed healthcare operators. Price discounting of medical charges is increasing, and 55% of hospitals are losing money on patient care. The situation is particularly tough in California, where University College of Los Angeles (UCLA) Medical Network is based.**
>
> **UCLA Medical Network has established four out-of-town storefront clinics, in upscale neighbourhoods. These are operated by physicians, and specialize. For instance the one in Fairfax district focuses on geriatrics for the area's middle-income retirees. These clinics not only deliver world-class medical programmes to suburbanites, but also generate revenue and feed the parent hospital. UCLA's hospital occupancy has increased as a result of these out-of-town clinics, and is now 80% while**

**outpatient visits have grown by 23% in the last two years.**[6]

A classic example of developing new marketing channels is the Irish pub phenomenon – well over 1,000 new Irish pubs have opened in some thirty-five countries since 1995, and one of the main beneficiaries is Guinness, whose beer exports have doubled since 1993.

**Guinness decided to export 'Irishness' in order to bolster exports of its dark brown stout. It has a staff of forty in its retail development unit, whose job is to help entrepreneurs open new Irish pubs. Guinness doesn't invest in the pubs itself, but helps select sites and provides advice on finance, staffing and décor.**

**The key elements in the Irish pub, as Guinness sees it are:**

- *Authentic design.* **The Irish Pub Company, Guinness's preferred pub specialist, builds and delivers three to four finished pubs monthly, to locations all over the world.**
- *Correct décor.* **The Irish Pub Company has a computerized bric-à-brac warehouse.**
- *Irish food and music.* **Specialized companies can provide live or piped Irish music, and, via satellite, Irish sports events to pubs around the world.**
- *Fully trained Irish bar staff.* **As a rule of thumb, half the staff should be Irish. There is an executive search company which specializes in finding them.**

**Around half the beer sold in these pubs is Irish, so Guinness benefits greatly. Will it last? Maybe, but there are already thirty Irish pubs in Berlin.**[7]

## Process for Offensive Channel Marketing

This section will outline how to translate the principles of Offensive Channel Marketing into action, by using a seven-step process. Steps 1–4 would be done by the Sales Director, working with his or her senior executives. Steps 5–7 would be led by the Sales Director, involving close interaction with the Marketing Department (Table 279).

**Table 279.  Seven-step process for Offensive Channel Marketing.**

|  |  |  |
|---|---|---|
| Step 1 | **Review, analyse existing channels** | ● Growth, profitability<br>● Competitive position |
| Step 2 | **Project future trends** | ● Long-term trends<br>● Emerging new channels |
| Step 3 | **Prioritize channels** | ● Use Quantified Portfolio Analysis |
| Step 4 | **Develop 3–5 year channel plan** | ● Objectives<br>● Strategies |
| Step 5 | **Synchronize channel and market plans** | ● Sales and Marketing Departments |
| Step 6 | **Convert to customer plans** | ● Major customers by channel<br>● Align with Brand Plans |
| Step 7 | **Monitor results** | ● Monitoring system |

## STEP 1:  REVIEW, ANALYSE EXISTING CHANNELS

This step involves defining channels, identifying total channel revenue and estimating your company's channel share, sales and profit margins. Channel definitions should be precise, and indicate how different channels interact, especially intermediaries and final channels to the consumer. It usually makes sense to define any individual outlet accounting for more than 10% of your total revenue as a channel. Boots would therefore qualify as a channel for cosmetics companies, B & Q for DIY producers, Sainsbury and Tesco for food manufacturers.

Channel profitability also needs to be studied carefully. In many companies, quality of channel profit data is poor, with major costs allocated on some arbitrary measure like channel share of total company revenue. Activity-based costing is necessary to determine the real cost of selling, supply chain and materials specifically produced for individual channels. Unless you fully understand your channel profitability, you cannot sensibly determine how to allocate investment between them.

Analysing profitability by trade channel enables you to get the right balance between profit levels and volume growth. All too often, the fastest-growing channels are the least profitable because they attract so much competition. A well-run company will review its profitability by channel at least every half year and take decisions on future balance by channel as a result.

Table 280 is a real-life example of such an analysis, which has to remain anonymous. The allocation of selling and distribution costs was based partly on activity-based costing.

| Table 280. Analysis of profitability by trade channel. | | | | |
|---|---|---|---|---|
| | **Distribution channel** | | | |
| | **A** | **B** | **C** | **D** |
| Channel volume trend | Flat | Down | Up | Up |
| Cases per delivery | 203 | 175 | 1125 | 37 |
| Gross margin (%) | 31.7 | 40.2 | 26.4 | 25.4 |
| Operating expenses (%) | 19.7 | 13.4 | 7.8 | 23.0 |
| Operating profit (%) | 12.0 | 26.8 | 18.6 | 2.4 |

Differences in margin by channel were very wide, and as a result of this analysis a number of decisions were made:

- On channel A, promotion spending was reduced as a percentage of sales, since it was expensive and not particularly effective.
- On Channel B, priority was increased, new account targets set and frequency of sales calls raised. Because of its declining trend, this channel had been somewhat neglected.
- On Channel D, delivery arrangements were renegotiated to achieve larger drops and a target was set to expand product range stocked, and so increase cases per drop. A hard line was to be taken on discount arrangements, and selling costs were to be reduced by changing to telesales.

Having collected relevant channel data, draw up a channel map. This summarizes by channel: total channel sales, your company's revenue, market share, share trend and profit margin. A simplified map of video games channels, ommitting intermediaries, is illustrated in Table 281.

**Table 281.  Video games: simplified channel map.**

| Channel | Electronics retailers | Other multiples | Mail order | Special-ists | Toys, Music |
|---|---|---|---|---|---|
| Channel sales £m | 190 | 92 | 81 | 75 | 100 |
| Company sales £m | 47 | 28 | 18 | 16 | 15 |
| Company share % | 25 | 30 | 22 | 21 | 15 |
| Share trend | Up | Down | Flat | Up | Down |
| Company profit % | 10 | 7 | 12 | 18 | 14 |
| | | | | | |
| Major Accounts | Dixons Comet | Woolworth WHS Boots | | | Toys R Us HMV Virgin |

The final stage of Step 1 is to summarize key needs for each channel; identify how well your company meets these needs; highlight current and potential channel conflicts (e.g. pricing); and evaluate how channels add value to your brands.

## STEP 2:  PROJECT FUTURE TRENDS

Look to the long term, 3–5–10 years ahead. Evaluate each major channel individually, covering the sort of issues illustrated in Table 282.

**Table 282.  Channel A: future trend projection.**

| Factor | Today | 5 years hence |
|---|---|---|
| 1.  Channel sales £m | 100 | 170 |
| 2.  Company sales £m | 10 | 22 |
| 3.  Company share % | 10 | 13 |
| 4.  Company profit % | 12 | 12 |
| 5.  Channel strategy | ● Expand store sizes<br>● Cut ranges and supplies | ● Increase in-store customer service<br>● Develop direct Marketing |
| 6.  Channel structure | ● Top 3 accounts do 40% total sales | ● Top 3 accounts do 65% of total sales. Mergers likely. |

| | | |
|---|---|---|
| 7. Key channel needs | • Strong brands<br>• Efficient supply | • Producer partnerships<br>• Joint direct marketing |
| 8. How company can meet needs | • Focus on fewer brands<br>• ECR supply chain plan | • Start first partnership *now*<br>• Build direct marketing skill *now* |
| 9. Channel conflicts | • Conflict on pricing with Channel C | • Channel C no longer a factor |
| 10. How channel adds value | • Breadth of coverage | • Direct joint customer contact<br>• Possibly co-branding[8] |

Major future marketing trends in most channels include:

• Growth of mass retail distribution at the expense of specialists.
• Reduction in number of channel steps, driven by need for greater speed and lower cost. Intermediaries are especially at risk, and some will secure their future position by buying retailers.
• Growth in direct selling to consumers, stimulated by desire of producers to increase their influence in order to gain a higher share of total channel profit margin. Financial services is an example, where forms of direct selling include telesales, direct mail and the Internet.
• 'Technology development accelerates channel evolution. Data networks are already enabling end-users to bypass traditional channels and deal directly with manufacturers and service providers.'[9]
• Regulation or deregulation of channels to spur competition. This has been of particular importance in the drinks, medicine, utilities and telecom markets.
• Cross-border involvement by retailers.
• More automated consumer access. This can range from vending machines, to hole-in-the-wall units, to interactive kiosks.
• Greater concentration of ownership within given channels, but increasing competition and cooperation *across* channels – supermarkets and banks.

## STEP 3: PRIORITIZE CHANNELS

Quantified Portfolio Analysis is the primary tool to use. Its application to prioritizing channels is described on pages 560–61 above.

## STEP 4:  DEVELOP THREE- OR FIVE-YEAR CHANNEL PLAN

Plan time-scale should fit with your corporate business plan, whether it be ten years, five or three. Similar principles and processes apply to channel plans as to market plans, and the two should be developed together. Follow the Marketing Planning Process described in Chapter 8 (pages 302–6).

This involves Business Analysis (Step 1 above), Anticipating the Future (Step 2 above), Opportunity Identification, Setting Objectives, Building Strategies and Developing Plans.

- In **opportunity identification**, you will focus on means to help build priority channels and to strengthen your position in them.
- **Setting objectives** means establishing short and long-term revenue, share and profit objectives by channel, just as you do by market.
- **Building strategies** involves exploiting opportunities in priority channels and determining how to achieve your channel objectives. You would also develop sub-strategies by channel, for topics like product or service range, presentation, pricing, consumer service levels – see Table 272 above (page 554) for full list.
- **Developing plans** would cover specific plans to support strategies, development projects and quarterly milestones.

The bulk of this work will be done by the Sales Department, but with full knowledge of market plans being developed concurrently by Marketing Department. Close cooperation between these departments, and constant mutual updating, is essential to ensure that channel and market plans are closely aligned, which leads to Step 5.

## STEP 5:  SYNCHRONIZE CHANNEL AND MARKET PLANS

It is highly inefficient for Marketing Departments to develop market plans, then throw them over the wall to Sales Department with the message attached: 'Now develop channel plans.' And the reverse also applies. No apology is made for hammering this basic principle, because so few companies get it right.

Market and channel plans should be developed concurrently and in concert. The main barrier to this is the involvement of two different departments. The best solution is for senior Marketing and Sales people to meet for half a day early in the planning process, and to exchange views at an opportunity workshop. For example, if a soft-drinks brand plans to greatly strengthen its position in the single-serve impulse sector, Sales Department will need to take this into account in developing its channel plans for convenience stores, garages and motorway outlets. Equally, if Sales Department sees great potential in a new direct channel, Marketing Department will need to consider which markets to focus on, and what direct products or services to develop.

Once overall objectives and strategies are developed in outline, Marketing and Sales Departments should exchange outline documents, and meet for a Strategy and Plans Workshop. Result should be **market** objectives, strategies, plans, broken down by channel, and **channel** objectives, strategies, plans broken down by market (Table 283).

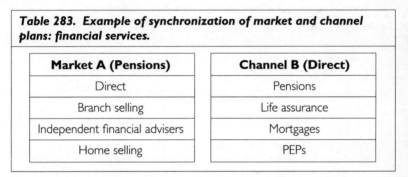

**Table 283. Example of synchronization of market and channel plans: financial services.**

| Market A (Pensions) | Channel B (Direct) |
| --- | --- |
| Direct | Pensions |
| Branch selling | Life assurance |
| Independent financial advisers | Mortgages |
| Home selling | PEPs |

## STEP 6: CONVERT TO CUSTOMER PLANS

Once channel plans have been agreed and thoroughly integrated with market plans, the next step is to develop plans for major customers or accounts. These would be done by national account managers. Sales Directors would use judgement as to who qualified as major customers. A toiletries company may decide to develop detailed plans for Boots, Sainsbury and Tesco, but only brief ones for Superdrug, Lloyds and Morrisons.

As with channel plans, **account** plans should be developed in close cooperation with Marketing, and integrated with **brand** plans. An outline format for a customer plan is shown in Table 284. It would be developed by the relevant National Account Manager, working closely with Brand Managers, and approved by the Sales Director. Copies would be given to any marketing people who needed them, though for confidentiality, profit margins by customer may be omitted.

---

**Table 284.  Outline format for customer plan, e.g. John Lewis.**

1. **Customer name**

2. **Customer facts:** Total sales, profits and trend. Number of outlets by type, trend. Major competitors.

3. **Customer strategies:** Overall, by major category. Attitudes to suppliers. Marketing, and consumer strategies. Key strengths, points of difference.

4. **Customer position in our categories:** Customer sales and share of total category in our main markets.

5. **Our position with customer:** By major market category, our sales, market share, net profit return. Trends. Our major brands and trends. Major competitor brands and trends.

6. **SWOT analysis of our company within customer.**

7. **Key future priorities and objectives with customer:** What future priority will we give this customer? What are our future objectives with customer over next 3 to 5 years in sales, profit, market share, partnership, joint activities, service levels, etc.?

8. **Key strategies for meeting objectives:** These would include sub-strategies for branding, key brand development, product range, supply chain, marketing support, customer service and so on.

9. **Next year's plan:** This would include total revenue by brand, marketing support spend specific to account and target profit margin. For each brand, the totality of its revenue by channel and major customer would be the same as the brand's revenue budget. (*In many companies, this exercise is either not done at all, or when done, fails to add up.*)

10. **Next year's activity:** Activities by major brand in each customer would be specified, and action milestones set. Things like joint sales forecasting, entry to a major new category or joint direct marketing initiatives would be included under this heading.

---

## STEP 7:  MONITOR RESULTS

Set up a simple monitoring system, measuring progress on the annual and three or five year plan.

# FLOW-CHART SUMMARY OF CHAPTER 15

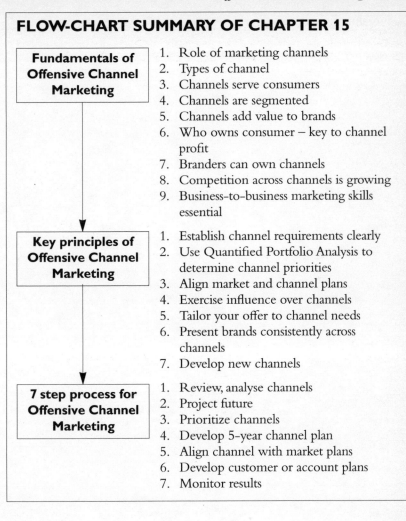

| **Fundamentals of Offensive Channel Marketing** | 1. Role of marketing channels<br>2. Types of channel<br>3. Channels serve consumers<br>4. Channels are segmented<br>5. Channels add value to brands<br>6. Who owns consumer – key to channel profit<br>7. Branders can own channels<br>8. Competition across channels is growing<br>9. Business-to-business marketing skills essential |
|---|---|
| **Key principles of Offensive Channel Marketing** | 1. Establish channel requirements clearly<br>2. Use Quantified Portfolio Analysis to determine channel priorities<br>3. Align market and channel plans<br>4. Exercise influence over channels<br>5. Tailor your offer to channel needs<br>6. Present brands consistently across channels<br>7. Develop new channels |
| **7 step process for Offensive Channel Marketing** | 1. Review, analyse channels<br>2. Project future<br>3. Prioritize channels<br>4. Develop 5-year channel plan<br>5. Align channel with market plans<br>6. Develop customer or account plans<br>7. Monitor results |

# PS Offensive Marketing: The Way Ahead

Congratulations on having completed the book!

You are the sort of person for whom this book is written . . .

The objectives of this book are to share practical learning, to communicate leading-edge approaches and to stimulate new thinking. Only you can say whether these objectives have been met. I hope the book will trigger new approaches and help you do an even better job next week and in three years' time. At most, I would be delighted if it enables you to unleash the full power of Offensive Marketing across the business you work in.

The book does not pretend to offer all the answers. After more than thirty years in marketing, I find the topic as fascinating now as the day I started and am still learning new things. You, I and others will continue to add refinement to the practice of marketing.

This brief *PS* is not intended to be a summary of *Even More Offensive Marketing*, since, as you can see, every chapter has an opening one-page summary and a closing flow chart. Its purpose is to evaluate the future vista for marketing, and to suggest how you, as a marketer, can take full advantage of the marketing approach in the future.

The UK is very well served with marketing institutions. The **Chartered Institute of Marketing** is easily the largest and highest-calibre professional marketing body in Europe. The **Marketing Society** is the leading association for senior practising marketers, and also runs many excellent events. The **Marketing Council** was formed to highlight the importance of the marketing approach to business success, and is targeted especially at Chief Executives and Boards who determine the environment in which marketers work. All these bodies have important roles to play. But the future success of the marketing approach depends critically on the effectiveness of individual marketers like yourself, and your ability to influence the thinking of your Board as well as colleagues in other departments.

Marketing and marketers have been extensively criticized in recent years, sometimes by people whose arrogance exceeds their ignorance, and sometimes constructively by those who really understand and care.

This book has taken justified criticisms into account, and a positive view of marketing's enormous future potential.

Anyone who attempts to undermine the strength of the marketing approach will lose the debate, since the arguments supporting it are unanswerable. There are a number of enduring truths about the power of the marketing approach which underpin business success, and drive the principles, processes and tools of *Even More Offensive Marketing*.

Here is a brief description of nine of these enduring truths of **marketing**:

## 1. Superior customer value is essential to corporate survival and success

In today's competitive markets, customers have an ever widening range of choice. They seek superior and constantly improving value. Companies failing to meet this standard, satisfied with providing mediocre products and services, won't survive in the long term, because customers won't need them. In your future career plans, be sure to spot and avoid such companies, or set up your own business in competition.

## 2. Superior or above-average profit growth is achieved by aligning strengths to opportunities, and by excellent cost management

You will recall the Marketing Alignment Process (MAP), which matched strengths – mainly assets and competencies – to opportunities; and how it optimized profit by prioritizing market segments and channels which were best *for you*, where you could compete most successfully. This is one key to above-average profit growth.

The other key is low-cost operation. You cannot deliver superior value if your costs are higher than competitors offering similar products and services. Excellent cost management requires close attention from everyone in the company and is often heavily dependent on the skills of Operations people.

However, marketers have a key role to play in cost management, through leading value engineering and relating every cost to the value it adds in customer satisfaction. Since most cost is designed into products or services when they are new, marketers need to pay particular attention to cost during new product development. When they develop a superior product or service, with a proven preference to competitors, their job is only half done. The other half is to design cost out, by trading off cost versus customer benefit while still retaining a strong preference. The West still appears to have a lot to learn from the Japanese in this area.

## 3. Everyone is a marketer and should think like one

Service marketers, some of them recent converts to the marketing approach, are leading the way in this area, and often seem to be closer to their customers than product marketers. Chapter 4, on Integrated Marketing, outlines a process for getting everyone to think like a marketer, through job objectives, appraisals and incentives geared to only two things – serving internal and external customers and managing cost in a customer-driven way (as in value engineering).

You will recall that these first three enduring 'truths' also comprise the definition of Offensive Marketing.

## 4. Quality is free

For many years, Philip Crosby[1] and other quality experts were voices crying in the wilderness. Buzzell and Gale's masterly analysis of the PIMS database provided authoritative support for their view. It showed that the additional cost necessary to achieve better quality was offset by avoidance of scrap, reprocessing and returns associated with lower-quality offerings. Superior quality also enhances the effectiveness of marketing spending, not least through high retention of customers gained.

This is an important finding which surprises many people, but not marketers, since it connects with our natural prejudices.

## 5. Closeness to customers is a key factor for success in any business

One of the means for achieving superior value is to understand customers' needs today, objectively monitor how well they are being met, and anticipate how they will change tomorrow.

In doing this, there is no substitute for direct face-to-face or phone contact with customers and consumers, not just by marketers, but also by people in Operations, R & D, Finance and Engineering. This can take the form of days with sales people, informal or formal customer contacts, Saturday-morning visits to retailers or distributors, and so on. Service marketers, like airlines, leisure operators, hotels and retailers, are often closer to their customers than manufacturers, because they have so many direct day-to-day dealings with them. Equally, fast-moving entrepreneurial companies may be closer to consumers than sophisticated corporations with professional marketers, who spend millions on market research and rarely talk to customers. Creative and well-planned customer research is certainly a good thing, but it needs to be supplemented with direct contact. 'The growth of advanced marketing research techniques in the USA, so much a part of the professionalization of marketing, has served to distance the company from the customers.'[2]

## 6. Differentiation, enhanced by strong branding, builds sustained competitive advantage

Marketers seek to deliver superior value in areas important to customers. This is good. But the ideal is to be differentiated as well, and to exploit this differentiation through strong branding.

## 7. Investment in strong and relevant customer communication usually pays

You rightly may think this is a sweeping statement. Of course, it is possible to spend too much on Communications, or the right amount in the wrong way. But if you have a distinctive and relevant customer proposition, well executed and effectively monitored, you also have a powerful engine for profitable growth worth investing in. To protect that opportunity, marketers need to agree with their colleagues in other departments, especially at Board level, on the best criteria for evaluating the profitability of communications investment, and to apply these rigorously.

## 8. The key decisions on marketing are taken by Boards, not by marketers

Boards take the critical decisions on stakeholder priorities, commitment to investment, long- versus short-term outlook, attitude to quality, service and cost. They are responsible for creating an environment in which marketing can prosper. Marketers can and must influence this.

## 9. Rigorous business analysis and purposeful testing greatly increase the effectiveness of marketing

Effective Business Analysis, covered in Chapter 5, is hard work, unglamorous and sometimes condemned as time-wasting by 'action-driven' managements, who expend enormous energy on doing the wrong things quickly. Thoughtful business analysis is a critical tool for the Offensive Marketer. By converting information into knowledge and understanding, so making decisions on facts with intuition added, you can unlock the secrets of the past. This will illuminate your journey into the future.

Unfortunately, high-quality business analysis is becoming something of a lost art, since, after the downsizing of the last decade, many line managers lack time, and the middle managers who used to emphasize its importance and provide training have disappeared. Consequently, much knowledge is lost because it is not recorded for the future. While the amount of information available in the last decade has increased enormously, the level of knowledge has not, and may well have declined.

Finally, testing, the importance of which has been emphasized above. Offensive Marketers must be prepared to take risks. Testing dramatically reduces the level of risk, and enables you to compare the potential of alternative options. It can be done quite inexpensively, in discussions with customers, or on a larger and more quantitative basis – the level of testing should be commensurate with the risk and the importance of the decision to be taken. Marketers should be like laboratory workers, continually checking out hypotheses and pushing forward the frontiers of knowledge through experimentation.

\*

Not many people would seriously challenge the substance of any of these nine enduring principles of marketing. So why do so few companies determinedly apply even half of them? Admittedly, they do require courage, determination, teamwork and clear future vision, none of which are easy. But I remain puzzled at the low level of application.

These enduring principles, and the fundamentals of the Offensive Marketing approach, certainly work, so this is your opportunity to change things in the future.

There's never been a better time to do it, with the future running in marketing's favour. Markets will continue to become even more competitive, and consumers more demanding. This will further increase the importance of the superior customer value and differentiation which Offensive Marketing can create. The emphasis in the City has already moved from downsizing to profitable growth, and is starting to creep towards more relevant performance measures like building shareholder value and the balanced scorecard.

This has been accompanied by a growing recognition of the importance of assets like brands, and customer databases, and of the marketing competencies which are necessary to get the most out of them.

Finally, the spread of best-practice benchmarking is bringing home to companies that many of the best-practice paragons they choose to benchmark against are customer-driven Offensive Marketers.

What do marketers like yourself need to do to exploit this future opportunity for marketing? You need to do six things:

(a) **Apply the full Offensive Marketing approach** rather than picking bits and pieces of it, because it works best as a totality.

(b) **Adopt a more process-driven approach to marketing.** You will have noticed that this book is full of sequential step-by-step processes for implementing principles and pro-grammes. Process management involves thinking through the best way of tackling a task, breaking it down into steps and applying the learning time after time. Compared to other departments, process management in marketing is in its infancy, but this will change, and rapidly too (Table 285).

**Table 285. Level of process management by department.**

| Finance | Operations | Sales | Marketing | (read across) |
|---------|-----------|-------|-----------|---------------|
| High | High | Medium | Low | ← Today |
| High | High | High | High | ← Tomorrow |

Process management in marketing will be less rigid than that applied in other departments. Creativity will be actively built into processes, which will have a strong customer focus and the necessary level of flexibility to respond to rapidly changing conditions. Marketing process management will bring with it many benefits, such as applying best practice in setting up processes; freeing up more time for long-term development; enhancing both creativity and speed to market; and spreading the marketing gospel *across* the company, because so many marketing processes are cross-departmental.

(c) **Spend more time on development, less on housekeeping.** Most marketers spend at least 80% of their time on tactics and administration – housekeeping – and less than 20% on the things that really count for the longer term, like customer franchise building. How can you raise the latter to 30% or even 40%? By restructuring the Marketing Department to create Brand Equity Managers, and by allocating more of the day-to-day tactical activities, like trade marketing or sales promotion, to specialists; by adopting marketing process management for greater efficiency; and by contracting out

non-core activities, or even returning them to other departments who have been using marketing as a dump-bin for
coordination.

(d) **Sharpen and broaden your competencies**. This book is
intended to help you to increase your competencies in
marketing. For the future, you will also need to broaden
your skills in the principles of Finance and Operations, in
understanding technology, and in project-managing cross-
departmental initiatives. This will enable you to spearhead the
corporate vision and strategies, and help make everyone think
like an offensive marketer.

(e) **Press for change in the way company performance is
evaluated**. While most marketers are aware that they need to
improve efficiencies, especially in accounting for marketing
spending, it is time to strongly question outdated financial
measures, and to press for more relevant indicators of company
performance to be published. The 'Offensive Marketing
Annual Report 2021' in Chapter 2 (page 74) is an example of
this approach.

Offensive Marketers are clearly profit-orientated, and have
skills in hitting both short- and long-term profit objectives.
However, archaic and backward-looking financial reports,
which blandly ignore those intangible assets and competencies
critical to future business success, deserve to be challenged by
non-financial people. The balanced scorecard has opened the
door a little – let's push it wide open.

(f) **Sell Offensive Marketing to non-marketers**. Historically,
Marketers have not spent enough time and effort selling the
merit of the marketing approach to their colleagues in other
departments. If marketing is to be a cross-departmental
process, and if everyone is to think like a marketer in future,
this is essential. Marketers need to inform, educate, persuade
and enthuse their colleagues about the marketing approach. A
good starting-point is the enduring principles of marketing
outlined earlier in this *PS*.

*

Thank you for reading the book. I hope it met your objectives. If you
have any queries, comments, suggestions or examples, please contact me
c/o Penguin Books, or take advantage of the opportunity to phone or
fax me in November 1997 or March 1998, using the numbers on page
586.

## After Sales Service
## How to get in touch with Hugh Davidson

1. You can always write to make suggestions for improvement or addition to *Even More Offensive Marketing*, or to raise questions. Write to Hugh Davidson (author), c/o Penguin Books, 27 Wrights Lane, London W8 5TZ. I welcome letters and you will, of course, receive a reply.

2. As a service to early readers, special phone, fax and e-mail lines will be available to enable you to contact me personally to discuss any queries, criticisms or suggestions about this book, *in November 1997 and March 1998 only*.

   Special line numbers are as follows:
   - Phone: 01865 326707
   - Fax:   01865 326341
   - E-mail: 101574.1027 @ compuserve.com

   Please note that these special numbers are available in November 1997 and March 1998 only. Outside that period, you should write to me as described in (1) above.

**J. Hugh Davidson**

# Recommended Reading List

There are many good books on business and marketing, a lot of them written in the 1990s.

This list contains those I have found most useful, in writing *Even More Offensive Marketing*, but it does not pretend to be comprehensive. None of Peter Drucker's books have been mentioned because there are so many. Most of these are well worth reading.

## Business Strategy and Principles

R. Buzzell and B. Gale, *The PIMS Principles,* Free Press, 1987.
● This is a most interesting and practical book – a 'must read' for all Marketers.

James Collins and Jerry Porras, *Built to Last*, Century, 1996.
● This book examines eighteen long-lasting American companies, many of them Offensive Marketers, and evaluates the reasons for their success.

Gary Hamel and P.K. Prahalad, *Competing for the Future*, Harvard Business School Press, 1996.
● Another 'must read' book for all marketers – it deals with developing core competencies, and how to anticipate and shape the future of your industry.

Johny Johansson and Ikujiro Nonaka, *Relentless – The Japanese Way of Marketing*, Butterworth-Heinemann, 1996.
● A very exciting book, full of interesting approaches.

John Kay, *Foundations of Corporate Success*, Oxford University Press, 1993.
● A readable and very intelligent book on business strategy.

David Packard, *The HP Way: How Bill Hewlett and I Built Our Company*, Harper Business, 1995.
● This describes the evolution of Hewlett Packard and its business principles.

Michael Porter, *Competitive Strategy*, Free Press, 1980.
                *Competitive Advantage*, Free Press, 1980.
● These books have influenced modern thinking on competitive analysis and competitive advantage. Neither is an easy read, but both repay the effort.

Alfred P. Sloan, Jr, *My Years with General Motors*, Pan, 1969.
● A fascinating account of the building of General Motors by one of the best early practitioners of market segmentation.

## Marketing Management

Michael Baker, *Marketing Strategy and Management*, Macmillan, 1992.
● Another good book by a well-known British author.

Kevin Clancy and Robert S. Shulman, *Marketing Myths That Are Killing the Business*, McGraw-Hill, 1994.
● Iconoclastic, but stimulating and full of well-supported practical thinking.

Peter Doyle, *Marketing Management and Strategy*, Prentice-Hall, 1994.
● A clear and well-written book by a leading UK authority.

Philip Kotler, *Marketing Management − Analysis, Planning, Implementation and Control*, Prentice-Hall, 1994. (Eighth edition.)
● The most widely used textbook on marketing, and deservedly so. It is very comprehensive, thoughtful and well presented.

## Performance Measurement, Costing and Finance

Robin Cooper, *When Lean Enterprises Collide − Competing Through Confrontation*, HBS Press, 1995.
● Based on a five-year study of management systems inside twenty Japanese companies, including Olympus, Nissan, Citizen and Komatsu. Covers target costing, value engineering, and a number of Marketing topics in an interesting way, with lots of examples.

Robert Kaplan and David Norton, *The Balanced Scorecard*, HBS Press, 1996.
● Sets out a new approach to corporate performance measurement to guide future strategic development. Rightly described as a landmark achievement.

Terry Smith, *Accounting for Growth*, Century Business, 1992.
● A penetrating analysis of accounting techniques, and how they can be manipulated legally.

## Marketing Planning

Malcolm McDonald, *Marketing Plans − How to Prepare Them: How to Use Them*, Butterworth-Heinemann, 1995.
● This is easily the leading book on a very important topic for marketers. Comprehensive, authoritative and full of examples, plus practical working tools.

## Communications and Advertising

Chris Baker, *Advertising Works 8*, NTC Publications Ltd, 1995.
- This contains the case histories for the winning entries in the IPA Advertising Effectiveness Awards Scheme. Each is well documented and presented. All eight books in this convincing series are worth reading or dipping into.

David Ogilvy, *Confessions of an Advertising Man*, Atheneum, NY, 1976.
- An entertaining and illuminating classic, and as well written as you would expect.

Jack Trout with Steve Rivkin, *The New Positioning*, McGraw-Hill, 1995.
- A follow-up book to the original *Positioning: The Battle for Your Mind*, by Ries and Trout.

## Customer Relationship Marketing

Garth Hallberg, *All Consumers Are Not Created Equal*, John Wiley, 1995.
- Written by a Director of Ogilvy & Mather. Provocative, balanced and full of convincing examples. Focuses mainly on fast-moving consumer goods.

Adrian Payne, Martin Christopher, Moira Clark and Helen Peck, *Relationship Marketing for Competitive Advantage*, Butterworth-Heinemann, 1995.
- An anthology of articles on winning and keeping customers, with a very good introduction.

Frederick Reichheld, *The Loyalty Effect*, HBS Press, 1996.
- Written by a Director of Bain & Co. An effective and practical book concentrating mainly on high ticket categories like cars, insurance, credit cards.

## Market Segmentation

Malcolm McDonald and Ian Dunbar, *Market Segmentation*, Macmillan Business, 1995.
- A practical and very useful contribution to an important topic that demystifies its complexities.

## Case Studies

Charles Baden-Fuller & Martyn Pitt, *Strategic Innovation*, Routledge, 1996.
- Sixteen case studies on companies like Swatch, Direct Line, Cartier, JCV, IKEA and Benetton, covering various aspects of strategic management. Well documented and an interesting read.

Sally Dibb & Lyndon Simkin, *The Marketing Casebook*, Routledge, 1996.
● Fifteen case studies and theory notes, including Heineken, JCB, TGI Friday and EuroDisney, from Warwick Business School.

Robert Thomas, *New Product Success Stories*, John Wiley & Sons, 1995.
● Twenty-four brief case studies, developed by MBA students at Georgetown University, USA, with two very good summaries of lessons learned.

# Notes and References

Chapter 1: **The Offensive Marketing Approach**

1. James Wallace and Jim Erikson, *Hard Drive*, John Wiley & Sons, 1992
2. ibid. Robert X. Cringley, *Accidental Empires*, Penguin, 1996; Bill Gates, *The Road Ahead*, Viking, 1995.
3. Speech by Peter Doyle, Professor of Marketing and Strategic Management, University of Warwick.
4. Frederick F. Reichheld, *The Loyalty Effect*, Harvard Business School Press, 1996.
5. J. Johansson and I. Nonaka, *Relentless – The Japanese Way of Marketing*, Butterworth-Heinemann, 1996.
6. J. Collins and J. Porras, *Built to Last*, Century Business, 1996. See especially Chapter 3, 'More Than Profits'.
7. *Note*: This table is similar to a P & L with one important exception – *depreciation*, a standard item in any P & L, has been replaced by *capital investment*, which does not appear in P & Ls. In the long-term, capex levels determine depreciation costs. Capex as a percentage of sales is an investment ratio often ignored by marketers, and it has been included in this table to emphasize its importance.
8. James Wallace and Jim Erikson, *Hard Drive*, John Wiley & Sons, 1992.
9. Theodore Levitt, *The Marketing Mode*, McGraw-Hill, 1969
10. Marketing Forum Report, December 1996.
11. Don Peppers and Martha Rogers, *The One to One Future*, Piatkus,1994.
12. Frederick F. Reichheld, *The Loyalty Effect*, Harvard Business School Press, 1996.
13. Peppers and Rogers, *The One to One Future*.
14. Garth Hallberg, *All Consumers Are Not Created Equal*, John Wiley, 1995.
15. *Financial Times*, 27 December 1996.
16. J. Johansson and I. Nonaka, *Relentless – The Japanese Way of Marketing*, Butterworth-Heinemann, 1996.

Chapter 2: **How Offensive Marketing Builds Above Average Profits**

1. Robert Kaplan and David Norton, *The Balanced Scorecard*, HBS Press, 1996.
2. *Fortune*, 23 December 1996.
3. Kazuo Inamori, *A Passion for Success*, McGraw-Hill, 1995.
4. See Ian Griffiths, *New Creative Accounting*, Macmillan, 1995; and Terry Smith, *Accounting for Growth*, Century Business, 1992.
5. Steve Lawrence, *International Accounting*, Thomson, 1996.
6. Derived from *Wall Street Journal, Europe report*, April 1996.
7. Steve Lawrence, *International Accounting*, Thomson, 1996.
8. Kazuo Inamori, *A Passion for Success*, McGraw-Hill, 1995.
9. Robert Kaplan and David Norton, *The Balanced Scorecard*, HBS Press, 1996.
10. Another recent measure is EVA – Economic Value Added – popularized by Stern Stewart, the US consultants. It deducts percent cost of capital from net percent profit after tax. From a marketing viewpoint, this offers little improvement compared with more conventional methods, since, as pointed out by the Lex Column in the *Financial Times* (23 December 1996), 'A business can boost EVA in any one year by running down the value of its assets – for example, by failing to invest in training, brand development and so forth.'

11. J.H. Davidson, series of articles in *Marketing Week*, 1979.
12. Alan Wolfe, *Profit from Strategic Marketing*, Pitman, 1993.
13. Gary Hamel and P.K. Prahalad, *Competing for the Future,* HBS Press, 1994.
14. ibid.
15. ibid
16. Real pricing is defined as price change, excluding effect of inflation.
17. *Fortune*, 11 November 1996.
18. *Fortune*, 23 December 1996.
19. Sony Annual Report, 1990.
20. *Fortune*, 14 October 1996.
21. This is a real-life example, based on a 1996 interview. Category and country have been disguised to protect confidentiality.
22. Robin Cooper, *When Lean Enterprises Collide*, Harvard Business School Press, 1995.
23. ibid
24. *Fortune*, 11 November 1996.
25. See Chapter 10 on 'Offensive Brand Development'.

## Chapter 3: **Offensive Vision and Attitudes**

1. Bill Gates, *The Road Ahead*, Viking, 1995.
2. Johnson & Johnson annual reports.
3. J. Collins and J. Porras, *Built to Last*. Century Business Books, 1996 and Warren Bennis, *On Becoming a Leader*, Addison-Wesley, 1989.
4. Robert Slater, *The New GE*, R. Irwin, 1996.
5. Collins and Porras, *Built to Last*.
6. The sweeping wording of AT&T's Vision is: 'We are dedicated to being the world's best at bringing people together – giving them easy access to each other and to the information and services they want and need – anytime, anywhere.'
7. *Financial Times*, 20 December 1996, article by Wolfgang Münchau.
8. Hamel and Prahalad, *Competing for the Future*.
9. *3M Annual Report*, 1994.
10. 'Triumph of the Nerds', Channel 4, April 1996.
11. Stratford Sharman, 'Eight Masters of Innovation', *Fortune Magazine*, 16 October 1984.
12. Bennett & Cooper, 'The Misuse of Marketing', *McKinsey Quarterly*, Fall, 1982.
13. Hamel and Prahalad, *Competing for the Future*.
14. Presentation to London Security Analysts, 1995.
15. *Toyota Annual Report*, 1996.
16. Nigel Hamilton, *Monty – The Making of a General, 1887–1942*, Hamish Hamilton, 1981.
17. This was an exaggeration. The tanks did not arrive until early September.
18. Hamilton, *Monty – The Making of a General*.

## Chapter 4: **The Integrated Marketing Approach**

1. 'The Total Marketing Approach' is another phrase sometimes used to describe Integrated Marketing.
2. *Duns Review*, December 1970.
3. Kotler, Fahey and Jatusripitak, *The New Competition*, Prentice-Hall, 1985.
4. Derived from article in *Wall Street Journal Europe*: Scott McCartney, 'Back on Course', 21 May 1996.
5. Iacocca, *Iacocca – An Autobiography*, Sidgwick & Jackson, 1985.
6. Sam Walton with John Huey, *Sam Walton – Made in America*, Doubleday, 1992.
7. J. Johansson and I. Nonaka, *Relentless – The Japanese Way of Marketing*, Butterworth-Heinemann, 1996.

## Chapter 5: **Offensive Business Analysis**

1. H. Golombek, *The Game of Chess*, Penguin, 1986.
2. SWOT = Strengths, Weaknesses, Opportunities, Threats.
3. These are obviously simplified calculations, since they ignore revenue from financing charges, sales of cars to spouses, and are not discounted into net present value. In addition, corporate fleet customers are not included.
4. Michael G. Allen, *Competitive Business Strategies*, McKinsey & Co. Inc. 1978.
5. Asahi Shimbun, *Japan Almanac*, 1995.

## Chapter 6: **Developing a Distinctive View of the Future**

1. This paragraph influenced by Hamel and Prahalad's *Competing for the Future*.
2. *Motorola: A Journey Through Time and Technology*, Motorola Museum of Electronics, 1994.
3. David Packard, *The HP Way – How Bill Hewlett and I Built Our Company*, Harper Business, 1995.
4. *3M Annual Report*, 1994.
5. Hamel and Prahalad, *Competing for the Future*, Harvard Business School, 1996.
6. *Strategic Innovation*, edited by Charles Baden-Fuller and Martyn Pitt, Routledge, 1996.
7. Hamel and Prahalad, *Competing for the Future*.

## Chapter 7: **Developing Winning Strategies**

1. Quoted by Robert Heller, 'The Making of Fortes', in *Management Today*, September 1969.
2. In practice, things do not seem to work out in such a neat and tidy way. (See R. Buzzell and B. Gale, *The PIMS Principles*, Free Press, 1987.) Buzzell and Gale conclude from their examination of the PIMS database, that 'many so-called dog, and ? businesses generate cash, whereas many cash cows are dry'. Their analysis showed that 74% of both 'Stars' and 'Cash Cows' were net cash generators, but as many as 59% of 'Dogs' and 54% of '?' were too.
3. Real pricing is defined as price change, excluding effect of inflation.
4. Robert C. Goizueta, Chairman, Coca-Cola, 1994.
5. Charles Baden-Fuller and Martyn Pitt, eds., *Strategic Innovation*, Routledge, 1996.
6. Buzzell and Gale, *The PIMS Principles*. Buzzell and Gale, using four-year averages of 2,611 business units, show that businesses with market shares over 30% achieve around three times the percent return on investment, versus those with a share of under 10%. They attribute this difference to scale economies and higher relative quality.
7. Buzzell and Gale, *The PIMS Principles*.
8. Charles Baden-Fuller and Martyn Pitt, eds, in *Strategic Innovation*, Routledge, 1996. See 'Case Study on Honda Motors' by Andrew Mair.
9. Robert J. Thomas, *New Product Success Stories*, John Wiley & Sons Inc., 1996.
10. Kotler, Fahey and Jatusripitak, *The New Competition*, Prentice-Hall, 1985.
11. *What Car?*, November 1985.
12. *What Car?*, December 1996.
13. Robert J. Thomas, *New Product Success Stories*, John Wiley & Sons Inc., 1996.
14. *Business Week,* 14 April 1997.
15. Robin Cooper, *When Lean Enterprises Collide*, Harvard Business School Press, 1995.
16. ibid.
17. ibid.

18. Che Guevara, *Guerrilla Warfare*, Penguin, 1969.
19. Article by Edmund O. Lawler, *Advertising Age*, 13 November 1995.
20. Article by Cecilie Rohwedder in *Wall Street Journal Europe*, 6 June 1996.

### Chapter 8:  **Offensive Marketing Planning**

1. Adapted from *3M Annual Report*, 1994.
2. Charles Baden-Fuller and Martyn Pitt, eds, *Strategic Innovation*, Routledge, 1996. See for interesting IKEA case study.
3. Frederick Reichheld, *The Loyalty Effect*, Harvard Business School Press, 1996, gives full treatment of this.
4. Carl Sewell, *Customers for Life*, Doubleday, 1990.
5. Mintel, Market Analysts.
6. *Market Line*, Gallup, 1995.
7. Calculated as regular users as percent of all using brand in past year.
8. Assumes a loyal customer is held for five years.

### Chapter 9:  **Offensive Segmentation**

1. See Reading List, page 588.
2. Kevin Clancy and Robert Shulman, *Marketing Myths That Are Killing The Business*, McGraw-Hill, 1995.
3. Alfred P. Sloan Jr., *My Years with General Motors*, Penguin, 1969.
4. ibid.
5. Jack Trout with Steve Rivkin, *The New Positioning*, McGraw-Hill, 1995.
6. *Advertising Age*, December 1996.
7. Robert Thomas, *New Product Success Stories*, John Wiley & Sons, 1995.
8. ibid.
9. *Advertising Age*, 9 December 1996.
10. *Ad Age International*, December 1996.
11. The area of 'consumers' and 'customers' is confusing due to differing use of language – Nestlé would regard a user of Nescafé as their *consumer*, while Tesco would describe the same person as their *customer*. We have defined consumers as people who use a product or service, and customers (buyers) as people with specialist knowledge who purchase for an organization.
12. Peter Sleight, *Targeting Customers*, NTC Publications, 1993, for detailed review.
13. ibid.
14. *Social Trends*. Central Statistical Office, London: The Stationery Office, published annually.
15. Peter Sleight, *Targeting Customers*, NTC Press, 1993. Detailed review.
16. ibid.
17. Xerox Corporation *Annual Report*, 1995.
18. This 63% comprises 40% + 15% + 8%, i.e. all the high loyalty level customers, where you have a high share of customers, total category purchases.

### Chapter 10:  **Offensive Brand Development**

1. Keynote speech to Annual Conference of Marketing Society, November 1989, by JHD.
2. Format for diagram originated by Saatchi & Saatchi.
3. Johansson and Nonaka, *Relentless – The Japanese Way of Marketing*.
4. ibid.
5. ibid.
6. 1995 has been used as the latest year for this trend comparison, since the basis of computation changed in 1996.

7. 'Brand Churn' – proliferating the number of products sold without significantly adding to volume.
8. Clancy and Shulman, *Marketing Myths That Are Killing Business*.
9. Betsy Boze and Charles Patton.
10. This section owes a particular acknowledgement to the SmithKline Beecham Consumer Health, 'Marketing Leadership Programme' – a set of best practice approaches and processes developed internally with contribution from Oxford Corporate Consultants.
11. IDVQ is a system developed by Novaction SA, Paris, France. It derives from research on thousands of brands.
12. Derived from Andrew Roberts, director of Taylor Nelson AGB.

## Chapter 11: **Offensive Product and Service Development**

1. Bob Beeby, formerly President, Pepsi-Cola International.
2. David Mahoney, quoted in J.T. Gerlach and C.A. Wainwright, *The Successful Management of New Products*, Pitman, 1970.
3. *Shell UK Review*, March 1995.
4. Booz Allen & Hamilton, *New Product Management for the 1980s*, Internal publication.
5. K. Clancy and R. Shulman, *The Marketing Revolution: A Radical Manifesto for Dominating the Marketplace*, Harper Business, 1991.
6. Cooper and Kleinschmidt, 'New Product Processes at Leading Industrial Firms', *Industrial Marketing Management*, May 1991.
7. Bill Ramsey, 'The New Product Dilemma', *Nielsen Marketing Trends*, January 1982. This study covered 1972–80, and used £4 million revenue per year as a criterion for successful advertised new products. Adjusting £4 million for inflation, the 1996 equivalent criterion would be £15 million, which looks reasonable if somewhat low. In the 1990s, success rates seem unlikely to be higher than in the 1970s.
8. Seizi Kato, *My Years with Toyota*, Toyota Motor Sales Co. Ltd, 1981.
9. Robert Heller, *The Supermanagers*, Sidgwick & Jackson, 1984.
10. David Packard, *The HP Way*, Harper Business, 1995.
11. Philip Kotler, *Marketing Management*, Prentice-Hall, 8th edition, 1994.

## Chapter 12: **Offensive Communications**

1. I am indebted for this analogy to Ries and Trout, *Positioning*, McGraw-Hill, 1981.
2. Kevin Tynan, *Multi-Channel Marketing*, Probus Publishing Company, 1994.
3. Garth Hallberg, *All Consumers Are Not Created Equal*, John Wiley, 1995.
4. Don Peppers and Martha Rogers, *The One to One Future*, Piatkus, 1993.
5. A study of 318 Marketers from the 1996 Marketing Forum showed that only 6% were currently using one major supplier for most or all of their communication needs. Sixty-two per cent believed 'that it is best to buy different expertise from different companies', while 29% said that they 'would like a one-stop solution – but don't believe it exists'.
6. The Marketing Forum, 1996: *Qualititative and Quantitative Research*, December 1996.
7. Garth Hallberg, *All Consumers Are Not Created Equal*, John Wiley, 1995.
8. Most frequently attributed to Lord Leverhulme.
9. James O. Peckham, *The Wheel of Marketing*, 1981.
10. Garth Hallberg, *All Consumers Are Not Created Equal*, John Wiley, 1995. Examples taken from this book.

11. ibid. Examples taken from this book.
12. *Advertising Works 8*, edited by Chris Baker, NTC Publications, 1995.
13. David Ogilvy, speech to ANA, reported in *Advertising Age*, 25 November 1991.
14. Adapted from *Advertising Works 7*, and *Advertising Works 8*, edited by Chris Baker, NTC, 1993, 1995.
15. ibid.
16. *Advertising Works 1–8*, NTC Publications, 1995.

## Chapter 13:　**Offensive Market Research**

1. *Admap* and JMRS are among the honourable exceptions.
2. *Journal of Market Research*, December 1995.
3. Adapted from 'How Intrapreneurs Innovate', in *Management Today*, December 1985, and from *3M Annual Report*, 1983.

## Chapter 14:　**Offensive Pricing**

1. Peter Doyle, *Marketing Management and Strategy*, Prentice-Hall, 1994.
2. Adapted from Figure 19–1 in Philip Kotler, *Marketing Management*, Prentice-Hall, 1994.
3. Will Hamilton, 'How manufacturers can stay ahead of the game,' *Admap*, March 1996.
4. ibid.
5. This entire section draws heavily from Clancy and Shulman, *Marketing Myths that are Killing Business*.
6. Justin Sargent, 'Strategies for Brand Success', *Admap*, March 1996.
7. K.K. Tse, *Marks & Spencer*, Pergamon Press Ltd, 1984.
8. John Millen, Procter & Gamble Vice-President of Sales, quoted in *EuroMarketing*, October 1996.

## Chapter 15:　**Offensive Channel Marketing**

1. C. Bucklin, S. DeFalco and Trip Levis, 'Are you tough enough to manage your own channels?', *McKinsey Quarterly*, vol 1, 1996.
2. Robert C. Goizueta, *Coca-Cola Annual Report*, 1995.
3. *Monopolies and Mergers Commission*, The Stationery Office, March 1995.
4. John Allen, Chief Executive, Ocean Group.
5. Peter Drucker, *Managing for Results*, Pan, 1970.
6. *Forbes*, 21 October 1996.
7. *Wall Street Journal Europe*, 23 October 1996.
8. Co-branding is where producer brand and channel brand (e.g. Boots) pool their brand strengths in joint marketing programmes to the consumer.
9. Bucklin, DeFalco and Trip Levis, 'Are you tough enough to manage your own channels?'.

## PS:　**Offensive Marketing: The Way Ahead**

1. Philip Crosby, *Quality Is Free*, McGraw-Hill, 1979.
2. J. Johansson and I. Nonaka, *Relentless – The Japanese Way of Marketing*.

# Index

Page references in *italic* are to figures, those in **bold** to tables.